Brief Contents

Contents

v

3 Improving Writing Techniques 56

4 Revising and Proofreading Business Messages 82

UNIT III

Routine Business Messages 101

5 Memorandums and E-Mail 102

UNIT IV

Negative, Persuasive, and Special Messages 165

UNIT V

Reporting Data 245

11 Proposals and Formal Reports 276

12 Oral Presentations, Meetings, and Telephone Communication 318

UNIT VI

Communicating for Employment 349

13 The Job Search, Résumés, and Cover Letters 350

14 Employment Interviewing and Follow-Up Messages 390

Contents

Preface

Thanks to the overwhelming support of students and instructors, *Essentials of Business Communication* has become the leading text/workbook in the field of business communication. The first four editions have been adopted in 546 colleges, universities, and vocational schools across the country. Because of its concise, efficient coverage, it has been especially appealing to students in a hurry to develop marketable skills.

Today's students will enter working environments with ever-increasing demands. As a result of growing emphasis on team management and employee empowerment, they will be expected to gather data, solve problems, and make decisions independently. They will be working with global trading partners and collaborating with work teams in an increasingly diverse workplace. And they will be using sophisticated technologies to communicate.

Surprisingly, writing skills are becoming more and more important. In the past, businesspeople may have written a couple of business letters a month, but now they receive and send hundreds of e-mail messages weekly. Their writing skills are showcased in every message they send. To help students develop the skills they need to succeed in today's technologically enhanced workplace, we have responded with a thoroughly revised Fifth Edition.

Effective Features That Remain Unchanged

In its first four editions, *Essentials* featured a practical teaching/learning program that helped students develop employment skills quickly. *Essentials* has been especially successful in developing communication skills for postsecondary, college, and adult students with outdated, inadequate, or weak language arts training. Writing skills receive special emphasis because these skills are increasingly important and because such skills require special training to develop.

Although the Fifth Edition represents a comprehensive revision, it retains the powerful foundation features that moved the first four editions to the head of the market. The following major features and effective strategies have helped thousands of students improve their communication skills.

- **Text/Workbook Format.** The convenient text/workbook format presents an all-in-one teaching-learning package that includes concepts, workbook application exercises, writing problems, and a combination handbook/reference manual.

Students work with and purchase only one volume for efficient, economical instruction.

- **Comprehensive But Concise Coverage.** An important reason for the enormous success of *Essentials of Business Communication* is that it practices what it preaches. The Fifth Edition follows the same strategy, concentrating on essential concepts presented without wasted words. The Fifth Edition still contains only 14 chapters, making it possible to cover easily in one quarter or semester.

- **Writing Plans and Writing Improvement Exercises.** Step-by-step writing plans structure the writing experience so that novice writers get started quickly—without struggling to provide unknown details to unfamiliar, hypothetical cases. Many revision exercises build confidence and skills.

- **Wide Coverage of Communication Technology.** All relevant chapters build technology skills by including discussions and applications involving e-mail, Web research, contemporary software, on-line employment, and electronic presentations.

- **Grammar/Mechanics Emphasis.** Each chapter features a systematic review of the Grammar/Mechanics Handbook. Readers take a short quiz to review specific concepts, and they also proofread business documents that provide a cumulative review of all concepts previously presented.

Revision Highlights

The following new features update the Fifth Edition:

- **Ampified Writing Process.** Chapter 2, "Writing for Business Audiences," has been totally revised so that it now introduces the writing process and places more emphasis on anticipating audience reaction so that students are better able to shape effective messages.

- **Strengthened Writing Techniques.** Three chapters are now devoted to writing techniques instead of two in the last edition. This change provides more opportunity for students to develop the basic and advanced writing skills that today's technology demands.

- **Integrated Internet Focus.** Internet concepts and applications are thoroughly integrated into chapters and case studies. Students learn about working in a technologically enhanced environment. Chapter 1 includes a workshop that tutors Internet novices and also challenges more advanced Web surfers. Chapter 8 teaches students how to write persuasive messages on-line, using Amazon.com as an example, and Chapter 11 helps readers locate and evaluate data on the Web.

- **Revised Communication Workshops.** Redesigned chapter workshops focus on technology, career skills, ethics, and multicultural issues. Information "chunking" and bulleting in the workshop text enhance readability and comprehension. "Your Task" and "Career Application" segments now provide consistent structure in guiding student responses.

- **Expanded Coverage of Career Skills.** Special workshop discussions focus on developing career skills that students need to succeed, such as using ethical tools, working collaboratively, observing business etiquette, and resolving workplace conflicts.

- **More Emphasis on E-Mail and the Web.** Reflecting business trends, this edition has fewer chapters devoted to letter writing and more discussions and assignments related to e-mail and the Web.

- **More Grammar/Mechanics.** As reviewers suggested, each chapter now includes an Advanced Grammar/Mechanics Review. Crammed with errors in grammar, punctuation, number expression, spelling, and capitalization, these exercises give instructors a challenging and exciting tool to help students recognize and avoid frequently made errors.

- **Amplified Oral Communication.** This edition moves speaking skills from Chapter 2 to Chapter 12 and greatly increases the coverage of electronic presentation software. Tips for planning and participating in meetings, as well as guidelines for improving telephone communication, complete the new chapter.

- **New End-of-Chapter Activities.** In some chapters as many as 80 percent of the activities are new, and many involve real problems from current events. All case studies now have "Your Task" segments that provide specific steps to follow in finishing the assignment.

- **More Cartoons!** Lightening the load and sharpening chapter concepts are many new cartoons, including Dilbert. His cubicle's-eye view of bosses, meetings, and management fads often features problems in communication.

- **New Video Case Studies.** A set of seven exciting videos, each about 8 minutes long, bridges the gap between textbook and the real world with case studies of such companies as Hudson's, Ben & Jerry's, Yahoo!, and World Gym.

- **Greater Use of Guffey Web Site.** To provide meaningful Web practice, this edition offers students rich resources at the Guffey Student Web site. Assignments using the Guffey Web site particularly effective for distance-learning classes and for intact classes with limited lecture time.

Other Features That Enhance Teaching and Learning

Although the Fifth Edition of *Essentials of Business Communication* packs considerable information into a small space, it covers all of the critical topics necessary in a comprehensive business communication course; and it also features many teaching-learning devices to facilitate instruction, application, and retention.

- **Focus on Writing Skills.** Most students need a great deal of instruction and practice in developing basic and advanced writing techniques, particularly in view of today's increased emphasis on communication by e-mail. Writing skills have returned to the forefront since so much of today's business is transacted through written messages. *Essentials* is the premier text/workbook in its focus on grammar and writing techniques.

- **E-Mail and Memo Emphasis.** *Essentials* is the only text/workbook that devotes an entire chapter to the writing of e-mail and memos, which have become the most used communication channels in the business world.

- **Listening, Speaking , and Nonverbal Skills.** Employers are increasingly seeking well-rounded individuals who can interact with fellow employees as well as represent the organization effectively. *Essentials* provides professional tips for managing nonverbal cues, overcoming listening barriers, developing speaking skills, planning and participating in meetings, and making productive telephone calls.

- **Coverage of Formal and Informal Reports.** Two chapters develop functional report-writing skills. Chapter 10 provides detailed instruction in the preparation of seven types of informal reports, while Chapter 11 covers proposals and formal reports. For quick comprehension all reports contain marginal notes that pinpoint writing strategies.

- **Employment Communication Skills.** Successful résumés, letters of application, and other employment documents are among the most important topics in a good business communication course. *Essentials* provides the most realistic and up-to-date résumés in the field. The models show chronological, functional, combination, and computer-friendly résumés.

- **Employment Interviewing.** *Essentials* devotes an entire chapter to effective interviewing techniques, including a discussion of screening interviews and hiring interviews. Chapter 14 also teaches techniques for fighting fear, answering questions, and following up.

- **Models Comparing Effective and Ineffective Documents.** To facilitate speedy recognition of good and bad writing techniques and strategies, *Essentials* presents many before-and-after documents. Marginal notes spotlight targeted strategies and effective writing.

- **Variety in End-of-Chapter Activities.** An amazing array of review questions, critical-thinking questions, writing improvement exercises, revision exercises, activities, and case problems hold student attention and help them apply chapter concepts meaningfully.

- **Diagnostic Test.** An optional grammar/mechanics diagnostic test helps students and instructors systematically determine specific student writing weaknesses. Students may be directed to the Grammar/Mechanics Handbook for remediation.

- **Grammar/Mechanics Handbook.** A comprehensive Grammar/Mechanics Handbook supplies a thorough review of English grammar, punctuation, capitalization style, and number usage. Its self-teaching exercises may be used for classroom instruction or for supplementary assignments. The handbook also serves as a convenient reference throughout the course and afterwards.

- **Textbook Coordination.** The principles of grammar and usage incorporated in *Essentials of Business Communication* coordinate with and reinforce those presented in Guffey's *Business English,* Guffey's *Essentials of College English,* and Clark and Clark's *Handbook for Office Workers.* This coordination means that students can move from one book to another without experiencing contradictory usage or style guidelines.

Unparalleled Instructor Support

The Fifth Edition of *Essentials* continues to set the standard for business communication support. Classroom success is easy to achieve because of the many practical ancillary items that supplement Guffey textbooks. No other author matches her level of support. Professor Melanie Young, Clark College, Vancouver, Washington, wrote,

> "*Essentials* is a big hit with my students. While they are working through all the exercises and sharing their completed case problems with each other, I'm enjoying the ease provided the instructor. The instructor's manual, electronic test bank, transparencies, and annotated teacher's text are wonderful tools. I'm amazed at the total number of items available to help me!"

The following time-saving ancillaries and resources accompany the Fifth Edition of *Essentials:*

- **Annotated Instructor's Edition** (0-324-01363-9). The Instructor's Edition includes a key so that teachers have an easy-to-read, all-in-one manual from which to teach. Answers to end-of-chapter review questions, writing improvement exercises, grammar/mechanics checkups, and the diagnostic test ensure classroom efficiency. Icons mark spots in the text where transparencies may be used to illustrate concepts and where supplementary lectures are available.

- **Instructor's Manual With Test Banks and Solutions Masters** (0-324-01367-1). The IM supplies general suggestions for teaching business communication, lesson plans for each chapter, test banks with 50 questions for each chapter, three unit tests, keys for all cumulative editing quizzes, and solutions transparency masters. In addition to ideas for course organization and evaluation, the IM provides many supplementary lectures on relevant topics not covered in the text.

- **Transparencies** (0-324-01382-5). Available to adopters is a remarkable collection of over 180 pages of transparency acetates that provide lecture summaries, additional examples, effective/ineffective documents, enrichment ideas, most problem solutions, and interactive quizzes. The transparency packet has been very popular in previous editions, but it is quite costly to mail because of the extraordinary number of sheets involved. With this edition, we're making the transparencies also available at the Guffey Instructor Web site. We encourage instructors to download them because the masters are immediately available, we save on mailing costs, and the masters are digital, which means instructors can customize them to fit their lectures.

- **PowerPoint® Slides** (0-324-01368-X). Summaries of important chapter concepts are professionally rendered in PowerPoint®. Instructors can use our chapter presentations or alter them for custom lectures. Our unique interactive program not only introduces concepts but also engages students in a dialogue that reviews and reinforces what they are seeing. This dynamic program captures attention, creates lively lectures, and, most important, enhances learning and retention.

- **ExamView Testing Software** (0-324-01383-3). All items from the printed test banks are available on disk with ExamView Testing Software, an automated testing program that allows instructors to create exams by selecting provided questions, modifying existing questions, and adding questions. It is available in Windows and MS-DOS versions and is provided free to instructors at educational institutions that adopt *Essentials of Business Communication*, 5e. Instructors can also have tests created and printed by calling Thomson Learning (South-Western) at 1-800-423-0563 between 8:30 a.m. and 6 p.m. EST.

- **BusinessLink Video Cases** (0-324-01364-7). Featuring real companies with real communication issues that managers and employees face, seven new videos (all about 8 minutes long) require student analysis, problem-solving skills, and application of communication concepts from the text. We've tried hard to provide a practical application for each video. For example in the Hudson video, students compare customer profiles with those developed by the trainees in the film. And your students will be as astonished as the Hudson trainees at the outcome!

- **Premier Web Site for Students.** Because of the heavy demand, we now operate identical versions of our student Web site at two locations. For *Essentials of Business Communication*, the primary site is located at **<http://www. westwords.com/guffey/students.html>.** The secondary site is located at **<http://www.meguffey.com>.** At either of these locations, students can test their knowledge of chapter concepts with interactive review exercises that provide immediate feedback electronically. They can see PowerPoint slides that review and emphasize chapter concepts. To expand their vocabulary, spelling, and sentence competency skills, students can use many self-paced skill-building drills written by the author. In addition to the text-specific items, students are offered links to the best search engines, employment and internship information sites, Web-site creation information, writing labs, electronic citation formats, on-line newspapers and magazines from around the world, and many other on-line resources of significance to business communication students. We provide over 3,000 student-oriented pages. No other Web site sponsored by an author matches our breadth of materials and speed of service!

- **Leading Web Site for Instructors.** The password-protected Instructors' site <http://www. westwords.com/instructor.html> supplies a remarkable collection of practical teaching materials such as downloadable modules on listening, peer editing, and report-writing projects. Instructors will also find discussion guides and bonus exercises. Passwords to the site can be found in the instructor's manual for *Essentials.*

- **Web Tutor** (0-324-06492-8). Web Tutor™ on WebCT is a content rich, web-based teaching and learning aid that reinforces and clarifies complex concepts. Web Tutor™ delivers innovative learning aids such as chapter reviews, flashcards, writing improvement exercises, spelling and vocabulary quizzes, and more. WebTutor™ also provides rich communication tools to instructors and students including a course calendar, chat, and e-mail. Instructors can incorporate Web Tutor as an integral part of the course or students can use it on their own as a study guide.

- **Print Newsletter.** *Business Communication News,* a twice-yearly newsletter, brings relevant business communication news, teaching tips, and announcements of new free materials. Instructors who have adopted *Essentials* may be placed on the mailing list by sending their names and addresses to Dr. Guffey at <meguffey@westwords.com> or by writing to the address shown at the end of the Preface.

- **E-Mail Newsletter.** *The On-Line Guffey Report* is a monthly electronic newsletter sent directly to instructors' e-mail boxes. Instructors may sign up at the Guffey Web site. The newsletter provides relevant news nuggets, classroom teaching tips, lecture ideas, and bonus case-study problems. Dr. Guffey remains the number one business communication author when it comes to accessibility, complimentary teaching materials, and on-line resources.

- **Distance Learning Resources.** Numerous distance learning instructors have made *Essentials* their textbook choice because of its comprehensive learning/ testing system, its technologically savvy approach, and its many on-line resources. Distance learning students have direct access to PowerPoint slides, interactive chapter review questions, interactive skill builders, electronic citation formats, and many other student-oriented electronic resources.

Acknowledgments

I gratefully acknowledge the following reviewers whose excellent advice and constructive suggestions helped shape the Fifth Edition of *Essentials of Business Communication:*

Christine Foster, Grand Rapids Community College
Nanette Clinch Gilson, San Jose State University
Tracey M. Harrison, Mississippi College
Jack Henson, Morehead State University
Karen A. Holtkamp, Xavier University
Mary E. Leslie, Grossmont College
Paul W. Murphey, Southwest Wisconsin Technical College
Jan Peterson, Anoka-Hennepin Technical College
Rose Ann Scala, Data Institute School of Business
Laurie Shapero, Miami-Dade Community College
Estelle Slootmaker, Aquinas College
Dana H. Swensen, Utah State University

For their contributions to previous editions, I warmly thank the following professionals:

Joyce M. Barnes, Texas A & M University–Corpus Christi
Patricia Beagle, Bryant & Stratton Business Institute
Nancy C. Bell, Wayne Community College
Ray D. Bernardi, Morehead State University
Karen Bounds, Boise State University
Jean Bush-Bacelis, Eastern Michigan University
Dee Anne Dill, Dekalb Technical Institute
Jeanette Dostourian, Cypress College
Nancy J. Dubino, Greenfield Community College
Cecile Earle, Heald College
Valerie Evans, Cuesta College
Pat Fountain, Coastal Carolina Community College
Marlene Friederich, New Mexico State University–Carlsbad
Margaret E. Gorman, Cayuga Community College
Judith Graham, Holyoke Community College
L. P. Helstrom, Rochester Community College
Rovena L. Hillsman, California State University, Sacramento
Michael Hricik, Westmoreland County Community College
Edna Jellesed, Lane Community College
Edwina Jordan, Illinois Central College
Diana K. Kanoy, Central Florida Community College
Ron Kapper, College of DuPage
Lydia Keuser, San Jose City College
Linda Kissler, Westmoreland County Community College
Keith Kroll, Kalamazoo Valley Community College
Richard B. Larsen, Francis Marion University
Nedra Lowe, Marshall University
Margarita Maestas-Flores, Evergreen Valley College
Jane Mangrum, Miami-Dade Community College
Maria Manninen, Delta College
Karen McFarland, Salt Lake Community College
Bonnie Miller, Los Medanos College
Mary C. Miller, Ashland University

Willie Minor, Phoenix College
Nancy Moody, Sinclair Community College
Nancy Mulder, Grand Rapids Junior College
Jackie Ohlson, University of Alaska–Anchorage
Carol Pemberton, Normandale Community College
Carl Perrin, Casco Bay College
Jeanette Purdy, Mercer County College
Carolyn A. Quantrille, Spokane Falls Community College
Susan Randles, Vatterott College
Ruth D. Richardson, University of North Alabama
Carlita Robertson, Northern Oklahoma College
Vilera Rood, Concordia College
Joseph Schaffner, SUNY College of Technology, Alfred
James Calvert Scott, Utah State University
Lance Shaw, Blake Business School
Cinda Skelton, Central Texas College
Clara Smith, North Seattle Community College
Marilyn St. Clair, Weatherford College
Judy Sunayama, Los Medanos College
David A. Tajerstein, SYRIT College
Marilyn Theissman, Rochester Community College
Lois A. Wagner, Southwest Wisconsin Technical College
Linda Weavil, Elan College
William Wells, Lima Technical College
Gerard Weykamp, Grand Rapids Community College
Beverly Wickersham, Central Texas College
Leopold Wilkins, Anson Community College
Almeda Wilmarth, State University of New York–Delhi
Barbara Young, Skyline College

In addition to honoring these friends and colleagues, I extend my warmest thanks to the many skillful professionals at South-Western College Publishing, including Pamela Person, Rob Bloom, Dave Shaut, Kelly Keeler, and Joe Devine. Special gratitude goes to my developmental editor, Mary Draper.

For preparing excellent new test questions, I salute Carolyn Seefer, Diablo Valley College; and for supervising all office functions I extend warm thanks to Lorraine Korkosz.

Finally, I express deep gratitude to my husband, Dr. George R. Guffey, professor emeritus of English, University of California, Los Angeles, for the creation and maintenance of our exceptional Web sites, for his development of an exciting PowerPoint program for *Essentials*, for his incredible technical and editorial skills, and, most of all, for his love, strength, and wisdom.

Each year I develop and distribute new classroom teaching materials for business communication instructors. To ensure that you receive notice of these materials, please send me your name and school address. And, of course, I am always delighted to receive comments about your course and suggestions for this book.

Dr. Mary Ellen Guffey
P.O. Box 6011
Malibu, CA 90264
E-mail: meguffey@westwords.com

Laying Communication Foundations

Facing Today's Communication Challenges

If I went back to college again, I'd concentrate on two areas: learning to write and to speak before an audience. Nothing in life is more important than the ability to communicate effectively.

GERALD R. FORD, *38th President of the United States*

LEARNING OBJECTIVES

1. Understand the importance of becoming an effective business communicator in today's changing workplace.
2. Examine the process of communication.
3. Discuss how to become an effective listener.
4. Analyze nonverbal communication and explain techniques for improving nonverbal communication skills.
5. Explain how culture affects communication and describe methods for improving cross-cultural communication.
6. Identify specific techniques that improve effective communication among diverse workplace audiences.

Becoming an Effective Business Communicator

Nearly three decades ago when he was president, Gerald Ford spoke about the importance of communication skills. If he had a second chance at college, he said, he'd concentrate on learning to write and learning to speak before an audience. Today, communication is even more important and more challenging than when President Ford spoke. We live in an information age that revolves around communication, a skill that is more challenging because of the tremendous changes in technology, the workforce, work environments, and the globalization of business.

The information revolution has made writing skills extremely important.

What's surprising about the information revolution, says one specialist, "is that the momentum has turned back to the written word."[1] Business communicators today are doing more writing than ever before. This book focuses on developing basic writing skills. But you will also learn to improve your listening, nonverbal, and speaking skills.

The abilities to read, listen, speak, and write effectively, of course, are not inborn. When it comes to communication, it's more *nurture* than *nature*. Good communicators are not born; they are made. Thriving in the dynamic and demanding new world of work will depend on many factors, some of which you cannot control. One factor that you do control, however, is how well you communicate.

The goals of this book are to teach you basic business communication skills, such as how to write a memo or letter and how to make a presentation. Anyone can learn these skills with the help of effective instructional materials and good model documents, all of which you'll find in this book. You also need practice—with meaningful feedback. You need someone such as your instructor to tell you how to modify your responses so that you can improve.

We've designed this book, its supplements, and our Web site to provide you and your instructor with everything necessary to make you a successful business communicator in today's dynamic workplace. Given the increasing emphasis on communication, many corporations are paying thousands of dollars to communication coaches and trainers to teach employees the very skills that you are learning in this course. Your coach is your instructor. Get your money's worth! Pick his or her brains.

With this book as your guide and your instructor as your coach, you may find this course to be the most important in your entire college curriculum. To get started, this first chapter presents an overview. You'll take a look at (1) the changing workplace, (2) the communication process, (3) listening, (4) nonverbal communication, (5) culture and communication, and (6) workplace diversity. The remainder of the book is devoted to developing specific writing and speaking skills.

Because communication skills are learned, you control how well you communicate.

This book and this course might well be the most important in your entire college career.

Succeeding in the Changing World of Work

The entire world of work is changing dramatically. The kind of work you'll do, the tools you'll use, the form of management you'll work under, the environment in which you'll work, the people with whom you'll interact—all are undergoing a pronounced transformation. Many of the changes in this dynamic workplace revolve around processing and communicating information. As a result, the most successful players in this new world of work will be those with highly developed communication skills. The following business trends illustrate the importance of excellent communication skills.

Trends in the new world of work emphasize the importance of communication skills.

- **Flattened management hierarchies.** To better compete and to reduce expenses, businesses have for years been trimming layers of management. This means that as a frontline employee, you will have fewer managers. You will be making decisions and communicating them to customers, to fellow employees, and to executives.
- **More participatory management.** Gone are the days of command-and-control management. Now, even new employees like you will be expected to understand and contribute to the big picture. Improving productivity and profitability will be everyone's job, not just management's.
- **Increased emphasis on self-directed work and project teams.** Businesses today are largely run by cross-functional teams of peers. You can expect to work with a team in gathering information, finding and sharing solutions, implementing decisions, and managing conflict. Good communication skills are extremely important in working together successfully in a team environment.
- **Heightened global competition.** Because American companies are moving beyond local markets, you may be interacting with people from many different cultures. As a successful business communicator, you will want to learn about other cultures. You'll also need to develop multicultural skills including sensitivity, flexibility, patience, and tolerance.

Today's employees must contribute to improving productivity and profitability.

- **Innovative communication technologies.** E-mail, fax, the Web, mobile technologies, audio and video conferencing—all of these technologies mean that you will be communicating more often and more rapidly than ever before. Your writing and speaking skills will be showcased as never before.
- **New work environments.** Mobile technologies and the desire for better work/family balance have resulted in flexible working arrangements. You may become part of the 33 percent of the workforce engaged in full or part-time telecommuting.[2] Working away from the office requires even more communication since staying connected means exchanging more messages.
- **Focus on information and knowledge as corporate assets.** Corporate America is increasingly aware that information is the key to better products and increased profitability. You will be expected to gather, sort, store, and disseminate data in a timely and accurate fashion. This is the new way of business life.[3]

Examining the Communication Process

As you can see, you can expect to be communicating more rapidly, more often, and with greater numbers of people than ever before. The most successful players in this new world of work will be those with highly developed communication skills. Since good communication skills are essential to your success, we need to take a closer look at the communication process.

Just what is *communication?* For our purposes communication is the *transmission of information and meaning from one individual or group to another.* The crucial element in this definition is *meaning.* Communication has as its central objective the transmission of meaning. The process of communication is successful only when the receiver understands an idea as the sender intended it. This process generally involves five steps, discussed here and shown in Figure 1.1.

Communication is the transmission of information and meaning from one individual or group to another.

FIGURE 1.1 Communication Process
Communication barriers and noise may cause the communication process to break down.

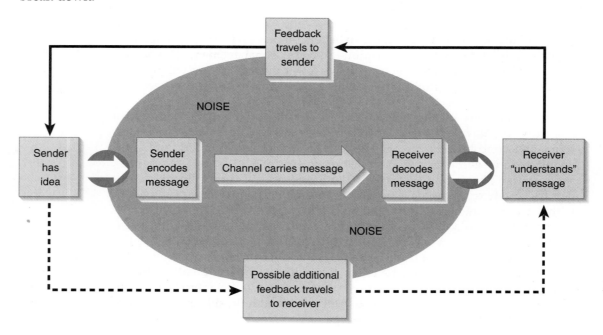

Chapter 1 Facing Today's Communication Challenges

1. **Sender has an idea.** The form of the idea may be influenced by the sender's mood, frame of reference, background, culture, and physical makeup, as well as the context of the situation.

2. **Sender encodes the idea in a message.** Encoding means converting the idea into words or gestures that will convey meaning. A major problem in communicating any message verbally is that words have different meanings for different people. That's why skilled communicators try to choose familiar words with concrete meanings on which both senders and receivers agree.

3. **Message travels over a channel.** The medium over which the message is transmitted is the *channel*. Messages may be sent by computer, telephone, letter, or memorandum. They may also be sent by means of a report, announcement, picture, spoken word, fax, or other channel. Because both verbal and nonverbal messages are carried, senders must choose channels carefully. Anything that disrupts the transmission of a message in the communication process is called *noise*. Channel noise ranges from static that disrupts a telephone conversation to spelling errors in an e-mail message. Such errors damage the credibility of the sender.

4. **Receiver decodes message.** The person for whom a message is intended is the *receiver*. Translating the message from its symbol form into meaning involves *decoding*. Successful communication takes place only when a receiver understands the meaning intended by the sender. Such success is often hard to achieve because no two people share the same backgrounds. Success is further limited because barriers and noise may disrupt the process.

5. **Feedback travels to sender.** The verbal and nonverbal responses of the receiver create feedback, a vital part of the entire communication process. Feedback helps the sender know that the message was received and understood. Senders can encourage feedback by asking questions such as *Am I making myself clear?* and *Is there anything you don't understand?* Senders can further improve feedback by delivering the message at a time when receivers can respond. Senders should also provide only as much information as a receiver can handle. Receivers can improve the process by paraphrasing the sender's message. They might say, *Let me try to explain that in my own words,* or *My understanding of your comment is . . .*

The communication process has five steps: idea formation, message encoding, message transmission, message decoding, and feedback.

Developing Better Listening Skills

An important part of the communication process is listening. By all accounts, however, most of us are not very good listeners. Do you ever pretend to be listening when you're not? Do you know how to look attentive in class when your mind wanders far away? How about "tuning out" people when their ideas are boring or complex? Do you find it hard to focus on ideas when a speaker's clothing or mannerisms are unusual?

You probably answered yes to one or more of these questions because many of us have developed poor listening habits. In fact, some researchers suggest that we listen at only 25 percent efficiency. Such poor listening habits are costly in business. Letters must be rewritten, shipments reshipped, appointments rescheduled, contracts renegotiated, and directions restated.

Most individuals listen at only 25 percent efficiency.

To improve listening skills, we must first recognize barriers that prevent effective listening. Then we need to focus on specific techniques that are effective in improving listening skills.

Barriers to Effective Listening

As you learned earlier, barriers and noise can interfere with the communication process. Have any of the following barriers and distractions prevented you from hearing what's said?

Barriers to listening may be physical, psychological, verbal, or nonverbal.

- **Physical barriers.** You cannot listen if you cannot hear what is being said. Physical impediments include hearing disabilities, poor acoustics, and noisy surroundings. It's also difficult to listen if you're ill, tired, uncomfortable, or worried.
- **Psychological barriers.** Everyone brings to the communication process a different set of cultural, ethical, and personal values. Each of us has an idea of what is right and what is important. If other ideas run counter to our preconceived thoughts, we tend to "tune out" the speaker and thus fail to hear.
- **Language problems.** Unfamiliar words can destroy the communication process because they lack meaning for the receiver. In addition, emotion-laden or "charged" words can adversely affect listening. If the mention of words such as *abortion* or *overdose* has an intense emotional impact, a listener may be unable to think about the words that follow.
- **Nonverbal distractions.** Many of us find it hard to listen if a speaker is different from what we view as normal. Unusual clothing, speech mannerisms, body twitches, or a radical hairstyle can cause enough distraction to prevent us from hearing what the speaker has to say.

Most North Americans speak at about 125 words per minute. The human brain can process information at least three times as fast.

- **Thought speed.** Because we can process thoughts over three times faster than speakers can say them, we can become bored and allow our minds to wander.
- **Faking attention.** Most of us have learned to look as if we are listening even when we're not. Such behavior was perhaps necessary as part of our socialization. Faked attention, however, seriously threatens effective listening because it encourages the mind to engage in flights of unchecked fancy. Those who practice faked attention often find it hard to concentrate even when they want to.
- **Grandstanding.** Would you rather talk or listen? Naturally, most of us would rather talk. Since our own experiences and thoughts are most important to us, we grab the limelight in conversations. We sometimes fail to listen carefully because we're just waiting politely for the next pause so that we can have our turn to speak.

Tips for Becoming an Active Listener

You can reverse the harmful effects of poor habits by making a conscious effort to become an active listener. This means becoming involved. You can't sit back and hear whatever a lazy mind happens to receive. The following techniques will help you become an active and effective listener.

To become an active listener, stop talking, control your surroundings, develop a positive mind-set, listen for main points, and capitalize on lag time.

- **Stop talking.** The first step to becoming a good listener is to stop talking. Let others explain their views. Learn to concentrate on what the speaker is saying, not on what your next comment will be.
- **Control your surroundings.** Whenever possible, remove competing sounds. Close windows or doors, turn off radios and noisy appliances, and move away from loud people or engines. Choose a quiet time and place for listening.
- **Establish a receptive mind-set.** Expect to learn something by listening. Strive for a positive and receptive frame of mind. If the message is complex, think of it as mental gymnastics. It's hard work but good exercise to stretch and expand the limits of your mind.
- **Keep an open mind.** We all sift and filter information through our own biases and values. For improved listening, discipline yourself to listen objectively. Be fair to the speaker. Hear what is really being said, not what you want to hear.
- **Listen for main points.** Concentration is enhanced and satisfaction is heightened when you look for and recognize the speaker's central themes.
- **Capitalize on lag time.** Make use of the quickness of your mind by reviewing the speaker's points. Anticipate what's coming next. Evaluate evidence the speaker has presented. Don't allow yourself to daydream.

- **Listen between the lines.** Focus both on what is spoken and what is unspoken. Listen for feelings as well as for facts.
- **Judge ideas, not appearances.** Concentrate on the content of the message, not on its delivery. Avoid being distracted by the speaker's looks, voice, or mannerisms.
- **Hold your fire.** Force yourself to listen to the speaker's entire argument or message before reacting. Such restraint may enable you to understand the speaker's reasons and logic before you jump to false conclusions.
- **Take selective notes.** For some situations thoughtful note-taking may be necessary to record important facts that must be recalled later. Select only the most important points so that the note-taking process does not interfere with your concentration on the speaker's total message.
- **Provide feedback.** Let the speaker know that you are listening. Nod your head and maintain eye contact. Ask relevant questions at appropriate times. Getting involved improves the communication process for both the speaker and the listener.

Listening actively may mean taking notes and providing feedback.

Improving Your Nonverbal Communication Skills

Understanding messages often involves more than merely listening to spoken words. Nonverbal clues, in fact, can speak louder than words. These clues include eye contact, facial expression, body movements, space, time, distance, and appearance. All these nonverbal clues affect how a message is interpreted, or decoded, by the receiver.

Nonverbal communication includes all unwritten and unspoken messages, intended or not.

Just what is nonverbal communication? It includes all unwritten and unspoken messages, whether intended or not. These silent signals have a strong effect on receivers. But understanding them is not simple. Does a downward glance indicate modesty? Fatigue? Does a constant stare reflect coldness? Dullness? Do crossed arms mean defensiveness? Withdrawal? Or do crossed arms just mean that a person is shivering?

Messages are even harder to decipher when the verbal and nonverbal codes do not agree. What would you think if Scott says he's not angry, but he slams the door when he leaves? What if Alicia assures the hostess that the meal is excellent, but she eats very little? The nonverbal messages in these situations speak more loudly than the words.

When verbal and nonverbal messages conflict, research shows that receivers put more faith in nonverbal cues. In one study speakers sent a positive message but averted their eyes as they spoke. Listeners perceived the total message to be negative. Moreover, they thought that averted eyes suggested lack of affection, superficiality, lack of trust, and nonreceptivity.[4]

When verbal and nonverbal messages clash, listeners tend to believe the nonverbal message.

Successful communicators recognize the power of nonverbal messages. Although it's unwise to attach specific meanings to gestures or actions, some cues broadcast by body language are helpful in understanding the feelings and attitudes of senders.

How the Eyes, Face, and Body Send Silent Messages

Words seldom tell the whole story. Indeed, some messages are sent with no words at all. The eyes, face, and body can convey a world of meaning without a single syllable being spoken.

Eye Contact. The eyes have been called the "windows to the soul." Even if they don't reveal the soul, the eyes are often the best predictor of a speaker's true feelings. Most of us cannot look another person straight in the eyes and lie. As a re-

The eyes are thought to be the best predictor of a speaker's true feelings.

sult, in American culture we tend to believe people who look directly at us. Sustained eye contact suggests trust and admiration; brief eye contact signals fear or stress. Good eye contact enables the message sender to see if a receiver is paying attention, showing respect, responding favorably, or feeling distress. From the receiver's viewpoint, good eye contact, in North American culture, reveals the speaker's sincerity, confidence, and truthfulness.

Facial Expression. The expression on a person's face can be almost as revealing of emotion as the eyes. Experts estimate that the human face can display over 250,000 expressions.[5] To hide their feelings, some people can control these expressions and maintain "poker faces." Most of us, however, display our emotions openly. Raising or lowering the eyebrows, squinting the eyes, swallowing nervously, clenching the jaw, smiling broadly—these voluntary and involuntary facial expressions can add to or entirely replace verbal messages.

Nonverbal messages often have different meanings in different cultures.

Posture and Gestures. A person's posture can convey anything from high status and self-confidence to shyness and submissiveness. Leaning toward a speaker suggests attraction and interest; pulling away or shrinking back denotes fear, distrust, anxiety, or disgust. Similarly, gestures can communicate entire thoughts via simple movements. However, the meanings of these movements differ in other cultures. Unless you know local customs, they can get you into trouble. In the United States and Canada, for example, forming the thumb and forefinger in a circle means everything's OK. But in Germany and parts of South America, the OK sign is obscene.

Tuning in on body language and other nonverbal messages requires that you be aware that they exist and that you value their importance. To take stock of the kinds of messages being sent by your body, ask a classmate to critique your use of eye contact, facial expression, and body movements. Another way to analyze your nonverbal style is to videotape yourself making a presentation and study your performance. This way you can make sure your nonverbal cues send the same message as your words.

How Time, Space, and Territory Send Silent Messages

People convey meaning in how they structure and organize time and how they order the space around themselves.

In addition to nonverbal messages transmitted by your body, three external elements convey information in the communication process: time, space, and distance.

Time. How we structure and use time tells observers about our personality and attitudes. For example, when Michelle Kwan, a banking executive, gives a visitor a prolonged interview, she signals her respect for, interest in, and approval of the visitor or the topic to be discussed.

Space. How we order the space around us tells something about ourselves and our objectives. Whether the space is a bedroom, a dorm room, an office, or a department, people reveal themselves in the design and grouping of their furniture. Generally, the more formal the arrangement, the more formal and closed the communication. The way office furniture is arranged sends cues on how communication is to take place. The late J. Edgar Hoover, director of the FBI, used to make his visitors sit at a small table below his large, elevated desk. Clearly, he did not want office visitors to feel equal to him.[6]

The distance required for comfortable social interaction is controlled by culture.

Territory. Each of us has certain areas that we feel are our own territory, whether it's a specific spot or just the space around us. Your father may have a favorite chair in which he is most comfortable, a cook might not tolerate intruders in his

"Sorry, Ridgely, but this area is my personal space."

© Sidney Harris.

or her kitchen, and veteran employees may feel that certain work areas and tools belong to them.

We all maintain zones of privacy in which we feel comfortable. Figure 1.2 categorizes the four zones of social interaction among Americans, as formulated by anthropologist Edward T. Hall.[7] Notice that Americans are a bit standoffish; only intimate friends and family may stand closer than about 1½ feet. If someone violates that territory, Americans feel uncomfortable and defensive and may step back to reestablish their space.

How Appearance Sends Silent Messages

The physical appearance of a business document, as well as the personal appearance of an individual, transmits immediate and important nonverbal messages.

The appearance of a message and of an individual can convey positive or negative nonverbal messages.

FIGURE 1.2 Four Space Zones for Social Interaction

Zone	Distance	Uses
Intimate	0 to 1½ feet	Reserved for members of the family and other loved ones.
Personal	1½ to 4 feet	For talking with friends privately. The outer limit enables you to keep someone at arm's length.
Social	4 to 12 feet	For acquaintances, fellow workers, and strangers. Close enough for eye contact yet far enough for comfort.
Public	12 feet and over	For use in the classroom and for speeches before groups. Nonverbal cues become important as aids to communication.

Appearance of Business Documents. The way a letter, memo, or report looks can have either a positive or a negative effect on the receiver. Sloppy e-mail messages send a nonverbal message that says you are in a terrific hurry or that the reader is not important enough for you to care. Envelopes—through their postage, stationery, and printing—can suggest routine, important, or junk mail. Letters and reports can look neat, professional, well organized, and attractive—or just the opposite. In succeeding chapters you'll learn how to create documents that send positive nonverbal messages through their appearance, format, organization, readability, and correctness.

Appearance of People. The way you look—your clothing, grooming, and posture—telegraphs an instant nonverbal message about you. Based on what they see, viewers make quick judgments about your status, credibility, personality, and potential. Because appearance is such a powerful force in business, some aspiring professionals are turning for help to image consultants (who charge up to $500 an hour!). As one human relations specialist observed, "If you don't look and act the part, you will probably be denied opportunities."[8]

Tips for Improving Your Nonverbal Skills

Because nonverbal clues can mean more than spoken words, learn to use nonverbal communication positively.

Nonverbal communication can outweigh words in the way it influences how others perceive us. You can harness the power of silent messages by reviewing the following tips for improving nonverbal communication skills:

- **Establish and maintain eye contact.** Remember that in the United States and Canada appropriate eye contact signals interest, attentiveness, strength, and credibility.
- **Use posture to show interest.** Encourage communication interaction by leaning forward, sitting or standing erect, and looking alert.
- **Improve your decoding skills.** Watch facial expressions and body language to understand the complete verbal and nonverbal message being communicated.
- **Probe for more information.** When you perceive nonverbal cues that contradict verbal meanings, politely seek additional clues (*I'm not sure I understand, Please tell me more about . . .,* or *Do you mean that . . .*).
- **Avoid assigning nonverbal meanings out of context.** Make nonverbal assessments only when you understand a situation or a culture.
- **Associate with people from diverse cultures.** Learn about other cultures to widen your knowledge and tolerance of intercultural nonverbal messages.
- **Appreciate the power of appearance.** Keep in mind that the appearance of your business documents, your business space, and yourself sends immediate positive or negative messages to receivers.
- **Observe yourself on videotape.** Ensure that your verbal and nonverbal messages are in sync by taping and evaluating yourself making a presentation.
- **Enlist friends and family.** Ask them to monitor your conscious and unconscious body movements and gestures to help you become a more effective communicator.

Understanding How Culture Affects Communication

Verbal and nonverbal meanings are even more difficult to interpret when people are from different cultures.

Comprehending the verbal and nonverbal meanings of a message is difficult even when communicators are from the same culture. But when they are from different cultures, special sensitivity and skills are necessary.

Negotiators for a North American company learned this lesson when they were in Japan looking for a trading partner. The North Americans were pleased after their first meeting with representatives of a major Japanese firm. The Japanese had nodded assent throughout the meeting and had not objected to a single proposal. The next day, however, the North Americans were stunned to learn that the Japanese had rejected the entire plan. In interpreting the nonverbal behavioral messages, the North Americans made a typical mistake. They assumed the Japanese were nodding in agreement as fellow North Americans would. In this case, however, the nods of assent indicated comprehension—not approval.

Every country has a unique culture or common heritage, joint experience, and shared learning that produce its culture. This experience gives members of that culture a complex system of shared values and customs. It teaches them how to behave; it conditions their reactions. Comparing traditional North American values with those in other cultures will broaden your world view. This comparison should also help you recognize some of the values that shape your actions and judgments of others.

Comparing Key Cultural Values

Until relatively recently, typical North Americans shared the same broad cultural values. Some experts identified them as "Anglo" or "mainstream" values.[9] These values largely represented white, male, Northern European views. Women and many minorities now entering the workforce may eventually modify these values. However, a majority of North Americans are still governed by these mainstream values.

Although North American culture is complex, we'll focus on four dimensions to help you better understand some of the values that shape your actions and judgments of others. These four dimensions are individualism, formality, communication style, and time orientation.

Individualism. One of the most identifiable characteristics of North Americans is their *individualism*. This is an attitude of independence and freedom from control. They think that initiative and self-assertion result in personal achievement. They believe in individual action, self-reliance, and personal responsibility; and they desire a large degree of freedom in their personal lives. Other cultures emphasize membership in organizations, groups, and teams; they encourage acceptance of group values, duties, and decisions. Members of these cultures typically resist independence because it fosters competition and confrontation instead of consensus.

While North Americans value individualism and personal responsibility, other cultures emphasize group- and team-oriented values.

Formality. A second significant dimension of North American culture is our attitude toward *formality*. Americans place less emphasis on tradition, ceremony, and social rules than do people in some other cultures. They dress casually and are soon on a first-name basis with others. Their lack of formality is often characterized by directness. In business dealings North Americans tend to come to the point immediately; indirectness, they feel, wastes time, a valuable commodity.

Communication Style. A third important dimension of our culture relates to *communication style*. North Americans value straightforwardness, are suspicious of evasiveness, and distrust people who might have a "hidden agenda" or who "play their cards too close to the chest."[10] North Americans also tend to be uncomfortable with silence and impatient with delays. Moreover, they tend to use and understand words literally. Latins, on the other hand, enjoy plays on words; and Arabs and South Americans sometimes speak with extravagant or poetic figures of speech (such as "the Mother of all battles").

North Americans tend to be direct and to understand words literally.

Time Orientation. A fourth dimension of our culture relates to *time orientation*. North Americans consider time a precious commodity to be conserved. They correlate time with productivity, efficiency, and money. Keeping people waiting for

North Americans correlate time with productivity, efficiency, and money.

FIGURE 1.3 Comparison of Cultural Values Ranked by Priority*

U.S. Americans	Japanese	Arabs
1. Freedom	1. Belonging	1. Family security
2. Independence	2. Group harmony	2. Family harmony
3. Self-reliance	3. Collectiveness	3. Parental guidance
4. Equality	4. Age/Seniority	4. Age
5. Individualism	5. Group consensus	5. Authority
6. Competition	6. Cooperation	6. Compromise
7. Efficiency	7. Quality	7. Devotion
8. Time	8. Patience	8. Patience
9. Directness	9. Indirectness	9. Indirectness
10. Openness	10. Go-between	10. Hospitality

*1 represents the most important value.
Source: F. Elashmawi and P. R. Harris, *Multicultural Management* (Houston: Gulf Publishing Co., 1998), 800-231-6275.

business appointments wastes time and is also rude. In other cultures, time may be perceived as an unlimited and never-ending resource to be enjoyed.

Figure 1.3 compares a number of cultural values for U.S. Americans, Japanese, and Arabs. Notice that belonging, group harmony, and collectiveness are very important to Japanese people, while family matters rank highest with Arabs. As we become aware of the vast differences in cultural values illustrated in Figure 1.3, we can better understand why communication barriers develop and how misunderstandings occur in cross-cultural interactions.

Controlling Ethnocentrism and Stereotyping

The process of understanding and accepting people from other cultures is often hampered by two barriers: ethnocentrism and stereotyping. These two barriers, however, can be overcome by developing tolerance, a powerful and effective aid to communication.

Ethnocentrism is the belief in the superiority of one's own culture and group.

Ethnocentrism. The belief in the superiority of one's own culture is known as *ethnocentrism.* This natural attitude is found in all cultures. Ethnocentrism causes us to judge others by our own values. If you were raised in North America, the values just described probably seem "right" to you, and you may wonder why the rest of the world doesn't function in the same sensible fashion. A North American businessperson in an Arab or Asian country might be upset at time spent over coffee or other social rituals before any "real" business is transacted. In these cultures, however, personal relationships must be established and nurtured before earnest talks may proceed.

A *stereotype* is an oversimplified behavioral pattern applied to entire groups.

Stereotypes. Our perceptions of other cultures sometimes cause us to form stereotypes about groups of people. A *stereotype* is an oversimplified behavioral pattern applied to entire groups. For example, the Swiss are hard-working, efficient, and neat; Germans are formal, reserved, and blunt; Americans are loud, friendly, and impatient; Canadians are polite, trusting, and tolerant; Asians are gracious, humble, and inscrutable. These attitudes may or may not accurately describe cultural norms. But when applied to individual business communicators, such stereotypes may create misconceptions and misunderstandings. Look beneath surface stereotypes and labels to discover individual personal qualities.

Tolerance. Working among people from other cultures demands tolerance and flexible attitudes. As global markets expand and as our society becomes increasingly multiethnic, tolerance becomes critical. *Tolerance,* here, does not mean "putting up with" or "enduring," which is one part of its definition. Instead, *tolerance* is used in a broader sense. It means having empathy for and appreciating beliefs and practices different from our own.

One of the best ways to develop tolerance is by practicing empathy. This means trying to see the world through another's eyes. It means being nonjudgmental, recognizing things as they are rather than as they "should be." It includes the ability to accept others' contributions in solving problems in a culturally appropriate manner. When Kal Kan Foods began courting the pet owners of Japan, for example, an Asian advisor suggested that the meat chunks in its Pedigree dog food be cut into perfect little squares. Why? Japanese pet owners feed their dogs piece by piece with chopsticks. Instead of insisting on what "should be" (feeding dogs chunky meat morsels), Kal Kan solved the problem by looking at it from another cultural point of view (providing neat small squares).[11]

The following tips provide specific suggestions for preventing miscommunication in oral and written transactions across cultures.

> **Developing intercultural tolerance means practicing empathy, being nonjudgmental, and being patient.**

Tips for Minimizing Oral Miscommunication Among Cross-Cultural Audiences

When you have a conversation with someone from another culture, you can reduce misunderstandings by following these tips:

- **Use simple English.** Speak in short sentences (under 15 words) with familiar, short words. Eliminate puns, sports and military references, slang, and jargon (special business terms). Be especially alert to idiomatic expressions that can't be translated, such as *burn the midnight oil* and *under the weather.*
- **Speak slowly and enunciate clearly.** Avoid fast speech, but don't raise your voice. Overpunctuate with pauses and full stops. Always write numbers for all to see.
- **Encourage accurate feedback.** Ask probing questions, and encourage the listener to paraphrase what you say. Don't assume that a yes, a nod, or a smile indicates comprehension or assent.

> **You can improve cross-cultural oral communication by using simple English, speaking slowly, enunciating clearly, encouraging feedback, observing eye messages, accepting blame, and listening without interruption.**

© 1989 by NEA, Inc.

"He doesn't understand you. Try shouting a little louder."

BERRY'S WORLD reprinted by permission of Newspaper Enterprise Association, Inc.

- **Check frequently for comprehension.** Avoid waiting until you finish a long explanation to request feedback. Instead, make one point at a time, pausing to check for comprehension. Don't proceed to B until A has been grasped.
- **Observe eye messages.** Be alert to a glazed expression or wandering eyes. These tell you the listener is lost.
- **Accept blame.** If a misunderstanding results, graciously accept the blame for not making your meaning clear.
- **Listen without interrupting.** Curb your desire to finish sentences or to fill out ideas for the speaker. Keep in mind that North Americans abroad are often accused of listening too little and talking too much.
- **Remember to smile!** Roger Axtell, international behavior expert, calls the smile the single most understood and most useful form of communication in either personal or business transactions.
- **Follow up in writing.** After conversations or oral negotiations, confirm the results and agreements with follow-up letters. For proposals and contracts, engage a translator to prepare copies in the local language.

Tips for Minimizing Written Miscommunication Among Cross-Cultural Audiences

When you write to someone from a different culture, you can improve your chances of being understood by following these tips:

You can improve cross-cultural written communication by adopting local styles, using short sentences and short paragraphs, avoiding ambiguous wording, and citing numbers carefully.

- **Adopt local styles.** Learn how documents are formatted and how letters are addressed and developed in the intended reader's country. Use local formats and styles.
- **Consider hiring a translator.** Engage a translator if (1) your document is important, (2) your document will be distributed to many readers, or (3) you must be persuasive.
- **Use short sentences and short paragraphs.** Sentences with fewer than 15 words and paragraphs with fewer than 5 lines are most readable.
- **Avoid ambiguous wording.** Include relative pronouns (*that, which, who*) for clarity in introducing clauses. Stay away from contractions (especially ones like *Here's the problem*). Avoid idioms (*once in a blue moon*), slang (*my presentation really bombed*), acronyms (*ASAP* for *as soon as possible*), abbreviations (*DBA* for *doing business as*), and jargon (*input, output, bottom line*). Use action-specific verbs (*purchase a printer* rather than *get a printer*).
- **Cite numbers carefully.** For international trade it's a good idea to learn and use the metric system. In citing numbers, use figures (*15*) instead of spelling them out (*fifteen*). Always convert dollar figures into local currency. Avoid using figures to express the month of the year. In North America, for example, March 5, 1998, might be written as 3/5/98, while in Europe the same date might appear as 5.3.98. For clarity, always spell the month out.

Capitalizing on Workforce Diversity

You can expect to be interacting with customers and colleagues who may differ from you in race, ethnicity, age, gender, national origin, physical ability, and many other characteristics.

As global competition opens world markets, North American businesspeople will increasingly interact with customers and colleagues from around the world. At the same time, the North American workforce is also becoming more diverse—in race, ethnicity, age, gender, national origin, physical ability, and countless other characteristics.

No longer, say the experts, will the workplace be predominantly male or Anglo-oriented. Nearly 85 percent of the new entrants to the workforce will be women, minorities, and immigrants, according to estimates from the U.S. Bureau of Labor Statistics. By the year 2005, groups now considered minorities (African Americans,

Hispanics, Asians, Native Americans, and others) will make up 27 percent of the workforce.[12] Women will make up 48 percent of the workforce. And more than 22 million workers will be 55 years or older.[13]

While the workforce is becoming more diverse, the structure of many businesses in North America is also changing. As you learned earlier, workers are now organized by teams. Organizations are flatter, and rank-and-file workers are increasingly making decisions among themselves. What does all this mean for you as a future business communicator? Simply put, your job may require you to interact with colleagues and customers from around the world. Your work environment will probably demand that you cooperate effectively with small groups of coworkers. And these coworkers may differ from you in race, ethnicity, gender, age, and other ways.

A diverse work environment has many benefits. Consumers want to deal with companies that respect their values and create products and services tailored to their needs. Organizations that hire employees with different experiences and backgrounds are better able to create the different products that these consumers desire. In addition, businesses with diverse workforces suffer fewer discrimination lawsuits, fewer union clashes, and less government regulatory action. That's why a growing number of companies view today's diversity movement as a critical bottom-line business strategy for improving employee relationships and increasing productivity.[14]

Diversity programs have become an important business strategy because of the benefits to consumers, work teams, and organizations.

GRANTLAND®

I DON'T UNDERSTAND WHY PEOPLE DISCRIMINATE AGAINST WOMEN OR MINORITIES OR THE DISABLED.

IT DOESN'T MAKE ANY SENSE!

IT'S LIKE THROWING AWAY A PRESENT BEFORE YOU'VE OPENED IT —

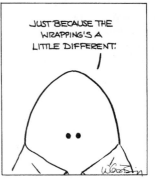
JUST BECAUSE THE WRAPPING'S A LITTLE DIFFERENT.

www.grantland.com

Tips for Effective Communication With Diverse Workplace Audiences

Capitalizing on workplace diversity is an enormous challenge for most organizations and individuals. Harmony and acceptance do not happen automatically when people who are dissimilar work together. The following suggestions can help you become a more effective communicator as you enter a rapidly evolving workplace with ethnically diverse colleagues and clients.

- **Understand the value of differences.** Diversity makes an organization innovative and creative. Sameness fosters "groupthink," an absence of critical thinking sometimes found in homogeneous groups. Case studies, for example, of the Kennedy administration's decision to invade Cuba and of the *Challenger* space shuttle disaster suggest that groupthink prevented alternatives from being considered.[15] Diversity in problem-solving groups encourages independent and creative thinking.

- **Don't expect conformity.** Gone are the days when businesses could say, "This is our culture. Conform or leave."[16] The CEO of athletic shoemaker Reebok stressed seeking people who have new and different stories to tell. "It accomplishes next to nothing to employ those who are different from us if the condition of their employment is that they become the same as us. For it is their differences that enrich us, expand us, provide us the competitive edge."[17]

- **Create zero tolerance for bias and stereotypes.** Cultural patterns exist in every identity group, but applying these patterns to individuals results in stereotyping. Assuming that African Americans are good athletes, that women are poor at math, that French Canadians excel at hockey, or that European American men are insensitive fails to admit the immense differences in people in each group. Check your own use of stereotypes and labels. Don't tell sexist or ethnic jokes at meetings. Avoid slang, abbreviations, and jargon that imply stereotypes. Challenge others' stereotypes politely but firmly.

- **Practice focused, thoughtful, and open-minded listening.** Much misunderstanding can be avoided by attentive listening. Listen for main points; take notes if necessary to remember important details. The most important part of listening, especially among diverse communicators, is judging ideas, not appearances or accents.

Successful communicators invite, use, and give feedback; make few assumptions; learn about their own cultures and other cultures; and seek common ground.

- **Invite, use, and give feedback.** As you learned earlier, a critical element in successful communication is feedback. You can encourage it by asking questions such as *Is there anything you don't understand?* When a listener or receiver responds, use that feedback to adjust your delivery of information. Does the receiver need more details? A different example? Slower delivery? As a good listener, you should also be prepared to give feedback. For example, summarize your understanding of what was said or agreed on.

- **Make fewer assumptions.** Be careful of seemingly insignificant, innocent workplace assumptions. For example, don't assume that everyone wants to observe the holidays with a Christmas party and a decorated tree. Celebrating only Christian holidays in December and January excludes those who honor Hanukkah, Kwanza, and the Chinese New Year. Moreover, in workplace discussions don't assume that everyone is married or wants to be or is even heterosexual, for that matter. For invitations, avoid phrases such as "managers and their *wives*." *Spouses* or *partners* is more inclusive. Valuing diversity means making fewer assumptions that everyone is like you or wants to be like you.

- **Learn about your cultural self.** Knowing your own cultural biases helps you become more objective and adaptable. Begin to recognize the stock reactions and thought patterns that are automatic to you as a result of your upbringing. Become more aware of your own values and beliefs. That way you can see them at work when you are confronted by differing values.

- **Seek common ground.** Look for areas where you and others not like you can agree or share opinions. Be prepared to consider issues from many perspectives, all of which may be valid. Accept that there is room for different points of view to coexist peacefully. Although you can always find differences, it's much harder to find similarities. Look for common ground in shared experiences, mutual goals, and similar values. Concentrate on your objective even when you may disagree on how to reach it.[18]

Summing Up and Looking Forward

This chapter described the importance of becoming an effective business communicator in this information economy. Many of the changes in today's dynamic workplace revolve around processing and communicating information. Flattened management hierarchies, participatory management, increased emphasis on work teams, heightened global competition, and innovative communication technologies are all trends that increase the need for good communication skills. To improve your skills, you should understand the communication process. Communication doesn't take place unless senders encode meaningful messages that can be decoded by receivers.

One important part of the communication process is listening. You can become a more active listener by keeping an open mind, listening for main points, capitalizing on lag time, judging ideas and not appearances, taking selective notes, and providing feedback.

The chapter also described ways to help you improve your nonverbal communication skills.

You learned the powerful effect that culture has on communication, and you became more aware of key cultural values for North Americans. Finally, the chapter discussed ways that businesses and individuals can capitalize on workforce diversity.

The following chapters present the writing process. You will learn specific techniques to help you improve your written and oral expression. Remember, communication skills are not inherited. They are learned. John Bryan, the highly respected CEO of Sara Lee, recognized this when he said that communication skills are "about 99 percent developed." Bryan contends that "the ability to construct a succinct memo, one that concentrates on the right issues, and the ability to make a presentation to an audience—these are skills that can be taught to almost anyone."[19]

Critical Thinking

1. Why should business and professional students strive to improve their communication skills, and why is it difficult or impossible to do so without help?
2. Recall a time when you experienced a problem as a result of poor communication. What were the causes of and possible remedies for the problem?
3. How are listening skills important to employees, supervisors, and executives? Who should have the best listening skills?
4. What arguments could you give for or against the idea that body language is a science with principles that can be interpreted accurately by specialists?
5. Since English is becoming the world's language and since the United States is a dominant military and trading force, why should Americans bother to learn about other cultures?

Chapter Review

6. Are communication skills acquired by *nature* or by *nurture?* Explain.

7. List seven trends in the workplace that affect business communicators. Be prepared to discuss how they might affect you in your future career.

8. Give a brief definition of the following words:
   a. Encode
   b. Channel
   c. Decode

9. List 11 techniques for improving your listening skills. Be prepared to discuss each.

10. What is nonverbal communication? Give several examples.

11. Why is good eye contact important for North American communicators?

12. Describe the concept of North American individualism. How does this concept set North Americans apart from people in some other cultures?

13. What is ethnocentrism, and how can it be reduced?

14. List seven suggestions for enhancing comprehension when you are talking with people for whom English is a second language. Be prepared to discuss each.

15. List eight suggestions for becoming a more effective communicator in a diverse workplace. Be prepared to discuss each.

Note to Students:
Check the Guffey Web site for updated EBC URLs (Web addresses).

Activities and Cases

1.1 Getting to Know You. Since today's work and class environments often involve cooperating in teams or small groups, getting to know your fellow classmates is important. To learn something about the people in this class and to give you practice in developing your communication skills, your instructor may choose one of the following techniques.

a. For larger classes your instructor may divide the class into groups of four or five. Take one minute to introduce yourself briefly (name, major interest, hobbies, goals). Spend five minutes in the first group session. Record the first name of each individual you meet. Then informally regroup. In new groups, again spend five minutes on introductions. After three or four sessions, study your name list. How many names can you associate with faces?

b. For smaller classes your instructor may ask each student to introduce himself or herself in a two-minute oral presentation while standing before the class at the rostrum. Where are you from? What are your educational goals? What are your interests? This informal presentation may serve as the first of two or three oral presentations correlated with Chapter 12.

1.2 Class Listening. Observe the listening habits of the students in one of your classes for a week. What barriers to effective listening did you observe? How many of the suggestions described in this chapter are being implemented by listeners in the class? Write a memo or an e-mail message to your instructor describing your observations. (See Chapter 5 to learn more about memos.)

1.3 Self-Listening. Analyze your own listening habits. What are your strengths and weaknesses? Decide on a plan for improving your listening skills. Write a memo or e-mail message to your instructor including your analysis and your improvement plan.

1.4 *Web* Extra Credit Listening. You are a student in a business management or another class. Your instructor notices that you have good listening habits. Disturbed by the poor listening skills of some other class members, your instructor asks you to do research and to present a program (for extra credit) to help students improve their listening skills. For this presentation do the following:

a. Write a specific statement of purpose.
b. Prepare a complete outline.
c. Write the introduction.
d. List visual aids that would be appropriate and describe their content.

Related Web Site: www.smartbiz.com/sbs/arts/bly55.htm

1.5 *Web* In-Service Listening Training. If you are now employed or have been employed, adapt the assignment in Activity 1.4 to your work. Assume that your supervisor has asked you to present an in-service training workshop that helps employees improve listening skills. Respond to the instructions in items (a) through (d).

Related Web Site: www.smartbiz.com/sbs/arts/bly55.htm

1.6 Silent Messages. Analyze the kinds of silent messages you send your instructor, your classmates, and your employer. How do you send these messages? Group them into categories, as suggested by what you learned in this chapter. What do these messages mean? Be prepared to discuss them in small groups or in a memo to your instructor.

1.7 Body Language. What attitudes do the following body movements suggest to you? Do these movements always mean the same thing? What part does context play in your interpretations?
a. **Whistling, wringing hands**
b. **Bowed posture, twiddling thumbs**
c. **Steepled hands, sprawling sitting position**
d. **Rubbing hand through hair**
e. **Open hands, unbuttoned coat**
f. **Wringing hands, tugging ears**

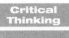

1.8 Universal Sign for "I Goofed." In an effort to promote peace and tranquillity on the highways, motorists submitted the following suggestions to a newspaper columnist.[20] In small groups consider the pros and cons for each of the following gestures intended as an apology when a driver makes a mistake. Why would some fail?
a. Lower your head slightly and bonk yourself on the forehead with the side of your closed fist. The message is clear: "I'm stupid. I shouldn't have done that."
b. Make a temple with your hands, as if you were praying.
c. Move the index finger of your right hand back and forth across your neck—as if you are cutting your throat.
d. Flash the well-known peace sign. Hold up the index and middle fingers of one hand, making a *V*, as in Victory.
e. Place the flat of your hands against your cheeks, as children do when they've made a mistake.
f. Clasp your hand over your mouth, raise your brows, and shrug your shoulders.
g. Use your knuckles to knock on the side of your head. Translation: "Oops! Engage brain."
h. Place your right hand high on your chest and pat a few times, like a basketball player who drops a pass or a football player who makes a bad throw. This says, "I'll take the blame."
i. Place your right fist over the middle of your chest and move it in a circular motion. This is universal sign language for "I'm sorry."
j. Open your window and tap the top of your car roof with your hand.
k. Smile and raise both arms, palms outward, which is a universal gesture for surrender or forgiveness.
l. Use the military salute, which is simple and shows respect.
m. Flash your biggest smile, point at yourself with your right thumb and move your head from left to right, as if to say, "I can't believe I did that."

1.9 Alice in Wonderland Travels to Tokyo. Analyze the following cross-cultural incident. Jeff Davis is the leader of a creative team representing a large American theme park company. The owners of a Japanese park rely on the American company to develop new attractions for their Tokyo park. But the Japanese own their park and must approve any new addition. Jeff and his team recently traveled to Japan to make an important presentation to the owners. His team had worked for the past year developing the concept of an outdoor garden maze with a network of hedge passageways for children to wander through. The concept was based on *Alice in Wonderland.*

The jobs of his entire team depended on selling the idea of this new attraction (including restaurants and gift shops) to the owners of the Tokyo park. Because the Japanese smiled and nodded throughout the presentation, Jeff assumed they liked the idea. When he pushed for final approval, the Japanese smiled and said that an outdoor garden attraction might be difficult in their climate. Jeff explained away that argument. Then he asked for a straightforward yes or no, but the Japanese answered, "We will have to study it very carefully." Thinking he had not made himself clear, Jeff began to review the strong points of the presentation. What cultural elements may be interfering with communication in this exchange?

1.10 Soup's On. Analyze the following cross-cultural incident. As a junior manager of Campbell Soup Company, you have been sent to Hong Kong to work on the development of new regional soup varieties to appeal to 2 billion Asian consumers. The Chinese are among the highest per capita soup eaters in the world, consuming an average of one bowl a day. In the Hong Kong taste kitchen, you are currently working on cabbage soup, scallop broth, and a special soup that combines watercress and duck gizzards. You've even tested exotic ingredients such as shark's fin and snake.[21] The supervisor of the taste kitchen understands English, but sometimes her eyes glaze over when you discuss procedures with her. What could you do to improve comprehension and minimize misunderstandings?

1.11 Translating Idioms. Explain in simple English what the following idiomatic expressions mean. Assume that you are explaining them to people for whom English is a second language.
a. let the cat out of the bag
b. take the bull by the horns
c. he is a tightwad
d. putting the cart before the horse
e. to be on the road
f. lend someone a hand
g. with flying colors
h. turn over a new leaf

1.12 *E-Mail* Analyzing Diversity at Reebok. Analyze the following diversity challenge. Reebok grew from a $12 million a year sport shoe company into a $3 billion footwear powerhouse without giving much thought to the hiring of employees. "When we were growing very, very fast, all we did was bring another friend into work the next day," recalled Sharon Cohen, Reebok vice president. "Everybody hired nine of their friends. Well, it happened that nine white people hired nine of their friends, so guess what? They were white, all about the same age. And then we looked up and said, 'Wait a minute. We don't like the way it looks here.' That's the kind of thing that can happen when you are growing very fast and thoughtlessly."[22]

Your Task. In what ways would Reebok benefit by diversifying its staff? What competitive advantages might it gain? Outline your reasoning in an e-mail message to your instructor.

1.13 Video Case Study: Diversity in Business at Dayton Hudson Department Stores. View the video describing Hudson's commitment to diversity. Stop the tape at the designated spot and break into small groups to analyze the pictures of potential customers No. 1 and No. 12.

Video

Your Task. In your group speculate about the person whose picture you have been assigned. What is that person's profession, interests and hobbies, family life, buying habits, and personal characteristics? Make lists of your group's profile of the targeted person. When the tape resumes, watch the profile developed by the Hudson's trainee group. How did your profile compare with that of the Hudson's trainee group? How close were you to describing the actual individual? What stereotypes were at work here? Why is it important to look beyond stereotypes in judging individuals? Your instructor may ask your group to submit its profile list.

Nouns

These checkups are designed to improve your control of grammar and mechanics. They systematically review all sections of the Grammar/Mechanics Handbook, which appears on pages 435–485. Answers are provided on page 486.

Review Sections 1.01–1.06 in the Grammar Review section of the Grammar/Mechanics Handbook. Then study each of the following statements. Underscore any inappropriate form, and write a correction in the space provided. Also record the appropriate G/M section and letter to illustrate the principle involved. If a sentence is correct, write C. When you finish, compare your responses with those provided. If your answers differ, study carefully the principles shown in parentheses.

companies   (1.05e)   **Example:**   Two surveys revealed that many companys will move to the new industrial park.

_____   1. Several attornies worked on the three cases simultaneously.
_____   2. Counter business is higher on Saturday's, but telephone business is greater on Sundays.
_____   3. Some of the citys in Kevin's report offer excellent opportunities.
_____   4. Frozen chickens and turkies are kept in the company's lockers.
_____   5. All secretaries were asked to check supplies and other inventorys.
_____   6. Only the Nashs and the Lopezes brought their entire families.
_____   7. In the 1980s profits grew rapidly; in the 1990's investments lagged.
_____   8. Both editor in chiefs instituted strict proofreading policies.

_____   9. Luxury residential complexs are part of the architect's plan.
_____   10. Voters in three countys are likely to approve new gas taxes.
_____   11. The instructor was surprised to find three Jennifer's in one class.
_____   12. Andre sent descriptions of two valleys in France to us via the Internet.
_____   13. How many copies of the statements showing your assets and liabilitys did you make?
_____   14. My monitor makes it difficult to distinguish between o's and a's.
_____   15. Both runner-ups complained about the winner's behavior.

The preceding exercises concentrated on a specific grammar area. The following exercise is packed with a variety of errors based on the grammar, punctuation, number style, capitalization, spelling words, and confusing words discussed in the Grammar/Mechanics Handbook. In the space provided write a corrected version of each sentence. Your instructor has the only key for this exercise.

Example: Before eating sixteen members of the Committee met in the sabin center.
Revision: Before eating, 16 members of the committee met in the Sabin Center.

1. At last Sundays graduation ceremonys Jennifer Rivers who uses a wheel-chair, was honored because she was the only graduate who had never missed a day of classes.

2. Please send photocopys of all european currencys that will be affected by the new euro.

3. If its not to late to register my brother and myself plan to take courses in History, Management, and English.

4. In just two hours time I was able to locate 9 excelent Web sites, containing relevant information for my report.

5. Mistakes are a fact of life, however it is the response to the error that really counts.

6. Complicating the problem is inefficent legislation, and lack of enforcement personel.

7. We cannot procede with the mailing, until the list of names and address are verified.

8. My new Sport Utility Vehicle came equiped with: antilock brakes, alloy wheels and a trip computer.

9. My bosses biggest computer worry is the possibility of us being hacked, and not knowing it.

10. Beside your résumé and cover letter you must submit a seperate employment application form.

11. Elizabeth was suprised that the Lopezes who once owned 2 popular resterants were now her neighbor.

12. Although the manufacture promised excelent milage my wife and me get only fifteen miles to the gallon.

13. Your bill of two hundred dollars is now ninety days overdue, therefore we are submitting it to a agency for collection.

14. If you have all ready sent your payment please disregard this notice.

15. Of the 350 letters mailed only five were returned as reported by Ms. Radfords assistant.

Grammar/Mechanics Challenge—1

Document for Revision

The following memo has many faults in grammar, spelling, punctuation, capitalization, word use, and number form. Use standard proofreading marks (see Appendix B) to correct the errors. Study the guidelines in the Grammar/Mechanics Handbook to sharpen your skills. When you finish, your instructor can show you the revised version of this memo.

TO: Tran Nguyen

FROM: Rachel Stivers, Manager

DATE: May 14, 200X

SUBJECT: WORK AT HOME GUIDELINES

Since you will be completeing most of your work at home for the next 4 months.
Follow these guidelines;

1. Check your message bored daily and respond promptly, to those who are trying to reach you.

2. Call the office at least twice a week to pick up any telephone messages, return these calls promply.

3. Transmit any work you do, on the computer to Jerry Gonzalez in our computer services department, he will analyze each weeks accounts, and send it to the proper Departments. .

4. Provide me with monthly reports' of your progress.

Chapter 1 Facing Today's Communication Challenges

We will continue to hold once a week staff meetings on Friday at 10 a.m. in the morning. Do you think it would be possible for you to attend 1 or 2 of these meeting. The next one is Friday May 17th.

I know you will work satisfactory at home Tran. Following these basic guidelines should help you accomplish your work, and provide the office with adequate contact with you.

Learning the Net to Boost Your Career Skills

As a business communicator in today's workplace, you must know your way around the Internet. In addition to using e-mail, you'll need to locate information on the Web—quickly and accurately. It's far too easy to waste time and money while roaming through cyberspace. Whether you're a novice or a surfing pro, this workshop will help you sharpen your Internet skills. A number of very important concepts are taught at a Web site called "Learn the Net."

- **Getting started.** Using your computer browser, type in this address: <www.learnthenet.com>. Here you will learn what *hypertext* is and how to know when images are hot. You will learn what a *URL* is and become familiar with your browser's toolbar. You will probably be using either a Netscape or an Explorer browser. Both toolbars are shown on the second screen at "Learn the Net."
- **Ten top tips for using the Web.** At "Learn the Net" click on "Ten Top Tips." Tip 1 discusses speeding up your Web browsing by turning off images. Most Web sites today, however, download graphics fairly quickly (depending on your setup and traffic). We recommend that you keep the images turned on; some images are actually hot links. Those of you who are beginners should focus on Tips 2, 4, 5, 6, and 9. More advanced Web surfers will find Tips 3, 7, 8, and 10 most interesting.
- **Reviewing basic functions.** Be sure you know how to use the *Stop, Back, Forward*, and *Refresh* (or *Reload*) buttons. Also be sure you know how to use the scroll bar at the top or bottom of the screen, as well as how to use the direction arrows and the *Page Up* and *Page Down* buttons. If you want another quick tutorial of basics, try <www.ithaca.edu/library/Training/ICYouSee.html>.
- **Searching the Web.** At the "Learn the Net" site, click on "Digging for Data." Learn about search engines and how to limit your search with quotation marks around your terms. Learn what kind of information you can expect to find on the Web. Find out what *Boolean logic* is.

Career Application

Assume that you are about to finish your degree program, and you are now looking for a job. The easiest way to job search today is on the Web. A terrific selection of Web job-search sites is available to students using Guffey textbooks. At the direction of your instructor, conduct a survey of electronic job advertisements in your field. What's available? How much is the salary? What are the requirements?

Your Task

- **Go to <meguffey.com>** and click on "Job Search." Scroll down to "Job Resources." You'll see many excellent job sites, but to get you started, click on "Monster.com." This is one of the most popular job sites with over 225,000 U.S. jobs.

- **Study the opening page.** Confusing, eh? Remember that all the free services on the Web are supported by advertisements. Try to ignore the clutter. Use your scroll bar to run up and down the page. At the very top you'll find the navigation buttons. Click on "Search Jobs."
- **Read "Tips for Searching."** This may take a few minutes, but it's well worth the time. Notice that you can limit your search to specific locations and categories. Under keyword search, you can further pinpoint your search with the title of the position you seek or terms that describe technical or professional experience.
- **Conduct a practice search.** Use the *Back* key (or click "Search Jobs" on the navigation bar at the top). On the opening page, find the "Location Search" box. Use the scroll button to highlight a geographical area. Just for fun, try "Honolulu, Hawaii." In the "Category Search" box, select "Administrative/ Clerical." In the "Keyword Search" box, type in "Administrative Assistant." Then press Enter in the "Search Jobs" box. You should see some actual job ads.
- **Conduct a real search.** Now conduct a job search in your career area and in geographical areas of your choice. If you don't find suitable jobs at Monster.com, use one of the other job sites. Select five ads and print them. If you cannot print, make notes on what you find.
- **Analyze the skills required.** How often do the ads mention communication, teamwork, and computer skills? What tasks do the ads mention? Is a salary given? Your instructor may ask you to submit your findings and/or report to the class.

Related Web Sites: You will use Learn the Net <www.learnthenet.com> and Monster.com <www.monster.com> in this workshop.

Web

Developing Writing Skills

2 Writing for Business Audiences

I wanted to know where they came from, what their interests were, and what I could talk to them about.

JOHN H. JOHNSON, *founder of* Ebony *and* Jet *magazines and* Fashion Fair *cosmetics, talking about customers*

LEARNING OBJECTIVES

1. Understand that business writing should be audience oriented, purposeful, and economical.
2. Identify and implement the three phases of the writing process.
3. Appreciate the importance of analyzing the task and profiling the audience for business messages.
4. Create messages that spotlight audience benefits and cultivate a "you" view.
5. Develop a conversational tone and use positive language.
6. Explain the need for inclusive language, plain expression, and familiar words.
7. List seven ways in which technology helps improve business writing.

Basics of Business Writing

Excellent communicators, like John H. Johnson, concentrate on the audience for their messages.

In communicating with others, newspaper founder and businessman John H. Johnson always concentrated on what *they* wanted rather than what *he* wanted. An exceedingly successful entrepreneur, Johnson was born in a tin-roof shack in Arkansas. Despite the odds, he became the first black on the *Forbes* magazine list of the 400 richest people in America. "Being poor made me run scared," he confessed. It also motivated him to find ways to succeed in publishing and in life. What is his greatest success secret? Focusing totally on his audience. With prospective advertisers, he always talked about what he could do for them. How could he help them improve their bottom line? How could he help them increase their sales? How could he make their lives easier?[1]

Audience awareness is one of the basics of business communication. This chapter focuses on writing for business audiences. Business writing may be different from other writing you have done. High school or college compositions and term papers may have required you to describe your feelings, display your knowledge, and meet a minimum word count. Business writing, however, has different goals. In preparing business messages and oral presentations, you'll find that your writing needs to be:

- **Audience oriented.** Like publisher John Johnson, you will concentrate on looking at a problem from the receiver's perspective instead of seeing it from your own.
- **Purposeful.** You will be writing to solve problems and convey information. You will have a definite purpose to fulfill in each message.
- **Economical.** You will try to present ideas clearly but concisely. Length is not rewarded.

> Business writing is audience oriented, purposeful, and economical.

These distinctions actually ease the writer's task. You won't be searching your imagination for creative topic ideas. You won't be stretching your ideas to make them appear longer. One writing consultant complained that "most college graduates entering industry have at least a subliminal perception that in technical and business writing, quantity enhances quality."[2] Wrong! Get over the notion that longer is better. Conciseness is what counts in business.

The ability to prepare concise, audience-centered, and purposeful messages does not come naturally. Very few people, especially beginners, can sit down and compose a terrific letter or report without training. But following a systematic process, studying model messages, and practicing the craft can make nearly anyone a successful business writer or speaker.

> Following a systematic process helps beginning writers create effective messages and presentations.

Writing Process for Business Messages and Oral Presentations

Whether you are preparing an e-mail message, memo, letter, or oral presentation, the process will be easier if you follow a systematic plan. Our plan breaks the entire task into three separate phases: prewriting, writing, and revising. As you can see in Figure 2.1, however, the process is not always linear.

To illustrate the writing process, let's say that you own a popular local McDonald's franchise. At rush times, you've got a big problem. Customers complain about the chaotic multiple waiting lines to approach the service counter. You once saw two customers nearly get into a fistfight over cutting into a line. And customers often are so intent on looking for ways to improve their positions in line that they fail to examine the menu. Then they are totally clueless when their turn arrives. You want to convince other franchise owners that a single-line (serpentine) system would work better. You could telephone everyone. But you want to present a serious argument with good points that owners will remember and be

> The writing process has three parts: prewriting, writing, and revising.

FIGURE 2.1 The Writing Process

willing to act on when they gather for their next district meeting. You decide to write a letter that you hope will win their support.

Prewriting

The first phase of the writing process involves analyzing and anticipating the audience and then adapting to that audience.

The first phase of the writing process prepares you to write. It involves *analyzing* the audience and your purpose for writing. The audience for your letter will be other franchise owners, some of whom are highly educated and some of whom are not. Your purpose in writing is to persuade them that a change in policy would improve customer service. You are convinced that a single-line system, such as that used in banks, would reduce chaos and make customers happier because they would not have to worry about where they are in line.

Prewriting also involves *anticipating* how your audience will react to your message. You're sure that some of the other owners will agree with you, but others might fear that customers seeing a long single line might go elsewhere. In *adapting* your message to the audience, you try to think of the right words and the right tone that will win approval.

Writing

The second phase of the writing process includes researching, organizing the message, and actually writing it.

The second phase involves researching, organizing, and then composing the message. In *researching* information for this letter, you would probably investigate other kinds of businesses that use single lines for customers. You might check out your competitors. What are Wendy's and Burger King doing? You might do some telephoning to see if other franchise owners are concerned about chaotic lines. Before writing to the entire group, you might brainstorm with a few owners to see what ideas they have for solving the problem.

Once you have collected enough information, you would focus on *organizing* your letter. Should you start out by offering your solution? Or should you work up to it slowly, describing the problem, presenting your evidence, and then ending with the solution? The final step in the second phase of the writing process is actually *composing* the letter. Naturally, you'll do it at your computer so that you can make revisions easily.

Revising

The third phase of the writing process includes revising for clarity and readability, proofreading for errors, and evaluating for effectiveness.

The third phase of the process involves revising, proofreading, and evaluating your letter. After writing the first draft, you'll spend a lot of time *revising* the message for clarity, conciseness, tone, and readability. Could parts of it be rearranged to make your point more effectively? This is the time when you look for ways to improve the organization and sound of your message. Next, you'll spend time *proofreading* carefully to ensure correct spelling, grammar, punctuation, and format. The final phase involves *evaluating* your entire message to decide whether it accomplishes your goal.

Scheduling the Writing Process

Although the writing process shows the three phases equally, the time you spend on each varies depending on the complexity of the problem, the purpose, the audience, and your schedule. One expert gives these rough estimates for scheduling a project:

- Prewriting—25 percent (planning and worrying)
- Writing—25 percent (organizing and composing)
- Revising—45 percent (40 percent revising and 5 percent proofreading)

These are rough guides, yet you can see that good writers spend most of their time on the final phase of revising and proofreading. Much depends, of course, on your project, its importance, and your familiarity with it. What's critical to remember, though, is that revising is a major component of the writing process.

It may appear that you perform one step and progress to the next, always following the same order. Most business writing, however, is not that rigid. Although writers perform the tasks described, the steps may be rearranged, abbreviated, or repeated. Some writers revise every sentence and paragraph as they go. Many find that new ideas occur after they've begun to write, causing them to back up, alter the organization, and rethink their plan.

Analyzing the Purpose for Writing and the Audience

We've just taken a look at the total writing process. As you begin to develop your business writing skills, you should expect to follow this process closely. With experience, though, you'll become like other good writers and presenters who alter, compress, and rearrange the steps as needed. But following a plan is very helpful at first. The remainder of this chapter covers the first phase of the writing process. You'll learn to analyze the purpose for writing, anticipate how your audience will react, and adapt your message to the audience.

Identifying Your Purpose

As you begin to compose a message, ask yourself two important questions: (1) Why am I sending this message? and (2) What do I hope to achieve? Your responses will determine how you organize and present your information.

Your message may have primary and secondary purposes. For college work your primary purpose may be merely to complete the assignment; secondary purposes might be to make yourself look good and to get a good grade. The primary purposes for sending business messages are typically to inform and to persuade. A secondary purpose is to promote goodwill: you and your organization want to look good in the eyes of your audience.

The primary purpose of most business messages is to inform or to persuade; the secondary purpose is to promote goodwill.

Selecting the Best Channel

After identifying the purpose of your message, you need to select the most appropriate communication channel. Some information is most efficiently and effectively delivered orally. Other messages should be written, and still others are best delivered electronically. Whether to set up a meeting, send a message by e-mail, or write a report depends on some of the following factors:

- Importance of the message
- Amount and speed of feedback required
- Necessity of a permanent record
- Cost of the channel
- Degree of formality desired

These five factors will help you decide which of the channels shown in Figure 2.2 is most appropriate for delivering a message.

Choosing an appropriate channel depends on the importance of the message, the feedback required, the need for a permanent record, the cost, and the formality needed.

Switching to Faster Channels

Technology and competition continue to accelerate the pace of business today. As a result, communicators are switching to ever-faster means of exchanging information. In the past business messages within organizations were delivered largely

FIGURE 2.2 Choosing Communication Channels

Channel	Best Use
E-mail	When you wish to deliver routine or urgent messages quickly and inexpensively across time zones or borders. Appropriate for small, large, local, or dispersed audiences. Quickly becoming preferred channel replacing hard-copy memos and many letters. Printout provides permanent record.
Face-to-face conversation	When you want to be persuasive, deliver bad news, or share a personal message.
Telephone call	When you need to deliver or gather information quickly, when nonverbal cues are unimportant, and when you cannot meet in person.
Voice mail message	When you wish to leave important or routine information that the receiver can respond to when convenient.
Fax	When your message must cross time zones or international boundaries, when a written record is significant, or when speed is important.
Face-to-face group meeting	When group decisions and consensus are important. Inefficient for merely distributing information.
Video or teleconference	When group consensus and interaction are important but members are geographically dispersed.
Memo	When you want a written record to explain policies clearly, discuss procedures, or collect information within an organization.
Letter	When you need a written record of correspondence with customers, the government, suppliers, or others outside an organization.
Report or proposal	When you are delivering considerable data internally or externally.

by hard-copy memos. Responses would typically take a couple of days. But that's too slow for today's communicators. They want answers and action now! Cell phones, faxes, Web sites, and especially e-mail can deliver that information much faster than can traditional channels of communication.

Within many organizations, hard-copy memos are still written, especially for messages that require persuasion, permanence, or formality. But the channel of choice for corporate communicators today is clearly e-mail. It's fast, cheap, and easy. Thus, fewer hard-copy memos are being written. Fewer letters are also being written. That's because many customer service functions can now be served through Web sites or by e-mail.

Whether your channel choice is e-mail, a hard-copy memo, or a report, you'll be a more effective writer if you spend sufficient time in the prewriting phase.

Anticipating the Audience

A good writer anticipates the audience for a message: What is the reader like? How will that reader react to the message? Although you can't always know exactly who the reader is, you can imagine some characteristics of the reader. Even writers of direct mail sales letters have a general idea of the audience they wish to target. Picturing a typical reader is important in guiding what you write. One copywriter at Lands' End, the catalog company, pictures his sister-in-law whenever he writes product descriptions for the catalog. By profiling your audience and shaping a message to respond to that profile, you are more likely to achieve your communication goals.

Profiling the Audience

Visualizing your audience is a pivotal step in the writing process. The questions in Figure 2.3 will help you profile your audience. How much time you devote to answering these questions depends greatly on your message and its context. An analytical report that you compose for management or an oral presentation before a big group would, of course, demand considerable audience anticipation. On the other hand, an e-mail message to a coworker or a letter to a familiar supplier might require only a few moments of planning. No matter how short your message, though, spend some time thinking about the audience so that you can tailor your words to your readers or listeners. "The most often unasked question in business and professional communication," claims a writing expert, "is as simple as it is important: *Have I thought enough about my audience?*"[3]

By profiling your audience before you write, you can identify the appropriate tone, language, and channel.

Responding to the Profile

Profiling your audience helps you make decisions about shaping the message. You'll discover what kind of language is appropriate, whether you're free to use specialized technical terms, whether you should explain everything, and so on. You'll decide whether your tone should be formal or informal, and you'll select the most desirable channel. Imagining whether the receiver is likely to be neutral, positive, or negative will help you determine how to organize your message.

Another advantage of profiling your audience is considering the possibility of a secondary audience. For instance, you might write a report that persuades your boss to launch a Web site for customers. Your boss is the primary reader, and he is familiar with many of the details of your project. But he will need to secure approval from his boss, and that person is probably unfamiliar with the project

After profiling the audience, you can decide whether the receiver will be neutral, positive, or hostile toward your message.

FIGURE 2.3 Asking the Right Questions to Profile Your Audience

Primary Audience

Who is my primary reader or listener?
What is my personal and professional relationship with that person?
What position does the individual hold in the organization?
How much does that person know about the subject?
What do I now about that person's education, beliefs, culture, and attitudes?
Should I expect a neutral, positive, or negative response to my message?

Secondary Audience

Who might see or hear this message in addition to the primary audience?
How do these people differ from the primary audience?

details. Because your report will be passed along to secondary readers, it must include more background information and more extensive explanations than you included for the primary reader, your boss. Analyzing the task and anticipating the audience assists you in adapting your message so that it will accomplish what you intend.

THE WALL STREET JOURNAL

"The tone of the letter is stern, almost threatening, but—see here?—He signs with a smiley face, so I think we may be all right."

Adapting to the Task and Audience

After analyzing your purpose and anticipating your audience, you must convey your purpose to that audience. Adaptation is the process of creating a message that suits your audience.

One important aspect of adaptation is *tone*. Conveyed largely by the words in a message, tone reflects how a receiver feels upon reading or hearing a message. Skilled communicators create a positive tone in their messages by using a number of adaptive techniques, some of which are unconscious. These include spotlighting audience benefits, cultivating a "you" attitude, sounding conversational, and using inclusive language. Additional adaptive techniques include using positive expression and preferring plain language with familiar words.

Writers improve the tone of a message by emphasizing reader benefits, cultivating a "you" attitude, and using a conversational tone and inclusive language.

Audience Benefits

Focusing on the audience sounds like a modern idea, but actually one of America's early statesmen and authors recognized this fundamental writing principle over 200 years ago. In describing effective writing, Ben Franklin observed, "To be good, it ought to have a tendency to benefit the reader."[4] These wise words have become a fundamental guideline for today's business communicators. Expanding on Franklin's counsel, a contemporary communication consultant gives this solid advice to his business clients: "Always stress the benefit to the readers of whatever it is you're trying to get them to do. If you can show them how you're going to save *them* frustration or help them meet their goals, you have the makings of a powerful message."[5]

Adapting your message to the receiver's needs means putting yourself in that person's shoes. It's called *empathy*. Empathic senders think about how a receiver will decode a message. They try to give something to the receiver, solve the receiver's problems, save the receiver's money, or just understand the feelings and position of that person. Which of the following messages is more appealing to the audience?

Empathy involves thinking of how the receiver feels and is likely to respond.

Sender focus	To enable us to update our stockholder records, we ask that the enclosed card be returned.
Audience focus	So that you may promptly receive dividend checks and information related to your shares, please return the enclosed card.
Sender focus	Our warranty becomes effective only when we receive an owner's registration.
Audience focus	Your warranty begins working for you as soon as you return your owner's registration.
Sender focus	We offer a CD-ROM language course that we have complete faith in.
Audience focus	The sooner you order the CD-ROM language program, the sooner the rewards will be yours.
Sender focus	The Human Resources Department requires that the enclosed questionnaire be completed immediately so that we can allocate our training resource funds.
Audience focus	By filling out the enclosed questionnaire, you can be one of the first employees to sign up for the new career development program.

The most successful messages focus on the audience.

"You" View

Notice how many of the previous audience-focused messages included the word *you*. In concentrating on receiver benefits, skilled communicators naturally develop the "you" view. They emphasize second-person pronouns (*you, your*) instead of first-person pronouns (*I/we, us, our*). Whether your goal is to inform, persuade, or promote goodwill, the catchiest words you can use are *you* and *your*. Compare the following examples.

Because receivers are most interested in themselves, emphasize *you* whenever possible.

"I/We" View	I have scheduled your vacation to begin May 1.
"You" View	You may begin your vacation May 1.
"I/We" View	We have shipped your order by UPS, and we are sure it will arrive in time for the sales promotion January 15.
"You" View	Your order will be delivered by UPS in time for your sales promotion January 15.
"I/We" View	I'm asking all employees to respond to the attached survey regarding working conditions.
"You " View	Because your ideas count, please complete the attached survey regarding working conditions.

To see if you're really concentrating on the reader, try using the "empathy index." In one of your messages, count all the second-person *you* references. Then, count all the first-person references. Your empathy index is low if the *I*'s and *we*'s outnumber the *you*'s and *your*'s.

But the use of *you* is more than merely a numbers game. Second-person pronouns can be overused and misused. Readers appreciate genuine interest; on the other hand, they resent obvious attempts at manipulation. Some sales messages, for example, are guilty of overkill when they include *you* dozens of times in a direct mail promotion. Furthermore, the word can sometimes create the wrong impression. Consider this statement: *You cannot return merchandise until you receive written approval. You* appears twice, but the reader feels singled out for criticism. In the following version the message is less personal and more positive: *Customers may return merchandise with written approval.* In short, avoid using *you* for general statements that suggest blame and could cause ill will.

Emphasize *you* but don't eliminate all *I* and *we* statements.

In recognizing the value of the "you" attitude, however, writers do not have to sterilize their writing and totally avoid any first-person pronouns or words that show their feelings. Skilled communicators are able to convey sincerity, warmth, and enthusiasm by the words they choose. Don't be afraid to use phrases such as *I'm happy* or *We're delighted,* if you truly are. When speaking face to face, communicators show sincerity and warmth with nonverbal cues such as a smile and pleasant voice tone. In letters, memos, and e-mail messages, however, only expressive words and phrases can show these feelings. These phrases suggest hidden messages that say to readers and customers "You are important, I hear you, and I'm honestly trying to please you."

Conversational but Professional

Strive for conversational expression, but also remember to be professional.

Most e-mail messages, business letters, memos, and reports replace conversation. Thus, they are most effective when they convey an informal, conversational tone instead of a formal, pretentious tone. But messages should not become so casual that they sound low-level and unprofessional. With the increasing use of e-mail, a major problem has developed. Sloppy, unprofessional expression appears in many e-mail messages. You'll learn more about e-mail in Chapter 5. At this point, though, we urge you to strive for a warm, conversational tone that does not include slang or low-level diction. The following examples should help you distinguish among three levels of diction.

Unprofessional	Conversational	Formal
(Low-level diction)	(Mid-level diction)	(High-level diction)
badmouth	criticize	denigrate
guts	nerve	courage
pecking order	line of command	dominance hierarchy
ticked off	upset	provoked
rat on	inform	betray
rip off	steal	expropriate

Unprofessional	If we just hang in there, we can snag the contract.
Conversational	If we don't get discouraged, we can win the contract.
Formal	If the principals persevere, they can secure the contract.

Your goal is a warm, friendly tone that sounds professional. Talk to the reader with words that are comfortable to you. Avoid long and complex sentences. Use familiar pronouns such *I, we,* and *you* and an occasional contraction, such as *we're* or *I'll.* Stay away from third-person constructions such as *the undersigned, the writer,* and *the affected party.* Also avoid legal terminology and technical words. Your writing will be easier to read and understand if it sounds like the following conversational examples:

Formal	All employees are herewith instructed to return the appropriately designated contracts to the undersigned.
Conversational	Please return your contracts to me.

Chapter 2 Writing for Business Audiences

Formal	Pertaining to your order, we must verify the sizes that your organization requires prior to consignment of your order to our shipper.
Conversational	We'll send your order as soon as we confirm the sizes you need.
Formal	The writer wishes to inform the above-referenced individual that subsequent payments may henceforth be sent to the address cited below.
Conversational	Your payments should now be sent to us in Lakewood.
Formal	To facilitate ratification of this agreement, your negotiators urge that the membership respond in the affirmative.
Conversational	We urge you to approve the agreement by voting yes.

Positive Language

The clarity and tone of a message are considerably improved if you use positive rather than negative language. Positive language generally conveys more information than negative language does. Moreover, positive messages are uplifting and pleasant to read. Positive wording tells what *is* and what *can be done* rather than what *isn't* and what *can't be done.* For example, *Your order cannot be shipped by January 10,* is not nearly as informative as *Your order will be shipped January 20.* Notice in the following examples how you can revise the negative tone to reflect a more positive impression.

Positive language creates goodwill and gives more options to receivers.

Negative	We are unable to send your shipment until we receive proof of your payment.
Positive	We look forward to sending your shipment as soon as we receive your payment.
Negative	We are sorry that we must reject your application for credit at this time.
Positive	At this time we can serve you on a cash basis only.
Negative	You will never regret opening a charge account with us.
Positive	Your new charge account enables you to purchase executive suits at reasonable prices.
Negative	If you fail to pass the exam, you will not qualify.
Positive	You'll qualify if you pass the exam.
Negative	Although I've never had a paid position before, I have worked as an intern in an attorney's office while completing my degree requirements.
Positive	My experience in an attorney's office and my recent training in legal procedures and computer applications can be assets to your organization.

Inclusive Language

A business writer who is alert and empathic will strive to use words that include rather than exclude people. Some words have been called *sexist* because they seem to exclude females. Notice the use of the masculine pronouns *he* and *his* in the following sentences:

Sensitive communicators avoid language that excludes people.

If a physician is needed, *he* will be called.
Every homeowner must read *his* insurance policy carefully.

These sentences illustrate an age-old grammatical rule called "common gender." When a speaker or writer did not know the gender (sex) of an individual, masculine pronouns (such as *he* or *his*) were used. Masculine pronouns were understood to indicate both men and women. Today, however, sensitive writers and speakers replace common-gender pronouns with alternate inclusive constructions. You can use any of four alternatives.

Sexist   Every attorney has ten minutes for *his* summation.

Alternative 1   All *attorneys* have ten minutes for *their* summations. (Use a plural noun and plural pronoun.)

Alternative 2   Attorneys have ten minutes for summations. (Omit the pronoun entirely.)

Alternative 3   Every attorney has ten minutes for *a* summation. (Use an article instead of a pronoun.)

Alternative 4   Every attorney has ten minutes for *his* or *her* summation. (Use both a masculine and a feminine pronoun.)

Note that the last alternative, which includes a masculine and a feminine pronoun, is wordy and awkward. Don't use it too frequently.

Other words are considered sexist because they suggest stereotypes. For example, the nouns *fireman* and *mailman* suggest that only men hold these positions. You can avoid offending your listener or reader by using neutral job titles or functions. Consider the following: *firefighter, letter carrier, salesperson, flight attendant, department head, committee chair, technician,* and *police officer.*

DILBERT   By Scott Adams

Plain Language

Inflated, unnatural writing that is intended to impress readers often confuses them.

Business communicators who are conscious of their audience try to use plain language that expresses clear meaning. They do not use showy words and ambiguous expressions in an effort to dazzle or confuse readers. They write to express ideas, not to impress others.

Some business, legal, and government documents are written in an inflated style that obscures meaning. This style of writing has been given various terms, such as *legalese, federalese, bureaucratese, doublespeak,* and the *official style.* It may be used intentionally to mask meaning. It may be an attempt to show off the writer's intelligence and education. Or it may result from lack of training. What do you think the manager's intention is in the following message?

> Personnel assigned vehicular space in the adjacent areas are hereby advised that utilization will be suspended temporarily Friday morning.

Employees will probably have to read that sentence several times before they understand that they are being advised not to park in the lot next door on Friday morning.

Legal documents, contracts, and government forms often suffer from this same ambiguous style. But the U.S. government wants this to change. At a well-publicized press conference, President Bill Clinton and Vice President Al Gore announced plans to require the use of plain language in government regulations.[6] This means a clear, simple style that uses everyday words. But the plain English movement goes beyond word choice. It also means writing that is easy to follow and organized into segments with appropriate headings. You are currently learning to apply many of the plain English movement recommendations, such as using familiar words, concise expression, active-voice verbs, and headings.

The important thing to remember is not to be impressed by high-sounding language and legalese, such as *herein, thereafter, hereinafter, whereas,* and similar expressions. Your writing will be better understood if you use plain language.

Familiar Words

Clear messages contain words that are familiar and meaningful to the receiver. How can we know what is meaningful to a given receiver? Although we can't know with certainty, we can avoid long or unfamiliar words that have simpler synonyms. Whenever possible in business communication, substitute short, common, simple words. Don't, however, give up a precise word if it says exactly what you mean.

Familiar words are more meaningful to readers and listeners.

Less Familiar Words	Simple Alternatives	Less Familiar Words	Simple Alternatives
ascertain	find out	perpetuate	continue
conceptualize	see	perplexing	troubling
encompass	include	reciprocate	return
hypothesize	guess	stipulate	require
monitor	check	terminate	end
operational	working	utilize	use
option	choice		

Technology Improves Your Business Writing

Thus far, we've concentrated on the basics of business writing, especially the prewriting phase of analyzing, anticipating, and adapting to the intended audience. Another basic for beginning business communicators is learning to use technology to enhance their writing efforts. Although computers and software programs cannot actually do the writing for you, they provide powerful tools that make the entire process easier and the results more professional. Here are seven ways your computer can help you improve written documents, oral presentations, and even Web pages.

Powerful writing tools can help you fight writer's block, collect information, outline and organize ideas, improve correctness and precision, add graphics, and design professional-looking documents.

1. **Fighting writer's block.** Because word processors enable ideas to flow almost effortlessly from your brain to a screen, you can expect fewer delays resulting from writer's block. You can compose rapidly, and you can experiment with structure and phrasing, later retaining and polishing your most promising thoughts. Many authors "sprint write," recording unedited ideas quickly, to start the composition process and also to brainstorm for ideas on a project. Then, they tag important ideas and use computer outlining programs to organize those ideas into logical sequences.

2. **Collecting information electronically.** Much of the world's information is now accessible by computer. You can locate many full-text articles from magazines, newspapers, and government publications. Massive amounts of information are available from the Internet, CD-ROMs, and on-line services. Through specialized information-retrieval services (such as ABI-INFORM or ProQuest), you can have at your fingertips up-to-the-minute business, legal, scientific, and scholarly information.

3. **Outlining and organizing ideas.** Most high-end word processors include some form of "outliner," a feature that enables you to divide a topic into a hierarchical order with main points and subpoints. Your computer keeps track of the levels of ideas automatically so that you can easily add, cut, or rearrange points in the outline. This feature is particularly handy when you're preparing a report or organizing a presentation. Some programs even enable you to transfer your outline directly to slide frames to be used as visual aids in a talk.

DILBERT   By Scott Adams

4. **Improving correctness and precision.** Nearly all word processing programs today provide features that catch and correct spelling and typographical errors. Poor spellers and weak typists universally bless their spell checkers for repeatedly saving them from humiliation. Most high-end word processing programs today also provide grammar checkers that are markedly improved over earlier versions. They now detect many errors in capitalization, word use (such as *it's, its*), double negatives, verb use, subject-verb agreement, sentence structure, number agreement, number style, and other writing faults. However, most grammar programs don't actually correct the errors they detect. You must know how to do that.

5. **Adding graphics for emphasis.** Your letters, memos, and reports may be improved by the addition of graphs and artwork to clarify and illustrate data. You can import charts, diagrams, and illustrations created in database, spread-

sheet, graphics, or draw-and-paint programs. Moreover, ready-made pictures, called clip art, can be used to symbolize or illustrate ideas.

6. **Designing and producing professional-looking documents, presentations, and Web pages.** Most high-end word processing programs today include a large selection of scalable fonts (for different character sizes and styles), italics, boldface, symbols, and styling techniques to aid you in producing consistent formatting and professional-looking results. Moreover, today's presentation software enables you to incorporate showy slide effects, color, sound, pictures, and even movies into your talks for management or customers. Web document builders also help you design and construct Web pages.

7. **Using collaborative software for team writing.** As part of today's team-based work environment, you can expect to work with others on projects. Special word processing programs with commenting and strikeout features allow you to revise easily and to identify each team member's editing. These collaborative programs, called groupware, also include decision-support tools to help groups generate, organize, and analyze ideas more efficiently than they could in traditional meetings.

Summing Up and Looking Forward

In this chapter you learned that good business writing is audience centered, purposeful, and economical. To achieve these results, business communicators typically follow a systematic writing process. This process includes three phases: prewriting, writing, and revising. In the prewriting phase, communicators analyze the task and the audience. They select an appropriate channel to deliver the message, and they consider ways to adapt their message to the task and the audience. Effective techniques include spotlighting audience benefits, cultivating the "you" view, striving to use conversational language, and expressing ideas positively. Good communicators also use inclusive language, plain expressions, and familiar words. Today's computer software provides wonderful assistance for business communicators. Technological tools help you fight writer's block, collect information, outline and organize ideas, improve correctness and precision, add graphics, design professional-looking documents and presentations, and collaborate on team writing projects.

The next chapter continues to examine the writing process. It presents additional techniques to help you become a better writer. You'll learn how to eliminate repetitious and redundant wording, as well as how to avoid wordy prepositional phrases, long lead-ins, needless adverbs, and misplaced modifiers. You'll also take a closer look at spell checkers and grammar checkers.

Critical Thinking

1. As a business communicator, you are encouraged to profile or "visualize" the audience for your messages. How is this possible if you don't really know the people who will receive a sales letter or who will hear your business presentation?

2. If adapting your tone to the receiving audience and developing reader benefits are so important, why do we see so much writing that fails to reflect these suggestions?

3. Discuss the following statement: "The English language is a landmine—it is filled with terms that are easily misinterpreted as derogatory and others that are blatantly insulting. . . . Being fair and objective is not enough; employers must also appear to be so."

4. Why is writing in a natural, conversational tone difficult for many people?

5. If computer software is increasingly able to detect writing errors, can business communicators stop studying writing techniques? Why?

Chapter Review

6. Name three ways in which business writing differs from other writing.

7. List the three phases of the writing process and summarize what happens in each phase. Which phase requires the most time?

8. What five factors are important in selecting an appropriate channel to deliver a message?

9. How does profiling the audience help a business communicator prepare a message?

10. What is meant by *audience benefit*? Give an original example.

11. List three specific techniques for developing a warm, friendly, and conversational tone in business messages.

12. Why does positive language usually tell more than negative language? Give an original example.

Chapter 2 Writing for Business Audiences

13. List five examples of sexist pronouns and nouns.

14. What does *plain language* mean in relation to the president's announced plans requiring the use of plain language in government regulations?

15. Name seven ways your computer can help you improve written documents.

Writing Improvement Exercises

Selecting Communication Channels. Using Figure 2.2, suggest the best communication channels for the following messages. Assume that all channels shown are available. Be prepared to explain your choices.

16. As department manager, you wish to inform four department members of a training session scheduled for three weeks from now.

17. As assistant to the vice president, you are to investigate the possibility of developing internship programs with several nearby colleges and universities.

18. You wish to send price quotes for a number of your products in response to a request from a potential customer in Taiwan.

19. You must respond to a notice from the Internal Revenue Service insisting that you did not pay the correct amount for last quarter's employer's taxes.

20. As a manager, you must inform an employee that continued tardiness is jeopardizing her job.

21. Members of your task force must meet to discuss ways to improve communication among 5,000 employees at 32 branches of your large company. Task force members are from Los Angeles, Orlando, San Antonio, White Plains, and Columbus (Ohio).

22. You need to know whether Paula in Printing can produce a special pamphlet for you within two days.

Audience Benefits and the "You" View. Revise the following sentences to emphasize the perspective of the audience and the "you" view.

23. To prevent us from possibly losing large sums of money, our bank now requires verification of any large check presented for immediate payment.

24. We take pride in announcing a new schedule of low-cost flights to Hawaii.

25. So that we may bring our customer records up to date and eliminate the expense of duplicate mailings, we are asking you to complete the enclosed card.

26. For just $300 per person, we have arranged a three-day trip to Las Vegas that includes deluxe accommodations, the "City Lights" show, and selected meals.

27. I give my permission for you to attend the two-day workshop.

28. We're requesting all employees to complete the enclosed questionnaire so that we may develop a master schedule for summer vacations.

29. I think my background and my education match the description of the manager trainee position you advertised.

30. We are offering an in-house training program for employees who want to improve their writing skills.

31. We are pleased to announce an arrangement with Compaq that allows us to offer discounted computers in the student bookstore.

Chapter 2 Writing for Business Audiences

32. We have approved your application for credit, and the account may be used immediately.

33. We are pleased to announce that we have selected you to join our trainee program.

34. Our safety policy forbids us from renting power equipment to anyone who cannot demonstrate proficiency in its use.

35. We will reimburse you for all travel expenses.

36. To enable us to continue our policy of selling name brands at discount prices, we cannot give cash refunds on returned merchandise.

Conversational, Professional Tone. Revise the following sentences to make the tone conversational yet professional.

Example: As per your recent request, the undersigned is happy to inform you that we are sending you forthwith the brochures you requested.
Revision: I'm happy to send you the brochures you requested.

37. Kindly inform the undersigned whether or not your representative will be making a visitation in the near future.

38. Pursuant to your letter of the 12th, please be advised that your shipment was sent 9 June 2000.

39. She was pretty ticked off because the manager accused her of ripping off office supplies.

40. Kindly be informed that your vehicle has been determined to require corrective work.

41. He didn't have the guts to badmouth her to her face.

42. The undersigned respectfully reminds affected individuals that employees desirous of changing their health plans must do so before December 30.

Positive Expression. Revise the following statements to make them more positive.

43. If you fail to pass the examination, you will not qualify.

44. In the message you left at our Web site, you claim that you returned a defective head-set.

45. We can't process your application because you neglected to insert your social security number.

46. Construction cannot begin until the building plans are approved.

47. It is impossible to move forward without community support.

48. Customers are ineligible for the 10 percent discount unless they show their membership cards.

49. Titan Insurance Company will not process any claim not accompanied by documented proof from a physician showing that the injuries were treated.

Inclusive Language. Revise the following sentences to eliminate terms that are considered sexist or that suggest stereotypes.

50. Any applicant for the position of fireman must submit a medical report signed by his physician.

51. Every employee is entitled to see his personnel file.

52. All conference participants and their wives are invited to the banquet.

53. At most hospitals in the area, a nurse must provide her own uniform.

54. Representing the community are a businessman, a lady attorney, and a female doctor.

55. A salesman would have to use all his skills to sell those condos.

56. Every doctor is provided with a parking place for his car.

Plain Language and Familiar Words. Revise the following sentences to use plain expression and familiar words.

57. Profits are declining because our sales staff is not cognizant of our competitor's products.

58. He hypothesized that the vehicle was not operational because of a malfunctioning gasket.

59. Because we cannot monitor all cash payments, we must terminate the contract.

60. The contract stipulates that management must perpetuate the retirement plan.

Plain, Positive Language. The following excerpt is from a Veterans Benefits Administration letter. Can you make it understandable? (*Evidence,* by the way, means "documents.")

61. If your evidence is not received before June 18, 2000, which is one year from the date of our first letter, your claim, if entitlement is established, cannot be processed before the date of the receipt of the evidence.

Grammar/Mechanics Checkup—2

Pronouns

Review Sections 1.07–1.09 in the Grammar Review section of the Grammar/ Mechanics Handbook. Then study each of the following statements. In the space provided, write the word that completes the statement correctly and the number of the G/M principle illustrated. When you finish, compare your responses with those provided on pages 486–487. If your responses differ, study carefully the principles in parentheses.

Example: The Recreation and Benefits Committee will be submitting (*its, their*)   <u>its</u>   **(1.09d)**
report soon.

1. I was expecting the manager to call. Was it (*he, him*) who left the message?   _____
2. Every one of the members of the men's soccer team had to move (*his car,*   _____
   their cars) before the game could begin.
3. A serious disagreement between management and (*he, him*) caused his res-   _____
   ignation.
4. Does anyone in the office know for (*who, whom*) this stationery was ordered?   _____
5. It looks as if (*her's, hers*) is the only report that cites electronic sources.   _____
6. Mrs. Simmons asked my friend and (*I, me, myself*) to help her complete the   _____
   work.
7. My friend and (*I, me, myself*) were also asked to work on Saturday.   _____
8. Both printers were sent for repairs, but (*yours, your's*) will be returned shortly.   _____
9. Give the budget figures to (*whoever, whomever*) asked for them.   _____
10. Everyone except the broker and (*I, me, myself*) claimed a share of the com-   _____
    mission.
11. No one knows that problem better than (*he, him, himself*).   _____
12. Investment brochures and information were sent to (*we, us*) shareholders.   _____
13. If any one of the women tourists has lost (*their, her*) scarf, she should see the   _____
    driver.
14. Neither the glamour nor the excitement of the position had lost (*its, it's, their*)   _____
    appeal.
15. Any new subscriber may cancel (*their, his or her*) subscription within the first   _____
    month.

The following sentences contain errors in grammar, punctuation, capitalization, number style, usage, and spelling. Below each sentence write a corrected version.

1. In the evening, each of the female nurses are escorted to their car.

2. It must have been him who received the highest score although its hard to understand how he did it.

3. The Manager asked Hilary and I to fill in for him for 4 hours on Saturday morning.

4. Working out at the Gym and jogging twenty miles a week is how she stays fit.

5. 3 types of costs must be considered for proper inventory controll, holding costs, ordering costs, and stocking costs.

6. If I was him I would fill out the questionaire immediately so that I would qualify for the drawing.

7. Higher engine revolutions per mile mean better acceleration, however lower revolutions mean better fuel economy.

8. Our teams day to day operations include: setting goals, improvement of customer service, manufacturing quality products and hitting sales targets.

9. If I had saw the shippers bill I would have payed it immediately.

10. Salary, hours, and benefits, these are 3 items about which most all job candidates ask.

11. Do you think it was him who left the package on the boss desk.

12.	About 1/2 of Pizza Huts six thousand outlets makes deliverys, the others concentrates on walk in customers.

13.	Every thing accept labor is covered in this 5 year warranty.

14.	Our Director of Human Resources felt nevertheless that the applicant should be given a interview.

15.	When Keisha completes her degree she plans to apply for employment in: Seattle, Dallas, or Atlanta.

Grammar/Mechanics Challenge—2

The e-mail message on the next page has many faults in grammar, spelling, punctuation, capitalization, word use, and number form. Pay attention to developing a conversational but professional tone, using familiar words, and striving for positive expression. Use standard proofreading marks (see Appendix B) to correct the errors. When you finish, your instructor can show you the revised version of this e-mail.

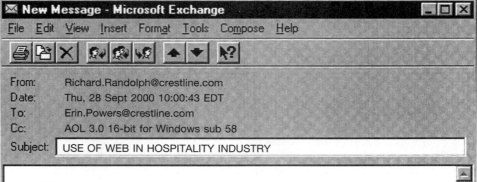

New Message - Microsoft Exchange

File Edit View Insert Format Tools Compose Help

From: Richard.Randolph@crestline.com
Date: Thu, 28 Sept 2000 10:00:43 EDT
To: Erin.Powers@crestline.com
Cc: AOL 3.0 16-bit for Windows sub 58
Subject: USE OF WEB IN HOSPITALITY INDUSTRY

Dear Erin:

Pertaining to your request I finalized some research on the utilization of the Web in hospitality operations. Perhaps the most extrordinary things that I learned are that the internet is considered the major driver of change in the lodging industry! Its allready changing the way we offer services, reshaping organizational structures and altaring the relationships between our guests and us.

In a survey of two thousand mangers the Hospitality information technology association uncovered some really weird findings. Hereinafter is a quick rundown of the survey results.

- Internet service is rapidly becoming the most sought-after amenity in Hotel Rooms.

- Two thirds of the respondents worked at propertys that had Web cites.

- A large majority said that a outside party had created there Web site.

- The average cost for creating a Web site was estimated at two thousand dollars and the cost of maintinance is two hundred and fifty dollars a month (requiring five man hours).

- 56% of the respondents said that there guests could make reservations using their Web site.

If we fail to develop our own Web cite, in my opinion I don't see how we can hope to compete in the rapidly-changing hospitality industry. Please advice me if you want me to begin preliminary plans for developing such a site.

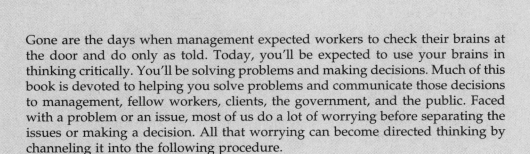

Sharpening Your Skills for Critical Thinking, Problem Solving, and Decision Making

Gone are the days when management expected workers to check their brains at the door and do only as told. Today, you'll be expected to use your brains in thinking critically. You'll be solving problems and making decisions. Much of this book is devoted to helping you solve problems and communicate those decisions to management, fellow workers, clients, the government, and the public. Faced with a problem or an issue, most of us do a lot of worrying before separating the issues or making a decision. All that worrying can become directed thinking by channeling it into the following procedure.

1. Identify and clarify the problem. Your first task is to recognize that a problem exists. Some problems are big and unmistakable, such as failure of an airfreight delivery service to get packages to customers on time. Other problems may be continuing annoyances, such as regularly running out of toner for an office copy machine. The first step in reaching a solution is pinpointing the problem area.

2. Gather information. Learn more about the problem situation. Look for possible causes and solutions. This step may mean checking files, calling suppliers, or brainstorming with fellow workers. For example, the air-freight delivery service would investigate the tracking systems of the commercial airlines carrying its packages to determine what is going wrong.

3. Evaluate the evidence. Where did the information come from? Does it represent various points of view? What biases could be expected from each source? How accurate is the information gathered? Is it fact or opinion? For example, it is a fact that packages are missing; it is an opinion that they are merely lost and will turn up eventually.

4. Consider alternatives and implications. Draw conclusions from the gathered evidence and pose solutions. Then weigh the advantages and disadvantages of each alternative. What are the costs, benefits, and consequences? What are the obstacles, and how can they be handled? Most important, what solution best serves your goals and those of your organization? Here's where your creativity is especially important.

5. Choose and implement the best alternative. Select an alternative and put it into action. Then, follow through on your decision by monitoring the results of implementing your plan. The freight company decided to give its unhappy customers free delivery service to make up for the lost packages and downtime. Be sure to continue monitoring and adjusting the solution to ensure its effectiveness over time.

Career Application

Let's return to the McDonald's problem (discussed on page 31) in which some franchise owners are unhappy with the multiple lines for service. Customers don't seem to know where to stand to be next served. Tempers flare when aggressive customers cut in line, and other customers spend so much time protecting their places in line that they fail to study the menu. Then they don't know what to order when they approach the counter. As a franchise owner, you would like to find a solution to this problem. Any changes in procedures, however, must be approved by all the McDonald's owners in a district. That means you'll have to get a majority to agree. You know that McDonald's management feels that the multiline system accommodates higher volumes of customers more quickly than a single-line system. Moreover, the problem of perception is important. What happens when customers open the door to a restaurant and see a long, single line? Do they stick around to learn how fast the line is moving?

Your Task

- Individually or with a team, use the critical thinking steps outlined here. Begin by clarifying the problem.
- Where could you gather information to help you solve this problem? Would it be wise to see what your competitors are doing? How do banks handle customer lines? Airlines? Sports events?
- Evaluate your findings and consider alternatives. What are the pros and cons of each alternative?
- Choose the best alternative. Present your recommendation to your class and give your reasons for choosing it.

Web

Related Web Site: Visit the McDonald's Web site <www.mcdonalds.com> to learn its policy toward listening to its franchisees. Do the opinions of franchisees really count?

> **Note to Students:**
> Check the Guffey Web site for updated EBC URLs (Web addresses).

3 Improving Writing Techniques

Be natural—write the way you talk. Business jargon too often is cold, stiff, unnatural. Don't put on airs. Pretense invariably impresses only the pretender.[1]

MALCOLM FORBES, *former president and editor in chief of* Forbes *magazine*

LEARNING OBJECTIVES

1. Contrast formal and informal methods of researching data and generating ideas for messages.
2. Specify how to organize information into outlines.
3. Compare direct and indirect patterns for organizing ideas.
4. Distinguish components of complete and effective sentences.
5. Emphasize important ideas and deemphasize unimportant ones.
6. Use active voice, passive voice, and parallelism effectively in messages.
7. Develop sentence unity by avoiding zigzag writing, mixed constructions, and misplaced modifiers.
8. Identify strategies for achieving paragraph coherence and composing the first draft of a message.

Writing naturally, as Malcolm Forbes advises, sounds easy. But it's not. It takes instruction and practice. You've already learned some techniques for writing naturally (using a conversational tone, positive language, plain expression, and familiar words). This chapter presents additional writing tips that make your communication not only natural but also effective.

Figure 3.1 reviews the entire writing process. In Chapter 2 we focused on the prewriting stage. This chapter addresses the second stage, which includes researching, organizing, and composing.

Researching

No smart businessperson would begin writing a message before collecting the needed information. We call this collection process *research*, a rather formal sounding term. For simple documents, though, the process can be quite informal. Research is necessary before beginning to write because the information you collect

FIGURE 3.1 The Writing Process

helps shape the message. Discovering significant data after a message is completed often means starting over and reorganizing. To avoid frustration and inaccurate messages, collect information that answers this primary question:

* What does the receiver need to know about this topic?

When the message involves action, search for answers to secondary questions:

* What is the receiver to do?
* How is the receiver to do it?
* When must the receiver do it?
* What will happen if the receiver doesn't do it?

Whenever your communication problem requires more information than you have in your head or at your fingertips, you must conduct research. This research may be formal or informal.

The second stage of the writing process involves research, which means collecting the necessary information to prepare a message.

Formal Research Methods

Long reports and complex business problems generally require some use of formal research methods. Let's say you are a market specialist for Coca-Cola, and your boss asks you to evaluate the impact on Coke sales of private-label or generic soft drinks (the bargain-basement-brand knockoffs sold at Kmart and other outlets). Or, let's assume you must write a term paper for a college class. Both tasks require more data than you have in your head or at your fingertips. To conduct formal research, you could:

Formal research may include searching libraries and electronic databases or investigating primary sources.

* **Search manually.** You'll find helpful background and supplementary information through manual searching of resources in public and college libraries. These traditional sources include books and newspaper, magazine, and journal articles. Other sources are encyclopedias, reference books, handbooks, dictionaries, directories, and almanacs.
* **Access electronically.** Much of the printed material just described is now available from the Internet, databases, or compact discs that can be accessed by computer. College and public libraries subscribe to retrieval services that permit you to access most periodic literature. You can also find extraordinary amounts of information by searching the Web. You'll learn more about using electronic sources in Chapters 10 and 11.
* **Go to the source.** For firsthand information, go directly to the source. For the Coca-Cola report, for example, you could find out what consumers really think by conducting interviews or surveys, by putting together questionnaires, or by organizing focus groups. Formal research includes structured sampling and controls that enable investigators to make accurate judgments and valid predictions.
* **Conduct scientific experiments.** Instead of merely asking for the target audience's opinion, scientific researchers present choices with controlled variables.

Good sources of primary information are interviews, surveys, questionnaires, and focus groups.

Let's say, for example, that Coca-Cola wants to determine at what price and under what circumstances consumers would switch from Coca-Cola to a generic brand. The results of such experimentation would provide valuable data for managerial decision making.

Because formal research techniques are particularly necessary for reports, you'll study resources and techniques more extensively in Chapters 10 and 11.

Informal Research and Idea Generation

Most routine tasks—such as composing e-mail messages, memos, letters, informational reports, and oral presentations—require data that you can collect informally. Here are some techniques for collecting informal data and for generating ideas:

- **Look in the files.** If you are responding to an inquiry, you often can find the answer to the inquiry by investigating the company files or by consulting colleagues.
- **Talk with your boss.** Get information from the individual making the assignment. What does that person know about the topic? What slant should be taken? What other sources would he or she suggest?
- **Interview the target audience.** Consider talking with individuals at whom the message is aimed. They can provide clarifying information that tells you what they want to know and how you should shape your remarks.
- **Conduct an informal survey.** Gather unscientific but helpful information via questionnaires or telephone surveys. In preparing a memo report predicting the success of a proposed fitness center, for example, circulate a questionnaire asking for employee reactions.
- **Brainstorm for ideas.** Alone or with others, discuss ideas for the writing task at hand, and record at least a dozen ideas without judging them. Small groups are especially fruitful in brainstorming because people spin ideas off one another.

Organizing Data

Once you've collected data, you must find some way to organize it. Organizing includes two processes: grouping and patterning. Well-organized messages group similar items together; ideas follow a sequence that helps the reader understand relationships and accept the writer's views. Unorganized messages proceed free-form, jumping from one thought to another. Such messages fail to emphasize important points. Puzzled readers can't see how the pieces fit together, and they become frustrated and irritated. Many communication experts regard poor organization as the greatest failing of business writers. Two simple techniques can help you organize data: the scratch list and the outline.

Outlining

Two simple ways to organize data are the scratch list and the outline.

In developing simple messages, some writers make a quick scratch list of the topics they wish to cover. They then compose a message at their computers directly from the scratch list.

Most writers, though, need to organize their ideas—especially if the project is complex—into a hierarchy, such as an outline. The beauty of preparing an outline is that it gives you a chance to organize your thinking before you get bogged down in word choice and sentence structure. Figure 3.2 shows a format for an outline.

FIGURE 3.2 Format for an Outline

          Title: Major Idea or Purpose
I.   First major component
     A.   First subpoint
          1.   Detail, illustration, evidence
          2.   Detail, illustration, evidence
     B.   Second subpoint
          1.
          2.
II. Second major component
     A.   First subpoint
          1.
          2.
     B.   Second subpoint
          1.
          2.

Tips for Making Outlines

• Define the main topic in the title.
• Divide the topic into main points, preferably three to five.
• Break the components into subpoints.
• Don't put a single item under a major component if you have only one subpoint; integrate it with the main item above it or reorganize.
• Strive to make each component exclusive (no overlapping).
• Use details, illustrations, and evidence to support subpoints.

The Direct Pattern

After preparing an outline, you will need to decide where in the message you will place the main idea. Placing the main idea at the beginning of the message is called the *direct pattern*. In the direct pattern the main idea comes first, followed by details, explanation, or evidence. Placing the main idea later in the message (after the details, explanation, or evidence) is called the *indirect pattern*. The pattern you select is determined by how you expect the audience to react to the message, as shown in Figure 3.3.

In preparing to write any message, you need to anticipate the audience's reaction to your ideas and frame your message accordingly. When you expect the reader to be pleased, mildly interested, or, at worst, neutral—use the direct pat-

Business messages typically follow either the (1) direct pattern, with the main idea first, or (2) the indirect pattern, with the main idea following explanation and evidence.

FIGURE 3.3 Audience Response Determines Pattern of Organization

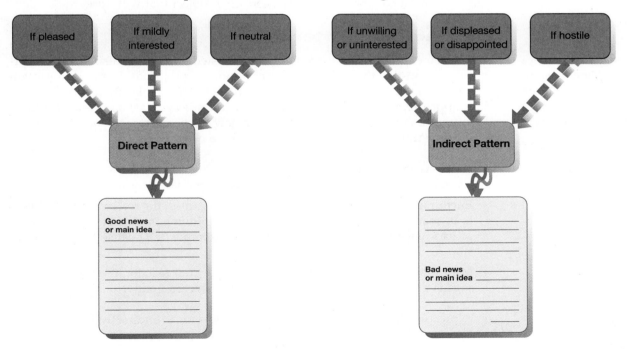

tern. That is, put your main point—the purpose of your message—in the first or second sentence. Compare the direct and indirect patterns in the following memo openings. Notice how long it takes to get to the main idea in the indirect opening.

Indirect Opening
Our company seeks to attract better-qualified job candidates. For this reason, the Management Council has been gathering information about an internship program for college students. After investigation, we voted to begin a pilot program next fall.

Direct Opening
The Management Council voted to begin a college internship pilot program next fall.

Frontloading saves the reader's time, establishes the proper frame of mind, and prevents frustration.

Explanations and details should follow the direct opening. What's important is getting to the main idea quickly. This direct method, also called *frontloading*, has at least three advantages:

- **Saves the reader's time.** Many of today's businesspeople can devote only a few moments to each message. Messages that take too long to get to the point may lose their readers along the way.
- **Sets a proper frame of mind.** Learning the purpose up front helps the reader put the subsequent details and explanations in perspective. Without a clear opening, the reader may be thinking, *Why am I being told this?*
- **Prevents frustration.** Readers forced to struggle through excessive verbiage before reaching the main idea become frustrated. They resent the writer. Poorly organized messages create a negative impression of the writer.

The direct pattern works best with audiences that are likely to be receptive.

This frontloading technique works best with audiences that are likely to be receptive to or at least not likely to disagree with what you have to say. Typical business messages that follow the direct pattern include routine requests and responses, orders and acknowledgments, nonsensitive memos, e-mail messages, informational reports, and informational oral presentations. All these tasks have one element in common: none has a sensitive subject that will upset the reader.

The Indirect Pattern

The indirect pattern works best when the audience may be uninterested, unwilling, displeased, or even hostile.

When you expect the audience to be uninterested, unwilling, displeased, or perhaps even hostile, the indirect pattern is more appropriate. In this pattern you don't reveal the main idea until after you have offered explanation and evidence. This approach works well with three kinds of messages: (1) bad news, (2) ideas that require persuasion, and (3) sensitive news, especially when being transmitted to superiors. The indirect pattern has these benefits:

- **Respects the feelings of the audience.** Bad news is always painful, but the trauma can be lessened when the receiver is prepared for it.
- **Encourages a fair hearing.** Messages that may upset the reader are more likely to be read when the main idea is delayed. Beginning immediately with a piece of bad news or a persuasive request, for example, may cause the receiver to stop reading or listening.
- **Minimizes a negative reaction.** A reader's overall reaction to a negative message is generally improved if the news is delivered gently.

Typical business messages that could be developed indirectly include letters and memos that refuse requests, deny claims, and disapprove credit. Persuasive requests, sales letters, sensitive messages, and some reports and oral presentations also benefit from the indirect strategy. You'll learn more about how to use the indirect pattern in Chapters 7 and 8.

In summary, business messages may be organized directly, with the main idea first, or indirectly, with the main idea delayed. Although these two patterns cover many communication problems, they should be considered neither universal nor inviolate. Every business transaction is distinct. Some messages are mixed: part good news, part bad; part goodwill, part persuasion. In upcoming chapters you'll practice applying the direct and indirect patterns in typical situations. Then, you'll have the skills and confidence to evaluate communication problems and vary these patterns depending on the goals you wish to achieve.

Effective Sentences

After deciding how to organize your message, you are ready to begin composing it. As you create your first draft, you'll be working at the sentence level of composition. Although you've used sentences all your life, you may be unaware of how they can be shaped and arranged to express your ideas most effectively. First, let's review some basic sentence elements.

Complete sentences have subjects and verbs and make sense.

Sentences must have subjects and verbs and must make sense.

SUBJECT VERB   SUBJECT   VERB
This report is clear and concise. Our employees write many reports.

Clauses and phrases, the key building blocks of sentences, are related groups of words. Clauses have subjects and verbs; phrases do not.

Clauses have subjects and verbs, but phrases do not.

PHRASE   PHRASE
The CEO of that organization sent a letter to our staff.

PHRASE   PHRASE
By reading carefully, we learned about the merger.

CLAUSE   CLAUSE
Because she writes well, Tracy answers most customer letters.

CLAUSE   CLAUSE
If you are going away, you should redirect your e-mail messages.

Clauses may be divided into two groups: independent and dependent. Independent clauses are grammatically complete. Dependent clauses depend for their meaning on independent clauses. In the two preceding examples, the clauses beginning with *If* and *Because* are dependent. Dependent clauses are often introduced by words such as *if, when, because,* and *as.*

Independent clauses may stand alone; dependent clauses may not.

INDEPENDENT CLAUSE
Tracy uses simple language.

DEPENDENT CLAUSE   INDEPENDENT CLAUSE
When she writes to customers, Tracy uses simple language.

By learning to distinguish phrases, independent clauses, and dependent clauses, you'll be able to punctuate sentences correctly and avoid three basic sentence faults: the fragment, the run-on sentence, and the comma splice.

Sentence Fragment

Fragments are broken-off parts of sentences and should not be punctuated as sentences.

One of the most serious errors a writer can make is punctuating a fragment as if it were a complete sentence. A fragment is a broken-off part of a sentence.

Fragment	Because most transactions require a permanent record. Good writing skills are critical.
Revision	Because most transactions require a permanent record, good writing skills are critical.
Fragment	The recruiter requested a writing sample. Even though the candidate seemed to communicate well.
Revision	The recruiter requested a writing sample, even though the candidate seemed to communicate well.

Fragments often can be identified by the words that introduce them—words such as *although, as, because, even, except, for example, if, instead of, since, so, such as, that, which,* and *when.* These words introduce dependent clauses. Make sure such clauses always connect to independent clauses.

Run-On (Fused) Sentence

When two independent clauses are run together without punctuation or a coordinating conjunction, a run-on (fused) sentence results.

A sentence with two independent clauses must be joined by a coordinating conjunction (*and, or, nor, but*) or by a semicolon (;). Without a conjunction or a semicolon, a run-on sentence results.

Run-on	Most job seekers present a printed résumé some are also using Web sites as electronic portfolios.
Revision 1	Most job seekers present a printed résumé, but some are also using Web sites as electronic portfolios.
Revision 2	Most job seekers present a printed résumé; some are also using Web sites as electronic portfolios.

Comma-Splice Sentence

When two independent clauses are joined by a comma without a conjunction, a comma splice results.

A comma splice results when a writer joins (splices together) two independent clauses with a comma. Independent clauses may be joined with a coordinating conjunction (*and, or, nor, but*) or a conjunctive adverb (*however, consequently, therefore,* and *others*). Notice that clauses joined by coordinating conjunctions require only a comma. Clauses joined by a coordinating adverb require a semicolon. Here are three ways to rectify a comma splice:

Comma Splice	Some employees responded by e-mail, others picked up the telephone.
Revision 1	Some employees responded by e-mail, and others picked up the telephone.
Revision 2	Some employees responded by e-mail; however, others picked up the telephone.
Revision 3	Some employees responded by e-mail; others picked up the telephone.

Sentence Length

Sentences of 20 or fewer words have the most impact.

Because your goal is to communicate clearly, you're better off limiting your sentences to about 20 or fewer words. The American Press Institute reports that reader comprehension drops off markedly as sentences become longer.[2] Thus, in craft-

Chapter 3 Improving Writing Techniques

ing your sentences, think about the relationship between sentence length and comprehension:

Sentence Length	Comprehension Rate
8 words	100%
15 words	90%
19 words	80%
28 words	50%

Instead of stringing together clauses with *and, but,* and *however,* break some of those complex sentences into separate segments. Business readers want to grasp ideas immediately. They can do that best when thoughts are separated into short sentences. On the other hand, too many monotonous short sentences will sound "grammar schoolish" and may bore or even annoy the reader. Strive for a balance between longer sentences and shorter ones.

Emphasis

When you are talking with someone, you can emphasize your main ideas by saying them loudly or by repeating them slowly. You could even pound the table if you want to show real emphasis! Another way you could signal the relative importance of an idea is by raising your eyebrows or by shaking your head or whispering in a low voice. But when you write, you must rely on other means to tell your readers which ideas are more important than others. Emphasis in writing can be achieved primarily in two ways: mechanically or stylistically.

Emphasis Through Mechanics

To emphasize an idea in print, a writer may use any of the following devices:

Underlining	<u>Underlining</u> draws the eye to a word.
Italics and boldface	Use *italics* or **boldface** for special meaning and emphasis.
Font changes	Changing from a large font to a small font or to a different font adds interest and emphasis.
All caps	Printing words in ALL CAPS is like shouting them.
Dashes	Dashes—if used sparingly—can be effective in capturing attention.
Tabulation	Listing items vertically makes them stand out: 1. First item 2. Second item 3. Third item

You can emphasize an idea mechanically by using underlining, italics, boldface, font changes, all caps, dashes, and tabulation.

Other means of achieving mechanical emphasis include the arrangement of space, color, lines, boxes, columns, titles, headings, and subheadings. Today's software and color printers provide a wonderful array of capabilities for setting off ideas.

Emphasis Through Style

Although mechanical means are occasionally appropriate, more often a writer achieves emphasis stylistically. That is, the writer chooses words carefully and constructs sentences skillfully to emphasize main ideas and deemphasize minor or negative ideas. Here are four suggestions for emphasizing ideas stylistically:

- **Use vivid words.** Vivid words are emphatic because the reader can picture ideas clearly.

You can emphasize ideas stylistically by using vivid words, labeling the main idea, and positioning the main idea strategically.

General	*One business* uses *personal* selling techniques.
Vivid	*Avon* uses *face-to-face* selling techniques.

General	A *customer said* that he wanted the contract returned *soon*.
Vivid	*Mr. Le Clerc* insisted that the contract be returned *by July 1*.

- **Label the main idea.** If an idea is significant, tell the reader.

Unlabeled	Explore the possibility of leasing a site, but also hire a consultant.
Labeled	Explore the possibility of leasing a site; but *most important*, hire a consultant.

- **Place the important idea first or last in the sentence.** Ideas have less competition from surrounding words when they appear first or last in a sentence. Observe how the concept of productivity is emphasized in the first and second examples:

Emphatic	*Productivity* is more likely to be increased when profit-sharing plans are linked to individual performance rather than to group performance.
Emphatic	Profit-sharing plans linked to individual performance rather than to group performance are more effective in increasing *productivity*.
Unemphatic	Profit-sharing plans are more effective in increasing *productivity* when they are linked to individual performance rather than to group performance.

- **Place the important idea in a simple sentence or in an independent clause.** Don't dilute the effect of the idea by making it share the spotlight with other words and clauses.

Emphatic	You are the first trainee that we have hired for this program. (Use a simple sentence for emphasis.)
Emphatic	Although we considered many candidates, you are the first trainee that we have hired for this program. (Independent clause contains main idea.)
Unemphatic	Although you are the first trainee that we have hired for this program, we had many candidates and expect to expand the program in the future. (Main idea is lost in a dependent clause.)

You can deemphasize ideas through word choice and placement.

Deemphasis. To deemphasize an idea, such as bad news, try one of the following stylistic devices:

- **Use general words.**

Vivid	Our records indicate that *you were recently fired*.
General	Our records indicate that *your employment status has changed recently*.

- **Place the bad news in a dependent clause connected to an independent clause with something positive.** In sentences with dependent clauses, the main emphasis is always on the independent clause.

Emphasizes bad news	We cannot issue you credit at this time, but we do have a plan that will allow you to fill your immediate needs on a cash basis.

Deemphasizes bad news   We have a plan that will allow you to fill your immediate needs on a cash basis since we cannot issue credit at this time.

Active and Passive Voice

In sentences with active-voice verbs, the subject is the doer of the action. In passive-voice sentences, the subject is acted upon.

Active-voice sentences are direct and easy to understand.

Active verb   Mr. Johnson *completed* the tax return before the April 15 deadline. (The subject, *Mr. Johnson*, is the doer of the action.)

Passive verb   The tax return *was completed* before the April 15 deadline. (The subject, *tax return*, is acted upon.)

In the first sentence, the active-voice verb emphasizes Mr. Johnson. In the second sentence, the passive-voice verb emphasizes the tax return. In sentences with passive-voice verbs, the doer of the action may be revealed or left unknown. In business writing, as well as in personal interactions, some situations demand tact and sensitivity. Instead of using a direct approach with active verbs, we may prefer the indirectness that passive verbs allow. Rather than making a blunt announcement with an active verb (*Tyler made a major error in the estimate*), we can soften the sentence with a passive construction (*A major error was made in the estimate*).

Here's a summary of the best use of active- and passive-voice verbs:

- **Use the active voice for most business writing.** It clearly tells what the action is and who is performing that action.

- **Use the passive voice to emphasize an action or the recipient of the action.** *You have been selected to represent us.*

- **Use the passive voice to deemphasize negative news.** *Your watch has not been repaired.*

- **Use the passive voice to conceal the doer of an action.** *A major error was made in the estimate.*

Although active-voice verbs are preferred in business writing, passive-voice verbs perform useful functions.

How can you tell if a verb is active or passive? Identify the subject of the sentence and decide whether the subject is doing the acting or being acted upon. For example, in the sentence *An appointment was made for January 1*, the subject is *appointment*. The subject is being acted upon; therefore, the verb (*was made*) is passive. Another clue in identifying passive-voice verbs is that they generally include a *to be* helping verb, such as *is, are, was, were, being,* or *been*.

Parallelism

Parallelism is a skillful writing technique that involves balanced writing. Sentences written so that their parts are balanced or parallel are easy to read and understand. To achieve parallel construction, use similar structures to express similar ideas. For example, the words *computing, coding, recording,* and *storing* are parallel because the words all end in *-ing*. To express the list as *computing, coding, recording,* and *storage* is disturbing because the last item is not what the reader expects. Try to match nouns with nouns, verbs with verbs, and clauses with clauses. Avoid mixing active-voice verbs with passive-voice verbs. Your goal is to keep the wording balanced in expressing similar ideas.

Balanced wording helps the reader anticipate and comprehend your meaning.

Lacks parallelism	The market for industrial goods includes manufacturers, contractors, wholesalers, and *those concerned with the retail function.*
Revision	The market for industrial goods includes manufacturers, contractors, wholesalers, and *retailers.* (Parallel construction matches nouns.)
Lacks parallelism	Our primary goals are to increase productivity, reduce costs, and *the improvement of product quality.*
Revision	Our primary goals are to increase productivity, reduce costs, and *improve product quality.* (Parallel construction matches verbs.)
Lacks parallelism	We are scheduled to meet in Dallas on January 5, *we are meeting in Montreal on the 15th of March,* and in Chicago on June 3.
Revision	We are scheduled to meet in Dallas on January 5, *in Montreal on March 15,* and in Chicago on June 3. (Parallel construction matches phrases.)
Lacks parallelism	Mrs. Horne audits all accounts lettered A through L; *accounts lettered M through Z are audited by Mr. Shapiro.*
Revision	Mrs. Horne audits all accounts lettered A through L; *Mr. Shapiro audits accounts lettered M through Z.* (Parallel construction matches active-voice verbs in balanced clauses.)

All items in a list should be expressed in balanced constructions.

In presenting lists of data, whether shown horizontally or tabulated vertically, be certain to express all the items in parallel form.

Parallelism in vertical list   Three primary objectives of advertising are as follows:
1. Increase the frequency of product use.
2. Introduce complementary products.
3. Enhance the corporate image.

Unity

Unified sentences contain thoughts that are related to only one main idea. The following sentence lacks unity because the first clause has little or no relationship to the second clause:

Unified sentences contain only related ideas.

Lacks unity	Our insurance plan is available in all the states and provinces, and you may name anyone as a beneficiary for your coverage.
Revision	Our insurance plan is available in all the states and provinces. What's more, you may name anyone as a beneficiary for your coverage.

The ideas are better expressed by separating the two dissimilar clauses and by adding a connecting phrase, as shown. Other writing faults that destroy sentence unity are zigzag writing, mixed constructions, and misplaced modifiers.

Zigzag Writing

Sentences that twist or turn unexpectedly away from the main thought are examples of zigzag writing. Such confusing writing may result when too many thoughts are included in one sentence or when one thought does not relate to another. To rectify a zigzag sentence, revise it so that the reader understands the relationship between the thoughts. If that is impossible, move the unrelated thoughts to a new sentence.

Zigzag sentences often should be broken into two sentences.

Zigzag writing	I appreciate the time you spent with me last week, and I have purchased a computer and software that generate graphics.
Revision	I appreciate the time you spent with me last week. As a result of your advice, I have purchased a computer and software that generate graphics.
Zigzag writing	The stockholders of a corporation elect a board of directors, although the chief executive officer is appointed by the board and the CEO is not directly responsible to the stockholders.
Revision	The stockholders of a corporation elect a board of directors, who in turn appoints the chief executive officer. The CEO is not directly responsible to the stockholders.

Mixed Constructions

Writers who fuse two different grammatical constructions destroy sentence unity and meaning.

Mixed constructions confuse readers.

Mixed construction	The reason I am late is *because* my car battery is dead.
Revision	The reason I am late is *that* my car battery is dead. (The construction introduced by *the reason is* should be a noun clause beginning with *that*, not an adverbial clause beginning with *because*.)
Mixed construction	When the stock market index rose five points was our signal to sell.
Revision	When the stock market index rose five points, we were prepared to sell. OR: Our signal to sell was an increase of five points in the stock market index.

Dangling and Misplaced Modifiers

Modifiers must be close to the words they describe or limit.

For clarity, modifiers must be close to the words they describe or limit. A modifier dangles when the word or phrase it describes is missing from its sentence. A modifier is misplaced when the word or phrase it describes is not close enough to be clear. In both instances, the solution is to position the modifier closer to the word(s) it describes or limits. Introductory verbal phrases are particularly dangerous; be sure to follow them immediately with the words they logically describe or modify.

Dangling modifier	To win the lottery, a ticket must be purchased. (The introductory verbal phrase must be followed by a logical subject.)
Revision	To win the lottery, you must purchase a ticket.
Dangling modifier	Driving through Malibu Canyon, the ocean suddenly came into view. (Is the ocean driving through Malibu Canyon?)
Revision	Driving through Malibu Canyon, we saw the ocean suddenly come into view.

Try this trick for detecting and remedying these dangling modifiers. Ask the question *who?* or *what?* after any introductory phrase. The words immediately following should tell the reader *who* or *what* is performing the action. Try the *who?* test on the previous danglers.

Misplaced modifier	Seeing his error too late, the envelope was immediately resealed by Matt (*Did the envelope see the error?*)
Revision	Seeing his error too late, Matt immediately resealed the envelope.
Misplaced modifier	A wart appeared on my left hand that I want removed. (*Is the left hand to be removed?*)
Revision	A wart that I want removed appeared on my left hand.
Misplaced modifier	The busy personnel director interviewed only candidates who had excellent computer skills in the morning. (*Were the candidates skilled only in the morning?*)
Revision	In the morning the busy personnel director interviewed only candidates who had excellent computer skills.

Paragraph Coherence

A paragraph is a group of sentences with a controlling idea, usually stated first. Paragraphs package similar ideas into meaningful groups for readers. Effective paragraphs are coherent; that is, they hold together. But coherence does not happen accidentally. It is achieved through effective organization and (1) repetition of key ideas, (2) use of pronouns, and (3) use of transitional expressions.

Three ways to create paragraph coherence are (1) repetition of key ideas, (2) use of pronouns, and (3) use of transitional expressions.

- **Repetition of key ideas or key words.** Repeating a word or key thought from a preceding sentence helps guide a reader from one thought to the next. This redundancy is necessary to build cohesiveness into writing.

Effective repetition	*Quality* problems in production are often the result of inferior raw materials. Some companies have strong programs for ensuring the *quality* of incoming production materials and supplies.

The second sentence of the preceding paragraph repeats the key idea of *quality.* Moreover, the words *incoming production materials and supplies* refer to *raw materials* mentioned in the preceding sentence. Good writers find similar words to describe the same idea, thus using repetition to clarify a topic for the reader.

- **Use of pronouns.** Pronouns such as *this, that, they, these,* and *those* promote coherence by connecting the thoughts in one sentence to the thoughts in a previous sentence. To make sure that the pronoun reference is clear, consider joining the pronoun with the word to which it refers, thus making the pronoun into an adjective.

Pronouns with clear antecedents can improve coherence.

Pronoun repetition	Xerox has a four-point program to assist suppliers. *This program* includes written specifications for production materials and components.

Be very careful, though, in using pronouns. A pronoun without a clear antecedent can be most annoying. That's because the reader doesn't know precisely to what the pronoun refers.

Faulty	When company profits increased, employees were given either a cash payment or company stock. *This* became a real incentive to employees.
Revision	When company profits increased, employees were given either a cash payment or company stock. *This profit-sharing plan* became a real incentive to employees.

- **Use of transitional expressions.** One of the most effective ways to achieve paragraph coherence is through the use of transitional expressions. These expressions act as road signs: they indicate where the message is headed, and they help the reader anticipate what is coming. Here are some of the most effective transitional expressions. They are grouped according to uses.

Transitional expressions build paragraph coherence.

Time Association	Contrast	Illustration
before, after	although	for example
first, second	but	in this way
meanwhile	however	
next	instead	
until	nevertheless	
when, whenever	on the other hand	

Cause, Effect	Additional Idea
consequently	furthermore
for this reason	in addition
hence	likewise
therefore	moreover

Paragraph Length

Although no rule regulates the length of paragraphs, business writers recognize the value of short paragraphs. Paragraphs with eight or fewer printed lines look inviting and readable. Long, solid chunks of print appear formidable. If a topic can't be covered in eight or fewer printed lines (not sentences), consider breaking it into smaller segments.

The most readable paragraphs contain eight or fewer printed lines.

Composing the First Draft

Create a quiet place in which to write.

Once you've researched your topic, organized the data, and selected a pattern of organization, you're ready to begin composing. Communicators who haven't completed the preparatory work often suffer from "writer's block" and sit staring at a piece of paper or at the computer screen. It's easier to get started if you have organized your ideas and established a plan. Composition is also easier if you have a quiet environment in which to concentrate. Businesspeople with messages to compose set aside a given time and allow no calls, visitors, or other interruptions. This is a good technique for students as well.

As you begin composing, keep in mind that you are writing the first draft, not the final copy. Experts suggest that you write quickly (*sprint writing*). Get your thoughts down now and refine them in later versions.[3] As you take up each idea, imagine that you are talking to the reader. Don't let yourself get bogged down. If you can't think of the right word, insert a substitute or type "find perfect word later."[4] Sprint writing works especially well for those composing on a computer because it's simple to make changes at any point of the composition process. If you are handwriting the first draft, double-space so that you have room for changes.

Summing Up and Looking Forward

This chapter explained the second phase of the writing process including researching, organizing, and composing. Before beginning a message, every writer collects data, either formally or informally. For most simple messages, you would look in the files, talk with your boss, interview the target audience, or possibly conduct an informal survey. Information for a message is then organized into a list or an outline. Depending on the expected reaction of the receiver, the message can be organized directly (for positive reactions) or indirectly (for negative reactions or when persuasion is necessary).

In composing the first draft, writers must be sure that sentences are complete. Emphasis can be achieved through mechanics (underlining, italics, font changes, all caps, and so forth) or through style (using vivid words, labeling the main idea, and positioning the important ideas). Important writing techniques include skillful use of active- and passive-voice verbs, developing parallelism, and achieving unity while avoiding zigzag writing, mixed constructions, and misplaced modifiers. Coherent paragraphs result from planned repetition of key ideas, proper use of pronouns, and inclusion of transitional expressions.

In the next chapter you'll learn helpful techniques for the third phase of the writing process, which includes revising and proofreading.

Critical Thinking

1. Why is audience analysis so important in choosing the direct or indirect pattern of organization for a business message?
2. In what ways do you imagine that writing on the job differs from the writing you do in your academic studies?
3. How are speakers different from writers in the manner in which they emphasize ideas?
4. Why are short sentences and short paragraphs appropriate for business communication?
5. When might it be unethical to use the indirect method of organizing a message?

6. What three steps are included in the second phase of the writing process?

7. Distinguish between formal and informal methods of researching data for a business message.

8. What is the difference between a list and an outline?

9. What is *frontloading* and what are its advantages?

10. When is the indirect method appropriate, and what are the benefits of using it?

11. List five techniques for achieving emphasis through mechanics.

12. List four techniques for achieving emphasis through style.

13. What is parallelism? Give an original example.

14. List three techniques for developing paragraph coherence.

15. What environment should you establish if you have something to write?

Writing Improvement Exercises

Revising Sentences. Revise the following sentences to remedy sentence fragments, run-on sentences, and comma splices.

16. When McDonald's tested pizza, Pizza Hut fought back. With aggressive ads ridiculing McPizza.

17. Companies sometimes sue their rivals they also may respond with counterattacks.

18. Aggressive advertisements can backfire that's why marketing directors consider them carefully.

19. Although Pizza Hut is the country's number one pizza chain. Domino's Pizza leads in deliveries.

20. About half of Pizza Hut's 6,600 outlets make deliveries, the others concentrate on walk-in customers.

Emphasis. For each of the following sentences, circle (a) or (b). Be prepared to justify your choice.
21. Which is more emphatic?
    (a) We need a faster, more efficient distribution system.
    (b) We need a better distribution system.
22. Which is more emphatic?
    (a) Increased advertising would improve sales.
    (b) Adding $50,000 in advertising would double our sales.
23. Which is more emphatic?
    (a) The committee was powerless to act.
    (b) The committee was unable to take action.
24. Which sentence places more emphasis on *product loyalty?*
    (a) Product loyalty is the primary motivation for advertising.
    (b) The primary motivation for advertising is loyalty to the product, although other purposes are also served.
25. Which sentence places more emphasis on the seminar?
    (a) An executive training seminar that starts June 1 will include four candidates.
    (b) Four candidates will be able to participate in an executive training seminar that we feel will provide a valuable learning experience.

26. Which sentence places more emphasis on the date?
    (a) The deadline is December 30 for applications for overseas assignments.
    (b) December 30 is the deadline for applications for overseas assignments.
27. Which is *less* emphatic?
    (a) Miss Curtis said that her financial status had worsened.
    (b) Miss Curtis said that she had lost her job and owed $2,000.
28. Which sentence *deemphasizes* the credit refusal?
    (a) We are unable to grant you credit at this time, but we will reconsider your application later.
    (b) Although we welcome your cash business, we are unable to offer you credit at this time; but we will be happy to reconsider your application later.
29. Which sentence gives more emphasis to *judgment?*
    (a) He has many admirable qualities, but most important is his good judgment.
    (b) He has many admirable qualities, including good judgment and patience.
30. Which is more emphatic?
    (a) Three departments are involved: (1) Legal, (2) Accounting, and (3) Distribution.
    (b) Three departments are involved:
        (1) Legal
        (2) Accounting
        (3) Distribution

Active-Voice Verbs. Business writing is more forceful if it uses active-voice verbs. Revise the following sentences so that verbs are in the active voice. Put the emphasis on the doer of the action. Add subjects if necessary.

Example: The computers were powered up each day at 7 a.m.

Revision: Kevin powered up the computers each day at 7 a.m.

31. Initial figures for the bid were submitted before the June 1 deadline.

32. New spices and cooking techniques were tried by McDonald's to improve its hamburgers.

33. Substantial sums of money were earned by employees who enrolled early in our stock option plan.

34. A significant financial commitment has been made by us to ensure that our customers can take advantage of our discount pricing.

Passive-Voice Verbs. When indirectness or tact is required, use passive-voice verbs. Revise the following sentences so that they are in the passive voice.

Example: Stacy did not submit the accounting statement on time.
Revision: The accounting statement was not submitted on time.

35. Bill made a computational error in the report.

36. We cannot ship your order for 10 monitors until June 15.

37. The government first issued a warning regarding the use of this pesticide over 15 months ago.

38. We will notify you immediately if we make any changes in your travel arrangements.

39. We cannot allow a cash refund unless you provide a register receipt.

Parallelism. Revise the following sentences so that their parts are balanced.

40. (Hint: Match verbs.) Some of our priorities include linking employee compensation to performance, keeping administrative costs down, the expansion of computer use, and the improvement of performance-review skills of supervisors.

41. (Hint: Match active voice of verbs.) Wendy Johnston, of the Red River office, will now supervise our Western Division; and the Eastern Division will be supervised by our Ottawa office manager, David Haskins.

42. (Hint: Match nouns.) Word processing software is used extensively in the fields of health care, by attorneys, by secretaries in insurance firms, for scripts in the entertainment industry, and in the banking field.

43. If you have decided to cancel our service, please cut your credit card in half, and the card pieces should be returned to us.

44. We need more laboratory space, additional personnel is required, and we also need much more capital.

45. The application for a grant asks for this information: funds required for employee salaries, how much we expect to spend on equipment, and what is the length of the project.

46. To lease an automobile is more expensive than buying one.

Chapter 3 Improving Writing Techniques

47. To use the copier, insert your meter, the paper trays must be loaded, indicate the number of copies needed, and your original sheet should be inserted through the feeder.

Sentence Unity. The following sentences lack unity. Rewrite, correcting the identified fault.

Example: (Dangling modifier) By advertising extensively, all the open jobs were filled quickly.
Revision: By advertising extensively, we were able to fill all the open jobs quickly.

48. (Dangling modifier) To open a money market account, a deposit of $3,000 is required.

49. (Mixed construction) The reason why Mrs. Harris is unable to travel extensively is because she has family responsibilities.

50. (Misplaced modifier) Identification passes must be worn at all times in offices and production facilities showing the employee's picture.

51. (Misplaced modifier) The editor in chief's rules were to be observed by all staff members, no matter how silly they seemed.

52. (Zigzag sentence) The business was started by two engineers, and these owners worked in a garage, which eventually grew into a million-dollar operation.

Coherence. Revise the following paragraphs to improve coherence. Study the example and review the chapter. But be aware that the transitional expressions and key words selected depend largely on the emphasis desired. Many possible revisions exist.

Example: Computer style checkers rank somewhere between artificial intelligence and artificial ignorance. Style checkers are like clever children: smart but not wise. Business writers should be cautious. They should be aware of the usefulness of style checkers. They should know their limitations.
Revision: Computer style checkers rank somewhere between artificial intelligence and artificial ignorance. *For example*, they are like clever children: smart but not wise. *For this reason*, business writers should be cautious. *Although* they should be aware of the usefulness of these software programs, business writers should *also* know their limitations.

53. Our computerized file includes all customer data. It provides space for name, address, and other vital information. It has an area for comments. The area for comments comes in handy. It requires more time and careful keyboarding, tho.

54. No one likes to turn out poor products. We began highlighting recurring problems. Employees make a special effort to be more careful in doing their work right the first time. It doesn't have to be returned to them for corrections.

55. Service was less than perfect for many months. We lacked certain intangibles. We didn't have the customer-specific data that we needed. We made the mistake of removing all localized, person-to-person coverage. We are returning to decentralized customer contacts.

Grammar/Mechanics Checkup—3

Verbs

Review Sections 1.10–1.15 in the Grammar Review section of the Grammar/ Mechanics Handbook. Then study each of the following statements. Underline any verbs that are used incorrectly. In the space provided, write the correct form (or C if correct) and the number of the G/M principle illustrated. When you finish, compare your responses with those provided on page 486. If your responses differ, study carefully the principles in parentheses.

| was | (1.10c) | **Example:** | Our inventory of raw materials <u>were</u> presented as collateral for a short-term loan. |

1. Located across town is a research institute and our product-testing facility.
2. Can you tell me whether a current list with all customers' names and addresses have been sent to marketing?
3. First Federal Savings, along with 20 other large national banks, offer a variety of savings plans.
4. Neither the plans that this bank offers nor the service just rendered by the teller are impressive.
5. Locating a bank and selecting a savings/checking plan often require considerable research and study.
6. The budget analyst wants to know whether the Equipment Committee are ready to recommend a printer.
7. Either of the printers that the committee selects is acceptable to the budget analyst.
8. If Mr. Davis had chose the Maximizer Plus savings plan, his money would have earned maximum interest.
9. Although the applications have laid there for two weeks, they may still be submitted.
10. Jessica acts as if she was the manager.
11. One of the reasons that our Alaskan sales branches have been so costly are the high cost of living.

In the space provided, write the letter of the sentence that illustrates consistency in subject, voice, and mood.

12. (a) If you will read the instructions, the answer can be found. _____
    (b) If you will read the instructions, you will find the answer.
13. (a) All employees must fill out application forms; only then will you be in- _____
        sured.
    (b) All employees must fill out application forms; only then will they be in-
        sured.
14. (a) First, take an inventory of equipment; then, order supplies _____
    (b) First, take an inventory of equipment; then, supplies must be ordered.
15. (a) Select a savings plan that suits your needs; deposits may be made im- _____
        mediately.
    (b) Select a savings plan that suits your needs; begin making deposits im-
        mediately.

Advanced Grammar/Mechanics Review—3

The following sentences contain errors in grammar, punctuation, capitalization, number style, usage, and spelling. Pay special attention to sentence fragments. Below each sentence write a corrected version. Check with your instructor for the solutions.

1. Although most of our capitol is tied up in equipment. We expect to purchase 2 vans in Febuary.
   [handwritten: SP, Two, February.]

2. During the Fall Erics schedule included classes in: Management, Marketing, and Spanish.
   [handwritten: full, M, M]

3. A list of resterants with dinners costing less than six dollars were given to my friend and I.
   [handwritten: SP, was, restaurants, me.]

4. Although we normally hire only experienced programmers, We occasionally consider well-trained individuals who lack experience.
   [handwritten: we]

5. All houses, accept your's has to be inspected for termite damage.
   [handwritten: except, have, yours]

6. The following 3 employees are indispensible Matt, Gabrielle, and Tyler.
   [handwritten: three]

7. Every classified employee, as well as all certified employees and members of management are eligible for new health benefits.

8. The 4 announcements from our human resources department surprised management as much as us.
   [handwritten: four]

9. Just between you and I, we expect to raise over two thousand dollars during the four week campaign.

10. Of course all of we homeowners are upset over this latest increase in property taxs.

Taxes

11. Opening his speech general colin powell said "The healthiest competition occurs when average people win by putting in above average effort.

12. If the President and Manager agree that next years sales campaign should emphasize customer service. Then we can procede.

13. Considering total sales Daphne is more of a team player than him. Which explains her recent promotion.

14. We trust that the New Year will be profitable for you, and that we may have many opportunitys to serve you.

15. Microsoft says, that they makes computing more accessable for every one because they offer: new ideas, new products, and services that are new for customers.

Grammar/Mechanics Challenge—3

Document for Revision

The following memo has many faults in grammar, spelling, punctuation, capitalization, word use, and number form. Use standard proofreading marks (see Appendix B) to correct the errors. Study the guidelines in the Grammar/Mechanics Handbook to sharpen your skills. When you finish, your instructor can show you the revised version of this memo.

DATE: July 24, 200X

TO: Jamal Wilkerson, Vice President

FROM: Roxanne Crosley, Manager, Payroll

SUBJECT: Departmental Error

This is to inform you that last month our central accounting department changed it's computer program for payroll processing. When this computer change was operationalized some of the stored information was not transfered to the new information database. As a consequence of this maneuver several errors occured in employee paychecks (1) medical benifits were not deducted (2) annuity deductions were not made and (3) errors occured in Federal witholding calculations.

Each and every one of the employees effected have been contacted; and this error has been elucidated. My staff and myself has been working overtime to replace all the missing data; so that corrections can be made by the August 30th payroll run.

Had I made a verification of the true facts before the paychecks were ran this slip-up would not have materialized. To prevent such an error in the future I decided to take the bull by the horns. At this point in time I have implemented a rigorous new verification system. I am of the firm opinion that utilization of the new system will definitely prevent this perplexing event from reoccuring.

Using Ethical Tools to Help You Do the Right Thing

In your career you will doubtless face times when you are torn by conflicting loyalties. Should you tell the truth and risk your job? Should you be loyal to your friends even if it means bending the rules? Should you be tactful or totally honest? Is it your duty to help your company make a profit, or should you be socially responsible?

Being ethical, according to the experts, means doing the right thing *given the circumstances*. Each set of circumstances requires analyzing issues, evaluating choices, and acting responsibly. Resolving ethical issues is never easy, but the task can be made less difficult if you know how to identify key issues. The following questions may be helpful.

- **Is the action you are considering legal?** No matter who asks you to do it or how important you feel the result will be, avoid anything that is prohibited by law. Giving a kickback to a buyer for a large order is illegal, even if you suspect that others in your field do it and you know that without the kickback you will lose the sale.
- **How would you see the problem if you were on the opposite side?** Looking at all sides of an issue helps you gain perspective. Consider the issue of mandatory drug testing among employees. From management's viewpoint such testing could stop drug abuse, improve job performance, and lower health insurance premiums. From the employees' viewpoint mandatory testing reflects a lack of trust of employees and constitutes an invasion of privacy. By weighing both sides of an issue, you can arrive at a more equitable solution.
- **What are the alternate solutions?** Consider all dimensions of other options. Would the alternative be more ethical? Under the circumstances, is the alternative feasible? Can an alternate solution be implemented with a minimum of disruption and with a high degree of probable success?
- **Can you discuss the problem with someone whose opinion you value?** Suppose you feel ethically bound to report accurate information to a client—even though your boss has ordered you not to do so. Talking about your dilemma with a coworker or with a colleague in your field might give you helpful insights and lead to possible alternatives.
- **How would you feel if your family, friends, employer, or coworkers learned of your action?** If the thought of revealing your action publicly produces cold sweats, your choice is probably not a wise one. Losing the faith of your friends or the confidence of your customers is not worth whatever short-term gains might be realized.

Career Application

After six months of job hunting, let's say you finally found a job with Company X. But it's in a city 700 miles from your home. A week after starting to work, you receive a job offer from Company Y that would increase your salary by 10 percent and would move you to a city closer to your home. You want very much to leave Company X to accept Company Y's offer. However, you are troubled because you told Company Y that you would stay and it has begun to train you. You feel particularly guilty because many nice people have made a special effort to welcome you and get you started in your new position.

Your Task

- In teams or individually, decide on an action to take. Begin by asking whether the action you are considering is legal.
- Looking at the problem from Company X's perspective, how much harm would be done by your leaving? What will Company X lose if you leave?
- What are alternate solutions? Is it entirely a money issue? Would you be happy with a higher salary at Company X?
- Can you discuss the problem with someone whose opinion you value? Should you consult someone at Company X? Your family? Friends?
- How would you feel if your family, friends, employer, or coworkers learned of your action?
- Present your decision in class discussion or in a memo to your instructor. Support your decision with your reasons.

Related Web Site: Visit the Texas Instruments ethics site <www.ti.com/corp/docs/company/citizen/ethics/quicktest.shtml> to see its Ethics Quick Test.

Web

Revising and Proofreading Business Messages

Vigorous writing is concise. A sentence should contain no unnecessary words . . . for the same reason that a drawing should have no unnecessary lines and a machine no unnecessary parts.

STRUNK AND WHITE, The Elements of Style

LEARNING OBJECTIVES

1. Understand the third phase of the writing process, revision.
2. Revise messages to achieve concise wording by eliminating wordy prepositional phrases, outdated expressions, long lead-ins, and needless adverbs.
3. Revise messages to eliminate fillers, repetitious words, and redundancies.
4. Revise messages to use jargon sparingly and avoid slang and clichés.
5. Revise messages to include precise verbs, concrete nouns, and vivid adjectives.
6. Describe effective techniques for proofreading routine and complex documents.

Understanding the Process of Revision

The third phase of the writing process includes revision, proofreading, and evaluating.

The best business writing is concise, clear, and vigorous. In this chapter you'll concentrate on techniques to achieve those qualities. These techniques are part of the third phase of the writing process, which centers on revising and proofreading. Revising means improving the content and sentence structure of your message. It may include adding, cutting, and recasting what you've written. Proofreading involves correcting the grammar, spelling, punctuation, format, and mechanics of your messages.

Both revising and proofreading require a little practice to develop your skills. That's what you will be learning in this chapter. Take a look at Figure 4.1. Notice how the revised version of this paragraph is clearer, more concise, and more vigorous because we removed a lot of dead wood. Major ideas stand out when they are not lost in a forest of words.

FIGURE 4.1 Revising for Conciseness

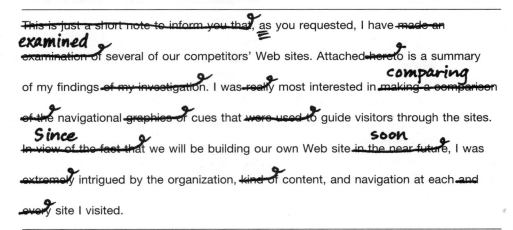

Rarely is the first or even the second version of a message satisfactory. One expert says, "Only amateurs expect writing perfection on the first try."[1] The revision stage is your chance to make sure your message says what you mean. It's also your chance to project a good image of yourself.

Many professional writers compose the first draft quickly without worrying about language, precision, or correctness. Then they revise and polish extensively. Other writers, however, prefer to revise as they go—particularly for shorter business documents. Whether you revise as you go or do it when you finish a document, you'll want to focus on concise wording. This includes eliminating wordy prepositional phrases, long lead-ins, outdated expressions, needless adverbs, fillers, and repetitious and redundant words. You'll also decide whether to include jargon, slang, and clichés. And you'll be looking for precise words that say exactly what you mean.

Some communicators write the first draft quickly; others revise and polish as they go.

Concise Wording

In business, time is indeed money. Translated into writing, this means that concise messages save reading time and, thus, money. In addition, messages that are written directly and efficiently are easier to read and comprehend. In the revision process look for shorter ways to say what you mean. Examine every sentence that you write. Could the thought be conveyed in fewer words? Notice how the following flabby expressions could be said more concisely.

Main points are easier to understand in concise messages.

Flabby	Concise	Flabby	Concise
at a later date	later	in the event that	if
at this point in time	now	in the amount of	for
afford an opportunity	allow	in the near future	soon
are of the opinion that	believe, think that	in view of the fact that	because
at the present time	now, presently	inasmuch as	since
despite the fact that	though	more or less	about
due to the fact that	because, since	until such time as	until
during the time	while		
feel free to	please		
for the period of	for		
fully cognizant of	aware of		
in addition to the above	also		
in spite of the fact that	even though		

Flabby phrases can often be reduced to a single word.

Wordy Prepositional Phrases

Replace wordy prepositional phrases with adverbs whenever possible.

Some wordy prepositional phrases may be replaced by single adverbs. For example, *in the normal course of events* becomes *normally* and *as a general rule* becomes *generally.*

Wordy	MCI approached the merger *in a careful manner.*
Concise	MCI approached the merger *carefully.*
Wordy	The merger will *in all probability* be effected.
Concise	The merger will *probably* be effected.
Wordy	We have taken this action *in very few cases.*
Concise	We have *seldom* taken this action.

Long Lead-Ins

Avoid long lead-ins that delay the reader from reaching the meaning of the sentence.

Delete unnecessary introductory words. The meat of the sentence often follows the words *that* or *because.*

Wordy	*I am sending you this announcement to let you all know that* the office will be closed Monday.
Concise	The office will be closed Monday.
Wordy	*You will be interested to learn that* you can now be served at our Web site.
Concise	You can now be served at our Web site.
Wordy	*I am writing this letter because* Dr. Steven Hunt suggested that your organization was hiring trainees.
Concise	Dr. Steven Hunt suggested that your organization was hiring trainees.

Outdated Expressions

Replace outdated expressions with modern, concise phrasing.

The world of business has changed greatly in the past century or two. Yet, some business writers continue to use antiquated phrases and expressions borrowed from a period when the "language of business" was exceedingly formal and flowery. In the 1800s, letter writers "begged to state" and "trusted to be favored with" and assured their readers that they "remained their humble servants." Such language suggests quill pens, sealing wax, green eyeshades, and sleeve guards. Avoid using time-worn, stale expressions that linger from the past. Replace outdated expressions such as those shown here with more modern phrasing:

Outdated Expressions	Modern Phrasing
are in receipt of	have received
as per your request	at your request
attached hereto	attached
enclosed please find	enclosed is/are
pursuant to your request	at your request
thanking you in advance	thank you
I trust that	I think, I believe
under separate cover	separately

Chapter 4 Revising and Proofreading Business Messages

Needless Adverbs

Eliminating adverbs such as *very, definitely, quite, completely, extremely, really, actually, somewhat,* and *rather* streamlines your writing. Omitting these intensifiers generally makes you sound more credible and businesslike.

Wordy	We *actually* did not *really* give his plan a *very* fair trial.
Concise	We did not give his plan a fair trial.
Wordy	Professor Susan Fagan offers an *extremely* fine course that students *definitely* appreciate.
Concise	Professor Susan Fagan offers a fine course that students appreciate.

Fillers

Avoid fillers that fatten sentences with excess words. Beginning an idea with *There is* usually indicates that writers are spinning their wheels until they decide where the sentence is going. Used correctly, *there* indicates a specific place (*I placed the box there*). Used as fillers, *there* and occasionally *it* merely take up space.

Wordy	There are three vice presidents who report directly to the president.
Concise	Three vice presidents report directly to the president.
Wordy	It is the client who should make application for licensing.
Concise	The client should apply for licensing.

Repetitious Words

Good communicators vary their words to avoid unintentional repetition. Not only does this shorten a message, but it also improves vigor and readability. Notice how leaden and monotonous the following personnel announcement sounds:

Avoid the monotony of unintentionally repeated words.

> Employees will be able to elect an additional six employees to serve with the four previously elected employees who currently comprise the employees' board of directors. To ensure representation, swing-shift employees will be electing one swing-shift employee as their sole representative.

The preceding version uses the word *employee* six times. In addition, the last sentence begins with the word *representation* and ends with the similar word *representative.* An easier-to-read version follows:

> Employees will be able to elect an additional six representatives to serve with the four previously elected members of the employees' board of directors. To ensure representation, swing-shift workers will elect their own board member.

In the second version synonyms (*representatives, members, workers*) replaced *employee.* The last sentence was reworked by using a pronoun (*their*) and by substituting *board member* for the repetitious *representative.* Variety of expression can be achieved by searching for appropriate synonyms and by substituting pronouns.

Good writers are also alert to the overuse of the articles *a, an,* and particularly *the.* Often the word *the* can simply be omitted, particularly with plural nouns.

Wordy	The committee members agreed on many rule changes.
Improved	Committee members agreed on many rule changes.

Redundant Words

Redundancies convey a meaning more than once.

Repetition of words to achieve emphasis or effective transition is an important writing technique discussed in the previous chapter. The needless repetition, however, of words whose meanings are clearly implied by other words is a writing fault called *redundancy*. For example, in the expression *final outcome*, the word *final* is redundant and should be omitted, since *outcome* implies finality. Learn to avoid redundant expressions such as the following:

absolutely essential	*final* outcome
adequate *enough*	*grateful* thanks
advance warning	*mutual* cooperation
basic fundamentals	*necessary* prerequisite
big *in size*	*new* beginning
combined *together*	*past* history
consensus *of opinion*	reason *why*
continue *on*	red *in color*
each *and every*	refer *back*
exactly identical	repeat *again*
few *in number*	*true* facts

Jargon

Jargon, which is terminology unique to a certain profession, should be reserved for individuals who understand it.

Except in certain specialized contexts, you should avoid jargon and unnecessary technical terms. Jargon is special terminology that is peculiar to a particular activity or profession. For example, geologists speak knowingly of *exfoliation, calcareous ooze,* and *siliceous particles.* Engineers are familiar with phrases such as *infrared processing flags, output latches,* and *movable symbology.* Telecommunication experts use such words and phrases as *protocol, mode,* and *asynchronous transmission.*

Every field has its own special vocabulary. Using that vocabulary within the field is acceptable and even necessary for accurate, efficient communication. Don't use specialized terms, however, if you have reason to believe that your reader may misunderstand them.

Slang

Slang sounds fashionable, but it lacks precise meaning and should be avoided in business writing.

Slang is composed of informal words with arbitrary and extravagantly changed meanings. Slang words quickly go out of fashion because they are no longer appealing when everyone begins to understand them. Consider the following statement of a government official who had been asked why his department was dropping a proposal to lease offshore oil lands: "The Administration has an awful lot of other things in the pipeline, and this has more wiggle room so they just moved it down the totem pole." He added, however, that the proposal might be offered again since "there is no pulling back because of hot-potato factors."

The meaning here, if the speaker really intended to impart any, is considerably obscured by the use of slang. Good communicators, of course, aim at clarity and avoid unintelligible slang.

Clichés

Clichés are expressions that have become exhausted by overuse. These expressions lack not only freshness but also clarity. Some have no meaning for people who are new to our culture. The following partial list contains clichés you should avoid in business writing.

Clichés are dull and sometimes ambiguous.

below the belt	keep your nose to the grindstone
better than new	last but not least
beyond the shadow of a doubt	make a bundle
easier said than done	pass with flying colors
exception to the rule	quick as a flash
fill the bill	shoot from the hip
first and foremost	stand your ground
hard facts	true to form

Precise Verbs

Effective writing creates meaningful images in the mind of the reader. Such writing is sparked by robust, concrete, and descriptive words. Ineffective writing is often dulled by insipid, abstract, and generalized words. The most direct way to improve lifeless writing is through effective use of verbs. Verbs not only indicate the action of the subject but also deliver the force of the sentence. Select verbs carefully so that the reader can visualize precisely what is happening.

Precise verbs make your writing forceful, clear, and lively.

General Our salesperson will *contact* you next week.
Precise Our salesperson will (*telephone, fax, e-mail, visit*) you next week.

General The CEO *said* that we should contribute.
Precise The CEO (*urged, pleaded, demanded*) that we contribute.

General We must *consider* this problem.
Precise We must (*clarify, remedy, rectify*) this problem.

General The newspaper was *affected* by the strike.
Precise The newspaper was (*crippled, silenced, demoralized*) by the strike.

The power of a verb is diminished when it is needlessly converted to a noun. This happens when verbs such as *acquire, establish,* and *develop* are made into nouns (*acquisition, establishment,* and *development*). These nouns then receive the central emphasis in the sentence. In the following pairs of sentences, observe how forceful the original verbs are as compared with their noun forms.

Weak	*Acquisition* of park lands was made recently by the city. (Noun centered)
Strong	The city *acquired* park lands recently. (Verb centered)
Weak	The webmaster and the designer had a *discussion* concerning graphics. (Noun centered)
Strong	The webmaster and the designer *discussed* graphics. (Verb centered)
Weak	Both companies must grant *approval* of the merger. (Noun centered)
Strong	Both companies must *approve* the merger. (Verb centered)

Concrete Nouns

Concrete nouns help readers visualize the meanings of words.

Nouns name persons, places, and things. Abstract nouns name concepts that are difficult to visualize, such as *automation, function, justice, institution, integrity, form, judgment,* and *environment.* Concrete nouns name objects that are more easily imagined, such as *desk, car,* and *lightbulb.* Nouns describing a given object can range from the very abstract to the very concrete—for example, *object, motor vehicle, car, convertible, Mustang.* All of these words or phrases can be used to describe a Mustang convertible. However, a reader would have difficulty envisioning a Mustang convertible when given just the word *object* or even *motor vehicle* or *car.*

In business writing, help your reader "see" what you mean by using concrete language.

General	a *change* in our budget
Concrete	a *10 percent reduction* in our budget
General	*that company's product*
Concrete	*NEC's Ultra Express pager*
General	*a person* called
Concrete	*Mrs. Swain, the administrative assistant,* called
General	we *improved* the assembly line
Concrete	we *installed 26 advanced Unimate robots* on the assembly line

Vivid Adjectives

A thesaurus (computer or printed) helps you select precise words and increase your vocabulary.

Including highly descriptive, dynamic adjectives makes writing more vivid and concrete. Be careful, though, neither to overuse them nor to lose objectivity in selecting them.

General	The report was on time.
Vivid	The *detailed 12-page* report was submitted on time.
General	Rick needs a better truck.
Vivid	Rick needs a *rugged, four-wheel-drive Dodge* truck.
General	We enjoyed the movie.
Vivid	We enjoyed the *entertaining* and *absorbing* movie.
Overkill	We enjoyed the *gutsy, exciting, captivating,* and *thoroughly marvelous* movie.

Understanding the Process of Proofreading

Once you have the message in its final form, it's time to proofread. Don't proofread earlier because you may waste time checking items that eventually are changed or omitted.

What to Watch for in Proofreading

Careful proofreaders check for problems in these areas:

- **Spelling.** Now's the time to consult the dictionary. Is *recommend* spelled with one or two *c*'s? Do you mean *affect* or *effect?* Use your computer spell checker, but don't rely on it totally. See the accompanying Communication Workshop to learn more about the benefits and hazards of computer spell checkers.
- **Grammar.** Locate sentence subjects; do their verbs agree with them? Do pronouns agree with their antecedents? Review the principles in the Grammar/Mechanics Handbook if necessary. Use your computer's grammar checker, but be suspicious. The Communication Workshop discusses grammar checkers more extensively.
- **Punctuation.** Make sure that introductory clauses are followed by commas. In compound sentences put commas before coordinating conjunctions (*and, or, but, nor*). Double-check your use of semicolons and colons.
- **Names and numbers.** Compare all names and numbers with their sources because inaccuracies are not immediately visible. Especially verify the spelling of the names of individuals receiving the message. Most of us immediately dislike someone who misspells our name.
- **Format.** Be sure that letters, printed memos, and reports are balanced on the page. Compare their parts and format with those of standard documents shown in Appendix A. If you indent paragraphs, be certain that all are indented.

> **Good proofreaders check spelling, grammar, punctuation, names, numbers, and format.**

How to Proofread Routine Documents

Most routine messages, including e-mails, require a light proofreading. Use the down arrow to reveal one line at a time, thus focusing your attention at the bottom of the screen. Read carefully for faults such as omitted or doubled words. Use the spell checker, if available.

For routine messages such as printed letters or memos, a safer proofreading method is reading from a printed copy. You're more likely to find errors and to observe the tone. "Things really look different on paper," observes veteran writer Louise Lague at *People* magazine. "Don't just pull a letter out of the printer and stick it in an envelope. Read every sentence again. You'll catch bad line endings, strange page breaks, and weird spacing. You can also get a totally different feeling about what you've said when you see it in print. Sometimes you can say something with a smile on your face; but if you put the same thing in print, it won't work."[2] Use standard proofreading marks, shown in Figure 4.2, to indicate changes.

> **Routine documents need a light proofreading.**

> **For both routine and complex documents, it's best to proofread from a printed copy, not on a computer screen.**

How to Proofread Complex Documents

Long, complex, or important documents demand more careful proofreading using the following techniques:

- Print a copy, preferably double-spaced, and set it aside for at least a day. You'll be more alert after a breather.
- Allow adequate time to proofread carefully. A common excuse for sloppy proofreading is lack of time.
- Be prepared to find errors. One student confessed, "I can find other people's errors, but I can't seem to locate my own." Psychologically, we don't expect to find errors, and we don't want to find them. You can overcome this obstacle by anticipating errors and congratulating, not criticizing, yourself each time you find one.

FIGURE 4.2 Proofreading Marks

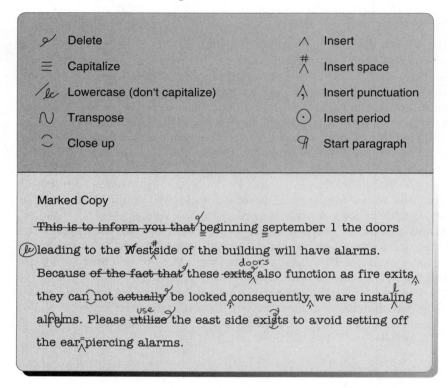

Read the message at least twice—once for word meanings and once for grammar/mechanics. For very long documents (book chapters and long articles or reports), read a third time to verify consistency in formatting.
- Reduce your reading speed. Concentrate on individual words rather than ideas.
- For documents that must be perfect, have someone read the message aloud. Spell names and difficult words, note capitalization, and read punctuation.
- Use standard proofreading marks, shown in Figure 4.2, to indicate changes.

Your computer word processing program may include a style or grammar checker. These programs generally analyze aspects of your writing style, including readability level and use of passive voice, trite expressions, split infinitives, and wordy expressions. Most programs use sophisticated technology (and a lot of computer memory) to identify significant errors. In addition to finding spelling and typographical errors, grammar checkers can find subject-verb lack of agreement, word misuse, spacing irregularities, punctuation problems, and many other faults. But they won't find everything, as you will see in the accompanying Communication Workshop. While grammar and spell checkers can help you a great deal, you are the final proofreader.

Summing Up and Looking Forward

Revision is the most important part of the writing process. To revise for clarity and conciseness, look for flabby phrases that can be shortened (such as *more* or *less*). Eliminate wordy prepositional phrases (*in all probability*), long lead-ins (*This is to inform you that*), outdated expressions (*pursuant to your request*), needless adverbs (*definitely, very*), and fillers (*There are*). Also watch for repetitious words and redundancies (*combined together*). Use jargon only when it is clear to receivers, and

Chapter 4 Revising and Proofreading Business Messages

avoid slang and clichés altogether. The best writing includes precise verbs, concrete nouns, and vivid adjectives. After revising a message, you're ready for the last step in the writing process: proofreading. Watch for irregularities in spelling, grammar, punctuation, names and numbers, and format. Although routine messages may be proofread on the screen, you will have better results if you proofread from a printed copy. Complex documents should be printed, put away for a day or so, and then proofread several times.

In these opening chapters you've studied the writing process. You've also learned many practical techniques for becoming an effective business communicator. Now it's time for you to put these techniques to work. Chapter 5 introduces you to writing e-mail messages and memorandums, the most frequently used forms of communication for most businesspeople. Later chapters present letters and reports.

Critical Thinking

1. "A real writer can sit down at a computer and create a perfect document the first time." Do you agree or disagree? Why?
2. Carefully written short messages often take longer to write than longer messages. Do you agree or disagree? Why?
3. Because clichés are familiar and have stood the test of time, do they help clarify writing?
4. If your boss writes in a flowery, formal tone and relies on outdated expressions, should you follow that style also?
5. Is it unethical to help a friend revise a report when you know that the friend will be turning that report in for a grade?

Chapter Review

6. How is revising different from proofreading?

7. Why is conciseness especially important in business?

8. What is a long lead-in? Give an original example.

9. What's wrong with using adverbs such as *very, really,* and *actually?*

10. What is a redundancy? Give an example.

11. What is jargon? When can it be used? What are examples in your field?

12. What happens when a verb (such as *describe*) is converted to a noun expression (*to make a description*)? Give an original example.

13. Should you proofread when you are writing or after you finish? Why?

14. What five areas should you especially pay attention to when you proofread?

15. How does the proofreading of routine and complex documents differ?

Writing Improvement Exercises

Wordiness. Revise the following sentences to eliminate flabby phrases, wordy prepositional phrases, outdated expressions, and long lead-ins.

Example: This is to notify you that at a later date we may be able to submit the report.
Revision: We may be able to submit the report later.

16. In the event that the response is at all favorable, we will in all probability start our Web site in the month of January.

17. This is to advise you that beginning with the date of April 1 all charges made after that date will be charged to your new credit card number.

18. Pursuant to your request, enclosed please find a copy of your August statement.

19. In view of the fact that our sales are increasing in a gradual manner, we must secure a loan in the amount of $50,000.

20. This is to let you know that you should feel free to use your credit card for the purpose of purchasing household items for a period of 60 days.

Needless Adverbs, Fillers, Repetitious Words. Revise the following sentences to eliminate needless adverbs, fillers (such as *there is* and *it is*), and unintentional repetition.

21. It is Web-based technology that is really streamlining administrative processes and reducing business costs for businesses.

22. It is certainly clear that there are many younger managers who are very eager but who are actually unprepared to assume management or leadership roles.

23. There are four employees who definitely spend more time in Internet recreational uses on the Internet than they spend on business-related Internet work.

24. There are definitely five advantages that computers have over a human decision maker.

Redundancies, Jargon, Slang, Clichés. Revise the following sentences to eliminate redundancies, jargon, slang, clichés, and any other wordiness.

Example: Last but not least, Troy collected together as much support material as possible to avoid getting burned in cash losses or bottom-line profits.

Revision: Finally, Troy collected as much support material as possible to avoid losing cash or profits.

25. First and foremost, we plan to emphasize an instructional training program.

26. It was the consensus of opinion of members of the committee that the committee should meet at 11 a.m. in the morning.

27. If you will refer back to the contract, you will definitely find that there are specific specifications to prevent anyone from blowing the budget.

28. This memorandum serves as an advance warning that all books and magazines borrowed from the library must be taken back to the library by June 1.

29. In view of the fact that our last presentation bombed, we are at this point in time convinced that we must include only the most absolutely essential selling points this time.

30. In the normal course of events, we would wait until such time as we had adequate enough credit reports.

Precise Verbs. Revise these sentences, centering the action in the verbs.

Example: Ms. Freeland gave an appraisal of the Web site.

Revision: Ms. Freeland appraised the Web site.

31. The webmaster made a description of the project.

32. Can you bring about a change in our company travel policy?

33. Web-based customer service will produce the effect of reduction in overall costs.

34. In writing this proposal, we must make application of new government regulations.

35. The board of directors made a recommendation affirming abandonment of the pilot project.

36. An investigator made a determination of the fire damages.

37. We hope to have production of our new line of products by January.

38. The duty of the comptroller is verification of departmental budgets.

39. Please make a correction in my account to reflect my late payment.

Vivid Words. Revise the following sentences to include vivid and concrete language. Add appropriate words.

Example: They said it was a long way off.
Revision: Management officials announced that the merger would not take place for two years.

40. Our new copier is fast.

41. An employee from that company notified us about the change in date.

42. Please contact them soon.

43. They said that the movie they saw was good.

44. Workers improved when they saw the big picture.

45. The report was weak.

Chapter 4 Revising and Proofreading Business Messages

Adjectives and Adverbs

Review Sections 1.16 and 1.17 of the Grammar Review section of the Grammar/Mechanics Handbook. Then study each of the following statements. Underscore any inappropriate forms. In the space provided, write the correct form (or C if correct) and the number of the G/M principle illustrated. You may need to consult your dictionary for current practice regarding some compound adjectives. When you finish, compare your responses with those provided at the end of the book. If your answers differ, study carefully the principles in parentheses.

Example: He was one of those individuals with a <u>live and let live</u> attitude.
live-and-let-live
_____ (1.17e)

1. Most of our long time customers have credit card accounts. _____
2. Many subscribers considered the $50 per year charge to be a bargain. _____
3. Other subscribers complained that $50 per year was exorbitant. _____
4. The Internet supplied the answer so quick that we were all amazed. _____
5. He only had $1 in his pocket. _____
6. Some experts predict that double digit inflation may return. _____
7. Jeremy found a once in a lifetime opportunity. _____

8. Although the car was four years old, it was in good condition. _____
9. Of the two colors, which is best for a Web background? _____
10. Professor Candace Carbone is well known in her field. _____
11. Channel 12 presents up to the minute news broadcasts. _____

12. Lower tax brackets would lessen the after tax yield of some bonds. _____
13. The conclusion drawn from the statistics couldn't have been more clearer. _____

14. This new investment fund has a better than fifty fifty chance of outperforming the older fund. _____
15. If you feel badly about the transaction, contact your portfolio manager. _____

Advanced Grammar/Mechanics Review—4

The following sentences contain errors in grammar, punctuation, capitalization, number style, usage, and spelling. Pay special attention to eliminating wordiness. Below each sentence write a corrected version.

Example: Inasmuch as our sales dropped fifty thousand dollars we are now fully cognizant of our competition.

Revision: Because our sales dropped $50,000, we are now aware of our competition.

1. This is to inform you that for a period of 2 weeks we must place a restriction on parking.

2. We made a plan to keep all our customers names and addresses in Mr. Betz database.

3. There are three laptop problems that have been solved, weight, size, and power consumption.

4. In view of the fact that the envelop was addressed to Manuel and I, him and me should receive the free gift.

5. Pursuant to your e-mail message of the 15th please be advised that your shipment was sent June 9.

6. Acting as President the budget was immediately signed by Rachel.

7. Although I'm sure it was him who sent the e-mail message the C.E.O. doesn't seem to care.

8. I am writing this e-mail to let you know that the meeting is May 15th.

9. The companys principle office is in Medford however, most shipments come from Portland.

10. If you are looking for a laptop that is small in size try the sony superslim 505 model.

11. We expect 17 employees to attend the 2 meetings on november 2nd.

12. To improve you're language skills the rules of grammar must be applied.

13. The Vice President and the Personnel Director made a distribution of complementary tickets to the concert.

14. New corporate taxes will effect all corporations in the near future.

15. Dr. Edward M. Shea who is one of the principle researchers sighted considerable evidence to support his arguement.

Document for Revision

The following letter has faults in grammar, punctuation, conversational language, outdated expressions, sexist language, concise wording, long lead-ins, and many other problems. Use standard proofreading marks (see Appendix B) to correct the errors. Study the guidelines in the Grammar/Mechanics Handbook to sharpen your skills. When you finish, your instructor may show you the revised version of this letter.

Ms. Kay Bradley

Title Guaranty & Abstract Company

2430 Providence Avenue

Anchorage, AK 99508

Dear Kay:

Pursuant to our telephone conversation this morning, this is to advise that two (2) agent's packages will be delivered to you next week. Due to the fact that new forms had to be printed; we do not have them immediately available.

Although we cannot offer a 50/50 commission split, we are able to offer new agents a 60/40 commission split. There are two new agreement forms that show this commission ratio. When you get ready to sign up a new agent have her fill in these up to date forms.

When you send me an executed agency agreement please make every effort to tell me what agency package was assigned to the agent. On the last form that you sent you overlooked this information. We need this data to distribute commissions in an expeditious manner.

If you have any questions, don't hesitate to call on me.

Yours very truly,

Grammar and Spell Checkers: They've Come a Long Way, Baby!

Nearly all high-end word processing programs now include sophisticated grammar and spell checkers to help writers with their proofreading chores.

Grammar Checkers

When first introduced, grammar and style checkers were not too helpful. They were limited in scope, awkward to use, and identified many questionable "errors." But today's grammar checkers detect an amazing number of legitimate writing lapses. Microsoft Word finds faults in word use (such as *there, their*) capitalization, punctuation, subject-verb agreement, sentence structure, singular and plural endings, repeated words, wordy expressions, gender-specific expressions, and many other problems.[3]

How does a grammar checker work? Let's say you typed the sentence, *The office and its equipment is for sale.* You would see a wavy green line appear under *is.* When you point your cursor at "Tools" in the tool bar and click on "Spelling and Grammar," a box opens up. It identifies the subject-verb agreement error and suggests the verb *are* as a correction. When you click on "Change," the error is corrected.

Spell Checkers

Spell checkers compare your typed words with those in the computer's memory. Microsoft Word uses a wavy red line to underline misspelled words caught "on the fly." Although some writers dismiss spell checkers as an annoyance, most of us are only too happy to have our typos and misspelled words detected. What's annoying is that spell checkers don't find all the problems. In the following poem, for example, only two problems were detected (*your* and *it's*).

> I have a spell checkers
>   That came with my PC.
> It plainly marks four my review
>   Mistakes I cannot sea.
> I've run this poem threw it,
>   I'm sure your pleased too no.
> Its letter perfect in it's weigh
>   My checker tolled me sew.
>   —Anonymous

The lesson to be learned here is that you can't rely totally on any spell checker. Misused words may not be highlighted because the spell checker doesn't know what meaning you have in mind. That's why you're wise to print out important messages and proofread them word by word.

Career Application

Your boss, Serena Johnson, is developing an in-service training program on word processing. She wants you to analyze the effectiveness of your computer's grammar and spell checkers. Your brief report will become part of a presentation to new employees.

Your Task

- You decide to try out your software with a set of test sentences. At a computer that has grammar and spell checking software, type the following four sentences, including all the errors. Print the sentences.
  1. Is the companys office located on riverside drive in new york city.
  2. The manger adviced her to make a consciensous effort to improve.
  3. There house and it's furniture was allready sold before they moved to miami.
  4. My friend and me was going to apply for the job in june but we were to late.
- For each sentence, underline the errors the software identified. Then circle the errors that the software missed. (A word may contain only one error.) Total your underlines and circles. Make notes on the kinds of errors identified and the kinds missed. Tip: You should find 20 errors.
- Based on your findings, how would you rate the usefulness of your computer's grammar and spell checkers? What are the strengths and weaknesses?
- What advice would you give to employees about relying on these programs for proofreading?
- In class discussion or in a memo, convey your findings and your advice to your boss, Serena Johnson.

Related Web Site: To learn what PCWeek Labs discovered in a test of grammar-checking programs, visit <www.zdnet.com/pcweek/reviews/0807/ tcheck.html>.

Web

Routine Business Messages

5 Memorandums and E-Mail

It's a continual challenge for us to keep our product groups small enough so that they feel empowered to make their stuff happen, rather than feeling like cogs in some giant machine. At the same time, we need to maintain a larger sense of community and allow a wide range of smart people within the company to provide thoughts and suggestions about product plans. E-mail is a great tool in enabling that sort of communication. It permits us to share technical strategy and vision across the entire company.[1]

BILL GATES, *Chairman, Microsoft*

LEARNING OBJECTIVES

1. Explain the importance of internal communication.
2. Analyze the writing process as it applies to e-mail messages and memorandums.
3. Understand how to use e-mail safely and effectively.
4. Explain and demonstrate a writing plan for memos and e-mail messages.
5. Demonstrate several ways to improve readability by using listing techniques.
6. Write memorandums and e-mail messages that inform.
7. Write memorandums and e-mail messages that make requests.
8. Write memorandums and e-mail messages that respond.

The Importance of Internal Communication

When Bill Gates was CEO of Microsoft, he wanted to be in constant contact with what was happening at his huge company. And he wanted his 33,000-plus employees to be in touch with each other exchanging information and ideas. He worried that Microsoft's size would work against excellence. But electronic mail has become an important tool in reducing barriers created by size and distance. Workers can almost instantly communicate with each other whether they are working in separate rooms, in separate buildings, or on separate continents.

At many companies today internal communication has become increasingly important. Organizations are downsizing, flattening chains of command, forming work teams, and empowering rank-and-file employees. Given more power in making decisions, employees find that they need more information. They must collect, exchange, and evaluate information about the products and services they offer. Management also needs input from employees to respond rapidly to global market actions.

This growing demand for information means increasing use of memorandums and e-mail. Until recently interoffice memos, such as that shown in Figure 5.1, were the most common channel for exchanging internal communication. Now, however, e-mail is the favored medium.

Developing skill in writing memos and e-mail brings you two important benefits. First, well-written documents are likely to achieve their goals. Second, such documents enhance your image within the organization. Individuals identified as competent, professional writers are noticed and rewarded; most often, they are the ones promoted into management positions.

This chapter concentrates on routine memos and e-mail messages. You'll study the writing process, as well as how to organize and format messages that inform, request, and respond. These straightforward messages follow the direct strategy because their topics are not sensitive and require little persuasion.

> **Downsized organizations, work teams, increased employee empowerment, and global competition mean more emphasis on internal communication.**

Writing Process

"One of the most amazing features of the information revolution," says one technology vice president, is that the "momentum has turned back to the written word."[2] Businesspeople are writing more messages than ever before, and many of them are e-mail messages and memos. Although routine, memos and e-mail messages require preparation because they may travel farther than you expect. A novice market researcher in Illinois, for example, was eager to please her boss. When asked to report on the progress of her project, she e-mailed a quick summary of her work. Later that week a vice president asked her boss how the project was progressing. Her boss forwarded the market researcher's hurried memo. Unfortunately, the resulting poor impression was difficult for the new employee to overcome.

Careful writing takes time—especially at first. By following a systematic plan and practicing your skill, however, you can speed up your efforts and greatly improve the product. The effort you make to improve your communication skills can pay big dividends. Frequently, your speaking and writing abilities determine how much influence you'll have in your organization. To make the best impression and to write the most effective messages, follow the three-phase writing process.

> **Businesspeople are writing more messages than ever before.**

> **A systematic plan helps you write faster and more effectively.**

Phase 1: Analysis, Anticipation, and Adaptation

In Phase 1 (prewriting) you'll need to spend some time analyzing your task. It's amazing how many of us are ready to put our pens or computers into gear before engaging our minds. Ask yourself three important questions:

- **Do I really need to write this memo or e-mail?** A phone call or a quick visit to a nearby coworker might solve the problem—and save the time and expense of a written message. On the other hand, some written messages are needed to provide a permanent record. Another decision is whether to write a hard-copy memo or send an electronic one.
- **Why am I writing?** Know why you are writing and what you hope to achieve. This will help you recognize what the important points are and where to place them.
- **How will the reader react?** Visualize the reader and the effect your message will have. Consider ways to shape the message to benefit the reader.

> **The first phase of the writing process focuses on prewriting: analyzing, anticipating, and adapting.**

FIGURE 5.1 Typical Hard-Copy Informational Memorandum

Aligns all information after longest guide word

Grabs attention and states purpose

Uses bulleted list and bold type for emphasis

Concludes with action request, deadline, and reason

↓ 2 inches   *Adecco, Inc.*
Interoffice Memorandom

DATE: November 8, 200X   ↓ 1 blank line

TO: All Staff Members

FROM: Serena Johnson, Manager
Human Resources Department

SUBJECT: RECOMMENDED OPTIONS FOR CHILD CARE BENEFITS

↓ 2 blank lines

We need your input! Members of your employee council and representatives from management recommend the following four options for child-care benefits. However, your feedback will determine the final choice.

- **On-site day-care centers.** This option accommodates employees' children on the premises. Weekly rates would be competitive with local day-care facilities. Although this option is most costly, it is worth pursuing if local facilities are deficient.

- **Off-site centers in conjunction with other local employers.** We are looking into the possibility of developing central facilities to be shared with nearby firms.

- **Neighborhood child-care centers.** We would contract with local centers to buy open slots for employees' children, perhaps at a discount.

- **Sick-child services.** This plan would provide employees with alternatives to missing work when children are ill. We are investigating sick-child programs at local hospitals, as well as services that send workers to employees' homes to look after sick children.

Before December 15 let your employee council representative know how you feel about these options. Once we have cost estimates and once we have your feedback, we can make a better decision. In January our benefits package will be negotiated.

Tips for Formatting Hard-Copy Memos

- Leave a 2-inch top margin.
- Set side margins at 1 to 1¼ inches.
- Leave a blank line between the heading guide words.
- Align the information following the headings.
- Leave two blank lines between SUBJECT and the first line of the memo.
- Single-space within the memo and double-space between paragraphs.

Phase 2: Research, Organization, and Composition

In Phase 2 (writing) you'll first want to check the files, gather documentation, and prepare your message. Make an outline of the points you wish to cover. For short messages you can jot down notes on the document you are answering. Be sure to prepare for revision, because excellence is rarely achieved on the first effort.

www.grantland.com

Phase 3: Revision, Proofreading, and Evaluation

Careful and caring writers revise their messages, proofread the final copy, and make an effort to evaluate the success of their communication.

- **Revise for clarity.** Viewed from the receiver's perspective, are the ideas clear? Do they need more explanation? If the memo is passed on to others, will they need further explanation? Consider having a colleague critique your message if it is an important one.
- **Proofread for correctness.** Are the sentences complete and punctuated properly? Did you overlook any typos or misspelled words? Remember to use your spell checker and grammar checker to proofread your message before sending it.
- **Plan for feedback.** How will you know if this message is successful? You can improve feedback by asking questions (such as *Do you agree with these suggestions?*) and by making it easy for the receiver to respond.

Using E-Mail Safely and Effectively

The stratospheric growth of e-mail continues unabated. At this writing about two thirds of American adults now use a computer, either at work or at home. And an incredible 46 percent of those who have on-line access use e-mail every day.[3] Suddenly, entire companies find that e-mail has become an indispensable means of internal communication as well as an essential link to customers and suppliers.

Early users were encouraged to ignore style and grammar. They thought that "words on the fly," as e-mail messages were considered, required little thought or editing. Correspondents used emoticons (such as sideways happy faces) to express their emotions. And some e-mail messages today are still quick and dirty. But as this communication channel matures, messages are becoming more proper and more professional.

Today, the average e-mail message may remain in the company's computer system for up to five years. And in some instances the only impression a person has of the e-mail writer is from a transmitted message. That's why it's important to take the time to organize your thoughts, compose carefully, and be concerned with correct grammar and punctuation.

> E-mail has become an essential means of communication within organizations as well as with customers and suppliers.

Savvy e-mail business communicators are also learning its dangers. They know that their messages can travel (intentionally or unintentionally) to unexpected destinations. A quickly drafted note may end up in the boss's mailbox or be forwarded to an adversary's box. Making matters worse, computers—like elephants and spurned lovers—never forget.[4] Even erased messages can remain on disk drives.

Smart E-Mail Practices

Despite its dangers and limitations, however, e-mail is increasingly the channel of choice for sending routine business messages. Other channels of communication are more effective for complex data or sensitive messages.

Getting Started. The following pointers will help you get off to a good start in using e-mail safely and effectively.

Composing with your word processing program generally produces better e-mail messages.

- **Compose off line.** Instead of dashing off hasty messages, take the time to compose off line. Consider using your word processing program and then uploading your message to the e-mail network. This avoids "self destructing" on line (losing all your writing through some glitch or pressing the wrong key).
- **Get the address right.** E-mail addresses are sometimes complex, often illogical, and always unforgiving. Omit one character or misread the letter l for the number 1, and your message bounces. Solution: Use your electronic address book for people you write to frequently. And double-check every address that you key in manually. Also be sure that you don't reply to a group of receivers when you intend to answer only one.
- **Avoid misleading subject lines.** With an abundance of spam (junk mail) clogging most inboxes, make sure your subject line is relevant and helpful. Generic tags such as *Hello* and *Great Deal* may cause your message to be deleted before it is opened.

Content, Tone, and Correctness. Although e-mail seems as casual as a telephone call, it's not. Because it produces a permanent record, think carefully about what you say and how you say it.

Avoid sending e-mail messages that are longer than three screens.

- **Be concise.** Don't burden readers with unnecessary information. Remember that monitors are small and typefaces are often difficult to read. Organize your ideas tightly. Messages over three screens in length would have to be very compelling to keep a reader's interest.
- **Don't send anything you wouldn't want published.** Because e-mail seems like a telephone call or a person-to-person conversation, writers sometimes send sensitive, confidential, inflammatory, or potentially embarrassing messages. Beware! E-mail creates a permanent record that often does not go away even when deleted. And every message is a corporate communication that can be used against you or your employer. Don't write anything that you wouldn't want your boss, your family, or a judge to read.

E-mail should not be used for bad news or angry messages.

- **Don't use e-mail to avoid contact.** E-mail is inappropriate for breaking bad news or for resolving arguments. For example, it's improper to fire a person by e-mail. It's also not a good channel for dealing with conflict with supervisors, subordinates, or others. If there's any possibility of hurt feelings, pick up the telephone or pay the person a visit.
- **Never respond when you're angry.** Always allow some time to cool off before shooting off a response to an upsetting message. You often come up with different and better alternatives after thinking about what was said. If possible, iron out differences in person.

- **Care about correctness.** People are still judged by their writing, whether electronic or paper-based. Sloppy e-mail messages (with missing apostrophes, haphazard spelling, and stream-of-consciousness writing) make readers work too hard. They resent not only the information but also the writer.
- **Resist humor and tongue-in-cheek comments.** Without the nonverbal cues conveyed by your face and your voice, humor can easily be misunderstood.

Avoid humorous or facetious expressions that may be misunderstood.

Netiquette. Although e-mail is a new communication channel, a number of rules of polite on-line interaction are emerging.

- **Limit any tendency to send blanket copies.** Send copies only to people who really need to see a message. It is unnecessary to document every business decision and action with an electronic paper trail.
- **Never send "spam."** Sending unsolicited advertisements ("spam") either by fax or e-mail is illegal in the United States.
- **Consider using identifying labels.** When appropriate, add one of the following labels to the subject line: ACTION (action required, please respond); FYI (for your information, no response needed); RE (this is a reply to another message); URGENT (please respond immediately).

DILBERT   By Scott Adams

- **Use capital letters only for emphasis or for titles.** Avoid writing entire messages in all caps, which is like SHOUTING!
- **Announce attachments.** If you're sending a lengthy attachment, tell your receiver. You might also ask what format is preferred.
- **Don't forward without permission.** Obtain approval before forwarding a message.

Replying to E-Mail. The following tips can save you time and frustration when answering messages.

- **Scan all messages in your inbox before replying to each individually.** Because subsequent messages often affect the way you respond, read them all first (especially all those from the same individual).
- **Don't automatically return the sender's message.** When replying, cut and paste the relevant parts. Avoid irritating your recipients by returning the entire "thread" (sequence of messages) on a topic.
- **Revise the subject line if the topic changes.** When replying or continuing an e-mail exchange, revise the subject line as the topic changes.

Personal Use. Remember that office computers are meant for work-related communication.

Cathy

- **Don't use company computers for personal matters.** Unless your company specifically allows it, never use your employer's computers for personal messages, personal shopping, or entertainment.
- **Assume that all e-mail is monitored.** Employers legally have the right to monitor e-mail, and many do.

Other Smart E-Mail Practices. Depending on your messages and audience, the following tips promote effective electronic communication.

- **Use design to improve readability of longer messages.** When a message requires several screens, help the reader with headings, bulleted listings, side headings, and perhaps an introductory summary that describes what will follow. Although these techniques lengthen a message, they shorten reading time.
- **Consider cultural differences.** When using this borderless tool, be especially clear and precise in your language. Remember that figurative clichés (*pull up stakes, playing second fiddle*), sports references (*hit a home run, play by the rules*), and slang (*cool, stoked*) cause confusion abroad.
- **Double-check before hitting the *Send* button.** Have you included everything? Avoid the necessity of sending a second message, which makes you look careless. Use spell-check and reread for fluency before sending.

Formatting E-Mail Messages

Because e-mail is a developing communication channel, its formatting and usage conventions are still fluid. Users and authorities, for instance, do not always agree on what's appropriate for salutations and closings. The following suggestions, however, can guide you in formatting most e-mail messages, but always check with your organization to observe its practices.

Although e-mail formatting style is still developing, all messages contain To, From, Date, and Subject lines.

Guide Words. Following the guide word *To,* some writers insert just the recipient's electronic address, such as *PWille@accountpro.com.* Other writers prefer to include the receiver's full name plus the electronic address, as shown in Figure 5.2. By including full names in the *To* and *From* slots, both receivers and senders are better able to identify the message. By the way, the order of *Date, To, From, Subject,* and other guide words varies depending on your e-mail program and whether you are sending or receiving the message.

Most e-mail programs automatically add the current date after *Date.* On the *Cc* line (which stands for *carbon* or *courtesy copy*) you can type the address of anyone who is to receive a copy of the message. Remember, though, to send copies only to those people directly involved with the message. Most e-mail programs also include a line for *Bcc* (*blind carbon copy*). This sends a copy without the addressee's knowledge. Many savvy writers today use *Bcc* for the names and addresses of a

FIGURE 5.2 Typical E-Mail Request Message

Tips for Formatting E-mail

- After *To,* type the receiver's electronic address. If you include the receiver's name, enclose the address in angle brackets.
- After *From,* type your name and electronic address, if your program does not insert it automatically.
- After *Subject,* provide a clear description of your message.
- Insert the addresses of anyone receiving carbon or blind copies.
- Include a salutation (such as *Dear Pat, Hi Pat, Greetings*) or weave the receiver's name into the first line. Some writers omit a salutation.
- Set your line length for no more than 80 characters. If you expect your message to be forwarded, set it for 60 characters.
- Use word wrap rather than pressing *Enter* at line ends.
- Double-space (press *Enter*) between paragraphs.
- Do not type in all caps or in all lowercase letters.
- Include a complimentary close, your name, and your address if you wish.

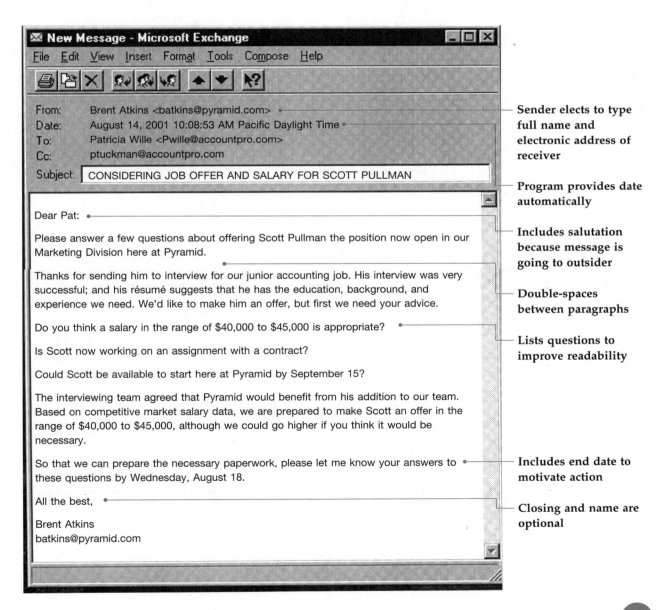

New Message - Microsoft Exchange

File   Edit   View   Insert   Format   Tools   Compose   Help

From: Brent Atkins <batkins@pyramid.com> —— Sender elects to type full name and electronic address of receiver
Date: August 14, 2001 10:08:53 AM Pacific Daylight Time
To: Patricia Wille <Pwille@accountpro.com>
Cc: ptuckman@accountpro.com
Subject: CONSIDERING JOB OFFER AND SALARY FOR SCOTT PULLMAN

—— Program provides date automatically

Dear Pat: •

Please answer a few questions about offering Scott Pullman the position now open in our Marketing Division here at Pyramid.

—— Includes salutation because message is going to outsider

Thanks for sending him to interview for our junior accounting job. His interview was very successful; and his résumé suggests that he has the education, background, and experience we need. We'd like to make him an offer, but first we need your advice.

—— Double-spaces between paragraphs

Do you think a salary in the range of $40,000 to $45,000 is appropriate?

Is Scott now working on an assignment with a contract?

Could Scott be available to start here at Pyramid by September 15?

—— Lists questions to improve readability

The interviewing team agreed that Pyramid would benefit from his addition to our team. Based on competitive market salary data, we are prepared to make Scott an offer in the range of $40,000 to $45,000, although we could go higher if you think it would be necessary.

So that we can prepare the necessary paperwork, please let me know your answers to these questions by Wednesday, August 18.

—— Includes end date to motivate action

All the best, •

Brent Atkins
batkins@pyramid.com

—— Closing and name are optional

---

list of receivers, a technique that avoids revealing the addresses to the entire group. On the subject line, identify the subject of the memo. Be sure to include enough information to be clear and compelling.

Salutations may be omitted in messages to close colleagues, but they are generally used in messages to others.

Salutation. What to do about a salutation is sticky. Many writers omit a salutation because they consider the message a memo. In the past, hard-copy memos were sent only to company insiders, and salutations were omitted. However, when e-mail messages travel to outsiders, omitting a salutation seems curt and unfriendly. Because the message is more like a letter, a salutation is appropriate (such as *Dear Jake; Hi, Jake; Greetings;* or just *Jake*). Including a salutation is also a visual cue to where the message begins. Many messages are transmitted or forwarded with such long headers that finding the beginning of the message can be difficult. A salutation helps, as shown in Figure 5.2. Other writers do not use a salutation; instead, they use the name of the recipient in the first sentence.

Body. The body of an e-mail message should be typed with upper- and lower-case characters—never in all uppercase or all lowercase characters. Cover just one topic, and try to keep the total message under three screens in length. To assist you, many e-mail programs have basic text-editing features, such as cut, copy, paste, and word-wrap. However, avoid boldface and italics because they may create a string of control characters that may cause chaos on the recipient's computer.

Closing lines (or a signature block) should name the writer and provide sufficient information for identification.

Closing Lines. Writers of e-mail messages sent within organizations may omit closings and even skip their names at the end of messages. They can omit these items because receivers recognize them from identification in the opening lines. But for outside messages, a writer might include a closing such as *Cheers* or *All the best* followed by the writer's name and e-mail address (because some systems do not transmit your address automatically). If the recipient is unlikely to know you, it's wise to include your title and organization. Some veteran e-mail users include a *signature file* with identifying information embellished with keyboard art. Use restraint, however, because signature files take up precious bandwidth (Internet capacity).

Developing a Writing Plan for Memos and E-Mail Messages

A writing plan helps you organize a complete message.

In this book you will be shown a number of writing plans appropriate for different messages. These plans provide a skeleton; they are the bones of a message. Writers provide the flesh. Simply plugging in phrases or someone else's words won't work. Good writers provide details and link their ideas with transitions to create fluent and meaningful messages. However, a writing plan helps you get started and gives you ideas about what to include. At first, you will probably rely on these plans considerably. As you progress, they will become less important. Later in the book no plans are provided.

Here is a general writing plan for a routine memo or e-mail message that is not expected to create displeasure or resistance.

WRITING PLAN FOR ROUTINE MEMOS AND E-MAIL MESSAGES

- **Subject line**—Summarize memo contents.
- **Opening**—State the main idea.
- **Body**—Provide background data and explain the main idea.
- **Closing**—Request action, summarize message, or present closing thought.

Writing the Subject Line

Probably the most important part of a memo or an e-mail message is the subject line. It should summarize the central idea and provide quick identification. It is usually written in an abbreviated style, often without articles (*a, an, the*). It need not be a complete sentence, and it does not end with a period. E-mail subject lines are particularly important, since meaningless ones may cause readers to delete a message without ever opening it. Good subject lines, such as the following, are specific, eye-catching, and talking (that is, they contain a verb form):

Subject: Three Promotional Items to Showcase at Our Next Trade Show (rather than *Trade Show*)

Subject: Beefing Up Our Messaging Capabilities (rather than *New Software*)

Subject: Staff Meeting to Discuss Summer Vacation Schedules (rather than *Meeting*)

A subject line must be concise but meaningful.

Beginning With the Main Idea

Most memos and e-mails cover routine, nonsensitive information that can be handled in a straightforward manner. Begin by frontloading; that is, reveal the main idea immediately. Even though the purpose of a memo or e-mail is summarized in the subject line, that purpose should be restated—and amplified—in the first sentence. Some readers skip the subject line and plunge right into the first sentence. Notice how the following indirect memo openers can be improved by frontloading.

Frontloading means revealing the main idea immediately.

Indirect Opening	**Direct Opening**
This is to inform you that for the past six months we have been examining benefits as part of our negotiation package under a contract that expires soon.	Please review the following four changes in our benefit package and let us know your preference by January 1.
As you may know, employees in Document Production have been complaining about eye fatigue as a result of the overhead fluorescent lighting in their center.	To improve lighting in Document Production, I recommend that we purchase high-intensity desk lamps.

Explaining Clearly in the Body

In the body of the message, explain the main idea. If you are asking for detailed information, arrange your questions in logical order. If you are providing information, group similar information together. When considerable data are involved, use a separate paragraph for each topic. Work for effective transitions between paragraphs.

Design your data for easy comprehension by using bulleted items, headings, tables, and lists. You'll learn more about writing lists shortly. All these techniques make readers understand important points quickly. Compare the following two versions of the same message. Notice how the graphic devices of bullets, columns, headings, and white space make the main points easier to comprehend.

Organize the message logically, keeping similar information grouped together.

Hard-to-Read Paragraph

Graphic highlighting (bullets, numbered lists, headings) makes information easier to read and review.

Effective immediately are the following air travel guidelines. Between now and December 31, only account executives may take company-approved trips. These individuals will be allowed to take a maximum of two trips per year, and they are to travel economy or budget class only.

Improved With Graphic Highlighting

Effective immediately are the following air travel guidelines:

* Who may travel: Account executives only
* How many trips: A maximum of two trips yearly
* By when: Between now and December 31
* Air class: Economy or budget class only

In addition to highlighting important information, pay attention to the tone of your message. Although memos are generally informal, they should also be professional. Remember that e-mail messages are not telephone conversations. Don't be overly casual, jocular, or blunt. Do attempt to establish a conversational tone by using occasional contractions (*won't, didn't, couldn't*) and personal pronouns (*I, me, we*).

Closing the Memo

The end of a memo should include action information (such as a deadline), a summarizing statement, or a closing thought.

Generally, end a memo or e-mail message with (1) action information, dates, or deadlines; (2) a summary of the message; or (3) a closing thought. Here again the value of thinking through the message before actually writing it becomes apparent. The closing is where readers look for deadlines and action language. An effective memo or e-mail closing might be, *Please submit your report by June 15 so that we can have your data before our July planning session.*

In more complex messages a summary of main points may be an appropriate closing. If no action request is made and a closing summary is unnecessary, you might end with a simple concluding thought (*I'm glad to answer your questions* or *This sounds like a useful project*). Although you needn't close messages to coworkers with goodwill statements such as those found in letters to customers or clients, some closing thought is often necessary to prevent a feeling of abruptness.

Closings can show gratitude or encourage feedback with remarks such as *I sincerely appreciate your cooperation* or *What are your ideas on this proposal?* Other closings look forward to what's next, such as *How would you like to proceed?* Avoid trite expressions, such as *Please let me know if I may be of further assistance.*

Whenever possible, the closing paragraph of a request should be *end dated*. An end date sets a deadline for the requested action and gives a reason for this action to be completed by the deadline. Such end dating prevents procrastination and allows the reader to plan a course of action to ensure completion by the date given. Giving a reason adds credibility to a deadline.

Please submit your order by December 1 so that sufficient labels will be on hand for mailing the year-end reports January 15.

Putting It All Together

The memo shown in Figure 5.3 is the first draft of a message Melissa Rivers wrote to her team leader. Although it contains solid information, the first version is so wordy and poorly organized that the reader has trouble grasping its significance. Melissa's revised message opens directly. Both the subject line and the first sentence explain the purpose for writing. Notice how much easier the revised ver-

FIGURE 5.3 Revising a Draft Memo

Ineffective First Draft

TO: George Wooldridge

This is in response to your recent inquiry about our customer database. Your message of May 9 said that you wanted to know how to deal with the database problems. ●————— Fails to reveal purpose quickly and concisely

I can tell you that the biggest problem is that it contains a lot of outdated information, including customers who haven't purchased anything in five or more years. Another problem is that the old database is not compatible with ●————— the new Access software that is being used by our mailing service, and this makes it difficult to merge files.

Does not help reader see the two problems or the three recommendations

I think I can solve both problems, however, by starting a new database. This would be the place where we put the names of all new customers. And we would have it keyed using Access software. The problem with outdated information could be solved by finding out if the customers in ●————— our old database wish to continue receiving our newsletter and product announcements. Finally, we would rekey the names of all active customers in the new database.

Forgets to conclude with next action and end date

Effective Final Draft

Interoffice Memorandum

DATE: May 15, 200X

TO: George Wooldridge, Team Leader

FROM: Melissa Rivers, Marketing

Subject line summarizes and identifies purpose ————— ● **SUBJECT:**   IMPROVING OUR CUSTOMER DATABASE

Opening states purpose concisely ————— ● As you requested, here are my recommendations for improving our customer database. The database has two major problems. First, it contains many names of individuals who have not made purchases in five or more years. Second, the format is not compatible with the new Access software used by our mailing service. The following procedures, however, should solve both problems:

Body organizes main points for readability ————— ● • **Start a new database.** Effective immediately, enter the names of all new customers in a new database using Access software.

• **Determine the status of customers in our old database.** Send out a mailing asking whether recipients wish to continue receiving our newsletter and product announcements.

• **Rekey the names of active customers in the new database.** Enter the names of all responding customers in our new database so that we have only one active database.

Closing mentions key benefit, provides deadline, and looks forward to next action ————— ● These changes will enable you, as team leader, to request mailings that go only to active customers. If you think these suggestions are workable, please respond by May 20. I will then investigate costs.

sion is to read. Bullets and boldfaced headings emphasize the actions necessary to solve the database problems. Notice, too, that the revised version ends with a deadline and refers to the next action to be taken.

Improving Memo and E-Mail Readability With Listing Techniques

Because readers of memos and e-mail messages are usually in a hurry, they want important information to stand out. One of the best ways to improve the readability of any message is by listing items. And the information in memos and e-mail messages often lends itself to listing. A list is a group or series of related items, usually three or more. Since lists require fewer words than complete sentences, they can be read and understood quickly and easily. In writing lists, keep these general points in mind.

You can improve the readability of a message by listing parallel items.

- **Make listed items parallel.** Listed items must all relate to the same topic, and they must be balanced grammatically. If one item is a single word but the next item requires a paragraph of explanation, the items are not suitable for listing.
- **Use bullets, numbers, or letters appropriately.** Numbers (*1, 2, 3*) and letters (*a, b, c*) suggest a hierarchy or sequence of operation; bullets merely separate.
- **Use generally accepted punctuation.** Most writers use a colon following the introduction to most lists. However, they don't use a colon if the listed items follow a verb or a preposition (for example, *the colors are red, yellow, and blue*). Use end punctuation only after complete sentences, and capitalize the first word of items listed vertically.

Parallelism

Instead of This	**Try This**
She likes *sleeping, eating,* and *to work.*	She likes *sleeping, eating,* and *working.*
We are hiring the following: *sales clerks, managers who will function as supervisors,* and *people to work in offices.*	We are hiring the following: *sales clerks, supervising managers,* and *office personnel.*

Instructions

Instead of This	**Try This**
Here are the instructions for operating the copy machine. First, you insert your meter in the slot. Then you load paper in the upper tray. Last, copies are fed through the feed chute.	Follow these steps to use the copy machine: 1. *Insert* your meter in the slot. 2. *Load* paper in the upper tray. 3. *Feed* copies through the feed chute.

Listed Items With Headings

Instead of This

On May 16 we will be in Albany, and Dr. Susan Dillon is the speaker. On June 20, we will be in Dallas and Dr. Diane Minger is the speaker.

Try This

Date	City	Speaker
May 16	Albany	Dr. Susan Dillon
June 20	Dallas	Dr. Diane Minger

Listed Items for Emphasis Within Sentences

Instead of This	**Try This**
To keep exercising, you should make a written commitment to yourself, set realistic goals for each day's workout, and enlist the support of a friend.	To keep exercising, you should (a) make a written commitment to yourself, (b) set realistic goals for each day's workout, and (c) enlist the support of a friend.

Bulleted Items

Instead of This	**Try This**
Our goal • Is to recruit intensely competitive sales reps • Is to use reps who know our products • Recruit intelligent reps who learn quickly	Our goal is to recruit sales reps who are • Intensely competitive • Familiar with our products • Intelligent and learn quickly

Memos and E-Mail Messages That Inform

You've now studied a basic plan for writing memos and e-mail messages, and you've learned how to highlight ideas with listing techniques. Now, you'll see how these techniques can be applied to specific situations. Most memos and e-mail messages can be divided into four groups: (1) those that inform, (2) those that request, (3) those that respond, and (4) those that persuade. In this chapter we will be concerned with the first three groups because they use the direct strategy. The fourth group, persuasive messages, uses the indirect strategy. They will be discussed in Chapter 8.

Memos that inform generally explain organization policies, procedures, and guidelines. As policy-making documents, these messages must be particularly clear and concise.

The e-mail message shown in Figure 5.4 informs department managers of a change in job-hiring procedures. The ineffective version begins negatively with an explanation of what went wrong with a new hiring procedure. Instead of starting directly, this message wanders through a maze of blame and incoherent explanation. The new procedure is stated negatively (*Do not submit your advertisements . . . .*) and is hidden inside two blocky paragraphs.

The effective version begins directly by telling readers immediately what the e-mail message is about. The next paragraph explains why the change is necessary. A list enumerates step-by-step procedures, thus making it easy for the reader to understand and follow the steps. The final paragraph restates the primary benefits of the new procedure and tells how more information may be obtained if necessary.

> **Memos and e-mail messages that inform often consist of policies, procedures, and guidelines.**

Memos and E-Mail Messages That Request

Messages that make requests are most effective when they use the direct approach. The reader learns immediately what is being requested. However, if you have any reason to suspect that the reader may resist the request, then an indirect approach would probably be more successful.

FIGURE 5.4 E-Mail Message That Informs

Ineffective First Draft

Vague, negative subject line ——

Fails to pinpoint main idea in opening ——

Rambling, negative explanation ——

New procedure is hard to follow ——

Uses threats instead of showing benefits to reader ——

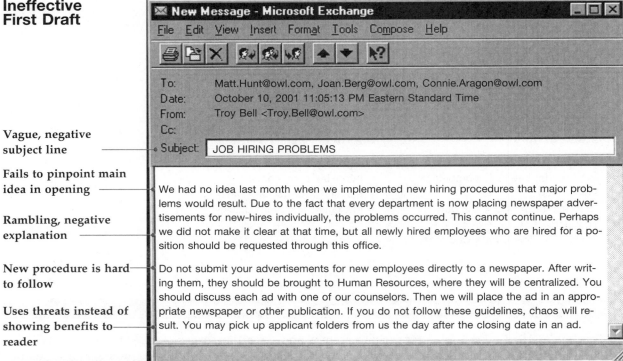

To: Matt.Hunt@owl.com, Joan.Berg@owl.com, Connie.Aragon@owl.com
Date: October 10, 2001 11:05:13 PM Eastern Standard Time
From: Troy Bell <Troy.Bell@owl.com>
Cc:
Subject: JOB HIRING PROBLEMS

We had no idea last month when we implemented new hiring procedures that major problems would result. Due to the fact that every department is now placing newspaper advertisements for new-hires individually, the problems occurred. This cannot continue. Perhaps we did not make it clear at that time, but all newly hired employees who are hired for a position should be requested through this office.

Do not submit your advertisements for new employees directly to a newspaper. After writing them, they should be brought to Human Resources, where they will be centralized. You should discuss each ad with one of our counselors. Then we will place the ad in an appropriate newspaper or other publication. If you do not follow these guidelines, chaos will result. You may pick up applicant folders from us the day after the closing date in an ad.

Effective Final Draft

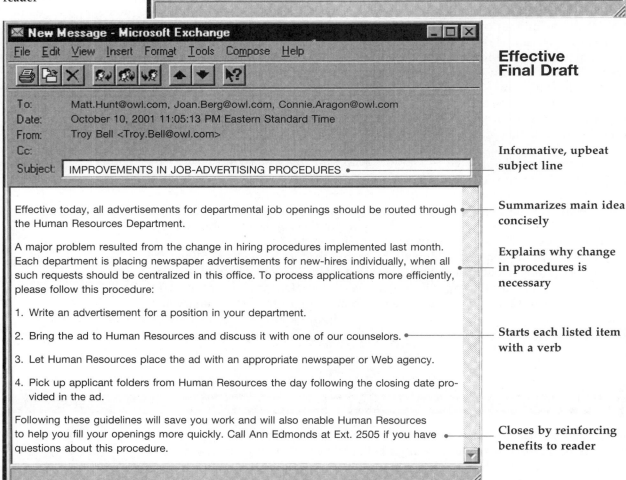

To: Matt.Hunt@owl.com, Joan.Berg@owl.com, Connie.Aragon@owl.com
Date: October 10, 2001 11:05:13 PM Eastern Standard Time
From: Troy Bell <Troy.Bell@owl.com>
Cc:
Subject: IMPROVEMENTS IN JOB-ADVERTISING PROCEDURES

Effective today, all advertisements for departmental job openings should be routed through the Human Resources Department.

A major problem resulted from the change in hiring procedures implemented last month. Each department is placing newspaper advertisements for new-hires individually, when all such requests should be centralized in this office. To process applications more efficiently, please follow this procedure:

1. Write an advertisement for a position in your department.

2. Bring the ad to Human Resources and discuss it with one of our counselors.

3. Let Human Resources place the ad with an appropriate newspaper or Web agency.

4. Pick up applicant folders from Human Resources the day following the closing date provided in the ad.

Following these guidelines will save you work and will also enable Human Resources to help you fill your openings more quickly. Call Ann Edmonds at Ext. 2505 if you have questions about this procedure.

Informative, upbeat subject line ——

Summarizes main idea concisely ——

Explains why change in procedures is necessary ——

Starts each listed item with a verb ——

Closes by reinforcing benefits to reader ——

Requests should be courteous and respectful, as illustrated in Figure 5.5. They should not be demanding or dictatorial. The tone of the following request would likely antagonize its recipient:

> I want you to find out why the Davis account was not included in this report, and I want this information before you do anything else.

The tone of a request message should encourage cooperation.

So that the intent of the message is not misunderstood, requests should be considered carefully and written clearly. What may seem clear to the writer may not always be clear to a reader. That's why it's always a good idea to have a fellow worker read an important message for clarity before it is sent out.

Notice in Figure 5.5 that the writer ends by asking that the responses be made before May 5 because the information will be used for a Management Council meeting May 8. Providing an end date helps the reader know how to plan a response so that action is completed by the date given. Expressions such as "do it whenever you can" or "complete it as soon as possible" make little impression on procrastinators or very busy people. It's always wise to provide a specific date for completion. Dates can be entered into calendars to serve as reminders.

FIGURE 5.5 E-Mail Message That Requests

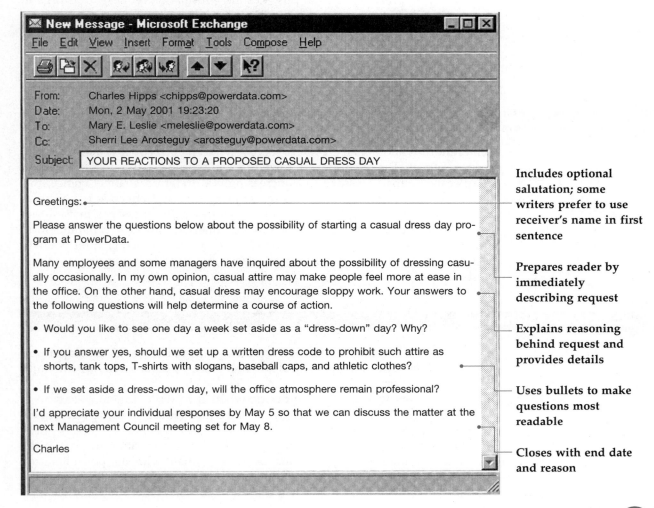

Includes optional salutation; some writers prefer to use receiver's name in first sentence

Prepares reader by immediately describing request

Explains reasoning behind request and provides details

Uses bullets to make questions most readable

Closes with end date and reason

Memos and E-Mail Messages That Respond

Much office correspondence reacts or responds to memos, e-mail messages, and other documents. When responding to a document, follow these preparatory steps:

1. Collect whatever information is necessary.
2. Organize your thoughts.
3. Make a brief outline of the points you plan to cover.

Begin the memo with a clear statement of the main idea, which often is a summary of the contents of the memo. Avoid wordy and dated openings such as *Pursuant to your request of January 20, I am herewith including the information you wanted.* Although many business messages actually sound like the preceding, they waste time and say little.

Notice in Figure 5.6 that Mary Leslie, manager of Legal Support Services, uses a straightforward opening in responding to her boss's request for information. She refers to his request, announces the information to follow, and identifies the date of the original message. Mary decides to answer with a standard hard-copy memo because she considers her reactions private and because she thinks that Vice President Hipps would like to have a permanent record of each manager's reactions to take to the Management Council meeting. She also knows that she is well within the deadline set for a response.

The body of a response memo provides the information requested. Its organization generally follows the sequence of the request. In Mary's memo she answers the questions as her boss presented them. However, she further clarifies the information by providing summarizing headings in bold type. These headings emphasize the groupings and help the reader see immediately what information is covered. The memo closes with a reassuring summary.

Summing Up and Looking Forward

Memorandums and e-mail messages serve as vital channels of information within business offices. They use a standardized format to request and deliver information. Because e-mail messages are increasingly a preferred channel choice, this chapter presented many techniques for sending safe and effective e-mail messages. You learned to apply the direct strategy in writing messages that inform, request, and respond. You also learned to use bullets, numbers, and parallel form for listing information so that main points stand out. In the next chapter you will extend the direct strategy to writing letters that make requests and respond to requests.

Critical Thinking

1. How can the writer of a business memo or an e-mail message develop a conversational tone and still be professional? Why do e-mail writers sometimes forget to be professional?
2. What factors would help you decide whether to write a memo, send an e-mail, make a telephone call, leave a voice mail message, or deliver a message in person?
3. Why are lawyers and technology experts warning companies to store, organize, and manage computer data, including e-mail, with sharper diligence?
4. Discuss the ramifications of the following statement: Once a memo or any other document leaves your hands, you have essentially published it.

Chapter 5 Memorandums and E-Mail

FIGURE 5.6 Memo That Responds

IntraData Associates
Interoffice Memo

DATE: May 4, 200X

TO: Charles Hipps, Vice President, Employee Relations

FROM: Mary E. Leslie, Manager, Legal Support Services   *M&L*

SUBJECT: REACTIONS TO PROPOSED CASUAL DRESS DAY PROGRAM   •————— **Announces main idea**

Here are my reactions, Charles, to your inquiry about a casual dress day   •————— **Summarizes main idea**
program made in your e-mail message of May 2.   **and refers to previous**
                                                                             message

- **Establish a dress-down day?** Yes, I would like to see such a day. In my
  department we now have a number of employees with flex schedules. They
  perform part of their work at home, where they can be as casual as they
  wish. Employees confined here in the office are a little resentful. I think a
  dress-down day could offer some compensation to those who come to the
  office daily.

- **Implement a dress code?** By all means! We definitely need a written   •————— **Arranges responses in**
  dress code not only to establish standards but also to protect the company   **order of original**
  from frivolous lawsuits.   **request and uses**
                                                                               boldface headings to
- **Professional office atmosphere?** I would hope that casual dress would   **emphasize and clarify**
  not promote casual work attitudes as well. We must establish that   **groupings**
  professionalism is non-negotiable. For example, we can't allow two-hour
  lunches or entire afternoons spent gossiping instead of working. Moreover,
  I think we should be careful in allowing casual dress only on the
  designated day, once a week.

I think a casual attire program can be beneficial and improve morale. But we   •————— **Closes with reassuring**
definitely need a dress code in place at the beginning of the program. Let me   **remark and offer of**
know if I may assist in implementing a casual-dress day program.   **further assistance**

5. Ethical Issue: Should managers have the right to monitor the e-mail messages of employees? Why or why not? What if employees are warned that e-mail could be monitored? If a company sets up an e-mail policy, should only in-house transmissions be monitored? Only outside transmissions?

Chapter Review

6. What three questions should a writer ask before beginning a memo or e-mail message?

7. Why are subject lines such as "Hello" or "Meeting" inappropriate?

8. Since e-mail messages are almost like telephone calls, why should one bother about correct spelling, grammar, punctuation, and expression?

9. In formatting e-mail messages, when should you include a salutation (*Dear Mark*)?

10. Should writers of e-mail messages include their names at the ends of messages?

11. What are the four parts of the writing plan for a routine memo or an e-mail message? What is included in each?

12. How can listed items improve memos and e-mail messages?

13. When are numbers appropriate for listing items? When are bullets appropriate?

14. What are four groups of memos? Which require a direct strategy?

15. What is *end dating?*

Writing Improvement Exercises

Message Openers. Compare the following sets of message openers. Circle the letter of the opener that illustrates a direct opening. Be prepared to discuss the weaknesses and strengths of each.

16. A letter to a security company inquiring about costs:
    a. We are considering keeping our facility open 24 hours a day because we can increase our profitability by running three shifts a day. We need some information.
    b. Please answer the following questions about the cost of adding security guards and electronic cameras to enable 24-hour operation of our facility.
17. An e-mail message announcing an in-service program:
    a. Employees interested in improving their writing and communication skills are invited to an in-service training program beginning October 4.
    b. For the past year we have been investigating the possibility of developing an in-service training program for some of our employees.
18. An e-mail message announcing a study:
    a. We have noticed recently a gradual but steady decline in the number of customer checking accounts. We are disturbed by this trend, and for this reason I am asking our Customer Relations Department to conduct a study and make recommendations regarding this important problem.
    b. Our Customer Relations Department will conduct a study and make recommendations regarding the gradual but steady decline of customer checking accounts.
19. A memo announcing a new procedure:
    a. Some customer representatives in the field have suggested that they would like to key their reports from the field instead of coming back to the office to enter them in their computers. That's why we have made a number of changes. We would like you to use the following procedures.
    b. Customer representatives may now key their field reports using the following procedures.

Opening Paragraphs. The following opening paragraphs to memos are wordy and indirect. After reading each paragraph, identify the main idea. Then, write an opening sentence that illustrates a more direct opening. Use a separate sheet if necessary.

20. Several staff members came to me and announced their interest in learning more about severance policies and separation benefits. As most of you know, these areas of concern are increasingly important for most Human Resources professionals. A seminar entitled "Severance & Separation Benefits" is being conducted February 11. I am allowing the following employees to attend the seminar: Terence Curran, Cindy Thompson, and Darlene McClure.

21. Your Intel Employees Association has secured for you discounts on auto repair, carpet purchases, travel arrangements, and many other services. These services are available to you if you have a Buying Power Card. All Intel employees are eligible for their own private Buying Power Cards.

Lists. Write lists as indicated below.

22. Use the following information to compose a single sentence that includes an introductory statement and a list with letters (*a, b, c*). Do not list the items vertically.

    The front page of a Web site should orient readers. This front page should tell them what the site is about. It should also tell about the organization of the site. Finally, it should tell them how to navigate the site.

23. Use the following information to compose a bulleted vertical list with an introductory statement.

To use the conventional Rollerblade heel brake, you should do these things. First, you should move one leg slightly forward. Then the ball of your foot should be lifted. Finally, the heel should be dragged to complete the braking action.

24. Use the following information to compose a sentence containing a list.

Your equipment lease will mature in a month. When it does, you must make a decision. Three options are available to you. If you like, you may purchase the equipment at fair market value. Or the existing lease may be extended, again at fair market value. Finally, if neither of these options is appealing, the equipment could be sent back to the lessor.

Activities and Cases

5.1 Memo That Informs: Sky-High Printing Bills. As Jeff Gordon, director of operations for DPI, a small software company, you are disturbed about some very large printing bills you've been receiving. DPI hires outside printers to prepare software manuals, marketing brochures, and sales materials. Printing is a necessary part of your business. But you hit the ceiling when you saw a recent bill from PrintMasters. Although all the bills seem high, those from PrintMasters are particularly suspicious.

You don't want to blame anyone, but you do want to inform all staff members that no printing bills will be paid in the future without careful scrutiny. In talking it over with Donna Graham, your colleague, you say, "We've got to make some changes. I can't plan my budget or control costs when these outrageous printing bills keep popping up. We're going to have to come up with some standardized procedure. Any ideas?" Donna responds, "One of the reasons that costs are so high is that some departments just don't think through their printing specifications before sending a job out. Maybe we should make departments write out their exact specifications and then get estimates and approvals—before they order any printing job."

You and she decide that two written estimates should be secured for any proposed printing job. You also decide that these estimates should be submitted to Donna for authorization. Only then can a department order any outside printing job. And this new procedure must start immediately. As Donna leaves, you remark, "You know, these new procedures mean that we'll probably get more competitive pricing. And they could even mean that departments will find better, more creative printing options!"

Your Task. Think through the process involved in creating a memo to the staff announcing the changes. To help you apply the principles you have learned in this chapter, read the options suggested here. Circle the most appropriate response for each question. If your instructor directs, compose the message as a memo addressed to all staff members or as an e-mail message addressed to your instructor.

Developing the Memo

1. What is the main idea in this memo?
   a. You are outraged at the high printing bills being received lately.
   b. You can't plan budgets or control costs when these unexpected bills keep coming in.
   c. The bills from PrintMasters are particularly suspicious.

d. A new procedure for submitting requests for outside printing jobs is being instituted immediately.

2. An effective opening sentence for your memo might be
　　a. Donna Graham and I have been concerned about the high printing bills we have received lately.
　　b. Please follow the new procedures listed below in submitting requests for outside printing jobs.
　　c. Very large expenditures for printing jobs have been submitted recently, some of which are quite suspicious.
　　d. Henceforth, no employee may send out a printing job without prior written approval.

3. The body of the memo should
　　a. Explain why the new procedure is necessary and how to follow it.
　　b. Recount the highlights of your conversation with Donna.
　　c. Identify the bills of the most offending printers, particularly PrintMasters.
　　d. Identify the departments and employees who have been responsible for most of the high costs.

4. In explaining the new procedure, you will probably want to list each step. Which of the following statements illustrates the best form?
　　a. Submission of all written estimates should be made to Donna Graham.
　　b. Written estimates should be submitted to Donna Graham.
　　c. Submit written estimates to Donna Graham.
　　d. Donna Graham will expect all written estimates to be submitted to her.

5. An effective closing for your memo might be
　　a. These procedures are effective immediately. Thank you for your cooperation in this matter.
　　b. Following these new procedures, which are effective immediately, will result in more competitive pricing and perhaps may even provide you with new creative printing options. If you have any questions, call Donna Graham at Ext. 556.
　　c. These procedures are effective immediately. By the way, don't forget to send me your ideas for equipping the new fitness center.
　　d. If I may be of assistance to you in any way, do not hesitate to call on me.

5.2 Memo That Requests: Making the Best of Temps. Analyze the following poorly written memo. List its faults in the space provided. Outline an appropriate plan for a memo that requests. Then, on a separate sheet or as an e-mail message, write an improved version of this memo.

DATE:　　　January 14, 200x
TO:　　　　Department Managers
FROM:　　 Ryan Crawford, Manager
　　　　　　Human Resources Department
SUBJECT:　TEMPORARY WORKERS

This is to inform you that we have not been totally happy with the quality of the temporary workers we are getting. We have trouble budgeting for them, their selection is difficult, and so is the hiring of these extra workers.

　Hoping to improve the problem, your help is requested. We need to know your past history in regard to the average number of temporary office workers in your department. This number would be based on how many you use each month. Your input is also requested in regard to the time a temporary worker remains in your employ. As a general rule, do you know the length of a temporary worker's work assignment? We're talking about your department only, of course. Another important bit of information revolves around the skills you need. To get you the best temps, your needs must be known. As a matter of fact, we also would like to know what temporary agencies you now use to supply temps to your department.

Pursuant to this request, we need your response by January 20. It would be advisable for you to write your answers on this sheet. Pending receipt of the return of this request, may we take the liberty of thanking you in advance. Through the use of the information you provide, we will make plans for an improved policy. That will help you fill your temporary employment needs pertaining to your department as efficiently as possible.

1. List at least five faults in this memo.

2. Outline a general writing plan for this memo.
   Subject line:
   Opening:
   Body:
   Closing:

5.3 Memo That Informs: Time Management Tips. Read the following poorly written memo, analyze its faults, outline a general writing plan, and then revise it.

DATE: Current
TO: Staff Members
FROM: Randy Eastman, Manager
SUBJECT: SUGGESTIONS

Recently I had the pleasure of attending an excellent time management seminar in which we managers were told about some interesting strategies for managing the glut of information from which we all suffer. Since many of you have been complaining about all the time you spend on e-mail and voice mail, I thought I would send you some of the best pointers we were given. These might help you increase your productivity and decrease your frustration.

When it comes to e-mail, we were urged to practice e-mail "triage." This means glancing through all incoming mail quickly and separating the messages you need to answer immediately, as well as determining which messages can wait and which ones can be deleted. Generally, you can do this by checking subject lines and the names of senders. To cut down on the amount of time you spend on your e-mail, you should check e-mail messages only once or twice each day and at specific times so that you develop a routine. This simple practice can save you a lot of wasted time. Another technique involves time management but also courtesy. Be sure to respond briefly to all important e-mails, even if you can say only that you are looking into a matter.

When it comes to voice mail, check it at least three times a day. This prevents "message bump"—having the same person call you several times with the same request. Another idea for saving time with voice mail is to try skipping to the beep when you want to leave a message. Hit the star or pound key on your phone.

By the way, we need a volunteer to attend a conference on preventing violence in the workplace. Thank you for your cooperation.

1. List at least five faults in this memo.

2. Outline a general writing plan for this memo.
    Subject line:
    Opening:
    Body:
    Closing:

5.4 Memo That Informs: What I Do on the Job. Some employees have remarked to the
boss that they are working more than other employees. Your boss has decided to study the
matter by asking all employees to describe exactly what they are doing. If some jobs are
found to be overly demanding, your boss may redistribute job tasks or hire additional employees.

Critical Thinking

Your Task. Write a well-organized memo describing your duties, the time you spend on
each task, and the skills needed for what you do. Provide enough details to make a clear
record of your job. Use actual names and describe actual tasks. Describe a current or previous job. If you have not worked, report to the head of an organization to which you belong.
Describe the duties of an officer or of a committee. Your boss or organization head appreciates brevity. Keep your memo under one page.

5.5 Memo That Informs: Party Time! Staff members in your office were disappointed that
no holiday party was given last year. They don't care what kind of party it is, but they do
want some kind of celebration this year.

Critical Thinking

Your Task. As Wendy Herman, you have been asked to draft a memo to the office staff
about a December holiday party. Decide what kind of party you would like. Include information about where the party will be held, when it is, what the cost will be, a description
of the food to be served, whether guests are allowed, and whom to make reservations with.

5.6 Reply Memo: Someone's Going to Get Dumped On. The IS (Information Systems)
network manager at Lionel Trains in Chesterfield, Michigan, worried that his company
would have to upgrade its Internet connection because operations were noticeably slower
than in the past. Upon checking, however, he discovered that extensive recreational Web
surfing among employees was the real reason for the slowdown.

Web

Team

Since the company needed a good policy on using e-mail and the Internet, he assigned
your team the task of investigating existing policies. Your team leader, Rick Rodriguez, who
has quite a sense of humor, said, "Adopting an Internet policy is a lot like hosting a convention of pigeons. Both will result in a lot of squawking, ruffled feathers, and someone getting dumped on." Right! No one is going to like having e-mail and Internet use restricted.
It is, indeed, a dirty job, but someone has to do it.

Your Task. Your team should first check Web sites to locate examples or models of company e-mail and Internet policies. For best results use several search engines and try variations of the search term "Company E-Mail Policy." Print any helpful material. Then meet
as a group and select six to eight major topics that you think should be covered in a company policy. Your investigation will act as a starting point in the long process of developing a policy that provides safeguards but is not overly restrictive. You are not expected to
write the policy at this time. But you could attach copies of anything interesting. Your boss

would especially like to know where he could see or purchase model company policies. As Thad Tucker send an e-mail message to Rick Rodriquez, your team leader.[5]

5.7 E-Mail Request Memo: Violent Video Games. Ever since the high-profile teenage shootings in Colorado and Georgia, you've been feeling pressure regarding violent video games. You own Wall's Camera and Video, and parents are increasingly getting on your case about restricting video rentals. One parent said, "Look, I have no idea what's in this video game because I can't play it." And you know that's true. A recent study revealed that only 5 percent of parents could identify a popular video game, "Duke Nukem," while 80 percent of junior high school students were familiar with the title. You also know that some video games are filled with violence, profanity, and sex.

You've heard that a new rating system is being considered in an attempt to prevent threatened state and federal regulation of movies and video games. This self-policing effort by the Video Software Dealers Association might help you respond to concerned parents. But you want to know more about it and how it will work. You remember an earlier effort to head off government regulation. Back in 1991 the video industry created a "Pledge to Parents" campaign, but it was intended largely to limit children's access to sexual content. You wonder what ever happened to that effort. By June 6 you would like to have some answers to your questions. At that time you will begin training a new summer crew.[6]

Your Task. As Sylvia Wall (swall@aol.com), write an e-mail message to Terry L. Buchanan, executive director of the Video Software Dealers Association (tlbuchanan@VSDA.org). Ask questions about the new rating system. Inquire about the Pledge to Parents campaign. You wonder whether you're the only dealer who is feeling parental pressure. Write a memo that lets him know whether you support or oppose a self-policing effort within the VSDA. Take advantage of this chance to ask more questions about video game ratings (use your imagination).

5.8 E-Mail Memo That Responds: Video Games Rating From _Early Childhood_ to _Adults Only._ The Video Software Dealers Association has been receiving a number of e-mails and letters from members inquiring about a new rating system for video games. As assistant to executive director Terry L. Buchanan, you've been asked to respond to Sylvia Wall's e-mail (Activity 5.7). Yes, a new rating system is being developed, and it will be released in January.

It goes something like this. Videos with content suitable for persons ages 3 and older will be rated "Early Childhood." Videos that may be watched by persons ages 6 and older will be rated "Everyone." "Teens" will be the rating for videos with content suitable for persons ages 13 and older. "Mature" is the rating for anyone 17 and older. The final rating is "Adults Only." Developed by the Entertainment Software Ratings Board, this rating system grew out of the original Pledge to Parents campaign introduced in 1991.

You asked your boss whether the ratings are mandatory, and he said, "Education and voluntary compliance with retailers are probably going to get us further than rigid mandates. As an industry, we'd have a tough time persuading retailers to stop selling some of their hottest products. Instead of enforcing rigid restrictions, we're going to develop educational material including posters and pamphlets that promote the new system." By the way, Sylvia Wall says that she supports the industry move toward more explicit ratings.

Your Task. In an e-mail to Sylvia Wall, explain the new rating system and answer her other inquiries. Show enthusiasm for her support of voluntary ratings. Decide whether and when to send her the new educational materials.

Web **5.9 Memo That Responds: What's New at the P.O.** Assume you are Leticia Lopez and you work for MagicMedia, Inc., a large software manufacturer. The office manager, Patricia Wildey, asks you to seek two kinds of information from the U.S. Postal Service. First, she wants to learn exactly how envelopes should be addressed according to U.S.P.S. guidelines. Second, she wants to know how to get a passport, since she will be traveling to Europe on business in the spring.

Your Task. To obtain both sets of information, visit the U.S.P.S. Web site. Write a one-page memo summarizing your findings.

Related Web Site: www.usps.gov/postofc/

5.10 Memo That Informs: Wilderness Retreat. Assume you are Mark Peters, president of a small printing operation employing 25 workers. On Friday, June 7, your print shop employees will join you at an expense-paid, one-day retreat that you hope will improve teamwork among the workers. The retreat will be led by Wilderness Retreats, which offers companies outdoor team training designed to build employee trust, teamwork, and loyalty. Employees will meet at work at 8 a.m., and a Wilderness Retreats van will pick them up and take them to a nearby National Forest. Employees will spend the day on team-building activities, including a map-reading exercise that will require employee teams to find their way through a wooded area to a "home base." The retreat will provide a catered picnic lunch and time for socializing. The group will return to work by 4 p.m.

Your Task. As Mark Peters, write a memo to employees announcing the retreat. Since the print shop will be closed during the retreat, you consider the retreat to be a work day and expect all employees to attend. Employees should dress casually. They'll be outside most of the day.

5.11 Memo That Responds: A Call for Cell Phone Etiquette. Have you ever been annoyed when the person at the table next to you in a restaurant carried on a loud conversation on her cell phone? Have you ever been frustrated to see the person in the car next to you chatting on his cell phone as his car drifts into your lane? Many people feel that cell phones are creating major problems because no sense of etiquette or proper use has developed to accompany their explosive growth. Some people simply do not use common sense when using them.

> **Critical Thinking**
> **Web**
> **Team**

Your Task. You've been hired by Cellular One as director of external affairs. Your first assignment is to form a team to produce a customer brochure that discusses proper cell phone etiquette. In a small group come up with several cell phone etiquette guidelines and submit these in a brief memo to your boss, Jeff Bowman, or in an e-mail to your instructor. You can read more details about this case and suggestions for relevant Web resources at the Guffey Web site.

Related Web Site: meguffey.com (Click on Book Support for Business Communication: Process and Product.)

5.12 Video Case Study: Innovation, Learning, and Communication at Yahoo! View the video describing the Internet company Yahoo. Assume you are an assistant to John Briggs, Senior Producer, who appeared in the video. John has just received a letter asking for permission from another film company to use Yahoo offices and personnel in an educational video, similar to the one you just saw. John wants you to draft an e-mail message for him to send to the operations manager, Ceci Lang, asking for permission for VX Studios to film. VX says it needs about 15 hours of filming time and would like to interview four or five managers as well as founders David Filo and Jerry Yang. VX would need to set up its mobile studio van in the parking lot and would need permission to use advertising film clips.

> **Video**

Although VX hopes to film in May, it is flexible about the date. John Briggs reminds you that Yahoo has participated in a number of films in the past two years, and some managers are complaining that they can't get their work done.

Your Task. Write a persuasive memo or e-mail message to Ceci Lang, Operations Manager, asking her to allow VX Studios to film at Yahoo. Your request memo should probably emphasize the value of these projects in enhancing Yahoo's image among future users. Provide any other details you think are necessary to create a convincing request memo that will win authorization from Ceci Lang to schedule this filming.

Prepositions and Conjunctions

Review Sections 1.18 and 1.19 in the Grammar Review section of the Grammar/
Mechanics Handbook. Then study each of the following statements. Write *a* or *b*
to indicate the sentence in which the idea is expressed more effectively. Also
record the number of the G/M principle illustrated. When you finish, compare
your responses with those provided. If your answers differ, study carefully the
principles shown in parentheses.

<u>b</u>   (1.18a)   **Example:**   (a)   Tiffany will graduate college this spring.
                                     (b)   Tiffany will graduate from college this spring.

1. (a) DataTech enjoyed greater profits this year then it expected.
    (b) DataTech enjoyed greater profits this year than it expected.
2. (a) I hate it when we have to work overtime.
    (b) I hate when we have to work overtime.
3. (a) Dr. Simon has a great interest and appreciation for the study of ro-
         botics.
    (b) Dr. Simon has a great interest in and appreciation for the study of ro-
         botics.
4. (a) Gross profit is where you compute the difference between total sales
         and the cost of goods sold.
    (b) Gross profit is computed by finding the difference between total sales
         and the cost of goods sold.
5. (a) We advertise to increase the frequency of product use, to introduce com-
         plementary products, and to enhance our corporate image.
    (b) We advertise to have our products used more often, when we have com-
         plementary products to introduce, and we are interested in making our
         corporation look better to the public.
6. (a) What type printer do you prefer?
    (b) What type of printer do you prefer?
7. (a) Where are you going to?
    (b) Where are you going?
8. (a) The sale of our San Antonio branch office last year should improve this
         year's profits.
    (b) The sale of our branch office in San Antonio during last year should im-
         prove the profits for this year.
9. (a) Do you know where the meeting is at?
    (b) Do you know where the meeting is?
10. (a) The cooling-off rule is an FTC rule that protects consumers from mak-
         ing unwise purchases at home.
    (b) The cooling-off rule is where the FTC has made a rule that protects con-
         sumers from making unwise purchases at home.
11. (a) Meetings can be more meaningful if the agenda is stuck to, the time
         frame is followed, and if someone keeps follow-up notes.
    (b) Meetings can be more meaningful if you stick to the agenda, follow the
         time frame, and keep follow-up notes.
12. (a) They printed the newsletter on yellow paper like we asked them to do.
    (b) They printed the newsletter on yellow paper as we asked them to do.
13. (a) A code of ethics is a set of rules spelling out appropriate standards of
         behavior.
    (b) A code of ethics is where a set of rules spells out appropriate standards
         of behavior.

14. (a) We need an individual with an understanding and serious interest in black-and-white photography.

    (b) We need an individual with an understanding of and serious interest in black-and-white photography.

15. (a) The most dangerous situation is when employees ignore the safety rules.

    (b) The most dangerous situation occurs when employees ignore the safety rules.

Advanced Grammar/Mechanics Review—5

The following sentences contain errors in grammar, punctuation, capitalization, number style, usage, and spelling. Below each sentence write a corrected version.

1. As a matter of fact the hawaiian alphabet has only twelve letters.

2. About one thousand of Burger Kings seven thousand four hundred u.s. resterants is serving the new coated fries.

3. Meanwhile the highly-advertised McDonald's 55-cent sandwich promotion which was pushed heavy by its Oak Brook Headquarters turned out to be a major dissappointment.

4. A powerful reason for Burger Kings new success is, a hefty 2 patty burger thats being promoted as an extra big Big Mac.

5. Experts say the 2 smartest dogs are scottish border collies and golden retrievers, on the other hand the dumbest are afghan hounds.

6. After listening carefully to your advise we paid several months rent in advance.

7. 2 sizes of batteries see Page Sixteen in the instruction booklet may be used in this flashlight.

8. When convenent will you please send me 3 copys of the companys color logo?

9. The first book ever wrote on a typewriter was: "Tom Sawyer."

10. A sign in the souvenir shop of Key west international airport reads "unattended children will be sold into slavery.

11. In Newsweek I saw an article titled *How to develop the exercise habit.*

12. Appearing next is the President and Sales Manager both of whom were personally invited by myself.

13. Production cost and markup is important to the manufacturer and to we vendors.

14. That stack of papers have been laying on your desk for at least three week's.

15. The only president to win a pulitzer prize is John F. Kennedy for Profiles in courage.

Grammar/Mechanics Challenge—5

Document for Revision

The following memo has faults in grammar, punctuation, spelling, capitalization, number form, repetition, wordiness, and other areas. Use standard proofreading marks (see Appendix B) to correct the errors. When you finish, your instructor can show you the revised version of this memo.

DATE: June 25, 200X

TO: Amy MacKenzie

FROM: Ira White

SUBJECT: COLLECTING DATA FOR ANNUAL REPORT

You have been assigned a special project, to collect information for next years annual report. You'll probably need to visit each department head personally to collect this information individually from them.

The Corporate Communications division which oversee the production of the annual report is of the opinion that you should concentrate on the following departmental data;

1. specific accomplishments of each department for the past year.

2. you must find out about goals of each department for the coming year.

3. in each department get names of interesting employees and events to be featured.

In view of the fact that this is a big assignment Maria Marquez has been assigned to offer assistance to you. Inasmuch as the annual report must be completed by September first; please submit your data in concise narrative form to me by August fifth.

Whose Computer Is It Anyway?

Many companies today provide their employees with computers and Internet access. Should employees be able to use those computers for on-line shopping, personal messages, personal work, and listening to music or playing games?

But It's Harmless

The *Wall Street Journal* reports that many office workers have discovered that it's far easier to do their shopping on-line than racing to malls and waiting in line. To justify her Web shopping at work, one employee, a recent graduate, says, "Instead of standing at the water cooler gossiping, I shop on-line." She went on to say, "I'm not sapping company resources by doing this."

Some office on-line shoppers say that what they're doing is similar to making personal phone calls. As long as they don't abuse the practice, they see no harm. And besides, shopping at the office is far faster than shopping from most dial-up home computer connections. Marketing director David Krane justifies his on-line shopping by explaining that his employer benefits because he is more productive when he takes minibreaks. "When I need a break, I just pull up a Web page and just browse," he says. "Ten minutes later, I'm all refreshed, and I can go back to business-plan writing."

Companies Urged to Crack Down

Employers are less happy about increasing use of bandwidth for personal on-line activities. UPS discovered an employee running a personal business from his office computer. And Lockheed Martin fired an employee who disabled its entire company network for six hours because of an e-mail message heralding a holiday event that the worker sent to 60,000 employees. One company found that people were downloading music from broadcast.com, using up 4 percent of the company's bandwidth.

Attorney Carole O'Blenes thinks that companies should begin cracking down. On-line shopping generates "junk e-mail" that could cause the company's server to crash. And what about productivity? "Whether they're checking their stocks, shopping, or doing research for their upcoming trip to Spain," she says, "that's time diverted from doing business."[7]

What's Reasonable?

Some companies try to enforce a "zero tolerance" policy, prohibiting any personal use of company equipment. Ameritech Corporation specifically tells employees that "computers and other company equipment are to be used only to provide service to customers and for other business purposes." Companies such as Boeing, however, allow employees to use faxes, e-mail, and the Internet for personal reasons. But it sets guidelines. Use has to be of "reasonable duration and frequency" and can't cause "embarrassment to the company."[8] Strictly prohibited are chain letters, obscenity, and political and religious solicitation.

Career Application

As an administrative assistant at Texas Technologies in Fort Worth, you have just received an e-mail from your boss asking for your opinion. It seems that many employees have been shopping on-line; one person actually received four personal packages from UPS in one morning. Although reluctant to do so, management is considering installing monitoring software that not only tracks Internet use but also allows extensive blocking of Web sites, such as porno, hate, and game sites.

Your Task

- In teams or as a class, discuss the problem of workplace abuse of e-mail and the Internet.
- Should full personal use be allowed?
- In terms of equipment, are computers and their links to the Internet similar to office telephones?
- Should employees be allowed to access the Internet for personal use if they use their own private e-mail accounts?
- Should management be allowed to monitor all Internet use?
- Should employees be warned if e-mail is to be monitored?
- What specific reasons can you give to support an Internet crackdown by management?
- What specific reasons can you give to oppose a crackdown?

Decide whether you support or oppose the crackdown. Explain your views in an e-mail or a memo to your boss, Arthur W. Rose <awrose@txtech.com>.

Related Web Site: Visit the Telemate.Net Software site <www.telemate.net> for an inner look at the nation's leading provider of Internet surveillance software.

Web

6 Routine Letters

Why do some people use a mystery-story approach when writing letters? They force you to read six or seven paragraphs before you begin to understand the point of the message.[1]

CATHY TRIMBLE, *Wellness Coordinator, Shore Memorial Hospital*

LEARNING OBJECTIVES

1. Write letters requesting information and action.
2. Write letters ordering merchandise.
3. Write letters making claims.
4. Write letters complying with requests.
5. Write letters responding to customer orders.
6. Write letters granting claims.

Letters that fail to get to the point are a pet peeve of Cathy Trimble, wellness coordinator at Shore Memorial Hospital. In her job she receives many requests for information about programs and services offered by the hospital. This state-of-the-art health-care facility serves residents and tourists visiting the Ocean City and Atlantic City, New Jersey, area. Mystery-story messages have no appeal for most of us. Readers want to know why a message was written and how it involves them. And they want that information up front.

Writing Everyday Business Letters

Letters communicate with outsiders and produce a formal record.

This chapter focuses on written messages that travel outside an organization. These messages generally take the form of letters. Although many businesspeople today seem to be writing fewer letters and more e-mail messages, you will still find many occasions when letters are required. When you need a formal record of an inquiry, response, or complaint, letters are the best communication channel.

Most business correspondence consists of routine letters. These everyday messages go to suppliers, government agencies, other businesses, and, most important, customers. Customer letters receive a high priority because these messages encourage product feedback, project a favorable image of the company, and promote future business.

Like memos, letters are easiest to write when you have a plan to follow. The plan for letters, just as for memos, is fixed by the content of the message and its expected effect on the receiver. Letters delivering bad news require an indirect approach, which you will learn about in Chapter 7. Most letters, however, carry good or neutral news. These letters should follow the direct strategy. You will recall that the main idea comes first in the direct strategy.

The content of a message and its anticipated effect on the reader determine the strategy you choose.

In this chapter you'll learn to apply the direct strategy in writing requests for information and action. You'll also learn how to respond to such requests.

Information Requests

Many business messages are written to request information. Although the specific subject of each inquiry may differ, the similarity of purpose in routine requests enables writers to use the following writing plan.

WRITING PLAN FOR AN INFORMATION REQUEST

- **Opening**—Ask the most important question first or express a polite command.
- **Body**—Explain the request logically and courteously. Ask other questions if necessary.
- **Closing**—Request a specific action with an end date, if appropriate, and show appreciation.

Opening Directly

The most emphatic positions in a letter are the openings and closings. Readers tend to look at them first. The writer, then, should capitalize on this tendency by putting the most significant statement first. The first sentence of an information request is usually a question or a polite command. It should not be an explanation or justification, unless resistance to the request is expected. When the information requested is likely to be forthcoming, immediately tell the reader what you want. This saves the reader's time and may ensure that the message is read. A busy executive who skims the mail, quickly reading subject lines and first sentences only, may grasp your request rapidly and act on it. A request that follows a lengthy explanation, on the other hand, may never be found.

Readers find the openings and closings of letters most interesting.

A letter inquiring about hotel accommodations, shown in Figure 6.1, begins immediately with the most important idea. Can the hotel provide meeting rooms and accommodations for 250 people? Instead of opening with an explanation of who the writer is or how the writer happens to be writing this letter, the letter begins more directly.

If several questions must be asked, you have two choices. You can ask the most important question first, as shown in Figure 6.1. An alternate opening begins with a summary statement, such as *Will you please answer the following questions about providing meeting rooms and accommodations for 250 people from May 25 through May 29.* Notice that the summarizing statement sounds like a question but has no question mark. That's because it's really a command disguised as a question. Rather than bluntly demanding information (*Answer the following questions*), we often prefer to soften commands by posing them as questions. Such statements, called rhetorical questions, should not be punctuated as questions because they do not require answers.

Begin an information request letter with the most important question or a summarizing statement.

FIGURE 6.1 Letter That Requests Information—Block Style

Letterhead ——————————————→ • # GEOTECH

770 Stewart Avenue
Garden City, NJ 11530   ↓ line 13 or 1 blank line below letterhead

Dateline ——————————————→ • August 20, 200X
                                          ↓ 1 to 9 blank lines

Inside address ————————→ • Ms. Jane Mangrum, Manager
Scottsdale Hilton Hotel
6333 North Scottsdale Road
Scottsdale, AZ 85253-4310   ↓ 1 blank line

Salutation ——————————————→ • Dear Ms. Mangrum: ↓ 1 blank line

Can the Scottsdale Hilton provide meeting rooms and accommodations for about 250 GeoTech sales representatives from May 25 through May 29?

Your hotel received strong recommendations because of its excellent resort and conference facilities. Our spring sales conference is scheduled for next May, and I am collecting information for our planning committee. Will you please answer these additional questions regarding the Scottsdale Hilton.

• Does the hotel have a banquet room that can seat 250?

Body ——————————————→ • • Do you have at least four smaller meeting rooms, each to accommodate a maximum of 75?

• What kind of computer facilities are available for power presentations?

• What is the nearest airport, and do you provide transportation to and from it?

Answers to these questions and any other information you can provide will help us decide which conference facility to choose. Your response before September 1 would be most appreciated since our planning committee meets September 4.

Sincerely yours,

Bobby Domathoti   ↓ 3 blank lines

Author's name and
identification ————————→ • Bobby Domathoti
Corporate Travel Department

Reference initials ——————→ • BD:gdr   ↓ 1 blank line

Tips for Formatting Letters

• Start the date on line 13 or 1 blank line below the letterhead.
• For block style, begin all lines at the left margin.
• For modified block style, begin the date and closing lines at the center.
• Leave side margins of 1 to 1½ inches depending on the length of the letter.
• Single-space the body and double-space between paragraphs.

Details in the Body

The body of a letter that requests information should provide necessary details. Remember that the quality of the information obtained from a request letter depends on the clarity of the inquiry. If you analyze your needs, organize your ideas, and frame your request logically, you are likely to receive a meaningful answer that doesn't require a follow-up message. Whenever possible, itemize the information to improve readability. Notice that the questions in Figure 6.1 are bulleted, and they are parallel. That is, they use the same balanced construction.

The body of a request letter may contain an explanation or a list of questions.

Closing With an Action Request

Use the final paragraph to ask for specific action, to set an end date if appropriate, and to express appreciation. As you learned in working with memos, a request for action is most effective when an end date and reason for that date are supplied, as shown in Figure 6.1.

The ending of a request letter should tell the reader what you want done and when.

It's always appropriate to end a request letter with appreciation for the action taken. However, don't fall into a cliché trap, such as *Thanking you in advance, I remain . . .* or the familiar *Thank you for your cooperation.* Your appreciation will sound most sincere if you avoid mechanical, tired expressions.

Order Requests

Most people generally order merchandise by telephone, catalog order form, fax, or Web page. Sometimes, though, you may not have a telephone number, order form, or Web address—only a street address. Other times you may wish to have a written record of the date and content of your order. When you must write a letter to order merchandise, use the direct strategy, beginning with the main idea.

To order merchandise, you may occasionally have to write a letter.

WRITING PLAN FOR AN ORDER REQUEST

- **Opening**—Authorize purchase and suggest method of shipping.
- **Body**—List items vertically; provide quantity, order number, description, and unit price; and show total price of order.
- **Closing**—Request shipment by a specific date, tell method of payment, and express appreciation.

To order items by letter, supply the same information that an order blank would require. In the opening let the reader know immediately that this is a purchase authorization and not merely an information inquiry. Instead of *I saw a number of interesting items in your catalog,* begin directly with order language such as *Please send me by UPS the following items from your fall merchandise catalog.*

If you're ordering many items, list them vertically in the body of your letter. Include as much specific data as possible: quantity, order number, complete description, unit price, and total price. Show the total amount, and figure the tax and shipping costs if possible. The more information you provide, the less likely that a mistake will be made.

In the closing tell how you plan to pay for the merchandise. Enclose a check, provide a credit card number, or ask to be billed. Many business organizations have credit agreements with their regular suppliers that enable them to send goods without prior payment. In addition to payment information, tell when the merchandise should be sent and express appreciation. The following letter from the human resources department of a business illustrates the pattern of an order letter.

Opens directly with
authorization for
purchase, method of
delivery, and catalog
source

Greetings:

Please send by express mail the following items from your summer catalog.

Uses columns to make
quantity, catalog
number, description,
and price stand out

Quantity	Catalog Number	Description	Price
250	OG44-18	Payroll greeting cards	$102.50
250	OG31-22	Payroll card envelopes	21.95
100	OM22-01	Performance greeting cards	80.00
	Subtotal		$204.45
	Tax at 7%		14.31
	Shipping		24.00
	Total		$242.76

Expresses appreciation
and tells when items
are expected. Identifies
method of payment

My company would appreciate receiving these cards immediately since we are starting an employee recognition program February 12. Enclosed is our check for $242.76. If additional charges are necessary, please bill my company.

Sincerely,

Simple Claim Requests

Claim letters register complaints and usually seek correction of a wrong.

In business many things can go wrong—promised shipments are late, warranted goods fail, or service is disappointing. When you as a customer must write to identify or correct a wrong, the letter is called a *claim.* Straightforward claims are those to which you expect the receiver to agree readily. But even these claims often require a letter. While your first action may be a telephone call or a visit to submit your claim, you may not get the results you seek. Written claims are often taken more seriously, and they also establish a record of what happened. Claims that require persuasion are presented in Chapter 8. In this chapter you'll learn to apply the following writing plan for a straightforward claim that uses a direct approach.

WRITING PLAN FOR A SIMPLE CLAIM

- **Opening**—Describe clearly the desired action.
- **Body**—Explain the nature of the claim, tell why the claim is justified, and provide details regarding the action requested.
- **Closing**—End pleasantly with a goodwill statement and include end dating if appropriate.

Opening With Action

The direct strategy is best for simple claims that require no persuasion.

If you have a legitimate claim, you can expect a positive response from a company. Smart businesses today want to hear from their customers. That's why you should open a claim letter with a clear statement of the problem or with the action you want the receiver to take. You might expect a replacement, a refund, a new order, credit to your account, correction of a billing error, free repairs, free inspection, or cancellation of an order.

When the remedy is obvious, state it immediately (*Please send us 24 Royal hot-air popcorn poppers to replace the 24 hot-oil poppers sent in error with our order shipped January 4*). When the remedy is less obvious, you might ask for a change in policy or procedure or simply for an explanation (*Because three of our employees with confirmed reservations were refused rooms September 16 in your hotel, would you please clarify your policy regarding reservations and late arrivals*).

Explaining in the Body

In the body of a claim letter, explain the problem and justify your request. Provide the necessary details so that the difficulty can be corrected without further correspondence. Avoid becoming angry or trying to fix blame. Bear in mind that the person reading your letter is seldom responsible for the problem. Instead, state the facts logically, objectively, and unemotionally; let the reader decide on the causes.

Include copies of all pertinent documents such as invoices, sales slips, catalog descriptions, and repair records. (By the way, be sure to send copies and *not* your originals, which could be lost.) When service is involved, cite names of individuals spoken to and dates of calls. Assume that a company honestly wants to satisfy its customers—because most do. When an alternative remedy exists, spell it out (*If you are unable to send 24 Royal hot-air popcorn poppers immediately, please credit our account now and notify us when they become available*).

Providing details without getting angry improves the effectiveness of a claim letter.

Closing Pleasantly

Conclude a claim letter with a courteous statement that promotes goodwill and expresses a desire for continued relations. If appropriate, include an end date (*We realize that mistakes in ordering and shipping sometimes occur. Because we've enjoyed your prompt service in the past, we hope that you will be able to send us the hot-air poppers by January 15*).

Finally, in making claims, act promptly. Delaying claims makes them appear less important. Delayed claims are also more difficult to verify. By taking the time to put your claim in writing, you indicate your seriousness. A written claim also starts a record of the problem, should later action be necessary. Be sure to keep a copy of your letter.

Written claims submitted promptly are taken more seriously than delayed ones.

Putting It All Together

Figure 6.2 shows a first draft of a hostile claim that vents the writer's anger but accomplishes little else. Its tone is belligerent, and it assumes that the company intentionally mischarged the customer. Furthermore, it fails to tell the reader how to remedy the problem. The revision tempers the tone, describes the problem objectively, and provides facts and figures. Most important, it specifies exactly what the customer wants done.

Notice that the letter in Figure 6.2 is shown with the return address typed above the date. This personal business style may be used when typing on paper without a printed letterhead. Notice, too, that this letter uses modified block style. The return address, date, and closing lines start at the center.

Information Response Letters

Often, your messages will respond favorably to requests for information or action. A customer wants information about a product. A supplier asks to arrange a meeting. Another business inquires about one of your procedures. But before responding to any inquiry, be sure to check your facts and figures carefully. Any letter written on company stationery is considered a legally binding contract. If a policy or procedure needs authorization, seek approval from a supervisor or executive before writing the letter. In complying with requests, you'll want to apply the same direct pattern you used in making requests.

Before responding to requests, gather facts, check figures, and seek approval if necessary.

FIGURE 6.2 Direct Claim Letter

Ineffective

Dear Good Vibes:

Sounds angry; jumps to conclusions → You call yourselves Good Vibes, but all I'm getting from your service is bad vibes! I'm furious that you have your salespeople slip in unwanted service warranties to boost your sales.

Forgets that mistakes happen → When I bought my Panatronic VCR from Good Vibes, Inc., in August, I specifically told the salesperson that I did NOT want a three-year service warranty. But there it is on my VISA statement this month! You people have obviously billed me for a service I did not authorize. I refuse to pay this charge.

Fails to suggest solution → How can you hope to stay in business with such fraudulent practices? I was expecting to return this month and look at CD players, but you can be sure I'll find an honest dealer this time.

Sincerely,

Keith Cortez

Effective

1201 Lantana Court
Lake Worth, FL 33461
September 3, 200X

Personal business letter style

Mr. Sam Lee, Customer Service
Good Vibes, Inc.
2003 53rd Street
West Palm Beach, FL 33407

Dear Mr. Lee:

Please credit my VISA account, No. 0000-0046-2198-9421, to correct an erroneous charge of $299.

States simply and clearly what to do

On August 8 I purchased a Panatronic VCR from Good Vibes, Inc. Although the salesperson discussed a three-year extended warranty with me, I decided against purchasing that service for $299. However, when my credit card statement arrived this month, I noticed an extra $299 charge from Good Vibes, Inc. I suspect that this charge represents the warranty I declined.

Explains objectively what went wrong

Doesn't blame or accuse

Enclosed is a copy of my sales invoice along with my VISA statement on which I circled the charge. Please authorize a credit immediately and send a copy of the transaction to me at the above address.

Documents facts

I'm enjoying all the features of my Panatronic VCR and would like to be shopping at Good Vibes for a CD player shortly.

Uses friendly tone

Suggests continued business once problem is resolved

Sincerely,

Keith Cortez
Keith Cortez

Enclosure

- **Subject line**—Identify previous correspondence.
- **Opening**—Deliver the most important information first.
- **Body**—Arrange information logically, explain and clarify it, provide additional information if appropriate, and build goodwill.
- **Closing**—End pleasantly.

Subject Line Efficiency

An information response letter might contain a subject line, which helps the reader recognize the topic immediately. Knowledgeable business communicators use a subject line to refer to earlier correspondence so that in the first sentence, the most emphatic spot in a letter, they are free to emphasize the main idea. Notice in Figure 6.3 that the subject line identifies the subject completely.

Use the subject line to refer to previous correspondence.

Opening Directly

In the first sentence of an information response, deliver the information the reader wants. Avoid wordy, drawn-out openings (*I have before me your letter of February 6, in which you request information about . . .*). More forceful and more efficient is an opener that answers the inquiry (*Here is the information you wanted about . . .*). When agreeing to a request for action, announce the good news promptly (*Yes, I will be happy to speak to your business communication class on the topic of . . .*).

Arranging Information Logically

When answering a group of questions or providing considerable data, arrange the information logically and make it readable by using lists, tables, headings, boldface, italics, or other graphic devices. When customers or prospective customers inquire about products or services, your response should do more than merely supply answers. You'll also want to promote your organization and products. Be sure to present the promotional material with attention to the "you" view and to reader benefits (*You can use our standardized tests to free you from time-consuming employment screening*). You'll learn more about special techniques for developing sales and persuasive messages in Chapter 8.

A good way to answer questions is to number or bullet each one.

Closing Pleasantly

To avoid abruptness, include a pleasant closing remark that shows your willingness to help the reader. Provide extra information if appropriate. Tailor your remarks to fit this letter and this reader. Since everyone appreciates being recognized as an individual, avoid form-letter closings such as *If we may be of further assistance, ...*

Customer Order Responses

Many companies acknowledge orders by sending a printed postcard that merely informs the customer that the order has been received. Other companies take advantage of this opportunity to build goodwill and to promote new products and services. A personalized letter responding to an order is good business, particularly for new accounts, large accounts, and customers who haven't placed orders recently. An individualized letter is also necessary if the order involves irregularities, such as delivery delays, back-ordered items, or missing items.

Letters that follow up orders create excellent opportunities to improve the company image and to sell products.

FIGURE 6.3 Information Response Letter

EXCALIBUR CREDIT SERVICE

301 N. International Parkway
Richardson, TX 75081

Voice: (800) 432-9587
Web: www.excalibur.com
Fax: (817) 683-2285

February 6, 200X

Ms. Hillary A. Roper
The Houston Post
4980 Washington Avenue
Houston, TX 77048

Identifies previous correspondence

SUBJECT: YOUR FEBRUARY 1 LETTER REQUESTING INFORMATION FOR AN ARTICLE TO APPEAR IN *THE HOUSTON POST*

Thanks for providing this excellent opportunity to answer frequently asked questions about the credit-reporting industry in general and about our company in particular. Below are my responses to the questions in your recent letter.

1. Excalibur is a credit-reporting agency that stores information about the credit history of consumers. Such agencies are necessary to help credit grantors evaluate the credit history of consumers in a timely manner so that creditworthy people can have ready access to credit.

Answers each inquiry fully and logically in list form

2. We do not collect or maintain information about race, religion, gender, salary, personal assets, checking or savings accounts, medical history, personal background, lifestyle, or criminal record.

3. The Fair Credit Reporting Act allows employers to access an applicant's credit report for employment purposes. We do not, however, make decisions about hiring applicants or denying employment.

4. A "risk score" is a numerical summary of the information in a consumer's file. It provides a credit grantor a nonjudgmental, empirically derived, and statistically correct tool to be used as part of the credit-evaluation process.

Builds goodwill by providing extra information and ends cordially without clichés

You'll find additional information in the enclosed booklet, "Understanding Excalibur's Credit-Reporting Service." If you would like to discuss my responses or ask additional questions, just call (414) 598-2302. We look forward to seeing your article in print.

Sincerely,

Debbie Wills-Garcia

Debbie Wills-Garcia
Consumer Services Division

DWG:rio
Enclosure

Letters that respond to orders should deliver the news immediately; therefore, the direct strategy is most effective. Here's a writing plan that will achieve the results you want in acknowledging orders.

WRITING PLAN FOR AN ORDER RESPONSE

- **Opening**—Tell when and how the shipment will be sent.
- **Body**—Explain the details of the shipment, discuss any irregularities in the order, include resale information, and promote other products and services if appropriate.
- **Closing**—Build goodwill and use a friendly, personalized closing.

Giving Delivery Information in the Opening

Customers want to know when and how their orders will be sent. Since that news is most important, put it in the first sentence. An inefficient opener such as *We have received your order dated June 20* wastes words and the reader's time by providing information that could be inferred from more effective openers. Instead of stating that an order has been received, imply it in a first sentence that provides delivery details, as shown in Figure 6.4 (*The books requested in your Order No. 2980 will be shipped . . .*).

The first sentence should tell when and how an order will be sent.

Putting Details in the Body

You should include details relating to an order in the body of a letter that acknowledges the order. You will also want to discuss any irregularities about the order. If, for example, part of the order will be sent from a different location or prices have changed or items must be back-ordered, present this information.

The body of an order response is also the appropriate place to include resale information. *Resale* refers to the process of reassuring customers that their choices were good ones. You can use resale in an order letter by describing the product favorably, as shown in Figure 6.4 (*The volumes you have ordered are among our best-selling editions*). You might mention its features or attributes, its popularity among customers, and its successful use in certain applications. Perhaps your competitive price recommends it.

When a sales clerk tells you how good you look in the new suit you just purchased, the clerk is practicing "resale."

Resale information confirms the discrimination and good judgment of your customers and encourages repeat business. After an opening statement describing delivery information, resale information such as the following is appropriate: *The multipurpose checks you have ordered allow you to produce several different check formats, including accounts payable and payroll. Customers tell us that these computerized checks are the answer to their check-writing problems.*

Order acknowledgment letters are also suitable channels for sales promotion material. An organization often has other products or services that it wishes to highlight and promote. For example, a computer supply house might include the following sales feature: *Another good buy from Quill is our popular $3\frac{1}{2}$-inch disk available in our "mini" bulk pack of 25 disks at only 99 cents each. And we will send you free a desk storage tray for your disks.* Use sales promotion material, however, in moderation. Too much can be a burden to read and therefore irritating.

Resale emphasizes a product already sold; promotion emphasizes additional products to be sold.

Showing Appreciation in the Closing

The closing should be pleasant, forward-looking, and appreciative. Above all, it should be personalized. That is, it should relate to the particular customer whose order you are acknowledging. Don't use all-purpose form-letter closings such as *We appreciate your interest in our company* or *Thank you for your order* or *We look forward to your continued business.*

The best closings are personalized; they relate to one particular letter.

FIGURE 6.4 Customer Order Response

Fails to address receiver by name

Opens with obvious statement

Sounds negative; uses outdated language

Misses chance to promote products

Dear Customer:

We are in receipt of your Purchase Order No. 2980 under date of March 15.

I'm sorry to report that the books you have ordered are selling so quickly that we cannot keep them in stock. Therefore, we will be forced to send them from our Toronto distribution centre. Pursuant to your request, every effort will be made to ship them as quickly as possible.

Attached please find a list of our contemporary issues. May I take the liberty to say that we thank you for allowing us to serve your book needs.

Sincerely,

Charles Bailey

Effective

Chartwell Publishers

1050 Birchmont Road
Scarborough, Ontario MIK 5G4

(416) 752-8900 FAX (416) 752-3966
Internet: http://www.chartwell.com

March 20, 200X

Ms. Sheila Miller
2569 Notre Dame Avenue
Winnipeg, MB R3H OJ9

Dear Ms. Miller:

SUBJECT: YOUR MARCH 15 BOOK ORDER NO. 2980

The books requested in your Order No. 2980 will be shipped from our Toronto distribution centre and should reach you by April 1.

The volumes you have ordered are among our best-selling editions and will certainly generate good sales for you at your spring book fair.

For your interest we are enclosing a list of contemporary issues recently released. If you place an order from this list or from our general catalogue, you will be eligible for special terms that we are offering for a limited time. For each $10 worth of books ordered at full list price, we will issue a $4 credit toward the purchase of additional books—as long as all the books are ordered at the same time.

Your book fair should be a resounding success, and we are genuinely pleased to supply these excellent editions. Please take advantage of our special terms and place your next order soon.

Sincerely,

Charles Bailey

Charles Bailey
Marketing Division

CB:wuh
Enclosure

Addresses receiver by name

Opens with information the reader wants most

Uses *resale* in reassuring reader of wise selections

Takes advantage of opportunity to promote new products

Ties in appreciation for order with content of letter

As you learned earlier, when an organization receives a claim, it usually means that something has gone wrong. In responding to a claim, you have three goals:

- To rectify the wrong, if one exists
- To regain the confidence of the customer
- To promote future business and goodwill

If you decide to grant the claim, your response letter will represent good news to the reader. Use the direct strategy described in the following writing plan.

- **Subject line (optional)**—Identify the previous correspondence.
- **Opening**—Grant request or announce the adjustment immediately. Include re-sale or sales promotion if appropriate.
- **Body**—Provide details about how you are complying with the request. Try to regain the customer's confidence, and include resale or sales promotion if appropriate.
- **Closing**—End positively with a forward-looking thought, express confidence in future business relations, and avoid referring to unpleasantness.

Revealing Good News in the Opening

Instead of beginning with a review of what went wrong, present the good news immediately. When Amy Hopkins responded to the claim of customer Electronic Warehouse about a missing shipment, her first draft, shown at the top of Figure 6.5, was angry. No wonder. Electronic Warehouse had apparently provided the wrong shipping address, and the goods were returned. But once Amy and her company decided to send a second shipment and comply with the customer's claim, she had to give up the anger and strive to retain the goodwill and the business of this customer. The improved version of her letter announces that a new shipment will arrive shortly.

If you decide to comply with a customer's claim, let the receiver know immediately. Don't begin your letter with a negative statement (*We are very sorry to hear that you are having trouble with your Sno-Flake ice crusher*). This approach reminds the reader of the problem and may rekindle the heated emotions or unhappy feelings experienced when the claim was written. Instead, focus on the good news. The following openings for various letters illustrate how to begin a message with good news.

> You may take your Sno-Flake ice crusher to Ben's Appliances at 310 First Street, Myrtle Beach, where it will be repaired at no cost to you.

> Thanks for your letter about your new Toyota Corolla tires. You are certainly justified in expecting them to last more than 12,000 miles.

> We agree with you that the warranty on your Turbo programmable calculator Model AI 25C should be extended for six months.

> The enclosed check for $325 demonstrates our desire to satisfy our customers and earn their confidence.

The writer responding to customer claims seeks to rectify the wrong, regain customer confidence, and promote future business.

Readers want to learn the good news immediately.

FIGURE 6.5

Customer Claim
Response

Fails to reveal good
news immediately;
blames customer

Creates ugly tone with
negative words and
sarcasm

Sounds grudging and
reluctant in granting
claim

Ineffective

Gentlemen:

In response to your recent complaint about a missing shipment, it's very difficult to deliver merchandise when we have been given an erroneous address.

Our investigators looked into your problem shipment and determined that it was sent immediately after we received the order. According to the shipper's records, it was delivered to the warehouse address given on your stationery: 3590 University Avenue, St. Paul, Minnesota 55114. Unfortunately, no one at that address would accept delivery, so the shipment was returned to us. I see from your current stationery that your company has a new address. With the proper address, we probably could have delivered this shipment.

Although we feel that it is entirely appropriate to charge you shipping and restocking fees, as is our standard practice on returned goods, in this instance we will waive those fees. We hope this second shipment finally catches up with you at your current address.

Sincerely,

Amy Hopkins

Effective

E<u>W</u> ELECTRONIC WAREHOUSE
930 Abbott Park Place
Providence, RI 02903-5309

February 21, 200X

Mr. Jeremy Garber
Sound Systems, Inc.
2293 Second Avenue
St. Paul, MN 55120

Dear Mr. Garber:

SUBJECT: YOUR FEBRUARY 28 LETTER ABOUT YOUR PURCHASE ORDER

You should receive by February 25 a second shipment of the speakers, VCRs, headphones, and other electronic equipment that you ordered January 20.

The first shipment of this order was delivered January 28 to 3590 University Avenue, St. Paul, Minnesota 55114. When no one at that address would accept the shipment, it was returned to us. Now that I have your letter, I see that the order should have been sent to 2293 Second Avenue, St. Paul, Minnesota 55120. When an order is undeliverable, we usually try to verify the shipping address by telephoning the customer. Somehow the return of this shipment was not caught by our normally painstaking shipping clerks. You can be sure that I will investigate shipping and return procedures with our clerks immediately to see if we can improve existing methods.

Your respect is important to us, Mr. Garber. Although our rock-bottom discount prices have enabled us to build a volume business, we don't want to be so large that we lose touch with valued customers like you. Over the years our customers' respect has made us successful, and we hope that the prompt delivery of this shipment will retain yours.

Sincerely,

Amy Hopkins
Amy Hopkins
Distribution Manager

c David Cole
  Shipping Department

Uses customer's name
in salutation

Announces good news
immediately

Regains confidence of
customer by
explaining what
happened and by
suggesting plans for
improvement

Closes confidently
with genuine appeal
for customer's respect

CATHY

In announcing that you will grant a claim, be sure to do so without a grudging tone—even if you have reservations about whether the claim is legitimate. Once you decide to comply with the customer's request, do so happily. Avoid half-hearted or reluctant responses (*Although the Sno-Flake ice crusher works well when it is used properly, we have decided to allow you to take yours to Ben's Appliances for repair at our expense*).

Be enthusiastic, not grudging, when granting a claim.

Explaining Compliance in the Body

In responding to claims, most organizations sincerely want to correct a wrong. They want to do more than just make the customer happy. They want to stand behind their products and services; they want to do what's right.

Most businesses comply with claims because they want to promote customer goodwill.

In the body of the letter, explain how you are complying with the claim. In all but the most routine claims, you should also seek to regain the confidence of the customer. You might reasonably expect that a customer who has experienced difficulty with a product, with delivery, with billing, or with service has lost faith in your organization. Rebuilding that faith is important for future business.

How to rebuild lost confidence depends on the situation and the claim. If procedures need to be revised, explain what changes will be made. If a product has defective parts, tell how the product is being improved. If service is faulty, describe genuine efforts to improve it. Notice in Figure 6.5 that the writer promises to investigate shipping procedures to see if improvements might prevent future mishaps.

Sometimes the problem is not with the product but with the way it's being used. In other instances customers misunderstand warranties or inadvertently cause delivery and billing mix-ups by supplying incorrect information. Remember that rational and sincere explanations will do much to regain the confidence of unhappy customers.

In your explanation avoid emphasizing negative words such as *trouble, regret, misunderstanding, fault, defective, error, inconvenience,* and *unfortunately*. Keep your message positive and upbeat.

Because negative words suggest blame and fault, avoid them in letters that attempt to build customer goodwill.

Deciding Whether to Apologize

Whether to apologize is a debatable issue. Some writing experts argue that apologies remind customers of their complaints and are therefore negative. These writers avoid apologies; instead they concentrate on how they are satisfying the customer. Real letters that respond to customers' claims, however, often include apologies.[2] If you feel that your company is at fault and that an apology is an appropriate goodwill gesture, by all means include it. Be careful, though, not to admit negligence. You'll learn more about responding to negative letters in Chapter 7.

Showing Confidence in the Closing

End your letter by looking ahead positively.

End positively by expressing confidence that the problem has been resolved and that continued business relations will result. You might mention the product in a favorable light, suggest a new product, express your appreciation for the customer's business, or anticipate future business. It's often appropriate to refer to the desire to be of service and to satisfy customers. Notice how the following closings illustrate a positive, confident tone.

> Your Sno-Flake ice crusher will help you remain cool and refreshed this summer. For your additional summer enjoyment, consider our Smoky Joe tabletop gas grill shown in the enclosed summer catalog. We genuinely value your business and look forward to your future orders.

> We hope that this refund check convinces you of our sincere desire to satisfy our customers. Our goal is to earn your confidence and continue to justify that confidence with quality products and matchless service.

> You were most helpful in telling us about this situation and giving us an opportunity to correct it. We sincerely appreciate your cooperation.

> In all your future dealings with us, you will find us striving our hardest to merit your confidence by serving you with efficiency and sincere concern.

Summing Up and Looking Forward

In this chapter you learned to write letters that respond favorably to information requests, orders, and customer claims. You also learned to write effective responses to these letters. All of these routine letters use the direct strategy. They open immediately with the main idea followed by details and explanations. But not all letters will carry good news. Occasionally, you must deny requests and deliver bad news. In the next chapter you will learn to use the indirect strategy in conveying negative news.

Critical Thinking

1. What's wrong with using the indirect pattern for writing routine requests and replies? If in the end the reader understands the message, why make a big fuss over the organization?
2. Since brevity is valued in business writing, is it ever wise to respond with more information than requested? Why or why not?
3. Is it insensitive to include resale or sales promotion information in a letter that responds to a claim letter from a customer?
4. Which is more effective in claim letters—anger or objectivity? Why?
5. Why is it important to regain the confidence of a customer when you respond to a claim letter?

Chapter Review

6. Why do businesspeople still write letters when e-mail is so much faster?

7. What determines whether you write a letter directly or indirectly?

8. What are the two most important positions in a letter?

9. List two ways that you could begin an inquiry letter that asks many questions.

10. What three elements are appropriate in the closing of a request for information?

11. What is a claim letter? Give an original example.

12. Name three kinds of customers for whom a personalized order acknowledgment makes sense.

13. How does *resale* differ from *sales promotion?* Give an original example of each.

14. What are the three goals of a writer responding to a customer claim letter?

15. Why do some companies comply with nearly all claims?

Writing Improvement Exercises

Letter Openers. Which of the following entries represents an effective direct opening?

16.a. Permit me to introduce myself. I am Alexa Alexander, and I represent TelCom. With the travel season approaching quickly, have you thought about upgrading your telecommunications system to meet the expected increased demand?

b. Have you thought about upgrading your telecommunications system to meet the expected increased demand in the upcoming travel season? _____

17.a. Thank you for your letter of December 2 in which you inquired about the availability of No. 19 bolts of fabric.
   b. We have an ample supply of No. 19 bolts in stock.

_____

18.a. Yes, the Princess Cruise Club is planning a 15-day Mediterranean cruise beginning October 20.
   b. This will acknowledge receipt of your letter of December 2 in which you ask about our Mediterranean cruise schedule.

_____

19.a. Your letter of July 9 requesting a refund has been referred to me because Mr. Halvorson is away from the office.
   b. Your refund check for $175 is enclosed.

_____

20.a. We sincerely appreciate your recent order for plywood wallboard panels.
   b. The plywood wallboard panels that you requested were shipped today by Coastal Express and should reach you by August 12.

_____

Direct Openings. Revise the following openings so that they are more direct. Add information if necessary.

21. Hello! My name is Todd Thompson, and I am the assistant manager of Body Trends, a fitness equipment center in Miami Shores. My manager has asked me to inquire about the upright and semirecumbent cycling machines that we saw advertised in the June issue of *Your Health* magazine. I have a number of questions.

22. Because I've lost your order blank, I have to write this letter. I hope that it's all right to place an order this way. I am interested in ordering a number of things from your summer catalog, which I still have although the order blank is missing.

23. Pursuant to your letter of January 15, I am writing in regard to your inquiry about whether we offer our European-style patio umbrella in colors. This unique umbrella is a very popular item and receives a number of inquiries. Its 10-foot canopy protects you when the sun is directly overhead, but it also swivels and tilts to virtually any angle for continuous sun protection all day long. It comes in two colors: off white and forest green.

24. I am pleased to receive your inquiry regarding the possibility of my acting as a speaker at the final semester meeting of your business management club on April 30. The topic of on-line résumés interests me and is one on which I think I could impart helpful information to your members. Therefore, I am responding in the affirmative to your kind invitation.

25. We have just received your letter of March 12 regarding the unfortunate troubles you are having with your Magnum videocassette recorder. In your letter you ask if you may send the flawed VCR to us for inspection. Although we normally handle all service requests through our local dealers, in your circumstance we are willing to take a look at your unit here at our Richmond plant. Therefore, please send it to us so that we may determine what's wrong.

Closing Paragraph. The following concluding paragraph to a claim letter response suffers from faults in strategy, tone, and emphasis. Revise and improve.

26. As a result of your complaint of June 2, we are sending a replacement shipment of laser printers by Atlantic Express. Unfortunately, this shipment will not reach you until June 5. We hope that you will not allow this troubling incident and the resulting inconvenience and lost sales you suffered to jeopardize our future business relations. In the past we have been able to provide you with quality products and prompt service.

Activities and Cases

6.1 Information Request: Résumé-Scanning at L. L. Bean. You're now in the job market, and you'd really like to apply for a job at L. L. Bean, the catalog superstore based in Freeport, Maine. But before you send your résumé, you want to know whether L. L. Bean scans incoming résumés. If it does, you'll have to make some changes in yours. But what changes? You decide to check the L. L. Bean Web site, but you don't see anything about résumés. You telephoned, but you didn't get a clear answer. You're still wondering about whether the company uses software to scan incoming résumés. If so, you wonder what you'll have to do to make your résumé scannable. And how about faxing your résumé? Or would it be better to send it by e-mail? Perhaps you should send two résumés—one that is impressive looking and one that is plain but scannable. And what about key words? You really don't have a clue about how to prepare a scannable résumé. You decide to write to L. L. Bean requesting information.

1. What should you include in the opening of an information request?

2. What should the body of your letter contain?

3. How can questions be handled most effectively?

4. How should you close the letter?

Your Task. Using your own return address, write a personal business letter to Ms. Ellen Wright, Human Resources Department, L. L. Bean, P.O. Box 403, Freeport, ME 04033. Inquire whether L. L. Bean scans incoming résumés. Ask specific questions about how to prepare and submit yours. Don't ask about jobs just yet!

6.2 Claim Request: Free Samples Are Surprisingly Costly. As marketing manager of West Palm Beach Travel, you are very ticked off at Quantum Enterprises. Quantum is a catalog company that provides imprinted promotional products for companies. Your travel company was looking for something special to offer in promoting its cruise ship travel packages. Quantum offered free samples of its promotional merchandise, under its "No Surprise" policy.

You figured, what could you lose? So on January 11 you placed a telephone order for a number of samples. These included three kinds of jumbo tote bags, a square-ended barrel bag with fanny pack, as well as a deluxe canvas attaché case and two colors of garment-dyed sweatshirts. All items were supposed to be free. You did think it odd that you were asked for your company's Master Card credit number, but Quantum promised to bill you only if you kept the samples.

When the items arrived, you weren't pleased, and you returned them all on January 21 (you have a postal receipt showing the return). But your February credit statement showed a charge of $239.58 for the sample items. You called Quantum in February and spoke to Diane, who assured you that a credit would be made on your next statement. However, your March statement showed no credit. You called again and received a similar promise. It's now April and no credit has been made. You decide to write and demand action. Circle the correct choice in the following items.

1. To open this claim letter, you should
   a. Provide a complete chronology of what happened with all the dates and facts.
   b. Tell Quantum how sick and tired you are of this game it is playing.
   c. Explain carefully how much of your valuable time you have spent on trying to resolve this matter.
   d. Describe the action you want taken.

2. In writing this claim letter, you should assume that Quantum
   a. Regularly uses this trick to increase its sales.
   b. Made an honest mistake and will rectify the problem.
   c. Has no intention of crediting your account.
   d. Reacts only when threatened seriously.

3. In the body of this claim letter, you should
   a. Describe briefly what has taken place.
   b. Refer to specific dates and names of people contacted.
   c. Enclose copies of any relevant documents.
   d. All of the above.

4. The closing of this claim letter should
   a. Refer to your attorney, whom Quatum will hear from if this matter is not settled.
   b. Explain what action you want taken and by when.
   c. Make sure that Quantum knows that you will *never* use their products again.
   d. Threaten to spread the word among the travel industry that Quantum can't be trusted.

Your Task. After circling your choices, write a claim letter that documents the problem and states the action you want taken. Add any information you feel is necessary. Address your letter to Ms. Cheryl Butler, Customer Services, Quantum Enterprises, 1505 State Highway 78, Kewanee, IL 61443.

6.3 Order Request: Camera Jumble. Analyze the following ineffective request for merchandise, and list its faults. Then outline a writing plan for an order request.

Dear Sir:

I saw a number of items in your summer/fall catalog that would fit my Lentax ME camera. I am particularly interested in your Super Zoom 55-200mm lens. Its number is SF39971, and it costs $139.95. To go with this lens I will need a polarizing filter. Its number is SF29032 and costs $22.95 and should fit a 52mm lens. Also include a 05CC magenta filter for a 52mm lens. That number is SF29036 and it costs $9.95. Please send also a Hikemaster camera case for $24.95. Its number is SF28355.

I am interested in having these items charged to my credit card. I'd sure like to get them quickly because my vacation starts soon.

Sincerely,

1. List at least five faults in this letter.

2. Outline a general writing plan for an order.
   Opening:
   Body:

   Closing:

Your Task. Rewrite this order request. Use modified block style, and place your return address above the date. Send the letter to Cameratone, Inc., 140 Northern Boulevard, Flushing, NY 11354-1400. Add any necessary information.

6.4 Information Request: Culture Vultures Seeking Adventure. You just saw a great TV program about cheap travel in Europe, and you think you'd like to try it next summer. The program described how some people want to get away from it all; others want to see a little of the world. Some want to learn a different language; some want to soak up a bit of culture. The "get-away" group, the program advised, should book a package trip to a Contiki resort where they relax and soak up the sun. But "culture vultures" and FITS (free independent travelers) should select the countries they want to visit and plan their own trips. You decide to visit France, Spain, and Portugal (or any other countries you select).

Begin planning your trip by gathering information from the country's tourist office. Many details need to be worked out. What about visas? How about inoculations (ouch!)? Since your budget will be limited, you need to stay in youth or elder hostels whenever possible. Where are they? Are they private? Some hostels accept only people who belong to their organization. You really need to get your hands on a list of hostels for every country before departure. You are also interested in any special transport passes for students, such as a Eurail Pass. And while you are at it, find out if they have any special guides for student travelers. All this information can be secured from a tourist office.

Your Task. Using the Internet, you found an address for information: France Tourist Office, 444 Madison Avenue, New York, NY 10020-2452 <http://www.fgtousa.org>. Write a letter requesting information. If you prefer another country, find its tourist office address. Because this is a personal business letter, include your return address above the date.

6.5 Information Request: Meeting in Las Vegas at the Fabulous Mandalay Bay. Your company, Software.com, has just had an enormously successful two-year sales period. The CEO has asked you, as marketing manager, to arrange a fabulous conference/retreat as a thank-you gift for all 75 engineers, product managers, and salespeople. He wants the company to host a four-day combination sales conference/vacation/retreat at some spectacular location. He suggests that you start by inquiring at the new Mandalay Bay Resort and Casino at Las Vegas. You check its Web site and get some good information. However, you decide to write a letter so that you can have a permanent, formal record of all the resorts you investigate. Thus, you decide to write a letter instead of inquiring by telephone. You estimate that your company will require about 75 rooms. You'll also need about three conference rooms for one and a half days. You want to know room rates, conference facilities, and entertainment possibilities for families. You have two times that would be possible: July 18–22 or August 4–8. You know that these are off-peak times, and you wonder if you can get a good room rate. What entertainment will be showing at the Mandalay Bay during these times? One evening you will want to host a banquet for about 140 people. The CEO wants a report from you by April 1.

Your Task. Write a well-organized information request to Ms. Carol Mintus, Manager, Convention Services, Mandalay Bay Resort and Casino, 240 Mandalay Bay Drive, Las Vegas, NV 87550.

Related Web Site: http://www.mandalaybay.com

Web

6.6 Information Request: Computer Code of Conduct. As an assistant in the campus computer laboratory, you have been asked by your boss to help write a code of conduct for use of the laboratory facilities. This code will spell out what behavior and activities are allowed in your lab. The first thing you are to do is conduct a search of the Internet to see what other college or university computing labs have written as conduct codes.

Your Task. Using at least two search engines, search the Web employing variations of the key words "computer code of conduct." Print two or three codes that seem appropriate. Write a letter (or e-mail message, if your instructor agrees) to the director of an educational computer laboratory asking for further information about its code and its effectiveness. Include at least five significant questions. Attach your printouts to your letter.

6.7 Information Request: Backpacking Cuisine. Assume that you are Benjamin Spring, manager of a health spa and also an ardent backpacker. You are organizing a group of hikers for a wilderness trip to Canada. One item that must be provided is freeze-dried food for the three-week trip. You are unhappy with the taste and quality of backpacking food products currently available. You expect to have a group of hikers who are older, affluent, and natural-food enthusiasts. Some are concerned about products containing preservatives, sugar, and additives. Others are on diets restricting cholesterol, fat, and salt.

You heard that Outfitters, Inc., offers a new line of freeze-dried products. You want to know what they offer and whether they have sufficient variety to serve all the needs of your group. You need to know where their products can be purchased and what the cost range is. You'd also like to try a few of their items before placing a large order. You are interested in how they produce the food products and what kinds of ingredients they use. If you have any items left over, you wonder how long they can be kept and still be usable.

Your Task. Write an information request letter to Tia Osborne, Outfitters, Inc., 1169 Willamette Street, Eugene, OR 97401.

6.8 Order Letter: Office Supplies to Go. As Hector Rivera, manager, Lasertronics, Inc., you want to order some items from an office supply catalog. But your catalog is one year old and you have lost the order form. Because you're in a hurry, you decide to place a fax order. Rather than write for a new catalog, you decide to take a chance and order items from the old catalog, realizing that prices may be somewhat different.

You want three Panasonic electric pencil sharpeners, Item 22-A, at $19.95 each. You want one steel desktop organizer, 60 inches long, Item No. 23-K. Its price is $117.50. Order two Roll-a-Flex files for 2- by 4-inch cards at $14.50 each. This is Item 23-G. The next item is No. 29-H, file folders, box of 100, letter size, at $5.29. You need ten boxes. You would like to be invoiced for this purchase, and you prefer UPS delivery. Even though the prices may be somewhat higher, you decide to list the prices shown in your catalog so that you have an idea of what the total order will cost.

Your Task. Write a letter to Monarch Discount Office Furniture, 2890 Monarch Road, Lethbridge, Alberta T1K 1L6. Between the date and the inside address, type TRANSMITTED BY FAX.

6.9 Claim Letter: Undersized French Doors. As Julie Chen, owner of Smart Interiors, you recently completed a kitchen remodel that required double-glazed, made-to-order oak French doors. You ordered them by telephone on July 2 from Custom Wood, Inc. When they arrived on July 25, your carpenter gave you the bad news: the doors were cut too small. Instead of measuring a total of 11 feet 8 inches, the doors measured 11 feet 4 inches. In your carpenter's words, "No way can I stretch those doors to fit these openings!" You waited three weeks for these doors, and your clients wanted them installed immediately. Your carpenter said, "I can rebuild this opening for you, but I'm going to have to charge you for my time." His extra charge came to $455.50.

You feel that the people at Custom Wood should reimburse you for this amount since it was their error. In fact, you actually saved them a bundle of money by not returning the doors. You decide to write to Custom Wood and enclose a copy of your carpenter's bill. You wonder whether you should also include a copy of Custom Wood's invoice, even though it does not show the exact door measurements. You are a good customer of Custom Wood, having used their quality doors and windows on many other jobs. You're confident that it will grant this claim.

Your Task. Write a claim letter to Jay Brandt, Marketing Manager, Custom Wood, Inc., 401 Main Street, Waterford, MI 48327.

6.10 Claim Letter: The Real Thing. Have you ever bought a product that didn't work as promised? Have you been disappointed in service at a bank, video store, restaurant, department store, or discount house? Have you had ideas about how a company or organization could improve its image, service, or product? Remember that smart companies want to know what their customers think, especially if a product could be improved.

Your Task. Select a product or service that has disappointed you. Write a claim letter requesting a refund, replacement, explanation, or whatever seems reasonable. For claims about food products, be sure to include bar-code identification from the package, if possible. Your instructor may ask you to actually mail this letter. When you receive a response, share it with your class.

6.11 Claim Letter: Deep Desk Disappointment. Assume that you are Monica Keil, President, Keil Consulting Services, 423 E. Willamette Avenue, Colorado Springs, CO 80903. Since your consulting firm was doing very well, you decided to splurge and purchase a fine executive desk for your own office. You ordered an expensive desk described as "North American white oak embellished with hand-inlaid walnut cross-banding." Although you would not ordinarily purchase large, expensive items by mail, you were impressed by the description of this desk and by the money-back guarantee promised in the catalog.

When the desk arrived, you knew that you had made a mistake. The wood finish was rough, the grain looked splotchy, and many of the drawers would not pull out easily. The advertisement had promised "full suspension, silent ball-bearing drawer slides." You are disappointed with the desk and decide to send it back, taking advantage of the money-back guarantee.

Your Task. Write a letter to Rodney Harding, Marketing Manager, Idaho Wood Products, P.O. Box 488, Sandpoint, ID 83864. You want your money refunded. You're not sure whether the freight charges can be refunded, but it's worth a try. Supply any details needed.

Web **6.12 Information Response: The Ski Club Wants to Go River Rafting.** As the program chair for the campus Ski Club, you have been asked by president Brian Krauss to investigate river rafting. The Ski Club is an active organization, and its members want to schedule a summer activity. A majority favored rafting. Use a browser to search the Web for relevant information. Select five of the most promising Web sites offering rafting. If possible, print a copy of your findings.

Your Task. Summarize your findings in a response letter to the Ski Club president. The next meeting is May 8, but you think it would be a good idea if you could discuss your findings with Brian before the meeting. Address your letter to Brian Krauss, President, SIU Ski Club, 303 Founders Hall, Carbondale, IL 62901.

Team

Critical
Thinking **6.13 Information Response Request: Scannable Résumés.** As part of a team of interns at the catalog store L. L. Bean, you have been asked to write a form letter to send to job applicants who inquire about your résumé-scanning techniques. The following poorly written response to an inquiry was pulled from the file.

Dear Mr. Madzar:

Your letter of April 11 has been referred to me for a response. We are pleased to learn that you are considering employment here at L. L. Bean, and we look forward to receiving your résumé, should you decide to send same to us.

You ask if we scan incoming résumés. Yes, we certainly do. Actually, we use SmartTrack, an automated résumé-tracking system. SmartTrack is wonderful! You know, we sometimes receive as many as 300 résumés a day, and SmartTrack helps us sort, screen, filter, and separate the résumés. It also processes them, helps us organize them, and keeps a record of all of these résumés. Some of the resumés, however, cannot be scanned, so we have to return those—if we have time.

The reasons that résumés won't scan may surprise you. Some applicants send photocopies or faxed copies, and these can cause misreading, so don't do it. The best plan is to send an original copy. Some people use colored paper. Big mistake! White paper (8 1/2 x 11-inch) printed on one side is the best bet. Another big problem is unusual type fonts, such as script or fancy gothic or antique fonts. They don't seem to realize that scanners do best with plain, readable fonts such as Helvetica or Arial in a 10- to 14-point size.

Other problems occur when applicants use graphics, shading, italics, underlining, horizontal and vertical lines, parentheses, and brackets. Scanners like plain "vanilla" résumés! Oh yes, staples can cause misreading. And folding of a résumé can also cause the scanners to foul up. To be safe, don't staple or fold, and be sure to use wide margins and a quality printer (no dot matrixes!!).

When a hiring manager within Bean decides to look for an appropriate candidate, he is told to submit key words to describe the candidate he has in mind for his opening. We tell him (or sometimes her) to zero in on nouns and phrases that best describe what they want. Thus, my advice to you is to try to include those words that highlight your technical and professional areas of expertise.

If you do decide to submit your résumé to us, be sure you don't make any of the mistakes described herein that would cause the scanner to misread it.

Sincerely,

Your Task. As a team, discuss how this letter could be improved. Decide what information is necessary to send to potential job applicants. Search for additional information that might be helpful. Then, submit an improved version to your instructor. Although the form letter should be written so that it can be sent to anyone who inquires, address this one to Daryl Black, 629 Massachusetts Avenue, Cambridge, MA 02139.

6.14 Information Response Request: Tell Me About Your Major. A friend in a distant city is considering moving to your area for more education and training in your field. This individual wants to know about your program of study.

Your Task. Write a letter describing a program in your field (or any field you wish to describe). What courses must be taken? Toward what degree, certificate, or employment position does this program lead? Why did you choose it? Would you recommend this program to your friend? How long does it take? Add any information you feel would be helpful.

6.15 Information Response Request: Backpacking Cuisine. As Tia Osborne, owner of Outfitters, Inc., producer of freeze-dried backpacking foods, answer the inquiry of Benjamin Spring (described in Activity 6.7). You are eager to have Mr. Spring sample your new all-natural line of products containing no preservatives, sugar, or additives. You want him to know that you started this company two years ago after you found yourself making custom meals for discerning backpackers who rejected typical camping fare. Some of your menu items are excellent for individuals on restricted diets. Some dinners are cholesterol-, fat-, and salt-free, but he'll have to look at your list to see for himself.

You will send him your complete list of dinner items and the suggested retail prices. You will also send him a sample "Saturday Night on the Trail," a four-course meal that comes with fruit candies and elegant appetizers. All your food products are made from choice ingredients in sanitary kitchens that you supervise personally. They are flash frozen in a new vacuum process that you patented. Although your dried foods are meant to last for years, you don't recommend that they be kept beyond 18 months because they may deteriorate. This could happen if a package were punctured or if the products became overheated.

Your Task. Respond to Benjamin Spring, 322 East Chapman, Fullerton, CA 92634. By the way, your products are currently available at Malibu Sports Center, 19605 Pacific Coast Highway, Malibu, CA 90265. Large orders may be placed directly with you, and you offer a 5 percent discount on direct orders.

6.16 Order Response: Office Supplies to Go. As the sales director of a discount office furniture supply, you'd like to be able to fill every order without difficulty. But sometimes that's impossible. You have received an order from Hector Rivera at Lasertronics (described in Activity 6.8). You must tell him that all of the prices listed in his old catalog have increased. That's the bad news. The good news is that you have in stock nearly everything he ordered. The only item not immediately available is the desktop organizer, Item No. 23-K. That has to be shipped from the manufacturer in Pittsburgh, Pennsylvania. You've been having trouble with that supplier lately, perhaps because of heavy demand. However, you think that the organizer will be shipped no later than three weeks from the current date.

You're pleased to have Lasertronics' order. You wonder if Lasertronics might be interested in your new line of office supply products at discount prices. Send Mr. Rivera a new catalog and call his attention to the low price on continuous-form computer paper. It's just $39.95 for a box containing 2,700 sheets of $9\frac{1}{2}$- by 11-inch, 20-pound printout paper.

Your Task. Write a customer order response letter to Hector Rivera, Manager, Lasertronics, Inc., 2004 Henrietta Road, Rochester, NY 14623. All the items he ordered, except the organizer, are on their way by UPS and should arrive in three days.

Critical Thinking **6.17 Claim Response: Undersized French Doors.** As Jay Brandt, manager of Custom Wood, Inc., you have a problem. Your firm manufactures quality precut and custom-built doors and frames. You have received a letter dated August 3 from Julie Chen (described in Activity 6.9). Ms. Chen is an interior designer, and she complains that the oak French doors she recently ordered for a client were made to the wrong dimensions.

Although they were the wrong size, she kept the doors and had them installed because her clients were without outside doors. However, her carpenter charged an extra $455.50 to install them. She claims that you should reimburse her for this amount, since your company was responsible for the error. You check her July 2 order and find that the order was filled correctly. In a telephone order, Ms. Chen requested doors that measured 11 feet 4 inches and that's what you sent. Now she says that the doors should have been 11 feet 8 inches.

Your policy forbids refunds or returns on custom orders. Yet, you remember that around July 2 you had two new people working the phones taking orders. It's possible that they did not hear or record the measurements correctly. You don't know whether to grant this claim or refuse it. But you do know that you must look into the training of telephone order takers and be sure that they verify all custom order measurements. It might also be a good idea to have your craftsmen call a second time to confirm custom measurements.

Ms. Chen is a successful interior designer and has provided Custom Wood with a number of orders. You value her business but aren't sure how to respond. You'd like to remind her that Custom Wood has earned a reputation as a premier manufacturer of wood doors and frames. Your doors feature prime woods, meticulous craftsmanship, and award-winning designs. And the engineering is ingenious.

Your Task. Decide how to treat this claim and then respond to Julie Chen, Smart Interiors, 3282 Richmond Road, Highland Hills Village, OH 44122. You might mention that you have a new line of greenhouse windows that are available in three sizes. Include a brochure describing these windows.

6.18 Claim Response: Deep Desk Disappointment. As Rodney Harding, marketing manager, Idaho Wood Products, it is your job to reply to customer claims, and today you must respond to Monica Keil, president, Keil Consulting Services (described in Activity 6.11). You are disturbed that she is returning the executive desk (Invoice No. 3499), but your policy is to comply with customer wishes. If she doesn't want to keep the desk, you will certainly return the purchase price plus shipping charges. Desks are occasionally damaged in shipping, and this may explain the marred finish and the sticking drawers.

You want Ms. Keil to give Idaho Wood Products another chance. After all, your office furniture and other wood products are made from the finest hand-selected woods by master artisans. Since she is apparently furnishing her office, send her another catalog and invite her to look at the traditional conference desk on page 10-E. This is available with a matching credenza, file cabinets, and accessories. She might be interested in your furniture-leasing plan, which can produce substantial savings.

Your Task. Write to Monica Keil, President, Keil Consulting Services, 423 E. Willamette Avenue, Colorado Springs, CO 80903. In granting her claim, promise that you will personally examine any furniture she may order in the future.

Video **6.19 Video Case Study: Responsibilities and Rewards at Ben & Jerry's.** View the Ben & Jerry's video either in the classroom or at the Guffey Web site <www.meguffey.com/small.html>. As you learn in the video, Ben & Jerry's changed its ice cream containers to use unbleached paper. The new packaging paper was chosen because chlorine is not used. What's wrong with chlorine? Although it makes paper white, chlorine contains dioxin, which is known to cause cancer, genetic and reproductive defects, and learning disabilities. In producing paper, pulp mills using chlorine are also adding to dioxin contamination of waterways. Finding a chlorine-free, unbleached paperboard for its packages delighted Ben & Jerry's. But the new process resulted in packages whose inner surfaces are brown, rather than white.

You've been hired at Ben & Jerry's to help answer incoming letters. Although you're fairly new, your boss gives you a letter from an unhappy customer. This customer opened a pint container of Ben & Jerry's "World's Best Vanilla" and then threw its contents out. He saw the brown inner lid and inner sides of the package, and he decided that his pint container must have been used for chocolate before it was used for vanilla. Or, he said, "The entire pint has gone bad and somehow turned the insides brown." Whatever the reason, he wasn't taking any chances. Although he's a long-time customer, he now wants his money back. The last comment in his letter was, "I like your stand on environmental and social issues, but I don't like getting my ice cream in used containers."

Your Task. Write a letter that explains the brown interior of the carton, justifies the use of the new packaging material, and retains the customer's business. How could you promote future business with this customer? Address your letter to Mr. Adam W. Johnson, 4030 West Griswold Road, Phoenix, AZ 85051.

Related Web Site: Visit the Ben & Jerry's Web site <www.benjerry.com/indexg.html> and look for information about dioxin. If the description is no longer on this page, search for helpful information on other pages.

Grammar/Mechanics Checkup—6

Commas 1

Review the Grammar Review section of the Grammar/Mechanics Handbook, Sections 2.01–2.04. Then study each of the following statements and insert necessary commas. In the space provided, write the number of commas that you add; write *0* if no commas are needed. Also record the number of the G/M principle illustrated. When you finish, compare your responses with those at the end of the book. If your answers differ, study carefully the principles shown in parentheses.

Example: In this class students learn to write clear and concise business letters, memos, and reports.   2   (2.01)

1. We do not as a rule allow employees to take time off for dental appointments.   _____
2. You may be sure Mrs. Schwartz that your car will be ready by 4 p.m.   _____
3. Anyone who is reliable conscientious and honest should be very successful.   _____
4. A conference on sales motivation is scheduled for May 5 at the Anaheim Marriott Hotel beginning at 2 p.m.   _____
5. As a matter of fact I just called your office this morning.   _____
6. We are relocating our distribution center from Memphis Tennessee to Des Moines Iowa.   _____
7. In the meantime please continue to send your orders to the regional office.   _____
8. The last meeting recorded in the minutes was on February 4 1998 in Chicago.   _____
9. Mr. Silver Mrs. Adams and Ms. Horne are our new representatives.   _____
10. The package mailed to Ms. Leslie Holmes 3430 Larkspur Lane San Diego CA 92110 arrived three weeks after it was mailed.   _____
11. The manager feels needless to say that the support of all employees is critical.   _____

12.	Eric was assigned three jobs: checking supplies replacing inventories and distributing delivered goods.
13.	We will work diligently to retain your business Mr. Lopez.
14.	The vice president feels however that all sales representatives need training.
15.	The name selected for a product should be right for that product and should emphasize its major attributes.

Advanced Grammar/Mechanics Review—6

The following sentences contain errors in grammar, punctuation, capitalization, number style, usage, and spelling. Below each sentence write a corrected version.

1. Every secretaries desk will be equipped with the most latest computer and printer.

2. We ordered new stationary about 2 months ago but I can find no correspondance or invoice related to our order.

3. Anyone of the Vice Presidents are authorized to sign checks, however for amounts that are over 10 thousand dollars 2 signatures are required.

4. To be admitted an application must be submitted before April 1st.

5. Although twenty percent of Campbell Soup Companys sales now come from outside the United States the Company expects to increase that number to thirty percent, by 2002.

6. The sierra club recommend investing in "socially responsible" companys such as the quaker oats company.

7. Some organizations worry that valueable company information may be stole over the internet.

8. Did you know that an ostriches eye is bigger than it's brain.

9. Jennifer completed a b.s. degree in Accounting, before taking a job with the boeing company.

10. Because he had took many computer courses Brandon had numerous job op-portunitys from which to chose.

11. The number of students taking Foreign Language courses are decreasing everyyear.

12. To ensure valid survey results each of the fortune 500 companies were sent a questionnaire by the researchers.

13. When Donna Sparks became Vice President of Customer Support at Xerox the support center was receiving more than ten thousand calls a month.

14. Amy miller president of quad graphics met privately with her director of marketing.

15. When president clinton met pope john in italy large crowds gathered.

Grammar/Mechanics Challenge—6

Document for Revision

The following letter has faults in grammar, punctuation, spelling, number form, and wordiness. Use standard proofreading marks (see Appendix B) to correct the errors. When you finish, your instructor can show you the revised version of this letter.

March 3, 200X

FAX TRANSMISSION

Ms. Susan Petty, Manager

Customer Service Department

Steel Cabinets, Inc.

Flint, MI 48433

Dear Ms. Petty:

Please rush a shipment of twenty-three No. 36-440 verticle file cabinets to us, to re-place those damaged in transit recently.

We appreciate you filling our order for 100 of these file cabinets as shown on the accompanying Invoice. Twenty-three of them however were damaged in transit and cannot be sold in there present condition. Because of the fact that 2 transit companies handled the shipment of the file cabinets we cannot determine whom is responsable for the damage.

These verticle files were featured in our newspaper add and we expect to sell a good many in our presale which is scheduled to begin 3/15. Therefore we would appreciate you rushing these cabinets by Red Dog Freight before 3/12. Moreover please let us know what should be done with the damaged cabinets.

Sincerely,

Kmart Cleans Up Its Act

For years Kmart has had a code of ethics for employees to sign and follow. Nevertheless, the scuttlebutt around the apparel industry was that at Kmart "they're all on the take."[3] Granted, Kmart's code said nothing about kickbacks, bribes, or gifts. In fact, no specific behavior at all was prohibited, and employees were even allowed to accept gifts worth $50 or less from outside vendors.

But all that changed after Michael Dowdle, Kmart's former director of shopping center development and marketing, was indicted for accepting kickbacks. The company immediately hired Kroll Associates to investigate Kmart's entire operation and recommend an ethics program to help clean up its act.

The new Kmart code of business conduct specifically forbids company employees from accepting any bribe, commission, kickback, payment, loan, gratuity (including travel and entertainment), gift sample, service, or promise of employment from any vendor, supplier, subcontractor, or competitor.[4] And every one of Kmart's 300,000 associates must sign the new oath. Even suppliers and vendors must sign statements pledging that they will abide by the new rules.

Other businesses are equally concerned about beefing up their ethics programs. Beall's department store chain, headquartered in Bradenton, Florida, requires all employees to read a 26-page handbook and sign a pledge regarding ethical conduct. Topics range from drug abuse, use of company resources, safety, employee fraternization, scheduling, and harassment to software piracy. Employees also complete annual questionnaires to reaffirm their commitment to ethical conduct.

Career Application

In class discussion consider these questions:

- Why are companies increasingly demanding that employees sign pledges of ethical conduct?
- Should employees be encouraged to report suspected unethical behavior of fellow workers?
- What are the advantages and disadvantages of detailed codes of conduct for employees?

Your Task

As Jason Hawkins, administrative assistant to the vice president of Nicolle, a chain of discount women's apparel shops, you have been asked to collect information about codes of conduct. This information will be discussed at the next Ethics Committee meeting February 14. Alarmed at Kmart's problems and suspecting pilferage among Nicolle employees, your boss and other members of management wish to implement a complete ethics program.

- Using the Web, locate Pryor & Associates, a company that specializes in employee support. It even offers sample employee conduct codes.

- Inquire about how specific a code should be. Should it get right down to naming prohibited deeds, or should it be general and thus more inclusive?

- Ask for advice on the best way to involve employees in the short term as well as over the long haul.

- Prepare a letter that requests samples of conduct codes as well as information about hotlines, in-service training programs, and successful programs at other retailers. Address your letter to David L. Pryor, Pryor & Associates, 3701 Bay Area Boulevard, Houston, TX 77062.

Web

Related Web Site: At the Applied Ethics Resources site <http://www.ethics. ubc.ca/resources/>, click on "Business Ethics." You'll find links to numerous business codes and creeds.

Negative, Persuasive, and Special Messages

Negative Messages

More thought goes into bad news messages. That's because we need to explain the whys and try to offer alternatives.[1]

CATHY DIAL, *manager, Consumer Affairs, Frito-Lay, a division of PepsiCo*

LEARNING OBJECTIVES

1. Describe a plan for resolving business problems.
2. List the four components of a bad-news message.
3. Distinguish between the direct and indirect pattern for business messages.
4. Discuss methods for applying the indirect pattern to bad-news messages, including buffering the opening, presenting the reasons, cushioning the bad news, and closing pleasantly.
5. Apply the indirect pattern in refusing requests, refusing claims, and announcing bad news to customers and employees.
6. Identify situations in which the direct pattern is appropriate for breaking bad news.
7. Explain when the indirect strategy may be unethical.

Strategies for Breaking Bad News

If your message delivers bad news, consider using the indirect strategy.

Breaking bad news is a fact of business life for Cathy Dial at Frito-Lay and for nearly every business communicator. Because bad news disappoints, irritates, and sometimes angers the receiver, such messages must be written carefully.

The direct strategy, which you learned to apply in earlier chapters, frontloads the main idea, even when it's bad news. The direct strategy appeals to efficiency-oriented writers who don't want to waste time with efforts to soften the effects of bad news.[2] Many business writers, however, prefer to use the indirect pattern in delivering negative messages. The indirect strategy is especially appealing to relationship-oriented writers. They care about how a message will affect its receiver.

Although the major focus of this chapter will be on developing the indirect strategy, you'll first learn the procedure that many business professionals follow in resolving business problems. It may surprise you. Then you'll study models of messages that use the indirect pattern to refuse requests, refuse claims, and announce bad news to customers and employees. Finally, you'll learn to identify instances in which the direct pattern may be preferable in announcing bad news.

Resolving Business Problems

In all businesses, things occasionally go wrong. Goods are not delivered, a product fails to perform as expected, service is poor, billing gets fouled up, or customers are misunderstood. All businesses offering products or services must sometimes deal with troublesome situations that cause unhappiness to customers and to employees. Whenever possible, these problems should be dealt with immediately and personally. One study found that a majority of business professionals resolve problems in the following manner:[3]

1. Call the individual involved.
2. Describe the problem and apologize.
3. Explain why the problem occurred, what you are doing to resolve it, and how you will prevent it from happening again.
4. Follow up with a letter that documents the phone call and promotes goodwill.

Dealing with problems immediately is very important in resolving conflict and retaining goodwill. Written correspondence is generally too slow for problems that demand immediate attention. But written messages are important (1) when personal contact is impossible, (2) to establish a record of the incident, (3) to formally confirm follow-up procedures, and (4) to promote good relations.

A bad-news follow-up letter is shown in Figure 7.1. Consultant Maris Richfield found herself in the embarrassing position of explaining why she had given out the name of her client to a salesperson. The client, Data.com, Inc., had hired her firm, Richfield Consulting Services, to help find an appropriate service for outsourcing its payroll functions. Without realizing it, Maris had mentioned to a potential vendor (Payroll Services, Inc.) that her client was considering hiring an outside service to handle its payroll. An overeager salesperson from Payroll Services immediately called on Data.com, thus angering the client. The client had hired the consultant to avoid this very kind of intrusion. Data.com did not want to be hounded by vendors selling their payroll services.

When she learned of the problem, the first thing consultant Maris Richfield did was call her client to explain and apologize. But she also followed up with the letter shown in Figure 7.1. The letter not only confirms the telephone conversation but also adds the right touch of formality. It sends the nonverbal message that the matter is being taken seriously and that it is important enough to warrant a written letter.

Problems with customers are generally resolved by first calling and then confirming with a follow-up letter.

Using the Indirect Pattern to Prepare the Reader

When sending a bad-news message that will upset or irritate the receiver, many business communicators use the indirect pattern. Revealing bad news indirectly shows sensitivity to your reader. Whereas good news can be announced quickly, bad news generally should be revealed gradually. By preparing the reader, you soften the impact. A blunt announcement of disappointing news might cause the receiver to stop reading and toss the message aside.

The indirect strategy enables you to keep the reader's attention until you have been able to explain the reasons for the bad news. The most important part of a

The indirect pattern softens the impact of bad news.

FIGURE 7.1 Bad-News Follow-Up Message

Richfield Consulting Services

4023 Rodeo Drive Plaza, Suite 404　　　　　　　　Voice: 213.499.8224
Beverly Hills, CA 90640　　　　　　　　　　　　Web: www.richfieldconsulting.com

October 23, 200X

Ms. Angela Ranier
Vice President, Human Resources
Data.com, Inc.
21067 Pacific Coast Highway
Malibu, CA 90265

Dear Angela:

Opens with agreement and apology →

You have every right to expect complete confidentiality in your transactions with an independent consultant. As I explained in yesterday's telephone call, I am very distressed that you were called by a salesperson from Payroll Services, Inc. This should not have happened, and I apologize to you again for inadvertently mentioning your company's name in a conversation with a potential vendor, Payroll Services, Inc.

Explains what caused problem and how it was resolved →

All clients of Richfield Consulting are assured that their dealings with our firm are held in the strictest confidence. Because your company's payroll needs are so individual and because you have so many contract workers, I was forced to explain how your employees differed from those of other companies. The name of your company, however, should never have been mentioned. I can assure you that it will not happen again. I have informed Payroll Services

Promises to prevent recurrence →

that it had no authorization to call you directly and its actions have forced me to reconsider using its services for my future clients.

Closes with forward look →

A number of other payroll services offer excellent programs. I'm sure we can find the perfect partner to enable you to outsource your payroll responsibilities, thus allowing your company to focus its financial and human resources on its core business. I look forward to our next appointment when you may choose from a number of excellent payroll outsourcing firms.

Sincerely yours,

Maris Richfield

Maris Richfield

Tips for Resolving Problems and Following Up

- Whenever possible, call or see the individual involved.
- Describe the problem and apologize.
- Explain why the problem occurred.
- Explain what you are doing to resolve it.
- Explain how it will not happen again.
- Follow up with a letter that documents the personal message.
- Look forward to positive future relations.

bad-news letter is the explanation, which you'll learn about shortly. The indirect plan consists of four main parts:

- Buffer
- Reasons
- Bad news
- Closing

Buffering the Opening

A buffer is a device to reduce shock or pain. To buffer the pain of bad news, begin with a neutral but meaningful statement that makes the reader continue reading. The buffer should be relevant and concise. Although it should avoid revealing the bad news immediately, it should not convey a false impression that good news follows. It should provide a natural transition to the explanation that follows. The individual situation, of course, will help determine what you should put in the buffer. Here are some possibilities for opening bad-news messages.

- **Best news.** Start with the part of the message that represents the best news. For example, in a memo that announces a new service along with a cutback in mail room hours, you might write, *To ensure that your correspondence goes out with the last pickup, we're starting a new messenger pickup service at 2:30 p.m. daily beginning June 1.*
- **Compliment.** Praise the receiver's accomplishments, organization, or efforts, but do so with honesty and sincerity. For instance, in a letter declining an invitation to speak, you could write, *The Thalians have my sincere admiration for their fund-raising projects on behalf of hungry children. I am honored that you asked me to speak Friday, November 5.*
- **Appreciation.** Convey thanks to the reader for doing business, for sending something, for showing confidence in your organization, for expressing feelings, or simply for providing feedback. In a letter responding to a complaint about poor service, you might say, *Thanks for telling us about your experience at our hotel and for giving us a chance to look into the situation.* Avoid thanking the reader, however, for something you are about to refuse.
- **Agreement.** Make a relevant statement with which both reader and receiver can agree. A letter that rejects a loan application might read, *We both realize how much the export business has been affected by the relative strength of the dollar in the past two years.*
- **Facts.** Provide objective information that introduces the bad news. For example, in a memo announcing cutbacks in the hours of the employees' cafeteria, you might say, *During the past five years the number of employees eating breakfast in our cafeteria has dropped from 32 percent to 12 percent.*
- **Understanding.** Show that you care about the reader. In announcing a product defect, the writer can still manage to express concern for the customer: *We know that you expect superior performance from all the products you purchase from OfficeCity. That's why we're writing personally about the Excell printer cartridges you recently ordered.*
- **Apology.** A study of actual letters responding to customer complaints revealed that 67 percent carried an apology of some sort.[4] If you do apologize, do it early, briefly, and sincerely. For example, a manufacturer of super premium ice cream might respond to a customer's complaint with, *We're genuinely sorry that you were disappointed in the price of the ice cream you recently purchased at one of our scoop shops. Your opinion is important to us, and we appreciate your giving us the opportunity to look into the problem you describe.*

A buffer opens a bad-news letter with a neutral, concise, relevant, and upbeat statement.

A good buffer may include the best news, a compliment, appreciation, facts regarding the problem, a statement indicating understanding, or an apology.

Presenting the Reasons

Bad-news messages should explain reasons before stating the negative news.

The most important part of a bad-news letter is the section that explains why a negative decision is necessary. Without sound reasons for denying a request or refusing a claim, a letter will fail, no matter how cleverly it is organized or written. As part of your planning before writing, you analyzed the problem and decided to refuse a request for specific reasons. Before disclosing the bad news, try to explain those reasons. Providing an explanation reduces feelings of ill will and improves the chances that the reader will accept the bad news.

- **Being cautious in explaining.** If the reasons are not confidential and if they will not create legal liability, you can be specific: *Growers supplied us with a limited number of patio roses, and our demand this year was twice that of last year.* In refusing a speaking engagement, tell why the date is impossible: *On January 17 we have a board of directors meeting that I must attend.*

Readers accept bad news more readily if they see that someone benefits.

- **Citing reader benefits.** Readers are more open to bad news if in some way, even indirectly, it may help them. In refusing a customer's request for free hemming of skirts and slacks, Lands' End wrote: *We tested our ability to hem skirts a few months ago. This process proved to be very time-consuming. We have decided not to offer this service because the additional cost would have increased the selling price of our skirts substantially, and we did not want to impose that cost on all our customers.*[5] Readers also accept bad news better if they recognize that someone or something else benefits, such as other workers or the environment: *Although we would like to consider your application, we prefer to fill managerial positions from within.* Avoid trying to show reader benefits, though, if they appear insincere: *To improve our service to you, we're increasing our brokerage fees.*

"Dear Valued Customer: We're sorry, but company policy forbids apologies. Sincerely yours . . . ."

- **Explaining company policy.** Readers resent blanket policy statements prohibiting something: *Company policy prevents us from making cash refunds* or *Contract bids may be accepted from local companies only* or *Company policy requires us to promote from within.* Instead of hiding behind company policy, gently explain why the policy makes sense: *We prefer to promote from within because it rewards* *the loyalty of our employees. In addition, we've found that people familiar with our organization make the quickest contribution to our team effort.* By offering explanations, you demonstrate that you care about readers and are treating them as important individuals.

- **Choosing positive words.** Because the words you use can affect a reader's response, choose carefully. Remember that the objective of the indirect pattern is to hold the reader's attention until you've had a chance to explain the reasons justifying the bad news. To keep the reader in a receptive mood, avoid expressions that might cause the reader to tune out. Be sensitive to negative words such as *claim, error, failure, fault, impossible, mistaken, misunderstand, never, regret, unwilling, unfortunately,* and *violate.*

"Dear Unhappy Customer: You claim that we made an error in your order. This is impossible. You must be mistaken and probably misunderstood the invoice. Unfortunately, we never issue refunds. If we may be of further service, do not hesitate to write . . . ."

- **Showing that the matter was treated seriously and fairly.** In explaining reasons, demonstrate to the reader that you take the matter seriously, have investigated carefully, and are making an unbiased decision. Consumers are more accepting of disappointing news when they feel that their requests have been heard and that they have been treated fairly. Avoid passing the buck or blaming others within your organization. Such unprofessional behavior makes the reader lose faith in you and your company.

Cushioning the Bad News

Although you can't prevent the disappointment that bad news brings, you can reduce the pain somewhat by breaking the news sensitively. Be especially considerate when the reader will suffer personally from the bad news. A number of thoughtful techniques can cushion the blow.

- **Positioning the bad news.** Instead of spotlighting it, sandwich the bad news between other sentences, perhaps among your reasons. Try not to let the refusal begin or end a paragraph—the reader's eye will linger on these high-visibility spots. Another technique that reduces shock is putting a painful idea in a subordinate clause: *Although another candidate was hired, we appreciate your interest in our organization and wish you every success in your job search.* Subordinate clauses often begin with words such as *although, as, because, if,* and *since.*

Techniques for cushioning bad news include positioning it strategically, using the passive voice, emphasizing the positive, implying the refusal, and suggesting alternatives or compromises.

- **Using the passive voice.** Passive-voice verbs enable you to depersonalize an action. Whereas the active voice focuses attention on a person (*We don't give cash refunds*), the passive voice highlights the action (*Cash refunds are not given because . . .*). Use the passive voice for the bad news. In some instances you can combine passive-voice verbs and a subordinate clause: *Although franchise scoop shop owners cannot be required to lower their ice cream prices, we are happy to pass along your comments for their consideration.*

- **Accentuating the positive.** As you learned earlier, messages are far more effective when you describe what you can do instead of what you can't do. Rather than *We will no longer allow credit card purchases,* try a more positive appeal: *We are now selling gasoline at discount cash prices.*

- **Implying the refusal.** It's sometimes possible to avoid a direct statement of refusal. Often, your reasons and explanations leave no doubt that a request has been denied. Explicit refusals may be unnecessary and at times cruel. In this refusal to contribute to a charity, for example, the writer never actually says no: *Because we will soon be moving into new offices in Glendale, all our funds are earmarked for moving and furnishings. We hope that next year we'll be able to support your worthwhile charity.* The danger of an implied refusal, of course, is that it can be so subtle that the reader misses it. Be certain that you make the bad news clear, thus preventing the need for further correspondence.

- **Suggesting a compromise or an alternative.** A refusal is not so depressing—for the sender or the receiver—if a suitable compromise, substitute, or alternative is available. In denying permission to a class to visit a historical private residence, for instance, this writer softens the bad news by proposing an alternative: *Although private tours of the grounds are not given, we do open the house and its gardens for one charitable event in the fall.*

You can further reduce the impact of the bad news by refusing to dwell on it. Present it briefly (or imply it), and move on to your closing.

Closing Pleasantly

Closings to bad-news messages might include a forward look, an alternative, good wishes, freebies, and resale or sales promotional information.

After explaining the bad news sensitively, close the message with a pleasant statement that promotes goodwill. The closing should be personalized and may include a forward look, an alternative, good wishes, freebies, resale information, or an off-the-subject remark.

- **Forward look.** Anticipate future relations or business. A letter that refuses a contract proposal might read: *Thanks for your bid. We look forward to working with your talented staff when future projects demand your special expertise.*

- **Alternative.** If an alternative exists, end your letter with follow-through advice. For example, in a letter rejecting a customer's demand for replacement of landscaping plants, you might say: *I will be happy to give you a free inspection and consultation. Please call 746-8112 to arrange a date for my visit.*

- **Good wishes.** A letter rejecting a job candidate might read: *We appreciate your interest in our company, and we extend to you our best wishes in your search to find the perfect match between your skills and job requirements.*

- **Freebies.** When customers complain—primarily about food products or small consumer items—companies often send coupons, samples, or gifts to restore confidence and to promote future business. In response to a customer's complaint about a frozen dinner, you could write, *Your loyalty and your concern about our frozen entrees is genuinely appreciated. Because we want you to continue enjoying our healthful and convenient dinners, we're enclosing a coupon that you can take to your local market to select your next Green Valley entree.*
- **Resale or sales promotion.** When the bad news is not devastating or personal, references to resale information or promotion may be appropriate: *The computer workstations you ordered are unusually popular because of their stain-, heat-, and scratch-resistant finishes. To help you locate hard-to-find accessories for these workstations, we invite you to visit our Web site where our on-line catalog provides a huge selection of surge suppressors, multiple outlet strips, security devices, and PC tool kits.*

Avoid endings that sound canned, insincere, inappropriate, or self-serving. Don't invite further correspondence (*If you have any questions, do not hesitate . . .*), and don't rehash the bad news.

Refusing Requests

Although the direct strategy is sometimes suitable, most of us prefer to be let down gently when we're being refused something we want. That's why the reasons-before-refusal pattern works well when you must turn down requests for favors, money, information, action, and so forth. The following writing plan is appropriate when you must deny a routine request or claim.

The indirect strategy is appropriate when refusing requests for favors, money, information, or action.

WRITING PLAN FOR REFUSING REQUESTS OR CLAIMS

- **Buffer:** Start with a neutral statement on which both reader and writer can agree, such as a compliment, appreciation, a quick review of the facts, or an apology.
- **Transition:** Try to include a key idea or word that acts as a transition to the explanation.
- **Reasons:** Present valid reasons for the refusal, avoiding words that create a negative tone. Include resale or sales promotion material if appropriate.
- **Bad news:** Soften the blow by deemphasizing the bad news, using the passive voice, accentuating the positive, or implying a refusal.
- **Alternative:** Suggest a compromise, alternative, or substitute if possible.
- **Closing:** Renew good feelings with a positive statement. Avoid referring to the bad news, and look forward to continued business.

Two versions of a request refusal are shown in Figure 7.2. A magazine writer requested salary information for an article, but this information could not be released. The ineffective version begins with needless information that could be implied. The second paragraph creates a harsh tone with such negative words as *sorry, must refuse, violate,* and *liable.* Since the refusal precedes the explanation, the reader probably will not be in a receptive frame of mind to accept the reasons for refusing. Notice, too, that the bad news is emphasized by its placement in a short sentence at the beginning of a paragraph. It stands out here and adds more weight to the rejection already felt by the reader.

FIGURE 7.2 Refusing a Request

Ineffective

States obvious information

Dear Ms. Brown:

I have your letter of October 21 in which you request information about the salaries and commissions of our top young salespeople.

Sounds harsh, blunt, and unnecessarily negative

I am sorry to inform you that we cannot reveal data of this kind. I must, therefore, refuse your request. To release this information would violate our private employee contracts. Such disclosure could make us liable for damages, should any employee seek legal recourse. I might say, however, that our salespeople are probably receiving the highest combined salary and commissions of any salespeople in this field.

Switches tone

If it were possible for us to help you with your fascinating research, we would certainly be happy to do so.

Sincerely yours,

Effective

CANON
ELECTRONICS

115 Fifth Avenue
New York, NY 10011-1010
(212) 593-1098
www.canon.com

January 15, 200X

Ms. Daniela Brown
1305 Elmwood Avenue
Buffalo, NY 14222-2240

Dear Ms. Brown:

The article you are now researching for *Business Management Weekly* sounds fascinating, and we are flattered that you wish to include our organization. We do have many outstanding young salespeople, both male and female, who are commanding top salaries.

Buffer shows interest, and transition sets up explanation

Each of our salespeople operates under an individual salary contract. During salary negotiations several years ago, an agreement was reached in which both sales staff members and management agreed to keep the terms of these individual contracts confidential. Although specific salaries and commission rates cannot be released, we can provide you with a ranked list of our top salespeople for the past five years. Three of the current top salespeople are under the age of thirty-five.

Explanation gives good reasons for refusing request

Refusal is softened by substitute

Enclosed is a fact sheet regarding our top salespeople. We wish you every success with your article, and we hope to see our organization represented in it.

Closing is pleasant and forward looking

Cordially,

Lloyd Kenniston

Lloyd Kenniston
Executive Vice President

LK:je
Enclosure: Sales Fact Sheet

Moreover, the refusal explanation is overly graphic, containing references to possible litigation. The tone at this point is threatening and unduly harsh. Then, suddenly, the author throws in a self-serving comment about the high salary and commissions of his salespeople. Instead of offering constructive alternatives, the ineffective version reveals only tiny bits of the desired data. Finally, the closing sounds syrupy and insincere.

In the more effective version of this refusal, the opening reflects the writer's genuine interest in the request. But it does not indicate compliance. The second sentence acts as a transition by introducing the words *salespeople* and *salaries*, repeated in the following paragraph. Reasons for refusing this request are objectively presented in an explanation that precedes the refusal. Notice that the refusal (*Although specific salaries and commission rates cannot be released*) is a subordinate clause in a long sentence in the middle of a paragraph. To further soften the blow, the letter offers an alternative. The cordial closing refers to the alternative, avoids mention of the refusal, and looks to the future.

It's always easier to write refusals when alternatives can be offered to soften the bad news. But often no alternatives are possible. The refusal shown in Figure 7.3 involves a delicate situation in which a manager has been asked by her superiors to violate a contract. Several of the engineers for whom she works have privately asked her to make copies of a licensed software program for them. They apparently want this program for their personal computers. Making copies is forbidden by the terms of the software licensing agreement, and the manager refuses

In refusing requests, avoid a harsh tone or being too explicit; offer constructive alternatives whenever possible.

FIGURE 7.3 E-Mail Memo That Refuses Request

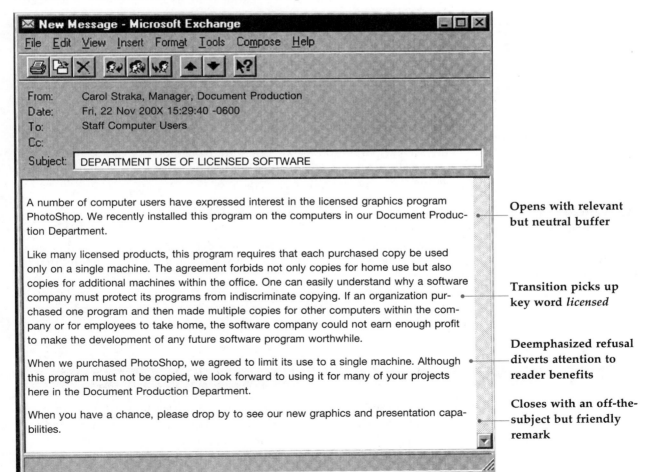

New Message - Microsoft Exchange

File Edit View Insert Format Tools Compose Help

From: Carol Straka, Manager, Document Production
Date: Fri, 22 Nov 200X 15:29:40 -0600
To: Staff Computer Users
Cc:
Subject: DEPARTMENT USE OF LICENSED SOFTWARE

A number of computer users have expressed interest in the licensed graphics program PhotoShop. We recently installed this program on the computers in our Document Production Department.

Opens with relevant but neutral buffer

Like many licensed products, this program requires that each purchased copy be used only on a single machine. The agreement forbids not only copies for home use but also copies for additional machines within the office. One can easily understand why a software company must protect its programs from indiscriminate copying. If an organization purchased one program and then made multiple copies for other computers within the company or for employees to take home, the software company could not earn enough profit to make the development of any future software program worthwhile.

Transition picks up key word licensed

When we purchased PhotoShop, we agreed to limit its use to a single machine. Although this program must not be copied, we look forward to using it for many of your projects here in the Document Production Department.

Deemphasized refusal diverts attention to reader benefits

When you have a chance, please drop by to see our new graphics and presentation capabilities.

Closes with an off-the-subject but friendly remark

to do this. Rather than saying no to each engineer who asks her, she sends all staff computer users the e-mail message shown in Figure 7.3.

The opening tactfully avoids suggesting that any engineer has actually asked to copy the software program. These professionals may prefer not to have their private requests made known. A transition takes the reader to the logical reasons against copying. Notice that the tone is objective, neither preaching nor condemning. The refusal is softened by being linked with a positive statement (*Although this program must not be copied, we look forward to using it for many of your projects here . . .*). To divert attention from the refusal, the memo ends with a friendly, off-the-subject remark.

Refusing Claims

Although most customer claims are granted, occasionally some must be refused.

All businesses offering products or services will receive occasional customer claims for adjustments. Claims may also arise from employees. Most of these claims are valid, and the customer or employee receives a positive response. Even unwarranted claims are sometimes granted because businesses genuinely desire to create a good public image and to maintain friendly relations with employees.

Some claims, however, cannot be approved because the customer or employee is mistaken, misinformed, unreasonable, or possibly even dishonest. Letters responding to these claims deliver bad news. And the indirect strategy breaks bad news with the least pain. It also allows the writer to explain why the claim must be refused before the reader realizes the bad news and begins resisting.

In the letter shown in Figure 7.4, the writer denies a customer's claim for the difference between the price the customer paid for speakers and the price he saw advertised locally (which would have resulted in a cash refund of $151). While Galaxy does match any advertised lower price, the price-matching policy applies *only* to exact models. This claim must be rejected because the advertisement the customer submitted shows a different, older speaker model.

The letter to Russell Chapman opens with a buffer that agrees with a statement in the customer's letter. It repeats the key idea of product confidence as a transition to the second paragraph. Next comes an explanation of the price-matching policy. The writer does not assume that the customer is trying to pull a fast one. Nor does the writer suggest that the customer is a dummy who didn't read or understand the price-matching policy.

When refusing customer claims, explain objectively and do not assume that the customer is an idiot or a crook.

The safest path is a neutral explanation of the policy along with precise distinctions between the customer's speakers and the older ones. The writer also gets a chance to resell the customer's speakers and demonstrate what a quality product they are. By the end of the third paragraph, it's evident to the reader that his claim is unjustified.

Notice how most of the components in an effective claim refusal are woven together in this letter: buffer, transition, explanation, and pleasant closing. The only missing part is an alternative, which was impossible in this situation.

Announcing Bad News to Customers and Employees

In addition to resolving claims, organizations occasionally must announce bad news to customers or to their own employees. Bad news to customers might involve rate increases, reduced service, changed procedures, new locations, or technical problems.

FIGURE 7.4 Refusing a Claim

Galaxy Sound Sales

3091 Geddes Road
Ann Arbor, Michigan 48104
Telephone: (313) 499-2341

Fax: (313) 499-5904
Web: www.galaxysound.com
E-mail: galaxy2@flash.com

May 24, 200X

Mr. Russell L. Chapman
4205 Evergreen Avenue
Dearborn, MI 48128

Dear Mr. Chapman:

You're absolutely right! We do take pride in selling the finest products at rock-bottom prices. The Boze speakers you purchased last month are premier concert hall speakers. They're the only ones we present in our catalog because they're the best.

> **Begins by agreeing with receiver**

We have such confidence in our products and prices that we offer the price-matching policy you mention in your letter of May 20. That policy guarantees a refund of the price difference if you see one of your purchases offered at a lower price for 30 days after your purchase. To qualify for that refund, customers are asked to send us an advertisement or verifiable proof of the product price and model. As our catalog states, this price-matching policy applies only to exact models with USA warranties.

> **Explains price-matching policy**

Our Boze AM-5 II speakers sell for $749. You sent us a local advertisement showing a price of $598 for Boze speakers. This advertisement, however, described an earlier version, the Boze AM-4 model. The AM-5 speakers you received have a wider dynamic range and smoother frequency response than the AM-4 model. Naturally, the improved model you purchased costs a little more than the older AM-4 model that the local advertisement describes. Your speakers have a new three-chamber bass module that virtually eliminates harmonic distortion. Finally, your speakers are 20 percent more compact than the AM-4 model.

> **Without actually saying no, shows why claim can't be honored**

You bought the finest compact speakers on the market, Mr. Chapman. If you haven't installed them yet, you may be interested in ceiling mounts, shown in the enclosed catalog on page 48. We value your business and invite your continued comparison shopping.

> **Renews good feelings by building confidence in wisdom of purchase**

Sincerely yours,

Mark L. Johnson

Mark L. Johnson

Bad news within organizations might involve declining profits, lost contracts, harmful lawsuits, public relations controversies, and changes in policy.

Whether you use a direct or an indirect pattern in delivering that news depends primarily on the anticipated reaction of the receiver. When the bad news affects customers or employees personally—such as cutbacks in pay, reduction of benefits, or relocation plans—you can generally lessen its impact and promote better relations by explaining reasons before revealing the bad news.

> **The choice of a direct or indirect strategy depends on the expected reaction of the receiver.**

- **Buffer:** Open with a compliment, appreciation, facts, or some form of good news.
- **Transition:** Include a key idea that leads from the opening to the reasons.
- **Reasons:** Explain the logic behind the bad news; use positive words and try to show reader benefits if possible.
- **Bad news:** Position the bad news so that it does not stand out. Consider implying the bad news.
- **Alternative:** Suggest a compromise or alternative, if possible.
- **Closing:** Look forward positively. Provide information about an alternative, if appropriate.

In many businesses today employees are being asked to pay more for their health care benefits. Midland Enterprises had to announce a substantial increase to its employees. Figure 7.5 shows two versions of its bad-news message. The first version opens directly with the bad news. No explanation is given for why health care costs are rising. Although Midland has been absorbing the increasing costs in the past and has not charged employees, it takes no credit for this. Instead, the tone of the memo is defensive and unsatisfying to receivers.

In announcing bad news to employees, consider starting with a neutral statement or something positive.

The improved version of this bad-news memo, shown at the bottom of Figure 7.5, uses the indirect pattern. Notice that it opens with a relevant, upbeat buffer regarding health care—but says nothing about increasing costs. For a smooth transition, the second paragraph begins with a key idea from the opening (*comprehensive package*). The reasons section discusses rising costs with explanations and figures. The bad news (*you will be paying $109 a month*) is clearly presented but embedded within the paragraph.

Throughout, the writer strives to show the fairness of the company's position. The ending, which does not refer to the bad news, emphasizes how much the company is paying and what a wise investment it is. Notice that the entire memo demonstrates a kinder, gentler approach than that shown in the first draft. Of prime importance in breaking bad news to employees is providing clear, convincing reasons that explain the decision.

When to Use the Direct Pattern

The direct pattern is appropriate when the bad news is not damaging, when the receiver might overlook the bad news, when the organization expects directness, when the receiver prefers directness, or when firmness is necessary.

Many bad-news letters are best organized indirectly, beginning with a buffer and reasons. The direct pattern, with the bad news first, may be more effective, though, in situations such as the following:

- **When the bad news is not damaging.** If the bad news is insignificant (such as a small increase in cost) and doesn't personally affect the receiver, then the direct strategy certainly makes sense.
- **When the receiver may overlook the bad news.** With the crush of mail today, many readers skim messages, looking only at the opening. If they don't find substantive material, they may discard the message. Rate increases, changes in service, new policy requirements—these critical messages may require boldness to ensure attention.
- **When organization policy suggests directness.** Some companies expect all internal messages and announcements—even bad news—to be straightforward and presented without frills.

FIGURE 7.5 Memo That Announces Bad News to Employees

Ineffective

MEMO TO: Staff

Beginning January 1 your monthly payment for health care benefits will be increased to $109 (up from $42 last year).

Every year health care costs go up. Although we considered dropping other benefits, Midland decided that the best plan was to keep the present comprehensive package. Unfortunately, we can't do that unless we pass along some of the extra cost to you. Last year the company was forced to absorb the total increase in health care premiums. However, such a plan this year is inadvisable.

We did everything possible to avoid the sharp increase in costs to you this year. A rate schedule describing the increases in payments for your family and dependents is enclosed.

- Hits readers with bad news without any preparation
- Does not explain why costs are rising
- Fails to take credit for absorbing previous increases
- Sounds defensive; fails to give reasons

Effective

DATE: November 6, 200X

TO: Fellow Employees

FROM: David P. Martinez, President   *DPM*

SUBJECT: MAINTAINING QUALITY HEALTH CARE

Begins with positive buffer

Health care programs have always been an important part of our commitment to employees here at Midland, Inc. We're proud that our total benefits package continues to rank among the best in the country.

Explains why costs are rising

Such a comprehensive package does not come cheaply. In the last decade health care costs alone have risen over 300 present. We're told that several factors fuel the cost spiral: inflation, technology improvements, increased cost of outpatient service, and "defensive" medicine practiced by doctors to prevent lawsuits.

Reveals bad news clearly but embeds it in paragraph

Just two years ago our monthly health care cost for each employee was $415. It rose to $469 last year. We were able to absorb that jump without increasing your contribution. But this year's hike to $539 forces us to ask you to share the increase. To maintain your current health care benefits, you will be paying $109 a month. The enclosed rate schedule describes the costs for families and dependents.

Ends positively by stressing the company's major share of the costs

Midland continues to pay the major portion of your health care program ($430 each month). We think it's a wise investment.

Enclosure

- **When the receiver prefers directness.** Busy managers may prefer directness. Such shorter messages enable the reader to get in the proper frame of mind immediately. If you suspect that the reader prefers that the facts be presented straightaway, use the direct pattern.

- **When firmness is necessary.** Messages that must demonstrate determination and strength should not use delaying techniques. For example, the last in a series of collection letters that seek payment of overdue accounts may require a direct opener.

Ethics and the Indirect Strategy

The indirect strategy is unethical only if the writer intends to deceive the reader.

You may worry that the indirect organizational strategy is unethical or manipulative because the writer deliberately delays the main idea. But consider the alternative. Breaking bad news bluntly can cause pain and hard feelings. By delaying bad news, you soften the blow somewhat, as well as ensure that your reasoning will be read while the receiver is still receptive. Your motives are not to deceive the reader or to hide the news. Rather, your goal is to be a compassionate, yet effective communicator.

The key to ethical communication lies in the motives of the sender. Unethical communicators *intend to deceive.* For example, Victoria's Secret, the clothing and lingerie chain, offered free $10 gift certificates. However, when customers tried to cash the certificates, they found that they were required to make a minimum purchase of $50 worth of merchandise.[6] For this misleading, deceptive, and unethical offer, the chain paid a $100,000 fine. Although the indirect strategy provides a setting in which to announce bad news, it should not be used to avoid or misrepresent the truth.

Summing Up and Looking Forward

When faced with delivering bad news, you have a choice. You can announce it immediately, or you can delay it by presenting a buffer and reasons first. Many business communicators prefer the indirect strategy because it tends to preserve goodwill. In some instances, however, the direct strategy is effective in delivering bad news.

In this chapter you learned to write follow-up bad-news messages as well as to apply the indirect strategy in refusing requests, denying claims, and delivering bad news to employees. This same strategy is appropriate when you make persuasive requests or when you try to sell something. Chapter 8 discusses how to apply the indirect strategy to persuasive and sales messages.

Critical Thinking

1. A survey of business professionals revealed that nearly every respondent said that every effort should be made to resolve business problems in person.[7] Why is this logical?
2. Does bad news travel faster and farther than good news? Why? What implications would this have for companies responding to unhappy customers?
3. Consider times when you have been aware that others have used the indirect pattern in writing or speaking to you. How did you react?
4. Why is the "reasons" section of a bad-news message so important?
5. Some people feel that all employee news, good or bad, should be announced directly. Do you agree or disagree? Why?

6. List the four steps that many business professionals follow in resolving business problems.

7. List the four main parts of the indirect pattern for revealing bad news.

8. What is a buffer?

9. List seven possibilities for opening bad-news messages.

10. Name at least five words that might affect readers negatively.

11. How can the passive voice be used effectively in bad-news messages? Provide an original example.

12. What is the danger in implying a refusal?

13. List five techniques for closing a bad-news message.

14. What determines whether you announce bad news to customers or employees directly or indirectly?

15. List five instances when bad news should be announced directly.

7.1 Subordinate Clauses. You can soften the effect of bad news by placing it in a subordinate clause that begins with *although, since,* or *because.* The emphasis in a sentence is on the independent clause. Instead of saying *We cannot serve you on a credit basis,* try *Since we cannot serve you on a credit basis, we invite you to take advantage of our cash discounts and sale prices.* Revise the following refusals so that the bad news appears in a subordinate clause.

16. We no longer print a complete catalog. However, we now offer all our catalog choices at our Web site, which is always current.

17. We hope to have our plant remodeling completed by June. We cannot schedule tours of the bottling plant until after we finish remodeling.

18. Island Airways cannot accept responsibility for expenses incurred indirectly from flight delays. However, we do recognize that this delay inconvenienced you.

7.2 Passive-Voice Verbs. Passive-voice verbs may be preferable in breaking bad news because they enable you to emphasize actions rather than personalities. Compare these two refusals:

Example: Active voice: I cannot authorize you to take three weeks of vacation in July.

Example: Passive voice: Three weeks of vacation in July cannot be authorized.

Revise the following refusals so that they use passive-voice instead of active-voice verbs.

19. We cannot refund cash for the items you purchased on credit.

A Cash refund for credit cannot be refunded ✓ for the items.

20. I have already filled my schedule on the date you wish me to speak.

My schedule is already filled on the date you wish me to speak,

21. We do not examine patients until we have verified their insurance coverage.

Insurance coverage is verified before we examine patients.

7.3 Implied Refusals. Bad news can be deemphasized by implying a refusal instead of stating it directly. Compare these refusals:

Example: Direct refusal: We cannot send you a price list nor can we sell our lawn mowers directly to customers. We sell only through dealers, and your dealer is HomeCo, Inc.

Example: Implied refusal: Our lawn mowers are sold only through dealers, and your dealer is HomeCo, Inc.

Revise the following refusals so that the bad news is implied.

22. We cannot give cash refunds for returned merchandise. Our policy enables us to give only store credit and only for merchandise that is returned in its original packaging and that is resalable.

23. I find it impossible to contribute to the fund-raising campaign this year. At present all the funds of my organization are needed to lease new equipment and offices for our new branch in Richmond. I hope to be able to support this fund in the future.

24. We cannot ship our fresh fruit baskets c.o.d. Your order was not accompanied by payment, so we are not shipping it. We have it ready, though, and will rush it to its destination as soon as you call us with your credit card number.

Our fresh fruit baskets are only sold by cash or credit card.

Activities and Cases

7.4 Follow-Up Apology: Million Dollar Upgrade Falls Short. As an Internet service provider, your company, WeConnect, is growing rapidly. To keep up with increased customer demand, you decided to install a million-dollar network upgrade. From USRobotics you bought what you thought were the finest modems on the market. They passed your rigorous lab tests with flying colors, but apparently some bugs in the operating system slipped through the cracks. The modems clearly were not "field ready" when they were installed. Now you are hearing from customers complaining of slower speeds in connecting to the Internet and even disconnections.

Derek Jones, manager, Information Systems, Big Dog Catalog Company, your most profitable local customer, is very upset. Jones says, "You promised a million-dollar upgrade, and now service is worse than ever!" You replied, "Look, we're very sorry. These bugs didn't show up in our lab tests. But USRobotics is providing excellent support for their hardware and we've cleared up most of the initial problems. Although we've fixed all the major technical problems, some other little things remain, and we're fully committed to a complete resolution." You ask for Big Dog's patience. Things will get better, you promise!

Discuss the following options in resolving this business problem.

1. Following a telephone call to this unhappy customer, what should you do next?
   a. Cool it. A telephone call is enough. You did what you could to explain the problem, and words will not solve the problem anyway.
   b. Wait to see whether this customer calls again. After all, the next move is up to him. Respond only after repeated complaints.
   c. Send a short e-mail message repeating your apology and explanation.
   d. Immediately send a letter that apologizes, explains, and shows how seriously you have taken the problem and the customer's complaint.
2. You decide to write a follow-up letter. To open this letter, you should begin with a(n)
   a. Neutral statement such as, *This letter is in response to your telephone complaint.*
   b. Defensive statement that protects you from legal liability (*As I mentioned on the telephone, you are the only customer who has complained about connection problems*).
   c. Apologetic statement that shows you understand and take responsibility for the problem.
   d. Off-the-subject remark such as *We're happy to hear that your company is increasing its catalog sales this quarter.*
3. In the body of the follow-up letter, you should
   a. Explain why the problem occurred.
   b. Describe what you are doing to resolve the problem.
   c. Promise that you will do everything possible to prevent the problem from happening again.
   d. All of the above.

4. In the closing of this letter, you should
   a. Avoid apologizing because it may increase your legal liabilities.
   b. Show appreciation for the customer's patience and patronage.
   c. Explain that company policy prohibits you from revealing the exact nature of the software and hardware problems.
   d. Provide an action deadline.

Your Task. After circling your choices and discussing them, write a follow-up letter to Mr. Derek Jones, Manager, Information Systems, Big Dog Catalog Company, 1308 East Tenth Street, Bloomington, IN 47405. You have set up a special Web site where customers can report any connection problems: **<http://home.weconnect.net/disconnect.html>**. However, you also want to assure customers that they can contact you personally with questions or comments. You promise that all their issues will be resolved as soon as possible. You might wish to write this letter so that you can use it to respond to other inquiries.

7.5 Request Refusal: Lease Payments Cannot Be Applied to Purchase. Analyze the following letter. List its weaknesses, and then revise it.

Dear Ms. Metzinger:

Unfortunately, we cannot permit you to apply the lease payments you've been making for the past ten months toward the purchase of your Sako 600 copier.

Company policy does not allow such conversion. Have you ever wondered why we can offer such low leasing and purchase prices? Converting lease payments to purchases would mean overall higher prices for our customers. Obviously, we couldn't stay in business long if we agreed to proposals such as yours.

You've had the Sako 600 copier for ten months now, Ms. Metzinger, and you say that you like its versatility and reliability. Perhaps we could interest you in another Sako model, such as the Sako 400 series. It may be closer to your price range. Do give us a call.

Sincerely,

1. List at least five faults in this letter.

2. Outline a plan for writing a refusal to a request.

Your Task. Revise this refusal. Send your letter to Ms. Kathy Metzinger, Copiers Plus, 320 Royal Poinciana Drive, Palm Bay, FL 32909. You might mention that many customers are pleased with the Sako copiers, including the Sako 400 series that has nearly as many features as the Sako 600 series. You'd like to demonstrate the Sako 400. Supply any additional information.

7.6 Bad News to Customers: J. Crew Goofs on Cashmere Turtleneck. Who wouldn't want a cashmere zip turtleneck sweater for $18? At the J. Crew Web site **<www.jcrew.com>**, many delighted shoppers scrambled to order the bargain cashmere. Unfortunately, the price should have been $218! Before J. Crew officials could correct the mistake, several hundred e-shoppers had bagged the bargain sweater for their digital shopping carts.

When the mistake was discovered, J. Crew immediately sent an e-mail message to the soon-to-be disappointed shoppers. The subject line shouted "Big Mistake!" Emily Woods, chairwoman of J. Crew, began her message with this statement: "I wish we could sell such an amazing sweater for only $18. Our price mistake on your new cashmere zip turtleneck probably went right by you, but rather than charge you such a large difference, I'm writing to alert you that this item has been removed from your recent order."

As an assistant in the communication department at J. Crew, you saw the e-mail message that was sent to customers and you tactfully suggested that the bad news might have been broken differently. Your boss says, "Okay, hot stuff. Give it your best shot."

Your Task. Although you have only a portion of the message, analyze the customer bad-news message sent by J. Crew. Using the principles suggested in this chapter, write an improved e-mail message. In the end, J. Crew decided to allow customers who ordered the sweater at $18 to reorder it for $118.80 to $130.80, depending on the size. Customers were given a special Web site to reorder (make up an address). Remember that J. Crew customers are youthful and hip. Keep your message upbeat.[8]

7.7 Request Refusal: Adieu to Cadillacs in Paris. "As I'm sure you've noticed, Cadillac has been on a bit of a roll lately with the worldwide launch of the all-new Seville and the much-awaited launch of the Escalade," began the GM invitation letter. This letter was sent to many of the top automotive journalists in the country inviting them to join GM's executives on a five-day all-expenses-paid press trip to Paris. Such junkets were not unusual. Big Three automakers routinely sponsored reporters' trips to ensure favorable local coverage from the big auto shows in Paris, Frankfurt, Geneva, and Tokyo.

GM particularly wanted reporters at the Paris show. This is the show where it hoped to position Cadillac as a global luxury car manufacturer. The invitation letter, mailed in July, promised a "sneak peak at Cadillac's first major concept vehicle in nearly 10 years." But GM had only 20 spots available for the trip, and journalists had to request one of the spots. Suddenly, in late July, GM found itself in the midst of an expensive strike. "All at once, what had seemed like a good idea started to look fiscally irresponsible," said J. Christopher Preuss, Cadillac spokesman. Although exact figures were not available, some estimates held that the Paris trip could easily cost $12,000 per reporter. That's a large bill for a company facing a prolonged, damaging strike.

Your Task. As part of a group of interns working in the communications division of GM, you and your team have been asked to draft a letter to the journalists who signed up for the trip. Announce that GM must back out. About the best thing they can expect now is an invitation to the gala unveiling and champagne reception GM will sponsor in January at the Detroit auto show. At that time GM will brief reporters about Cadillac's "new vision" and unveil the eye-popping Escalade. Mr. Preuss is embarrassed about canceling the Paris trip, but he feels GM must do what is financially prudent. Prepare a draft of the letter for the signature of J. Christopher Preuss. Address the first letter to Rodney M. Puckett, 18543 Haggerty Road, Livonia, MI 48152.[9]

7.8 Request Refusal: The End of Free Credit Reports. You are part of the customer service team at Experian, the largest supplier of consumer and business credit information in the world. Experian took over TRW Information Systems & Services back in 1996. Experian currently employs over 11,000 people in the United States, United Kingdom, Continental Europe, Africa, and Asia Pacific. As a service to consumers, Experian at one time provided complimentary credit reports. However, it now offers them only in certain states and to certain groups of people.

Experian's Web site explains its new policy in its FAQs (Frequently Asked Questions). Your boss says to you, "I guess not everyone is able to learn about our new policy by going to our Web site because we still receive bundles of requests for free reports. I'm unhappy with a letter we've been using to respond to these requests. I want you to compose a draft of a new form letter that we can send to people who inquire. You should look at our Web site to see who gets free reports and in what states."

Because you are fairly new to Experian, you ask your boss what prompted the change in policy. She sighs and says, "It was a good idea, but it got out of hand. So-called 'credit repair' companies would refer their clients to us for free credit reports, and then they advised their clients to dispute every item on the report. The Federal Trade Commission actually called these companies *fraudulent.* We had to change our policy. But you can read more about it at our Web site."

Your Task. You resolve to study the Experian Web site <**http://www.experian.com/**> closely. Your task is to write a letter refusing the requests of people who want free credit reports. But you must also explain the reasons for the change in policy, as well as its exceptions. Decide whether you should tell consumers how to order a copy and how to pay for it. Although your letter will be used repeatedly for such requests, address your draft to Mrs. Sherry Bennett, 250 Bruce Street, Morrilton, AR 72110. Sign it with your boss's name, Elizabeth Buerkle.

7.9 Bad News for Customers: Changing Our Credit Policy. Analyze the following ineffective letter.

Dear Charge Customers:

This letter is being sent to you to announce the termination of in-house charge accounts at Golden West Print and Frame Shop. We are truly sorry that we can no longer offer this service.

Because some customers abused the privilege, we must eliminate local charge accounts. We regret that we must take this action, but we found that carrying our own credit had become quite costly. To continue the service would have meant raising our prices. As a small but growing business, we decided it was more logical to drop the in-house charges. As a result, we are forced to begin accepting bank credit cards, including VISA and MasterCard.

Please accept our apologies in trimming our services somewhat. We hope to see you soon when we can show you our new collection of museum-quality gilded wood frames.

Sincerely,

Your Task. In teams or individually, discuss the weaknesses in this letter. Revise the letter so that it follows the indirect pattern of development.

7.10 Claim Refusal: Wilted Landscaping. As Kissandra Powell, owner of Town & Country Landscaping, you must refuse the following request. Mr. and Mrs. Paul Alexander have asked that you replace the landscaping in the home they recently purchased in Kettering. You had landscaped that home nearly a year ago for the former owner, Mrs. Hunter, installing a sod lawn and many shrubs, trees, and flowers. It looked beautiful when you finished, but six months later, Mrs. Hunter sold the property and moved to Dayton. Four months elapsed before the new owners moved in. After four months of neglect and a hot, dry summer, the newly installed landscaping suffered.

You guarantee all your work and normally would replace any plants that do not survive. Under these circumstances, however, you do not feel justified in making any refund because your guarantee necessarily presumes proper maintenance on the part of the property owner. Moreover, your guarantee is made only to the individual who contracted with you—not to subsequent owners. You would like to retain the goodwill of the new owners, since this is an affluent neighborhood and you hope to attract additional work here. On the other hand, you can't afford to replace the materials invested in this job. You believe that the lawn could probably be rejuvenated with deep watering and fertilizer.

Your Task. Write to Mr. and Mrs. Paul Alexander, 3318 Clearview Drive, Kettering, OH 45429 refusing their claim. You would be happy to inspect the property and offer suggestions to the Alexanders. In reality, though, you wonder whether the Alexanders might not have a claim against the former owner or the escrow agency for failing to maintain the property. Clearly, however, the claim is not against you.

7.11 Refusing a Claim: Evicting a Noisy Neighbor. As Arman Aryai, you must deny the request of Robert Brockway, one of the tenants in your three-story office building. Mr. Brockway, a CPA, demands that you immediately evict a neighboring tenant who plays loud music throughout the day, interfering with Mr. Brockway's conversations with clients and with his concentration. The noisy tenant, Ryan McInnis, seems to operate an entertainment booking agency and spends long hours in his office.

Critical Thinking

You know you can't evict Mr. McInnis immediately because of his lease. Moreover, you hesitate to do anything drastic because paying tenants are hard to find. You called your attorney, and he said that the first thing you should do is talk to the noisy tenant or write him a letter asking him to tone it down. If this doesn't work within 30 days, you could begin the eviction process.

Your Task. Decide on a course of action. Because Mr. Brockway doesn't seem to answer his telephone, you must write him a letter. You need a permanent record of this decision anyway. Write to Robert Brockway, CPA, Suite 203, Pico Building, 1405 Wilshire Boulevard, Santa Monica, CA 90405. Deny his request, but tell him how you plan to resolve the problem.

7.12 Customer Bad News: Kodak Refuses Customer's Request to Repeat World Trip. Kodak Customer Service Manager Charlie Smith can't believe what he reads in a letter from Brian P. Coyle. This 27-year-old Orlando resident actually wants Kodak to foot the bill for a repeat round-the-world trip because his Advantix camera malfunctioned and he lost 12 rolls of film!

As soon as Smith saw the letter and the returned camera, he knew what was wrong. Of the 2 million Advantix cameras made last year, 20,000 malfunctioned. A supplier squirted too much oil in the shutter mechanism, and the whole lot was recalled. In fact, Kodak spent almost $1 million to remove these cameras from store shelves. Kodak also contacted all customers who could be reached. In addition to the giant recall, the company quickly redesigned the cameras so that they would work even if they had excess oil. But somehow Coyle was not notified of the recall. When Smith checked the warranty files, he learned that this customer had not returned his warranty. Had the customer done so, he would have been notified in August, well before his trip.

Although Customer Service Manager Smith is sorry for the mishap, he thinks that a request for $20,000 to replace "lost memories" is preposterous. Kodak has never assumed any responsibility beyond replacing a camera or film. This customer, however, seems to have suffered more than a routine loss of snapshots. Therefore, Smith decides to sweeten the deal by offering to throw in a digital camera valued at $225, more than double the cost of the Advantix. One of the advantages of a digital camera is that it contains an LCD panel that enables the photographer to view stored images immediately. No chance of losing memories with this digital camera!

Your Task. As the assistant to Customer Service Manager Smith, you must write a letter that refuses the demand for $20,000 but retains the customer's goodwill. Tell this customer what you will do, and be sure to explain how Kodak reacted immediately when it discovered the Advantix defect. Write a sensitive refusal to Brian P. Coyle, 5942 Bear Crossing Drive, Orlando, FL 32746.[10]

7.13 Employee Bad News: Strikeout for Expanded Office Teams. Assume you are Hank James, vice president of Human Resources at Tissue Mills Paper Co., 508 W. Inverary Road, Kingston, Ontario K2G 1V8. Recently several of your employees requested that their spouses or friends be allowed to participate in Tissue Mills' intramural sports teams. Although the teams play only once a week during the season, these employees claim that they can't afford more time away from friends and family. Over 100 employees currently participate in the eight coed volleyball, softball, and tennis teams, which are open to company employees only. The teams were designed to improve employee friendships and to give employees a regular occasion to have fun together.

If nonemployees were to participate, you're afraid that employee interaction would be limited. And while some team members might have fun if spouses or friends were included, you're not so sure all employees would enjoy it. You're not interested in turning intramural sports into "date night." Furthermore, the company would have to create additional teams if many nonemployees joined, and you don't want the administrative or equipment costs of more teams. Adding teams also would require changes to team rosters and game schedules, which could be a problem for some employees. You do understand the need for social time with friends and families, but guests are welcome as spectators at all intramural games. Besides, the company already sponsors a family holiday party and an annual company picnic.

Your Task. Write an e-mail or hard-copy memo to the staff denying the request of several employees to include nonemployees on Tissue Mills' intramural sports teams.

7.14 Employee Bad News: Refusing Christmas. In the past your office has always sponsored a Christmas party at a nice restaurant. As your company has undergone considerable downsizing and budget cuts during the past year, you know that no money is available for holiday entertaining. Moreover, the staff has become more diverse, and you decide that it might be better to celebrate a "holiday" party instead of a Christmas event.

Your Task. As executive vice president, send an e-mail or hard-copy memo to Dina Gillian, office manager. Dina asked permission to make restaurant reservations for this year's Christmas party. Refuse Dina, but offer some alternatives. How about a potluck dinner?

Web

Team

Critical Thinking

7.15 Customer Bad News: Telephone Company Makes Giant Boo-Boo. GTE, one of the largest regional telephone companies, recently made a horrendous blunder. Inadvertently, it released thousands of unlisted residential telephone numbers and addresses in directories leased to telemarketers. "This is a boo-boo of giant proportions," said consumer advocate Beth Givens.[11]

Your Task. Read the complete case at <http://www.westwords.com/guffey/eager.html>. Answer the four critical thinking questions. Then, as an assistant to the regional GTE president, work with a team to hammer out the first draft of a letter to be sent to GTE customers. By the way, your boss decided to assign 500 employees the task of personally telephoning each affected customer to announce the error and offer remedies. You and your team are to draft a letter to the other customers—those whose unlisted numbers were not released. GTE knows that they will hear rumors and be worried about their privacy. He wants your letter to assure them that GTE cares and that the mistake will not happen again.

Grammar/Mechanics Checkup—7

Commas 2

Review the Grammar/Mechanics Handbook Sections 2.05–2.09. Then study each of the following statements and insert necessary commas. In the space provided write the number of commas that you add; write *0* if no commas are needed. Also record the number of the G/M principle(s) illustrated. When you finish, compare your responses with those provided at the end of the book. If your answers differ, study carefully the principles shown in parentheses.

Example: When businesses encounter financial problems, they often reduce their administrative staffs.

1   2.06a

1. As stated in the warranty this printer is guaranteed for one year.
2. Today's profits come from products currently on the market and tomorrow's profits come from products currently on the drawing boards.

3. Companies introduce new products in one part of the country and then watch how the product sells in that area. _____

4. One large automobile manufacturer which must remain nameless recognizes that buyer perception is behind the success of any new product. _____

5. The imaginative promising agency opened its offices April 22 in Cambridge. _____

6. The sales associate who earns the highest number of recognition points this year will be honored with a bonus vacation trip. _____

7. Darren Wilson our sales manager in the Panama City area will present the new sales campaign at the June meeting. _____

8. Our new product has many attributes that should make it appealing to buyers but it also has one significant drawback. _____

9. Although they have different technical characteristics and vary considerably in price and quality two or more of a firm's products may be perceived by shoppers as almost the same. _____

10. To motivate prospective buyers we are offering a cash rebate of $2. _____

Review of Commas 1 and 2

11. When you receive the application please fill it out and return it before Monday January 3. _____

12. On the other hand we are very interested in hiring hard-working conscientious individuals. _____

13. In March we expect to open a new branch in Concord which is an area of considerable growth. _____

14. As we discussed on the telephone the ceremony is scheduled for Thursday June 9 at 3 p.m. _____

15. Dr. Adams teaches the morning classes and Mrs. Wildey is responsible for evening sections. _____

Advanced Grammar/Mechanics Review—7

The following sentences contain errors in grammar, punctuation, capitalization, number style, usage, and spelling. Below each sentence write a corrected version.

1. The first state by state report describing the nations tobacco use and tobacco control laws were recently released.

2. The report which was compiled by the centers for disease control and prevention showed adult smoking rates that varied from 15% of the population in utah, to thirty percent in neighboring nevada.

3. As expected nevadas pattern of deaths related to smoking was nearly twice that of utahs.

4. Hailed by anti-tobacco groups as proof of the need for more stricter National regulations the report was dismissed by the tobacco industry as "old news".

5. The food and drug administration said that the comparisons might stimulate changes in some states, but that the report was not part of any particular policy drive.

6. "This is a snapshot not an evaluation of what reduces tobacco use" said Michael P. Eriksen director of the office on smoking and health which is a federal agency with headquarters in atlanta.

7. Most likely to attract attention, are data related to smoking among High School students.

8. 8 of the 10 states with the lowest cigarette taxs has a higher than average number of smokers.

9. The state of washington which has the highest taxes at $.81 a pack ranks in the middle on percentage of smokers.

10. 1/3 of the states now has laws banning citys and towns, from imposing tobacco restrictions.

11. Walker Merryman a spokesman for the tobacco institute said "This report is more rehash than research, it is not terribly useful for understanding why kids smoke".

12. Anti-tobacco supporters are urging congress to support the FDAs proposal to severely restrict: advertising marketing and distribution of tobacco products.

13. The state of west virginia, however faces the biggest problem, nearly thirty-nine percent of it's students who were 16 to 18 years of age, reported smoking within the month in which they were surveyed.

14. Only 17% of the children of high school age in Washington D.C. however had smoked.

15. Willie Davis Nevadas tobacco education and information officer explained that its hard to restrict smoking when the states economy is linked so close to gaming which is linked to tobacco.

Grammar/Mechanics Challenge—7

Document for Revision

The following letter has faults in grammar, punctuation, spelling, number form, and negative words. Use standard proofreading marks (see Appendix B) to correct the errors. When you finish, your instructor can show you the revised version of this letter.

May 3, 200X

Mr. Ragu Raghavan

Medical Supplies, Inc.

P.O. Box 489

Missouri City, TX 77489

Dear Mr. Raghavan:

You will be recieving shortly the rubbermaid service and utility carts you ordered along with 5 recycling stack bins. Unfortunately, the heavy duty can crusher is not available but it will be sent from the factory in Albany New York and should reach you by May 31st.

You may place any future orders, by using our toll free telephone number (1-800-577-9241), or our toll free fax number (1-800-577-2657). If you need help with any items ask for one of the following sales representives, Bill Small, Susan Freed, or Rick Woo. When the items you order are in our currant catalog it will be shipped the same day you place you're order. For products to be custom imprinted please provide a typed or printed copy with your order.

Remember we are the only catalog sales company that guarantees your full satisfaction. If you are not pleased we'll arrange for a prompt refund, credit or replacement. We'll also refund or credit all shipping costs associated with the returned items. We want your business!

Sincerely,

Presenting Bad News in Other Cultures

To minimize disappointment, Americans generally prefer to present negative messages indirectly. Other cultures may treat bad news differently.

- In Germany business communicators occasionally use buffers but tend to present bad news directly.

- British writers also tend to be straightforward with bad news, seeing no reason to soften its announcement.

- In Latin countries the question is not how to organize negative messages but whether to present them at all. It's considered disrespectful and impolite to report bad news to superiors. Thus, reluctant employees may fail to report accurately any negative messages to their bosses.

- In Thailand the negativism represented by a refusal is completely alien; the word *no* does not exist. In many cultures negative news is offered with such subtleness or in such a positive light that it may be overlooked or misunderstood by literal-minded Americans.

- In many Asian and some Latin cultures, one must look beyond an individual's actual words to understand what's really being communicated. One must consider the communication style, the culture, and especially the context.

  "I agree" might mean "I agree with 15 percent of what you say."
  "We might be able to" could mean "Not a chance."
  "We will consider" could mean "WE will, but the real decision maker will not."
  "That is a little too much" might equate to "That is outrageous."[12]

Career Application

Interview fellow students or work colleagues who are from other cultures. Collect information regarding the following.

- How is negative news handled in their cultures?

- How would typical business communicators refuse a request for a business favor (such as a contribution to a charity)?

- How would typical business communicators refuse a customer's claim?

- How would an individual be turned down for a job?

Your Task

Report the findings of your interviews in class discussion or in a memo report. In addition, collect samples of foreign business letters. You might ask foreign students, your campus admissions office, or local export/import companies if they would be willing to share business letters from other countries. Compare letter styles, formats, tone, and writing strategies. How do these elements differ from those in typical North American business letters?

8

Letters and Memos That Persuade

Facts and figures alone will never convince anyone. If you can't connect your facts to the dreams of the client, then all the statistics and charts in the world won't make any impression.[1]

RENÉ NOURSE, *vice president, Investments, Prudential Securities Incorporated*

LEARNING OBJECTIVES

1. Use the indirect strategy to persuade.
2. Write convincing claim request letters.
3. Request favors persuasively.
4. Present new ideas in persuasive memos.
5. Analyze techniques used in sales letters.
6. Compose carefully planned sales letters.

The ability to persuade is a key factor in the success you achieve in your business messages, in your career, and in your interpersonal relations. Persuasive individuals, like René Nourse at Prudential Securities Incorporated, are those who present convincing arguments that influence or win over others.

The ability to persuade is a primary factor in personal and business success.

René Nourse persuades people to invest in stocks and bonds. She knows that facts and figures alone are not convincing; they must be connected to people's desires and needs. Applying this persuasive technique and many others can help you become a persuasive communicator. Because their ideas generally prevail, persuasive individuals become decision makers—managers, executives, and entrepreneurs. This chapter will examine techniques for presenting ideas persuasively.

Persuasive Requests

Persuasion is necessary when resistance is anticipated or when ideas require preparation before they can be presented effectively. For example, let's say you bought a new car and the transmission repeatedly required servicing. When you finally got tired of taking it in for repair, you decide to write to the car manufacturer's district office asking that the company install a new transmission in your car. You know that your request will be resisted. You must convince the manufacturer that replacement, not repair, is needed. Routine claim letters, such as those you wrote in Chapter 6, are straightforward and direct. Persuasive requests, on the other hand, are generally more effective when they are indirect. Reasons and explanations should precede the main idea. To overcome possible resistance, the writer lays a logical foundation before the request is delivered. A writing plan for a persuasive request requires deliberate development.

Use persuasion when you must change attitudes or produce action.

WRITING PLAN FOR A PERSUASIVE REQUEST

- **Opening:** Obtain the reader's attention and interest.
- **Body:** Explain logically and concisely the purpose of the request and prove its merit.
- **Closing:** Ask for a particular action and show courtesy and respect.

Persuasive Claims

The organization of an effective persuasive claim centers on the closing and the persuasion. First, decide what action you want taken to satisfy the claim. Then, decide how you can prove the worth of your claim. Plan carefully the line of reasoning you will follow in convincing the reader to take the action you request. If the claim is addressed to a business, the most effective appeals are generally to the organization's pride in its products and its services. Refer to its reputation for integrity and your confidence in it. Show why your claim is valid and why the company will be doing the right thing in granting it. Most organizations are sincere in their efforts to produce quality products that gain consumer respect.

The most successful appeals are to a company's pride in its products and services.

Although claim letters are often complaint letters, try not to be angry. Hostility and emotional threats toward an organization do little to achieve the goal of a claim letter. Claims are usually referred to a customer service department. The claims adjuster answering the claim probably had nothing to do with the design, production, delivery, or servicing of the product. An abusive letter may serve only to offend the claims adjuster, thus making it hard for the claims adjuster to evaluate the claim rationally.

The most effective claim quickly captures the reader's attention in the opening and sets up the persuasion that follows. In the body of the claim, convincing reasons should explain and justify the claim. Try to argue without overusing negative words, without fixing blame for the problem, and without becoming emotional. That's not easy to do. You'll be most successful if you arrange objective reasons in an orderly manner with appropriate transitions to guide the reader through the persuasion.

Claim letters should avoid negative and emotional words and should not attempt to fix blame.

Following the persuasion, spell out clearly the desired action in the closing. Remember, the best claims show respect and courtesy.

Observe how the claim letter shown in Figure 8.1 illustrates the preceding suggestions. When Champion Automotives bought several new enhanced telephones, it discovered that they would not work when the fluorescent lights were on. The company's attempt to return the telephones had been refused by the retailer. Notice that the opening statement captures attention with a compliment about the product. The second paragraph describes the problem without rancor or harsh words. The letter goes on to suggest the responsibility of the manufacturer while stressing the disappointment of the writer. The final paragraph tells exactly what action should be taken.

FIGURE 8.1 Claim Request (Complaint Letter)

CHAMPION AUTOMOTIVES
309 Porterville Plaza, Lansing, Michigan 48914 (517) 690-3500

November 21, 200X

Customer Service
Raytronic Electronics
594 Stanton Street
Mobile, AL 36617

Uses simplified letter style when name of receiver is unknown

SUBJECT: CODE-A-PHONE MODEL 100S

Begins with compliment

Your Code-A-Phone Model 100S answering unit came well recommended. We liked our neighbor's unit so well that we purchased three for different departments in our business.

Describes problem calmly

After the three units were unpacked and installed, we discovered a problem. Apparently our office fluorescent lighting interferes with the electronics in these units. When the lights are on, heavy static interrupts every telephone call. When the lights are off, the static disappears.

We can't replace the fluorescent lights; thus we tried to return the Code-A-Phones to the place of purchase (Office Mart, 2560 Haslett Avenue, Lansing, MI 48901). A salesperson inspected the units and said they could not be returned since they were not defective and they had been used.

Suggests responsibility

Stresses disappointment

Because the descriptive literature and instructions for the Code-A-Phones say nothing about avoiding use in rooms with fluorescent lighting, we expected no trouble. We were quite disappointed that this well-engineered unit—with its time/date stamp, room monitor, and auto-dial features—failed to perform as we hoped it would.

Tells what action to take

Appeals to company's desire to preserve good reputation

If you have a model with similar features that would work in our offices, give me a call. Otherwise, please authorize the return of these units and refund the purchase price of $519.45 (see enclosed invoice). We're confident that a manufacturer with your reputation for excellent products and service will want to resolve this matter quickly.

Janet K. Booth

JANET K. BOOTH, PRESIDENT

JKB:ett
Enclosure

Tips for Making Claims

- Begin with a compliment, point of agreement, statement of the problem, or brief review of action you have taken to resolve the problem.
- Provide identifying data.
- Prove that your claim is valid; explain why the receiver is responsible.
- Enclose document copies supporting your claim.
- Appeal to the receiver's fairness, ethical and legal responsibilities, and desire for customer satisfaction.
- Describe your feelings and your disappointment.
- Avoid sounding angry, emotional, or irrational.
- Close by telling exactly what you want done.

Favor Requests

Asking for a favor implies that you want someone to do something for nothing—or for very little. Common examples are requests for the donation of time, money, energy, a name, resources, talent, skills, or expertise. On occasion, everyone needs to ask a favor. Small favors, such as asking a coworker to lock up the office for you on Friday, can be straightforward and direct. Little resistance is expected. Larger favors, though, require careful planning and an indirect strategy. A busy executive is asked to serve on a committee to help disadvantaged children. A florist is asked to donate table arrangements for a charity fund-raiser. A well-known author is asked to speak before a local library group. In each instance persuasion is necessary to overcome natural resistance.

Requests for large favors generally require persuasive strategies.

The letters shown in Figure 8.2 illustrate two versions of a favor request. In a nutshell, an organization without funds hopes to entice a well-known authority to speak before its regional conference. Such a request surely requires indirectness and persuasion, but the ineffective version begins with a direct appeal. Even worse, the reader is given an opportunity to refuse the request before the writer has a chance to present reasons for accepting. Moreover, this letter fails to convince the reader that she has anything to gain by speaking to this group. Finally, the closing suggests no specific action to help her accept, should she be so inclined.

A favor request is doomed to failure if the writer does not consider its effect on the reader. In the more effective version, notice how the writer applies the indirect strategy. The opening catches the reader's interest and makes her want to read more regarding the reaction to her article. By showing how Dr. Ward's interests are related to the organization's, the writer lays a groundwork of persuasion before presenting the request. The request is then followed by reasoning that shows Dr. Ward how she will benefit from accepting this invitation. This successful letter concludes with an action closing.

Persuasive Memos

Within an organization the indirect strategy is useful when persuasion is needed in presenting new ideas to management or to colleagues. It's also useful in requesting action from employees and in securing compliance with altered procedures. Whenever resistance is anticipated, a sound foundation of reasoning should precede the main idea. This foundation prevents the idea from being rejected prematurely.

Presenting reasons first avoids premature rejection of a new idea.

You should expect new ideas to create resistance. It doesn't matter whether the ideas are moving downward as orders from management, moving upward as suggestions to management, or moving laterally among coworkers. Resistance to change is natural. When asked to perform differently or to try something new, some individuals resist because they are lazy. Others resist because they fear failure. Still others resist because they feel threatened—the proposed changes may encroach on their status or threaten their security. Some people resist new ideas because they are jealous of the person making the proposal.

Whatever the motivation, resistance to new ideas and altered procedures should be expected. You can prepare for this resistance by anticipating objections, offering counterarguments, and emphasizing benefits. Don't assume that the advantages of a new plan are obvious and therefore may go unmentioned. Use concrete examples and familiar illustrations in presenting arguments.

Offering counterarguments helps overcome resistance.

In the memo shown in Figure 8.3, John Pease, supervisor, argues for the purchase of a new scanner and software. He expects the director to resist this request because the budget is already overextended. John's memo follows the writing plan for a persuasive request. It begins by describing a costly problem in which John knows the reader is interested. To convince the director of the need for these

FIGURE 8.2 Persuasive Favor Request

Ineffective

Provides easy excuse for refusal

Sounds writer-centered instead of reader-centered

Closes negatively and fails to tell how to respond

Dear Dr. Ward:

Although your research, teaching, and consulting must keep you extremely busy, we hope that your schedule will allow you to be the featured speaker at the American Personnel Managers Association's regional conference in Boston March 23.

We are particularly interested in the article that appeared in the *Harvard Business Review*. A number of our members indicated that your topic, "Cost/Benefit Analysis for Human Resources," is something we should learn more about.

We have no funds to pay you, but we would like to invite you and your spouse to be our guests at the banquet following the day's sessions. We hope that you will be able to speak before our group.

Sincerely,

Effective

American Personnel Managers Association
P.O. Box 5893
Boston, Massachusetts 02148
(617) 543-8922

January 4, 200X

Professor Edna C. Ward
Winthrop University
Rock Hill, SC 29733

Dear Dr. Ward:

Cost/benefit analysis applied to human resources is a unique concept. Your recent article on that topic in the *Harvard Business Review* ignited a lively discussion at the last meeting of the Boston chapter of the American Personnel Managers Association.

Many of the managers in our group are experiencing the changes you describe. Functions in the personnel area are now being expanded to include a wide range of salary, welfare, benefit, and training programs. These new programs can be very expensive. Our members are fascinated by your cost/benefit analysis that sets up a formal comparison of the costs to design, develop, and implement a program idea against the costs the idea saves or avoids.

The members of our association have asked me to invite you to be the featured speaker March 23 when we hold our annual East Coast regional conference in Boston. About 150 personnel management specialists will attend the all-day conference at the Park Plaza Hotel. We would like you to speak at 2 p.m. on the topic of "Applying Cost/Benefit Analysis in Human Resources Today."

Although an honorarium is not provided, we can offer you an opportunity to help human resources managers apply your theories in solving some of their most perplexing problems. You will also meet managers who might be able to supply you with data for future research into personnel functions. In addition, the conference includes two other sessions and a banquet, to which you and a guest are invited.

Please call me at (617) 543-8922 to allow me to add your name to the program as the featured speaker before the American Personnel Managers Association March 23.

Respectfully yours,

Ellen Benowitz

Ellen Benowitz
Executive Secretary

Grabs attention of reader by appealing to her interests

Persuades reader that her expertise is valued

Softens negative aspects of request with reader benefits

Ends confidently with specific action to be taken

FIGURE 8.3 Persuasive Memo

Amdahl & Findley, Inc.
Interoffice Memorandum

DATE: March 7, 200X

TO: Beverly M. Wingard, Director, Operations

FROM: John Pease, Supervisor, Central Services

SUBJECT: REDUCING OVERTIME AND IMPROVING TURNAROUND TIME

We have a problem in Central Services. Last month we paid nearly $5,400 in overtime to our document specialists who were forced to work 50- and 60-hour weeks to keep up with the heavy demand for printed documents. Despite this overtime the average turnaround time for documents submitted to Central Services is now five working days, which is too long.

The major cause of our problem is a backlog of engineering reports. These old reports are available only in print form, and they must now be digitized to be accessible and searchable. This means that our document specialists have been rekeying hundreds of pages of reports.

We could solve this problem with the addition of a scanning system. I estimate that we could eliminate at least 40 percent of our overtime and also reduce turnaround time on documents by two days if our operators had a scanning system to convert our engineering reports to an electronic format. To accomplish this, we need a high-end scanner linked to a computer using a database known as Application Extender.

Two alternatives are available in relation to scanning services. We could purchase the equipment ourselves, or we could outsource the job to a service bureau to make our digital conversions. Service bureaus, however, are expensive and slow. Moreover, we face a security problem whenever our reports leave our premises. Because of the sensitive nature of most of our work, keeping the reports on site makes the most sense.

Purchasing a high-end scanner plus the necessary software promises three significant benefits:

1. Savings of at least $2,500 in overtime each month by reducing the rekeying of printed documents.

2. Reduction of turnaround time from five days to a maximum of three days.

3. Improved morale among our document specialists.

Emphasizes reader benefits

Captures attention with a problem that can be solved

Begins each paragraph with a topic sentence

Explains background before making proposal

Anticipates objections and answers them

Summarizes benefits in a list

Delays mention of price until after convincing arguments are presented

Ends with explicit request and provides end dating

For these reasons, I recommend that we purchase a Fujitso Turbo Scanner, Model SL2000, plus Digital's Application Extender software. The purchase price of these two items, approximately $5,000, will be recovered within two months as a result of reduced overtime payments.

Enclosed are details of the recommended scanner and conversion software. Please give me authorization to submit a purchase order for these two items by April 1 so that Central Services can improve turnaround time before we are asked to begin work on the fiscal year-end reports in July.

Enclosure

purchases, John must first explain the background of his request. Because John knows that the director values brevity, he tries to focus on the main points. To further improve readability, John begins every paragraph with a topic sentence.

After reviewing background information and the cause of the problem, John brings up the request for a new scanning system. He discusses it in terms of benefits to the reader and the company (eliminating 40 percent of overtime and reducing turnaround time). John also anticipates objections (outsourcing as an alternative) but counters this possible objection by pointing out that outsourcing is expensive, slow, and insecure. In the closing John asks for a specific action and provides support documentation to speed his request. He also includes end dating, which prompts the director to act by a certain date.

Sales Letters

Direct mail marketing accounts for 44 percent of all mail delivered.

Despite all the hype about e-business and the Internet, sales letters remain the "simplest and most effective sales tool to [reach] customers and prospects."[2] Sales letters are usually part of direct mail marketing efforts that many people consider "junk mail." An incredible 44 percent of all mail delivered is made up of direct mail marketing.[3] This includes all sales letters, packets, brochures, and catalogs sent directly to consumers.

The professionals who specialize in direct mail marketing have made a science of analyzing a market, developing an appropriate mailing list, studying the product, preparing a comprehensive presentation that appeals to the needs of the target audience, and motivating the reader to act. This carefully orchestrated presentation typically concludes with a sales letter accompanied by a brochure, a sales list, illustrations of the product, testimonials, and so forth.

Sales letters are written by professionals in large firms, but in small firms people must write their own.

We are most concerned here with the sales letter: its strategy, organization, and appeals. You'll want to learn the secrets of these messages for many reasons. Although the sales letters of big organizations are usually written by professionals, many smaller companies cannot afford such specialized services. Entrepreneurs and employees of smaller businesses may be called on to write their own sales messages. For example, one recent graduate started a graphics/secretarial service and immediately had to write a convincing letter offering her services. Another graduate went to work for a small company that installs security systems. Because of his recent degree (other employees were unsure of their skills), he was asked to draft a sales letter outlining specific benefits for residential customers.

Recognizing and applying the techniques of sales writing can be helpful even if you never write an actual sales letter.

From a broader perspective nearly every letter we write is a form of sales. We sell our ideas, ourselves, and our organizations. Learning the techniques of sales writing will help you be more effective in any communication that requires persuasion and promotion. Moreover, recognizing the techniques of selling will enable you to respond to such techniques more rationally. You will be a better-educated consumer of ideas, products, and services if you understand how sales appeals are made.

The following writing plan for a sales letter attempts to overcome anticipated reader resistance by creating a desire for the product and by motivating the reader to act.

WRITING PLAN FOR A SALES LETTER

- **Opening:** Capture the attention of the reader.
- **Body:** Emphasize a central selling point, appeal to the needs of the reader, create a desire for the product, and introduce price strategically.
- **Closing:** Stimulate the reader to act.

Analyzing the Product and the Reader

Before implementing the writing plan, it's wise to study the product and the target audience so that you can emphasize features with reader appeal.

Know Your Product. To sell a product effectively, learn as much as possible about its construction, including its design, raw materials, and manufacturing process. Study its performance, including ease of use, efficiency, durability, and applications. Consider warranties, service, price, and special appeals. Know your own product but also that of your competitor. In this way, you can emphasize your product's strengths against the competitor's products' weaknesses.

Know the Culture. If a product is being developed and marketed for consumers in different cultures, learn as much as possible about the targeted cultures. Although companies would like to use the same products and advertising campaigns as they push into global markets, most find that a "one size fits all" approach falls flat. They may think globally, but they must execute locally. For example, in producing and selling dishwasher soap and fabric softeners in Europe, Unilever discovered amazing differences in cultural preferences. Germans demanded products that were gentle on lakes and rivers. Spaniards wanted cheaper products that made shirts white and soft. And Greeks asked for smaller packages that kept the cost of each store visit low.[4]

In Britain consumers are put off by American "hard-sell" ads. Instead, they prefer to be approached gently, entertained, and charmed. In reality, most American advertisements don't cross the Atlantic or Pacific very well. Products and persuasive strategies must be crafted for each particular culture group.

Knowing the audience and adapting your message to it is important for any communication. But it's especially true for sales letters. That's why the most effective sales letters are sent to targeted audiences. Mailing lists for selected groups can be purchased or compiled. For example, the manufacturer of computer supplies would find an appropriate audience for its products in the mailing list of subscribers to a computer magazine.

Target the Audience. By using a selected mailing list, a sales letter writer is able to make certain assumptions about the readers. Readers may be expected to have similar interests, abilities, needs, income, and so forth. The sales letter, then, can be adapted to appeal directly to this selected group. Whenever possible, work

> **Both the product and the reader require careful analysis before a successful sales letter can be written.**

> **A target audience is one that is preselected for characteristics that make it a good market for a particular product.**

"I find it hard to believe that we've actually won 20 million dollars when they send the letter bulk mail."

From *The Wall Street Journal*—permission, Cartoon Features Syndicate.

from databases that enable you to personalize your letters so that you can use the receiver's name.[5] When aiming at a less specific audience, the writer can make only general assumptions and must use a shotgun approach, hoping to find some appeal that motivates the reader.

Capturing the Reader's Attention

Gaining the attention of the reader is essential in unsolicited or uninvited sales letters. In solicited sales letters, individuals have requested information; thus, attention-getting devices are less important.

Attention-getting devices are especially important in unsolicited sales letters.

Provocative messages or unusual formats may be used to attract attention in unsolicited sales letters. These devices may be found within the body of a letter or in place of the inside address.

Offer	Your free calculator is just the beginning!
Product feature	Your vacations—this year and in the future—can be more rewarding thanks to an exciting new book from *National Geographic.*
Inside-address opening	We Wonder, Mrs. Crain, If You Would Be Interested In Losing 5 Pounds This Week.
Startling statement	Extinction is forever. That's why we need your help in preserving many of the world's endangered species.
Story	On a beautiful late spring afternoon, 25 years ago, two young men graduated from the same college. They were very much alike, these two young men. . . . Recently, these men returned to their college for their 25th reunion. They were still very much alike. . . . But there was a difference. One of the men was manager of a small department of [a manufacturing company]. The other was its president.

Other effective openings include a bargain, a proverb, a solution to a problem, a quotation from a famous person, an anecdote, and a question.

Appealing to the Reader

Persuasive appeals generally fall into two broad groups: emotional appeals and rational appeals. Emotional appeals are those associated with the senses; they include how we feel, see, taste, smell, and hear. Strategies that arouse anger, fear, pride, love, and satisfaction are emotional.

Emotional appeals relate to the senses; rational appeals relate to reasoning and intellect.

Rational strategies are those associated with reason and intellect; they appeal to the mind. Rational appeals include references to making money, saving money, increasing efficiency, and making the best use of resources. Generally you should use rational appeals when a product is expensive, long-lasting, or important to health and security. Use emotional appeals when a product is inexpensive, short-lived, or nonessential.

Banks selling checking and savings services frequently use rational appeals. They emphasize saving money in checking fees, earning interest on accounts, receiving free personalized checks, and saving time in opening the account. In contrast, a travel agency selling a student tour to the Mexican Riviera uses an emotional strategy by describing the "sun, fun, rockin' and partying" to be enjoyed. Many successful selling campaigns combine appeals, emphasizing perhaps a rational appeal while also including an emotional appeal in a subordinated position.

Emphasizing Central Selling Points

Although a product may have a number of features, concentrate on just one or two of those features. Don't bewilder the reader with too much information. Analyze the reader's needs and tailor your appeal directly to the reader. The letter selling a student tour to the Mexican Riviera emphasized two points:

In sales letters develop one or two central selling points and stress them.

> 1. We see to it that you have a great time. Let's face it. By the end of the semester, you've earned your vacation. The books and jobs and stress can all be shelved for a while.
> 2. We keep our trips cheap. Mazatlan 1A is again the lowest-priced adventure trip offered in the entire United States.

The writer analyzed the student audience and elected to concentrate on two appeals: (1) an emotional appeal to the senses (having a good time) and (2) a rational appeal to saving money (paying a low price).

Creating a Desire for the Product

In convincing readers to purchase a product or service, you may use a number of techniques:

Create a desire for a product through reader benefits, concrete and objective language, product confidence, or testimonials.

- **Reader benefit.** Discuss product features from the reader's point of view. Remember the advice of René Nourse at Prudential Securities: facts and figures alone will sell nothing. They must be connected to the dreams and needs of the receiver. Show how the reader will benefit from the product:

  You'll be able to extend your summer swim season by using our new solar pool cover.

- **Concrete language.** Use concrete words instead of general or abstract language:

  Our Mexican tour provides more than just a party. Maybe you've never set eyes on a giant 60-foot saguaro cactus . . . or parasailed 1,000 feet above the Pacific Ocean . . . or watched a majestic golden sunset from your own private island.

- **Objective language.** Avoid language that sounds unreasonable. Overstatements using words like *fantastic, without fail, foolproof, amazing, astounding,* and so forth do not ring true. Overblown language and preposterous claims may cause readers to reject the entire sales message.

- **Product confidence.** Build confidence in your product or service by assuring customer satisfaction. You can do this by offering a free trial, money-back guarantee, free sample, or warranty. Another way to build confidence is to associate your product with respected references or authorities:

  Our concept of economical group travel has been accepted and sponsored by five city recreation departments. In addition, our program has been featured in *Sunset Magazine,* the *Los Angeles Times,* the *San Francisco Chronicle,* and the *Oakland Tribune.*

- **Testimonials.** The statements of satisfied customers are effective in creating a desire for the product or service:

  A student returning from Mazatlan's cruise last year said, "I've just been to paradise."

Introducing Price Strategically

Introduce price early if it is a sales feature; otherwise, delay mentioning it.

If product price is a significant sales feature, use it early in your sales letter. Otherwise, don't mention price until after you have created the reader's desire for the product. Some sales letters include no mention of price; instead, an enclosed order form shows the price. Other techniques for deemphasizing price include the following:

- **Show the price in small units.** For instance, instead of stating the total cost of a year's subscription, state the magazine's price in terms of each issue. Or describe insurance premiums in terms of their cost per day.

- **Show how the reader is saving money by purchasing the product.** In selling solar heating units, for example, explain how much the reader will save on heating-fuel bills.

- **Compare your prices with those of competitors.** Describe the savings to be realized when your product is purchased.

- **Make your price a bargain.** For instance, point out that the special introductory offer is one third off the regular price. Or say that that price includes a special discount if the reader acts immediately.

- **Associate the price with reader benefits.** Note, for example, that *for as little as $3 a month, you'll enjoy emergency road and towing protection, emergency trip-interruption protection, and nine other benefits.*

Notice in Figure 8.4 how price is directly linked to customer benefits. Century Federal Bank opens its promotional letter by telling the reader how much money can be saved on its checking account. This central selling feature is then emphasized throughout the letter, although other selling points are also mentioned.

Stimulating Action

Close a sales letter by telling the reader exactly what to do.

The closing of a sales letter has one very important goal: stimulating the reader to act. A number of techniques help motivate action:

- **Make the action clear.** Use specific language to tell exactly what is to be done:

  Submit your request at our Web site <www.johnson.com>.
  Call this toll-free number.
  Send the enclosed reservation card along with your check.

- **Make the action easy.** Highlight the simple steps the reader needs to take:

  Just use the enclosed pencil to indicate the amount of your gift. Drop the postage-paid card in the mail, and we'll handle the details.

- **Offer an inducement.** Encourage the reader to act while low prices remain in effect. Offer a gift or a rebate for action:

  Now is a great time to join the Radisson Travel Club. By joining now, you'll receive a handsome black and gold-tone cell phone case that's shock-, water-, and idiotproof.

- **Limit the offer.** Set a specific date by which the reader must act in order to receive a gift, a rebate, benefits, low prices, or a special offer:

  Act quickly, because I'm authorized to make this special price on solar greenhouses available only until May 1.

FIGURE 8.4 Sales Letter

Century Federal Bank
3200 East 30th Avenue, Eugene, OR 97405-3201

Teresa Sekine
AVP & Manager
Personal Financial Center

April 3, 200X

Mr. Frank Lawrence
1045 Redwood Drive
Eugene, OR 97431

Dear Mr. Lawrence:

Why pay $50, $100, or even $150 a year in checking account service charges when Century Federal has the right price for checking—FREE! •——— **Captures attention with appealing offer**

At Century Federal we want your business. That's why we're offering "Totally Free Checking." Compare the cost of your present checking account. We know you'll like the difference. We also have six other personalized checking plans, one of which is certain to be right for you. •——— **Emphasizes central selling point but also introduces other services**

In addition to the best price on checking accounts, we provide a variety of investment • opportunities and two hassle-free credit-line programs. Once you qualify, you can use your credit line at any time without applying for a new loan each time you need money. With one of our credit-line programs, you can write a check for just about anything, including a vacation, home improvements, major purchases, unexpected medical bills, or • investment opportunities.

Focuses on rational appeals

Suggests specific reader benefits

If you have not yet heard about Century Federal, you'll find that we have eight convenient locations to serve you.

Check out the details of our services described in the enclosed pamphlets or at our Web site <www.centuryfed.com>. Then check us out by stopping in to open your free • checking account at one of our eight convenient locations. You can also open your account by simply filling out the enclosed postage-paid card and returning it to us. **Makes it easy for reader to open account**

If you open your Century Federal checking account before June 15, we'll give you 200 • free checks and we'll buy back any unused checks you have from your present checking account. Act now to start saving money. We look forward to serving you.

Offers incentive for action before given date

Sincerely yours,

Teresa Sekine

Teresa Sekine
Accounts Vice President

TS:egh
Enclosures

- **Make payment easy.** Encourage the reader to send a credit card number or to return a card and be billed later.

The sales letter for the Legal Services Institute shown in Figure 8.5 sounds quite casual. However, it actually required considerable planning on the part of the writer. This letter announces a newsletter of legal tips to help managers avoid conduct that might result in expensive lawsuits. The letter concentrates on a central selling point (the need for current legal information) as it leads up to the action to be taken (returning a reservation form). Notice how the writer uses both emotional and rational appeals. Emotional appeals refer to a fear that managers might accidentally stumble into messy lawsuits. Rational appeals center on the

FIGURE 8.5 Successful Sales Letter

LEGAL SERVICES INSTITUTE, INC.

533 Meadowridge Drive
Lynchburg, VA 24503

February 13, 200X

Mr. C. D. Avery, President
Avery Enterprises, Inc.
2043 Powers Ferry
Marietta, GA 30067

Dear Mr. Avery:

Attracts attention with startling statement

If you had told me a couple of years ago that any time I hired, fired, or appraised an employee I could be facing a million-dollar lawsuit, I'd have said you were crazy.

Builds interest with emotional appeals

Just last October, though, I read about an employee who claimed that he had been fired because he had complained that his company had not kept its promises to him. A Wisconsin jury dropped a $12.1 million award in his lap! You're probably as alarmed as I am at the exploding number of lawsuits for hiring discrimination, libel, wrongful termination, sexual harassment, and employee testing. Employees are demanding their rights more than ever, often using the courts to support their claims.

As a business owner, you may know about these dangerous litigious topics. But what about all the managers in your company who aren't as knowledgeable? How can you train them to avoid stumbling accidentally into expensive lawsuits?

Announces product and creates desire

Associates price with reader benefit

The best way to prepare your managers is with our easy-to-read newsletter called the MANAGER'S LEGAL UPDATE. Twice a month, this four-page letter delivers valuable advice to the managers you pick. They will learn to avoid those "red flag" promises, practices, and actions that a hungry lawyer can use to bring legal action against your firm. And with legal fees starting at $200 and $300 an hour, you know how costly it is to defend against any claim. That's where MANAGER'S LEGAL UPDATE can save you thousands of dollars—and at a cost of less than 85 cents a copy.

Makes it easy to respond

To start your protection immediately, just sign the enclosed reservation form. Fill in the number of copies you want, and return the form in the postage-paid envelope. I'll take care of the rest.

Sincerely,

Winston M. Bacon

Winston M. Bacon, President

WMB:rjt

Motivates action with free gift

P.S. Respond within ten days and we'll rush you at no charge THE EMPLOYER'S LEGAL HANDBOOK, a special reference book selling for $39.95 in bookstores.

---

cost of attorneys' fees compared with the low cost of the newsletter. The price of the newsletter subscription is linked with reader benefits, followed by a satisfaction guarantee. In the closing the writer requests action and makes it easy to take. A strategic postscript offers a final incentive: a free gift for prompt action. This letter typifies successful sales letters. It sounds conversational, it offers reader benefits, and it motivates action.

Writing On-Line Sales Letters

Consumers can expect to be receiving more on-line sales letters as e-business grows.

As consumers become more comfortable with on-line shopping, they will be receiving more e-mail sales letters, such as that shown in Figure 8.6. Amazon.com started as an on-line bookseller, but it has become the largest mail-order store

FIGURE 8.6 Amazon On-Line Sales Message

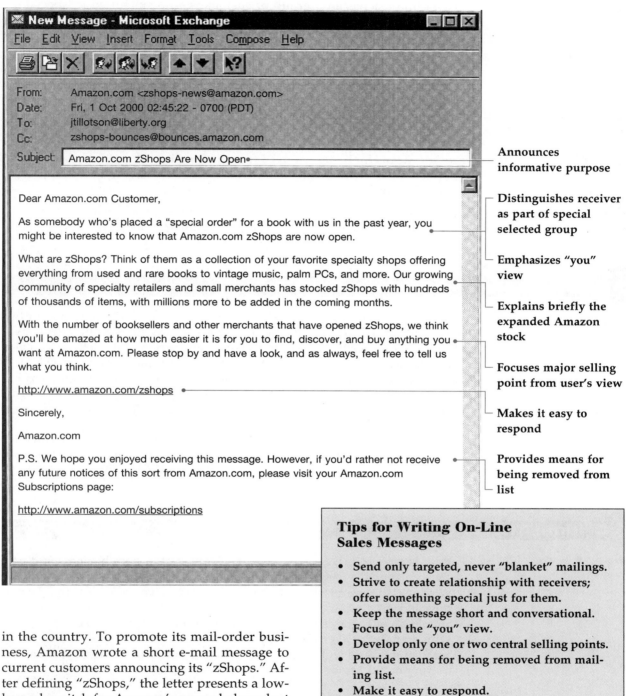

Subject: Amazon.com zShops Are Now Open	Announces informative purpose
As somebody who's placed a "special order" for a book with us in the past year, you might be interested to know that Amazon.com zShops are now open.	Distinguishes receiver as part of special selected group
What are zShops? Think of them as a collection of your favorite specialty shops offering everything from used and rare books to vintage music, palm PCs, and more.	Emphasizes "you" view
Our growing community of specialty retailers and small merchants has stocked zShops with hundreds of thousands of items, with millions more to be added in the coming months.	Explains briefly the expanded Amazon stock
With the number of booksellers and other merchants that have opened zShops, we think you'll be amazed at how much easier it is for you to find, discover, and buy anything you want at Amazon.com.	Focuses major selling point from user's view
http://www.amazon.com/zshops	Makes it easy to respond
P.S. We hope you enjoyed receiving this message. However, if you'd rather not receive	Provides means for being removed from list

Tips for Writing On-Line Sales Messages

- Send only targeted, never "blanket" mailings.
- Strive to create relationship with receivers; offer something special just for them.
- Keep the message short and conversational.
- Focus on the "you" view.
- Develop only one or two central selling points.
- Provide means for being removed from mailing list.
- Make it easy to respond.
- Convey a tone of sincerity.

in the country. To promote its mail-order business, Amazon wrote a short e-mail message to current customers announcing its "zShops." After defining "zShops," the letter presents a low-key sales pitch for Amazon's expanded product offerings.

Although short, this message contains some important lessons for writers of on-line sales messages.

- **Be selective.** Send messages only to targeted, preselected customers. E-mail users detest "spam" (unsolicited sales and other messages). However, receivers are surprisingly receptive to offers specifically for them. Remember that today's customer is *somebody*—not *anybody*.

- **Make the recipient feel special.** Notice that the Amazon message begins by placing the receiver in a group of customers who submitted a "special or-der" for a book in the past year. Although this message may have been sent to hundreds of thousands of customers, they felt that they were not part of a herd.
- **Keep the message short and conversational.** The Amazon message contains only three short paragraphs. Because on-screen text is taxing to read, be brief. Also make the message sound like casual conversation.
- **Focus on one or two central selling points.** In the Amazon sales message, the only real pitch is how much easier it is to buy everything at Amazon.
- **Provide means for being removed from mailing list.** It's polite and good busi-ness tactics to include a statement that tells receivers how to be removed from the sender's mailing database.
- **Project sincerity.** Sending a simple, low-key message and encouraging feed-back help establish a tone of sincerity in the Amazon message.

Summing Up and Looking Forward

The ability to persuade is a powerful and versatile communication tool. In this chapter you learned to apply the indirect strategy in writing claim letters, mak-ing favor requests, writing persuasive memos, and writing sales letters. You also learned techniques for developing successful on-line sales messages. The tech-niques suggested here will be useful in many other contexts beyond the writing of these business documents. You will find that logical organization of arguments is also extremely effective in expressing ideas orally or anytime you must over-come resistance to change.

In coming chapters you will learn how to modify and generalize the techniques of direct and indirect strategies in preparing goodwill messages as well as writ-ing short and long reports.

Critical Thinking

1. Why is the ability to persuade a significant trait in both business and per-sonal relations?
2. Why does the organization of a successful persuasive claim center on the rea-sons and the closing?
3. Should favor requests be written directly or indirectly? Discuss.
4. Why do individuals resist change?
5. Some individuals will never write an actual sales letter. Why is it neverthe-less important for them to learn the techniques for doing so?

Chapter Review

6. In the indirect strategy, what should precede the main idea?

7. List at least four examples of favor requests.

Chapter 8 Letters and Memos That Persuade

8. Name at least eight items a salesperson should know about a product before attempting to sell it.

9. The most effective sales letters are sent to what kind of audience?

10. What is an unsolicited sales letter? Give an example.

11. What is a solicited sales letter? Give an example.

12. List at least five ways to gain a reader's attention in the opening of a sales letter.

13. In selling a product, when are rational appeals most effective?

    When are emotional appeals most effective?

14. Name six writing techniques that stimulate desire for a product.

15. How are on-line sales letters different from and similar to hard-copy sales letters?

Direct Strategy   **Indirect Strategy**

8.1 Strategies. For each of the following situations, check the appropriate writing strategy.

_____ 16. An appeal for a contribution to Children's World, a charity

_____ 17. An announcement that henceforth all dental, health, and life insurance benefits for employees will be reduced

_____ 18. A request to another company for verification of employment regarding a job applicant

_____ 19. A letter to a painting contractor demanding payment for replacing office floor tiles damaged by sloppy painters

_____ 20. A request for information about an oak desk and computer workstation

_____ 21. A letter to a grocery store asking for permission to display posters advertising a school fund-raising car wash

_____ 22. A request for a refund of the cost of a computer program that does not perform the functions it was expected to do

_____ 23. A request for a refund of the cost of a hair dryer that stopped working after a month's use (the hair dryer carries a one-year warranty)

_____ 24. An invitation to a prominent author to speak before a student rally

_____ 25. A memo to employees describing the schedule and selections of a new mobile catering service

Acitivities and Cases

8.2 Persuasive Claim: Exchanging Copiers. Analyze the following poorly written claim. List its weaknesses and outline a writing plan. If your instructor directs, revise it.

Gentlemen:

Three months ago we purchased four of your CopyMaster Model S-5 photocopiers, and we've had nothing but trouble ever since.

Our salesperson, Kevin Woo, assured us that the S-5 could easily handle our volume of 3,000 copies a day. This seemed strange since the sales brochure said that the S-5 was meant for 500 copies a day. But we believed Mr. Woo. Big mistake! Our four S-5 copiers are down constantly; we can't go on like this. Because they're still under warranty, they eventually get repaired. But we're losing considerable business in downtime.

Your Mr. Woo has been less than helpful, so I telephoned the district manager, Keith Sumner. I suggested that we trade in our S-5 copiers (which we got for $2,500 each) on two S-55 models (at $13,500 each). However, Mr. Sumner said he would have to charge 50 percent depreciation on our S-5 copiers. What a ripoff! I think that 20 percent depreciation is more reasonable since we've had the machines only three months. Mr. Sumner said he would get back to me, and I haven't heard from him since.

I'm writing to your headquarters because I have no faith in either Mr. Woo or Mr. Sumner, and I need action on these machines. If you understood anything about business, you would see what a sweet deal I'm offering you. I'm willing to stick with your company and purchase your most expensive model—but I can't take such a loss on the S-5 copiers. The S-5 copiers are relatively new; you should be able to sell them with no trouble. And think of all the money you'll save by not having your repair technicians making constant trips to service our S-5 copiers! Please let me hear from you immediately.

1. List at least five faults.

2. Outline a writing plan for a persuasive request.
   Opening:
   Body:
   Closing:

8.3 Favor Request: Inviting a Speaker. Analyze the following poorly written invitation. List its weaknesses and outline a writing strategy. If your instructor directs, revise it.

Dear Dr. Thomas:

Because you're a local Atlanta author, we thought it might not be too much trouble for you to speak at our GSU Management Society banquet May 5.

Some of us business students here at Georgia State University admired your book *Beyond Race and Gender,* which appeared last spring and became such a hit across the nation. One of our professors said you were now the nation's diversity management guru. What exactly did you mean when you said that America is no longer a melting pot of ethnic groups—it's now an "American mulligan stew"?

Because we have no funds for honoraria, we have to rely on local speakers. The Reverend James R. Jones and Vice Mayor Rebecca A. Timmons were speakers in the past. Our banquets usually begin at 6:30 with a social hour, followed by dinner at 7:30 and the speaker from 8:30 until 9:00 or 9:15. We can arrange transportation for you and your wife if you need it.

We realize that you must be very busy, but we hope you'll agree. Please let our advisor, Professor Alexa North, have the favor of an early response.

1. List at least five weaknesses.

2. Outline a writing plan for a favor request.
   Opening:
   Body:
   Closing:

8.4 Persuasive Memo: Asking for Tuition Reimbursement. Analyze the following poorly written memo. List its weaknesses. If your instructor directs, revise it.

TO: Jay S. Jacobs, VP, Human Resources

Sue Simmons and I, along with other Intercontinental employees, have been eager to return to college, but we can't afford the costs of tuition and books.

Many of us were forced to go to work before we could complete our college degrees. We know that the continuing education divisions of some universities provide good courses that we could take at night. Sue and I—and we think many other employees as well—would like to enroll in these courses. Would Intercontinental be interested in helping us with a tuition-reimbursement program?

We've heard about other local companies (Bank of America, First Federal, GE, and others) that offer reimbursement for fees and books when employees complete approved courses with a C or higher. Sue and I have collected information, including a newspaper clipping that we're enclosing. Surveys show that tuition-reimbursement programs help improve employee morale and loyalty. They also result in higher productivity because employees develop improved skills.

We'd like a chance to talk over this worthwhile employee program with you at your convenience.

1. List the weaknesses in this memo.

2. Outline a writing plan for this memo.
   Opening:

   Body:

   Closing:

8.5 Sales Letters: Analyzing the Pitch. Select a one- or two-page sales letter received by you or a friend. (If you are unable to find one, your instructor may have a collection.) Study the letter and then answer these questions:

a. What techniques capture the reader's attention?
b. Is the opening effective? Explain.
c. What are the central selling points?
d. Does the letter use rational, emotional, or a combination of appeals? Explain.
e. What reader benefits are suggested?
f. How does the letter build interest in the product or service?
g. How is price handled?
h. How does the letter anticipate reader resistance and offer counterarguments?
i. What action is the reader to take? How is the action made easy?
j. What motivators spur the reader to act quickly?

8.6 Persuasive Claim: Kodak Ruins His Round-the-World Trip. Pictures of himself in front of the Great Pyramids of Giza, shots of the famous Blue Mosque in Istanbul, and photographs of himself dancing with children around a fire in a Thailand village—all lost because of a faulty shutter mechanism on his camera. (See Activity 7.11 in Chapter 7.) Brian P. Coyle, a 27-year-old resident of Orlando, Florida, made a once-in-a-lifetime trip around the world last fall. To record the sights and adventures, he invested in a Kodak Advantix camera. This is the camera featured by Eastman Kodak Company in television ads showing an American tourist snapping a shot of his gorgeous Italian date in Venice. When she is gone, he discovers that he misloaded the film, and he shouts, "I should have had a Kodak Advantix camera!"

In fact, Coyle selected the Advantix because of this easy-load feature, which worked well. But when he returned, he discovered that 12 of the 15 rolls of film he shot were ruined. He learned later that the camera shutter had malfunctioned. Needless to say, Coyle is very unhappy. After all, half of the fun of a trip lies in the memories summoned forth by photographs that can be enjoyed years after one returns. The emotional value of his pictures is far greater than the film on which they are recorded. He decides that he won't settle for 12 rolls of new film and perhaps replacement of the camera. He wants Kodak to send him around the world to repeat his trip. He figures that it is the only way he can recapture and record his lost adventure. He figures it would cost him about $20,000 to repeat his 27-day trip.

Coyle asks you, who he knows is studying business communication, to help him write a convincing letter to Kodak. You respond that it's highly unlikely that Kodak will grant this claim, and Coyle says, "Hey, what have I got to lose? Kodak ruined my trip, and I think a lot of travelers would be interested in hearing about my troubles with Kodak's Advantix camera."

Your Task. Help your friend Brian P. Coyle write a persuasive letter to Kodak. Send the defective camera, purchase papers, and 12 rolls of ruined film. (Should you send it by Certified Mail with a return receipt requested?) Address your letter to Mr. Charles Smith, Customer Relations, Eastman Kodak Company, 258 West Main Street, Rochester, NY 14605.[6]

8.7 Persuasive Claim: Excessive Attorney Fees.
You are the business manager for McConnell's, a producer of gourmet ice cream. McConnell's has 12 ice cream parlors in the San Francisco area and a reputation for excellent ice cream. Your firm was approached by an independent ice cream vendor who wanted to use McConnell's name and recipes for ice cream to be distributed through grocery stores and drugstores. As business manager you worked with a law firm, Lancomb, Pereigni, and Associates, to draw up contracts regarding the use of McConnell's name and quality standards for the product.

When you received the bill from Louis Lancomb, you couldn't believe it. The bill itemized 38 hours of attorney preparation, at $300 per hour, and 55 hours of paralegal assistance, at $75 per hour. The bill also showed $415 for telephone calls, which might be accurate because Mr. Lancomb had to converse with McConnell's owners, who were living in Ireland at the time. However, you doubt that an experienced attorney would require 38 hours to draw up the contracts in question.

Perhaps some error was made in calculating the total hours. Moreover, you have checked with other businesses and found that excellent legal advice can be obtained for $150 per hour. McConnell's would like to continue using the services of Lancomb, Pereigni, and Associates for future legal business. Such future business is unlikely if an adjustment is not made on this bill.

Your Task. Write a persuasive request to Louis Lancomb, Attorney at Law, Lancomb, Pereigni, and Associates, 2690 Mission Street, San Francisco, CA 94103.

8.8 Persuasive Favor/Action Request: Dining Gratuity Guidelines.
As a server in the Tejas Grill, you have occasionally been "stiffed" by a customer who left no tip. You know your service is excellent, but some customers just don't get it. They seem to think that tips are optional, a sign of appreciation. For servers, however, tips are 80 percent of their income. In a recent *New York Times* article, you learned that some restaurants—like the new 16-32 Coach House in New York—automatically add a 15 percent tip to the bill. In Santa Monica the Lula restaurant prints "gratuity guidelines" on checks, showing customers what a 15 or 20 percent tip would be. You also know that American Express recently developed a gratuity calculation feature on its terminals. This means that diners don't even have to do the math!

Your Task. Your fellow servers have asked you, who they know is studying business communication, to write a serious letter to Doug Young, general manager of Tejas (3210 Congress Avenue, Austin, TX 78704), persuading him to adopt mandatory tipping guidelines. Talk with fellow servers (classmates) to develop logical persuasive arguments.

8.9 Persuasive Favor Request: Inviting the Diva of Retail.
As program chair of the National Association of Retail Merchandisers, you must find a speaker for your annual

meeting in April. In *Inc.* magazine you saw an impressive article about J'Amy Owens, president of the Retail Group Inc., a Seattle-based strategic retail consulting firm. Owens has become the guru of retail makeovers with a client list of over 400 companies. She believes that the retail economy will increasingly be driven by *experience* as opposed to transactions. "Retail has to feel relevant or it's dead," she says.

Driving the shift in retail focus is Generation Y (those born between 1977 and 1994). They will represent 41 percent of the U.S. population in 10 years. And only 15 percent of this group frequent department stores. Besides being the place where parents shop, department stores specialize in *products* as opposed to *customers,* Owens believes. The store of the future will provide in-store Web access; give environmental controls to customers; furnish lots of sunlight, water, and vegetation; and offer "safe dangers," such as climbing walls and skateboard ramps.

Owens is very much in demand. She has been credited with helping many well-known brands regain lost luster, including McDonald's, Blockbuster Video, Sears, and Starbucks. When Nike lost the devotion of Generation Y, it commissioned her to figure out how to win them back. After her startling redesign of Mega Mart, a consumer electronics firm, it became one of the highest-grossing sellers of consumer electronics in North America.[7]

Your Task. Write a persuasive letter inviting J'Amy Owens, president, Retail Group Inc., 240 Pacific Avenue, Seattle, WA 98303. Invite her to be the keynote speaker. You know that she generally earns $5,000 a pop for industry presentations, but your budget allows only $3,000. You hope, however, that she'll be receptive since you expect about 1,500 of the top retailers to attend the conference April 6 in New Orleans.

8.10 Persuasive Favor Request: Cultivating an Internship. Your school has no internship program in your field. You realize that work experience is invaluable both to acquaint you with the field and to help you find employment. You decide to write to Rancho Enterprises, Inc., asking this company to hire you as an intern.

Although you're taking a full load of courses, you feel you could work 12 to 15 hours per week for one semester. You would have to arrange the internship hours around your existing class schedule. Describe your desire to function in a specific capacity, but express your willingness to serve wherever the company can accommodate you. Of course, you expect no remuneration, but you will be receiving up to three units of credit if Rancho can take you for one semester.

Your Task. Write a persuasive letter to Phyllis Laranjo, Manager, Human Resources, Rancho Enterprises, 1901 San Antonio Avenue, Houston, TX 77027.

8.11 Personal Persuasive Memo: We Need a Change. In your own work or organization experience, identify a problem for which you have a solution. Should a procedure be altered to improve performance? Would a new or different piece of equipment help you perform your work better? Could some tasks be scheduled more efficiently? Are employees being used most effectively? Could customers be better served by changing something? Do you want to work other hours or perform other tasks?

Your Task. Once you have identified a situation requiring persuasion, write a memo to your boss or organization head. Use actual names and facts. Employ the concepts and techniques in this chapter to help you convince your boss that your idea should prevail. Include concrete examples, anticipate objections, emphasize reader benefits, and end with a specific action to be taken.

8.12 Persuasive E-Mail: Overusing Overnight Shipments. As office manager of Cambridge Software, write a memo persuading technicians, engineers, programmers, and other employees to reduce the number of overnight or second-day mail shipments. Your Federal Express and other shipping bills have been sky high, and you feel that staff members are overusing these services.

Encourage employees to send messages by fax. Sending a fax costs only about 35 cents a page to most long-distance areas and nothing to local areas. There's a whopping difference between 35 cents and $15 for FedEx service! Whenever possible, staff members should obtain the FedEx account number of the recipient and use it for charging the shipment. If staff members plan ahead and allow enough time, they can use UPS ground service, which takes three to five days.

Your Task. Ask the staff to consider whether the recipient is *really* going to use the message as soon as it arrives. Does it justify an overnight shipment? You'd like to reduce overnight delivery services voluntarily by 50 percent over the next two months. Unless a sizable reduction occurs, the CEO is threatening severe restrictions in the future. Address your e-mail to all employees.

8.13 Web Video, Persuasive Request: World Gym. Many San Franciscans think that World Gym is the best gym in the city for the money. The physical plant is huge, containing over 35,000 square feet of space stocked with free weights, treadmills, lifecycles, Stairmasters, recumbent bikes, rowing machines, and other equipment. But World Gym finds that most of its members come at the same time, from 4 p.m. to 8 p.m. The owners think they could increase profitability and improve service by installing additional security cameras so that members will feel safe in coming at later hours.

Web

Your Task. See the complete case at **<http://www.westwords.com/guffey/role.html>**. (If you cannot view the case, you can read the complete transcript that is provided.) Answer the critical thinking questions. Then draft a letter to members that will persuade them to fill out a simple questionnaire regarding proposed additional security cameras. Although you're new to the gym world, the owners value your recent training in business communication.

8.14 Persuasive Letter or E-Mail: Persuading Your Congressperson. Assume you are upset about an issue, and you want your representative or senator to know your position. Choose a national issue about which you feel strongly: student loans, Social Security depletion, human rights in other countries, federal safety regulations for employees, environmental protection, affirmative action, gun control, taxation of married couples, the federal deficit, or some other area regulated by Congress. Then write to your congressperson explaining your views.

Web

For best results, consider these tips: (1) Use the proper form of address (*The Honorable John Smith, Dear Senator Smith* or *The Honorable Joan Doe, Dear Representative Doe*). (2) Identify yourself as a member of his or her state or district. (3) Immediately state your position (*I urge you to support/oppose . . . because*). (4) Present facts and illustrations and how they affect you personally. If legislation were enacted, how would you or your organization be better off or worse off? Avoid generalities. (5) Offer to provide further information. (6) Keep the letter polite, constructive, and brief (one page tops).

Your Task. Obtain your congressperson's address by using a Web search engine (such as www.altavista.com). Use search terms such as "U.S. Senators" or "Congressional Representatives." Enclosing your search terms in quotation marks ensures that the words will be searched as a unit. Decide whether you should write an e-mail or a letter. Remember that although e-mail messages are fast, they don't carry as much influence as personal letters.

8.15 Sales Letter: Fitness at Miller Brewing Company. Health research shows that 34 million Americans are overweight, and estimated costs for the nation in deaths related to obesity exceed $39 million. Employers and employees could save $1,200 a year for each person's medical costs if overweight employees shed their excess weight.

As a sales representative for Fitness Associates, you think your fitness equipment and programs could be instrumental in helping people lose weight. With regular exercise at an on-site fitness center, employees lose weight and improve overall health. As employee health improves, absenteeism is reduced and overall productivity increases. And employees love working out before or after work. They make the routine part of their workday, and they often have work buddies who share their fitness regimen.

Though many companies resist spending money to save money, fitness centers need not be large or expensive to be effective. Studies show that moderately sized centers coupled with motivational and training programs yield the greatest success. For just $30,000, Fitness Associates will provide exercise equipment including stationary bikes, weight machines, and treadmills. Their fitness experts will design a fitness room, set up the fitness equipment, and design appropriate programs. Best of all, the one-time cost is usually offset by cost savings within one year of center installation. For additional fees FA can also provide fitness consultants for employee fitness assessments. FA specialists will also train employees on proper use of equipment, and they will clean and manage the facility—for an extra charge, of course.

Your Task. Write a sales letter to Ms. Kathleen Stewart, Human Resources Vice President, Miller Brewing Company, 3939 West Highland Blvd., Milwaukee, WI 53208. Assume you are writing on company letterhead paper. Ask for an appointment to meet with her. Send her a brochure detailing the products and services that Fitness Associates provides. As an incentive, offer a free fitness assessment for all employees if Miller Brewing installs a fitness facility by December 1.

8.16 Sales Letter: Promoting Your Product or Service. Identify a situation in your current job or a previous one in which a sales letter is (was) needed. Using suggestions from this chapter, write an appropriate sales letter that promotes a product or service. Use actual names, information, and examples. If you have no work experience, imagine a business you'd like to start: Web site design, word processing, student typing, pet grooming, car detailing, tutoring, specialty knitting, balloon decorating, delivery service, child care, gardening, lawn care, or something else.

Your Task. Write a letter selling your product or service to be distributed to your prospective customers. Be sure to tell them how to respond.

Grammar/Mechanics Checkup—8

Commas 3

Review the Grammar/Mechanics Handbook Sections 2.10–2.15. Then study each of the following statements and insert necessary commas. In the space provided write the number of commas that you add; write *0* if no commas are needed. Also record the number of the G/M principle(s) illustrated. When you finish, compare your responses with those provided at the end of the book. If your answers differ, study carefully the principles shown in parentheses.

<u>2</u>   (2.12)   **Example:**   It was Glynna Lee, not Melinda Harris, who was given the Kirkland account.

     1. "The choice of a good name" said President Zajdel "cannot be overestimated."

     2. Donna H. Cox Ph.D. and Catherine Merrikin M.B.A. were hired as consultants.

     3. Their August 15 order was shipped on Monday wasn't it?

     4. The Web is most useful in providing customer service such as on-line catalog information and verification of shipping dates.

     5. The bigger the investment the greater the profit.

Review Commas 1, 2, 3

6. As you requested your order for cartridges file folders and copy paper will be sent immediately. _____

7. We think however that you should reexamine your Web site and that you should consider redesigning its navigation system. _____

8. Within the next eight-week period we hope to hire Brenda Woodward who is currently CEO of a small consulting firm. _____

9. Our convention will attract more participants if it is held in a resort location such as San Diego Monterey or Las Vegas. _____

10. If everyone who applied for the position were interviewed we would be overwhelmed. _____

11. In the past ten years we have employed over 30 well-qualified individuals many of whom have selected banking as their career. _____

12. Sylvia A. Wall who spoke to our class last week is the author of a book entitled *Writing Winning Résumés.* _____

13. A recent study of productivity that was conducted by authoritative researchers revealed that U.S. workers are more productive than workers in Europe or Japan. _____

14. The report concluded that America's secret productivity weapon was not bigger companies more robots or even brainier managers. _____

15. As a matter of fact the report said that America's productivity resulted from the rigors of unprotected hands-off competition. _____

Advanced Grammar/Mechanics Review—8

The following sentences contain errors in grammar, punctuation, capitalization, number style, usage, and spelling. Below each sentence write a corrected version.

1. Not one of the job candidates who we interviewed last week have written a thank you letter.

2. You would of laughed if you could of saw Kevin and I fixing the bosses printer.

3. Either the Marketing Director or the Sales Manager have to approve our departments budget for the next fiscal year.

4. Looking into the mirror of his new jeep grand cherokee Brian slipped on his ray-ban sunglasses, and thought that he looked very cool.

5. Most wifes are listed as beneficiarys on insurance policys of their husbands'.

6. The CEO hisself is willing to support whomever we nominate as our repre-senative.

7. Our salesperson told Ryan and I that a wide range of services are available if we sign up.

8. Somebody on the boys team left their shoes on the bus.

9. $600 are more than I can afford to pay for rent although I do like that 3 bed-room apartment.

10. Flying over the rain forests of indonesia the trees formed a menacing, green carpet.

11. 4 candidates submitted applications, however only one had the neccessary skills.

12. Our Manager cautioned Yvette and I not to take the C.E.O.s angry remarks personal.

13. Every employee who completes the course satisfactory, are entitled to have their fees reimbursed.

14. The following benefits are available to cardholders; travel planning, free checking account and low monthly interest.

15. Tornado warnings has been posted for the residence of: oklahoma arkansas and missouri.

cause, for the third time in as many weeks, she was forced to give up part of her weekend for work. This time it was for a black-tie affair that everyone in the office tried to duck. Laura is particularly angry with Bob, who should have represented the team at this awards dinner. But he uttered the magic word: *family*. "Bob says he has plans with his family, and it's like a get-out-of-jail-free card," Laura complains to you. "I don't resent him or his devotion to his family. But I do resent it when my team constantly expects me to give up my personal time because I don't have kids. That's my choice, and I don't think I should be punished for it."[11]

Your Task

Using the principles outlined here, work out a conflict resolution plan for Laura and Bob. Your instructor may wish to divide your class into three-person teams to role-play Laura, Bob, and the team leader. Add any details to make a realistic scenario.

- What are the first steps in resolving this conflict?
- What arguments might each side present?
- What alternatives might be offered?
- What do you think is the best solution?
- How could it be implemented with the least friction?

9 Goodwill and Special Messages

There are no economic constraints that prevent you from thanking people for their efforts. But keep in mind that a mere thank-you, accompanied by general comments, is pretty hollow. . . . Specificity, warmth, and sincerity are as important as the difference between a personal note and a computerized form letter.[1]

ANDREW S. GROVE, *founder, Intel Corporation, the world's largest chip manufacturer*

LEARNING OBJECTIVES

1. Recognize opportunities for writing goodwill messages.
2. Appreciate how special messages can build goodwill.
3. Write messages of appreciation, congratulations, and sympathy.
4. Write letters of recommendation.
5. Write form and guide letters.

This chapter presents a diverse group of goodwill and special messages requiring you to adapt the strategies and writing techniques you have learned in previous chapters. Some of the messages convey personal goodwill, and others carry business information of a special nature.

The messages in this chapter do not have specific writing plans. You will find, as you progress in your development of the craft of writing, that you are less dependent on writing plans to guide you. Although you will not be provided with detailed writing plans here, we will point out similarities between situations and make suggestions regarding appropriate strategies. This chapter will be helpful not only for its opportunities to adapt strategies but also for the models provided.

Goodwill Messages

Goodwill messages carry good wishes, warm feelings, and sincere thoughts to friends, customers, and employees. These are messages that do not have to be written—and often are not written for a number of reasons. Because goodwill messages are not urgent and because words do not come readily to mind, it's easy to procrastinate. People may feel an urge to express thanks or congratulations or sympathy, but they put it off until the moment passes. Then it's too late.

Yet, nearly everyone appreciates receiving sincere thanks or words of congratulations. Human nature creates within us a desire for social approval: we want to be accepted, remembered, consoled, appreciated, and valued. Although busy or unsure businesspeople may avoid writing goodwill messages, these letters and memos are worth the effort because they gratify both senders and receivers and because they fulfill important human needs.

Letters that convey social approval satisfy deep human needs for both the sender and the receiver.

Greeting cards and commercial thank-you notes provide ready-made words, but these messages cannot express your own personal thoughts. When you receive a card, what do you read first—the printed words of the card maker or the penned-in remarks of the sender? The personal sentiments of the sender are always more expressive and more meaningful to the reader than is the printed message. In the opening quotation Andrew Grove, founder of the giant chipmaker Intel, recognizes that goodwill messages must be specific, sincere, and warm. Without these elements, he feels, you might as well send a computerized form letter.

Goodwill messages are most effective when they are written immediately and follow this strategy:

- Identify the situation.
- Include specific details and personal thoughts.
- Close with a forward-looking thought or a concluding remark.

Messages of Appreciation

Extend thanks and show appreciation when someone has done you a favor or whenever an action merits praise. Letters of appreciation may also be written to customers for their business, as shown in Figure 9.1. Relationships with customers and suppliers are the cornerstone of successful enterprises. Common business wisdom dictates sending letters of appreciation, cards, and sometimes gifts during the December holiday period. But it's also important to express appreciation all year round. Notice that the message in Figure 9.1 begins by identifying the situation. The body provides specific details, while the closing looks forward to continued profitable dealings.

Send words of appreciation for favors and to praise actions.

Letters of appreciation should be written when someone has done you a favor. The letter to Sandra Scott in Figure 9.2 expresses the gratitude of a class for a guided tour of a corporate communication center. Thanks and compliments fill the opening, body, and closing of this message. It's no secret that readers rarely tire of sincere praise, so be sure to include many specific references to the reader and to the service rendered. Notice that a copy (expressed by *c*) of this thank-you letter was sent to Ms. Scott's boss. In this way, the letter becomes more than a routine thank-you. Not only is her boss made aware of her excellence, but also the letter will probably be placed in her personnel file and be useful in future performance evaluations and promotions.

In expressing appreciation, remember that thanks and compliments are more powerful when they are written rather than spoken. People know that it takes much more effort to sit down and write a note. And written messages are tangible and lasting. The receiver might hang your letter or note prominently as a continuing reminder of your thoughtfulness.

Letters or notes of appreciation for hospitality are generally handwritten, but they may also be printed, particularly if one's handwriting is not terrific. Two versions of a thank-you letter for a dinner at a professor's home are shown in Figure 9.3. The ineffective message fails because of its generalities and its overemphasis on *I*. Thank-yous should be about the reader, not the writer.

A good letter of appreciation for a dinner generally refers to the (1) fine food, (2) warm hospitality, and (3) pleasant company. Notice in the more effective

FIGURE 9.1 Appreciation for a Customer's Business

STAFFING RESOURCE NETWORK

302 N.E. Third Avenue
Miami, FL 33158
Phone: (305) 320-4491   FAX: (305) 320-3591
WEB: http://www.staffresource.com

January 3, 200X

Mrs. Billie Tomlin, Vice President
First American Bank and Trust
4549 Miramar Center
Fort Lauderdale, FL 33519

Dear Mrs.Tomlin:

Expresses appreciation immediately

Staffing your organization with temporary office workers for the past six years has been our pleasure, and we are grateful for your business.

Reminds and assures customer of services

As we begin the new year, I want you to know that you may continue to count on us for temporary staff members who are as productive as your permanent personnel. As a regular user of our services, you know how cost-effective it is to keep a lean staff, calling on us to help you fill in with temporaries during peak periods and for special projects.

Closes with forward-looking thought

Thank you for allowing us to send you our qualified temporaries. We appreciate the confidence you have shown in our agency for these past six years, and we look forward to many more years of mutually profitable dealings.

Sincerely,

Thomas Rees

Thomas Rees
President

Thank-you letters generally refer to the fine food, warm hospitality, and good company provided.

thank-you in Figure 9.3 that the writer includes all three of these elements. And he makes his appreciation especially meaningful by remembering a number of specifics, such as the delicious trout dinner and the superb chocolate mousse dessert. By highlighting specifics, the writer not only personalizes the letter but also decreases the use of *I*.

Messages of Congratulations

Messages of congratulations deliver recognition for a special event, such as a promotion, appointment, award, graduation, or significant honor. They also mark personal events, such as an engagement, marriage, anniversary, or birth.

FIGURE 9.2 Appreciation for Favor

Berkeley College
40 West Red Oak Lane
White Plains, NY 10604-3602

February 18, 200X

Ms. Sandra Scott, Manager
Information Support Services
Atlantic Labs
6398 Darien Boulevard
Stamford, CT 06059

Dear Ms. Scott:

Your excellent guided tour of the Communications Services Center at Atlantic Labs was the highlight of the semester for our class.

Your lucid description of the Center's operations and equipment enabled our business communication class to better understand some of the technology being used in this field. We very much appreciated, Ms. Scott, learning how work groups compose and edit reports using software to keep track of individual comments and multiple versions of report drafts. Equally interesting was your explanation and demonstration of desktop videoconferencing.

Your careful preparation for our group and your painstaking organization of the tour schedule allowed our class to see numerous operations in a short time. Many students commented on your enthusiastic and knowledgeable presentation.

Our trip to Atlantic was entertaining and instructive. We enjoyed the modern interior design, the "urban Eden" of indoor plants and trees, the colorful artwork and furniture, and the lovely employee lounges. Most important, though, we appreciated your tour because it helped bridge the gap between classroom information and real-world applications in the field of communications. On behalf of our entire class, I thank you.

Sincerely,

Robin A. Gottesman

Robin A. Gottesman
Student, Communication 202 Class

c Mr. Raymond T. LaManna
  Vice President, Information Services

Opens with enthusiastic appreciation for favor

Recalls details and specifics for personal touch

Summarizes and highlights most important reason for appreciation

---

These messages should contain warmth, approval, and praise. Avoid mechanical phrases such as *Congratulations on your promotion. You certainly deserve it.*

Try to include personal references and specific details that make your thoughts different from the bland and generalized expressions in greeting cards. Often brief and conversational, congratulatory letters may be handwritten or keyboarded. If a news clipping announced the good news, it's a nice touch to attach the article to your congratulatory letter. Smart managers know that recognition is the most powerful motivator of all.[2] Managers can lift employee morale with recognition in the form of awards, words of encouragement, and notes, such as the following memo congratulating an employee on her promotion.

Although many good-will letters and notes are handwritten, they may be printed—particularly if your handwriting is poor.

FIGURE 9.3 Appreciation for Hospitality

Ineffective

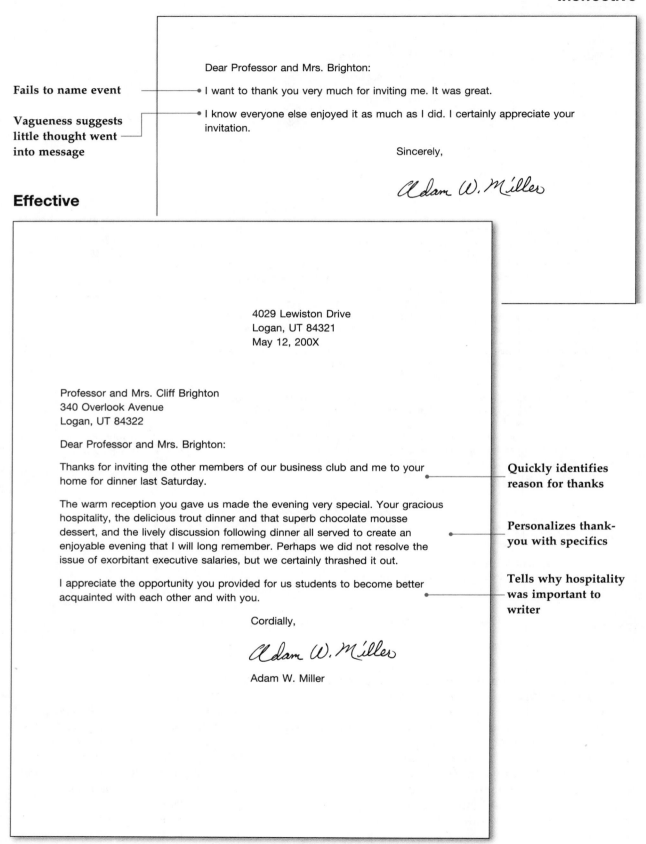

Fails to name event

Vagueness suggests little thought went into message

Dear Professor and Mrs. Brighton:

I want to thank you very much for inviting me. It was great.

I know everyone else enjoyed it as much as I did. I certainly appreciate your invitation.

Sincerely,

Adam W. Miller

Effective

4029 Lewiston Drive
Logan, UT 84321
May 12, 200X

Professor and Mrs. Cliff Brighton
340 Overlook Avenue
Logan, UT 84322

Dear Professor and Mrs. Brighton:

Thanks for inviting the other members of our business club and me to your home for dinner last Saturday.

The warm reception you gave us made the evening very special. Your gracious hospitality, the delicious trout dinner and that superb chocolate mousse dessert, and the lively discussion following dinner all served to create an enjoyable evening that I will long remember. Perhaps we did not resolve the issue of exorbitant executive salaries, but we certainly thrashed it out.

I appreciate the opportunity you provided for us students to become better acquainted with each other and with you.

Cordially,

Adam W. Miller

Adam W. Miller

Quickly identifies reason for thanks

Personalizes thank-you with specifics

Tells why hospitality was important to writer

FIGURE 9.4 Message of Sympathy

> *Dear Jane,*
>
> *We were deeply saddened to learn of your loss. Although words are seldom adequate to express sympathy, I want you to know that I count myself among your many friends who share your grief and understand the profound loss that you are experiencing.*
>
> *Henry's kind nature, his patience, and his devotion to you were apparent to all. He will be missed. If there is any way that we may ease your sorrow, you know that we are here and eager to assist.*
>
> *Sincerely,*
>
> *Christopher*

Messages of Sympathy

Grief is easier to bear when we know others care. Whatever the misfortune, show your concern with sympathetic words. Depending on the situation, express the loss that you feel, console the reader, and extend your willingness to help in any way possible. You'll want to recognize virtues in the loved one and assure the reader that he or she is not alone in this unhappy moment.

> A letter of sympathy should console the reader, point out virtues in the loved one, and express a willingness to help.

If you need ideas regarding what to say in a message of sympathy, examine the model here. Inspiration can also be gleaned from the thoughts expressed in commercially prepared cards. Study the cards, adapt some of the ideas, and then write your own individual message. The handwritten note in Figure 9.4 was written by a manager to an administrative assistant who lost her husband.

Special Information Letters

As a businessperson, you may occasionally need to write special information letters, such as those asking for or giving recommendations. Other special messages include form and guide letters. All these letters employ the direct strategy and the same emphasis on specifics that you learned in writing goodwill messages.

Letters Requesting Recommendations

When you apply for employment, for admission to special programs, or for acceptance to some social organizations, you may need to request letters of recommendation.

DATE:	January 25, 200X
TO:	Sherrie Hickox
FROM:	Donna Faber, Manager
SUBJECT:	CONGRATULATIONS ON YOUR PROMOTION!

Your promotion to the position of supervisor of Document Services, Sherrie, is wonderful news! It seems only yesterday that you were an inexperienced part-time assistant who came to my office with excellent skills, bubbling enthusiasm, and a desire to succeed.

We missed you when you left our department, but we take great pride in your accomplishments and wish you every success in your new position.

> Congratulations should be sent promptly, and they should focus on the reader.

FIGURE 9.5 Letter Requesting Permission for Recommendation

3219 Crest Hill Drive
Joliet, IL 60469
May 19, 200X

Professor Pat McMahon
South Suburban College
15800 South State
South Holland, IL 60573

Dear Professor McMahon:

Opens with compliment and explanation

Your course in office information technology was my introduction to the field, and your instruction provided an excellent background in this career area. Because you know this field well and because you also know my work as a student, may I use your name as a reference when I apply for employment?

Provides information to help reader comply with request

As I will complete my course work at South Suburban College in June, I will be looking for employment shortly. Being able to list your name as a reference would assist my efforts greatly. Enclosed is a fact sheet listing information that may be helpful to you when you write about me.

Expresses appreciation and supplies postcard for quick reply

I am grateful to you for the excellent foundation you provided in office technology and for any help you can provide in my job search. Please indicate your willingness to serve as a reference by mailing the enclosed postage-paid card.

Sincerely yours,

Shandela W. Atkins

Shandela W. Atkins

Enclosures

Always ask permission before listing someone as a reference.

Naturally, before you list anyone as a reference, you will ask for permission. This is not only courteous but also prudent. By offering the opportunity to accept or refuse, you can find individuals who will write favorable recommendations.

A letter asking for permission to list an instructor as a reference, such as that shown in Figure 9.5, should be persuasive. Notice that the writer provides explanations and kind words before announcing her request. The writer also makes it easy for the receiver to agree to the request by including an addressed postcard.

Help your recommender by supplying data about the job and about you.

If an instructor or someone else agrees to write a recommendation, you can assist that person by supplying a résumé, data sheet, or fact sheet. If you know the position for which you are applying, furnish specifics about what the job requires and what you would like the recommender to cover. Your recommender wants to help you succeed. Give that person details about the job requirements and your qualifications. For example, if the job description states "must have strong interpersonal skills and excellent written and oral communication skills," tell your recommenders of these specifications. Also provide concrete examples explaining how you feel that you meet the specifications so that your recommenders can write a targeted recommendation.

Letters of Recommendation

A letter of recommendation evaluates an individual. Recommendations may be written to nominate people for awards and for membership in organizations. Most often, however, they are written by employers to appraise the performance of current or past employees. As you progress in your career into supervisory and management roles, you can expect to write such recommendations.

Using Caution in Writing Recommendations. Many companies today, fearing lawsuits, prohibit their managers from recommending ex-employees. Instead, when these companies are asked about former employees, they provide only the essentials, such as date of employment and position held. Employers are gun-shy because former employees have sued—and won—charging defamation of character. Letters of recommendation carrying negative statements can damage reputations, thus preventing former employees from gaining employment.

Employers are afraid to write letters of recommendation because of lawsuits.

Yet, companies that no longer allow recommendations to be written for former employees face still another legal problem. Because silence can lead to bad hiring decisions, former employers can be sued for withholding pertinent information (if, for example, a past employer did not reveal information about a child molester who applied for work at a school).

Despite all the news about employment lawsuits, research suggests that the fear of litigation over recommendations is exaggerated. One law professor stated that "job discrimination cases remain one of the single most unsuccessful classes of litigation for plaintiffs."[3] Many states have passed laws protecting employers who provide truthful information.[4] Businesspeople today are still writing recommendations because they recognize the value of such messages in conveying personnel data. Yet, they are cautious in writing them. Observing the following guidelines can help you stay out of trouble:

- **Write only in response to requests.** Don't volunteer information, particularly if it's negative.
- **State that your remarks are confidential.** While such a statement does not prevent legal review, it does suggest the intentions of the writer.
- **Provide only job-related information.** Avoid commenting on behavior or activities away from the job.
- **Avoid vague or ambiguous statements.** Keep in mind that imprecise, poorly explained remarks (*She left the job suddenly*) may be made innocently but could be interpreted quite differently.
- **Supply specific evidence for any negatives.** Support any damaging information with verifiable facts (*We can document serious problems with Lisa's work* rather than *She robbed us blind*).[5]
- **Stick to the truth.** Report facts (*Troy had an accident*) rather than speculations (*He may have had too much to drink*). Truth is always a valid defense against libel or slander.

Writing Effective Recommendations. If you decide to write a letter of recommendation for a job applicant, ask the candidate to supply you with personal and professional data. Request a data sheet or a résumé, and ask what information

You'll be expected to write recommendations as you progress in your career.

the applicant wants emphasized. Recommendations often have three parts: opening, body, and conclusion.

The opening of a recommendation names the candidate, states that the message is confidential, and describes your relationship.

Opening. In the opening of an employment recommendation, you should give the name of the candidate and the position sought, if it is known. State that your remarks are confidential, and suggest that you are writing at the request of the applicant. Describe your relationship with the candidate, as shown here:

> Ms. Cindy Rosales, whom your organization is considering for the position of media trainer, requested that I submit confidential information on her behalf. Ms. Rosales worked under my supervision for the past two years in our Video Training Center.

Letters that recommend individuals for awards may open with more supportive statements, such as *I'm very pleased to nominate Robert Walsh for the Employee-of-the-Month award. For the past sixteen months, Mr. Walsh served as staff accountant in my division. During that time he distinguished himself by . . . .*

The body describes the applicant's job performance and employment traits.

Try to provide specifics rather than generalities.

Body. The body of an employment recommendation letter should describe the applicant's job performance and characteristics. Employers are particularly interested in such traits as communication, organizational, and people skills. They're also eager for comments about ability to work both with a team and independently, honesty, dependability, ambition, loyalty, and initiative. In describing these traits, though, be sure to back them up with evidence. One of the biggest weaknesses in letters of recommendation is that writers tend to make global, nonspecific statements (*He was careful and accurate* versus *He completed eight financial statements monthly with about 99 percent accuracy*). Employers prefer definite, task-related descriptions:

> As a training development specialist, Ms. Rosales demonstrated superior organizational and interpersonal skills. She started as a Specialist I, writing scripts for interactive video modules. After six months she was promoted to team leader. In that role she supervised five employees who wrote, produced, evaluated, revised, and installed 14 computer/videodisc training courses over a period of eighteen months.

Be especially careful to support any negative comments with verification (not *He was slower than other customer service reps* but *He answered 25 calls an hour, while most service reps average 40 calls an hour*). In reporting deficiencies be sure to describe behavior (*Her last two reports were late and had to be rewritten by her supervisor*) rather than evaluate it (*She is unreliable and her work is careless*).

Provide an overall evaluation in the closing.

Closing. In the final paragraph of a letter of recommendation, you should offer an overall evaluation. Indicate how you would rank this person in relation to others in similar positions. Many managers add a statement indicating whether they would rehire the applicant, given the chance. If you are strongly supportive, summarize the candidate's best qualities. In the closing you might also offer to answer questions by telephone. Such a statement, though, could suggest that the candidate has weak skills and that you will make damaging statements orally but not in print. Here's how our sample letter might close:

> Ms. Rosales is one of the most productive employees I have supervised. I would rank her in the top 10 percent of all the media specialists with whom I have worked. Were she to return to Bridgeport, we would be pleased to rehire her. If you need additional information, call me at (517) 443-9902.

General letters of recommendation, written when the candidate has no specific position in mind, often begin with the salutation TO PROSPECTIVE EMPLOYERS. More specific recommendations, to support applications to known positions, address an individual. When the addressee's name is unknown, consider using the simplified letter format, shown in Figure 9.6, which avoids a salutation.

FIGURE 9.6 Letter of Recommendation

St. Elizabeth's Hospital

4230 North Clark Street
Chicago, Illinois 60640

January 9, 200X

Director, Human Resources
MedicPlan Health Services
5440 Memorial Highway
Tampa, FL 33634

RECOMMENDATION OF GREGORY M. MAY   •————— **Uses simplified letter style**

At the request of Gregory M. May, I submit this confidential information in support of his application for the position of assistant director of your Human Resources Department. Mr. May served under my supervision as assistant director of Guest Relations at St. Elizabeth's Hospital for the past four years. •————— **Identifies applicant, cites confidentiality, and tells relationship of writer**

Mr. May was in charge of many customer service programs for our 550-bed hospital. A large part of his job involved monitoring and improving patient satisfaction. Because of his personable nature and superior people skills, he got along well with fellow employees, patients, and physicians. His personnel record includes a number of "Gotcha" citations, given to employees caught in the act of performing exemplary service. •————— **Supports general qualities with specific details**

Mr. May works well with a team, as evidenced by his participation on the steering committee to develop our "Service First Every Day" program. His most significant contributions to our hospital, though, came as a result of his own creativity and initiative. He developed and implemented a patient hotline to hear complaints and resolve problems immediately. This enormously successful telephone service helped us improve our patient satisfaction rating from 7.2 last year to 8.4 this year. That's the highest rating in our history, and Mr. May deserves a great deal of the credit. •————— **Describes and interprets accomplishments**

We're sorry to lose Mr. May, but we recognize his desire to advance his career. I am confident that his resourcefulness, intelligence, and enthusiasm will make him successful in your organization. I recommend him without reservation. •————— **Summarizes main points and offers evaluation**

Suzanne M. Lindsey

SUZANNE M. LINDSEY, SUPERVISOR, GUEST RELATIONS

SML:egi

Tips for Writing Recommendations

- Identify the reason for writing.
- Suggest the confidentiality of the recommendation.
- Establish your relationship with the applicant.
- Identify the length of employment and job duties.
- Describe the applicant's professional qualities.
- Include specific details that illustrate the applicant's personality, performance, and ability to work with others.
- Compare the applicant with others in his or her field.
- Offer an overall rating of the applicant.
- Summarize the applicant's significant attributes.
- Draw a conclusion regarding the recommendation.

Figure 9.6 illustrates a complete letter of recommendation for employment. After naming the applicant and the position sought, the letter describes the applicant's present duties. Instead of merely naming positive qualities (*personable, superior people skills, works well with a team,* and *creative*), the writer demonstrates these attributes with specific examples and details.

Form and Guide Letters

Form letters are prewritten, printed messages used to deliver repetitious and routine information. To save the expense of composing, evaluating, revising, and printing individual letters, many organizations prepare standardized form letters for recurring situations.

Form letters contain blanks to be filled in.

Form letters can be personalized with blanks for such variables as names and addresses, dates, balances, and other specific data. These letters are efficient for sales messages, personnel policy announcements, procedural explanations for customers and suppliers, order acknowledgments, and other repetitive information.

Guide letters use prewritten sentences and paragraphs. Insurance companies, for example, send thousands of guide letters to policyholders to answer routine questions regarding their coverage. Rather than compose individual responses, company representatives select appropriate paragraphs from a book of ready-made answers and instruct a word processing specialist to use these paragraphs in preparing a letter on word processing equipment.

When used properly, form and guide letters are efficient and cost-effective.

Form and guide letters unquestionably save time and money. Well-written repetitive messages used appropriately are expedient and accepted by readers. Poorly written or misused letters, on the other hand, are doubly offensive. Readers' feelings are hurt because they are treated mechanically, and they are also confused because the letter doesn't apply to them or doesn't answer their questions.

Word processing software makes the preparation and processing of form and guide letters simple. If you decide to use this means of delivering messages, follow these guidelines:

- Be certain that your form and guide letters are appropriate to the situation for which they will be used.
- Compose your letters so that they are responsive and yet require insertion of a minimum number of variables.
- Test your form and guide letters over a long period to see if they are effective.
- Revise your letters based on reader reactions.

Personalized form letters, such as that shown in Figure 9.7, can be tailored to individual circumstances by inserting variable data in the places provided. Word processing software merges a shell or main document with variable data to produce individually printed letters quickly and economically.

Summing Up and Looking Forward

Goodwill and special messages can be among the most important that you write because they build solid relationships with employees, customers, and suppliers. To be effective, they should be written immediately, sound sincere, and include specifics about the reader. Letters of recommendation are written by many employers despite legal perils. They should describe performance objectively and be honest. Form and guide letters are special messages that deliver routine, repetitious information. They can save time and effort for companies, but each one must be written carefully so that it is responsive to the situation.

FIGURE 10.7 Personalized Form Letter

Connections International

18210 Ventura Boulevard, Suite 303
Encino, CA 91436
Voice: (818) 455-9328   FAX: (818) 458-3321

{Current date}

{Title} {First name} {Last name}
{Street address}
{City}, {State} {Zip}

Dear {Title} {Last name}:

We appreciate your interest in our English/American study program offered to Japanese students. The enclosed pamphlet describes the program in detail and shows pictures of students who have participated in the past.

In brief, our organization, Connections International, supplies transportation, tours, and cultural/social programs for Japanese students coming to America to study the English language and American culture.

Our next group is scheduled to arrive {date}, and the tentative cost is {price} per student per week. This payment covers transportation, travel, and entertainment as outlined in the enclosed pamphlet. An advance payment of {deposit} is required at least three weeks before departure. This deposit is necessary in order to set the program in operation, retain proper vehicles, and make necessary lodging reservations. The amount will be deducted from the total payment for the group.

Thank you very much for considering the cultural immersion programs of Connections International. We look forward to providing warm and rewarding experiences for your students.

Sincerely yours,

CONNECTIONS INTERNATIONAL

Melissa M. Hashimoto

Melissa M. Hashimoto
Senior Coordinator

Enclosure

> Word processing software enables you to merge main document with mailing list

> Variable data fields provide individual information for each message

Now that you have completed your instruction in writing letters and memos, you're ready to learn about writing reports. Chapter 10 introduces informal reports, and Chapter 11 discusses formal reports.

Critical Thinking

1. How are goodwill messages important to a businessperson's career?
2. Why write a letter of sympathy or congratulations when a greeting card would accomplish the same end?
3. Why should an applicant ask permission before listing an individual's name as a reference?

4. As a means of screening candidates, are letters of recommendation a valid source of information?

5. Is it ethical to write a positive recommendation for an employee who has not been cooperative but whom the entire office would like to see leave?

Chapter Review

6. In goodwill messages following the direct strategy, what does the writer include in the opening, body, and close?

7. Name three instances in which letters of appreciation are appropriate.

8. Why should a copy of a letter of appreciation be sent to an employee's supervisor?

9. What four kinds of information or topics can you include in a letter of sympathy?

10. Name three instances in which letters of recommendation, other than for employment, might be written.

11. What six guidelines can help you stay out of dangerous territory in writing employment letters of recommendation?

12. List ten suggestions for information to be included in a letter of recommendation.

13. How can the writer of a letter of recommendation avoid generalities?

14. When are form letters useful?

15. Name four guidelines for preparing the most helpful form and guide letters.

Activities and Cases

9.1 Employment Recommendation: Sorry to See You Go. Assume that you are Ross Neil, manager of Builder's City. Alan B. Khory, one of your favorite department managers, has now completed his college education and will be leaving the store. Mr. Khory asks you to write a recommendation for him to enter a management trainee program for a large retailer. You know that he is a quiet, unassertive individual; but he has been an excellent hardware manager for you these past three years.

You ask Mr. Khory to refresh your memory about his performance at Builder's City. He reminds you that he started as a clerk and became department manager at the Winnetka store within six months, while at the same time working toward a college degree. His department has five employees. Within his department he tried to streamline operations. He reduced crowded displays so that the store wasn't so cluttered. He tried to increase inventory turnarounds so that fewer duplicate items were stored in the retail display area. He solved some problems that increased sales and, of course, increased profits. When the new computerized inventory system was introduced, he was very interested in it; his department was operational long before some others.

You feel that Mr. Khory has been one of your most enterprising and responsible department managers. You hate to lose him, but you can understand his desire to achieve his long-term goal in administrative management. In your letter you want to show that he has the traits necessary to be a good manager. Your opinion is that he will be an excellent management trainee. Instead of saying that Mr. Khory is able to solve problems and possesses initiative, you want to show how he demonstrates these qualities. You also want to present a fair picture. You feel that you should mention that Mr. Khory is quiet, though he gets along well both with customers and with the employees he supervises. He was, after all, responsible for training all new employees hired for the hardware department. He was also responsible for planning a work schedule that kept the employees happy and provided adequate sales coverage.

Your Task. Before you begin writing this letter of recommendation, outline a plan. The information presented here is unorganized and poorly expressed. Improve it. Add any realistic data necessary to create a good letter. Conclude your letter with a statement regarding the potential success of Mr. Khory. Use block style. Address your letter to Ms. Jane Bennett, Personnel Director, Federated Stores, Inc., 3900 East Carson Street, Long Beach, CA 90808.

9.2 Letter of Appreciation: Thanks for Saving Our Trade Show Exhibit. Your company manufactures gifts and toys, and it hired Exhibitors, Inc., to produce a razzle-dazzle exhibit for the Atlantic City Gift and Toy Show. The day before the show was to open, you arrived at the convention center and found that nothing had been set up. Bill Roever, the technician from Exhibitors, Inc., whose job was setting up your exhibit, appeared frantic. After several telephone calls, he discovered that the freight carrying the exhibit was sitting in a warehouse 80 miles away in Philadephia, with no chance of delivery this weekend. However, the warehouse manager said he would open up the warehouse if someone would pick up the freight.

Bill rented a truck and drove the 80 miles to Philadelphia. Since he was unfamiliar with the turnpikes, the trip took many hours; and by the time he arrived, the warehouse manager had gone. Luckily, Bill had asked for the man's home phone number. When he called, the warehouse manager's wife said he had gone to a hockey game. Instead of giving up, Bill went back to the warehouse and waited. After several hours, the warehouse manager arrived, unlocked the warehouse, and helped load the freight onto the rental truck. Bill drove back to the convention center, arriving in the middle of the night. The next morning he got up early, unloaded the exhibit, returned the truck, and set up a terrific exhibit before the show opened at 9 a.m.

Your Task. Write a letter of appreciation to Mr. Bill Roever, Exhibitors, Inc., 2501 Corprew Avenue, Norfolk, VA 23504. Praise his extraordinary effort, and be sure to send a copy to Ms. Karen H. Perry, president, Exhibitors, Inc.

9.3 Letter of Sympathy: For a Friend. Assume that the spouse of a colleague or friend has died.

Your Task. Write a letter of sympathy. Include enough detail to make your letter significantly different from greeting card messages.

9.4 Letter of Appreciation: For Your Boss. You've just been entertained at an elegant dinner at the home of your boss during the winter holiday season. Other members of your immediate staff also came to the party.

Your Task. Write a letter of appreciation to your boss (supervisor, manager, vice president, president, or chief executive officer) and his or her spouse. Include specific details that make your letter personal, sincere, and concrete.

9.5 Request for Recommendation: For You. You're about to start your job search, and you know that you will need good letters of reference.

Your Task. Write to an instructor or a previous employer asking for permission to use that individual as a reference. Supply whatever details are necessary.

Critical Thinking **9.6 Letter of Recommendation: By You and For You.** You are about to leave your present job. When you ask your boss for a letter of recommendation, to your surprise he tells you to write it yourself and then have him sign it. Actually, this is not an unusual practice today. Many businesspeople find that employees are very perceptive and accurate when they evaluate themselves.

Your Task. Use specifics from a current or previous job. Assume that you are the boss. In writing the letter of recommendation, speak of yourself in the third person (*Lisa worked under my supervision during the summer of . . . . Lisa was in charge of . . . . I consider her to be reliable . . . .*).

9.7 Letter of Appreciation: Thanks for Speaking. As program chair of the National Association of Retail Merchandisers, you must send a thank-you letter to your keynote speaker, J'Amy Owens (see Chapter 8, Activity 8.9). She gave the keynote address at your annual conference April 6, and she was enthusiastically received.

Your Task. Write to Ms. J'Amy Owens, President, Retail Group Inc., 240 Pacific Avenue, Seattle, WA 98303. Enclose her $3,000 check, along with a copy of the NARM *Retail Rap* newsletter, in which an article about her appeared. The article contains a picture showing her delivering her speech before your group.

9.8 Letter of Congratulation: For an Employee. Shinya Ouchi, a part-time worker in the Human Resources Department for the past three years, has just completed the requirements for a B.S. in computer science.

Your Task. As manager of the department, write him a letter of congratulations. Although he will probably be leaving, you are very happy for him.

9.9 Undirected Letter of Recommendation: For an Employee. As office manager of the law firm of Ernst, Katz, and Ernst, you have supervised the work of Wendy White, who is moving to another city with her husband. Wendy has been a fine legal secretary. She asks you to write a general letter of recommendation that she can use when she applies for a job.

Your Task. Write an undirected letter of recommendation for Wendy White. Since she has not asked you to address the letter to a specific individual, use an appropriate opening.

9.10 Letter of Appreciation: To an Instructor. After finishing the course of instruction at your school, you have taken a job in your field. One of your instructors was especially kind to you when you were a student. This instructor also wrote an effective letter that helped you obtain your job.

Your Task. Write a letter thanking your instructor.

9.11 Form Letter: To Students. When students are about to graduate, they must fill out applications so that their records can be checked to see if they have completed all the requirements. If the computer search of their records indicates that they are missing some requirements, they must be notified.

Your Task. As an assistant in the Student Services office, you have been asked to write a personalized form letter to those students who are missing some requirements. Leave a blank space to fill in the missing requirement(s). Tell these students that a mistake may have been made; perhaps their records have an error or are not up to date. Regardless, the students must come in for a conference with a records officer. Since time is limited, the conferences have already been scheduled. Leave a blank space for the date of the conference to be filled in for each student. Prepare the form letter for the signature of Dean Janet A. Brashars.

9.12 Connecting With E-Mail: Letter of Recommendation. One of your instructors has been nominated for a teaching award. Selected students have been asked to write letters in support of the nomination. However, the deadline for submitting the letters is just one day away. Thus, the chairperson of the teaching committee asks you to send your recommendation by e-mail, with a hard copy to follow later.

Your Task. Write an e-mail message recommending an instructor of your choice. Send it to your instructor.

9.13 Goodwill Messages From the Web: Free Cyber Greeting Cards. You just heard a huge belly laugh coming from the boss's office, and he yells, "Come look at this!" On his monitor you see an animated cartoon showing a bulging mailbox that opens to reveal eyes that dart back and forth and a leering grin on a faceless monster with the caption, "Long time, no e-mail." You and your boss have a good laugh, and your boss says, "Hey, are these e-mail greeting cards free? We could use something like this around here to lighten the mood or to stay in touch with clients." Because your boss knows nothing about electronic greeting cards, he asks you to locate a few card services on the Web and tell him what you find. Are cards available that would be appropriate for maintaining contact with clients and for motivating employees?

Your Task. Locate three of the best Web sites offering free business greeting cards or postcards. You can begin with bluemountain.com, which is a premier on-line greeting card site. To find other Web sites, use a search engine such as <www.altavista.com>. Try search terms such as "business greeting cards" or "virtual business cards." Remember that adding quotation marks generally limits the search to the exact expression wanted, rather than finding each word separately. You'll find many greeting card sites. To select the best ones, look at the date when the site was last updated. Then judge how professional the site looks. Does it show categories of cards? Can you find several good examples of business cards? Write a brief e-mail report to your boss, Doug Rincon. List three sites, summarize key features, and describe examples of cards in which your boss might be interested.

Web **Related Web site: To reach the premier greeting card site on the Web, visit <bluemountain.com>.**

Team **9.14 Thanks for a Favor: The Century's Biggest Change in Job Finding.** Your business communication class was fortunate to have author Joyce Lain Kennedy speak to you. She has written many books including *Electronic Job Search Revolution, Hook Up, Get Hired!,* and *Electronic Résumé Revolution.* Ms. Kennedy talked about writing a scannable résumé, using keywords to help employers hire you, keeping yourself visible in databases on the Internet, and how to find on-line classified ads. The class especially liked hearing the many examples of real people who had found jobs on the Internet.

Ms. Kennedy shared many suggestions from human resources people, and she described how large and small employers are using computers to read résumés and track employees. You know that she did not come to plug her books, but when she left, most class members wanted to head straight for a bookstore to get some of them. Her talk was a big hit.

Your Task. Your professor asks the class to break into small groups so that each team can draft a thank-you letter. Address your letter to Joyce Lain Kennedy, P.O. Box 3502, Carlsbad, CA 92009.

Grammar/Mechanics Checkup—9

Semicolons and Colons

Review Sections 2.16–2.19 in the Grammar/Mechanics Handbook. Then study each of the following statements. Insert any necessary punctuation. Use the delete sign to omit unnecessary punctuation. In the space provided indicate the number of changes you made and record the number of the G/M principle(s) illustrated. (When you replace one punctuation mark with another, count it as one change.) If you make no changes, write 0. This exercise concentrates on semicolon and colon use, but you will also be responsible for correct comma use. When you finish, compare your responses with those shown at the end of the book. If your responses differ, study carefully the specific principles shown in parentheses.

2   (2.16a)   **Example:** The job of Mr. Wellworth is to make sure that his company has enough cash to meet its obligations moreover he is responsible for locating credit when needed.

1. Short-term financing refers to a period of under one year long-term financing on the other hand refers to a period of ten years or more.
2. Cash resulting from product sales does not arrive until December therefore our cash flow becomes critical in October and November.
3. We must negotiate short-term financing during the following months September October and November.

4. Large American corporations that offer huge amounts of trade credit are, _____ Ford Motor Company, General Electric Company, Gulf Oil Company, and Microsoft.

5. Although some firms rarely, if ever, need to borrow short-term money many _____ businesses find that they require significant credit to pay for current production and sales costs.

6. A supermarket probably requires no short-term credit, a greeting card man- _____ ufacturer however typically would need considerable short-term credit.

7. We offer three basic types of credit open-book accounts promissory notes and _____ trade acceptances.

8. Speakers at the conference on credit include the following businesspeople Mary _____ Ann Mahan financial manager Holmes Industries Terry L. Buchanan comptroller Metropolitan Bank and Mark Kendall legal counsel Security Federal Bank.

9. The prime interest rate is set by one or more of the nation's largest banks and _____ this rate goes up or down as the cost of money to the bank itself fluctuates.

10. Most banks are in business to lend money to commercial customers for ex- _____ ample retailers service companies manufacturers and construction firms.

11. Avionics, Inc., which is a small electronics firm with a solid credit rating re- _____ cently applied for a loan but First Federal refused the loan application because the bank was short on cash.

12. When Avionics, Inc., was refused by First Federal its financial managers sub- _____ mitted applications to: Fidelity Trust, Farmers Mutual, and Mountain Federal.

13. The cost of financing capital investments at the present time is very high there- _____ fore Avionics' managers may elect to postpone certain expansion projects.

14. If interest rates reach as high as 18 percent the cost of borrowing becomes _____ prohibitive and many businesses are forced to reconsider or abandon projects that require financing.

15. Several investors decided to pool their resources then they could find at- _____ tractive investments.

Advanced Grammar/Mechanics Review—9

The following sentences contain errors in grammar, punctuation, capitalization, number style, usage, and spelling. Below each sentence write a corrected version.

1. On the basis of the Presidents recommendation the Senior Vice President and the Manager were promoted, however there new salarys don't become effective until January 1st.

2. The 2 biggest sellers of blue jeans are finding there market invaded by hotter more fashion conscious manufacturers.

3. Will you please call me before 5 pm EST?

4. Cybertec, Inc. does send items c.o.d. doesn't it.

5. In the not too distant future my friend and me hope to open a clothing out-let in the bahamas.

6. To start a business at least fifty thousand dollars is needed by us.

7. I bought the book titled On-line Job searches, and read the chapter called Keyword Strategies.

8. If your not on the internet your missing a world of opportunity, and knowl-ege.

9. If possible send the contract by fax before 6 o'clock p.m.

10. When we analyzed customers complaints we realized that technical support and delivery was responsible for most of the problems.

11. 35 1999 graduates indicated that they would attend the reunion.

12. All things considered the show will be canceled because it's ratings have sank so low.

13. Northwest airlines offer special menus including: hindu, muslim, and "refugee" meals served to asian refugee passengers flying from southeast asia.

14. Men can read smaller print better then women; but women can hear better then men.

15. If I was you I would take my father-in-laws advise.

Document for Revision

The following letter has faults in grammar, punctuation, spelling, number form, wordiness, and repetition. Use standard proofreading marks (see Appendix B) to correct the errors. When you finish, your instructor can show you the revised version of this letter.

October, 200X

Ms. Christie Young

637 Elkhart Street

Aurora, CA 80011

Dear Ms. Young:

Enclosed are copies of this years Sportour ski brochure. This year, in addition to our charter program (which include all our charter trips to the rockies and Europe and canada we are introducing a new program in conjunction with western airlines.

The combination of these 2 programs, offer our customers the most complete ski package we have every created. Value, flexability and variety are all amalgamated in this years program.

Due to the fact that many dates and destinations are all ready begining to fillup please select your trip and complete and fill out the reservation form included in the brochure. Send your deposit of two hundred dollars and forward to the Sportours Main Office as soon as possible.

We invite you to ski with us this comming season, and look forward to serving you, as a special incentive we're taking fifty dollars off the complete package price against the first 25 people who send in there reservations.

Sincerely,

Etiquette 101: A Crash Course in Business Social Skills

Etiquette, civility, and sensitivity may seem out of place in today's fast-moving and fiercely competitive global economy. But lately we're seeing signs that etiquette is returning to fashion in the world of commerce and industry. More and more employers are recognizing that good manners are good for business.

Schools offering management programs often now include a short course in manners. And companies are conducting manners seminars for trainee and veteran managers. Why is politeness regaining legitimacy as a leadership tool? Primarily because courtesy works. Good manners convey a positive image of an organization. People like to do business with people who show respect and treat others with civility.

Etiquette is more about attitude than about formal rules of behavior. That attitude is a desire to make others feel comfortable. You don't have to become a "sissy" or an etiquette nut, but you might need to polish your social competencies a little to be an effective businessperson today. Here are some time-honored classic tips for communicators.[6]

- Smile and greet coworkers in passing.
- Return phone calls and e-mail messages promptly.
- Share recognition for joint projects.
- Use titles for higher-ranking coworkers; avoid the use of first names unless you are asked to be less formal.
- Be on time for meetings, and don't leave early.
- Pay attention during meetings. Save Walkmans, knitting, or "busy work" for breaks or after work. Refrain from doodling.
- Contribute your fair share for office treats, gifts, or housekeeping duties.
- Pay attention to people's names so that you can remember them.
- Don't discuss sensitive topics (such as sex, religion, and politics) with people you don't know.
- Respect other people's space.
- Show interest in other people. Look at them; make eye contact. Ask questions. Laugh at others' jokes.
- Don't use social/business occasions to lobby for a raise, bonus, promotion, and so forth.
- Keep your hands to yourself. Some people don't like to be touched.
- Hold doors for men or women entering with you.
- Remember that "please" and "thank you" are always in style.[7]

Chapter 9 Goodwill and Special Messages

Career Application

You're part of a team of interns that is ending a two-month assignment at a large local firm. With graduation just around the corner, everyone has been looking for permanent jobs. One team member announces that he has been invited for a job interview that includes dinner. He wants to make a good impression, but he confides that he has had very few opportunities to eat at fine restaurants and he's feeling uneasy. He asks for advice.

Your Task

- What general tips of etiquette can you give regarding such things as appropriate dress, arriving at the restaurant, conversation, body language, napkins, and being introduced to people?

- What specific tips can you give regarding the use of silverware, what to order, when to begin eating, and how to eat?

- What should the guest do to express appreciation after a dinner meeting?

- List your suggestions and bring them to class to discuss in teams.

Related Web Site: Visit the Virtual Career Center, Dining Etiquette <http://mba.bus.msu.edu/vcc/VCC/Interview/DINING.HTM> for a list of dining guidelines. If this site is unavailable, search for relevant information by using one or more search engines with the term "dining etiquette."

Reporting Data

10 Informal Reports

Great leaders are always great simplifiers who can cut through argument, debate, and doubt to offer a solution everybody can understand.[1]

GENERAL COLIN POWELL, *former Chairman of the Joint Chiefs of Staff and White House national security advisor*

LEARNING OBJECTIVES

1. Identify seven kinds of informal reports and four report formats.

2. Define a report project and gather data.

3. Organize report data using effective headings.

4. Present data objectively to gain credibility.

5. Write information and recommendation reports.

6. Write justification and progress reports.

7. Write formal and informal minutes of meetings.

8. Write summaries and to-file reports.

Informal reports are relatively short (under ten pages) and are usually written in memo or letter format.

Good report writers, like the great leaders Gen. Colin Powell describes, are good at simplifying facts so that anyone can understand them. Collecting information and organizing it clearly and simply into meaningful reports are skills that all successful businesspeople today require. In this age of information, reports play a significant role in helping decision makers solve problems. You can learn to write good reports by examining basic techniques and by analyzing appropriate models. In this chapter we'll concentrate on informal reports. These reports tend to be short (usually under ten pages), use memo or letter format, and are personal in tone.

Seven Kinds of Informal Reports

You are about to examine seven categories of informal reports frequently written in business. In many instances the boundaries of the categories overlap; distinctions are not always clear-cut. Individual situations, goals, and needs may make one report take on some characteristics of a report in another category. Still, these general categories, presented here in a brief overview, are helpful to beginning writers. Later in the chapter the reports will be illustrated and discussed in more detail.

- **Information reports.** Reports that collect and organize information are informative or investigative. They may record routine activities such as daily, weekly, and monthly reports of sales or profits. They may investigate options, performance, or equipment. Although they provide information, they do not analyze that information.

- **Recommendation reports.** Recommendation reports are similar to information reports in that they present information. However, they offer analysis in addition to data. They attempt to solve problems by evaluating options and offering recommendations. These reports are solicited; that is, the writer has been asked to investigate and report.

- **Justification reports.** Like recommendation reports, justification reports attempt to solve problems. However, they are unsolicited; that is, the writer generates the report on his or her own. He or she observes a problem, analyzes alternatives, and describes a potential solution.

- **Progress reports.** Progress reports monitor the headway of unusual or non-routine activities. For example, progress reports would keep management informed about a committee's preparations for a trade show 14 months from now. Such reports usually answer three questions: (1) Is the project on schedule? (2) Are corrective measures needed? (3) What activities are next?

- **Minutes of meetings.** A record of the proceedings of a meeting is called "the minutes." This record is generally kept by a secretary. Minutes may be kept for groups that convene regularly, such as the monthly meeting of a club, or for groups that meet irregularly, such as committees.

- **Summaries.** A summary condenses the primary ideas, conclusions, and recommendations of a longer report or publication. Employees may be asked to write summaries of technical reports. Students may be asked to write summaries of periodical articles or books to sharpen their writing skills.

- **To-file reports.** Reports prepared to document an idea or action are called "to-file" reports. These useful reports provide a written record of conversations, directives, and decisions. In today's often litigious business world, such reports are becoming increasingly important.

Reports that provide data are informational; reports that draw conclusions and make recommendations are analytical.

Report Formats

How should a report look? The following four formats are used frequently.

- **Letter format** is appropriate for informal reports prepared by one organization for another. These reports are much like letters except that they are more carefully organized, using headings and lists where appropriate.

- **Memo format** is common for informal reports written for circulation within an organization. These internal reports follow the conventions of memos that you learned in Chapter 5—with the addition of headings.

- **Report format** is used for longer and somewhat more formal reports. Printed on plain paper (instead of letterhead or memo forms), these reports begin with a title followed by carefully displayed headings and subheadings. (See an illustration of report format in Figure 10.7, formal minutes of a meeting.)

- **Prepared forms** are useful in describing routine activities such as police arrest reports or merchandise inventories. Standardized headings on these forms save time for the writer; forms also make similar information easy to locate.

Informal reports may appear in four formats: in letter, memo, or report form or on prepared forms.

FIGURE 10.1 Ten Tips for Designing Better Documents

Desktop publishing packages, high-level word processing programs, and laser printers now make it possible for you to turn out professional-looking documents. The temptation, though, is to overdo it by incorporating too many features in one document. Here are ten tips for applying good sense and good design principles in "publishing" your documents:

- **Analyze your audience.** Avoid overly flashy type, colors, and borders for conservative business documents. Also consider whether your readers will be reading painstakingly or merely browsing. Lists and headings help those readers who are in a hurry.

- **Choose an appropriate type size.** For most business memos, letters, and reports, the body text should be 10 to 12 points tall (a point is 1/72 of an inch). Larger type looks amateurish, and smaller type is hard to read.

- **Use a consistent type font.** Although your software may provide a variety of fonts, stay with a single family of type within one document. The most popular fonts are Times Roman and Helvetica. For emphasis and contrast, you may vary the font size and weight with **bold**, *italic*, *bold italic*, and other selections.

- **Generally, don't justify right margins.** Textbooks, novels, newspapers, magazines, and other long works are usually set with justified (even) right margins. However, for shorter works ragged-right margins are recommended because such margins add white space and help readers locate the beginnings of new lines. Slower readers find ragged-right copy more legible.

- **Separate paragraphs and sentences appropriately.** The first line of a paragraph should be indented or preceded by a blank line. To separate sentences, typists have traditionally left two spaces. This spacing is still acceptable for most business documents. If you are preparing a newsletter or brochure, however, you may wish to adopt printer's standards, leaving one space after end punctuation.

- **Design readable headlines.** Use upper- and lowercase letters for the most readable headlines. All caps is generally discouraged because solid blocks of capital letters interfere with recognition of word patterns. To further improve readability, select a sans serif typeface (one without cross strokes or embellishment), such as Helvetica or Arial.

- **Strive for an attractive page layout.** In designing title pages or visual aids, provide for a balance between print and white space. Also consider placing the focal point (something that draws the reader's eye) at the optical center of a page—about three lines above the actual center. Moreover, remember that the average reader scans a page from left to right and top to bottom in a Z pattern. Plan your visuals accordingly.

- **Use graphics and clip art with restraint.** Images created with spreadsheet or graphics programs can be imported into documents. Original drawings, photographs, and clip art can also be scanned into documents. Use such images, however, only when they are well drawn, relevant, purposeful, and appropriately sized.

- **Avoid amateurish results.** Many beginning writers, eager to display every graphic device a program offers, produce busy, cluttered documents. Too many typefaces, ruled lines, images, and oversized headlines will overwhelm readers. Strive for simple, clean, and forceful effects.

- **Develop expertise.** Learn to use the desktop publishing features of your current word processing software, or investigate one of the special programs, such as Ventura, PageMaker, Harvard Graphics, PowerPoint, or CorelDraw. Although the learning curve for many of these programs is steep, such effort is well spent if you will be producing newsletters, brochures, announcements, visual aids, and promotional literature.

Today's reports and other business documents are far more sophisticated than typewritten documents of the past. If you've worked with a computer and a laser printer, you know how easy it is to make your documents look as if they were professionally printed. In fact, reports are no longer merely *keyboarded*; today, they are *designed*. As a report writer, you have a wide selection of type sizes, fonts, and formats from which to choose plus a host of word processing capabilities to fashion attractive documents. Figure 10.1, "Ten Tips for Designing Better Documents," offers suggestions to help you use these capabilities wisely.

Your natural tendency in preparing a report is to sit down and begin writing immediately. If you follow this urge, however, you will very likely have to backtrack and start again. Reports take planning, beginning with defining the project and gathering data. The following guidelines will help you plan your project.

Defining the Project

Begin the process of report writing by defining your project. This definition should include a statement of purpose. Ask yourself: Am I writing this report to inform, to analyze, to solve a problem, or to persuade? The answer to this question should be a clear, accurate statement identifying your purpose. In informal reports the statement of purpose may be only one sentence; that sentence usually becomes part of the introduction. Notice how the following introductory statement describes the purpose of the report:

> This report presents data regarding in-service training activities coordinated and supervised by the Human Resources Department between the first of the year and the present.

After writing a statement of purpose, analyze who will read your report. If your report is intended for your immediate supervisors and they are supportive of your project, you need not include extensive details, historical development, definition of terms, or persuasion. Other readers, however, may require background data and persuasive strategies.

The expected audience for your report influences your writing style, research method, vocabulary, areas of emphasis, and communication strategy. Remember, too, that your audience may consist of more than one set of readers. Reports are often distributed to secondary readers who may need more details than the primary reader.

Begin a report by formulating a statement of purpose. Explain why you are writing the report.

Gathering Data

A good report is based on solid, accurate, verifiable facts. Typical sources of factual information for informal reports include (1) company records; (2) observation; (3) surveys, questionnaires, and inventories; (4) interviews; and (5) research.

Company Records. Many business-related reports begin with an analysis of company records and files. From these records you can observe past performance and methods used to solve previous problems. You can collect pertinent facts that will help determine a course of action.

Observation. Another logical source of data for many problems lies in personal observation and experience. For example, if you were writing a report on the need for additional computer equipment, you might observe how much the current equipment is being used and for what purpose.

Surveys, Questionnaires, and Inventories. Data from groups of people can be collected most efficiently and economically by using surveys, questionnaires, and inventories. For example, if you were part of a committee investigating the success of a campus recycling program, you might begin by using a questionnaire to survey use of the program by students and faculty.

The facts for reports are often obtained from company records, observation, surveys, interviews, and research.

Interviews. Talking with individuals directly concerned with the problem produces excellent firsthand information. Interviews also allow for one-on-one communication, thus giving you an opportunity to explain your questions and ideas in eliciting the most accurate information.

Electronic and Other Research. An extensive source of current and historical information is available electronically by using a computer to connect to databases and other on-line resources. From a personal or office computer you can access storehouses of information provided by the government, newspapers, magazines, and companies. For short, informal reports the most usable data will probably be found in periodicals and on-line resources. Chapter 11 contains more detailed suggestions about on-line research.

Determining Organization

The difference between an inductive and deductive strategy is the placement of conclusions and recommendations.

Like correspondence, reports may be organized inductively (indirectly) or deductively (directly). Placement of the main idea (recommendations or conclusions) is delayed in the inductive approach. Figure 10.2 shows the same material for a report organized two different ways. Only the skeleton of facts representing a complex problem are shown. However, you can see the effects of organization.

The inductive approach brings the reader through the entire process of analyzing a problem. It mirrors our method of thinking: problem, facts, analysis, recommendation. As you learned earlier, this strategy is successful when persuasion is necessary. It's also useful when the reader lacks knowledge and must be informed. However, busy executives or readers already familiar with the problem may want to get to the point more quickly.

The deductive approach is more direct; recommendations and conclusions are presented first so that readers have a frame of reference for the following dis-

FIGURE 10.2 Comparing Inductive and Deductive Organization Methods

Inductive (Indirect) Method

Problem	Inadequate student parking on campus during prime class times.
Facts	10,000 permits sold for 3,000 parking spaces; some parking lots unusable in bad weather; large numbers of visitors without permits fill parking spaces; no land for new lots.
Discussion	Carpool? Try shuttles from distant parking lots? Enforce current regulations more strictly? Charge premium for parking in prime locations or during prime times? Build double-deck parking structures? Restrict visitors?
Recommendations	Short term: begin shuttle program. Long term: solicit funds for improving current lots and building new multistory structures.

Deductive (Direct) Method

Problem	Inadequate student parking on campus during prime class times.
Recommendations	Short term: begin shuttle program. Long term: solicit funds for improving current lots and building new multistory structures.
Facts	10,000 permits sold for 3,000 parking spaces; some lots unusable in bad weather; large numbers of visitors without permits fill spaces; no land for new lots.
Discussion	Carpool? Try shuttles from distant parking lots? Enforce current regulations more strictly? Charge premium for parking in prime locations or during prime times? Build double-deck parking structures? Restrict visitors?

cussion and analysis. Business reports are commonly organized deductively. Analyze your audience and purpose to determine the best overall strategy.

Using Effective Headings

Good headings are helpful to both the report reader and the writer. For the reader they serve as an outline of the text, highlighting major ideas and categories. They also act as guides for locating facts and pointing the way through the text. Moreover, headings provide resting points for the mind and for the eye, breaking up large chunks of text into manageable and inviting segments. For the writer headings force organization of the data into meaningful blocks.

You may choose functional or talking heads. Functional heads (such as *Introduction, Discussion of Findings,* and *Summary*) help the writer outline a report. Functional heads are used in the information report shown in Figure 10.3. But talking heads (such as *Students Perplexed by Shortage of Parking* or *Short-Term Parking Solutions*) provide more information to the reader. Many of the examples in this chapter use functional heads for the purpose of instruction. To provide even greater clarity, you can make headings both functional and descriptive, such as *Recommendations: Shuttle and New Structures.* Whether your heads are talking or functional, keep them brief and clear. Here are general tips on displaying headings effectively:

(margin note) **Functional heads show the outline of a report; talking heads provide more information.**

- **Use appropriate heading levels.** The position and format of a heading indicate its level of importance and relationship to other points.
- **Strive for parallel construction.** Use balanced expressions such as *Visible Costs* and *Invisible Costs* rather than *Visible Costs* and *Costs That Don't Show.*
- **For short reports use first- and second-level headings.** Many business reports contain only one or two levels of headings. For such reports use first-level headings (centered, bolded) and/or second-level headings (flush left, bolded).
- **Capitalize and underline carefully.** Most writers use all capital letters (without underlines) for main titles, such as the report, chapter, and unit titles. For first- and second-level headings, they capitalize only the first letter of main words. For additional emphasis, they use a bold font.
- **Keep headings short but clear.** Try to make your headings brief (no more than eight words) but understandable. Experiment with headings that concisely tell who, what, when, where, and why.
- **Don't enclose headings in quotation marks.** Quotation marks are appropriate only for marking quoted words or words used in a special sense, such as slang. They are unnecessary in headings.
- **Don't use headings as antecedents for pronouns** such as *this, that, these,* and *those.* For example, when the heading reads *Laser Printers,* don't begin the next sentence with *These are often used with desktop publishing software.*

Being Objective

Reports are convincing only when the facts are believable and the writer is credible. You can build credibility in a number of ways:

(margin note) **Reports are more believable if the author is impartial, separates fact from opinion, uses moderate language, and cites sources.**

- **Present both sides of an issue.** Even if you favor one possibility, discuss both sides and show through logical reasoning why your position is superior. Remain impartial, letting the facts prove your point.
- **Separate fact from opinion.** Suppose a supervisor wrote, *Our department works harder and gets less credit than any other department in the company.* This opinion

FIGURE 10.3 Information Report—Letter Format

STEFFINS RESEARCH SERVICES
1366 Wakefield Circle
Virginia Beach, VA 23455
(804) 571-3302

August 4, 200X

Ms. Jean Sturgill, Promotions Manager
Wilkes Recording Studios
4453 Fairfax Boulevard
Alexandria, VA 22341

Dear Ms. Sturgill:

SUBJECT: AVAILABILITY OF NAMES FOR NEW RECORDING SERIES

Identifies report and authorization — Here is the report you requested regarding the availability of names for use in a new recording series under the Wilkes Recording Studios label.

Introduction

Discusses research methods — The following information is based on trademark searches of the U.S. Patent and Trademark Office, the Copyright Office, several other sources of patent data within the music industry, and the services of our attorneys. Using the latest digital search tools, my staff conducted a full search of the five names you submitted. Of the group, we find that two names are possible for your use.

Discussion of Findings

Below are summaries of the results of our digital search of the five specific titles you suggested.

Enumerates research findings — 1. **Gold Label.** Our research disclosed one recording company using the "Gold Label" name, and this causes us some concern. However, our outside counsel advises us that the name "Gold Label" is available for Wilkes's use in light of the trademark registrations for "Gold Note" currently owned by your affiliated companies.

2. **The Master Series.** Several registrations containing the word "Master" appear in the Patent and Trademark Office. Since many registrations exist, no one can assert exclusive rights to that word. Therefore, Wilkes's use of the name "The Master Series" is not precluded.

---

is difficult to prove, and it damages the credibility of the writer. A more convincing statement might be, *Our productivity has increased 6 percent over the past year, and I'm proud of the extra effort my employees are making.* After you've made a claim or presented an important statement in a report, ask yourself, Is this a verifiable fact? If the answer is no, rephrase your statement to make it sound more reasonable.

- **Be sensitive and moderate in your choice of language.** Don't exaggerate. Instead of saying *most people think . . .*, it might be more accurate to say *some people think . . . .* Obviously, avoid using labels and slanted expressions. Calling someone a *turkey,* an *egghead,* or an *elitist* demonstrates bias. If readers suspect that a writer is prejudiced, they may discount the entire argument.

FIGURE 10.3 Information Report—Page 2

Ms. Jean Sturgill   Page 2   August 4, 200X

3. **Heavenly Voices.** Our search of copyright records disclosed that approximately seven songs were recorded in 1999 on the "Heavenly Voices" record label, with an address in Sausalito, California. Repeated attempts to reach this business have been unsuccessful. • ——— **Bold headings improve readability**

4. **Celestial Sounds.** A record label using this name produced 12 titles in 1998. Apparently the recording company is now defunct, but the trademark registration, No. 1,909,233, persists.

5. **Cherubim.** This name has at least one currently operating outstanding trademark, Trademark Registration No. 2,109,900 for "Cherubim Music."

Summary

Of the five names discussed here, the first two appear to be open to you: "Gold Label" and "The Master Series." The names "Heavenly Voices" and "Celestial Sounds" require additional research. Since "Cherubim" is trademarked, it is unavailable for your consideration. • ——— **Summarizes significant findings**

Should you have any other names you would like us to check, please call me at (804) 571-3302. It's always a pleasure to serve you.

Sincerely yours,

Ellie Steffins

Ellie Steffins
President

ES:jer

- **Cite sources.** Tell your readers where the information came from. For example, *In a telephone interview with Blake Spence, director of transportation, October 15, he said . . . OR: The Wall Street Journal (August 10, p. 40) reports that . . . .* By referring to respected sources, you lend authority and credibility to your statements. Your words become more believable and your argument, more convincing.

Information Reports

Writers of information reports provide information without drawing conclusions or making recommendations. Some information reports are highly standardized, such as police reports, hospital admittance reports, monthly sales reports, or government regulatory reports. Essentially, these are fill-in reports using prepared forms for recurring data. Other information reports are more personalized, as illustrated in Figure 10.3. They often include these sections:

Introduction

Information reports usually contain three parts: *introduction, findings,* and *summary.*

The introduction to a report may be called *Introduction* or *Background.* In this section do the following: (1) explain why you are writing, (2) describe what methods and sources were used to gather information and why they are credible, (3) provide any special background information that may be necessary, (4) give the purpose of the report, if known, and (5) offer a preview of your findings.

Findings

The findings section of a report may also be called *Observations, Facts, Results,* or *Discussion.* Important points to consider in this section are organization and display. Since information reports generally do not include conclusions or recommendations, inductive or deductive organization may be less appropriate. Instead, consider one of these methods of organization: (1) chronological, (2) alphabetical, (3) topical, or (4) most to least important.

To display the findings effectively, number the paragraphs, underline or boldface the key words, or indent the paragraphs. Be sure that words used as headings are parallel in structure. If the findings require elaboration, either include this discussion with each segment of the findings or place it in a separate section entitled *Discussion.*

Summary

A summary section is optional. If it is included, use it to synopsize your findings objectively and impartially.

The information report shown in Figure 10.3 describes names available for a new recording series. The writer, an information specialist and consultant, used functional headings (*Introduction, Discussion of Findings,* and *Summary*). Although these headings immediately announce the report's organization, they give no hint of what the sections actually reveal.

Notice how easy this information report is to read. Short paragraphs, ample use of headings, white space, concise writing, and an enumerated list all contribute to improved readability.

Recommendation Reports

Unlike information reports, recommendation reports include conclusions and recommendations.

Recommendation reports present information and analysis meant to solve a problem. These reports are usually written in response to requests by superiors. Writers are expected to analyze data, draw conclusions, and make recommendations. These reports may be arranged inductively (indirectly) or deductively (directly), depending on the problem, audience, and purpose. To arrange a report deductively, place the conclusions and recommendations near the beginning. For inductive arrangement, place them toward the end.

The recommendation report shown in Figure 10.4 presents information about procedures for hiring and using temporary employees. Organized inductively, this report begins with a description of the background and problem. Conclusions and recommendations follow. Because the writer thought the reader would require persuasion, she arranged the report to follow logical thought processes.

In addition to illustrating inductive organization, the recommendation report in Figure 10.4 shows the memo format. This report was internal; therefore, it used company memo stationery.

FIGURE 10.4 Recommendation Report—Memo Format

Pyramid Industries

Internal Memorandum

DATE: June 3, 200X

TO: Brenda Hardin, Director
              Human Resources Services

FROM: Laurie Glaze, Manager   *Laurie*
              Information Services

SUBJECT: DEVELOPING PROCEDURES FOR USING TEMPORARY
              EMPLOYEES

At your request I am submitting this report detailing my recommendations for
improving the use of temporary employees in all departments within Pyramid.
My recommendations are based on my own experience with hundreds of temporary employees and on my interviews with other department managers.

Background

Pyramid has increased its number of service accounts from 58 to 97 over the
past three years. During that same period the number of permanent employees has increased only 12 percent. Because we have not been able to find
qualified individuals to hire as full-time employees, we have been forced to rely
on temporary employees more heavily than ever before. During the past year
Pyramid has required the services of 189 temporary employees.

Joe Hernandez in Human Resources reports that he does not expect the employment picture to improve in the future. He feels that Pyramid will probably
continue to hire large numbers of temporary employees for the next two years.

Problem

Temporary employees are hired by department managers who have little experience in acquiring temps, planning their work, or supervising them. As a result, the productivity of the temps is not always as great as it could be.
Moreover, we sometimes hire expensive, highly skilled individuals for routine
tasks. These workers are bored with their assigned tasks and dissatisfied with
their experience at Pyramid; hence they refuse to return.

- *Includes signature here rather than at end*
- *Announces report and establishes sources of data*
- *Presents facts that suggest significance of problem*
- *Provides details that justify need for change*

Tips for Formatting Memo Reports

- Use memo format for internal reports.
- Include DATE, TO, FROM, and SUBJECT.
- Start on line 13 to leave a 2-inch top margin.
- Single-space paragraphs but leave one to two blank lines before a side heading.
- Use side headings when report has only one heading level.
- Bold the side headings and capitalize initial letters of important words.
- Decide whether to use functional headings, as shown here, or talking headings.
- Use ragged right margins, as shown here. Do not justify the margins.

FIGURE 10.4 Recommendation Report—Page 2

Brenda Hardin   Page 2   June 3, 200X

Conclusions

Draws conclusions from preceding facts ——

Pyramid could improve the productivity, effectiveness, and morale of its temporary employees by instituting changes in three areas: (1) establishing standardized procedures for departments requesting temps, (2) introducing techniques for department managers to follow when temps first arrive, and (3) providing suggestions for adequate supervision after temps are on the job.

Recommendations

System for Requesting Temps. I recommend that Human Resources prepare a form that supervisors complete when they need temporary employees. The form will require department managers to indicate precisely what skills are required for the tasks to be completed. We should not request an administrative assistant for a task that a clerk could perform. Requests for temps should then be channeled through one office, such as Human Resources.

Procedures for Introducing Temps to Workforce. When temps are hired, department managers can improve their productivity by following these suggestions:

Itemizes specific actions to solve problem ——

1. Lay out and organize the work to be completed.
2. Simplify the tasks as much as possible.
3. Ensure that supplies and operating equipment are available.
4. Encourage the temp to ask questions clarifying tasks.

Follow-Up Supervision. Probably the most important suggestion involves supervision. As soon as a temp starts on the job, assign a nearby supervisor. Spot-check the temp an hour after work is begun and at other intervals. Don't wait until a task is completed to discover a misunderstanding.

Limitations

Gains credibility by acknowledging limitations of recommendations ——

The success of these recommendations is limited by two factors. First, Human Resources must agree to assume the task of regulating the hiring of all temporary employees. Second, department managers must be supportive of the new procedures. To secure their cooperation, an in-service training workshop should be provided to instruct managers in working with temps.

The headings in the report shown in Figure 10.4 include *Background, Problem, Conclusions, Recommendations,* and *Limitations.* Other possible section headings for a recommendation report follow:

Introduction	Analysis of Facts
Background	Options
Problem	Rejected Alternatives
Method of Collecting Data	Limitations
Findings	Conclusions
Presentation of Facts	Recommendations

FIGURE 10.5 Justification Report

MEMORANDUM

DATE: June 11, 200X

TO: James C. Downs, Vice President
          Operations Division

FROM: Sally Stouder, Office Manager
          Accounting Department

SUBJECT: INSTALLATION OF FLAT, UNDERCARPET WIRING TO UPDATE
          CURRENT ELECTRICAL WIRING SYSTEM

Proposal

Because the Accounting Department of Hershey Chocolate Company needs a
flexible, economical wiring system that can accommodate our ever-changing
electrical, communication, and data processing needs, I propose that we install a flat, undercarpet wiring system.

> *Presents main idea (proposal) immediately*

Present System

At present our department has an outdated system of floor ducts and power
poles and a network of surface wiring that is overwhelmed by the demands we
are now placing on it. The operation of 27 pieces of equipment (including
computers, printers, modems, faxes, and copiers), plus 34 telephones requires
extensive electrical circuits and cabling. In addition, our overhead lighting,
consisting of fluorescent fixtures in a suspended egg-crate structure, contains
excessive wiring above the drop ceiling.

> *Describes problem, emphasizing current deficiencies*

We have outgrown our present wiring system, and future growth is contingent
on the availability of power. Since Hershey's goal is to have a computer terminal and modem at every workstation, we must find a better way to service our
power needs than through conventional methods.

Advantages of Proposed System

Power, telephone, and data cables are now available in a flat form only .043
inches thick. This flat, flexible cable can be installed underneath existing car-
peting, thus preventing costly and disruptive renovation necessary for in-

> *Shows how new system would solve problems*

Justification Reports

Justification reports include information, analysis, and recommendations. Unlike
recommendation reports, however, they are *unsolicited*—that is, the idea for a justification report starts with the writer instead of with a superior. The writer may
wish to purchase equipment, change a procedure, or revise existing policy. Typically, the desired change will be obvious to the reader. Therefore, persuasion
should not be a primary goal. Start directly with the proposal or problem. Follow
this with some or all of the following topics: Present System, Proposed System,
Advantages, Cost and Savings, Methods or Procedures, Conclusion, and Discussion. Figure 10.5 shows a justification report within Hershey Chocolate Company.

FIGURE 10.5 Justification Report—Page 2

stalling additional round cables. Because flat cables can be moved easily, an undercarpet system would provide great flexibility. Whenever we move a computer or add a printer or a fax machine, we can easily make necessary changes in the wiring.

Offers convincing arguments for undercarpet wiring

Undercarpet wiring would allow us to eliminate all power poles. These poles break up the office landscaping and create distracting shadows about which employees complain.

Installation of an undercarpet wiring system in the Accounting Department would enable Hershey to evaluate the system's effectiveness before considering it for other areas, such as sales, customer services, and field warehousing.

Cost and Savings

Relates costs to savings and benefits

The AMP Products Corporation of Harrisburg estimates that undercarpet wiring for the Accounting Department would cost about $29,000. If we were to use conventional methods to install round wiring, we would have to renovate our entire department, costing over $200,000. Undercarpet wiring, then, saves Hershey over $170,000. Equally important, however, is the savings in terms of productivity and employee satisfaction, which would deteriorate if renovation were required.

Progress Reports

Progress reports tell management whether nonroutine projects are on schedule.

Progress reports describe the headway of unusual or nonroutine projects. Most progress reports include these four parts:

• The purpose and nature of the project

• A complete summary of the work already completed

• A thorough description of work currently in progress, including personnel, methods, obstacles, as well as attempts to remedy obstacles

• A forecast of future activities in relation to the scheduled completion date, including recommendations and requests

FIGURE 10.6 Progress Report

MEMORANDUM

DATE: April 20, 200X

TO: Dorothy Prevatt, President

FROM: Maria Robinson, Development Officer   *MR*

SUBJECT: CONSTRUCTION PROGRESS OF MIAMI BRANCH OFFICE

Construction of Prevatt Realty's Miami branch office has entered Phase 3. Although we are one week behind the contractor's original schedule, the building should be ready for occupancy August 15. — *Introduces report with a summary*

Past Progress

Phase 1 involved development of the architect's plans; this process was completed February 5. Phase 2 involved submission of the plans for county building department approval. The plans were then given to four contractors for estimates. The lowest bidder was Holst Brothers Contractors. This firm began construction on March 25. — *Describes completed work concisely*

Present Status

Phase 3 includes initial construction procedures. The following steps have been completed as of April 20:

1. Demolition of existing building 11485 NW 27 Avenue
2. Excavation of foundation footings for the building and for the surrounding wall
3. Installation of steel reinforcing rods in building pad and wall
4. Pouring of concrete foundation

— *Itemizes current activities*

The contractor indicated that he was one week behind schedule for the following reasons. The building inspectors required additional steel reinforcement not shown on the architect's blueprints. Further, excavation of the footings required more time than the contractor anticipated because the 18-inch footings were all below grade.

Future Schedule

Despite some time lost in Phase 3, we are substantially on target for the completion of this office building by August 1. Phase 4 includes framing, drywalling, and plumbing. — *Projects future activities*

In Figure 10.6 Maria Robinson explains the construction of a realty company branch office. She begins with a statement summarizing the construction progress in relation to the expected completion date. She then updates the reader with a brief recap of past progress. She emphasizes the present status of construction and concludes by describing the next steps to be taken.

Some business communicators use progress reports to do more than merely report progress. These reports can also be used to offer ideas and float "trial balloons." Let's say you are reporting on the progress of redesigning the company Web site. You might suggest a different way to handle customer responses. Instead of making an official recommendation, which might be rejected, you can lay the foundation for a change within your progress report. Progress reports can also be used to build the image of a dedicated, conscientious employee.

FIGURE 10.7 Minutes of Meeting, Formal—Report Format

Professional Secretaries Association
Planning Committee Meeting
October 23, 200X, 10 a.m.
Conference Room A, Century Towers

Present: Marilyn Andrews, Melody Franklin, June Gonzales, Brenda Miller, Margaret Zappa, Martha Zebulski

Absent: Amy Costello

The meeting was called to order by Chair Margaret Zappa at 10:05 a.m. Minutes from the June 22 meeting were read and approved.

Old Business

Brenda Miller and Martha Zebulski reviewed the information distributed at the last meeting about hotels being considered for the Houston conference. Brenda said that the Hilton Regency has ample conference rooms and remodeled interiors. Martha reported that the Embassy Suites Houston also has excellent banquet facilities, adequate meeting facilities, and rooms at $82 per night. Melody Franklin moved that we hold the PSA International Convention at the Embassy Suites Houston. Brenda Miller seconded the motion. The motion passed 5–1.

New Business

The chair announced three possible themes for the convention, all of which focused on technology and the changing role of the secretary. June Gonzales suggested the following possible title: "The New, the Tried and True, and the Unusual." Martha Zebulski suggested a communication theme. Several other possibilities were discussed. The chair appointed a subcommittee of June and Martha to bring to the next committee meeting two or three concrete theme ideas.

Reports

Brenda Miller reported on convention exhibits and her desire to involve more companies and products. Discussion followed regarding how this might be accomplished. Brenda Miller moved that the PSA office staff develop a list of possible exhibitors. Marilyn Andrews seconded the motion. It passed 6–0.

The meeting was adjourned at 11:45 by Margaret Zappa.

Respectfully submitted,

Melody Franklin

Melody Franklin, Secretary

Annotations (left margin):
- Shows attendees and absentees
- Describes disposition of previous minutes and old business
- Summarizes new business and announcements
- Records discussion, motions, votes, and action taken
- Shows name and signature of person recording minutes

Formal Minutes

Minutes provide a summary of the proceedings of meetings. Formal, traditional minutes, illustrated in Figure 10.7, are written for large groups and legislative bodies. The following items are usually included in the sequence shown:

- Name of group, date, time, place, name of meeting
- Names of attendees and absentees, if appropriate
- Old business, new business, announcements, reports
- Motions, vote, action taken
- Name and signature of individual recording minutes

FIGURE 10.8 Minutes of Meeting, Informal—Report Format

Malibu Beach Homeowners' Association

Board of Directors Meeting
April 12, 200X

MINUTES

Directors Present: S. Stallone, A. McGraw, J. Carson, W. Goldberg, A. Pettus
Directors Absent: B. Streisand

Summary of Topics Discussed

- Report from Architectural Review Committee. Copy attached.
- Landscaping of center divider on Paseo Canyon. Three options considered: hiring private landscape designer, seeking volunteers from community, assigning association handyman to complete work.
- Collection of outstanding assessments. Discussion of delinquent accounts and possible actions. *— Summarizes discussion*
- Use of beach club by film companies. Pros: considerable income. Cons: damage to furnishings, loss of facility to homeowners.
- Nomination of directors to replace those with two-year appointments.

Decisions Reached

- Hire private landscaper to renovate and plant center divider on Paseo Canyon.
- Attach liens to homes of members with delinquent assessments. *— Capsulizes decisions rather than showing motions and voting*
- Submit to general membership vote the question of renting the beach club to film companies.

Action Items

Item	Responsibility	Due Date
1. Landscaping bid	J. Carson	May 1
2. Attorney for liens	B. Streisand	April 20
3. Creation of nominating committee	A. Pettus	May 1

— Highlights items for action

Informal Minutes

The minutes of business meetings and small organizations may be recorded informally, as illustrated in Figure 10.8. They may be distributed in hard-copy form or by e-mail. Informal minutes are usually shorter and easier to read than formal minutes. Informal minutes place less emphasis on the conventions of reporting and do not attempt to record the exact wording of individual statements. Instead, informal minutes concentrate on the following:

- Summaries of important discussions
- Decisions reached
- Items on which action must be taken, including people responsible and due dates

FIGURE 10.9 Summary of Article—Memo Format

DATE: November 18, 200X

TO: Professor Valerie Evans

FROM: Edwin Hwang   *EH*

SUBJECT: ANALYSIS OF COMPUTER MAINTENANCE ARTICLE

Introduces report

In response to your request, here is an analysis of "Taking the Sting Out of Computer Repair," which appeared in the July 1999 issue of *Office Administration and Automation*.

Major Points

The author, Michael B. Chamberlain, discusses three alternatives available to computer users seeking service. Each has advantages and disadvantages.

Summarizes primary ideas and conclusions

- **Factory service.** The user sends the equipment back to the factory for repairs. Expert service is provided, but generally the time required is impossibly long.

- **Customer self-service.** Large companies may maintain in-house repair departments, but their technicians find it difficult to keep abreast of changing hardware and software.

- **Third-party service.** Independent computer maintenance organizations offer convenience, but they can't always handle multivendor systems.

Omits examples, illustrations, and references

The author favors the third option and provides many tips on how to work with third-party maintenance companies. Before choosing such an organization, he warns, make sure that it has experts who can work with your configuration.

Reveals evaluation of writer

Strengths and Weaknesses

The strength of this article lies in the discussion on how to choose a service organization. The author also provides helpful preventive maintenance tips.

This article had two weaknesses. First, the author failed to support his choice of third-party maintenance companies effectively. Second, the article was poorly organized. It was difficult to read because it was not developed around major ideas. Better headings would have helped readers recognize significant data.

Summaries

A summary condenses the primary ideas, conclusions, and recommendations of a longer publication.

A summary compresses essential information from a longer publication. An *executive summary* generally summarizes a long report or proposal. It concentrates on what management needs to know from a longer report.

Employees are sometimes asked to write executive summaries that condense technical reports, periodical articles, or books so that their staffs or superiors may grasp the main ideas quickly. Students are often asked to write summaries of articles, chapters, or books to sharpen their writing skills and to confirm their knowledge of reading assignments.

FIGURE 10.10 To-File Report

Informatics, Inc.

Internal Memo

DATE: February 4, 200X

TO: Kimberlee Bartel
            Chief Counsel

FROM: Judith Bynum   JB
            Business Manager

SUBJECT: DISPOSITION OF UNORDERED MERCHANDISE

This confirms our telephone conversation today in which you advised me
regarding the disposition of unordered merchandise sent to my office by ven-   • ——— **Provides record of**
dors. It is my understanding that I am under no obligation to return this mer-   **conversation**
chandise since its delivery was unauthorized. I further understand that
after reasonable time has elapsed, we may use this merchandise or dispose   • ——— **Repeats major ideas**
of it as we see fit.

Please let me hear from you by February 10 if this record of our conversation   • ——— **Requests correction if**
is inaccurate.   **necessary**

A summary should highlight primary ideas, conclusions, and recommendations.
It usually omits examples, illustrations, and references. Organized for readability,
a summary often includes headings and bulleted or enumerated lists. It may also
contain the reactions or recommendations of the reader, as shown in Figure 10.9.
A clearly stated purpose and a summary of main points along with itemized conclusions and recommendations give readers a quick overview of the entire article.

To-File Reports

To-file reports document oral decisions, directives, and discussions. They create
a concise, permanent record that may be important for future reference. Because
individuals may forget, alter, or retract oral commitments, a written record should
often be established. However, to-file reports should not be made for minor events.

To-file reports typically include the names and titles of involved individuals,
along with a summary of the decision. A copy of the report is sent to involved
individuals so that corrections or amendments may be made before the report is
filed. Figure 10.10 shows a to-file report in memo format.

Summing Up and Looking Forward

This chapter presented seven types of informal business reports: information reports, recommendation reports, justification reports, progress reports, minutes of meetings, summaries, and to-file reports. Information reports generally provide data only. But recommendation and justification reports are more analytical in that they also evaluate the information, draw conclusions, and make recommendations. This chapter also discussed four formats for reports. Letter format is used for reports sent outside an organization; memo format is used for internal reports. More formal reports are formatted on plain paper with a manuscript design, while routine reports may be formatted on prepared forms. The chapter presented numerous model documents illustrating the many kinds of reports and their formats. Readers also were given tips for designing reports with desktop publishing programs to enhance their appearance.

All of the examples in this chapter are considered relatively informal. Longer, more formal reports are necessary for major investigations and research. These reports and proposals, along with suggestions for research methods, are presented in Chapter 11.

Critical Thinking

1. How do business reports differ from business letters?
2. Of the reports presented in this chapter, discuss those that require inductive (indirect) development versus those that require deductive (direct) development.
3. How are the reports that you write for your courses similar to those presented here? How are they different?
4. Compare and contrast formal and informal minutes of meetings. Why would some organizations require more formal minutes?
5. Compare and contrast recommendation and justification reports.

Chapter Review

6. List seven kinds of short reports. Be prepared to describe each.

7. List four formats suitable for reports. Be prepared to discuss each.

Chapter 10 Informal Reports

8. From the lists you made in Questions 6 and 7, select a report category and appropriate format for each of the following situations.
   a. Your supervisor asks you to read a long technical report and write a report that condenses the important points.

   b. You want to tell management about an idea you have for improving a procedure that you think will increase productivity.

   c. You just completed a telephone conversation with a union representative detailing your rights in a disagreement you had with your supervisor.

   d. You are asked to record the proceedings of a meeting of your school's student association.

   e. As Engineering Department office manager, you have been asked to describe your highly regarded computer system for another department.

   f. As a police officer, you are writing a report of an arrest.

   g. At a mail-order catalog company, your boss asks you to investigate ways to reduce the time that customers are kept waiting for service representatives to take their telephone orders. He wants your report to examine the problem and offer solutions.

9. If you were about to write the following reports, where would you gather information? Be prepared to discuss the specifics of each choice.
   a. You are a student representative on a curriculum committee. You are asked to study the course requirements in your major and make recommendations.

   b. As department manager, you must write job descriptions for several new positions you wish to establish in your department.

   c. You are proposing to management the replacement of a copier in your department.

   d. You must document the progress of a 12-month campaign to alter the image of Levi-Strauss jeans.

10. What three questions do progress reports typically address?

11. What one factor distinguishes reports developed inductively from those developed deductively?

12. What is the purpose of a to-file report?

13. Information reports generally contain what three parts?

14. Why are informal minutes usually easier to read than formal minutes?

15. An article summary that your employer asks you to write should include what items?

Team

10.1 Evaluating Headings and Titles. Identify the following report headings and titles as "talking" or "functional/descriptive." Discuss the usefulness and effectiveness of each.

a. Problem

b. Need for Tightening Computer ID System

c. Annual Budget

d. How Direct Mail Can Deliver Profits for Your Business

e. Case History: Buena Vista Palace Hotel Focuses on Improving Service to Customers

f. Solving Our Networking Problems With an Extranet

g. Comparing Copier Volume, Ease of Use, and Speed

h. Alternatives

10.2 Information Report: Describing Your Job. Your instructor wants to learn about your employment. Select a position you now hold or one that you have held in the past. If you have not been employed, choose an organization to which you belong.

Your Task. Write an information report describing your employment. As an introduction describe the company and its products or services, its ownership, and its location. As the main part of the report, describe your position, including its tasks and the skills required to perform these tasks. Summarize by describing the experience you gained. Your memo report should be single-spaced and 1 1/2 to 2 pages long and should be addressed to your instructor.

Web

10.3 Information Report: Learning About a Position. Gather information about a position in which you might be interested. Learn about the nature of the job. Discover whether certification, licenses, or experience is required. One of the best places to search is the latest *Occupational Outlook Handbook* (see the Web site address at the end of this case).

Your Task. Write an information report that characterizes the working conditions in your target career area. Describe typical entry-level salaries and the potential for advancement. If your instructor wishes to make this an extended report, collect information about two companies where you might apply. Investigate each company's history, products and/or services, size, earnings, reputation, and number of employees. Describe the functions of an employee working in the position you have investigated. To do this, interview one or more individuals who are working in that position. Devote several sections of your report to the specific tasks, functions, duties, and opinions of these individuals. You can make this into a recommendation report by drawing conclusions and making recommendations. One conclusion that you could draw relates to success in this career area. Who might be successful in this field?

Related Web Site: The government's premier career reference book on occupations and tomorrow's job market is available on-line at <http://stats.bls.gov/ocohome.htm>.

10.4 Recommendation Report: Retaining Employees. An employer for whom you worked last year regarded you highly. Although you are no longer employed there, this individual called to ask your candid opinion on how to retain employees. He is concerned about the high rate of turnover. What advice can you offer? How do similar businesses recruit and retain their employees?

Critical
Thinking

Your Task. Using actual experiences, write a recommendation report with your suggestions for retaining employees. Use letter format and organize your remarks under a number of descriptive headings, such as *Problem, Possible Causes, Suggestions for Retaining Staff.*

10.5 Recommendation Report: Expanding the Company Library. Despite the interest in on-line publications, managers and employees at your company still like to browse through magazines in the company library. Bonnie Finley, the company librarian, wants to add business periodicals to the library subscription list and has requested help from various company divisions.

Critical
Thinking

Your Task. You've been asked to recommend four periodicals in your particular specialty (accounting, marketing, or whatever). Visit your library and use appropriate indexes and guides to select four periodicals to recommend. Write a memo report to Ms. Finley describing the particular readership, usual contents, and scope of each periodical. To judge each adequately, you should examine several issues. Explain why you think each periodical should be ordered and who would read it. Convince the librarian that your choices would be beneficial to your department.

10.6 Justification Report: Evaluating Your Curriculum. You have been serving as a student member of a college curriculum advisement committee. The committee is expected to examine the course requirements for a degree or certificate in your major.

Team

Your Task. In teams of three to five, decide whether the requirements are realistic and practical. What improvements can your team suggest? Interview other students and faculty members for their suggestions. Prepare a justification report in letter or memo format to send to the dean of your college proposing your suggestions. You anticipate that the dean may need to be persuaded to make any changes. Consider delaying your recommendations until after you have developed a foundation of explanation and reasons.

10.7 Justification Report: Purchasing New Equipment. In your work or your training, identify equipment that needs to be purchased or replaced (computer, printer, modem, VCR, copier, digital camera, etc.). Gather information about two different models or brands.

Your Task. Write a justification report comparing the two items. Establish a context by describing the need for the equipment. Discuss the present situation, emphasizing the current deficiencies. Describe the advantages of acquiring the new equipment.

10.8 Progress Report: Making Headway Toward Your Degree. You made an agreement with your parents (or spouse, relative, or significant friend) that you would submit a progress report at this time describing headway toward your educational goal (employment, certificate, or degree).

Your Task. In memo format write a progress report that fulfills your promise to describe your progress toward your educational goals. Address your progress report to your parents, spouse, relative, or significant friend. In your memo (1) describe your goal; (2) summarize the work you have completed thus far; (3) discuss thoroughly the work currently in progress, including your successes and anticipated obstacles; and (4) forecast your future activities in relation to your scheduled completion date.

10.9 Minutes: Recording the Proceedings of a Meeting. Attend an open meeting of an organization at your school or elsewhere. Assume that you are asked to record the proceedings.

Your Task. Record the meeting proceedings in formal or informal minutes. Review the chapter to be sure you include all the data necessary for minutes. Focus on motions, votes, decisions reached, and action taken.

10.10 Summary: Condensing an Article About E-Mail Privacy. Your boss is worried because the company has no formal e-mail policy. Should employees be allowed to use e-mail for personal messages? May management monitor the messages of employees? He asks you to research this topic (or another topic on which you and your instructor agree).

Your Task. Find a good article (at least 1,000 words) in a magazine, journal, or electronic database. In a one- or two-page memo, summarize the major points of the article. Evaluate the strengths and weaknesses of the article. Address your memo summary to Justin Bridges, division manager.

10.11 To-File Report: Remembering a Decision. You just saw the vice president of operations in the hall and reminded him that your department needs a new copier. He told you to go ahead and get estimates from three sources. You know what a faulty memory he has, and you don't want him to forget or renege on this decision.

Your Task. Write a to-file report addressed to Vice President A. M. Miller. Be careful of the tone. Don't sound as if you are badgering.

10.12 Longer Report: Solving a Problem. Choose a business or organization with which you are familiar and identify a problem such as sloppy workmanship, indifferent service, poor attendance at organization meetings, uninspired cafeteria food, antique office equipment, arrogant management, lack of communication, underappreciated employees, wasteful procedures, or a similar problem.

Your Task. Describe the problem in detail. Assume you are to report to management (or to the leadership of an organization) about the nature and scope of the problem. Decide which kind of report to prepare (information, recommendation, justification), and choose the format. Naturally, you will gather data from reputable sources to lend authority to your conclusions and recommendations. Determine the exact topic and report length after consultation with your instructor.

Web **10.13 Code of Ethics for Ruby's Natural by Nature.** You and another recent graduate were hired by Ruby's Natural by Nature, a small premium ice cream company in Brooklyn, New York. It makes terrific ice cream that contains no pesticides, hormones, or antibodies and is certified to be organic. Your boss, Ruby Fowler, not only wants to produce wholesome ice cream products, but she also wants to ensure that her company and employees act ethically.

She thinks that Ruby's Natural by Nature needs some kind of code of ethics, credo, or mission statement. She asks you and your partner to search the Web for anything you can find that might help her write a code, credo, or mission statement for the company. She is most interested, of course, in companies that are in the food industry. You immediately think of Ben & Jerry's, which probably has a code of ethics or mission statement since social responsibility is high on its list of priorities.

Your Task. Use one or two search engines to look for codes of ethics. Print three or four codes, credos, or mission statements. Individually or as a team, write an information report in memo format to CEO Ruby Fowler summarizing the topics covered in the codes. Be sure to include the Web addresses of the codes you cite.

Related Web Sites: To find the Web site addresses of many well-known companies, search the database of Hoovers <hoovers.com>. For a selected list of corporate codes of ethics, try "Business Ethics Resources on WWW" <www.ethics.ubc.ca/resources>.

10.14 Connecting With E-mail: Progress Report. If you are working on a long report for either this chapter or Chapter 11, keep your instructor informed of your progress.

Your Task. Send your instructor a report detailing the progress you are making on your long report assignment. Discuss (1) the purpose of the report, (2) the work already completed, (3) the work currently in progress, and (4) your schedule for completing the report.

Grammar/Mechanics Checkup—10

Possessives

Review Sections 2.20–2.22 in the Grammar/Mechanics Handbook. Then study each of the following statements. Underscore any inappropriate form. Write a correction in the space provided, and record the number of the G/M principle(s) illustrated. If a sentence is correct, write C. When you finish, compare your responses with those at the back of the book. If your answers differ, study carefully the principles shown in parentheses.

Example:	In just two <u>years</u> time, the accountants and managers devised an entirely new system.	years'	(2.20b)

1. Two supervisors said that Mr. Wilsons work was excellent. _____
2. In less than a years time, the offices of both attorneys were moved. _____
3. None of the employees in our Electronics Department had taken more than two weeks vacation. _____
4. All the secretaries agreed that Ms. Lanhams suggestions were practicable. _____
5. After you obtain your boss approval, send the application to Human Resources. _____
6. We tried to sit at our favorite waitress station, but all her tables were filled. _____
7. Despite Kevin grumbling, his wife selected two bonds and three stocks for her investments. _____
8. The apartment owner requires two months rent in advance from all applicants. _____
9. Four companies buildings were damaged in the fire. _____
10. In one months time we hope to be able to complete all the address files. _____
11. Only one ladies car had its engine running. _____
12. One secretaries desk will have to be moved to make way for the computer. _____

_____ 13. Several sellers permits were issued for two years.

14. Marks salary was somewhat higher than David.

_____ 15. Lisas job in accounts receivable ends in two months.

The following sentences contain errors in grammar, punctuation, capitalization, number style, usage, and spelling. Pay special attention to eliminating expletives (*there is, there are*). Below each sentence write a corrected version.

Example: There were 2 employees who volunteered to head the united way campaign.
Revision: Two employees volunteered to head the United Way campaign.

1. There are three Vice Presidents who report directly to the company President.

2. Although the meeting was first scheduled for May 2nd its been rescheduled for May 10th.

3. As a matter of fact there are figures that suggest that a medium size dog costs exactly six thousand four hundred dollars to raise for eleven years.

4. There were exhibitors at the Trade Show, who came from as far as australia and japan, to promote there products.

5. If there have been many customers who are complaining we must revamp delivery schedules.

6. Would you please remove the charge of 78 dollars from my July statement?

7. "Large companies," says Ted Stank professor of transportation at iowa state university "are looking for ways to shrink shipping costs.

8. There were 25 Kodak Cameras awarded as prizes at the end of the year awards' ceremony.

9. Because there are so many midwesterners and northerners who flock to florida the price of rental units inflates in the winter.

10. After traveling north on highway 101 exit at paradise valley road, and follow the signs to vista parkway estates.

11. In north america thirty-eight percent of the land is wilderness, however in africa only twenty-eight percent is wilderness.

12. On december 21st did we pay forty-two dollars a share to acquire 1/4th of the stocks in biogenetics, inc.

13. By eliminating 1 olive from each salad served in the first class section american airlines saved forty thousand dollars.

14. There are many foreign language software programs that we stock including: russian, chinese, japanese, and dutch programs.

15. There is no national football league team that plays it's home games in a domed stadium that have ever won a superbowl.

Grammar/Mechanics Challenge—10

Document for Revision

The following progress report has faults in grammar, punctuation, spelling, number form, wordiness, and word use. Use standard proofreading marks (see Appendix B) to correct the errors. When you finish, your instructor can show you the revised version of this report.

TO:	Jon Peterson	DATE:	January 6, 200X
	Executive Producer		

FROM: Tiffany Taylor-Payton   *TTP*

Location Manager

SUBJECT: SITE FOR "REDWOOD BAY" TELEFILM

This memo describes the progress of my exploration for an appropriate rustic home, villa or ranch to be used in connection with the wine country sequences in the telefilm "Redwood Bay".

Work Completed: To prepare for this assignment several sites in the Russian River area were visited. Possible locations include turn of the century estates, victorian mansions and rustic farmhouses. One acceptional cite is the country meadow inn a 97 year old farmhouse nestled amoung vine yards with a breath taking view of vallies, redwoods, and distant mountains.

Work To Be Completed: In the next 5 days I'll search the sonoma county countryside including winerys at Korbel, Field Stone, and Napa. Many old winerys contain charming structures that may present exactly the degree of atmosphere and mystery we seek, these winerys have the added advantage of easy acess.

My final report in regards to the 3 most promising locations are nearly completed. You will in all probability be able to visit these cites January 21st.

Laying the Groundwork for Team Writing Projects

The chances are that you can look forward to some kind of team writing in your future career. You may collaborate voluntarily (seeking advice and differing perspectives) or involuntarily (through necessity or by assignment). Working with other people can be frustrating, particularly when some team members don't carry their weight or when conflict breaks out. Team projects, though, can be harmonious and productive when members establish ground rules at the outset and adhere to guidelines such as the following.

Preparing to Work Together. Before you discuss the project, talk about how your group will function.

- Limit the size of your team, if possible, to three or four members. Larger groups have more difficulties. An odd number is usually preferable to avoid ties in voting.

- Name a meeting leader (to plan and conduct meetings), a recorder (to keep a record of group decisions), and an evaluator (to determine if the group is on target and meeting its goals).

- Decide whether your team will be governed by consensus (everyone must agree) or by majority rule.

- Compare schedules of team members, and set up the best meeting times. Plan to meet often. Avoid other responsibilities during meetings.

- Discuss the value of conflict. By bringing conflict into the open and encouraging confrontation, your team can prevent personal resentment and group dysfunction. Confrontation can actually create better final documents by promoting new ideas and avoiding "group think."

- Discuss how you will deal with members who are not pulling their share of the load.

Planning the Document. Once you've established ground rules, you're ready to discuss the project and resulting document. Be sure to keep a record of the decisions your team makes.

- Establish the document's specific purpose and identify the main issues involved.

- Decide on the final form of the document. What parts will it have?

- Discuss the audience(s) for the document and what appeal would help it achieve its purpose.

- Develop a work plan. Assign jobs. Set deadlines.

- Decide how the final document will be written: individuals working separately on assigned portions, one person writing the first draft, the entire group writing the complete document together, or some other method.

Collecting Information. The following suggestions help teams gather accurate information:

- Brainstorm for ideas as a group.
- Decide who will be responsible for gathering what information.
- Establish deadlines for collecting information.
- Discuss ways to ensure the accuracy of the information collected.

Organizing, Writing, and Revising. As the project progresses, your team may wish to modify some of its earlier decisions.

- Review the proposed organization of your final document, and adjust it if necessary.
- Write the first draft. If separate team members are writing segments, they should use the same word processing program to facilitate combining files.
- Meet to discuss and revise the draft(s).
- If individuals are working on separate parts, appoint one person (probably the best writer) to coordinate all the parts, striving for consistent style and format.

Editing and Evaluating. Before the document is submitted, complete these steps:

- Give one person responsibility for finding and correcting grammatical and mechanical errors.
- Meet as a group to evaluate the final document. Does it fulfill its purpose and meet the needs of the audience?

Career Application

Select a report topic from this chapter or Chapter 11. Assume that you must prepare the report as a team project. If you are working on a long report, your instructor may ask you to prepare individual progress reports as you develop your topic.

Your Task

- Form teams of three to five members.
- Prepare to work together by using the suggestions provided here.
- Plan your report by establishing its purpose, identifying the main issues, developing a work plan, and assigning tasks.
- Collect information, organize the data, and write the first draft.
- Decide how the document will be revised, edited, and evaluated.

Your instructor may assign grades not only on the final report but also on your team effectiveness and your individual contribution, as determined by fellow team members.

11 Proposals and Formal Reports

Today, more than ever, success in business requires knowing how to write powerful, persuasive proposals and reports. From large corporations to the smallest entrepreneurial operations, businesspeople are demanding proposals so that they can compare apples to apples.[1]

THOMAS SANT, *consultant and author of over $11 billion worth of business reports and proposals*

LEARNING OBJECTIVES

1. Identify and explain the parts of informal and formal proposals.

2. Describe the preparatory steps for writing a formal report.

3. Collect data from secondary sources including print and electronic sources.

4. Understand how to use Web browsers and search engines to locate reliable data.

5. Discuss how to generate primary data from surveys, interviews, observation, and experimentation.

6. Understand the need for accurate documentation of data.

7. Describe how to organize report data, create an outline, and make effective titles.

8. Illustrate data using tables, charts, and graphs.

9. Sequence 13 parts of a formal report.

Proposals are persuasive offers to solve problems, provide services, or sell equipment.

Proposals are written offers to solve problems, provide services, or sell equipment. Let's say that sports shoe manufacturer Nike wants to upgrade the computers and software in its human resources department. If it knows exactly what it wants, it would prepare a request for proposals (RFP) specifying its requirements. It then publicizes this RFP, and companies interested in bidding on the job submit proposals. Both large and small companies, as proposal consultant Tom Sant says, are increasingly likely to use RFPs to solicit competitive bids on their projects. This enables them to compare "apples to apples." That is, they can compare prices from different companies on their projects. They also want the legal protection offered by proposals, which are legal contracts.

Many companies earn a sizable portion of their income from sales resulting from proposals. That's why creating effective proposals is especially important today. In writing proposals, the most important thing to remember is that proposals are sales presentations. They must be persuasive, not merely mechanical descriptions of what you can do. You may recall from Chapter 8 that effective persuasive sales messages (1) emphasize benefits for the reader, (2) "toot your horn" by detailing your expertise and accomplishments, and (3) make it easy for the reader to understand and respond.

Both large and small companies today often use requests for proposals (RFPs) to solicit competitive bids on projects.

Informal Proposals

Proposals may be informal or formal; they differ primarily in length and format. Informal proposals are often presented in two- to four-page letters. Sometimes called letter proposals, they contain six principal parts: introduction, background, proposal, staffing, budget, and authorization. The informal letter proposal shown in Figure 11.1 illustrates all six parts of a letter proposal. This proposal is addressed to a Logan, Utah, dentist who wants to improve patient satisfaction.

Informal proposals may contain an introduction, background information, the proposal, staffing requirements, a budget, and an authorization request.

Introduction

Most proposals begin by explaining briefly the reasons for the proposal and by highlighting the writer's qualifications. To make your introduction more persuasive, you need to provide a "hook" to capture the reader's interest. One proposal expert suggests these possibilities:[2]

- Hint at extraordinary results with details to be revealed shortly.
- Promise low costs or speedy results.
- Mention a remarkable resource (well-known authority, new computer program, well-trained staff) available exclusively to you.
- Identify a serious problem (worry item) and promise a solution, to be explained later.
- Specify a key issue or benefit that you feel is the heart of the proposal.

Effective proposal openers "hook" readers by promising extraordinary results or resources or by identifying key benefits, issues, or outcomes.

For example, Dana Swensen, in the introduction of the proposal shown in Figure 11.1, focused on a key benefit. In this proposal to conduct a patient satisfaction survey, Dana thought that the client, Dr. Peters, would be most interested in specific recommendations for improving service to his patients. But Dana didn't hit on this hook until after the first draft had been written. Indeed, it's often a good idea to put off writing the introduction to a proposal until after you have completed other parts. For longer proposals the introduction also describes the scope and limitations of the project, as well as outlining the organization of the material to come.

Background, Problem, Purpose

The background section identifies the problem and discusses the goals or purposes of the project. Your aim is to convince the reader that you understand the problem completely. Thus, if you are responding to an RFP, this means repeating its language. For example, if the RFP asks for the *design of a maintenance program for high-speed mail-sorting equipment,* you would use the same language in explaining the purpose of your proposal. This section might include segments entitled *Basic Requirements, Most Critical Tasks,* and *Most Important Secondary Problems.*

FIGURE 11.1 Informal Proposal

SWENSEN RESEARCH ASSOCIATES

One Providence Plaza
Ogden, Utah 84404
(801) 628-3011

May 15, 200X

Dr. Michael Peters
1789 Clarkston Avenue
Logan, UT 84322

Dear Dr. Peters:

Grabs attention with "hook" that focuses on key benefit

Helping you improve your practice is of the highest priority to us at Swensen Research Associates. We are pleased to submit the following proposal outlining our plan to help you more effectively meet your patient's needs by analyzing their views about your practice.

Background and Goals

We understand that you have been incorporating a total quality management system in your practice. Although you have every reason to believe your patients are pleased with the service you provide, you would like to give them an opportunity to discuss what they like and possibly don't like about your service. Based on our conversations, we understand that you would like the patient surveys to allow you to do the following:

Identifies four goals of survey

- Determine the level of their satisfaction with you and your staff
- Elicit suggestions for improvement
- Learn more about how your patients discovered you
- Compare your "preferred" and "standard" patients

Proposed Plan

Announces heart of proposal

To help you achieve your goals, Swenson Research proposes the following plan:

Survey. A short but thorough questionnaire will probe the data you desire. This questionnaire will measure your patients' reactions to such elements as courtesy, professionalism, accuracy of billing, friendliness, and waiting time. After you approve it, the questionnaire will be sent to a carefully selected sample of 300 patients whom you have separated into groupings of "preferred" and "standard."

Divides total plan into logical segments for easy reading

Analysis. Survey data will be analyzed by demographic segments, such as patient type, age, and gender. Our experienced team of experts, using state-of-the-art computer systems and advanced statistical measures, will study the (1) degree of patient satisfaction, (2) reasons for satisfaction or dissatisfaction, and (3) relationship between your "preferred" and "standard" patients. Moreover, our team will give you specific suggestions for making patient visits more pleasant.

Report. You will receive a final report with the key findings outlined here. The report will include tables summarizing all responses categorized by "preferred" and "standard" clients. Our staff will also draw conclusions based on these findings.

Proposal, Plan, Schedule

The proposal section must give enough information to secure the contract but not so much detail that the services are not needed.

In the proposal section itself, you should discuss your plan for solving the problem. In some proposals this is tricky because you want to disclose enough of your plan to secure the contract without giving away so much information that your services aren't needed. Without specifics, though, your proposal has little chance, so you must decide how much to reveal. Tell what you propose to do and how it will benefit the reader. Remember, too, that a proposal is a sales presentation. Sell your methods, product, and "deliverables"—items that will be left with the client. In this section some writers specify how the project will be managed and how its progress will be audited. Most writers also include a schedule of activities or a timetable showing when events take place.

FIGURE 11.1 Continued

Dr. Michael Peters   Page 2   May 15, 200X

Schedule. With your approval, the following schedule has been arranged for your patient satisfaction survey:

Questionnaire development and mailing	June 1–16
Deadline for returning questionnaire	June 24
Data tabulation and processing	June 24–26
Completion of final report	July 1

Staffing

Swensen Research Associates is a nationally recognized, experienced research consulting firm specializing in survey investigation. I have assigned your customer satisfaction survey to Dr. Kelly Miller, our director of research. Dr. Miller was trained at Utah State University and has successfully supervised our research program for the past nine years. Before joining SRA, she was a marketing analyst with Procter & Gamble Company.

Assisting Dr. Miller will be a team headed by James Wilson, our vice president for operations. Mr. Wilson earned a bachelor's degree in computer science and a master's degree in marketing from the University of Michigan. Within our organization he supervises our computer-aided telephone interviewing (CAT) system and manages our 30-person professional interviewing staff.

Budget

	Estimated Hours	Rate	Total
Professional and administrative time			
Questionnaire development	3	$150/hr.	$ 450
Data processing and tabulation	16	50/hr.	800
Analysis of findings	15	150/hr.	2,250
Preparation of final report	5	150/hr.	750
Mailing costs			390
Total costs			$4,640

Authorization

Patient satisfaction is vital to the success of your practice. Our professionally designed and administered client survey will help you determine how best to meet the needs of your patients, thereby assuring the success of your practice. Specific results from your survey can be ready for you by July 1. Please sign the enclosed duplicate copy of this letter and return it to us with a retainer of $2,320 so that we may begin developing your survey immediately. The rates in this offer are in effect only until September 1. Thank you for giving us this chance to help you better serve your patients.

Sincerely,

Dana H. Swensen

Dana H. Swensen, President

DHS:pem
Enclosure

Uses past-tense verbs to show that work has already started on the project

Builds credibility by describing outstanding staff and facilities

Itemizes costs carefully because a proposal is a contract offer

Summarizes benefits, makes response easy, and provides deadline

Staffing

The staffing section of a proposal describes the credentials and expertise of the project leaders. It may also identify the size and qualifications of the support staff, along with other resources such as computer facilities and special programs for analyzing statistics. In longer proposals, résumés of key people may be provided. The staffing or personnel section is a good place to endorse and promote your staff.

Budget

A central item in most proposals is the budget, a list of project costs. You need to prepare this section carefully because it represents a contract; you can't raise

www.grantland.net

Because a proposal is a legal contract, the budget must be researched carefully.

the price later—even if your costs increase. You can—and should—protect yourself with a deadline for acceptance. In the budget section some writers itemize hours and costs; others present a total sum only. A proposal to install a complex computer system might, for example, contain a detailed line-by-line budget. In the proposal shown in Figure 11.1, Dana Swensen felt that she needed to justify the budget for her firm's patient satisfaction survey, so she itemized the costs. But the budget included for a proposal to conduct a one-day seminar to improve employee communication skills might be a lump sum only. Your analysis of the project will help you decide what kind of budget to prepare.

Authorization

Informal proposals often close with a request for approval or authorization. In addition, the closing should remind the reader of key benefits and motivate action. It might also include a deadline date beyond which the offer is invalid. At some companies, such as Hewlett-Packard, authorization to proceed is not part of the proposal. Instead, it is usually discussed after the customer has received the proposal. In this way the customer and the sales account manager are able to negotiate terms before a formal agreement is drawn.

Formal Proposals

Formal proposals respond to big projects and may contain 200 or more pages.

Formal proposals differ from informal proposals not in style but in size and format. Formal proposals respond to big projects and may range from 5 to 200 or more pages. To facilitate comprehension and reference, they are organized into many parts. In addition to the six basic parts just described, formal proposals contain some or all of the following additional parts: copy of the RFP, letter of transmittal, abstract and/or executive summary, title page, table of contents, figures, and appendix.

Well-written proposals win contracts and business for companies and individuals. In fact, many companies depend entirely on proposals to generate their income. Companies such as Microsoft, Hewlett-Packard, and IBM employ staffs of people that do nothing but prepare proposals to compete for new business. For more information about industry standards and resources, visit the Web site of the Association of Proposal Management Professionals <www.apmp.org>.

Preparing to Write Formal Reports

Formal reports, whether they offer only information or whether they also analyze that information and make recommendations, typically have three characteristics: formal tone, traditional structure, and length. Although formal research reports in business are seen infrequently, they serve a very important function. They provide management with vital data for decision making. In this section we will consider the entire process of writing a formal report: preparing to write; collecting, documenting, organizing, and illustrating data; and presenting the final report.

Like proposals and informal reports, formal reports begin with a definition of the project. Probably the most difficult part of this definition is limiting the scope of the report. Every project has limitations. Decide at the outset what constraints influence the range of your project and how you will achieve your purpose. How much time do you have for completing your report? How much space will you be allowed for reporting on your topic? How accessible are the data you need? How thorough should your research be?

If you are writing about low morale among swing-shift employees, for example, how many of your 475 employees should you interview? Should you limit your research to company-related morale factors, or should you consider external factors over which the company has no control? In investigating variable-rate mortgages, should you focus on a particular group, such as first-time homeowners in a specific area, or should you consider all mortgage holders? The first step in writing a report, then, is determining the precise boundaries of the topic.

Once you have defined the project and limited its scope, write a statement of purpose. The statement of purpose should describe the goal, significance, and limitations of the report. Notice how the following statement pinpoints the research and report:

> The purpose of this report is to explore employment possibilities for entry-level paralegal workers in the city of San Francisco. It will consider typical salaries, skills required, opportunities, and working conditions. This research is significant because of the increasing number of job openings in the paralegal field. This report will not consider legal secretarial employment, which represents a different employment focus.

The primary differences between formal and informal reports are tone, structure, and length.

The planning of every report begins with a statement of purpose explaining the goal, significance, and limitations of the report.

Researching Secondary Data

One of the most important steps in the process of writing a report is that of research. Because a report is only as good as its data, you'll want to spend considerable time collecting data before you begin writing.

Data fall into two broad categories, primary and secondary. Primary data result from firsthand experience and observation. Secondary data come from reading what others have experienced and observed. Coca-Cola and Pepsi-Cola, for example, produce primary data when they stage taste tests and record the reactions of consumers. These same sets of data become secondary after they have been published and, let's say, a newspaper reporter uses them in an article about soft drinks. Secondary data are easier and cheaper to develop than primary data, which might involve interviewing large groups or sending out questionnaires.

You're going to learn first about secondary data because that's where nearly every research project should begin. Often, something has already been written about your topic. Reviewing secondary sources can save time and effort and prevent you from "reinventing the wheel." Most secondary material is available either in print or electronically.

Primary data come from firsthand experience and observation; secondary data, from reading.

Print Resources

Although we're seeing a steady movement away from print to electronic data, much information is available only in print.

> Although researchers are increasingly turning to electronic data, much data is available only in print.

If you are an infrequent library user, begin your research by talking with a reference librarian about your project. These librarians won't do your research for you, but they will steer you in the right direction. And they are very accommodating. Several years ago a *Wall Street Journal* poll revealed that librarians are among the friendliest, most approachable people in the working world. Many libraries help you understand their computer, cataloging, and retrieval systems by providing brochures, handouts, and workshops.

> Books provide historical, in-depth data; periodicals provide limited but current coverage.

Books. Although quickly outdated, books provide excellent historical, in-depth data on subjects. Books can be located through print catalogs or on-line catalogs. Most automated systems today enable you to learn not only whether a book is in the library but also whether it is currently available.

Periodicals. Magazines, pamphlets, and journals are called *periodicals* because of their recurrent or periodic publication. Journals, by the way, are compilations of scholarly articles. Articles in journals and other periodicals will be extremely useful to you because they are concise, limited in scope, current, and can supplement information in books.

Print, CD-ROM, and Web-based Bibliographic Indexes. *The Readers' Guide to Periodical Literature* is a valuable index of general-interest magazine article titles. It includes such magazines as *Time, Newsweek, The New Yorker,* and *U.S. News & World Report.* More useful to business writers, though, will be the titles of articles appearing in business and industrial magazines (such as *Forbes, Fortune,* and *Business Week*). For an index of these publications, consult the *Business Periodicals Index.* Most indexes today are available in print, CD-ROM, and Web versions for easy searching.

Electronic Databases

As a writer of business reports today, you will probably begin your secondary research with electronic resources. Most writers turn to them first because they are fast, cheap, and easy to use. Some are even accessible from remote locations. This means that you can conduct detailed searches without ever leaving your office, home, or dorm room. Although some databases are still offered on CD-ROM, information is increasingly available in on-line databases. They have become the staple of secondary research.

> Most researchers today begin by looking in electronic databases.

> A database stores information so that it is accessible by computer and digitally searchable.

A database is a collection of information stored electronically so that it is accessible by computer and digitally searchable. Databases provide both bibliographic (titles of documents and brief abstracts) and full-text documents. Most researchers prefer full-text documents. Various databases contain a rich array of magazine, newspaper, and journal articles, as well as newsletters, business reports, company profiles, government data, reviews, and directories.

The Internet

The best-known area of the Internet is the World Wide Web. Growing at a dizzying pace, the Web includes an enormous collection of specially formatted documents called Web pages located at Web sites around the world. Web offerings include on-line databases, magazines, newspapers, library resources, job and résumé banks, sound and video files, and many other information resources. Creators of Web pages use a special system of codes (HTML, i.e., Hypertext Markup

> The World Wide Web is a collection of hypertext pages that offer information and links.

Language) to format their offerings. The crucial feature of these hypertext pages is their use of links to other Web pages. Links are identified by underlined words and phrases or, occasionally, images. When clicked, links connect you to related Web pages. These pages immediately download to your computer screen, thus creating a vast web of resources at your fingertips.

Web Opportunities and Challenges. To a business researcher, the Web offers a wide range of organizational information. You can expect to find such items as product facts, public relations material, mission statements, staff directories, press releases, current company news, government information, selected article reprints, collaborative scientific project reports, and employment information. The Web is unquestionably one of the greatest sources of information now available to anyone needing facts quickly and inexpensively. But the information is not always reliable. Check out the Communication Workshop at the end of this chapter to learn more about sorting the legitimate sites from the hoaxes and hucksters.

In addition to being uneven, information on the Web can be frustrating and time-consuming to locate. The constantly changing contents of the Web and its lack of organization make it more problematic for research than searching commercial databases. Moreover, the quality of Web content is often questionable. You'll learn more about evaluating Web sources shortly.

Web Browsers and URLs. Searching the Web requires a Web browser, such as Netscape Navigator or Microsoft Internet Explorer. Browsers are software programs that enable you to view the graphics and text of, as well as access links to, Web pages. To locate the Web page of a specific organization, you need its URL (Uniform Resource Locator). URLs are case and space sensitive, so be sure to type the address exactly as it is printed. For most companies, the URL is http://www.xyzcompany.com (Tip: You can save some keystrokes by omitting "http://"; this portion of the URL is usually unnecessary.) Your goal is to locate the top-level Web page of an organization's site. On this page you'll generally find an overview of the site contents or a link to a site map. If you can't guess a company's URL, you can usually find it quickly at Hoover's **<www.hoovers.com>**.

> Web browsers are software programs that access Web pages and their links.

Search Tools. Finding what you are looking for on the Web is like searching for a library book without using the card catalog. Fortunately, a number of search tools—such as Yahoo!, AltaVista, and HotBot—are available at specialized Web sites. These search tools look up words in their indexes. But because of the vastness of the Web, many Web pages are not indexed. Even though search tools don't survey everything that's out there on the Web, they usually turn up more information than you want.

> Search tools such as Yahoo!, AltaVista, and HotBot help you locate specific Web sites and information.

Like everything else about the Web, search tools are constantly evolving as developers change their features to attract more users. Check the Guffey Web site **<www.westwords.com/guffey/students.html>** to find links to up-to-date reviews of search engines. And always read the help sections of any search engine when you first use it.

Dumb as Rocks? Internet Search Tips and Techniques. "Search engines are dumber than a box of rocks," claims one Web veteran. For example, he says, "If you ask one to look up *bathing suits,* it will find sites on *bathing* and on *suits,*"[3] but not necessarily on the combined concept of *bathing suits.* The researcher must enclose the phrase in quotation marks so that the search engine will look for the words together. Knowing how to use search engines can transform that dumb box of rocks into a jewel case bulging with gems of useful information. Here are a few tips to make you a savvy Internet researcher:[4]

> You must know how to use search engines to make them most effective.

- **Use two or three search tools.** Different Internet search engines turn up different results. One expert wisely observed: "Every search engine will give you good results some of the time. Every search engine will give you surprisingly bad results some of the time. No search engine will give you good results all of the time."[5]

- **Understand case sensitivity.** Generally use lowercase for your searches, unless you are searching for a term that is typically written in upper- and lowercase, such as a person's name.

- **Understand the AND/OR default and quotation marks.** When searching for a phrase, such as *cost benefit analysis,* most search tools will retrieve documents having all or some of the terms. This AND/OR strategy is the default of most search tools. To locate occurrences of the complete phrase, enclose it in quotation marks.

- **Prefer uncommon words.** Commonly used words make poor search keywords. For example, instead of *keeping employees,* use *employee retention.*

- **Omit articles and prepositions.** These are known as "stop words," and they do not add value to a search. Instead of *request for proposal,* use *proposal request.*

- **Use wild cards.** Most search engines support wild cards, such as asterisks. For example, the search term *cent** will retrieve *cents,* while *cent*** will retrieve both *center* and *centre.*

- **Know your search tool.** When connecting to a search service for the first time, always read the description of its service, including its FAQs (Frequently Asked Questions), Help, and How to Search sections.

"Wow! Bookmark this site!"

- **Bookmark the best.** To keep better track of your favorite Internet sites, save them on your browser as bookmarks.

- **Be persistent.** If a search produces no results, check your spelling. Try synonyms and variations on words. Try to be less specific in your search term. If your search produces too many hits, try to be more specific. Think of words that uniquely identify what you're looking for. And use as many relevant keywords as possible. Repeat your search a few days later.

Chapter 11 Proposals and Formal Reports

Although you'll begin a business report by probing for secondary data, you'll probably need primary data to give a complete picture. Business reports that solve specific current problems typically rely on primary, firsthand data. If, for example, management wants to discover the cause of increased employee turnover in its Seattle office, it must investigate conditions in Seattle by collecting recent information. Providing answers to business problems often means generating primary data through surveys, interviews, observation, or experimentation.

Primary data come from firsthand experience.

Surveys

Surveys collect data from groups of people. When companies develop new products, for example, they often survey consumers to learn their needs. The advantages of surveys are that they gather data economically and efficiently. Mailed surveys reach big groups nearby or at great distances. Moreover, people responding to mailed surveys have time to consider their answers, thus improving the accuracy of the data.

Surveys yield efficient and economical primary data for reports.

Mailed surveys, of course, have disadvantages. Most of us rank them with junk mail, so response rates may be no higher than 10 percent. Furthermore, those who do respond may not represent an accurate sample of the overall population, thus invalidating generalizations from the group. Let's say, for example, that an insurance company sends out a survey questionnaire asking about provisions in a new policy. If only older people respond, the survey data cannot be used to generalize what people in other age groups might think. A final problem with surveys has to do with truthfulness. Some respondents exaggerate their incomes or distort other facts, thus causing the results to be unreliable. Nevertheless, surveys may be the best way to generate data for business and student reports.

Although mailed surveys may suffer low response rates, they are still useful in generating primary data.

Interviews

Some of the best report information, particularly on topics about which little has been written, comes from individuals. These individuals are usually experts or veterans in their fields. Consider both in-house and outside experts for business reports. Tapping these sources will call for in-person or telephone interviews. To elicit the most useful data, try these techniques:

Interviews with experts produce useful report data, especially when little has been written about a topic.

- **Locate an expert.** Ask managers and individuals working in an area whom they consider to be most knowledgeable. Check membership lists of professional organizations, and consult articles about the topic or related topics. Most people enjoy being experts or at least recommending them. You could also post an inquiry to an Internet newsgroup. An easy way to search newsgroups in a topic area is through Deja News **<www.deja.com>**.

- **Prepare for the interview.** Learn about the individual you're interviewing as well as the background and terminology of the topic. Let's say you're interviewing a corporate communication expert about producing an in-house newsletter. You ought to be familiar with terms such as *font* and software such as PhotoShop, PaintShop Pro, and Adobe Illustrator. In addition, be prepared by making a list of questions that pinpoint your focus on the topic. Ask the interviewee if you may record the talk.

- **Make your questions objective and friendly.** Don't get into a debating match with the interviewee. And remember that you're there to listen, not to talk! Use open-ended, rather than yes-or-no, questions to draw experts out.

- **Watch the time.** Tell interviewees in advance how much time you expect to need for the interview. Don't overstay your appointment.

- **End graciously.** Conclude the interview with a general question, such as, *Is there anything you'd like to add?* Express your appreciation, and ask permission to telephone later if you need to verify points.

Observation and Experimentation

Some of the best report data come from firsthand observation and investigation.

Some kinds of primary data can be obtained only through firsthand observation and investigation. How long does a typical caller wait before a customer service rep answers the call? How is a new piece of equipment operated? Are complaints of sexual harassment being taken seriously? Observation produces rich data, but that information is especially prone to charges of subjectivity. One can interpret an observation in many ways. Thus, to make observations more objective, try to quantify them. For example, record customer telephone wait-time for 60-minute periods at different times throughout a week. Or compare the number of sexual harassment complaints made with the number of investigations undertaken and resulting actions.

Experimentation produces data suggesting causes and effects. Informal experimentation might be as simple as a pretest and posttest in a college course. Did students expand their knowledge as a result of the course? More formal experimentation is undertaken by scientists and professional researchers who control variables to test their effects. Assume, for example, that the Hershey Company wants to test the hypothesis (which is a tentative assumption) that chocolate lifts people out of the doldrums. An experiment testing the hypothesis would separate depressed individuals into two groups: those who ate chocolate (the experimental group) and those who did not (the control group). What effect did chocolate have? Such experiments are not done haphazardly, however. Valid experiments require sophisticated research designs and careful attention to matching the experimental and control groups.

Documenting Data

Whether you collect data from primary or secondary sources, the data must be documented; that is, you must indicate where the data originated. Careful documentation in a report serves three purposes:

- **Strengthens your argument.** Including good data from reputable sources will convince readers of your credibility and the logic of your reasoning.
- **Protects you.** Acknowledging your sources keeps you honest. It's unethical and illegal to use others' ideas without proper documentation.
- **Instructs the reader.** Citing references enables readers to pursue a topic further and make use of the information themselves.

Using the ideas of someone else without giving credit is called plagiarism and is unethical. Even if you paraphrase (put the information in your own words), the ideas must be documented. You can learn more about documenting sources by studying the formal report in Figure 11.15 and by consulting Appendix C.

Citing Electronic Sources. Standards for researchers using electronic sources are still evolving. When citing electronic media, you should hold the same goals as for print sources. That is, you want to give credit to the authors and to allow others to locate the same or updated information easily. However, traditional formats for identifying authors, publication dates, and page numbers become confusing when applied to sources on the Internet. Strive to give correct credit for electronic sources by including the author's name (when available), document title, Web page title, access date, and Web address (in angle brackets). Here's an example of an Internet bibliographic citation:

Jacobson, Trudi and Laura Cohen. "Evaluating Internet Resources." University at Albany Libraries. Retrieved 13 January 2000 <http://www.albany.edu/library/internet/evaluate.html>

Formats for some electronic sources are shown in Appendix C. For more comprehensive electronic citation formats, visit the Guffey Web site.

Organizing and Outlining Data

Once you've collected the data for a report and recorded that information on notes or printouts, you're ready to organize it into a coherent plan of presentation. First, you should decide on an organizational strategy, and then you'll want to outline the report following your plan.

Organizational Strategies

The readability of a report is greatly enhanced by skillful organization of the facts presented. You have already studied numerous strategies or plans of organization for shorter documents. Here is a brief overview of possible plans for the organization of formal reports:

- **Deductive strategy.** As you recall from earlier instruction, the deductive strategy presents main ideas first. In formal reports that would mean beginning with proposals or recommendations. For example, if you were studying five possible locations for a proposed shopping center, you would begin with the recommendation of the best site and follow with a discussion of other sites. Use this strategy when the reader is supportive and knowledgeable.

- **Inductive strategy.** Inductive reasoning presents facts and discussion first, followed by conclusions and recommendations. Since formal reports generally seek to educate the reader, this order of presentation is often most effective. Following this sequence, a study of possible locations for a shopping center would begin with data regarding all proposed sites followed by analysis of the information and conclusions drawn from that analysis.

- **Chronological sequence.** Information sequenced along a time frame is arranged chronologically. This plan is effective for presenting historical data or for describing a procedure. A description of the development of a multinational company, for example, would be chronological. A report explaining how to obtain federal funding for a project might be organized chronologically. Often topics are arranged in a past-to-present or present-to-past sequence.

- **Geographical or spatial arrangement.** Information arranged geographically or spatially is organized by physical location. For instance, a report analyzing a company's national sales might be divided into sections representing different geographical areas such as the East, South, Midwest, West, and Northwest.

- **Topical or functional arrangement.** Some subjects lend themselves to arrangement by topic or function. A report analyzing changes in the management hierarchy of an organization might be arranged in this manner. First, the report would consider the duties of the CEO followed by the functions of the general manager, business manager, marketing manager, and so forth.

In organizing a formal report, you may find that you combine some of the preceding plans. However it's done, you must break your topic into major divisions,

The overall presentation of a topic may be inductive or deductive, while parts of the report may be chronological (such as the background) or topical (such as a discussion of findings).

FIGURE 11.2 Outline Format

```
                    FORMS OF BUSINESS OWNERSHIP

        I. Sole proprietorship (first main topic)
           A. Advantages of sole proprietorship (first subdivision of Topic I)
              1. Minimal capital requirements (first subdivision of Topic A)
              2. Control by owner (second subdivision of Topic A)
           B. Disadvantages of sole proprietorship (second subdivision of Topic I)
              1. Unlimited liability (first subdivision of Topic B)
              2. Limited management talent (second subdivision of Topic B)
       II. Partnership (second main topic)
           A. Advantages of partnership (first subdivision of Topic II)
              1. Access of capital (first subdivision of Topic A)
              2. Management talent (second subdivision of Topic A)
              3. Ease of formation (third subdivision of Topic A)
           B. Disadvantages of partnership (second subdivision of Topic II)
              1. Unlimited liability (first subdivision of Topic B)
              2. Personality conflicts (second subdivision of Topic B)
```

usually three to six. These major divisions then can be partitioned into smaller subdivisions. To identify these divisions, you may use functional heads (such as *Introduction, Findings, Discussion, Conclusions, Recommendations*) or talking heads that explain the contents of the text. You may want to review the suggestions for writing effective headings in Chapter 10, page 251.

Outlines and Headings

Most writers agree that the clearest way to show the organization of a report topic is by recording its divisions in an outline. Although the outline is not part of the final report, it is a valuable tool of the writer. It reveals at a glance the overall organization of the report. As you learned in Chapter 3, outlining involves dividing a topic into major sections and supporting those with details. Figure 11.2 shows an abbreviated outline of a report about forms of business ownership. Rarely is a real outline so perfectly balanced; some sections are usually longer than others. Remember, though, not to put a single topic under a major component. If you have only one subpoint, integrate it with the main item above it or reorganize. Use details, illustrations, and evidence to support subpoints.

The main points used to outline a report often become the main headings of the written report. In Chapter 10 you studied tips for writing talking and functional headings. Formatting those headings depends on what level they represent. Major headings, as you can see in Figure 11.3, are centered and typed in bold font. Second-level headings start at the left margin, and third-level headings are indented and become part of a paragraph.

Illustrating Data

Effective graphics clarify numerical data and simplify complex ideas.

Tables, charts, graphs, illustrations, and other visual aids can play an important role in clarifying, summarizing, and emphasizing information. Numerical data become meaningful, complex ideas are simplified, and visual interest is provided by the appropriate use of graphics. Here are general tips for making the most effective use of visual aids:

FIGURE 11.3 Levels of Headings in Reports

2-inch top margin

REPORT, CHAPTER, AND PART TITLES

2 blank lines

The title of a report, chapter heading, or major part (such as CONTENTS or NOTES) should be centered in all caps. If the title requires more than one line, arrange it in an inverted triangle with the longest lines at the top. Begin the text a triple space (two blank lines) below the title, as shown here.

2 blank lines

First-Level Subheading

1 blank line

Headings indicating the first level of division are centered and bolded. Capitalize the first letter of each main word. Whether a report is single-spaced or double-spaced, most typists triple-space (leaving two blank lines) before and double-space (leaving one blank line) after a first-level subheading.

1 blank line

Every level of heading should be followed by some text. For example, we could not jump from "First-Level Subheading," shown above, to "Second-Level Subheading," shown below, without some discussion between.

Good writers strive to develop coherency and fluency by ending most sections with a lead-in that introduces the next section. The lead-in consists of a sentence or two announcing the next topic.

2 blank lines

Second-Level Subheading

Headings that divide topics introduced by first-level subheadings are bolded and begin at the left margin. Use a triple space before and a double space after a second-level subheading. If a report has only one level of heading, use either first- or second-level subheading style.

Always be sure to divide topics into two or more subheadings. If you have only one subheading, eliminate it and absorb the discussion under the previous major heading. Try to make all headings within a level grammatically equal. For example, all second-level headings might use verb forms (*Preparing*, *Organizing*, and *Composing*) or noun forms (*Preparation*, *Organization*, and *Composition*).

1 blank line

Third-level subheading. Because it is part of the paragraph that follows, a third-level subheading is also called a "paragraph subheading." Capitalize only the first word and proper nouns in the subheading. Bold the subheading and end it with a period. Begin typing the paragraph text immediately following the period, as shown here. Double-space before a paragraph subheading.

Places major headings in the center. Capitalizes initial letters of main words

Starts at left margin

Makes heading part of paragraph

- Clearly identify the contents of the visual aid with meaningful titles and labels.
- Refer the reader to the visual aid by discussing it in the text and mentioning its location and figure number.
- Locate the visual aid close to its reference in the text.
- Strive for vertical placement of visual aids. Readers are disoriented by horizontal pages in reports.
- Give credit to the source if appropriate.

The tips presented here for generating and implementing graphics in formal reports are useful in other presentations as well.

Tables

Tables permit systematic presentation of large amounts of data, while charts enhance visual comparisons.

Probably the most frequently used visual aid in reports is the table. A table presents quantitative information in a systematic order of columns and rows. Here are tips for making good tables, one of which is illustrated in Figure 11.4:

- Provide clear heads for the rows and columns.
- Identify the units in which figures are given (percentages, dollars, units per worker hour, and so forth) in the table title, in the column or row head, with the first item in a column, or in a note at the bottom.
- Arrange items in a logical order (alphabetical, chronological, geographical, highest to lowest) depending on what you need to emphasize.
- Use *N/A* (not available) for missing data.
- Make long tables easier to read by shading alternate lines or by leaving a blank line after groups of five.

Bar Charts

Bar charts enable readers to compare related items, see changes over time, and understand how parts relate to a whole.

Although they lack the precision of tables, bar charts enable you to make emphatic visual comparisons. Bar charts can be used to compare related items, illustrate changes in data over time, and show segments as part of a whole. Figures 11.5 through 11.8 show vertical, horizontal, grouped, and segmented bar charts that highlight some of the data shown in the MPM Entertainment Company table (Figure 11.4). Note how the varied bar charts present information in different ways.

Many suggestions for tables also hold true for bar charts. Here are a few additional tips:

- Keep the length of each bar and segment proportional.
- Include a total figure in the middle of a bar or at its end if the figure helps the reader and does not clutter the chart.
- Start dollar or percentage amounts at zero.
- Avoid showing too much information, thus producing clutter and confusion.

FIGURE 11.4 Table Summarizing Precise Data

Figure 1
MPM ENTERTAINMENT COMPANY
Income by Division (in millions of dollars)

	Theme Parks	Motion Pictures	Video	Total
1997	$15.8	$39.3	$11.2	$66.3
1998	18.1	17.5	15.3	50.9
1999	23.8	21.1	22.7	67.6
2000	32.2	22.0	24.3	78.5
2001 (projected)	35.1	21.0	26.1	82.2

Source: *Industry Profiles* (New York: DataPro, 2000), 225.

FIGURE 11.5 Vertical Bar Chart

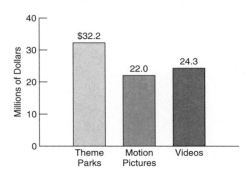

Figure 1
2000 MPM INCOME BY DIVISION

Source: *Industry Profiles* (New York: DataPro, 2000), 225.

FIGURE 11.6 Horizontal Bar Chart

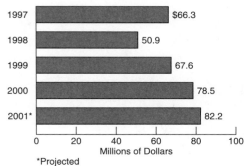

Figure 2
TOTAL MPM INCOME, 1997 TO 2001

*Projected
Source: *Industry Profiles*.

FIGURE 11.7 Grouped Bar Chart

Figure 3
**MPM INCOME BY DIVISION
1998, 1999, AND 2000**

* Projected
Source: *Industry Profiles*.

FIGURE 11.8 Segmented 100% Bar Chart

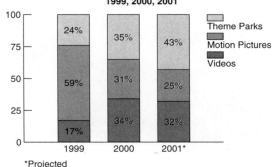

Figure 4
**PERCENTAGE OF TOTAL INCOME BY DIVISION
1999, 2000, 2001**

*Projected
Source: *Industry Profiles*.

Line Charts

The major advantage of line charts is that they show changes over time, thus indicating trends. Figures 11.9 through 11.11 show line charts that reflect income trends for the three divisions of MPM. Notice that line charts do not provide precise data, such as the 2000 MPM Videos income. Instead, they give an overview or impression of the data. Experienced report writers use tables to list exact data; they use line charts or bar charts to spotlight important points or trends.

Simple line charts (Figure 11.9) show just one variable. Multiple line charts combine several variables (Figure 11.10). Segmented line charts (Figure 11.11), also called surface charts, illustrate how the components of a whole change over time. Notice that Figure 11.11 helps you visualize the shift in total MPM income from motion pictures to videos and theme parks. By contrast, tables don't permit such visualization.

Here are tips for preparing line charts:

- Begin with a grid divided into squares.

- Arrange the time component (usually years) horizontally across the bottom; arrange values for the other variable vertically.

- Draw small dots at the intersections to indicate each value at a given year.

Line charts illustrate trends and changes in data over time.

FIGURE 11.9 Simple Line Chart

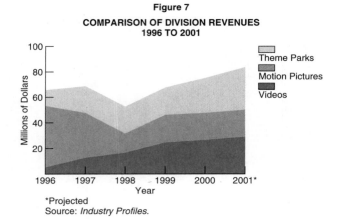

Figure 5
MOTION PICTURE REVENUES
1996 TO 2001

*Projected
Source: *Industry Profiles.*

FIGURE 11.10 Multiple Line Chart

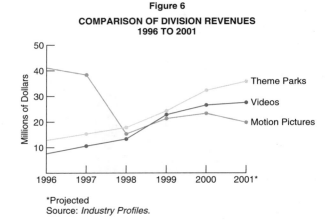

Figure 6
COMPARISON OF DIVISION REVENUES
1996 TO 2001

*Projected
Source: *Industry Profiles.*

FIGURE 11.11 Segmented Line (Surface) Chart

Figure 7
COMPARISON OF DIVISION REVENUES
1996 TO 2001

*Projected
Source: *Industry Profiles.*

FIGURE 11.12 Pie Chart

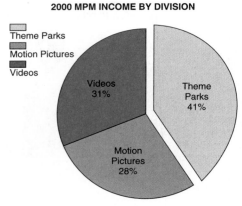

Figure 8
2000 MPM INCOME BY DIVISION

Source: *Industry Profiles.*

- Connect the dots and add color if desired.
- To prepare a segmented (surface) chart, plot the first value (say, video income) across the bottom; add the next item (say, motion picture income) to the first figures for every increment; for the third item (say, theme park income) add its value to the total of the first two items. The top line indicates the total of the three values.

Pie Charts

Pie charts are most useful in showing the proportion of parts to a whole.

Pie, or circle, charts enable readers to see a whole and the proportion of its components, or wedges. Although less flexible than bar or line charts, pie charts are useful in showing percentages, as Figure 11.12 illustrates. Notice that a wedge can be "exploded" or popped out for special emphasis, as seen in Figure 11.12. For the most effective pie charts, follow these suggestions:

- Begin at the 12 o'clock position, drawing the largest wedge first. (Computer software programs don't always observe this advice, but if you're drawing your own charts, you can.)

Chapter 11 Proposals and Formal Reports

- Include, if possible, the actual percentage or absolute value for each wedge.
- Use four to eight segments for best results; if necessary, group small portions into one wedge called "Other."
- Distinguish wedges with color, shading, or cross-hatching.
- Keep all labels horizontal.

Flow Charts

Procedures are simplified and clarified by diagramming them in a flow chart, as shown in Figure 11.13. Whether you need to describe the procedure for handling a customer's purchase order or outline steps in solving a problem, flow charts help the reader visualize the process. Traditional flow charts use the following symbols:

Flow charts use standard symbols to illustrate a process or procedure.

- Ovals to designate the beginning and end of a process
- Diamonds to denote decision points
- Rectangles to represent major activities or steps.

Organization Charts

Many large organizations are so complex that they need charts to show the chain of command, from the boss down to line managers and employees. The chart in Figure 11.14 defines the hierarchy of authority from the board of directors to individual managers.

Organization charts show the line of command and thus the flow of official communication from management to employees.

Using Your Computer to Produce Charts

Designing effective bar charts, pie charts, figures, and other graphics is easy with today's software. Spreadsheet programs—such as Lotus 1-2-3, Excel, and QuattroPro—as well as presentation graphics programs—such as Harvard Graphics and Microsoft PowerPoint—allow even nontechnical people to design

FIGURE 11.13 Flow Chart

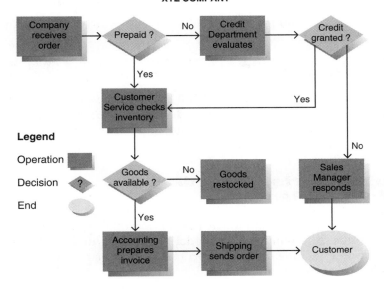

FLOW OF CUSTOMER ORDER THROUGH
XYZ COMPANY

Flow charts are useful for clarifying procedures.

FIGURE 11.14 Organization Chart

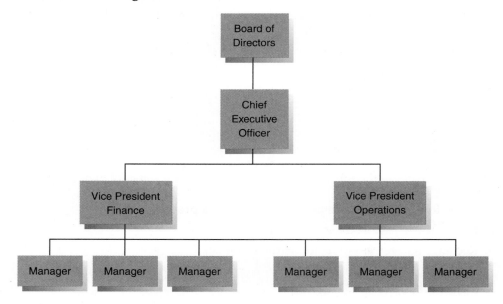

quality graphics. These graphics can be printed directly on paper for written reports or used for transparency masters and slides for oral presentations. The benefits of preparing visual aids on a computer are near-professional quality, shorter preparation time, and substantial cost savings. To prepare computer graphics, follow these steps:

- Assemble your data, usually in table form (such as that in Figure 11.4).
- Choose a chart type, such as a pie chart, grouped bar chart, vertical bar chart, horizontal bar chart, organization chart, or some other graphic.
- To make a pie chart, key in the data or select the data from an existing file.
- Add a title for the chart as well as any necessary labels.
- To make a bar or line chart, indicate the horizontal and vertical axes (reference lines or beginning points).
- Verify the legend, which your program may generate automatically.
- Print the final chart on paper or import into another program.

Presenting the Final Report

Long reports are generally organized into three major divisions: (1) prefatory parts, (2) body, and (3) supplementary parts. Following is a description of the order and content of each part. Refer to the model formal report in Figure 11.15 for illustrations of most of these parts.

Prefatory Parts (Preceding the Body of Report)

- **Title fly.** A single page with the title begins a formal report. In less formal reports, the title fly is omitted. Our model report does not include this optional part. Compose the title of your report carefully so that it shows immediately what the report covers and what it does not cover.

- **Title page.** In addition to the title, the title page shows the author, the individual or organization who authorized the report, the recipient of the report, and the date.

- **Letter of authorization.** If a letter or memo authorized the report, it may be included in the prefatory material. This optional part is omitted from the model in Figure 11.15.

- **Letter of transmittal.** This is the first impression the reader receives of the report; as such, it should be given serious consideration. Use the direct strategy and include some or all of the suggestions here:

  1. Deliver the report ("Here is the report you authorized").
  2. Present an overview of the report.
  3. Suggest how to read or interpret it.
  4. Describe limitations, if they exist.
  5. Acknowledge those who assisted you.
  6. Suggest follow-up studies, if appropriate.
  7. Express appreciation for the assignment.
  8. Offer to discuss the report personally.

  A letter or memo of transmittal presents an overview of the report, suggests how to read it, describes limitations, acknowledges assistance, and expresses appreciation.

- **Table of contents.** Identify the name and location of every part of the report except the title fly, title page, and table of contents itself. Use spaced periods (leaders) to join each part with its page number.

- **Executive summary, abstract, synopsis, or epitome.** A summary condensing the entire report may carry any of these names. This time-saving device summarizes the purpose, findings, and conclusions.

Body of Report

- **Introduction or background.** After the prefatory parts, begin the body of the report with an introduction that includes any or all of the following items:

  1. Explanation of how the report originated and why it was authorized
  2. Description of the problem that prompted the report and the specific research questions to be answered
  3. Purpose of the report
  4. Scope (boundaries) and limitations or restrictions of the research
  5. Sources and methods of collecting data
  6. Summary of findings, if the report is written deductively
  7. Preview of the major sections of the report to follow, thus providing coherence and transition for the reader

  The body of a report includes an introduction; discussion of findings; and summary, conclusions, or recommendations.

- **Discussion of findings.** This is the main section of the report and contains numerous headings and subheadings. It is unnecessary to use the title *Discussion of Findings*; many business report writers prefer to begin immediately with the major headings into which the body of the report is divided. As with short reports, you may organize the body deductively, inductively, chronologically, geographically, or topically. Present your findings objectively, avoiding the use of first-person pronouns (*I, we*). Include tables, charts, and graphs if necessary to illustrate findings. Analytic and scientific reports may include another section entitled *Implications of Findings*, in which the findings are analyzed and related to the problem. Less formal reports contain the author's analysis of the research findings within the *Discussion* section.

- **Summary, conclusions, recommendations.** If the report has been largely informational, it ends with a summary of the data presented. If the report analyzes research findings, then it ends with conclusions drawn from the analyses. An analytic report frequently poses research questions. The conclusion to such a report reviews the major findings and answers the research questions.

FIGURE 11.15 Model Formal Report

Title Page

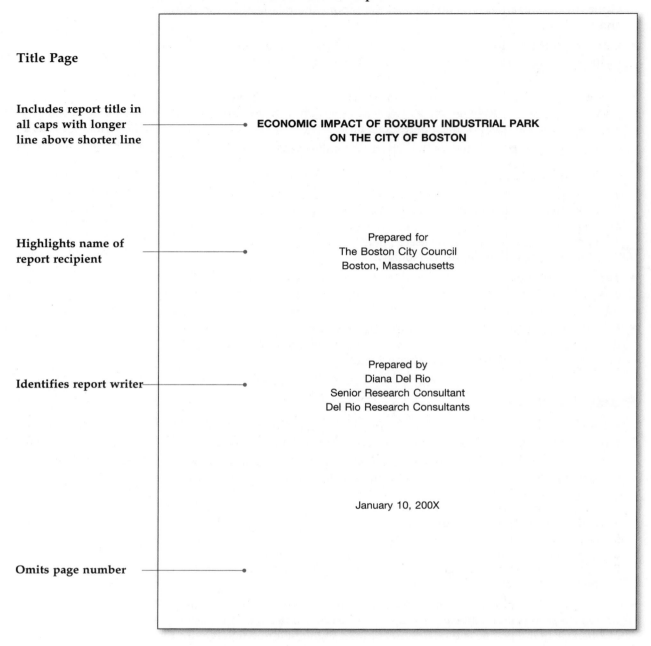

Includes report title in all caps with longer line above shorter line

ECONOMIC IMPACT OF ROXBURY INDUSTRIAL PARK ON THE CITY OF BOSTON

Highlights name of report recipient

Prepared for
The Boston City Council
Boston, Massachusetts

Identifies report writer

Prepared by
Diana Del Rio
Senior Research Consultant
Del Rio Research Consultants

January 10, 200X

Omits page number

The title page is usually arranged in four evenly balanced areas. If the report is to be bound on the left, move the left margin and center point ¼ inch to the right. Notice that no page number appears on the title page, although it is counted as page i. In designing the title page, be careful to avoid anything unprofessional—such as too many type fonts, italics, oversized print, and inappropriate graphics. Keep the title page simple and professional.

FIGURE 11.15 Continued

DEL RIO INDUSTRIAL CONSULTANTS

588 Park Avenue   www.delrio.com
Boston, Massachusetts 02116   (617) 549-1101

January 12, 200X

City Council
City of Boston
Boston, MA 02290

Dear Council Members:

The attached report, requested by the Boston City Council in a letter to Goldman-Lyon & Associates dated May 20, describes the economic impact of Roxbury Industrial Park on the city of Boston. We believe you will find the results of this study useful in evaluating future development of industrial parks within the city limits.

This study was designed to examine economic impact in three areas:

(1) Current and projected tax and other revenues accruing to the city from Roxbury Industrial Park

(2) Current and projected employment generated by the park

(3) Indirect effects on local employment, income, and economic growth

Primary research consisted of interviews with 15 Roxbury Industrial Park tenants and managers, in addition to a 2000 survey of over 5,000 RIP employees. Secondary research sources included the Annual Budget of the City of Boston, county and state tax records, government publications, periodicals, books, and on-line resources. Results of this research, discussed more fully in this report, indicate that Roxbury Industrial Park exerts a significant beneficial influence on the Boston metropolitan economy.

We would be pleased to discuss this report and its conclusions with you at your request. My firm and I thank you for your confidence in selecting our company to prepare this comprehensive report.

Sincerely,

Diana Del Rio

Diana Del Rio
Senior Research Consultant

DDR:mef
Attachment

Letter of Transmittal

Announces report and identifies authorization

Gives broad overview of report purposes

Describes primary and secondary research

Offers to discuss report; expresses appreciation

A letter or memo of transmittal announces the report topic and explains who authorized it. It describes the project briefly and previews the conclusions, if the reader is supportive. Such messages generally close by expressing appreciation for the assignment, suggesting follow-up actions, acknowledging the help of others, or offering to answer questions. The margins for the transmittal should be the same as for the report, about $1\frac{1}{4}$ inches on all sides.

FIGURE 11.15 Continued

Table of Contents and List of Figures

Uses leaders to guide eye from heading to page number

Indents secondary headings to show levels of outline

Includes tables and figures in one list for simplified numbering

Because the table of contents and the list of figures for this report are small, they are combined on one page. Notice that the titles of major report parts are in all caps, while other headings are a combination of upper- and lowercase letters. The style duplicates those within the report. Advanced word processing capabilities enable you to generate a contents page automatically, including leaders and accurate page numbering—no matter how many times you revise.

FIGURE 11.15 Executive Summary

EXECUTIVE SUMMARY

The city of Boston can benefit from the development of industrial parks like the Roxbury Industrial Park. Both direct and indirect economic benefits result, as shown by this in-depth study conducted by Del Rio Industrial Consultants. The study was authorized by the Boston City Council when Goldman-Lyon & Associates sought the City Council's approval for the proposed construction of a G-L industrial park. The City Council requested evidence demonstrating that an existing development could actually benefit the city.

Our conclusion that the city of Boston benefits from industrial parks is based on data supplied by a survey of 5,000 Roxbury Industrial Park employees, personal interviews with managers and tenants of RIP, city and state documents, and professional literature.

Analysis of the data revealed benefits in three areas:

(1) Revenues. The city of Boston earned nearly $1 million in tax and other revenues from the Roxbury Industrial Park in 1994. By 2001 this income is expected to reach $1.7 million (in constant 1994 dollars).

(2) Employment. In 1994 RIP businesses employed a total of 7,035 workers, who earned an average wage of $24,920. By 2001 RIP businesses are expected to employ directly nearly 15,000 employees who will earn salaries totaling over $450 million.

(3) Indirect benefits. Because of the multiplier effect, by 2001 Roxbury Industrial Park will directly and indirectly generate a total of 38,362 jobs in the Boston metropolitan area.

On the basis of these findings, it is recommended that development of additional industrial parks be encouraged to stimulate local economic growth.

iii

Opens directly with major research findings

Identifies data sources

Summarizes organization of report

Condenses recommendations

An executive summary or abstract highlights report findings, conclusions, and recommendations. Its length depends on the report it summarizes. A 100-page report might require a 10-page summary. Shorter reports may contain 1-page summaries, as shown here. Unlike letters of transmittal (which may contain personal pronouns and references to the writer), summaries are formal and impersonal. They use the same margins as the body of the report.

FIGURE 11.15 Continued

Page 1

Lists three problem questions

Describes authorization for report and background of study

ECONOMIC IMPACT OF ROXBURY INDUSTRIAL PARK

PROBLEM

This study was designed to analyze the direct and indirect economic impact of Roxbury Industrial Park on the city of Boston. Specifically, the study seeks answers to these questions:

(1) What current tax and other revenues result directly from this park? What tax and other revenues may be expected in the future?

(2) How many and what kind of jobs are directly attributable to the park? What is the employment picture for the future?

(3) What indirect effects has Roxbury Industrial Park had on local employment, incomes, and economic growth?

BACKGROUND

The development firm of Goldman-Lyon & Associates commissioned this study of Roxbury Industrial Park at the request of the Boston City Council. Before authorizing the development of a proposed Goldman-Lyon industrial park, the City Council requested a study examining the economic effects of an existing park. Members of the City Council wanted to determine to what extent industrial parks benefit the local community, and they chose Roxbury Industrial Park as an example.

For those who are unfamiliar with it, Roxbury Industrial Park is a 400-acre industrial park located in the city of Boston about 4 miles from the center of the city. Most of the area lies within a specially designated area known as Redevelopment Project No. 2, which is under the jurisdiction of the Boston Redevelopment Agency. Planning for the park began in 1986; construction started in 1988.

1

The first page of a formal report contains the title printed 2 inches from the top edge. Titles for major parts of a report (such as *PROBLEM, BACKGROUND, FINDINGS,* and *CONCLUSIONS*) are centered in all caps. First-level headings (such as *Employment* on page 302) are printed with bold upper- and lowercase letters. Second-level headings (such as *Distribution* on page 302) begin at the side. See Figure 11.3 for an illustration of heading formats.

FIGURE 11.15 Continued

The park now contains 14 building complexes with over 1.25 million square feet of completed building space. The majority of the buildings are used for office, research and development, marketing and distribution, or manufacturing uses. Approximately 50 acres of the original area are yet to be developed.

Data for this report came from a 2000 survey of over 5,000 Roxbury Industrial Park employees, interviews with 15 RIP tenants and managers, the Annual Budget of the City of Boston, county and state tax records, current books, articles, journal, and on-line resources. Projections for future revenues resulted from analysis of past trends and "Estimates of Revenues for Debt Service Coverage, Redevelopment Project Area 2" (Miller 79).

Page 2

Provides specifics for data sources

DISCUSSION OF FINDINGS

The results of this research indicate that major direct and indirect benefits have accrued to the city of Boston and surrounding metropolitan areas as a result of the development of Roxbury Industrial Park. The research findings presented here fall into three categories: (a) revenues, (b) employment, and (c) indirect effects.

Previews organization of report

Revenues

Roxbury Industrial Park contributes a variety of tax and other revenues to the city of Boston. Figure 1 summarizes revenues.

Figure 1

Places figure close to textual reference

REVENUES RECEIVED BY THE CITY OF BOSTON
FROM ROXBURY INDUSTRIAL PARK

Current Revenues and Projections to 2005

	2000	2005
Sales and use taxes	$604,140	$1,035,390
Revenues from licenses	126,265	216,396
Franchise taxes	75,518	129,424
State gas tax receipts	53,768	92,134
Licenses and permits	48,331	82,831
Other revenues	64,039	111,987
Total	$972,061	$1,668,162

Source: State Board of Equalization *Bulletin*. Boston: State Printing Office, 2000, 103.

2

Notice that this formal report is single-spaced. Many businesses prefer this space-saving format. However, some organizations prefer double-spacing, especially for preliminary drafts. If you single-space, do not indent paragraphs. If you double-space, do indent the paragraphs. Page numbers may be centered 1 inch from the bottom of the page or placed 1 inch from the upper right corner at the margin. Strive to leave a minimum of 1 inch for top, bottom, and side margins. References follow the parenthetical citation style of the Modern Language Association (MLA). Notice that the author's name and a page reference appear in parentheses.

FIGURE 11.15 Continued

Page 3

Continues interpreting figures in table

Includes ample description of electronic reference

Sets stage for next topics to be discussed

Sales and Use Revenues

As shown in Figure 1, the city's largest source of revenues from RIP is the sales and use tax. Revenues from this source totaled $604,140 in 2000, according to figures provided by the Massachusetts State Board of Equalization (26). Sales and use taxes accounted for more than half of the park's total contribution to the city of $972,061.

Other Revenues

Other major sources of city revenues from RIP in 2000 include alcohol licenses, motor vehicle in lieu fees, trailer coach licenses ($126,265), franchise taxes ($75,518), and state gas tax receipts ($53,768).

Projections

Total city revenues from RIP will nearly double by 2005, producing an income of $1.7 million. This estimate is based on an annual growth rate of 1.4 percent, as projected by the Bureau of Labor Statistics and reported at the Web site of Infoplease.com ("Economic Outlook Through 2008").

Employment

One of the most important factors to consider in the overall effect of an industrial park is employment. In Roxbury Industrial Park the distribution, number, and wages of people employed will change considerably in the next five years.

Distribution

A total of 7,035 employees currently work in various industry groups at Roxbury Industrial Park, as shown in Figure 2. The largest number of workers (58 percent) is employed in manufacturing and assembly operations. In the next largest category, the computer and electronics industry employs 24 percent of the workers. Some overlap probably exists because electronics assembly could be included in either group. Employees also work in publishing (9 percent), warehousing and storage (5 percent), and other industries (4 percent).

Although the distribution of employees at Roxbury Industrial Park shows a wide range of employment categories, it must be noted that other industrial parks would likely generate an entirely different range of job categories.

3

Only the most important research findings are interpreted and discussed for readers. The depth of discussion depends on the intended length of the report, the goal of the writer, and the expectations of the reader. Because the writer wants this report to be formal in tone, she avoids *I* and *we* in all discussions.

FIGURE 11.15 Continued

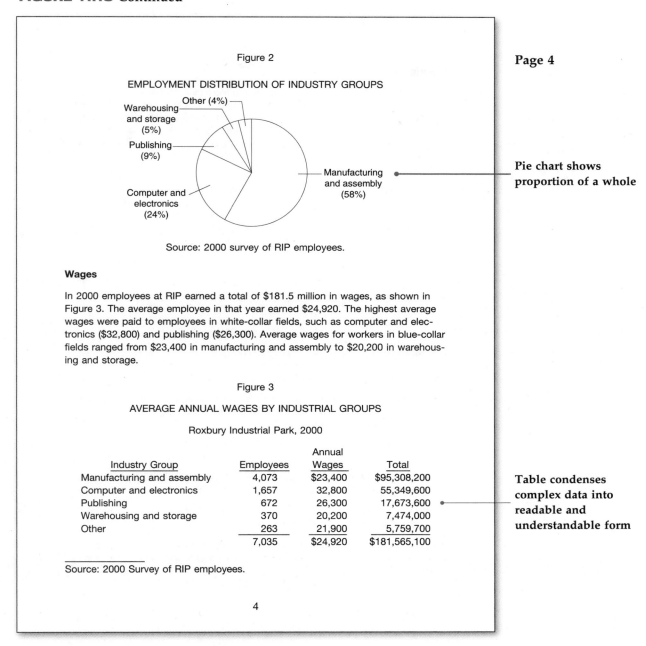

Figure 2

EMPLOYMENT DISTRIBUTION OF INDUSTRY GROUPS

Other (4%)
Warehousing and storage (5%)
Publishing (9%)
Computer and electronics (24%)
Manufacturing and assembly (58%)

Source: 2000 survey of RIP employees.

Pie chart shows proportion of a whole

Page 4

Wages

In 2000 employees at RIP earned a total of $181.5 million in wages, as shown in Figure 3. The average employee in that year earned $24,920. The highest average wages were paid to employees in white-collar fields, such as computer and electronics ($32,800) and publishing ($26,300). Average wages for workers in blue-collar fields ranged from $23,400 in manufacturing and assembly to $20,200 in warehousing and storage.

Figure 3

AVERAGE ANNUAL WAGES BY INDUSTRIAL GROUPS

Roxbury Industrial Park, 2000

Industry Group	Employees	Annual Wages	Total
Manufacturing and assembly	4,073	$23,400	$95,308,200
Computer and electronics	1,657	32,800	55,349,600
Publishing	672	26,300	17,673,600
Warehousing and storage	370	20,200	7,474,000
Other	263	21,900	5,759,700
	7,035	$24,920	$181,565,100

Table condenses complex data into readable and understandable form

Source: 2000 Survey of RIP employees.

4

If you use figures or tables, be sure to introduce them in the text (for example, *as shown in Figure 3*). Although it's not always possible, try to place them close to the spot where they are first mentioned. To save space, you can print the title of a figure at its side. Because this report contains few tables and figures, the writer named them all "Figures" and numbered them consecutively.

FIGURE 11.15 Continued

Page 5

Clarifies information
and tells what it
means in relation to
original research
questions

Projections

By 2005 Roxbury Industrial Park is expected to more than double its number of employees, bringing the total to over 15,000 workers. The total payroll in 2001 will also more than double, producing over $450 million (using constant 1996 dollars) in salaries to RIP employees. These projections are based on an 8 percent growth rate (Miller 78), along with anticipated increased employment as the park reaches its capacity.

Future development in the park will influence employment and payrolls. One RIP project manager stated in an interview that much of the remaining 50 acres is planned for medium-rise office buildings, garden offices, and other structures for commercial, professional, and personal services (Novak). Average wages for employees are expected to increase because of an anticipated shift to higher-paying white-collar jobs. Industrial parks often follow a similar pattern of evolution (Badri 41). Like many industrial parks, RIP evolved from a warehousing center into a manufacturing complex.

Summarizes
conclusions and
recommendations

CONCLUSIONS AND RECOMMENDATIONS

Analysis of tax revenues, employment data, personal interviews, and professional literature leads to the following conclusions and recommendations about the economic impact of Roxbury Industrial Park on the city of Boston:

1. Sales tax and other revenues produced nearly $1 million in income to the city of Boston in 2000. By 2005 sales tax and other revenues are expected to produce $1.7 million in city income.

2. RIP currently employs 7,035 employees, the majority of whom are working in manufacturing and assembly. The average employee in 2000 earned $24,920.

3. By 2005 RIP is expected to employ more than 15,000 workers producing a total payroll of over $450 million.

4. Employment trends indicate that by 2005 more RIP employees will be engaged in higher-paying white-collar positions.

On the basis of these findings, we recommend that the City Council of Boston authorize the development of additional industrial parks to stimulate local economic growth.

5

After discussing and interpreting the research findings, the writer articulates what she considers the most important conclusions and recommendations. Longer, more complex reports may have separate sections for conclusions and resulting recommendations. In this report they are combined. Notice that it is unnecessary to start a new page for the conclusions.

FIGURE 11.15 Continued

WORKS CITED

Badri, Masood A. "Infrastructure, Trends, and Economic Effects of Industrial Parks." Industry Week 1 April 2000: 38–45.

"Economic Outlook Through 2008." Bureau of Labor Statistics. Retrieved Infoplease.com 24 Nov. 2000 <http://www.infoplease.com/ipa/A0300371.html>.

Cohen, Allen P. "Industrial Parks Invade Suburbia." The New York Times 10 Dec. 1999, sec. C: 1.

Massachusetts State Board of Equalization Bulletin. Boston: State Printing Office, 2000. 26–29.

Miller, Arthur M. "Estimates of Revenues for Debt Service Coverage, Redevelopment Project Area No. 2." Miller and Schroeder Municipals. New York: Rincon Press, 1999. 78–79.

Novak, Ivan M. Personal interview with author. 30 Sept. 2000.

U. S. Bureau of the Census. "Travel to Work Characteristics for the 50 Largest Metropolitan Areas by Population in the United States: 1990 Census." Retrieved 15 Dec. 2000 <http://www.census.gov/population/socdemo/journey/ustime90.dat>.

Arranges references in alphabetical order

Follows Modern Language Association documentation style

If a report seeks to determine a course of action, it may end with conclusions and recommendations. Recommendations regarding a course of action may be placed in a separate section or incorporated with the conclusions.

Supplementary Parts of Report

- **Footnotes or endnotes.** See Appendix C for details on how to document sources. In the footnote method the source notes appear at the foot of each page. In the endnote method they are displayed immediately after the text on a page called *Notes*.

- **Bibliography.** Most formal reports include a bibliography that lists all sources consulted in the report research. Our model report follows the Modern Language Association (MLA) documentation style; thus its *Works Cited* functions as a bibliography. See Appendix C for more information on documentation formats.

- **Appendix.** The appendix contains any supplementary information needed to clarify the report. Charts and graphs illustrating significant data are generally part of the report proper. However, extra information that might be included in an appendix are such items as a sample survey, a survey cover letter, correspondence relating to the report, maps, other reports, and optional tables.

Endnotes, a bibliography, and appendixes may appear after the body of the report.

Summing Up and Looking Forward

Proposals are offers to solve problems, provide services, or sell equipment. Both small and large businesses today write proposals to generate income. Informal proposals may be as short as two pages; formal proposals may be 200 pages or more. Regardless of the size, proposals contain standard parts that must be developed persuasively.

Formal reports present well-organized information systematically. The information may be collected from primary or secondary sources. All ideas borrowed from others must be documented. Good reports contain appropriate headings and illustrations.

Written reports are vital to decision makers. But oral reports can be equally important. In the next chapter you will learn how to organize and make oral presentations, as well as how to conduct meetings and communicate effectively on the telephone.

Critical Thinking

1. Why is the writing of proposals an important function in many businesses?
2. Discuss this statement, made by three well-known professional business writers: "Nothing you write will be completely new."[6]
3. Is information obtained on the Web as reliable as information obtained from journals, newspapers, and magazines? Explain.
4. Should all reports be written so that they follow the sequence of investigation—that is, description of the initial problem, analysis of issues, data collection, data analysis, and conclusions? Why or why not?
5. Distinguish between primary and secondary data. Which data are more likely to be useful in a business report?

Chapter Review

6. What are the six principal parts of an informal proposal? Be prepared to explain each.

7. How are formal proposals different from informal proposals?

8. What is the first step in writing a formal report?

9. Do formal business reports generally rely more heavily on primary or secondary data?

10. List four sources of secondary information, and be prepared to discuss how valuable each might be in writing a formal report about updating your company's accounting procedures.

11. Define these terms: browser, URL, search tool.

12. List four levels of headings, and explain how they are different.

13. Pie charts are most helpful in showing what?

    Line graphs are most effective in showing what?

14. List three reasons for documenting data in a business report.

15. List the parts of a formal report. Be prepared to discuss each.

Activities and Cases

11.1 Researching Secondary and Primary Data. In teams, discuss how you would collect information for each of the following report topics. Would your research be primary, secondary, or a combination of methods? What resources would be most useful—books, articles, the Web, interviewing?

Team

a. The history of unions

b. Which public relations firm will best improve the image of a company so that its stock price increases

c. The cause of the high absenteeism in one department of a company

d. The latest Occupational Safety and Health Administration (OSHA) rulings that might affect your small business

e. The traffic count at a possible location for a fast-food restaurant

f. What the heads of three departments think about changing the official routine for developing each year's budget in your company

g. The costs and features of a new telephone/voice mail system for your company

h. How users are reacting to a new accounting software program recently released

i. How to meet international quality standards (ISO certification) so that you can sell your products in Europe

11.2 Outlining. You work for a recruiting firm that helps businesses find candidates for jobs. Over the years, many clients have asked for suggestions on the best way to interview job candidates. Your boss asks you to write a short report on how to become a great interviewer. Here are some ideas you gathered from your own experience and that of other recruiters:

One of the most important qualities of a successful interview is efficient use of the interview time. Most businesspeople hate the hiring process because it interrupts their daily routine and throws off their schedules. But you have found that if you block out an afternoon or a whole day, you don't feel so frustrated. In addition, shutting out all interruptions and setting aside 45 minutes for each interview can also be helpful.

Interviewing is an inexact art because judging the talents and abilities of people is very subjective. To select the best candidate, you must begin with a list of all the job duties. Then you select the three duties with the highest priorities. Naturally, you would then ask questions to discover what candidate can perform those duties best.

Every interview should have objectives. What do you want to achieve? One of the most important goals is uncovering the experience that qualifies the candidate to do the job. Another important element is the correlation you see between the candidate and your company's values. A major final objective is selling the candidate on the opportunity with your company.

Your Task. Select the most important information and organize it into an outline such as that shown in Figure 11.2. You should have three main topics with three subdivisions under each. Assume that you would gather more information later. Add a title.

Team

11.3 Selecting Visual Aids. In teams identify the best visual aid (table, bar chart, line chart, pie chart, flow chart, organization chart) to illustrate the following data:

a. Instructions for workers telling them how to distinguish between worker accidents that must be reported to state and federal agencies and those that need not be reported

b. Figures showing what proportion of every state tax dollar is spent on education, social services, transportation, debt, and other expenses

c. Data showing the academic, administrative, and operation divisions of a college, from the president to department chairs and division managers

d. Figures showing the operating profit of a company for the past five years

e. Figures comparing the sales of VCRs, color TVs, and personal computers for the past five years

f. Percentages showing the causes of forest fires (lightning, 73 percent; arson, 5 percent; campfires, 9 percent; and so on) in the Rocky Mountains

g. Figures comparing the cost of basic TV cable service in ten areas of the United States for the past ten years (the boss wants to see exact figures)

11.4 Evaluating Visual Aids. From *U.S. News & World Report, USA Today, Business Week,* a textbook, or some other publication, locate one example each of a table, a pie chart, a line chart, a bar chart, and an organization chart. Bring copies of these visual aids to class. How effectively could the data have been expressed in words, without the graphics? Is the appropriate graphic form used? How is the graphic introduced in the text? Your instructor may ask you to submit a memo discussing visual aids.

11.5 Studying Visual Aids in Annual Reports. In a memo to your instructor, evaluate the effectiveness of visual aids in three to five corporation annual reports. Critique their readability, clarity, and success in visualizing data. How were they introduced in the text? What suggestions would you make to improve them?

11.6 Library Recommendation. You have been asked to recommend a library to fellow students who have little library experience. Visit your school or public library. Observe its resources, method of operation, shelf lists, electronic capabilities, and personnel. Write a one-page memo report describing your findings.

11.7 Bibliography. Select a business topic that interests you. Prepare a bibliography of at least five current magazine articles, three books, and five other references that contain relevant information regarding the topic. Your instructor may ask you to divide your bibliography into sections: *Books, Periodicals, Other Resources.* You may also be asked to annotate your bibliography, that is, to compose a brief description of each reference, such as this:

Rash, Wayne, Jr. "Dawn of the Dead Disk." *Byte,* July 2000, 137–140. This article discusses the need for timely, complete backups of data stored on hard disks so that when a hard disk crashes, a business may continue with the least interruption.

11.8 Proposal: Don't Give Up Your Day Job. As a struggling student, single parent, or budding entrepreneur, you decide to start your own part-time business (Web site design, word processing, or something similar). Select a company or professional in your city that

Critical Thinking

might need your services. Assess your expertise and equipment. Check out the competition. What are competitors offering, and what do they charge?

Your Task. Prepare a letter proposal offering your services to a specific individual.

Critical Thinking

11.9 Formal Report: Readability of Insurance Policies. The 21st Century Insurance Company is concerned about the readability of its policies. State legislators are beginning to investigate complaints of policyholders who say they can't understand their insurance policies. One judge lambasted insurers, saying, "The language in these policies is bureaucratic gobbledygook, jargon, double-talk, a form of officialese, federalese, and insurancese that does not qualify as English. The burden upon organizations is to write policies in a manner designed to communicate rather than to obfuscate." Taking the initiative in improving its policies, 21st Century hires you as a consultant to study its standard policy and make recommendations.

Examine a life, fire, or health insurance policy that you or a friend or relative holds. Select one that is fairly complex. Study the policy for jargon, confusing language, long sentences, and unclear antecedents. Evaluate its format, print size, paper and print quality, amount of white space, and use of headings. Does it have an index or glossary? Are difficult terms defined? How easy is it to find specifics, should a policyholder want to check something?

In addition to the data you collect from your own examination of the policy, 21st Century gives you the following data from a recent policyholder survey:

Response to statement: "I am able to read and understand the language and provisions of my policy."

Age Group	Strongly Agree	Agree	Undecided	Disagree	Strongly Disagree
18–34	2%	9%	34%	41%	14%
35–49	2	17	38	33	10
50–64	1	11	22	35	31
65+	1	2	17	47	33

Your Task. Prepare a report for Heather Garcia, vice president, 21st Century Insurance Company, discussing your analysis, conclusions, and recommendations for improving its basic policy.

11.10 Formal Report: Fast-Food Checkup. The national franchising headquarters for a fast-food chain has received complaints about the service, quality, and cleanliness of one of its restaurants in your area. You have been sent to inspect and to report on what you see.

Your Task. Select a nearby fast-food restaurant. Visit on two or more occasions. Make notes about how many customers were served, how quickly they received their food, and how courteously they were treated. Observe the number of employees and supervisors working. Note the cleanliness of observable parts of the restaurant. Inspect the restroom as well as the exterior and surrounding grounds. Sample the food. Your boss is a stickler for details; he has no use for general statements such as *The restroom was not clean.* Be specific. Draw conclusions. Are the complaints justified? If improvements are necessary, make recommendations. Address your report to Lawrence C. Kelsey, President.

11.11 Formal Report: Consumer Product Investigation. Study a consumer product that you might consider buying. Are you (or your family) interested in purchasing a VCR, computer, digital camera, microwave, car, van, camcorder, or some other product? Your investigation should include primary data collected from interviews with users, owners, salespersons, service technicians, and so forth. You'll also find rich resources on the Web and in sales brochures and pamphlets. Conduct secondary research by studying (and citing) magazine articles in such publications as *Consumer Reports.* Be sure to narrow your topic by setting boundaries on your search. For example, are you interested in an economy van with good mileage that will be driven 50 miles daily? Are you in the market for an economical auto-focus camera?

Your Task. In your report include an introduction that discusses why you selected this product and for whom it is intended (for example, a VCR for a middle-class family who would use it primarily for watching rented videocassettes and for time-shift recording of television programs). Perhaps provide some background data about the product gleaned from your reading. In the findings section you might discuss such topics as price, warranty, specific features, and service reputation. Draw conclusions from your data, and make a recommendation. Address the report to your instructor. Your instructor may ask your class to work in pairs on this project.

11.12 Formal Report: Communication Skills on the Job. Collect information regarding communication skills used by individuals in a particular career field (accounting, management, marketing, office administration, paralegal, and so forth). Interview three or more individuals in a specific occupation in that field. Determine how much and what kind of writing they do. Do they make oral presentations? How much time do they spend in telephone communication? Do they use e-mail? If so, how much and for what? What recommendations do they have for training for this position?

Your Task. Write a report that discusses the findings from your interviews. What conclusions can you draw regarding communication skills in this field? What recommendations would you make for individuals entering this field? Your instructor may ask you to research the perception of businesspeople over the past ten years regarding the communication skills of employees. To gather such data, conduct library or on-line research.

11.13 Searching the Internet: Proposal for Setting Up a Web Site. As a consultant, you have been asked to investigate the cost of setting up a World Wide Web site for Kevin St. John, who owns a travel agency (or a florist shop, party-planning service, secretarial service, automotive parts store, teddy bear gift shop, car dealership, or any other reasonable community organization or business). He hopes to begin with a simple, basic Web site.

Web

Critical
Thinking

Your Task. Use search engines on the Internet to locate information. Try "Web Site Construction" as a search term. Visit several sites that offer to build Web sites. Focus on those that seem most professional. Look to see when the site was last updated. Read the promotional material and decide whether it is well written. Remember, anyone can post a Web site. Investigate the general characteristics of a Web site, how to create and promote a site, and how to maintain a Web server. Mr. St. John wants a low-cost but high-quality site. Develop cost figures. Draw conclusions and make recommendations in a letter proposal to Mr. St. John.

Related Web Site: <http://coytecom.com/webdevo/construct.html>

11.14 Connecting With E-Mail: Reporting on Your Report. Send an e-mail message to your instructor summarizing your report topic, outlining your work plan, and showing your work schedule. Be concise but specific.

11.15 BusinessLink Video Case Study—Technology in Communication at Burke Marketing Research. Burke Marketing Research is one of the premier international marketing research and consulting firms in the industry. It's the world's seventh largest research company with offices in 40 countries around the world. For it to remain successful, effective internal and external communication is vital.

Video

Your Task. After viewing the Burke video, discuss these questions:

- What technological tools does Burke use for written communication?
- What are the advantages and disadvantages of e-mail for Burke?
- Why is Burke moving from paper to paperless reports?
- What technological tools does Burke use for oral communication?
- Why has videoconferencing been less successful than teleconferencing? (Videoconferencing involves the transmission of images; teleconferencing generally means the transmission of voice only.)
- How does Burke use the Internet to collect and deliver information?

Grammar/Mechanics Checkup—11

Other Punctuation

Although this checkup concentrates on Sections 2.23–2.29 in the Grammar/Mechanics Handbook, you may also refer to other punctuation principles. Insert any necessary punctuation. In the space provided, indicate the number of changes you make and record the number of the G/M principle(s) illustrated. Count each mark separately; for example, a set of parentheses counts as 2. If you make no changes, write *0*. When you finish, compare your responses with those provided at the end of the book. If your responses differ, study carefully the specific principles shown in parentheses.

2 _____ (2.27)   **Example:**   (De-emphasize.) The consumption of Mexican food products is highest in certain states (California, Arizona, New Mexico, and Texas), but this food trend is spreading to other parts of the country.

_____ 1. (Emphasize.) The convention planning committee has invited three managers   Jim Lowey, Frank Beyer, and Carolyn Wong   to make presentations.

_____ 2. Would you please Miss Sanchez use your computer to recalculate these totals

_____ 3. (Deemphasize.) A second set of demographic variables see Figure 13 on page 432 includes nationality, religion, and race.

_____ 4. Because the word recommendation is frequently misspelled we are adding it to our company style book.

_____ 5. Recruiting, hiring, and training   these are three important functions of a personnel officer.

_____ 6. The office manager said, Who placed an order for two dozen printer cartridges

_____ 7. Have any of the research assistants been able to locate the article entitled How Tax Reform Will Affect You

_____ 8. (Emphasize.) The biggest oil-producing states Texas, California, and Alaska   are experiencing severe budget deficits.

_____ 9. Have you sent invitations to Mr Ronald E Harris, Miss Michelle Hale, and Ms Sylvia Mason

_____ 10. Dr. Y. W. Yellin wrote the chapter entitled Trading on the Options Market that appeared in a book called Securities Markets.

_____ 11. James said, "I'll be right over" however he has not appeared yet.

_____ 12. In business the word liability may be defined as any legal obligation requiring payment in the future.

_____ 13. Because the work was scheduled to be completed June 10; we found it necessary to hire temporary workers to work June 8 and 9.

_____ 14. Did any c o d shipments arrive today

_____ 15. Hooray I have finished this checkup haven't I

The following sentences contain errors in grammar, punctuation, capitalization, number style, usage, and spelling. Below each sentence write a corrected version.

1. Each of our applicants are rated on the following factors; skills, experience, education, and people skills.

2. Although Tonya and him agreed to pay two months rent in advance the landlord refused to rent to them.

3. The nations airlines threatened to stop service on Monday at 5 p.m..

4. Our 3 top sales reps, Lucinda, Keith, and Michael—received cash bonus's of one thousand dollars each.

5. Did we send 2 copies of the proposal to SuperCom, Inc?

6. If you were me would you step into the managers shoes at this time.

7. Matt wondered whether all two hundred of our brochures would be delivered within the 2 week mailing period?

8. A complete glossary of terms, see page 200 are available to help readers' understand difficult terms.

9. In The New York Times you will find an article titled The Blossoming of Internet Chat, however we could not locate it on-line.

10. Mr Ferranto, Ms Elliott, and Miss Simons has each recieved a new computer.

11. (Direct quotation) The teacher said, A clear conscious is usually the sign of a bad memory.

12. Would you please send me this years rankings of all your stock funds?

13. A host of ethical issues surround business including economic justice, corporate morality and whistleblowing.

14. Texas Instruments developed it's own code of ethics however its difficult to inforce such a code.

15. For those whom are interested the on-line version of U. S. News and World Reports college rankings are now available.

Grammar/Mechanics Challenge—11

Document for Revision

The following report executive summary has faults in grammar, punctuation, spelling, number form, wordiness, and word use. Use standard proofreading marks (see Appendix B) to correct the errors. When you finish, your instructor can show you the revised version of this summary.

EXECUTIVE SUMMARY

Problem

The U.S. tuna industry must expand it's markets abroad particularly in regard to Japan. Although consumption of tuna is decreasing in the United States they are increasing in Japan. The problem that is for the american tuna industry is developing apropriate marketing strategies to boost its current sale in Japanese markets.

Summary of Findings

This report analyzes the Japanese market which currently consumes six hundred thousand tons of tuna per year, and is growing rapidly. Much of this tuna is supplied by imports which at this point in time total about 35% of sales. Our findings indicate that not only will this expand, but the share of imports will continue to grow. The trend is alarming to Japanese tuna industry leaders, because this important market, close to a $billion a year, is increasingly subject to the influence of foreign imports. Declining catches by Japans own Tuna fleet as well as a sharp upward turn in food preference by affluent Japanese consumers, has contributed to this trend.

Recommendations

Based on our analisys we reccommend the following 5 marketing strategys for the U.S. Tuna industry.

Kevin Wilson

You are a mid-manager for an insurance company; Stella Sharp is your administrative assistant. Your boss is Mrs. Carol Smith, vice-president for administrative services. Mrs. Smith has just sent you a memo informing you that your assistant, Stella, is being fired because she is living with a man without being married, which is against company policy. Take a stand on this issue. Either write your boss defending Stella's right to chose her own lifestyle and remain working for the company or write Stella and inform her that she is being fired for violating a valid company policy.

Laura Huckley > Dealing w/ Person's Anger Situation

How to Mediate

1. Farm greater supplys of bluefin tuna to export.

2. We should market our own value added products.

3. Sell fresh tuna direct to the Tokyo Central Wholesale market.

4. Sell to other Japanese markets also.

5. Direct sales should be made to Japanese Supermarket chains.

Web Evaluation: Hoax? Scholarly Research? Advocacy?

Most of us tend to think that any information turned up via a Web search engine has somehow been evaluated as part of a valid selection process.[7] Wrong! The truth is that the Internet is rampant with unreliable sites that reside side by side with reputable sites. Anyone with a computer and an Internet connection can publish anything on the Web.

Unlike library-based research, information at many sites has not undergone the editing or scrutiny of scholarly publication procedures. The information we read in journals and most reputable magazines is reviewed, authenticated, and evaluated. That's why we have learned to trust these sources as valid and authoritative. But information on the Web is much less reliable. Some sites are obvious hoaxes. Others exist to distribute propaganda. Still others want to sell you something. To use the Web meaningfully, you must scrutinize what you find. For comprehensive, updated information and links to guide you in evaluating Web sources, check the Guffey Web site **<www.westwords.com/guffey/students. html>.** Here are specific questions to ask as you examine a site:

- **Currency.** What is the date of the Web page? When was it last updated? Is some of the information obviously out of date? If the information is time sensitive and the site has not been updated recently, the site is probably not reliable.

- **Authority.** Who publishes or sponsors this Web page? What makes the presenter an authority? Is a contact address available for the presenter? Learn to be skeptical about data and assertions from individuals whose credentials are not verifiable.

- **Content.** Is the purpose of the page to entertain, inform, convince, or sell? Who is the intended audience, based on content, tone, and style? Can you judge the overall value of the content compared with the other resources on this topic? Web presenters with a slanted point of view cannot be counted on for objective data.

- **Accuracy.** Do the facts that are presented seem reliable to you? Do you find errors in spelling, grammar, or usage? Do you see any evidence of bias? Are footnotes provided? If you find numerous errors and if facts are not referenced, you should be alert that the data may be questionable.

Career Application

Your boss wants to see how good your Web assessment skills are. You've been asked to conduct research at three of the following sites:

Families Against Internet Censorship **<shell.rmi.net/~fagin/faic/>**
Edmunds—Where Smart Car Buyers Start **<www.edmunds.com>**
Mankato, Minnesota, Home Page **<www.lme.mankato.msus.edu/mankato/ mankato.html>**

EarthSave International **<www.earthsave.org/>**
The True But Little Known Facts About Women and Aids **<http://147.129.10/**
library/research/AIDSFACTS.htm>

Your Task. Answer the following questions:

- What evidence can you find to determine whether these sites represent hoaxes, personal opinion, or reliable information?
- Are the sources for factual information clearly listed so that they can be verified?
- Can you tell who publishes or sponsors the page?
- Are the organization's biases clearly stated?
- Is advertising clearly differentiated from informational content?
- Would you use these sites for scholarly research? Why or why not?

Oral Presentations, Meetings, and Telephone Communication

Public speaking skills have risen to the top of nearly every company's wish list of executive attributes.[1]

HAL LANCASTER, Wall Street Journal *columnist*

LEARNING OBJECTIVES

1. Discuss two important first steps in preparing an effective oral presentation.
2. Explain the major elements in the introduction, body, and conclusion of an oral presentation and discuss the importance of verbal signposts.
3. Identify appropriate visual aids and handouts for a presentation.
4. Review techniques for designing an electronic presentation.
5. Specify delivery techniques for use before, during, and after a presentation.
6. List techniques for improving telephone and voice mail effectiveness.
7. Plan and participate in productive and efficient business meetings.

Many businesspeople must make presentations as part of their careers.

Organizations today are increasingly interested in hiring people with speaking skills. Why? "As organizations are downsizing, we need more well-rounded people," says Hollis Church, communications specialist.[2] "They may not only be the technical expert, but the spokesperson for a product."

At some point everyone in business has to sell an idea, and such persuasion is often done in person. Speaking skills play an important role in a successful career. You might, for example, need to describe your company's expansion plans to your banker, or you might need to persuade management to support your proposed marketing strategy. You might have to make a sales pitch before customers or speak to a professional gathering. This chapter will help you develop speaking skills in making oral presentations and in using the telephone and voice mail to advantage. You'll also learn to plan and participate in efficient business meetings.

Preparing an Effective Oral Presentation

Most of us experience a certain amount of fear before making an oral presentation. You should expect to get butterflies in your stomach. It's quite normal. When you feel those butterflies, though, speech coach Dianna Booher advises getting

A letter must be written to all present holders of safety deposit boxes. There has never been a rent fee before, but the bank has now decided to charge rent for the safety deposit boxes because of the long waiting list for them and the low supply. Some customers have had a box for fifty years and have never paid a cent. There will now be a yearly fee of $10 to $50 depending on the size of the box. As manager of customer relations, write a letter to your safety deposit box customers informing them of the new fee.

You are an executive for a large, local corporation and well known for your work with charitable organizations. During the year, you have spent most of your time on the road helping charities establish effective public relations campaigns. As a result of this effort, you ignored your own work and spent little time with your family—you even missed Christmas! Your boss and your spouse have praised your devotion to help the needy, but they have also tactfully let you know that you must take care of your other obligations by the end of the year.

This morning, you received a request from Homes For Kids, an organization that finds foster families for abused, abandoned, and orphaned children. They do good work and are nationally known. They have begged you to help organize and appear on a three-day national telethon during Easter, April 19-20, assuring you that your presence will result in at least an additional $250,000 for their fund raising. The request is well written and assumes you will agree. Write Homes For Kids and say no. Try not to appear selfish or egotistical.

them in formation and visualizing the swarm as a powerful push propelling you to a peak performance.[3] In other words, you can capitalize on the adrenaline that is coursing through your body by converting it to excitement and enthusiasm for your performance. But you can't just walk in and "wing it." People who don't prepare suffer the most anxiety and give the worst performances. You can learn to make effective oral presentations by focusing on four areas: preparation, organization, visual aids, and delivery.

Knowing Your Purpose

The most important part of your preparation is deciding what you want to accomplish. Do you want to sell a health care program to a prospective client? Do you want to persuade management to increase the marketing budget? Do you want to inform customer service reps of three important ways to prevent miscommunication? Whether your goal is to persuade or to inform, you must have a clear idea of where you are going. At the end of your presentation, what do you want your listeners to remember or do?

Eric Evans, a loan officer at First Fidelity Trust, faced such questions as he planned a talk for a class in small business management. Eric's former business professor had asked him to return to campus and give the class advice about borrowing money from banks in order to start new businesses. Because Eric knew so much about this topic, he found it difficult to extract a specific purpose statement for his presentation. After much thought he narrowed his purpose to this: *To inform potential entrepreneurs about three important factors that loan officers consider before granting start-up loans to launch small businesses.* His entire presentation focused on ensuring that the class members understood and remembered the three principal ideas.

Preparing for an oral presentation means identifying the purpose and knowing the audience.

Knowing Your Audience

A second key element in preparation is analyzing your audience, anticipating its reactions, and making appropriate adaptations. Many factors influence a presentation. A large audience, for example, usually requires a more formal and less personalized approach. Other audience characteristics, such as age, gender, education, experience, and attitude toward the subject, will also affect your style and message content. Analyze these factors to determine your strategy, vocabulary, illustrations, and level of detail. Here are specific questions to consider:

Audience characteristics to analyze include size, age, gender, experience, attitude, and expectations.

- *How will this topic appeal to this audience?*
- *How can I relate this information to their needs?*
- *How can I earn respect so that they accept my message?*
- *Which of the following would be most effective in making my point? Statistics? Graphic illustrations? Demonstrations? Case histories? Analogies? Cost figures?*
- *What measures must I take to ensure that this audience remembers my main points?*

Organizing the Content

Once you have determined your purpose and analyzed the audience, you're ready to collect information and organize it logically. Good organization and conscious repetition are the two most powerful keys to audience comprehension and retention. In fact, many speech experts recommend the following admittedly repetitious, but effective, plan:

- **Step 1:** Tell them what you're going to say.
- **Step 2:** Say it.
- **Step 3:** Tell them what you've just said.

In other words, repeat your main points in the introduction, body, and conclusion of your presentation. Although it sounds deadly, this strategy works surprisingly well. Let's examine how to construct the three parts of a presentation and add appropriate verbal signposts to ensure that listeners understand and remember.

Introduction

The opening of your presentation should strive to accomplish three specific goals:

- Capture listeners' attention and get them involved
- Identify yourself and establish your credibility
- Preview your main points

Attention-grabbing openers include questions, startling facts, jokes, anecdotes, and quotations.

If you're able to appeal to listeners and involve them in your presentation right from the start, you're more likely to hold their attention until the finish. Consider some of the same techniques that you used to open sales letters: a question, a startling fact, a joke, a story, or a quotation. Some speakers achieve involvement by opening with a question or command that requires audience members to raise their hands or stand up.

To establish your credibility, you need to describe your position, knowledge, or experience—whatever qualifies you to speak. Try also to connect with your audience. Listeners are particularly drawn to speakers who reveal something of themselves and identify with them. A consultant addressing office workers might reminisce about how she started as a clerk-typist; a CEO might tell a funny story in which the joke is on himself.

After capturing attention and establishing yourself, you'll want to preview the main points of your topic, perhaps with a visual aid. You may wish to put off actually writing your introduction, however, until after you have organized the rest of the presentation and crystallized your principal ideas.

Take a look at Eric Evans' introduction, shown in Figure 12.1, to see how he integrated all the elements necessary for a good opening.

Body

The best oral presentations focus on a few key ideas.

The biggest problem with most oral presentations is a failure to focus on a few principal ideas. Thus, the body of your short presentation (20 or fewer minutes) should include a limited number of main points, say, two to four. Develop each main point with adequate, but not excessive, explanation and details. Because too many details can obscure the main message, keep your presentation simple and logical. Remember, listeners have no pages to leaf back through should they become confused.

When Eric Evans began planning his presentation, he realized immediately that he could talk for hours on his topic. He also knew that listeners are not good at separating major and minor points. Thus, instead of submerging his listeners in a sea of information, he sorted out a few principal ideas. In the mortgage business, loan officers generally ask the following three questions of each applicant

FIGURE 12.1 Oral Presentation Outline

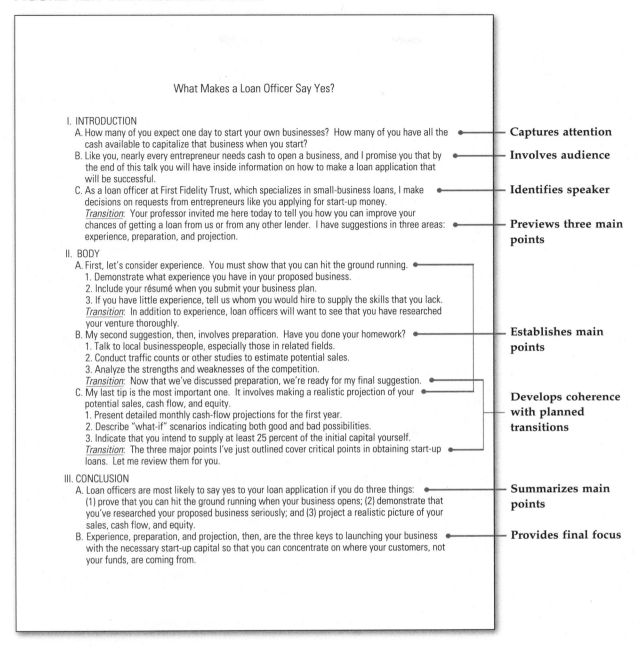

What Makes a Loan Officer Say Yes?

I. INTRODUCTION
   A. How many of you expect one day to start your own businesses? How many of you have all the — **Captures attention**
      cash available to capitalize that business when you start?
   B. Like you, nearly every entrepreneur needs cash to open a business, and I promise you that by — **Involves audience**
      the end of this talk you will have inside information on how to make a loan application that
      will be successful.
   C. As a loan officer at First Fidelity Trust, which specializes in small-business loans, I make — **Identifies speaker**
      decisions on requests from entrepreneurs like you applying for start-up money.
      Transition: Your professor invited me here today to tell you how you can improve your
      chances of getting a loan from us or from any other lender. I have suggestions in three areas: — **Previews three main points**
      experience, preparation, and projection.

II. BODY
   A. First, let's consider experience. You must show that you can hit the ground running.
      1. Demonstrate what experience you have in your proposed business.
      2. Include your résumé when you submit your business plan.
      3. If you have little experience, tell us whom you would hire to supply the skills that you lack.
      Transition: In addition to experience, loan officers will want to see that you have researched
      your venture thoroughly.
   B. My second suggestion, then, involves preparation. Have you done your homework? — **Establishes main points**
      1. Talk to local businesspeople, especially those in related fields.
      2. Conduct traffic counts or other studies to estimate potential sales.
      3. Analyze the strengths and weaknesses of the competition.
      Transition: Now that we've discussed preparation, we're ready for my final suggestion.
   C. My last tip is the most important one. It involves making a realistic projection of your — **Develops coherence with planned transitions**
      potential sales, cash flow, and equity.
      1. Present detailed monthly cash-flow projections for the first year.
      2. Describe "what-if" scenarios indicating both good and bad possibilities.
      3. Indicate that you intend to supply at least 25 percent of the initial capital yourself.
      Transition: The three major points I've just outlined cover critical points in obtaining start-up
      loans. Let me review them for you.

III. CONCLUSION
   A. Loan officers are most likely to say yes to your loan application if you do three things: — **Summarizes main points**
      (1) prove that you can hit the ground running when your business opens; (2) demonstrate that
      you've researched your proposed business seriously; and (3) project a realistic picture of your
      sales, cash flow, and equity.
   B. Experience, preparation, and projection, then, are the three keys to launching your business — **Provides final focus**
      with the necessary start-up capital so that you can concentrate on where your customers, not
      your funds, are coming from.

for a small business loan: (1) Are you ready to "hit the ground running" in starting your business? (2) Have you done your homework? and (3) Have you made realistic projections of potential sales, cash flow, and equity investment?

These questions would become his main points, but Eric wanted to streamline them further so that his audience would be sure to remember them. He capsulized the questions in three words: *experience, preparation,* and *projection.* As you can see in Figure 12.1, Eric prepared a sentence outline showing these three main ideas. Each is supported by examples and explanations.

How to organize and sequence main ideas may not be immediately obvious when you begin working on a presentation. Let's review the five organizational methods employed for written reports in Chapter 11, because those methods are equally appropriate for oral presentations. You could structure your ideas by the following elements:

Main ideas can be organized according to time, component, importance, criteria, or conventional groupings.

- **Time.** Example: A presentation describing the history of a problem, organized from the first sign of trouble to the present.
- **Component.** Example: A sales report organized by divisions or products.
- **Importance.** Example: A report describing operating problems arranged from the most important to the least important.
- **Criteria.** Example: A presentation evaluating equipment by comparing each model against a set of specifications.
- **Conventional groupings.** Example: A report comparing asset size, fees charged, and yields of mutual funds arranged by these existing categories.

In his presentation Eric arranged the main points by importance, placing the most important point last where it had maximum effect.

In organizing any presentation, prepare a little more material than you think you will actually need. Savvy speakers always have something useful in reserve (such as an extra handout, transparency, or idea)—just in case they finish early.

Conclusion

Effective conclusions summarize main points and focus on a goal.

You should prepare the conclusion carefully because this is your last chance to drive home your main points. Don't end limply with comments such as "I guess that's about all I have to say." Skilled speakers use the conclusion to review the main themes of the presentation and focus on a goal. They concentrate on what they want the audience to do, think, or remember. Even though they were mentioned earlier, important ideas must be repeated. Notice how Eric Evans, in the conclusion shown in Figure 12.1, summarized his three main points and provided a final focus to listeners.

When they finish, most speakers encourage questions. If silence ensues, you can prime the pump with "One question that I'm frequently asked is . . . ." You can also remark that you will be happy to answer questions individually after the presentation is completed.

Verbal Signposts

Knowledgeable speakers provide verbal signposts to spotlight organization and key ideas.

Speakers must remember that listeners, unlike readers of a report, cannot control the rate of presentation or flip back through pages to review main points. As a result, listeners get lost easily. Knowledgeable speakers help the audience recognize the organization and main points in an oral message with verbal signposts. They keep listeners on track by including helpful previews, summaries, and transitions, such as these:

- **To Preview**

  The next segment of my talk presents three reasons for . . .

  Let's now consider the causes of . . .

- **To Summarize**

  Let me review with you the major problems I've just discussed . . .

  You see, then, that the most significant factors are . . .

- **To Switch Directions**

   Thus far we've talked solely about . . .; now let's move to . . .

   I've argued that . . . and . . ., but an alternate view holds that . . . .

You can further improve any oral presentation by including appropriate transitional expressions such as *first, second, next, then, therefore, moreover, on the other hand, on the contrary*, and *in conclusion*. These expressions lend emphasis and tell listeners where you are headed. Notice in Eric Evans's outline, in Figure 12.1, the specific transitional elements designed to help listeners recognize each new principal point.

Planning Visual Aids and Handouts

Before you make a business presentation, consider this wise Chinese proverb: "Tell me, I forget. Show me, I remember. Involve me, I understand." Because your goals as a speaker are to make listeners understand, remember, and act on your ideas, include visual aids to get them interested and involved. Some authorities suggest that we acquire 85 percent of all our knowledge visually. Therefore, an oral presentation that incorporates visual aids is far more likely to be understood and retained than one lacking visual enhancement.

> **Visual aids clarify points, improve comprehension, and aid retention.**

Good visual aids have many purposes. They emphasize and clarify main points, thus improving comprehension and retention. They increase audience interest, and they make the presenter appear more professional, better prepared, and more persuasive. Furthermore, research shows that the use of visual aids actually shortens meetings.[4] Visual aids are particularly helpful for inexperienced speakers because the audience concentrates on the aid rather than on the speaker. Good visuals also serve to jog the memory of a speaker, thus improving self-confidence, poise, and delivery.

Fortunately for today's speakers, many forms of visual media are available to enhance a presentation. Figure 12.2 describes a number of visual aids and compares their cost, degree of formality, and other considerations. Three of the most popular visuals are overhead transparencies, computer visuals, and handouts.

Overhead Transparencies. Student and professional speakers alike rely on the overhead projector for many reasons. Most meeting areas are equipped with projectors and screens. Moreover, acetate transparencies for the overhead are cheap, easily prepared on a computer or copier, and simple to use. And, because rooms need not be darkened, a speaker using transparencies can maintain eye contact with the audience. However, transparencies are definitely "low-tech" and avoided by many businesspeople today because they give the impression that the speaker is not up to date. If you do use transparencies, be sure to stand to the side of the projector so that you don't obstruct the audience's view.

Handouts. You can enhance and complement your presentations by distributing pictures, outlines, brochures, articles, charts, summaries, or other supplements. Speakers who use computer presentation programs often prepare a set of their slides along with notes to hand out to viewers. Timing the distribution of any handout, though, is tricky. If given out during a presentation, your handouts tend to distract the audience, causing you to lose control. Thus, it's probably best to discuss most handouts during the presentation but delay distributing them until after you finish.

Computer Visuals. With today's excellent software programs—such as PowerPoint, Freelance Graphics, and Corel Presentations—you can create dynamic,

FIGURE 12.2 Presentation Enhancers

Medium	Cost	Audience Size	Formality Level	Advantages and Disadvantages
Overhead projector	Low	2–200	Formal or informal	Transparencies are easy and inexpensive to produce. Speaker keeps contact with audience.
Flipchart	Low	2–200	Informal	Easels and charts are readily available and portable. Speaker can prepare the display in advance or on the spot.
Write-and-wipe board	Medium	2–200	Informal	Procelain-on-steel surface replaces messy chalkboard. Speaker can wipe clean with cloth.
Slide projector	Medium	2–500	Formal	Slides provide excellent graphic images. Darkened room may put audience to sleep. Slides demand expertise, time, and equipment to produce.
Video monitor	Medium	2–100	Formal or informal	A VCR display features motion and sound. Videos require skill, time, and equipment to prepare.
Computer slides	Low	2–200	Formal or informal	Computers generate slides, transparencies, or multimedia visuals. Presentation software programs are easy to use, and they create dazzling results.
Handouts	Varies	Unlimited	Formal or informal	Audience appreciates take-home items such as outlines, tables, charts, reports, brochures, or summaries. However, handouts can divert attention from speaker.

colorful presentations with your PC. The output from these programs is generally shown on a PC monitor, a TV monitor, an LCD (liquid crystal display) panel, or a screen. With a little expertise and advanced equipment, you can create a multimedia presentation that includes stereo sound, videos, and hyperlinks, as described in the following discussion of electronic presentations.

Designing an Electronic Presentation

Computer-aided presentations are economical, flexible, professional, and easy to prepare.

The content of most presentations today hasn't changed, but the medium certainly has. At meetings and conferences smart speakers now use computer programs, such as PowerPoint, to present, defend, and sell their ideas most effectively. Business speakers have switched to computer presentations because they are economical, flexible, and easy to prepare. Changes can be made right up to the last minute. Most important, though, such presentations make even amateurs look like real pros.

Using Templates

Many novice presenters begin by using one of the professionally designed templates that come with a software program such as PowerPoint. These templates combine harmonious colors, borders, and fonts for pleasing visual effects. Tem-

FIGURE 12.3 Selecting a Slide Layout

You may choose from a variety of slide layout plans, or you may design your own slide to fit your material.

plates also provide guidance in laying out each slide, as shown in Figure 12.3. You can select a layout for a title page, a bulleted list, a bar chart, a double-column list, an organization chart, and so on.

www.grantland.net

Working With Color

You don't need training in color theory to create presentation images that impress your audience rather than confuse them. You can use the color schemes from the design templates that come with your presentation program, or you can alter them. Here are some pointers in choosing a color scheme for visuals:

Background and text colors depend on lightness of room.

- Develop a color palette of five or fewer colors.
- Use warm (red, orange) colors to highlight important elements.
- Use the same color for similar elements.

FIGURE 12.4 Preparing a PowerPoint Presentation

Tips for Preparing and Using Slides

- Keep all visuals simple; spotlight major points only.
- Use the same font size and style for similar headings.
- Apply the Rule of Seven: No more than seven words on a line, seven total lines, and 7 × 7 or 49 total words.
- Be sure that everyone in the audience can see the slides.
- Show a slide, allow audience to read it, then paraphrase it. Do NOT read from a slide.
- Rehearse by practicing talking to the audience, not to the slides.
- Bring back-up transparencies in case of equipment failure.

- Use dark text on a light background for presentations in bright rooms.
- Use light text on a dark background for presentations in darkened rooms.
- Use dark text on a light background for transparencies.
- Beware of light text on light backgrounds and dark text on dark backgrounds.

Building Bullet Points

Incremental bullet points enable a speaker to animate the presentation and control the flow of ideas.

When you prepare your slides, translate the major headings in your presentation outline into titles for slides. For example, Figure 12.4 represents portions of a long report. The major topics of the report outline became the titles of slides. Major subpoints became bullet items. As you learned earlier, bulleted items must be constructed in parallel form. They should be phrases or key words, not complete sentences.

One of the best features about electronic presentation programs is the "build" capability. You can focus the viewer's attention on each specific item as you add bullet points line by line. The bulleted items may "fly" in from the left, right, top, or bottom. They can also build or dissolve from the center. As each new bullet point is added, leave the previous ones on the slide but show them in lightened text. In building bulleted points or in moving from one slide to the next, you can use slide transition elements, such as "wipe outs," glitter, ripple, liquid, and vortex effects. But don't overdo it. Experts suggest choosing one transition effect and applying it consistently.[5]

For the most readable slides, apply the Rule of Seven. Each slide should include no more than seven words in a line, no more than seven total lines, and no more than 7×7 or 49 total words. And remember that presentation slides summarize; they don't tell the whole story. That's the job of the presenter.

Adding Multimedia and Other Effects

Many presentation programs also provide libraries of multimedia features to enhance your content. These include sound, animation, and video elements. For example, you could use sound effects to "reward" correct answers from your audience. But using the sound of screeching tires in a Department of Motor Vehicles presentation is probably unwise. Similarly, video clips—when used judiciously— can add excitement and depth to a presentation. You might use video to capture attention in a stimulating introduction, to show the benefits of a product in use, or to bring the personality of a distant expert or satisfied customer right into the meeting room.

Another way to enliven a presentation is with real-life photographic images, which are now easy to obtain thanks to the prevalence of new low-cost scanners and digital cameras. Some programs are also capable of generating hyperlinks ("hot" spots on the screen) that allow you to jump instantly to relevant data or multimedia content.

Multimedia elements include sound, animation, and video features.

Producing Speaker's Notes and Handouts

Most electronic presentation programs offer a variety of presentation options. In addition to printouts of your slides, you can make speaker's notes, as shown in Figure 12.5. These are wonderful aids for practicing your talk; they remind you of the supporting comments for the abbreviated material in your slides. Many programs allow you to print miniature versions of your slides with numerous slides to a page, if you wish. These miniatures are handy if you want to preview your talk to a sponsoring organization or if you want to supply the audience with a summary of your presentation.

Developing Web-Based Presentations and Electronic Handouts

Because of recent technological improvements, you can now give a talk without even traveling off-site. In other words, you can put your slides "on the road." Web presentations with slides, narration, and speaker control are emerging as a less expensive alternative to videoconferencing, which involves special equipment for sending images. For example, as a Web presenter you could initiate a meeting via a conference call, narrate using a telephone, and have participants see your slides from the browsers on their computers. If you prefer, you could skip the narration and provide a prerecorded presentation.

Web presentations are less expensive than videoconferencing.

Web-based presentations have many applications, including providing access to updated training or sales data whenever needed.[6] Larry Magid, computer expert and noted speaker, suggests still another way that speakers can use the Web.

FIGURE 12.5 Making Speaker's Notes for an Electronic Presentation

Speaker's notes enable you to print discussion items beneath each slide, thus providing handy review material for practice.

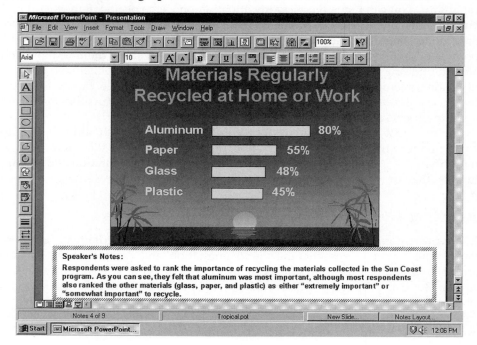

He recommends posting your slides on the Web even if you are giving a face-to-face presentation. Attendees prefer electronic handouts to paper handouts because they don't have to lug the printed handouts home.[7]

Avoiding Being Upstaged by Your Slides

Although electronic presentations supply terrific sizzle, they cannot replace the steak. In developing a presentation, don't expect your slides to carry the show. They merely summarize important points. As the speaker, you must explain the analyses leading up to the major points. You must explain what the major points mean.

Slides provide you with talking points. For each slide you should have one or more paragraphs of narration to present to your audience. Make use of the speaker's notes feature to capture your supporting ideas while you make the slides. And don't let a PowerPoint presentation "steal your thunder." You must maintain control of the presentation rather than allowing the electronics to take over. In addition to your narration, you can maintain control by using a laser pen or pointer to connect you with the screen. Keep in mind that your slides and transparencies merely supply a framework for your presentation. Your audience came to see and hear you.

Polishing Your Delivery

Once you've organized your presentation and prepared visuals, you're ready to practice delivering it. Here are suggestions for selecting a delivery method, along with specific techniques to use before, during, and after your presentation.

Stage Fright

Stage fright is both natural and controllable.

Nearly everyone experiences some degree of stage fright when speaking before a group. Being afraid is quite natural and results from actual physiological changes occurring in your body. Faced with a frightening situation, your body responds with the fight-or-flight response. This response provides you with increased energy to deal with threatening situations. It also creates those sensations—dry mouth, sweaty hands, increased heartbeat, and stomach butterflies—that we associate with stage fright.

Although it's impossible to eliminate these physiological symptoms altogether, you can reduce their effects with the following techniques:

- **Use deep breathing.** Inhale to a count of ten, hold this breath to a count of ten, and exhale to a count of ten. Concentrate on your counting and your breathing; both activities reduce your stress.

- **Feel confident about your topic.** Select a topic that you know well and that is relevant to your audience.

- **Use positive self-talk.** Remind yourself that you know your topic and are prepared. Tell yourself that your audience is on your side—because it is.

- **Shift the spotlight to your visuals.** At least some of the time the audience will be focusing on your slides, transparencies, handouts, or whatever you have prepared—and not on you.

- **Ignore any stumbles.** Don't apologize or confess your nervousness. If you keep going, the audience will forget any mistakes quickly.

Delivery Techniques

Inexperienced speakers often feel that they must memorize an entire presentation to be effective. Unless you're an experienced performer, however, you will sound wooden and unnatural. Moreover, forgetting your place can be disastrous! That's why memorizing an entire oral presentation is not recommended. However, memorizing significant parts—the introduction, the conclusion, and perhaps a meaningful quotation—can be dramatic and impressive.

www.grantland.net

If memorizing won't work, you may wonder if reading your presentation is the best plan. Definitely not! Reading to an audience is boring and ineffective. Because reading suggests that you don't know your topic very well, the audience loses confidence in your expertise. Reading also prevents you from maintaining eye contact. You can't see audience reactions; consequently, you can't benefit from feedback.

Neither the memorizing nor the reading method creates very convincing presentations. The best plan, by far, is a "notes" method. Plan your presentation carefully and talk from note cards or an outline containing key sentences and major ideas. By preparing and then practicing with your notes, you can talk to your audience in a conversational manner. Your notes should be neither entire paragraphs nor single words. Instead, they should contain a complete sentence or two to introduce each major idea. Below the topic sentence(s), outline subpoints and illustrations. Note cards will keep you on track and prompt your memory, but only if you have rehearsed the presentation thoroughly.

Before Your Presentation

Instead of worrying about everything that could go wrong during your presentation, get ready by doing the following:

Thorough preparation, extensive rehearsal, and stress-reduction techniques can lessen stage fright.

- **Prepare thoroughly.** One of the most effective strategies for reducing stage fright is knowing your subject thoroughly. Research your topic diligently and prepare a careful sentence outline. Those who try to "wing it" usually suffer the worst butterflies—and make the worst presentations.

- **Rehearse repeatedly.** When you rehearse, practice your entire presentation, not just the first half. Place your outline sentences on separate cards. You may also want to include transitional sentences to help you move to the next topic. Use these cards as you practice, and include your visual aids in your rehearsal. Record your rehearsal on audio- or videotape so that you can evaluate your effectiveness.

- **Time yourself.** Most audiences tend to get restless during longer talks. Thus, try to complete your presentation in no more than 20 minutes. Set a timer during your rehearsal to measure your speaking time.

- **Request a lectern.** Every beginning speaker needs the security of a high desk or lectern from which to deliver a presentation. It serves as a note holder and a convenient place to rest wandering hands and arms.

- **Check the room.** Before you talk, make sure that a lectern has been provided. If you are using sound equipment or a projector, be certain they are operational. Check electrical outlets and the position of the viewing screen. Ensure that the seating arrangement is appropriate to your needs.

- **Practice stress reduction.** If you feel tension and fear while you are waiting your turn to speak, use stress-reduction techniques, such as deep breathing discussed earlier.

During Your Presentation

After preparing thoroughly and checking the room, you're ready to step before your audience. The following techniques can help you make a good impression during your presentation:

- **Begin with a pause.** When you first approach the audience, take a moment to adjust your notes and make yourself comfortable. Establish your control of the situation.

- **Present your first sentence from memory.** By memorizing your opening, you can immediately establish rapport with the audience through eye contact. You'll also sound confident and knowledgeable.

- **Maintain eye contact.** If the size of the audience overwhelms you, pick out two individuals on the right and two on the left. Talk directly to these people.

- **Control your voice and vocabulary.** This means speaking in moderated tones but loudly enough to be heard. Eliminate verbal static, such as *ah, er, you know,* and *um*. Silence is preferable to meaningless fillers when you are thinking of your next idea.

- **Put the brakes on.** Many novice speakers talk too rapidly, displaying their nervousness and making it very difficult for audience members to understand their ideas. Slow down and listen to what you are saying.

- **Move naturally.** You can use the lectern to hold your notes so that you are free to move about casually and naturally. Avoid fidgeting with your notes, your clothing, or items in your pockets. Learn to use your body to express a point.

- **Use visual aids effectively.** You should discuss and interpret each visual aid for the audience. Move aside as you describe it so that it can be seen fully. Use a pointer if necessary.

- **Avoid digressions.** Stick to your outline and notes. Don't suddenly include clever little anecdotes or digressions that occur to you on the spot. If it's not part of your rehearsed material, leave it out so that you can finish on time. Remember, too, that your audience may not be as enthralled with your topic as you are.

- **Summarize your main points.** Conclude your presentation by reiterating your main points or by emphasizing what you want the audience to think or do. Once you have announced your conclusion, proceed to it directly. Don't irritate the audience by talking for five or ten more minutes.

> Eye contact, a moderate tone of voice, and natural movements enhance a presentation.

After Your Presentation

Most presentations involve interaction with the audience once the speaker finishes. Use this time to do the following:

- **Distribute handouts.** If you prepared handouts with data the audience will need, pass them out when you finish.

- **Encourage questions.** If the situation permits a question-and-answer period, announce it at the beginning of your presentation. Then, when you finish, ask for questions. Set a time limit for questions and answers.

- **Repeat questions.** Although the speaker may hear the question, audience members often do not. Begin each answer with a repetition of the question. This also gives you thinking time. Then, direct your answer to the entire audience.

- **Reinforce your main points.** You can use your answers to restate your primary ideas ("I'm glad you brought that up because it gives me a chance to elaborate on . . ."). In answering questions, avoid becoming defensive or debating the questioner.

- **Keep control.** Don't allow one individual to take over. Keep the entire audience involved.

- **End with a summary and appreciation.** To signal the end of the session before you take the last question, say something like "We have time for just one more question." As you answer the last question, try to work it into a summary of your main points. Then, express appreciation to the audience for the opportunity to talk with them.

> The time to answer questions, distribute handouts, and reiterate main points is after a presentation.

Telephones and Voice Mail

Although we often get stressed over oral presentations, we sometimes take other speaking tasks too lightly—such as talking on the telephone. The telephone is the most universal—and, some would say, the most important—piece of equipment in offices today.[8] The telephone has spawned an entire new industry—voice mail systems, which are rapidly replacing switchboards and receptionists. These computerized message systems greatly reduce labor costs and provide sophisticated capabilities and flexibility unavailable in the past.

Telephones and voice mail should promote goodwill and increase productivity.

Regardless of their advanced technology, though, telephones and voice mail are valuable business tools only when they generate goodwill and increase productivity. Poor communication techniques can easily offset any benefits arising from improved equipment. What good is an extensive voice mail system if callers hang up in frustration after waiting through a long list of menu options without hearing what they need? Here are suggestions aimed at helping business communicators make the best use of telephone and voice mail equipment.

Making Productive Telephone Calls

Making productive telephone calls means planning an agenda, identifying the purpose, being courteous and cheerful, and avoiding rambling.

Before making a telephone call, decide whether the intended call is really necessary. Could you find the information yourself? If you wait a while, would the problem resolve itself? Perhaps your message could be delivered more efficiently by some other means. One West Coast company found that telephone interruptions consumed about 18 percent of staff members' workdays. Another study found that two thirds of all calls were less important than the work they interrupted.[9] Alternatives to telephone calls include e-mail, memos, or calls to voice mail systems. If a telephone call must be made, consider using the following suggestions to make it fully productive:

- **Plan a mini-agenda.** Have you ever been embarrassed when you had to make a second telephone call because you forgot an important item the first time? Before placing a call, jot down notes regarding all the topics you need to discuss. Following an agenda guarantees not only a complete call but also a quick one. You'll be less likely to wander from the business at hand while rummaging through your mind trying to remember everything.

- **Use a three-point introduction.** When placing a call, immediately (1) name the person you are calling, (2) identify yourself and your affiliation, and (3) give a brief explanation of your reason for calling. For example: "May I speak to Larry Lopez? This is Hillary Dahl of Sebastian Enterprises, and I'm seeking information about a software program called Power Presentations." This kind of introduction enables the receiving individual to respond immediately without asking further questions.

- **Be cheerful and accurate.** Let your voice show the same kind of animation that you radiate when you greet people in person. In your mind try to envision the individual answering the telephone. A smile can certainly affect the tone of your voice, so smile at that person. Moreover, be accurate about what you say. "Hang on a second; I'll be right back" rarely is true. Better to say, "It may take me two or three minutes to get that information. Would you prefer to hold or have me call you back?"

- **Bring it to a close.** The responsibility for ending a call lies with the caller. This is sometimes difficult to do if the other person rambles on. You may need to use suggestive closing language, such as "I've certainly enjoyed talking with you," "I've learned what I needed to know, and now I can proceed with my work," "Thanks for your help," or "I must go now, but may I call you again in the future if I need . . .?"

- **Avoid telephone tag.** If you call someone who's not in, ask when it would be best for you to call again. State that you will call at a specific time—and do it. If you ask a person to call you, give a time when you can be reached—and then be sure you are in at that time.

- **Leave complete voice mail messages.** Remember that there's no rush when you leave a voice mail message. Always enunciate clearly. And be sure to provide a complete message, including your name, telephone number, and the time and date of your call. Explain your purpose so that the receiver can be ready with the required information when returning your call.

Receiving Productive Telephone Calls

With a little forethought you can make your telephone a productive, efficient work tool. Developing good telephone manners also reflects well on you and on your organization.

Receiving productive telephone calls means identifying oneself, being responsive and helpful, and taking accurate messages.

- **Identify yourself immediately.** In answering your telephone or someone else's, provide your name, title or affiliation, and, possibly, a greeting. For example, "Larry Lopez, Proteus Software. How may I help you?" Force yourself to speak clearly and slowly. Remember that the caller may be unfamiliar with what you are saying and fail to recognize slurred syllables.

- **Be responsive and helpful.** If you are in a support role, be sympathetic to callers' needs. Instead of "I don't know," try "That's a good question; let me investigate." Instead of "We can't do that," try "That's a tough one; let's see what we can do." Avoid "No" at the beginning of a sentence. It sounds especially abrasive and displeasing because it suggests total rejection.

- **Be cautious when answering calls for others.** Be courteous and helpful, but don't give out confidential information. Better to say, "She's away from her desk" or "He's out of the office" than to report a colleague's exact whereabouts.

- **Take messages carefully.** Few things are as frustrating as receiving a potentially important phone message that is illegible. Repeat the spelling of names and verify telephone numbers. Write messages legibly and record their time and date. Promise to give the messages to intended recipients, but don't guarantee return calls.

- **Explain what you're doing when transferring calls.** Give a reason for transferring, and identify the extension to which you are directing the call in case the caller is disconnected.

Making the Best Use of Voice Mail

Voice mail links a telephone system to a computer that digitizes and stores incoming messages. Some systems also provide functions such as automated attendant menus, allowing callers to reach any associated extension by pushing specific buttons on a touch-tone telephone. Interactive systems allow callers to receive verbal information from a computer database. For example, a ski resort in Colorado uses voice mail to answer routine questions that once were routed through an operator: "Welcome to Snow Paradise. For information on accommodations, touch 1; for snow conditions, touch 2; for ski equipment rental, touch 3," and so forth.

Voice mail serves many functions, but the most important is message storage. Because half of all business calls require no discussion or feedback (according to AT&T estimates), the messaging capabilities of voice mail can mean huge savings for businesses. Incoming information is delivered without interrupting potential receivers and without all the niceties that most two-way conversations require. Stripped of superfluous chitchat, voice mail messages allow communicators to focus on essentials. Voice mail also eliminates telephone tag, inaccurate message-taking, and time-zone barriers. Critics complain, nevertheless, that automated systems seem cold and impersonal and are sometimes confusing and irritating.

Voice mail eliminates telephone tag, inaccurate message-taking, and time-zone barriers; it also allows communicators to focus on essentials.

In any event, here are some ways that you can make voice mail work more effectively for you:

- **Announce your voice mail.** If you rely principally on a voice mail message system, identify it on your business stationery and cards. Then, when people call, they will be ready to leave a message.

- **Prepare a warm and informative greeting.** Make your mechanical greeting sound warm and inviting, both in tone and content. Identify yourself and your organization so that callers know they have reached the right number. Thank the caller and briefly explain that you are unavailable. Invite the caller to leave a message or, if appropriate, call back. Here's a typical voice mail greeting: "Hi! This is Larry Lopez of Proteus Software, and I appreciate your call. You've reached my voice mailbox because I'm either working with customers or talking on another line at the moment. Please leave your name, number, and reason for calling so that I can be prepared when I return your call." Give callers an idea of when you will be available, such as "I'll be back at 2:30" or "I'll be out of my office until Wednesday, May 20." If you screen your calls as a time-management technique, try this message: "I'm not near my phone right now, but I should be able to return calls after 3:30."

- **Test your message.** Call your number and assess your message. Does it sound inviting? Sincere? Understandable? Are you pleased with your tone? If not, says one consultant, have someone else, perhaps a professional, record a message for you.

Planning and Participating in Productive Meetings

Because you can expect to attend many meetings, learn to make them efficient, satisfying, and productive.

As businesses become more team oriented and management becomes more participatory, people are attending more meetings than ever. One survey of managers found that they were devoting as many as two days a week to various gatherings.[10] Yet, meetings are almost universally disliked. Typical comments include "We have too many of them," "They don't accomplish anything," and "What a waste of time!" In spite of employee reluctance and despite terrific advances in communication and team technology, face-to-face meetings are not going to disappear.

In discussing the future of meetings, Akio Morita, chairman of the Sony Corporation, said that he expects "face-to-face meetings will still be the number one form of communication in the twenty-first century."[11] So, get used to them. Meetings are here to stay. Our task, then, as business communicators, is to learn how to make them efficient, satisfying, and productive.

Meetings, by the way, consist of three or more individuals who gather to pool information, solicit feedback, clarify policy, seek consensus, and solve problems. But meetings have another important purpose for you. They represent opportunities. Because they are a prime tool for developing staff, they are career-critical. "If you can't orchestrate a meeting, you're of little use to the corporation," says Morris Schechtman, head of a leadership training firm.[12] At meetings judgments are formed and careers are made. Therefore, instead of treating them as thieves of your valuable time, try to see them as golden opportunities to demonstrate your leadership, communication, and problem-solving skills. The following techniques for planning and conducting successful meetings will help you make the most of these opportunities.

Call meetings only when ideas must be exchanged, and invite only key people.

Deciding Whether a Meeting Is Necessary

No meeting should be called unless the topic is important, can't wait, and requires an exchange of ideas. If the flow of information is strictly one way and no immediate feedback will result, then don't schedule a meeting. For example, if people are merely being advised or informed, send an e-mail, memo, or letter. Leave a telephone or voice mail message, but don't call a costly meeting.

Remember, the real expense of a meeting is the lost productivity of all the people attending. To decide whether the purpose of the meeting is valid, it's a good idea to consult the key people who will be attending. Ask them what outcomes are desired and how to achieve those goals. This consultation also sets a collaborative tone and encourages full participation.

Selecting Participants

The number of meeting participants is determined by the purpose of the meeting, as shown in Figure 12.6. If the meeting purpose is motivational, such as an awards ceremony for sales reps of Mary Kay Cosmetics, then the number of participants is unlimited. But to make decisions, according to studies at 3M Corporation, the best number is five or fewer participants.[13] Ideally, those attending should be people who will make the decision and people with information necessary to make the decision. Also attending should be people who will be responsible for implementing the decision and representatives of groups who will benefit from the decision.

Distributing Advance Information

At least two days in advance of a meeting, distribute an agenda of topics to be discussed. Include any reports or materials that participants should read in advance. For continuing groups, you might also include a copy of the minutes of the previous meeting. To keep meetings productive, limit the number of agenda items. Remember, the narrower the focus, the greater the chances for success. A good agenda, as illustrated in Figure 12.7, covers the following information:

Pass out a meeting agenda showing topics to be discussed and other information.

- Date and place of meeting
- Start time and end time
- Brief description of each topic, in order of priority, including the names of individuals who are responsible for performing some action
- Proposed allotment of time for each topic
- Any pre-meeting preparation expected of participants

Getting the Meeting Started

To avoid wasting time and irritating attendees, always start meetings on time—even if some participants are missing. Waiting for latecomers causes resentment and sets a bad precedent. For the same reasons, don't give a quick recap to any-

Start meetings on time and open with a brief introduction.

FIGURE 12.6 Meeting Purpose and Number of Participants

Purpose	Ideal Size
Intensive problem solving	5 or fewer
Problem identification	10 or fewer
Information reviews and presentations	30 or fewer
Motivational	Unlimited

FIGURE 12.7 Typical Meeting Agenda

AGENDA

Quantum Travel International

Staff Meeting September 4, 200X

10 to 11 a.m.

Conference Room

		Person	Proposed Time
I.	Call to order; roll call		
II.	Approval of agenda		
III.	Approval of minutes from previous meeting		
IV.	Committee reports		
	A. Web site update	Kevin	5 minutes
	B. Tour packages	Lisa	10 minutes
V.	Old business		
	A. Equipment maintenance	John	5 minutes
	B. Client escrow accounts	Alicia	5 minutes
	C. Internal newsletter	Adrienne	5 minutes
VI.	New business		
	A. New accounts	Sarah	5 minutes
	B. Pricing policy for trips	Marcus	15 minutes
VII.	Announcements		
VIII.	Chair's summary, adjournment		

one who arrives late. At the appointed time, open the meeting with a three- to five-minute introduction that includes the following:

- Goal and length of the meeting
- Background of topics or problems
- Possible solutions and constraints
- Tentative agenda
- Ground rules to be followed

A typical set of ground rules might include arriving on time, communicating openly, being supportive, listening carefully, participating fully, confronting conflict frankly, following the agenda, and adhering to Robert's Rules of Order. At this point, ask if participants agree with you thus far. The next step is to assign one attendee to take minutes and one to act as a recorder. The recorder stands at a flipchart or whiteboard and lists the main ideas being discussed and agreements reached.

Moving the Meeting Along

After the preliminaries, the leader should say as little as possible. Like a talk show host, an effective leader makes "sure that each panel member gets some air time while no one member steals the show."[14] Remember that the purpose of a meeting is to exchange views, not to hear one person, even the leader, do all the talking. If the group has one member who monopolizes, the leader might say, "Thanks, Kurt, for that perspective, but please hold your next point while we hear how Ann would respond to that." This technique also encourages quieter participants to speak up.

To avoid allowing digressions to sidetrack the group, try generating a "Parking Lot" list. This is a list of important but divergent issues that should be discussed at a later time. Another way to handle digressions is to say, "Folks, we are getting off track here. Forgive me for pressing on, but I need to bring us back to the central issue of . . . ."[15] It's important to adhere to the agenda and the time schedule. Equally important, when the group seems to have reached a consensus, is summarizing the group's position and checking to see whether everyone agrees.

Keep the meeting moving by avoiding issues that sidetrack the group.

Dealing With Conflict

Many meetings experience some form of conflict. Although such conflict is natural and even desirable, it can cause awkwardness and uneasiness. Conflict typically develops when people feel unheard or misunderstood.

If two people are in conflict, the best approach is to encourage each to make a complete case while group members give their full attention. Let each one question the other. Then, the leader should summarize what was said, and the group should offer comments. The group may modify a recommendation or suggest alternatives before reaching consensus on a direction to follow.

Ending With a Plan

End the meeting at the agreed time. The leader should summarize what has been decided, who is going to do what, and by what time. It may be necessary to ask people to volunteer to take responsibility for completing action items agreed to in the meeting. No one should leave the meeting without a full understanding of what was accomplished.

One effective closure technique that encourages full participation is "once around the table." Everyone is asked to summarize briefly his or her interpretation of what was decided and what happens next. Of course, this closure technique works best with smaller groups. The leader should conclude by asking the group to set a time for the next meeting. He or she should also assure the group that a report will follow and thank participants for attending.

End the meeting with a summary of accomplishments.

Following Up Actively

If minutes were taken, they should be distributed within a couple of days after the meeting. It is up to the leader to see that what was decided at the meeting is accomplished. The leader may need to call people to remind them of their assignments and also to volunteer to help them if necessary.

Follow up by reminding participants of their assigned tasks.

This chapter presented techniques for making effective oral presentations. Good presentations begin with analysis of your purpose and your audience. Organizing the content involves preparing an effective introduction, body, and closing. Verbal signposts help listeners recognize the organization and main points in an oral message. Visual aids are important in emphasizing and clarifying points. Because today's speakers are increasingly using presentation software, you learned how to develop a PowerPoint presentation.

The best method for delivering a presentation is with note cards, although significant parts could be memorized. You learned special techniques for reducing stage fright as well as effective strategies to be used before, during, and after your presentation.

This chapter also presented techniques for making and receiving telephone calls and for using voice mail effectively. Finally, you learned how to plan and participate in productive meetings.

The final two chapters of this book focus on your ultimate goal—getting a job. You'll learn how to write a persuasive résumé and how to ace an employment interview.

Critical Thinking

1. Why is it necessary to repeat key points in an oral presentation?
2. How can a speaker make the most effective use of visual aids?
3. How can speakers prevent electronic presentation software from stealing their thunder?
4. Why are callers often unhappy with voice mail menu systems? What techniques can individuals use to make the best use of voice mail?
5. Comment on the following statement: "If you can't orchestrate a meeting, then you are of little use to an organization."

Chapter Review

6. The planning of an oral presentation should begin with serious thinking about what two factors?

7. Name three goals to be achieved in the introduction of an oral presentation.

8. What should the conclusion to an oral presentation include?

9. Name three ways for a speaker to use verbal signposts in a presentation. Illustrate each.

10. Why are visual aids particularly useful to inexperienced speakers?

11. Name three advantages of electronic presentation software.

12. What delivery method is most effective for speakers?

13. What is a three-point introduction for a telephone call?

14. What is an agenda and what should it include?

15. How can meeting leaders and participants deal with conflict?

Activities and Cases

12.1 Critiquing a Speech. Visit your library and select a speech from *Vital Speeches of Our Day.* Write a memo report to your instructor critiquing the speech in terms of the following:
a. Effectiveness of the introduction, body, and conclusion
b. Evidence of effective overall organization
c. Use of verbal signposts to create coherence
d. Emphasis of two to four main points
e. Effectiveness of supporting facts (use of examples, statistics, quotations, and so forth)

12.2 Preparing an Oral Presentation from an Article. Select a newspaper or magazine article and prepare an oral report based on it. Submit your outline, introduction, and conclusion to your instructor, or present the report to your class.

12.3 Overcoming Stage Fright. Nearly everyone feels fear before making an oral presentation. Discussing those fears can sometimes change your perception and help you overcome stage fright.

Team

Your Task. In teams develop a list of reasons for being fearful when making a presentation. What makes you nervous? Being tongue-tied? All eyes on you? Messing up? Forgetting your ideas and looking silly? Then, in groups of three or four discuss ways to overcome these fears. Your instructor may ask you to write a memo (individual or collective) summarizing your suggestions, or you may break out of your small groups and report your best ideas to the entire class.

12.4 Investigating Oral Communication in Your Field. Oral communication plays a surprisingly important role in the lives of most businesspeople.

Your Task. Interview one or two individuals in your professional field. How is oral communication important in this profession? Does the need for oral skills change as one advances? What suggestions can these people make to newcomers to the field for developing proficient oral communication skills? Discuss your findings with your class.

12.5 Outlining an Oral Presentation. One of the hardest parts of preparing an oral presentation is developing the outline.

Your Task. Select an oral presentation topic from the list in Activity 12.8 or suggest an original topic. Prepare an outline for your presentation using the following format.

Title _____

Purpose _____

	I.	INTRODUCTION
Gain attention of audience		A.
Involve audience		B.
Establish credibility		C.
Preview main points		D.
Transition		
Main point	II.	BODY
Illustrate, clarify, contrast		A.
		1.
		2.
		3.
Transition		
Main point		B.
Illustrate, clarify, contrast		1.
		2.
		3.
Transition		
Main point		C.
Illustrate, clarify, contrast		1.
		2.
		3.
Transition		
	III.	CONCLUSION
Summarize main points		A.
Provide final focus		B.
Encourage questions		C.

Web

12.6. Discovering Presentation Tips on the Internet. A number of Web sites offer interesting advice for speakers.

Your Task. Using your favorite search engine and the search term "presentation tips," visit at least three Web sites that provide suggestions for giving presentations. If possible, print the most relevant findings. Select at least eight good tips or techniques *that you did not learn from this chapter*. Your instructor may ask you to bring them to class for discussion or submit a short memo report outlining your tips.

Web

12.7 Learning About Toastmasters. By becoming members of Toastmasters, many businesspeople have developed their speaking skills and gained confidence. Toastmasters is an organization devoted to improving listening, thinking, and speaking skills.

Your Task. Visit the Toastmasters' Web site and become familiar with its member services. Study the ten tips it provides for successful public speaking. In an e-mail message to your instructor, explain how Toastmasters could help you improve your communication skills. Also compare its speaking tips with those in this chapter. How were they similar or dissimilar?

Related Web Site: <www.toastmasters.org>

12.8 Choosing a Topic for an Oral Presentation. As an expert in your field, you have been called in to explain some aspect of a topic of your choice to an interested audience. Since your time is limited, prepare a concise yet forceful presentation with effective visual aids.

Your Task. Select a topic from the list below or from the report topics offered in Activity 11.1 at the end of Chapter 11. Develop a five- to ten-minute oral presentation.

a. What time-management techniques can managers use to improve efficiency and reduce stress?
b. Should job candidates post their résumés at job sites on the Web?
c. Do you agree with some observers who complain that PowerPoint is contributing to the "debasement of rhetoric"? (L. Zuckerman, *The New York Times,* 17 April 1999, A17)
d. What is the employment outlook in three career areas of interest to you?
e. What is telecommuting, and for what kind of workers is it an appropriate work alternative?
f. How much choice should parents have in selecting schools for their young children (parochial, private, and public)?
g. What travel location would you recommend for college students at Christmas (or another holiday or in summer)?
h. What is the economic outlook for a given product (such as domestic cars, laptop computers, digital cameras, fitness equipment, or a product of your choice)?
i. How can your organization or institution improve its image?
j. Why should people invest in a company or scheme of your choice?
k. What brand and model of computer and printer represent the best buy for college students today?
l. What franchise would offer the best investment opportunity for an entrepreneur in your area?
m. How should a job candidate dress for an interview?
n. Why should you be hired for a position for which you have applied?
o. How do the accounting cycles in manual and computerized systems compare?
p. How is an administrative assistant different from a secretary?
q. Where should your organization hold its next convention?
r. What is your opinion of the statement "Advertising steals our time, defaces the landscape, and degrades the dignity of public institutions"?[16]
s. How can individuals reduce their income tax responsibilities?
t. What is the outlook for real estate (commercial or residential) investment in your area?
u. What do the personal assistants for celebrities do, and how does one become a personal assistant? (Investigate the Association of Celebrity Personal Assistants.)
v. What kinds of gifts are appropriate for businesses to give clients and customers during the holiday season?
w. What scams are on the Federal Trade Commission's List of Top 10 Consumer Scams, and how can consumers avoid falling for them?
x. How are businesses and conservationists working together to protect the world's dwindling tropical forests?
y. Should employees be able to use computers in a work environment for anything other than work-related business?
z. What suggestions can you offer to your school's athletic department to increase attendance at minor sports events?

12.9 Improving Telephone Skills by Role Playing. Acting out the roles of telephone caller and receiver is an effective technique for improving skills. To give you such practice, your instructor will divide the class into pairs.

Your Task. For each scenario take a moment to read and rehearse your role silently. Then play the role with your partner. If time permits, repeat the scenarios, changing roles.

Partner 1	Partner 2
A. You are the personnel manager of Data-tronics, Inc. Call Elizabeth Franklin, office manager at Computers Plus. Inquire about a job applicant, Chelsea Chavez, who listed Ms. Franklin as a reference.	You are the receptionist for Computers Plus. The caller asks for Elizabeth Franklin, who is home sick today. You don't know when she will be able to return. Answer the call appropriately.
B. Call Ms. Franklin again the following day to inquire about the same job applicant, Chelsea Chavez. Ms. Franklin answers today, but she talks on and on, describing the applicant in great detail. Tactfully close the conversation.	You are now Ms. Franklin, office manager. Describe Chelsea Chavez, an imaginary employee. Think of someone with whom you've worked. Include many details, such as her ability to work with others, her appearance, her skills at computing, her schooling, her ambition, and so forth.
C. You are now the receptionist for Tom Wing, of Wing Imports. Answer a call for Mr. Wing, who is working in another office, at ext. 134, where he will accept calls.	You are now an administrative assistant for attorney Michael Murphy. Call Tom Wing to verify a meeting date Mr. Murphy has with Mr. Wing. Use your own name in identifying yourself.
D. You are now Tom Wing, owner of Wing Imports. Call your attorney, Michael Murphy, about a legal problem. Leave a brief, incomplete message.	You are now the receptionist for attorney Michael Murphy. Mr. Murphy is skiing in Aspen and will return in two days, but he doesn't want his clients to know where he is. Take a message.
E. Call Mr. Murphy again. Leave a message that will prevent telephone tag.	Take a message again.

12.10 Analyzing a Meeting. You've learned a number of techniques in this chapter for planning and participating in meetings. Here's your chance to put your knowledge to work.

Your Task. Attend a structured meeting of a college, social, business, or other organization. Compare the manner in which the meeting is conducted with the suggestions presented in this chapter. Why did the meeting succeed or fail? Prepare a memo for your instructor or be ready to discuss your findings in class.

12.11 BusinessLink Video Case Study: Designing and Delivering Effective Business Presentations at Burke Marketing Research. The consultants at Burke Marketing investigate marketing problems brought to them by clients. A client may want to know, for example, whether their new nacho-flavored popcorn will appeal to consumers. Burke specialists conduct the research, analyze the findings, and report those findings to the business owners. Although written reports are provided, oral presentations usually receive the most attention.

Your Task. After viewing the Burke video, respond to these questions:

- What are the four main steps that Burke consultants follow in creating an effective oral presentation?

- What tips do Burke consultants mention for improving the delivery of a presentation?
- How can unfavorable results be presented successfully?
- What is the worst presentation error a presenter can make?

Grammar/Mechanics Checkup—12

Capitalization

Review Sections 3.01–3.16 in the Grammar/Mechanics Handbook. Then study each of the following statements. Circle any lowercase letter that should be capitalized. Draw a slash (/) through any capital letter that you wish to change to lowercase. Indicate in the space provided the number of changes you made in each sentence and record the number of the G/M principle(s) illustrated. If you made no changes, write *0*. When you finish, compare your responses with those provided at the back of the book. If your responses differ, study carefully the principles in parentheses.

Example: After consulting our Attorneys for legal advice, Vice president Mills signed the contract.   4   (3.01, 3.06a)

1. All american passengers from Flight 402 must pass through Customs Inspection at Gate 17 upon arrival at Baltimore international airport.   _____
2. Personal tax rates for japanese citizens are low by International standards; rates for japanese corporations are high, according to Iwao Nakatani, an Economics Professor at Osaka university.   _____
3. In the end, Business passes on most of the burden to the Consumer: What looks like a tax on Business is really a tax on Consumption.   _____
4. Lisa enrolled in courses in History, Sociology, Spanish, and Computer Science.   _____
5. Did you see the *Forbes* article entitled "Careers in horticulture are nothing to sneeze at"?   _____
6. Although I recommend the Minex Diskettes sold under the brandname Maxidisk, you may purchase any Diskettes you choose.   _____
7. According to a Federal Government report, any regulation of State and County banking must receive local approval.   _____
8. The vice president of the united states said, "this country continues to encourage Foreign investments."   _____
9. The Comptroller of Ramjet International reported to the President and the Board of Directors that the internal revenue service was beginning an investigation of their Company.   _____
10. My Mother, who lives near St. Petersburg, reports that protection from the Sun's rays is particularly important in the South.   _____
11. Our Managing Editor met with Leslie Hawkins, Manager of the Advertising Sales Department, to plan an Ad Campaign for our special issue.   _____
12. In the fall, Editor in Chief Porter plans an article detailing the astounding performance of the austrian, West german, and italian currencies.   _____
13. To reach Belle Isle park, which is located on an Island in the Detroit river, tourists pass over the Douglas MacArthur bridge.   _____
14. On page 6 of the catalog you will see that the computer science department is offering a number of courses in programming.   _____
15. Please consult figure 3.2 in chapter 5 for U.S. census bureau figures regarding non-english-speaking residents.   _____

The following sentences contain errors in grammar, punctuation, capitalization, number style, usage, and spelling. Below each sentence write a corrected version.

1. The five top food service franchisors in the country are the following, mc-donald's, subway sandwiches & salads, burger king, 7-eleven, and international dairy queen.

2. Middleby Corporation which is based in elgin illinois and it's german partner has developed a commercial size cooker to make french fries that taste greasy but are not.

3. Although the time and temperature is set by the user the cooker adjusts itself automatically.

4. The President and Chief Executive of Middleby said, "this machine is programmed to learn.

5. We rented the 4,000 sq. foot building in new yorks times square to many small space tenants.

6. As a manager the most important task is planning.

7. Proper tools and modern equipment makes business's run smooth.

8. Looking back through history, no Presidency raises deeper philosophical issues than Bill Clinton.

9. Last Fall, the seattle based bicycle manufacturer TiCycle installed a network to link 5 PC's in it's factory and retail store.

10. Drove by a series of decisive actions AOLs membership grew by nearly two and a half million.

11. At the marriott residence inn in fairfax virginia a 1 bedroom suite costs about ninety dollars a night.

12. One of the most popular amenities offerred by top tier extended stay hotels are the free Buffet breakfast.

13. Just between you and I do you prefer a backpacking trip to canada or river rafting down the snake river.

14. We had less than fifteen items but others in the grocery store line were over the limit.

15. The President, Ceo, and 3 Managers will tour our facilitys in florida and texas.

Grammar/Mechanics Challenge—12

Document for Revision

The following executive summary of a report has faults in grammar, punctuation, spelling, number form, wordiness, and word use. Use standard proofreading marks (see Appendix B) to correct the errors. When you finish, your instructor can show you the revised version of this abstract.

EXECUTIVE SUMMARY

Purpose of Report

The purposes of this report is (1) To determine the Sun coast university campus communitys awareness of the campus recycling program and (2) To recommend ways to increase participation. Sun Coasts recycling program was intended to respond to the increasing problem of waste disposal, to fulfil it's social responsibility as an educational institution, and to meet the demands of legislation that made it a requirement for individuals and organizations to recycle.

A Survey was conducted in an effort to learn about the campus communities recycling habits and to make an assessment of the participation in the recycling program that is current. 220 individuals responded to the Survey but twenty-seven Surveys could not be used. Since Sun coast universitys recycling program include only aluminum, glass, paper and plastic at this point in time these were the only materials considered in this Study.

Recycling at Sun coast

Most Survey respondants recognized the importance of recycling, they stated that they do recycle aluminum, glass, paper and plastic on a regular basis either at home or at work. However most respondants displayed a low-level of awareness, and use of the on campus program. Many of the respondants was unfamilar with the location of the bins around campus; and therefore had not participated in the Recycling Program. Other responses indicated that the bins were not located in convenent locations.

Reccommendations for increasing recycling participation

Recommendations for increasing participation in the Program include the following;

1. relocating the recycling bins for greater visability

2. development of incentive programs to gain the participation of on campus groups

3. training student volunteers to give on campus presentations that give an explaination of the need for recycling, and the benefits of using the Recycling Program

4. we should increase Advertising in regard to the Program

Nine Techniques for Gaining and Keeping Audience Attention

Experienced speakers know how to capture the attention of an audience and how to maintain that attention during a presentation. Here are nine proven techniques:

- **A promise.** Begin with a promise that keeps the audience expectant (for example, "In this presentation I will show you how you can increase your sales by 50 percent.").

- **Drama.** Open by telling an emotionally moving story or by describing a serious problem that involves the audience. Throughout your talk include other dramatic elements, such as a long pause after a key statement. Change your vocal tone or pitch. Professionals use high-intensity emotions such as anger, joy, sadness, and excitement.

- **Eye contact.** As you begin, command attention by surveying the entire audience to take in all listeners. Take two to five seconds to make eye contact with as many people as possible.

- **Movement.** Leave the lectern area whenever possible. Walk around the conference table or between the aisles of your audience. Try to move toward your audience, especially at the beginning and end of your talk.

- **Questions.** Keep listeners active and involved with rhetorical questions. Ask for a show of hands to get each listener thinking. The response will also give you a quick gauge of audience attention.

- **Demonstrations.** Include a member of the audience in a demonstration (for example, "I'm going to show you exactly how to implement our four-step customer courtesy process, but I need a volunteer from the audience to help me.").

- **Samples/gimmicks.** If you're promoting a product, consider using items to toss out to the audience or to award as prizes to volunteer participants. You can also pass around product samples or promotional literature. Be careful, though, to maintain control and to regain your handouts.

- **Visuals.** Give your audience something to look at besides yourself. Use a variety of visual aids in a single session. Also consider writing the concerns expressed by your listeners on a flipchart or on the board as you go along.

- **Self-interest.** Review your entire presentation to ensure that it meets the critical What's-in-it-for-me? audience test. Remember that people are most interested in things that benefit them.

Career Application

As an intern in a large organization, you have been asked to demonstrate the use of PowerPoint. Many members of the staff have not used it, and they would like a quick introduction. Because your boss knows that you have studied PowerPoint recently, she asks you to make a presentation.

Your Task

- List the techniques discussed here that would be useful in gaining and keeping audience attention.

- Describe how you could involve the audience.

- Discuss how you could bring drama to the presentation.

- Compare the techniques that might be effective for a business group with those that might be effective for a classroom presentation.

6

Communicating for Employment

13 The Job Search, Résumés, and Job Application Letters

If your résumé isn't a winner, it's a killer.

JOYCE LAIN KENNEDY, *renowned careers author and nationally syndicated columnist*

LEARNING OBJECTIVES

1. Prepare for employment by identifying your interests, evaluating your assets, recognizing the changing nature of jobs, choosing a career path, and studying traditional and electronic job search techniques.

2. Compare and contrast chronological, functional, and combination résumés.

3. Organize and format the parts of a résumé to produce a persuasive product.

4. Identify techniques that prepare a résumé for computer scanning, posting at a Web site, faxing, and e-mailing.

5. Write a persuasive job application letter to accompany your résumé.

Whether you are applying for your first permanent position, competing for promotion, or changing careers, you'll be more successful if you understand employment strategies and how to promote yourself with a winning résumé. This chapter provides expert current advice in preparing for employment, searching the job market, writing a persuasive résumé, and developing an effective job application letter.

Preparing for Employment

Finding a satisfying career means learning about oneself, the job market, and the employment process.

You may think that the first step in finding a job is writing a résumé. Wrong! The job search process actually begins long before you are ready to prepare your résumé. Regardless of the kind of employment you seek, you must invest time and effort getting ready. You can't hope to find the position of your dreams without (1) knowing yourself, (2) knowing the job market, and (3) knowing the employment process.

In addition to searching for career information and choosing a specific job objective, you should be studying the job market and becoming aware of the substantial changes in the nature of work. You'll also want to understand how to use the latest Internet resources in your job search. When you have finished all this preparation, you're ready to design a persuasive résumé and job application letter. These documents should be appropriate for small businesses as well as for larger organizations that may be using résumé-scanning programs. Following these steps, summarized in Figure 13.1 and described in this chapter, gives you a master plan for landing a job you really want.

www.grantland.net

Identifying Your Interests

The employment process begins with introspection. This means looking inside yourself to analyze what you like and dislike so that you can make good employment choices. Career counselors charge large sums for helping individuals learn about themselves. You can do the same kind of self-examination—without

Analyzing your likes and dislikes helps you make wise employment decisions.

FIGURE 13.1 The Employment Search

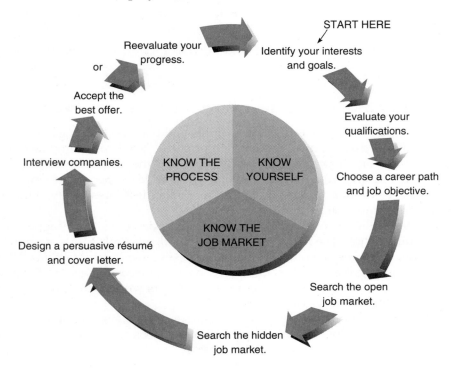

spending a dime. For guidance in choosing a field that eventually proves to be satisfying, answer the following questions. If you have already chosen a field, think carefully about how your answers relate to that choice.

Answering specific questions can help you choose a career.

- Do I enjoy working with people, data, or things?
- How important is it to be my own boss?
- How important are salary, benefits, and job stability?
- How important are working environment, colleagues, and job stimulation?
- Would I rather work for a large or small company?
- Must I work in a specific city, geographical area, or climate?
- Am I looking for security, travel opportunities, money, power, or prestige?
- How would I describe the perfect job, boss, and coworkers?

Evaluating Your Qualifications

Assessing your skills and experience prepares you to write a persuasive résumé.

In addition to your interests, assess your qualifications. Employers today want to know what assets you have to offer them. Your responses to the following questions will target your thinking as well as prepare a foundation for your résumé. Remember, though, that employers seek more than empty assurances; they will want proof of your qualifications.

- What computer skills can I offer? (What specific software programs can I name?)
- What other skills have I acquired in school, on the job, or through activities? How can I demonstrate these skills?
- Do I work well with people? What proof can I offer? (Consider extracurricular activities, clubs, and jobs.)
- Am I a leader, self-starter, or manager? What evidence can I offer?
- Do I speak, write, or understand another language?
- Do I learn quickly? Am I creative? How can I demonstrate these characteristics?
- Do I communicate well in speech and in writing? How can I verify these talents?

Recognizing the Changing Nature of Jobs

Downsizing and flatter organizations have resulted in people feeling less secure in their jobs.

As you learned in Chapter 1, the nature of the workplace is changing. One of the most significant changes involves the concept of the "job." Following the downsizing in many organizations in the early 1990s and the movement toward flattened organizations throughout the rest of the decade, fewer people are employed in permanent positions. Many employees are feeling less job security, although they are doing more work.

In his best-selling book *JobShift*, William Bridges describes the disappearance of the traditional job. The notion of a full-time permanent job with a specific job description, he claims, is giving way to more flexible work arrangements. Work is completed by teams assigned to projects or outsourced to a group that's not even part of an organization.[1] He sees the migration of work away from the fixed "boxes" that we've always called jobs.

"Jobs" are becoming more flexible and less permanent.

At the same time that work is becoming more flexible, big companies are no longer the main employers. Only 20 percent of new jobs are created by big companies.[2] And only one third of people currently employed work for companies with 500 or more employees.[3] People seem to be working for smaller companies, or they are becoming consultants or specialists who work on tasks or projects under arrangements too fluid to be called "jobs." And because new technologies can spring up overnight making today's skills obsolete, employers are less willing to hire people into jobs with narrow descriptions.

What do these changes mean for you? For one thing, you should probably no longer think in terms of a lifelong career with a single company. In fact, you can't even expect reasonably permanent employment for work well done. This social contract between employer and employee is no longer a given. And predictable career paths within companies have largely disappeared. Career advancement, therefore, is in your own hands.[4] In the new workplace you can expect to work for multiple employers on flexible job assignments associated with teams and projects.

Because of this changing nature of work, you can never become complacent about your position or job skills. Be prepared for constant retraining and updating of your skills. People who learn quickly and adapt to change are "high-value-added" individuals who will always be in demand even in a climate of surging change.

Choosing a Career Path

There's no escaping the fact that the employment picture today is much different from that of a decade or two ago. As a new college graduate, you can expect to have eight to ten jobs in as many as three different careers during your lifetime.[5] Some of you probably have not yet settled on your first career choice; others are returning to college to retrain for a new career. Although you may be changing jobs in the future, you still need to train for a specific career area now. In choosing an area, you'll make the best decisions when you can match your interests and qualifications with the requirements and rewards in specific careers. But where can you find career data? Here are some suggestions:

College graduates can expect to have eight to ten jobs in three or more different careers in a lifetime.

- **Visit your campus career center.** Most have literature, inventories, software programs, and Internet connections that allow you to investigate such fields as accounting, finance, office technology, information systems, hotel management, and so forth.

- **Search the Web.** Many job search sites on the Web offer career planning information and resources. For example, at JobWeb you can link to Career/Life Planning sites for college students. Updated descriptions of and links to the best career counseling and job search Web sites may be found at the Guffey Student Web site **<http://www.westwords.com/guffey/students.html>**. Click on "Jobs."

- **Use your library.** Many print and on-line resources are especially helpful. Consult the latest edition of the *Dictionary of Occupational Titles, Occupational Outlook Handbook,* and *The Jobs Rated Almanac* for information about career duties, qualifications, salaries, and employment trends.

Career information can be obtained at campus career centers and libraries, from the Internet, in classified ads, and from professional organizations.

- **Take a summer job, internship, or part-time position in your field.** Nothing is better than trying out a career by actually working in it or an allied area. Many companies offer internships and temporary jobs to begin training college students and to develop relationships with them. These relationships sometimes blossom into permanent positions.

Summer and part-time jobs and internships are good opportunities to learn about different careers.

- **Interview someone in your chosen field.** People are usually flattered when asked to describe their careers. Inquire about needed skills, required courses, financial and other rewards, benefits, working conditions, future trends, and entry requirements.

- **Monitor the classified ads.** Early in your college career, begin monitoring want ads and Web sites of companies in your career area. Check job availability, qualifications sought, duties, and salary range. Don't wait until you're about to graduate to see how the job market looks.

- **Join professional organizations in your field.** Frequently, they offer student membership status and reduced rates. You'll get inside information on issues, career news, and possible jobs.

Using Traditional Job Search Techniques

A traditional job search campaign might include checking classified ads and announcements in professional publications, contacting companies, and developing a network of contacts.

Finding the perfect job requires an early start and a determined effort. Whether you use traditional or on-line job search techniques, you should be prepared to launch an aggressive campaign. And you can't start too early. Some universities now require first- and second-year students to take an employment seminar called "Reality 101." Students are told early on that a college degree alone doesn't guarantee a good job. They are cautioned that grade-point averages make a difference to employers. And they are advised of the importance of experience. Here are some traditional steps that job candidates take:

- **Check classified ads in local and national newspapers.** Be aware, though, that classified ads are only one small source of jobs.

- **Check announcements in publications of professional organizations.** If you do not have a student membership, ask your professors to share current copies of professional journals, newsletters, and so on. Your college library is another good source.

- **Contact companies in which you're interested, even if you know of no current opening.** Write an unsolicited letter and include your résumé. Follow up with a telephone call. Check the company's Web site for employment possibilities and procedures.

- **Sign up for campus interviews with visiting company representatives.** Campus recruiters may open your eyes to exciting jobs and locations.

- **Ask for advice from your instructors.** They often have contacts and ideas for expanding your job search.

- **Develop your own network of contacts.** Networking still accounts for most of the jobs found by candidates. Therefore, plan to spend a considerable portion of your job search time developing a personal network. The Communication Workshop on page 387 gives you step-by-step instructions for traditional networking as well as some ideas for on-line networking.

Using Electronic Job Search Techniques

An electronic job search campaign includes searching career and company Web sites for job listings.

Just as the Internet has changed the way the world works, it's also changing the nature of the job search. One software maker observed, "Employers are more proactive now, and there's less 'pounding the pavement' for job seekers."[6] Increasing numbers of employers are listing their job openings at special Web sites that are similar to newspaper classified ads. Companies are also listing job openings at their own Web sites, providing a more direct connection to employment opportunities. Although we will describe six of the best Internet job sites here, you can find a more extensive and continuously updated list with clickable hot links at the Guffey Student Web site **<http://www.westwords.com/guffey/students.html>**. Our site includes many job lists for recent college graduates and entry-level positions.

- **America's Job Bank** is a partnership between the U.S. Department of Labor and the state-operated Public Employment Service. It lists more than 1.5 million job opportunities across the country, and its service is free.

- **Career Mosaic** offers a jobs database, employer profiles, information about on-line job fairs, résumés posted by job seekers, and tips on improving résumés. You can see the results of a job search for an administrative assistant position in Figure 13.2.

- **CareerPath.com** allows you to search help-wanted ads from the nation's leading newspapers. It also presents relevant news and advice articles.

- **College Grad Job Hunter** offers job postings and helpful hints for novices to the job market, such as how to write a résumé, how to interview, and how to negotiate.

- **Monster Board** offers access to information on more than 290,000 jobs worldwide. It publishes a free newsletter, arranges chat sessions on helpful topics for job seekers, and posts over 1,500 pages of targeted career advice.

Perhaps even better are the job openings listed at company Web sites. Check out your favorite companies to see what positions are open. What's the fastest way to find a company's Web address? We recommend Hoover's **<www.hoovers.com>** for quick company information and Web site links. If that fails, use your favorite search engine to learn whether a company has its own

FIGURE 13.2 Results From On-Line Job Search

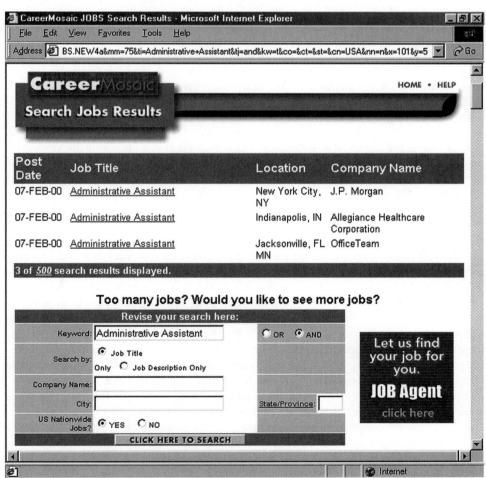

Web site. Some companies even have on-line résumé forms that encourage job candidates to sub mit their qualifications immediately. For example, Texas Instruments provides a form called "TI Resume Builder" at **<http://www.ti.com/recruit/docs/resume-form.shtml>**.

Hundreds of job sites now flood the Internet, and increasing numbers of companies offer on-line recruiting. However, the harsh reality is that landing a job still depends largely on personal contacts. One employment expert said, "On-line recruiting is a little like computer dating. People may find dates that way, but they don't get married that way."[7] Another professional placement expert said, "If you think just [posting] your résumé will get you a job, you're crazy. [Electronic services are] just a supplement to a core strategy of networking your buns off."[8]

The Persuasive Résumé

After using both traditional and on-line resources to learn about the employment market and to develop job leads, you'll focus on writing a persuasive résumé. Such a résumé does more than merely list your qualifications. It packages your assets into a convincing advertisement that sells you for a specific job. The goal of a persuasive résumé is winning an interview. Even if you are not in the job market at this moment, preparing a résumé now has advantages. Having a current résumé makes you look well organized and professional should an unexpected employment opportunity arise. Moreover, preparing a résumé early can help you recognize weak areas and give you time to bolster them.

Choosing a Résumé Style

Your qualifications and career goal will help you choose from among three résumé styles: chronological, functional, and combination.

Chronological. Most popular with recruiters is the chronological résumé, shown in Figure 13.3. It lists work history job by job, starting with the most recent position. Recruiters favor the chronological format because such résumés quickly reveal a candidate's education and experience record. One corporate recruiter said, "I'm looking for applicable experience; chronological résumés are the easiest to assess."[9] The chronological style works well for candidates who have experience in their field of employment and for those who show steady career growth. But for many college students and others who lack extensive experience, the functional résumé format may be preferable.

Chronological résumés focus on past employment; functional résumés focus on skills.

Functional. The functional résumé, shown in Figure 13.4, focuses attention on a candidate's skills rather than on past employment. Like a chronological résumé, the functional résumé begins with the candidate's name, address, telephone number, job objective, and education. Instead of listing jobs, though, the functional résumé groups skills and accomplishments in special categories, such as *Supervisory and Management Skills* or *Retailing and Marketing Experience.* This résumé style highlights accomplishments and can de-emphasize a negative employment history. People who have changed jobs frequently or who have gaps in their employment records may prefer the functional résumé. Recent graduates with little employment experience often find the functional résumé useful.

Functional résumés are also called *skill* résumés. Although the functional résumé of Donald Vinton shown in Figure 13.4 concentrates on skills, it does include a short employment section because recruiters expect it. Notice that Donald breaks his skills into three categories. An alternative—and easier—method is to make one large list, perhaps with a title such as *Areas of Accomplishment, Summary of Qualifications,* or *Areas of Expertise and Ability.*

Chapter 13 The Job Search, Résumés, and Job Application Letters

FIGURE 13.3 Chronological Résumé

ROBERTA M. SANCHEZ
1148 Lambert Road
Naperville, IL 60144

Phone: (708) 814-9322   E-mail: rsanchez@sprint.com

OBJECTIVE   Position with financial services organization installing accounting software and
                     providing user support, where computer experience and proven communication
                     and interpersonal skills can be used to improve operations.

EXPERIENCE   **Accounting software consultant,** Financial Specialists, Elmhurst, Illinois
                     June 2000 to present
                     ● Design and install accounting systems for businesses such as 21st Century
                       Real Estate, Illini Insurance, Aurora Lumber Company, and others.
                     ● Provide ongoing technical support and consultation for regular clients.
                     ● Help write proposals, such as recent one that won $250,000 contract.

                     Office manager (part-time), Post Premiums, Naperville, Illinois
                     June 1996 to May 2000
                     ● Conceived and implemented improved order processing and filing system.
                     ● Managed computerized accounting system; trained new employees to use it.
                     ● Helped install local area network.

                     Bookkeeper (part-time), Sunset Avionics, Downers Grove, Illinois
                     August 1994 to May 1998
                     ● Kept books for small airplane rental and repair service.
                     ● Performed all bookkeeping functions including quarterly internal audit.

EDUCATION   **College of DuPage,** Glen Ellyn, Illinois
                     Associate of Arts degree in business administration, June 2000
                     GPA in major 3.6/4.0

                     Computer Associates training seminars, summer and fall 2000
                     Certificates of completion
                     Seminars in consulting ethics, marketing, and ACCPAC accounting software

SPECIAL SKILLS   ● Proficient in Word 98, PageMaker, Lotus 97, and Excel.
                     ● Skilled in ACCPAC Plus, MAS90, and Solomon IV accounting software.
                     ● Trained in technical writing, including proposals and documentation.
                     ● Experienced in office administration and management.
                     ● Competent at speaking and writing Spanish.

HONORS AND   Dean's list, 3 semesters
ACTIVITIES   Member, Beta Alpha Gamma (business student honorary)
                     Member, Academic Affairs Advisory Committee, College of DuPage, 1997–99

Includes detailed objective in response to advertisement

Uses present-tense verbs for current job

Shows job title in bold for readability

Chronological format arranges jobs and education by dates

White space around headings creates open look

Highlights technical, management, and communication skills

Roberta Sanchez uses a chronological résumé to highlight her work experience, most of which is related directly to the position she seeks. Although she is a recent graduate, she has accumulated experience in two part-time jobs and one full-time job. If she had wished to emphasize her special skills (which is not a bad idea considering her heavy computer expertise), she could have placed the special skills section just after her objective.

FIGURE 13.4 Functional Résumé

Uses general objective
for all-purpose résumé

Avoids dense look by
starring items on
separate lines (could
have used bullets,
dashes, periods, or
boxes)

Emphasizes relevant
skills for
sales/marketing
position

Employs action
verbs to describe
skills

Uses periods at ends
of lines only after
complete statements

DONALD W. VINTON
2250 Turtle Creek Drive
Monroeville, Pennsylvania 15146
PHONE: (412) 724-4981   E-mail: dwvinton@aol.com

OBJECTIVE   Position in sales or marketing with opportunity for advancement and travel.

SALES/   *Demonstrated lawn-care equipment in central and western Pennsylvania.
MARKETING   *Achieved product sales amounting to 120 percent of forecast in competitive
SKILLS   field.
                      *Personally generated over $25,000 in telephone subscriptions as part of
                       President's Task Force for the Penn Foundation.
                      *Conducted telephone survey of selected businesses in two counties to deter-
                       mine potential users of farm equipment and to promote company services.
                      *Successfully served 40 or more retail customers daily as clerk in electrical
                       appliance department of national home hardware store.

COMMUNICATION   *Conducted survey, analyzed results, and wrote a 20-page report regarding
SKILLS   the need for developing a recycling program at Penn State.
                      *Presented talks before selected campus classes and organizations encourag-
                       ing students to participate in recycling program.
                      *Spoke for award-winning delegation defending U.S. policies before mock
                       U.N. meeting.
                      *Announced sports news for WGNF, college radio station.

ORGANIZATIONAL/   *Helped conceptualize, organize, and conduct highly successful campus
MANAGEMENT   campaign to register student voters.
SKILLS   *Scheduled events and arranged weekend student retreat for Newman Club.
                      *Trained and supervised two counter employees at Pizza Bob's.
                      *Organized courses, extracurricular activities, and part-time employment
                       to graduate in seven semesters. Earned 3.4 grade-point average (A = 4.0).

EDUCATION   Pennsylvania State University, State College, PA. B.S., 2000
                         Major: Business Administration with sales and marketing emphasis
                         GPA in major: 3.6 (A = 4.0)

                      Community College of Allegheny County, Monroeville, PA
                         Courses in General Studies and Business Administration

EMPLOYMENT   1998–2000, Pizza Bob's, State College, Pennsylvania
                      Summer 1997, Bellefonte Manufacturers Representatives, Pittsburgh
                      Summer 1994, Home Depot, Inc., Pittsburgh

INTERESTS   Basketball, soccer, mountain biking, skiing

Donald Vinton, a recent graduate, chose this functional format to de-emphasize his
meager work experience and emphasize his potential in sales and marketing. Within
each of the three major categories, he lists specific achievements, all of which are
introduced by action verbs. He has also included a number of keywords that could be
helpful if his résumé is scanned. He included an employment section to satisfy
recruiters.

Combination. The combination résumé style, shown in Figure 13.5, draws on the best features of the chronological and functional résumés. It emphasizes a candidate's capabilities while also including a complete job history. The combination résumé is a good choice for recent graduates because it enables them to profile what they can do for a prospective employer. If the writer has a specific job in mind, the items should be targeted to that job description.

Arranging the Parts

Although résumés have standard parts, their arrangement and content should be strategically planned. The most persuasive résumés emphasize skills and achievements aimed at a particular job or company. They show a candidate's most important qualifications first, and they de-emphasize any weaknesses. In arranging the parts, try to create as few headings as possible; more than six generally looks cluttered. No two résumés are ever exactly alike, but most writers consider the following parts.

Résumés should be arranged with the most important qualifications first.

Main Heading. Your résumé should always begin with your name, address, telephone number, and e-mail address, if available. If possible, include a telephone number where messages may be left for you. Don't give a number that is always busy because you're using a modem on that line. Prospective employers tend to call the next applicant when no one answers. Avoid showing both permanent and temporary addresses; some specialists say that dual addresses immediately identify about-to-graduate college students. Keep the main heading as uncluttered and simple as possible. And don't include the word *résumé*; it's like putting the word *letter* above correspondence.

Career Objective. Opinion is divided on the effect of including a career objective on a résumé. Recruiters think such statements indicate that a candidate has made a commitment to a career. Moreover, career objectives make recruiters' lives easier by allowing them to classify the résumé quickly. But such declarations can also disqualify a candidate if the stated objective doesn't match a company's job description.[10] One expert warned that putting a job objective on a résumé has "killed more opportunities for candidates . . . than typos."[11]

You have four choices regarding career objectives.

Include a career objective for a specific, targeted position; omit an objective on a general résumé.

1. Include a career objective only when applying for a specific, targeted position. For example, the following responds to an advertised position: *Objective: To work in the health care industry as a human resources trainee with exposure to recruiting, training, and benefits administration.*
2. Omit a career objective, especially if you are preparing an all-purpose résumé.
3. Include a general statement, such as *Objective: Challenging position in urban planning* or *Job Goal: Position in sales/marketing.*
4. Omit an objective on the résumé but include it in the application letter, where it can be tailored to a specific position.[12]

Some consultants warn against using the words *entry-level* in your objective, as these words emphasize lack of experience. Many aggressive job applicants today prepare individual résumés that are targeted for each company or position sought. Thanks to word processing, the task is easy.

Education. The next component on your résumé is your education—if it is more noteworthy than your work experience. In this section you should include the name and location of schools, dates of attendance, major fields of study, and degrees received. Your grade-point average and/or class ranking are important to prospective employers. One way to enhance your GPA is to calculate it in your

FIGURE 13.5 Combination Résumé

Omits objective to keep all options open

Focuses on skills and aptitudes that employers seek

Arranges employment by job titles for easy reading

Combines activities and awards to fill out section

Includes references because local employers expect them (most résumés today omit references)

SUSAN R. SNOW
Route 2, Box 180
Dodgeville, Wisconsin 53533
Residence: (608) 935-3196   Messages: (608) 935-4399

SKILLS AND CAPABILITIES
- Keyboard 70 wpm with accuracy.
- Take symbol shorthand at 90 wpm with accurate transcription.
- Skilled in the production of legal documents and correspondence.
- Competent in producing mailable copy from machine transcription.
- Experienced in personal computer use, including the following software: Word 98, Lotus 97, and Excel.
- Ability to perform office tasks and interact effectively using excellent written and oral communication skills.

EXPERIENCE
Word Processing Operator 1, Limited-term employee
University of Wisconsin-Madison, May 2000 to August 2000
- Transcribed confidential letters, memos, reports, and other documents from machine dictation using Word 98.
- Proofread documents for other operators, marking grammar and content errors.

Student Assistant
Southwest Wisconsin Technical College, Fennimore, WI 53809, June 1999 to August 1999
- Typed memos and input financial aid data on terminal to mainframe; printed and verified monthly report totals for $70,000 budget.
- Helped financial aid applicants understand and complete five-page form.
- Screened incoming telephone calls for supervisor and three counselors.

Part-Time Cook and Cashier
Souprrr Subs, Fennimore, WI 53809, May 1998 to May 1999
- Prepared menu items, accepted customer payments, and balanced cash drawer.

EDUCATION
Southwest Wisconsin Technical College, Fennimore, WI 53809
Major: Office assistant and word processing specialist programs
AA degree expected May 2001. GPA in major: 3.6 (4.0 = A)

ACTIVITIES AND AWARDS
- Received the _Fennimore Times_ award from Southwest Wisconsin Technical College Foundation for academic excellence and contribution to campus life.
- Elected secretary of Business Professionals of America Club. Represented SWTC chapter at state and national competitions.

REFERENCES

Ms. Shirley A. Yost	Professor Lois Wagner	Mr. James W. Loy
College of Letters & Science	SW Wisconsin Technical College	SW Wisconsin Technical College
University of Wisconsin	Highway 18 East	Highway 18 East
Madison, WI 53489	Fennimore, WI 53809	Fennimore, WI 53809
(413) 390-4491	(608) 822-8931	(608) 822-8749

Because Susan Snow wanted to highlight her skills and capabilities along with her experience, she combined the best features of functional and traditional résumés. This résumé style is becoming increasingly popular. Although it's not standard practice, Susan included references because employers in her area expect them.

Note: For more résumé models, see Figures 13.10–13.13.

major courses only (for example, *3.6/4.0 in major*). By the way, it is not unethical to showcase your GPA in your major—so long as you clearly indicate what you are doing.

Under *Education* you might be tempted to list all the courses you took, but such a list makes for very dull reading. Refer to courses only if you can relate them to the position sought. When relevant, include certificates earned, seminars attended, and workshops completed. Because employers are interested in your degree of self-sufficiency, you might want to indicate the percentage of your education for which you paid. If your education is incomplete, include such statements as *B.S. degree expected 6/02* or *80 units completed in 120-unit program*. Entitle this section *Education, Academic Preparation,* or *Professional Training.*

Work Experience or Employment History. If your work experience is significant and relevant to the position sought, this information should appear before education. List your most recent employment first and work backwards, including only those jobs that you think will help you win the targeted position. A job application form may demand a full employment history, but your résumé may be selective. (Be aware, though, that time gaps in your employment history will probably be questioned in the interview.) For each position show the following:

The work experience section of a résumé should list specifics and quantify achievements.

- Employer's name, city, and state
- Dates of employment
- Most important job title
- Significant duties, activities, accomplishments, and promotions

Describe your employment achievements concisely but concretely. Avoid generalities such as *Worked with customers*. Be more specific, with statements such as *Served 40 or more retail customers a day; Successfully resolved problems about custom stationery orders;* or *Acted as intermediary among customers, printers, and suppliers*. If possible, quantify your accomplishments, such as *Conducted study of equipment needs of 100 small businesses in Phoenix; Personally generated orders for sales of $90,000 annually; Keyboarded all the production models for a 250-page employee procedures manual;* or *Assisted editor in layout, design, and news writing for 12 issues of division newsletter*. One professional recruiter said, "I spend a half hour every day screening 50 résumés or more, and if I don't spot some [quantifiable] results in the first 10 seconds, the résumé is history."[13]

In addition to technical skills, employers seek individuals with communication, management, and interpersonal capabilities. This means you'll want to select work experiences and achievements that illustrate your initiative, dependability, responsibility, resourcefulness, and leadership. Employers also want people who can work in teams. Thus, include statements such as *Collaborated with interdepartmental task force in developing 10-page handbook for temporary workers* and *Headed student government team that conducted most successful voter registration in campus history.*

Statements describing your work experience can be made forceful and persuasive by using action verbs, such as those listed in Figure 13.6 and illustrated in Figure 13.7.

Capabilities and Skills. Recruiters want to know specifically what you can do for their companies. Therefore, list your special skills, such as *Proficient in preparing correspondence and reports using Word 98*. Include your ability to use computer programs, office equipment, foreign languages, or sign language. Describe proficiencies you have acquired through training and experience, such as *Trained in computer accounting, including general ledger, accounts receivable, accounts payable, and payroll*. Use expressions such as *competent in, skilled in, proficient with, experienced*

Emphasize the skills and aptitudes that recommend you for a specific position.

FIGURE 13.6 Action Verbs for Persuasive Résumés*

Management Skills	Communication Skills	Research Skills	Technical Skills	Teaching Skills
administered	addressed	clarified	assembled	adapted
analyzed	arbitrated	collected	built	advised
consolidated	arranged	critiqued	calculated	clarified
coordinated	collaborated	diagnosed	computed	coached
delegated	convinced	evaluated	designed	communicated
developed	developed	examined	devised	coordinated
directed	drafted	extracted	engineered	developed
evaluated	edited	identified	executed	enabled
improved	explained	inspected	fabricated	encouraged
increased	formulated	interpreted	maintained	evaluated
organized	interpreted	interviewed	operated	explained
oversaw	negotiated	investigated	overhauled	facilitated
planned	persuaded	organized	programmed	guided
prioritized	promoted	summarized	remodeled	informed
recommended	publicized	surveyed	repaired	instructed
scheduled	recruited	systematized	solved	persuaded
strengthened	translated		upgraded	set goals
supervised	wrote			trained

*The underlined words are especially good for pointing out **accomplishments.**

in, and *ability to;* for example, *Competent in typing, editing, and/or proofreading reports, tables, letters, memos, manuscripts, and business forms.*

You'll also want to highlight exceptional aptitudes, such as working well under stress and learning computer programs quickly. If possible, provide details and evidence that back up your assertions; for example, *Mastered PhotoShop in 25 hours with little instruction.* Search for examples of your writing, speaking, man-

FIGURE 13.7 Using Action Verbs to Strengthen Your Résumé

Identified weaknesses in internship program and **researched** five alternate programs.

Reduced delivery delays by an average of three days per order.

Streamlined filing system, thus reducing 400-item backlog to 0.

Organized holiday awards program for 1,200 attendees and 140 awardees.

Created a 12-point checklist for managers to use when requesting temporary workers.

Designed five posters announcing new employee suggestion program.

Calculated shipping charges for overseas deliveries and **recommended** most economical rates.

Managed 24-station computer network linking data and employees in three departments.

Distributed and **explained** voter registration forms to over 500 prospective student voters.

Praised by top management for enthusiastic teamwork and achievement.

Secured national recognition from National Arbor Foundation for tree project.

FIGURE 13.6 Continued

Financial Skills	Creative Skills	Helping Skills	Clerical or Detail Skills	More Verbs for Accomplishments
administered	acted	assessed	approved	achieved
allocated	conceptualized	assisted	catalogued	expanded
analyzed	created	clarified	classified	improved
appraised	customized	coached	collected	pioneered
audited	designed	counseled	compiled	reduced (losses)
balanced	developed	demonstrated	generated	resolved (problems)
budgeted	directed	diagnosed	inspected	restored
calculated	established	educated	monitored	spearheaded
computed	founded	expedited	operated	transformed
developed	illustrated	facilitated	organized	
forecasted	initiated	familiarized	prepared	
managed	instituted	guided	processed	
marketed	introduced	motivated	purchased	
planned	invented	referred	recorded	
projected	originated	represented	screened	
researched	performed		specified	
	planned		systematized	
	revitalized		tabulated	

Source: Adapted from Yana Parker, *The Damn Good Résumé Guide* (Berkeley, CA: Ten Speed Press). Reprinted with permission.

agement, organizational, and interpersonal skills—particularly those talents that are relevant to your targeted job.

For recent graduates, this section can be used to give recruiters evidence of your potential. Instead of *Capabilities*, the section might be called *Skills and Abilities*.

CATHY © Cathy Guisewite. Reprinted with permission of UNIVERSAL PRESS SYNDICATE. All rights reserved.

Awards, Honors, and Activities. If you have three or more awards or honors, highlight them by listing them under a separate heading. If not, put them with activities. Include awards, scholarships (financial and other), fellowships, honors, recognition, commendations, and certificates. Be sure to identify items clearly. Your reader may be unfamiliar, for example, with Greek organizations, honoraries, and awards; tell what they mean. Instead of saying *Recipient of Star award*, give more details: *Recipient of Star award given by Pepperdine University to outstanding graduates who combine academic excellence and extracurricular activities.*

Awards, honors, and activities are appropriate for résumés; most personal data are not.

It's also appropriate to include school, community, and professional activities. Employers are interested in evidence that you are a well-rounded person. This section provides an opportunity to demonstrate leadership and interpersonal skills. Strive to use action statements. For example, instead of saying *Treasurer of business club*, explain more fully: *Collected dues, kept financial records, and paid bills while serving as treasurer of 35-member business management club.*

Personal Data. Today's résumés omit personal data, such as birth date, marital status, height, weight, and religious affiliation. Such information doesn't relate to genuine occupational qualifications, and recruiters are legally barred from asking for such information. Some job seekers do, however, include hobbies or interests (such as skiing or photography) that might grab the recruiter's attention or serve as conversation starters. Naturally, you wouldn't mention dangerous pastimes (such as bungee jumping or sports car racing) or time-consuming interests. But you should indicate your willingness to travel or to relocate, since many companies will be interested.

References are unnecessary for the résumé, but they should be available for the interview.

References. Listing references on a résumé is favored by some recruiters and opposed by others.[14] Such a list takes up valuable space. Moreover, it is not normally instrumental in securing an interview—few companies check references before the interview. Instead, they prefer that a candidate bring to the interview a list of individuals willing to discuss her or his qualifications. If you do list them, use parallel form. For example, if you show a title for one person (*Professor, Dr., Mrs.*), show titles for all. Include addresses and telephone numbers.

Whether or not you include references on your résumé, you should have their names available when you begin your job search. Ask three to five instructors or previous employers whether they will be willing to answer inquiries regarding your qualifications for employment. Be sure, however, to provide them with an opportunity to refuse. No reference is better than a negative one. Do not include personal or character references, such as friends or neighbors, because recruiters rarely consult them. Companies are more interested in the opinions of objective individuals.

One final note: human resources officers see little reason for including the statement *References furnished upon request.* "It's like saying the sun comes up every morning," remarked one human resources professional.[15]

Making Your Résumé Computer Friendly

Increasing use of scanners requires job candidates to prepare computer-friendly résumés.

Thus far our résumé advice aimed at human readers. However, the first reader of your résumé may well be a computer. Hiring companies now use computer programs to reduce hiring costs and make résumé information more accessible. The process of a résumé-scanning program is shown in Figure 13.8

Before you send your résumé, you should learn whether the recipient uses scanning software. One simple way to find out is to call any company where you plan to apply and ask if it scans résumés electronically. If you can't get a clear answer and you have even the slightest suspicion that your résumé might be read electronically, you'll be smart to prepare a plain, scannable version.

A scannable résumé must sacrifice many of the graphics possibilities that savvy writers employ. Computers aren't impressed by graphics; they prefer "vanilla" résumés—free of graphics and fancy fonts. To make a computer-friendly "vanilla" résumé, you'll want to apply the following suggestions about its physical appearance.

Computer-friendly résumés are free of graphics and fancy fonts.

- **Avoid unusual typefaces, underlining, and italics.** Moreover, don't use boxing, shading, or other graphics to highlight text. These features don't scan well. Most applicant-tracking programs, however, can accurately read bold print, solid bullets, and asterisks.

FIGURE 13.8 What a Résumé-Scanning Program Does

| Reads résumé with scanner | Identifies job categories and ranks applicants | Generates letters of rejection or interview offers | Stores information or actual résumé image for future searches |

- **Use 10- to 14-point type.** Because touching letters or unusual fonts are likely to be misread, it's safest to use a large, well-known font, such as 12-point Times Roman or Helvetica. This may mean that your résumé will require two pages. After printing, inspect your résumé to see if any letters touch—especially in your name.

- **Use smooth white paper, black ink, and quality printing.** Avoid colored and textured papers as well as dot-matrix printing.

- **Be sure that your name is the first line on the page.** Don't use fancy layouts that may confuse a scanner.

- **Provide white space.** To ensure separation of words and categories, leave plenty of white space. For example, instead of using parentheses to enclose a telephone area code, insert blank spaces, such as 212 799-2415. Leave blank lines around headings.

- **Avoid double columns.** When listing job duties, skills, computer programs, and so forth, don't tabulate items into two- or three-column lists. Scanners read across and may convert tables into gobbledygook.

- **Don't fold or staple your résumé.** Send it in a large envelope so that you can avoid folds. Words that appear on folds may not be scanned correctly. Avoid staples because the indentions left after they are removed may cause pages to stick.

- **Use abbreviations carefully.** Minimize unfamiliar abbreviations, but maximize easily recognized abbreviations—especially those within your field, such as CAD, COBRA, or JIT. When in doubt, though, spell out! Computers are less addled by whole words.

- **Include all your addresses and telephone numbers.** Be sure your résumé contains your e-mail address, as well as your land address, telephone numbers, and fax number, if available.

- **Be prepared to send your résumé in ASCII.** Pronounced "AS kee," this format offers text only and is immediately readable by all computer programs. It eliminates italics, bold, underlining, and unusual keyboard characters.

Emphasizing Keywords

In addition to paying attention to the physical appearance of your résumé, you must also be concerned with keywords. These are usually nouns that describe what an employer wants. Suppose a supervisor at Nike wants to hire an administrative assistant with special proficiencies. That supervisor might submit the fol-

Keywords are nouns that describe specific candidate traits or job requirements.

lowing keywords to the Nike applicant-tracking system: *Administrative Assistant, Computer Skills, Word 2000, Self-Starter, Report Writing, Proofreading, Communication Skills.* The system would then search through all the résumés on file to see which ones best match the requirements.

A computer-friendly résumé may contain a keyword summary filled with words (usually nouns) that describe the job or candidate.

Joyce Lain Kennedy, nationally syndicated career columnist and author of *Electronic Résumé Revolution*,[16] suggests using a keyword summary. This list of keyword descriptors immediately follows your name and address on your résumé. A keyword summary, as illustrated in Figure 13.13, should contain your targeted job title and alternative labels, as well as previous job titles, skills, software programs, and selected jargon known in your field. It concentrates on nouns rather than on verbs or adjectives.

To construct your summary, go through your core résumé and mark all relevant nouns. Also try to imagine what eight to ten words an employer might use to describe the job you want. Then select the 25 best words for your summary. Because interpersonal traits are often requested by employers, consult Figure 13.9. It shows the most frequently requested interpersonal traits, as reported by Resumix, one of the leaders in résumé-scanning software.

You may entitle your list *Keyword Summary, Keyword Profile,* or *Keyword Index.* Here's an example of a possible keyword summary for a junior accountant:

Keyword Summary

Accountant: Public. Junior. Staff. AA, Delgado Community College—Business Administration. BA, Nicholls State University—Accounting. Payables. Receivables. Payroll Experience. Quarterly Reports. Unemployment Reports. Communication Skills. Computer Skills. Excel. Word 2000. PCs. Mainframes. Internet. Web. Networks. J. D. Edwards Software. Ability to learn software. Accurate. Dean's List. Award of Merit. Team player. Willing to travel. Relocate.

After an introductory keyword summary, your résumé should contain the standard parts discussed in this chapter. Remember that the keyword section merely helps ensure that your résumé will be selected for inspection. Then human eyes take over. Therefore, you'll want to observe the other writing tips you've learned to make your résumé attractive and forceful. Figures 13.10 through 13.12 show additional examples of chronological and combination résumés. Notice that the scannable résumé in Figure 13.13 is not drastically different from the others. It does, however, include a keyword summary.

FIGURE 13.9 Interpersonal Keywords Most Requested by Employers Using Résumé-Scanning Software*

Ability to delegate	Creative	Leadership	Self-accountable
Ability to implement	Customer oriented	Multitasking	Self-managing
Ability to plan	Detail minded	Open communication	Setting priorities
Ability to train	Ethical	Open minded	Supportive
Accurate	Flexible	Oral communication	Takes initiative
Adaptable	Follow instructions	Organizational skills	Team building
Aggressive worker	Follow through	Persuasive	Team player
Analytical ability	Follow up	Problem solving	Tenacious
Assertive	High energy	Public speaking	Willing to travel
Communication skills	Industrious	Results oriented	
Competitive	Innovative	Safety conscious	

*Reported by Resumix, a leading producer of résumé-scanning software.
Source: Joyce Lain Kennedy and Thomas J. Morrow, *Electronic Résumé Revolution* (New York: John Wiley & Sons), 70. Reprinted by permission of John Wiley & Sons, Inc.

FIGURE 13.10 Enhanced Résumé

Jeffrey V. O'Neill

2590 Roxbury Drive
Montpelier, Vermont 05602
(802) 672-5590
joneill@aol.com

Objective	To obtain a challenging position using my financial education and experience.
Education	• Millikin School of Commerce, University of Virginia Bachelor of Science in Commerce, May 2000. GPA: 3.8 Concentrations in Finance and Management Information Systems • University of Vermont, Burlington, VT, 1996–2000
Honors	Golden Key National Honor Society Dean's List 1996–2000 Phi Eta Sigma Freshman Honor Society Vermont State Scholarship
Experience	**Kraft General Foods International,** Ryebrook, New York (Summer 1999) Systems Engineer • Independently analyzed and documented purchasing system and reengineered procedures to improve efficiency. • Evaluated use of 25 PCs and made recommendations to CIO that would save over $30,000. • Conducted cost-benefit study to update PCs and improve network integration for 150 users. **Millikin Computer Lab,** Charlottesville, Virginia (Fall 1998 to present) Lab Consultant • Solve problems and maintain LAN of the Commerce School. • Provide technical assistance to over 300 students and 25 faculty members in the use of lab hardware and software. **Shearson-Lehman Brothers,** Stamford, Connecticut (March 1998) Extern • Gained valuable insights into U.S. capital markets while assisting financial consultants. • Analyzed equity-options trades to determine how financial securities are evaluated.
Computer Experience	Languages: TruBasic, COBOL Environments: Microsoft Windows, DOS, UNIX Applications: Lotus, Excel, Word, WordPerfect, PowerPoint
Activities	• Student Council Representative to Admissions Committee, Fall 1999 • Commerce School Representative to Student Council, Spring 1999 to present • Finance Society Executive Board, Chairman for Investments Game, Spring 1999 • Intramural soccer and basketball, tennis, guitar

Annotations:
— Places honors first for emphasis
— Quantifies many experiences
— Organizes computer skills into three categories
— Shows leadership qualities and well-rounded personality

Although Jeffrey O'Neill had little paid work experience off campus, his résumé looks impressive because of his relevant summer, campus, and extern experiences. He describes specific achievements related to finance, his career goal. This version of his résumé is enhanced with desktop publishing features because he knows it will not be scanned.

FIGURE 13.11 Combination Résumé

Responds to specific job advertisement

Highlights skills named in advertisement

Combines skills and experience for most forceful appeal

Quantifies descriptions of experience

Includes activities and awards with education because of limited space

RICK M. JAMESON

4938 Mountain View Avenue
Sunnyvale, CA 94255
(415) 479-1982
Messages: (415) 412-5540

Objective: Position as Staff Accountant with progressive Bay Area firm, where my technical, computer, and communication skills will be useful in managing accounts and acquiring new clientele.

SKILLS AND CAPABILITIES

Accounting
- Ability to journalize entries accurately in general and specialized journals.
- Proficient in posting to general ledger, preparing trial balance, and detecting discrepancies.
- Trained in preparing and analyzing balance sheet and other financial statements.

Computer
- Experienced in using Lotus, dBASE, and WordPerfect for Windows.
- Comfortable in personal computer (MS-DOS), mainframe, or network environments.
- Ability to learn new computer programs and applications quickly, with little instruction.

Communication and Interpersonal
- Enjoy working with details and completing assignments accurately and on time.
- Demonstrate sound writing and speaking skills acquired and polished in business letter writing, report writing, and speech classes.
- Interact well with people as evidenced in my successful sales, volunteer, and internship work.

EXPERIENCE

Tax Preparer, Volunteer Income Tax Assistance program (VITA)
Sponsored by the Internal Revenue Service and California State University, San Jose. Prepared state and federal tax returns for individuals with incomes under $25,000. Conducted interviews with over 50 individuals to elicit data regarding taxes. Determined legitimate tax deductions and recorded them accurately. (Tax seasons, 1998 to present)

Accounting Intern, Software, Inc., Accounting Department, Santa Clara, CA
Assisted in analyzing data for weekly accounts payable aging report. Prepared daily cash activity report for sums up to $10,000. Calculated depreciation on 12 capital asset accounts with a total valuation of over $900,000. Researched and wrote report analyzing one division's budget of $150,000. (Spring 1998)

Salesperson, Kmart, Santa Clara, CA
Helped customers select gardening and landscaping supplies. Assisted in ordering merchandise, stocking the department, and resolving customer problems. (Summers 1998, 1999)

EDUCATION

California State University, San Jose. B.S. degree expected 6/00
Major: Business Administration
Specialization: Accounting Theory and Practice. GPA: 3.2 (A = 4.0)
Participated as member of Accounting Club for two years.
San Jose Community College. A.A. degree 6/97
Major: Business Administration and Accounting. GPA: 3.4 (A = 4.0)
Received Award of Merit for volunteer work as orientation guide and peer tutor.

Rick Jameson's résumé responds to an advertisement specifying skills for a staff accountant. He uses the combination format to allow him to highlight the skills his education and limited experience have provided. To make the résumé look professional, he uses the italics, bold, and scalable font features of his word processing program.

FIGURE 13.12 Chronological Résumé

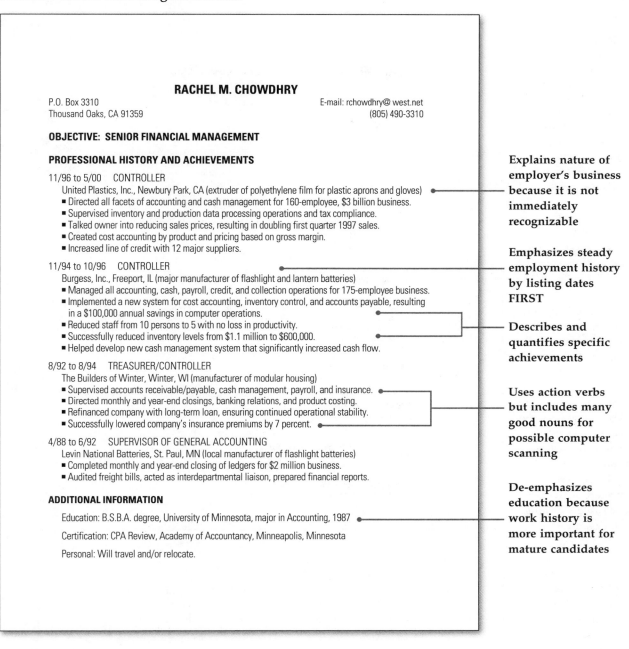

RACHEL M. CHOWDHRY

P.O. Box 3310
Thousand Oaks, CA 91359

E-mail: rchowdhry@ west.net
(805) 490-3310

OBJECTIVE: SENIOR FINANCIAL MANAGEMENT

PROFESSIONAL HISTORY AND ACHIEVEMENTS

11/96 to 5/00   CONTROLLER
    United Plastics, Inc., Newbury Park, CA (extruder of polyethylene film for plastic aprons and gloves)
    ■ Directed all facets of accounting and cash management for 160-employee, $3 billion business.
    ■ Supervised inventory and production data processing operations and tax compliance.
    ■ Talked owner into reducing sales prices, resulting in doubling first quarter 1997 sales.
    ■ Created cost accounting by product and pricing based on gross margin.
    ■ Increased line of credit with 12 major suppliers.

11/94 to 10/96   CONTROLLER
    Burgess, Inc., Freeport, IL (major manufacturer of flashlight and lantern batteries)
    ■ Managed all accounting, cash, payroll, credit, and collection operations for 175-employee business.
    ■ Implemented a new system for cost accounting, inventory control, and accounts payable, resulting
      in a $100,000 annual savings in computer operations.
    ■ Reduced staff from 10 persons to 5 with no loss in productivity.
    ■ Successfully reduced inventory levels from $1.1 million to $600,000.
    ■ Helped develop new cash management system that significantly increased cash flow.

8/92 to 8/94   TREASURER/CONTROLLER
    The Builders of Winter, Winter, WI (manufacturer of modular housing)
    ■ Supervised accounts receivable/payable, cash management, payroll, and insurance.
    ■ Directed monthly and year-end closings, banking relations, and product costing.
    ■ Refinanced company with long-term loan, ensuring continued operational stability.
    ■ Successfully lowered company's insurance premiums by 7 percent.

4/88 to 6/92   SUPERVISOR OF GENERAL ACCOUNTING
    Levin National Batteries, St. Paul, MN (local manufacturer of flashlight batteries)
    ■ Completed monthly and year-end closing of ledgers for $2 million business.
    ■ Audited freight bills, acted as interdepartmental liaison, prepared financial reports.

ADDITIONAL INFORMATION

    Education: B.S.B.A. degree, University of Minnesota, major in Accounting, 1987

    Certification: CPA Review, Academy of Accountancy, Minneapolis, Minnesota

    Personal: Will travel and/or relocate.

Annotations (right margin):

Explains nature of employer's business because it is not immediately recognizable

Emphasizes steady employment history by listing dates FIRST

Describes and quantifies specific achievements

Uses action verbs but includes many good nouns for possible computer scanning

De-emphasizes education because work history is more important for mature candidates

Because Rachel Chowdhry has many years of experience and seeks high-level employment, she focuses on her experience. Notice how she includes specific achievements and quantifies them whenever possible.

FIGURE 13.13 Computer-Friendly Résumé

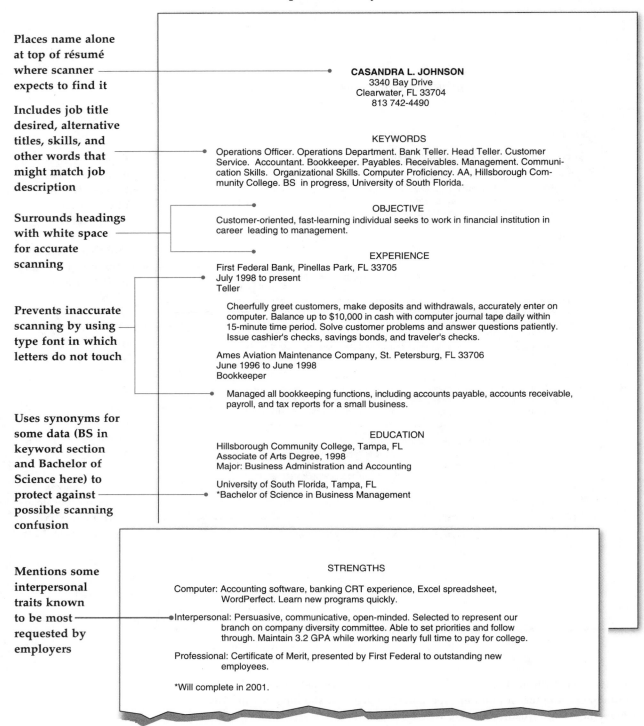

Places name alone at top of résumé where scanner expects to find it

Includes job title desired, alternative titles, skills, and other words that might match job description

Surrounds headings with white space for accurate scanning

Prevents inaccurate scanning by using type font in which letters do not touch

Uses synonyms for some data (BS in keyword section and Bachelor of Science here) to protect against possible scanning confusion

Mentions some interpersonal traits known to be most requested by employers

CASANDRA L. JOHNSON
3340 Bay Drive
Clearwater, FL 33704
813 742-4490

KEYWORDS

Operations Officer. Operations Department. Bank Teller. Head Teller. Customer Service. Accountant. Bookkeeper. Payables. Receivables. Management. Communication Skills. Organizational Skills. Computer Proficiency. AA, Hillsborough Community College. BS in progress, University of South Florida.

OBJECTIVE

Customer-oriented, fast-learning individual seeks to work in financial institution in career leading to management.

EXPERIENCE

First Federal Bank, Pinellas Park, FL 33705
July 1998 to present
Teller

Cheerfully greet customers, make deposits and withdrawals, accurately enter on computer. Balance up to $10,000 in cash with computer journal tape daily within 15-minute time period. Solve customer problems and answer questions patiently. Issue cashier's checks, savings bonds, and traveler's checks.

Ames Aviation Maintenance Company, St. Petersburg, FL 33706
June 1996 to June 1998
Bookkeeper

Managed all bookkeeping functions, including accounts payable, accounts receivable, payroll, and tax reports for a small business.

EDUCATION

Hillsborough Community College, Tampa, FL
Associate of Arts Degree, 1998
Major: Business Administration and Accounting

University of South Florida, Tampa, FL
*Bachelor of Science in Business Management

STRENGTHS

Computer: Accounting software, banking CRT experience, Excel spreadsheet, WordPerfect. Learn new programs quickly.

Interpersonal: Persuasive, communicative, open-minded. Selected to represent our branch on company diversity committee. Able to set priorities and follow through. Maintain 3.2 GPA while working nearly full time to pay for college.

Professional: Certificate of Merit, presented by First Federal to outstanding new employees.

*Will complete in 2001.

Casandra Johnson prepared this "vanilla" résumé (free of graphics and fancy formatting) so that it would scan well if read by a computer. Notice that she begins with a keyword summary that contains job titles, skills, traits, and other descriptive words. She hopes that some of these keywords will match those submitted by an employer. To improve accurate scanning, she avoids italics, vertical and horizontal lines, and double columns.

Preparing an On-Line, Hypertext Résumé

To give your résumé life and make it stand out from others, you might wish to prepare an on-line résumé. This is actually an HTML (Hypertext Markup Language) document located at a Web site. Posting an on-line résumé has some distinct advantages—and a few disadvantages.

On the plus side, merely preparing an on-line résumé suggests that you have exceptional technical savvy. (You would, of course, give credit for any borrowed graphics or code.) An on-line résumé can be viewed whenever it is convenient for an employer, and it can be seen by many individuals in an organization without circulating a paper copy. But the real reason for preparing an on-line résumé is that it can become an electronic portfolio with links to examples of your work.

You could include clickable links to reports you have written, summaries of projects completed, a complete list of your course work, letters of recommendation (with permissions from your recommenders), and extra information about your work experience. An advanced portfolio might include links to electronic copies of your artwork, film projects, blueprints, and photographs of classwork that might otherwise be difficult to share with potential employers. Moreover, you can include razzle-dazzle effects such as color, animation, sound, and graphics. An on-line résumé provides ample opportunity to show off your creative talents, but only if the position calls for creativity.

On the minus side, on-line résumés must be more generic than print résumés. They cannot be altered easily if you apply for different positions. Moreover, they present a security problem unless password protected. You may want to include only an e-mail address instead of offering your address and telephone number.

Perhaps the best approach is to submit a traditional résumé and letter of application and treat your on-line résumé only as a portfolio of your work. Don't confuse a computer-friendly résumé with a hypertext résumé. The former is one that can be easily scanned; while the latter is essentially a dedicated Web site with your résumé information and work samples.

> An on-line résumé contains hypertext links to work samples or a portfolio of additional information.

Risking Your Future With an Inflated Résumé

A résumé is expected to showcase a candidate's strengths and minimize weaknesses. For this reason, recruiters expect a certain degree of self-promotion. But some résumé writers step over the line that separates honest self-marketing from deceptive half-truths and flat-out lies. Distorting facts on a résumé is unethical; lying is illegal. And either practice can destroy a career.

Although recruiters can't check everything, most will verify previous employment and education before hiring candidates. Over half will require official tran-

> Even if discovered much later, deception on a résumé can result in firing.

GRANTLAND®

www.grantland.net

scripts. And after hiring, the checking process may continue. At one of the nation's top accounting firms, the human resources director described the posthiring routine: "If we find a discrepancy in GPA or prior experience due to an honest mistake, we meet with the new hire to hear an explanation. But if it wasn't a mistake, we terminate the person immediately. Unfortunately, we've had to do that too often."[17]

No job seeker wants to be in the unhappy position of explaining résumé errors or defending misrepresentation. Avoiding the following common problems can keep you off the hot seat:

- **Inflated education, grades, or honors.** Some job candidates claim degrees from colleges or universities when in fact they merely attended classes. Others increase their grade-point averages or claim fictitious honors. Any such dishonest reporting is grounds for dismissal when discovered.

- **Enhanced job titles.** Wanting to elevate their status, some applicants misrepresent their titles. For example, one technician called himself a "programmer" when he had actually programmed only one project for his boss. A mail clerk who assumed added responsibilities conferred upon herself the title of "supervisor." Even when the description seems accurate, it's unethical to list any title not officially granted.

- **Puffed-up accomplishments.** Some job seekers inflate their employment experience or achievements. One clerk, eager to make her photocopying duties sound more important, said that she assisted the *vice president in communicating and distributing employee directives.* An Ivy League graduate who spent the better part of six months watching rented videos on his VCR described the activity as *Independent Film Study.* The latter statement may have helped win an interview, but it lost him the job.[18] In addition to avoiding puffery, guard against taking sole credit for achievements that required many people. When recruiters suspect dubious claims on résumés, they nail applicants with specific—and often embarrassing—questions during their interviews.[19]

- **Altered employment dates.** Some candidates extend the dates of employment to hide unimpressive jobs or to cover up periods of unemployment and illness. Let's say that several years ago Cindy was unemployed for fourteen months between working for Company A and being hired by Company B. To make her employment history look better, she adds seven months to her tenure with Company A and seven months to Company B. Now her employment history has no gaps, but her résumé is dishonest and represents a potential booby trap for her.

Applying the Final Touches

In addition to being well written, a résumé must be carefully formatted and meticulously proofread.

Because your résumé is probably the most important document you will ever write, you should expect to revise it many times. With so much information in concentrated form and with so much riding on its outcome, your résumé demands careful polishing, proofreading, and critiquing.

As you revise, be certain to verify all the facts, particularly those involving your previous employment and education. Don't be caught in a mistake, or worse, distortion of previous jobs and dates of employment.

As you continue revising, look for other ways to improve your résumé. For example, consider consolidating headings. By condensing your information into as few headings as possible, you'll produce a clean, professional-looking document. Study other résumés for valuable formatting ideas. Ask yourself what graphics highlighting techniques you can use to improve readability: capitalization, underlining, indenting, and bulleting. Experiment with headings and styles to achieve a pleasing, easy-to-read message. Moreover, look for ways to eliminate wordiness. For example, instead of *Supervised two employees who worked at the counter*, try *Supervised two counter employees*. Review Chapter 4 for more tips on writing concisely.

Above all, make your résumé look professional. Avoid anything humorous or "cute," such as a help-wanted poster with your name or picture inside. Eliminate the personal pronoun *I*. The abbreviated, objective style of a résumé precludes the use of personal pronouns. Use white, off-white, or buff-colored heavy bond paper (24-pound) and a first-rate printer.

After revising, proofread, proofread, and proofread again: for spelling and mechanics, for content, and for format. Then, have a knowledgeable friend or relative proofread it again. This is one document that must be perfect.

By now you may be thinking that you'd like to hire someone to write your résumé. Don't. First, you know yourself better than anyone else could know you. Second, you'll end up with either a generic or a one-time résumé. A generic résumé in today's highly competitive job market will lose out to a targeted résumé nine times out of ten. Equally useless is a one-time résumé aimed at a single job. What if you don't get that job? Because you will need to revise your résumé many times as you seek a variety of jobs, be prepared to write (and rewrite) it yourself.

A final word about résumé-writing services. Some tend to produce eye-catching, elaborate documents with lofty language, fancy borders, and fuzzy thinking. Here's an example of empty writing: "Seeking a position which will utilize academic achievements and hands-on experience while providing for career-development opportunities."[20] Save your money and buy a good interview suit instead.

> Because résumés must be perfect, they should be proofread many times.

Faxing or E-Mailing Your Résumé

In this hurry-up world, employers increasingly want information immediately. If you must fax or e-mail your résumé, take a second look at it. The key to success is SPACE. Without it, letters and character blur. Underlines blend with the words above, and bold print may look like an ink blot.[21] How can you improve your chances of making a good impression when you must fax or e-mail your résumé?

If you are faxing your printed résumé, select a font with adequate space between each character. Thinner fonts—such as Times, Palatino, New Century Schoolbook, Courier, and Bookman—are clearer than thicker ones. Use a 12-point or larger font, and avoid underlines, which may look broken or choppy when faxed. To be safe, get a transmission report to ensure that all pages were transmitted satisfactorily. Finally, follow up with your polished, printed résumé.

If you are e-mailing your résumé, you may wish to prepare an ASCII version (text only). It will eliminate bold, italics, underlining, tabulated indentions, and unusual characters. To prevent lines from wrapping at awkward spots, keep your line length to 65 characters or less. You can, of course, transmit a fully formatted, attractive résumé if you send it as an attachment and your receiver is using a compatible e-mail program.

Nearly everyone writes a résumé by adapting a model, such as those in Figures 13.3 through 13.5 and 13.10 through 13.13. The chronological résumé for Rachel Chowdhry shown in Figure 13.12 is typical of candidates with considerable working experience. Although she describes four positions that span a 14-year period, she manages to fit her résumé on one page. However, two-page résumés are justified for people with long work histories.

> Résumés to be faxed should have ample space between letters, be printed in 12-point or larger font, and avoid underlines.

> Résumés that are sent by e-mail transmit best as ASCII (text-only) files without tabs or underlines, and without italic, bold, or unusual characters.

The Persuasive Job Application Letter

To accompany your résumé, you'll need a persuasive job application letter (also called a cover letter). The job application letter has three purposes: (1) introducing the résumé, (2) highlighting your strengths in terms of benefits to the

Job application letters introduce résumés, relate writer strengths to reader benefits, and seek an interview.

reader, and (3) gaining an interview. In many ways your application letter is a sales letter; it sells your talents and tries to beat the competition. It will, accordingly, include many of the techniques you learned for sales presentations in Chapter 8.

Human resources professionals disagree on how long to make job application letters. Many prefer short letters with no more than four paragraphs; instead of concentrating on the letter, these readers focus on the résumé. Others desire longer letters that supply more information, thus giving them a better opportunity to evaluate a candidate's qualifications. The latter human resources professionals argue that hiring and training new employees is expensive and time-consuming; therefore, they welcome extra data to guide them in making the best choice the first time. Follow your judgment in writing a brief or a lengthier letter. If you feel, for example, that you need space to explain in more detail what you can do for a prospective employer, do so.

Regardless of its length, an application letter should have three primary parts: (1) an opening that gains attention, (2) a body that builds interest and reduces resistance, and (3) a closing that motivates action.

Gaining Attention in the Opening

The opener in a letter of application gains attention by addressing the receiver by name.

The first step in gaining the interest of your reader is addressing that individual by name. Rather than sending your letter to the "Personnel Manager" or "Human Resources Department," try to identify the name of the appropriate individual. Make it a rule to call the organization for the correct spelling and the complete address. This personal touch distinguishes your letter and demonstrates your serious interest.

How you open your letter of application depends largely on whether the application is solicited or unsolicited. If an employment position has been announced and applicants are being solicited, you can use a direct approach. If you do not know whether a position is open and you are prospecting for a job, use an indirect approach. Whether direct or indirect, the opening should attract the attention of the reader. Strive for openings that are more imaginative than *Please consider this letter an application for the position of . . .* or *I would like to apply for. . . .*

Openings for Solicited Jobs. Here are some of the best techniques to open a letter of application for a job that has been announced:

Openers for solicited jobs refer to the source of the information, the job title, and qualifications for the position.

- **Refer to the name of an employee in the company.** Remember that employers always hope to hire known quantities rather than complete strangers:

  Mitchell Sims, a member of your Customer Service Department, told me that IntriPlex is seeking an experienced customer service representative. The attached summary of my qualifications demonstrates my preparation for this position.

  At the suggestion of Ms. Jennifer Larson of your Human Resources Department, I submit my qualifications for the position of staffing coordinator.

- **Refer to the source of your information precisely.** If you are answering an advertisement, include the exact position advertised and the name and date of the publication. For large organizations it's also wise to mention the section of the newspaper where the ad appeared:

  Your advertisement in Section C-3 of the June 1 *Daily News* for an accounting administrator greatly appeals to me. With my accounting training and computer experience, I believe I could serve Quad Graphics well.

The September 10 issue of *The Washington Post* reports that you are seeking a mature, organized, and reliable administrative assistant with excellent communication skills.

Susan Butler, placement director at Sierra University, told me that DataTech has an opening for a technical writer with knowledge of Web design and graphics.

- **Refer to the job title and describe how your qualifications fit the requirements.** Human resources directors are looking for a match between an applicant's credentials and the job needs:

Will an honors graduate with a degree in recreation and two years of part-time experience organizing social activities for a convalescent hospital qualify for your position of activity director?

Because of my specialized training in computerized accounting at Boise State University, I feel confident that I have the qualifications you described in your advertisement for a cost accountant trainee.

Openings for Unsolicited Jobs. If you are unsure whether a position actually exists, you may wish to use a more persuasive opening. Since your goal is to convince this person to read on, try one of the following techniques:

- **Demonstrate interest in and knowledge of the reader's business.** Show the human resources director that you have done your research and that this organization is more than a mere name to you:

Since Signa HealthNet, Inc., is organizing a new information management team for its recently established group insurance division, could you use the services of a well-trained information systems graduate who seeks to become a professional systems analyst?

- **Show how your special talents and background will benefit the company.** Human resources directors need to be convinced that you can do something for them:

Could your rapidly expanding publications division use the services of an editorial assistant who offers exceptional language skills, an honors degree from the University of Maine, and two years' experience in producing a campus literary publication?

In applying for an advertised job, Kendra A. Hawkins wrote the solicited letter of application shown in Figure 13.14. Notice that her opening identifies the position and the newspaper completely so that the reader knows exactly what advertisement Kendra refers to. Using features on her word processing program, Kendra designed her own letterhead that uses her name and looks like professionally printed letterhead paper.

More challenging are unsolicited letters of application, such as Donald Vinton's shown in Figure 13.15. Because he hopes to discover or create a job, his opening must grab the reader's attention immediately. To do that, he capitalizes on company information appearing in the newspaper. Donald purposely kept his application letter short and to the point because he anticipated that a busy executive would be unwilling to read a long, detailed letter. Donald's unsolicited letter "prospects" for a job. Some job candidates feel that such letters may be even more productive than efforts to secure advertised jobs, since "prospecting" candidates face less competition. Notice that Donald's letter uses a standard return address consisting of his street, city, and the date.

Openers for unsolicited jobs show interest in and knowledge of the company, as well as spotlighting reader benefits.

FIGURE 13.14 Solicited Application Letter

Kendra A. Hawkins

1770 Hawthorne Place, Boulder CO 80304

May 23, 2000

Ms. Courtney L. Donahue
Director, Human Resources
Del Rio Enterprises
Denver, CO 82511

Dear Ms. Donahue:

Your advertisement for an assistant product manager, appearing May 22 in Section C of the *Denver Post,* immediately caught my attention because my education and training closely parallel your needs.

According to your advertisement, the job includes "assisting in the coordination of a wide range of marketing programs as well as analyzing sales results and tracking marketing budgets." A recent internship at Ventana Corporation introduced me to similar tasks. Assisting the marketing manager enabled me to analyze the promotion, budget, and overall sales success of two products Ventana was evaluating. My ten-page report examined the nature of the current market, the products' life cycles, and their sales/profit return. In addition to this research, I helped formulate a product merchandising plan and answered consumers' questions at a local trade show.

Intensive course work in marketing and management, as well as proficiency in computer spreadsheets and databases, has given me the kind of marketing and computer training that Del Rio probably demands in a product manager. Moreover, my recent retail sales experience and participation in campus organizations have helped me develop the kind of customer service and interpersonal skills necessary for an effective product manager.

After you have examined the enclosed résumé for details of my qualifications, I would be happy to answer questions. Please call me to arrange an interview at your convenience so that we may discuss how my marketing experience, computer training, and interpersonal skills could contribute to Del Rio Enterprises.

Sincerely,

Kendra A. Hawkins

Kendra A. Hawkins

Enclosure

Building Interest in the Body

The body of a letter of application should build interest, reduce resistance, and discuss relevant personal traits.

Once you have captured the attention of the reader, you can use the body of the letter to build interest and reduce resistance. Keep in mind that your résumé emphasizes what you have *done*; your application letter stresses what you *can do* for the employer.

Your first goal is to relate your remarks to a specific position. If you are responding to an advertisement, you'll want to explain how your preparation and experience fill the stated requirements. If you are prospecting for a job, you may not know the exact requirements. Your employment research and knowledge of your field, however, should give you a reasonably good idea of what is expected for this position.

FIGURE 13.15 Unsolicited Letter of Application

2250 Turtle Creek Drive
Monroeville, PA 15146
May 29, 2000

Mr. Richard M. Jannis
Vice President, Operations
Sports World, Inc.
4907 Allegheny Boulevard
Pittsburgh, PA 16103

Dear Mr. Jannis:

Today's Pittsburgh *Examiner* reports that your organization plans to expand its operations to include national distribution of sporting goods, and it occurs to me that you will be needing highly motivated, self-starting sales representatives and marketing managers. Here are three significant qualifications I have to offer:

- Four years of formal training in business administration, including specialized courses in sales management, retailing, marketing promotion, and consumer behavior.

- Practical experience in demonstrating and selling consumer products, as well as successful experience in telemarketing.

- Good communication skills and a strong interest in most areas of sports (which helped me become a sportscaster at Penn State radio station WGNF).

May we talk about how I can put these qualifications, and others summarized in the enclosed résumé, to work for Sports World as it develops its national sales force? I'll call during the week of June 5 to discuss your company's expansion plans and the opportunity for an interview.

Sincerely yours,

Donald W. Vinton

Donald W. Vinton

Enclosure

Annotations:
- Uses standard return address format, but could have designed his own letterhead
- Shows knowledge of company and resourcefulness
- Keeps letter brief to retain reader's attention
- Refers to résumé
- Takes initiative for follow-up

It's also important to emphasize reader benefits. In other words, you should describe your strong points in relation to the needs of the employer. In one employment survey many human resources professionals expressed the same view: "I want you to tell me what you can do for my organization. This is much more important to me than telling me what courses you took in college or what 'duties' you performed on your previous jobs."[22] Instead of *I have completed courses in business communication, report writing, and technical writing,* try this:

Courses in business communication, report writing, and technical writing have helped me develop the research and writing skills required of your technical writers.

Spotlighting reader benefits means matching one's personal strengths to an employer's needs.

Choose your strongest qualifications and show how they fit the targeted job. And remember, students with little experience are better off spotlighting their education and its practical applications, as these candidates did:

> Because you seek an architect's apprentice with proven ability, I submit a drawing of mine that won second place in the Sinclair College drafting contest last year.

> Successfully transcribing over 100 letters and memos in my college transcription class gave me experience in converting the spoken word into the written word, an exacting communication skill demanded of your administrative assistants.

In the body of your letter, you'll also want to discuss relevant personal traits. Employers are looking for candidates who, among other things, are team players, take responsibility, show initiative, and learn easily. Finally, in this section or the next, you should refer the reader to your résumé. Do so directly or as part of another statement, as shown here:

> Please refer to the attached résumé for additional information regarding my education, experience, and references.

> As you will notice from my résumé, I will graduate in June with a bachelor's degree in business administration.

Motivating Action in the Closing

The closing of a letter of application should include a request for an interview.

After presenting your case, you should conclude with a spur to action. This is where you ask for an interview. If you live in a distant city, you may request an employment application or an opportunity to be interviewed by the organization's nearest representative. However, never ask for the job. To do so would be presumptuous and naive. In requesting an interview, suggest reader benefits or review your strongest points. Sound sincere and appreciative. Remember to make it easy for the reader to agree by supplying your telephone number and the best times to call you. And keep in mind that some human resources directors prefer that you take the initiative to call them. Here are possible endings:

> I hope this brief description of my qualifications and the additional information on my résumé indicate to you my genuine desire to put my skills in accounting to work for you. Please call me at (405) 488-2291 before 10 a.m. or after 3 p.m. to arrange an interview.

> To add to your staff an industrious, well-trained administrative assistant with proven word processing and communication skills, call me at (350) 492-1433 to arrange an interview. I can meet with you at any time convenient to your schedule.

> Next week, after you have examined the attached résumé, I will call you to discuss the possibility of arranging an interview.

Avoiding "I" Dominance

As you revise your application letter, notice how many sentences begin with *I*. Although it's impossible to talk about yourself without using *I*, you can reduce the number of sentences beginning with this pronoun by using two techniques. First, place *I* in the middle of sentences instead of dominating the opening. Instead of *I was the top salesperson in my department*, try *While working in X department, I did Y and Z and among 15 coworkers, I received top ratings from my managers.* Incorporating *I* into the middle of sentences considerably reduces its domination.

Another technique for avoiding "I" dominance involves making activities and outcomes, and not yourself, the subjects of sentences. For example, rather than *I took classes in business communication and computer applications,* say *Classes in business communication and computer applications prepared me to. . . .* Instead of *I enjoyed helping customers,* say *Helping customers was a real pleasure.*

Final Tips

Like the résumé, your application letter must look professional and suggest quality. This means using a traditional letter style, such as block or modified block. Also, be sure to print it on the same bond paper as your résumé. More and more writers today are designing their own letterhead paper, or they adapt one of the "wizards" available with their word processing programs. Be sure to use restraint, though, so that your letterhead looks truly professional, such as that shown in Figure 13.14. Finally, proofread your application letter several times; then, have a friend read it for content and mechanics.

A letter of application should look professional and suggest quality.

Summing Up and Looking Forward

In today's competitive job market, an employment search begins with identifying your interests, evaluating your qualifications, and choosing a career path. Finding the perfect job will mean a concentrated effort devoted to checking classified advertisements, networking, and studying on-line job possibilities. In applying for jobs, you'll want to submit a persuasive résumé that sells your skills and experience. Whether you choose a chronological, functional, or combination résumé style, you should tailor your assets to fit the position sought. If you think your résumé might be scanned, emphasize keywords and keep the format simple. A persuasive application letter should introduce your résumé and describe how your skills and experiences match those required.

Now, if your résumé and application letter have been successful, you'll proceed to the employment interview, one of life's most nerve-wracking experiences. The last chapter in this book provides helpful suggestions for successful interviewing and follow-up communication.

Critical Thinking

1. How has the concept of the job changed, and how will it affect your employment search?
2. How is a résumé different from a company employment application?
3. Some job candidates think that applying for unsolicited jobs can be more fruitful than applying for advertised openings. Discuss the advantages and disadvantages of letters that "prospect" for jobs.
4. What are the advantages and disadvantages of developing a hypertext résumé?
5. Ethical Issue: At work fellow employee Kevin lets it slip that he did not complete the degree he claims on his résumé. You have never liked Kevin, but he does satisfactory work. You are both competing for the same promotion. You are considering writing an anonymous note to the boss telling him to verify Kevin's degree. Use the tools on page 80 to decide whether this is an ethical action.

6. List at least five questions that you should ask yourself to identify your employment interests.

7. List five or more sources of career information.

8. How are most jobs likely to be found? Through the classified ads? Employment agencies? Networking? Explain.

9. What is the goal of your résumé?

10. Describe a chronological résumé and discuss its advantages.

11. Describe a functional résumé and discuss its advantages.

12. What are the disadvantages of a functional résumé?

13. When does it make sense to include a career objective on your résumé?

14. On a chronological résumé what information should you include for the jobs you list?

15. In addition to technical skills, what traits and characteristics do employers seek?

16. List some suggestions for making a résumé easily scannable by a computer.

17. What are keywords and why are they important in résumé scanning? Give examples.

18. If you are e-mailing your résumé, why is it wise to send a text-only version?

19. What are the three purposes of a job application letter?

20. How can you make it easy for a recruiter to reach you?

Activities and Cases

13.1 Identifying Your Employment Interests. In a memo addressed to your instructor, answer the questions in the section "Identifying Your Interests" at the beginning of the chapter. Draw a conclusion from your answers. What kind of career, company, position, and location seem to fit your self-analysis?

13.2 Evaluating Your Qualifications. Prepare four worksheets that inventory your qualifications in the areas of employment, education, capabilities and skills, and honors and activities. Use active verbs when appropriate.

a. *Employment.* Begin with your most recent job or internship. For each position list the following information: employer; job title; dates of employment; and three to five duties, activities, or accomplishments. Emphasize activities related to your job goal. Strive to quantify your achievements.

b. *Education.* List degrees, certificates, and training accomplishments. Include courses, seminars, or skills that are relevant to your job goal. Calculate your grade-point average in your major.

c. *Capabilities and skills.* List all capabilities and skills that recommend you for the job you seek. Use words such as *skilled, competent, trained, experienced,* and *ability to.* Also list five or more qualities or interpersonal skills necessary for a successful individual in your chosen field. Write action statements demonstrating that you possess some of these qualities. Empty assurances aren't good enough; try to show evidence (*Developed teamwork skills by working with a committee of eight to produce a . . .*).

d. *Awards, honors, and activities.* Explain any awards so that the reader will understand them. List campus, community, and professional activities that suggest you are a well-rounded individual or possess traits relevant to your target job.

13.3 Choosing a Career Path. Visit your college library, local library, or campus career center. In bound form or on CD-ROM, consult the *Dictionary of Occupational Titles*. Find the description for a position for which you could apply in two to five years. Photocopy or print the pages from the *Occupational Outlook Handbook* that describe employment in the area in which you are interested. If your instructor directs, attach these copies to the letter of application you will write in Activity 13.9.

13.4 Searching the Job Market. Clip a job advertisement from the classified section of a newspaper or print one from a career site on the Web. Select an ad describing the kind of employment you are seeking now or plan to seek when you graduate. Save this advertisement to attach to the résumé you will write in Activity 13.8.

Web **13.5 Posting a Résumé on the Web.** Prepare a list of at least three on-line employment sites where you could post your résumé. Describe the procedure involved and the advantages for each site.

13.6 Draft Document: Résumé. Analyze the following résumé. Discuss its strengths and weaknesses. Your instructor may ask you to revise sections of this résumé before showing you an improved version.

Wendy Lee Cox
5349 East Zion Place
Tulsa, OK 74115-3394
Phone: (d) (918) 834-4583 (n) (918) 594-2985

Seeking to be hired at Mead Products as an intern in Accounting

SKILLS: Accounting, Internet, Windows 98, Excel, PowerPoint, Freelance Graphics

EDUCATION
Now working on B.S. in Business Administration. Major, Management and Accounting; GPA is 3.5. Expect to graduate in June, 2001.

EXPERIENCE:
Assistant Accountant, 1996 to present. March and McLennan, Inc., Bookkeeping/Tax Service, Tulsa. I keep accounting records for several small businesses accurately. I prepare 150 to 200 individual income tax returns each year. For Hill and Hill Truck Line I maintain accurate and up-to-date A/R records. And I prepare payroll records for 16 employees at three firms.

Peterson Controls Inc., Tulsa. Data Processing Internship, 2000 to present. I design and maintain spreadsheets and also process weekly and monthly information for production uptime and downtime. I prepare graphs to illustrate uptime and downtime data.

Tulsa Country Club. Accounts Payable Internship, 1999 to 2000. Took care of accounts payable including filing system for the club. Responsible for processing monthly adjusting entries for general ledger. Worked closely with treasurer to give the Board budget/disbursement figures regularly.

Langston University, Tulsa. I marketed the VITA program to Langston students and organized volunteers and supplies. Official title: Coordinator of Volunteer Income Tax Assistance Project.

COMMUNITY SERVICE: March of Dimes Drive, Central Park High School; All Souls Unitarian Church, coordinator for Children's Choir

13.7 Draft Document: Letter of Application. Analyze each section of the following letter of application written by an accounting major about to graduate.

Dear Human Resources Director:

Please consider this letter as an application for the position of staff accountant that I saw advertised in the *Houston Post*. Although I have had no paid work experience in this field, accounting has been my major in college and I'm sure I could be an asset to your company.

For four years I have studied accounting, and I am fully trained for full-charge bookkeeping as well as electronic accounting. I have taken 36 units of college accounting and courses in business law, economics, statistics, finance, management, and marketing. In addition to my course work, during the tax season I have been a student volunteer for VITA. This is a project to help individuals in the community prepare their income tax returns, and I learned a lot from this experience. I have also received some experience in office work and working with figures when I was employed as an office assistant for Copy Quick, Inc.

I am a competent and responsible person who gets along pretty well with others. I have been a member of some college and social organizations and have even held elective office.

I feel that I have a strong foundation in accounting as a result of my course work and my experience. Along with my personal qualities and my desire to succeed, I hope that you will agree that I qualify for the position of staff accountant with your company.

Sincerely,

13.8 Résumé. Using the data you developed in Activity 13.2, write your résumé. Aim it at a full-time job, part-time position, or internship. Attach a job listing for a specific position (from Activity 13.4). Use a computer. Revise your résumé until it is perfect.

13.9 Job Application Letter. Write an application letter introducing your résumé. Again, use a computer. Revise your application letter until it is perfect.

Grammar/Mechanics Checkup—13

Number Style

Review Sections 4.01–4.13 in the Grammar/Mechanics Handbook. Then study each of the following pairs. Assume that these expressions appear in the context of letters, reports, or memos. Write *a* or *b* in the space provided to indicate the preferred number style and record the number of the G/M principle illustrated. When you finish, compare your response with those at the end of the book. If your responses differ, study carefully the principles in parentheses.

Example: (a) six investments (b) 6 investments   a _____ (4.01a)

1. (a) sixteen credit cards	(b) 16 credit cards	_____
2. (a) Fifth Avenue	(b) 5th Avenue	_____
3. (a) 34 newspapers	(b) thirty-four newspapers	_____
4. (a) July eighth	(b) July 8	_____
5. (a) twenty dollars	(b) $20	_____
6. (a) on the 15th of June	(b) on the fifteenth of June	_____
7. (a) at 4:00 p.m.	(b) at 4 p.m.	_____
8. (a) 3 200-page reports	(b) three 200-page reports	_____
9. (a) over 18 years ago	(b) over eighteen years ago	_____
10. (a) 2,000,000 people	(b) 2 million people	_____
11. (a) fifteen cents	(b) 15 cents	_____
12. (a) a thirty-day warranty	(b) a 30-day warranty	_____
13. (a) 2/3 of the e-mails	(b) two thirds of the e-mails	_____
14. (a) two telephones for 15 employees	(b) 2 telephones for 15 employees	_____
15. (a) 6 of the 130 letters	(b) six of the 130 letters	_____

The following sentences contain errors in grammar, punctuation, capitalization, number style, usage, and spelling. Below each sentence write a corrected version.

1. Please send the softwear to myself or whomever submitted the order.

2. All committe members except Tracy and he knew the assignment, and were prepared with there reports when they were do.

3. Was any of the managers absent on the Monday following the 4 day week-end.

4. The U.S. Governments crash-worthiness standards all call for the use of five feet 9 inch 179 pound dummys.

5. The makers of Saturn however decided to use dummys ranging from forty-five pound children to 112 pound females to burly 234 pound males.

6. The president made an off the record comment but members of congress soon heard it repeated.

7. We retained only a 4 year old printer, however it will be inspected year-by-year.

8. Before five p.m. we must return all 3 computers to our 7th Avenue office.

9. The U.S. postal service announced on July 1st that it would increase rates by 4.5%.

10. The three Cs of credit is the following, character, capacity, and capitol.

11. James Roosevelt said that his Father gave him the following advice on making speeches—"Be sincere, be breif; and be seated.

12. Some trucks acceded the 5,000 pound weight limit, others were under it.

13. Each of the quickly-printed computer books have been priced to sell at ten dollars and ninety-five cents.

14. If you will send the shipment to Elizabeth or I; it's contents will be inspected throughly.

15. The itinerary for Luke and he included 3 countrys holland france and germany.

Grammar/Mechanics Challenge—13

Document for Revision

The following résumé (shortened for this exercise) has faults in grammar, punctuation, spelling, number form, verb form, wordiness, and word use. Use standard proofreading marks (see Appendix B) to correct the errors. When you finish, your instructor can show you the revised version of this résumé.

MEGAN A. RYAN

2450 1st Street

Miami, Flor., 33133

EDUCATION

Coastal Community College, Miami, Florida. Degree expected in June 2001. Major

Word Processing.

EXPERIENCE:

- **Office Assistant.** Host Systems, Miami. 1999 too pressent. Responsible for entering data on Macintosh computer. I had to insure accuracy and completness of data that was to be entered. Another duty was maintaining a clean and well-organized office. I also served as Office Courier.

- **Lechter's Housewares.** Miami Shorés. 2nd Asst. Mgr I managed store in absence of mgr. and asst. mgr. I open and close registers. Ballanced daily reciepts. Ordered some mds. I also had to supervise 2 employes, earning rabid promotion.

- **Clerk typist.** Caribean Cruises Miami. 1996-97. (part time) Entered guest data on IBM PC. Did personalized followup letters to customer inquirys. Was responsible for phones. I also handled all errands as courier.

STRENGTHS

IBM PC, transcription, poofreading.

Can type 50 words/per/minute.

I am a fast learner, and very accurate.

Word-perfect, Excell, InterNet

How to Use Traditional and On-Line Networking to Explore the Hidden Job Market

Not all jobs are advertised in classified ads or listed in job databases. The "hidden" job market, according to some estimates, accounts for as much as two thirds of all positions available. Companies don't always announce openings publicly because it's time-consuming to interview all the applicants, many of whom are not qualified. But the real reason that companies resist announcing a job is that they dislike hiring "strangers." One recruiter explains, "If I'm in a hiring position, I'm first going to look around among my friends and acquaintances. If I can't find anybody, I'll look around for their friends and acquaintances. Only if I can't find anybody will I advertise."[23] Employers are much more comfortable hiring a person they know.

The key to finding a good job, then, is converting yourself from a "stranger" into a known quantity. One way to become a known quantity is by networking. You can use either traditional methods or on-line resources.

Traditional Networking

You may not have thought of it in this way, but you have a network of friends and relatives. When you are looking for a job, you need to extend this network beyond your normal circle of friends. Here's how to do it systematically.

Step 1: Develop a List. Make a list of anyone who would be willing to talk with you about finding a job. List your friends, relatives, former employers, former coworkers, classmates from grade school and high school, college friends, members of your church, people in social and athletic clubs, present and former teachers, neighbors, and friends of your parents.

Step 2: Make Contacts. Call the people on your list or, even better, try to meet with them in person. To set up a meeting, say, "Hi, Aunt Martha! I'm looking for a job and I wonder if you could help me out. When could I come over to talk about it?" During your visit be friendly, well organized, polite, and interested in what your contact has to say. Provide a copy of your résumé, and try to keep the conversation centered on your job search area. Your goal is to get two or more referrals. In pinpointing your request, ask two questions: "Do you know of anyone who might have an opening for a person with my skills?" If the person does not, then ask, "Do you know of anyone else who might know of someone who would?"

Step 3: Follow Up on Your Referrals. Call the people whose names are on your referral list. You might say something like, "Hello. I'm Carlos Ramos, a friend of Connie Cole. She suggested that I call and ask you for help. I'm looking for a position as a marketing trainee, and she thought you might be willing to see me and give me a few ideas." Don't ask for a job. During your referral interview ask how the individual got started in this line of work, what he or she likes best (or least) about the work, what career paths exist in the field, and what problems must be overcome by a newcomer. Most important, ask how a person with your background and skills might get started in the field. Send an informal thank-you note to anyone who helps you in your job search, and stay in touch with the most promising contacts. Ask if you may call every three weeks or so during your job search.

On-Line Networking

Like traditional networking, the goal with on-line networking is to make connections with people who are advanced in their field. Ask for their advice about finding a job. Most people like talking about themselves, and asking them about their experiences is an excellent way to begin an on-line correspondence. "Hanging out" at an on-line forum or newsgroup where industry professionals can be found is also a great way to keep tabs on the latest business trends and potential job leads.

- **Web-based forums.** Forum One <www.forumone.com> is a Web site that allows you to search over 310,000 Web forum discussion groups. For example, the search term "business" brings up hundreds of groups where professionals are discussing their fields. Other topics include recreation, hobbies, science, health, sports, and the arts.
- **Mailing lists.** LISZT <www.liszt.com> is the premier directory of publicly accessible mailing lists, with over 90,000 listings, 178 of which are devoted to business topics. Other topic areas include arts, books, computers, music, recreation, health, Internet, nature, and religion.

Career Application

Everyone who goes out on the job market needs to develop his or her own network. Assume you are ready to change jobs or look for a permanent position. Begin developing your personal network.

Your Task

- Conduct at least one referral interview and report on it to your class.
- Join one professional mailing list. Ask your instructor to recommend an appropriate list for your field.
- Take notes on discussions at your mailing list and report your reactions and findings to your class.

Employment Interviewing and Follow-Up Messages

Very often the difference between the person hired and the person rejected is not who is the better candidate but who is better prepared for the interview. Careers can be made and lost at that point alone.[1]

JOHN D. SHINGLETON, *former placement director, Michigan State University*

LEARNING OBJECTIVES

1. Distinguish between screening interviews and hiring/placement interviews.
2. Identify information resources in investigating target employers.
3. Explain how to prepare for employment interviews.
4. Recognize how to control nonverbal messages and how to fight interview fears.
5. Be prepared to answer favorite interview questions and know how to close an interview.
6. Itemize topics and behaviors to avoid in interviews.
7. Write follow-up letters and other employment messages.

Job interviews, for most of us, are intimidating; no one enjoys being judged and, possibly, rejected. Should you expect to be nervous about an upcoming job interview? Of course! Everyone is uneasy about being scrutinized and questioned. But think of how much *more* nervous you would be if you had no idea what to expect in the interview and if you were unprepared.

This chapter presents different kinds of interviews and shows you how to prepare for them. You'll learn how to gather information about an employer, as well as how to reduce nervousness, control body language, and fight fear during an interview. You'll pick up tips for responding to recruiters' favorite questions and learn how to cope with illegal questions and salary matters. Moreover, you'll receive pointers on significant questions you can ask during an interview. Finally, you'll learn what you should do as a successful follow-up to an interview.

Yes, you can expect to be nervous. But you can also expect to ace an interview when you know what's coming and when you prepare thoroughly. Remember, it's often the degree of preparation that determines who gets the job.

Job applicants generally face two kinds of interviews: screening interviews and hiring/placement interviews. You must succeed in the first to proceed to the second.

Screening Interviews

Screening interviews do just that—they screen candidates to eliminate those who fail to meet minimum requirements. Initial screening may be done by telephone or by computer.[2]

A telephone screening interview may be as short as five minutes. But don't treat it casually. It's not just another telephone call. If you don't perform well during the telephone interview, it may be your last interview with that organization. Here's how you can be prepared:

- Keep a list near the telephone of positions for which you have applied.
- Have your résumé, references, a calendar, and a notepad handy.
- If caught off guard, ask if you can call back in a few minutes from the telephone in your office. Organize your materials and yourself.
- Sell your qualifications, and, above all, sound enthusiastic!

One recruiter said that the mistakes most often made in telephone screening interviews were bringing up money too soon and exhibiting disinterest by typing on a keyboard. Another mistake, made by individuals using company telephones for their job search, was whispering so that coworkers would not hear them.[3]

A new trend in screening interviews involves computers. Many well-known retailers—such as Target, Macy's, Hollywood Video, and Longs Drug Stores—are replacing paper applications and in-person interviews with computer kiosks for the initial screening of applicants.[4] Athletic shoe manufacturer Nike used computer interviews to select 2,500 candidates from the 6,000 who responded to ads for workers at its Las Vegas Niketown.[5]

Hiring/Placement Interviews

The most promising candidates selected from screening interviews will be invited to hiring/placement interviews. Although these interviews are the real thing, in many ways they are like a game. Trained interviewers try to uncover any negative information that will eliminate a candidate. The candidate, of course, tries to minimize faults and emphasize strengths to avoid being eliminated. Like most games, the more practice you get, the better you perform because you know what to expect. Conducted in depth, hiring/placement interviews may take many forms.

- **One-on-one interviews** are most common. You can expect to sit down with a company representative and talk about the job and your qualifications. If the representative is the hiring manager, questions will be specific and job-related. If the representative is from human resources, the questions will probably be more general.
- **Sequential and group interviews** are common with companies that rule by consensus. You may face many interviewers in sequence, all of whom you must listen to carefully and respond to positively. Many group interviews are conducted by teams. With team interviews, begin to think in terms of "we" in-

Screening interviews are intended to eliminate those who fail to meet minimum requirements.

In hiring/placement interviews, recruiters try to uncover negative information while candidates try to minimize faults and emphasize strengths.

stead of "I." Explain how you contributed to a team effort instead of emphasizing individual achievements.[6] Strive to stay focused, summarize important points, and ask good questions.

- **Stress interviews** are meant to test your reactions. If asked rapid-fire questions from many directions, take the time to slow things down. For example, *I would be happy to answer your question, Ms. X, but first I must finish responding to Mr. Z.* If greeted with silence, another stress technique, you might say, *Would you like me to begin the interview? Let me tell you about myself.* Or ask a question such as *Can you give me more information about the position?* A stress interviewer might confront a job candidate with, *It's obvious your background makes you totally unqualified for this position. Why should we even waste our time talking?* The best way to handle stress questions is to remain calm and give carefully considered answers.

Investigating the Target

One of the most important steps in winning the interview game is gathering information about a prospective employer. In learning about a company, you may uncover information that convinces you that this is not the company for you. It's always better to learn about negatives early in the process. More likely, though, the information you collect will help you tailor your application and interview responses to the organization's needs. Recruiters are impressed by candidates who have done their homework.

Digging for Company Information

Researching an organization enlightens candidates and impresses recruiters.

For companies that are publicly held, you can generally learn a great deal from annual reports and financial disclosure reports. Company information is also available in *Gale's Job Seeker's Guide to Private and Public Companies, Hoover's Handbook of American Companies, The Million Dollar Directory, Moody's Complete Corporate Index,* and *Standard and Poor's Registry of Corporations.* Some of these resources are now available on the Internet. Many big and small companies today maintain Web sites bursting with juicy information. Another way to learn about an organization is to call the receptionist or the interviewer directly. Ask what you can read to prepare you for the interview. Here are some specifics to research:

- Find out all you can about company leaders. Their goals, ambitions, and values often are adopted by the entire organization—including your interviewer.

Study company leaders, organizational strategies, finances, products, customers, competition, and advertising.

- Investigate the business philosophy of the leaders, such as their priorities, strategies, and managerial approaches. Are you a good match with your target employer? If so, be sure to let the employer know that there is a correlation between their needs and your qualifications.

- Learn about the company's accomplishments and setbacks. This information should help you determine where you might make your best contribution.

- Study the company's finances. Are they so shaky that a takeover is imminent? If so, look elsewhere. Try to get your hands on an annual report. Many larger companies now post them at their Web sites.

- Examine its products and customers. What excites you about this company?

- Check out the competition. What are its products, strengths, and weaknesses?

- Analyze the company's advertising, including sales and marketing brochures. One candidate, a marketing major, spent a great deal of time poring over brochures from an aerospace contractor. During his initial interview, he shocked and impressed the recruiter with his knowledge of the company's guidance systems. The candidate had, in fact, relieved the interviewer of his least-favorite task—explaining the company's complicated technology.[7]

Learning About Smaller Companies

For smaller companies and those that are not publicly owned, you'll probably have to do a little more footwork. You might start with the local library. Ask the reference librarian to help you locate information. Newspapers might contain stories or press releases with news of an organization. Visit the Better Business Bureau to discover whether the company has had any difficulties with other companies or consumers. Investigate the chamber of commerce to see what you can learn about the target company.

Talking with company employees is always a good idea, if you can manage it. They are probably the best source of inside information. Try to be introduced to someone who is currently employed—but not working in the immediate area where you wish to be hired. Be sure to seek out someone who is discreet.

The best source of inside information is company employees.

You know how flattered you feel when an employer knows about you and your background. That feeling works both ways. Employers are pleased when job candidates take an interest in them. Be ready to put in plenty of effort in investigating a target employer because this effort really pays off at interview time.

Preparing and Practicing

After you have learned about the target organization, study the job description. It not only helps you write a focused résumé but also enables you to match your education, experience, and interests with the employer's position. Finding out the duties and responsibilities of the position will help you practice your best response strategies.

One of the best ways to prepare involves itemizing your (1) most strategic skills, (2) greatest areas of knowledge, (3) strongest personality traits, and (4) key accomplishments. Write this information down and practice relating these strengths to the kinds of questions frequently asked in interviews. Here are some specific tips for preparation:

- Practice, practice, practice. Recite answers to typical interview questions in a mirror, with a friend, while driving in your car, or in spare moments. Keep practicing until you have the best responses down pat.

Practice success stories that emphasize your most strategic skills, areas of knowledge, strongest personality traits, and key accomplishments.

- Consider videotaping or tape recording a practice session to see and hear how you really come across. Do you look and sound enthusiastic?

- Be ready to answer questions about alcohol and drug use. It is legal to ask if a candidate drinks alcohol, but it is not legal to ask how much. If you take a job with a large company, you can count on being asked to take a drug test.

- Expect to explain problem areas on your résumé. For example, if you have little or no experience, you might emphasize your recent training and up-to-date skills. If you have gaps in your résumé, be prepared to answer questions about them positively and truthfully.

- Try to build interviewing experience with less important jobs first. You will become more confident and better able to sell your strengths with repeated interviewing exposure. Think of it as a game that requires practice.

Send positive nonverbal messages by arriving on time, being courteous, dressing professionally, greeting the interviewer confidently, controlling your body movements, making eye contact, and smiling.

What comes out of your mouth and what's written on your résumé are not the only messages an interviewer receives about you. Nonverbal messages also create powerful impressions on people. Here are suggestions that will help you send the right nonverbal messages during interviews:

- Arrive on time or a little early. If necessary, find the location on a trial run a few days before the interview so that you know where to park, how much time the drive takes, and what office to find.

www.grantland.net

- Be courteous and congenial to everyone. Remember that you are being judged not only by the interviewer but by the receptionist and anyone else who sees you before and after the interview. They will notice how you sit, what you read, and how you look.
- Introduce yourself to the receptionist and wait to be invited to sit.
- Dress professionally. Even if some employees in the organization dress casually, you should look qualified, competent, and successful. One young applicant complained to his girlfriend about having to wear a suit for an interview when everyone at the company dressed casually. She replied, "You don't get to wear the uniform, though, until you make the team!"
- Greet the interviewer confidently. Extend your hand, look him or her directly in the eye, and say, "I'm pleased to meet you, Mr. X. I am Z." In this culture a firm, not crushing, handshake sends a nonverbal message of poise and assurance.
- Wait for the interviewer to offer you a chair. Make small talk with upbeat comments, such as "This is a beautiful headquarters. How many employees work here?" Don't immediately begin rummaging in your briefcase for your résumé. Being at ease and unrushed suggest that you are self-confident.
- Control your body movements. Keep your hands, arms, and elbows to yourself. Don't lean on a desk. Sit erect, leaning forward slightly. Keep your feet on the floor.
- Make eye contact frequently but don't get into a staring contest. A direct eye gaze, at least in North America, suggests interest and trustworthiness.

- Smile enough to convey a positive attitude. Have a friend give you honest feed-back on whether you generally smile too much or not enough.
- Sound enthusiastic and interested—but sincere.

Fighting Fear

Expect to be nervous. It's natural! Other than public speaking, employment interviews are the most dreaded events in people's lives. One of the best ways to overcome fear is to know what happens in a typical interview. Figure 14.1 describes how a recruiter usually structures an interview. You can further reduce your fears by following these suggestions:

- Practice interviewing as much as you can—especially with real companies. The more times you experience the interview situation, the less nervous you will be.
- Prepare 110 percent! Know how you will answer the most frequently asked questions. Be ready with success stories. Rehearse your closing statement. One of the best ways to reduce butterflies is to know that you have done all you can to be ready for the interview.
- Take deep breaths, particularly if you feel anxious while waiting for the interviewer. Deep breathing makes you concentrate on something other than the interview and also provides much-needed oxygen.
- Remember that the interviewer isn't the only one who is gleaning information. You have come to learn about the job and the company. In fact, during some parts of the interview, you will be in charge. This should give you courage.

Fight fear by practicing, preparing 110 percent, breathing deeply, and knowing that you are in charge for part of the interview.

FIGURE 14.1 Steps in an Employment Interview From a Recruiter's Perspective

Step 1	Step 2	Step 3
Before interview, review candidate's résumé.	Check career objective. Look for skills; note items to pursue.	Greet candidate. Introduce self. Make candidate feel comfortable.

Step 4	Step 5	Step 6
Describe open position. Confirm candidate's interest in position.	Give brief overview of organization.	Using résumé, probe for evidence of relevant skills and traits.

Step 7	Step 8	Step 9
Solicit questions from candidate.	Close interview by promoting organization and explaining next step.	Fill out evaluation form.

How you answer questions can be as important as the answers themselves.

The way you answer questions can be almost as important as what you say. Use the interviewer's name and title from time to time when you answer: *Ms. Lyon, I would be pleased to tell you about . . . .* People like to hear their own names. But be sure you are pronouncing the name correctly!

Occasionally it may be necessary to refocus and clarify vague questions. Some interviewers are inexperienced and ill at ease in the role. You may even have to ask your own question to understand what was asked: *By _____ do you mean _____?*

Consider closing out some of your responses with *Does that answer your question?* or *Would you like me to elaborate on any particular experience?*

Stay focused on the skills and traits that employers seek; don't reveal weaknesses.

Always aim your answers at the key characteristics interviewers seek: expertise and competence, motivation, interpersonal skills, decision-making skills, enthusiasm for the job, and a pleasing personality. And remember to stay focused on your strengths. Don't reveal weaknesses, even if you think they make you look human. You won't be hired for your weaknesses, only for your strengths.

Use good English and enunciate clearly. Remember, you will definitely be judged by how well you communicate. Avoid slurred words such as *gonna* and *din't*, as well as slangy expressions such as *yeah, like,* and *you know*. Also eliminate verbal static (*ah, and, uhm*). As you practice answering expected interview questions, it's always a good idea to make a tape recording. Is your speech filled with verbal static?

You can't expect to be perfect in an employment interview. No one is. But you can avert sure disaster by avoiding certain topics and behaviors such as those described in Figure 14.2.

FIGURE 14.2 Ten Interview Actions to Avoid

1. Don't ask for the job. It's naive, undignified, and unprofessional. Wait to see how the interview develops.

2. Don't trash your previous employer, supervisors, or colleagues. The tendency is for interviewers to wonder if you would speak about their companies similarly.

3. Don't be a threat to the interviewer. Avoid suggesting directly or indirectly that your goal is to become head honcho, a path that might include the interviewer's job.

4. Don't be late or too early for your appointment. Arrive five minutes before you are scheduled.

5. Don't discuss controversial subjects, and don't use profanity.

6. Don't smoke unless the interviewer smokes.

7. Don't emphasize salary or benefits. If the interview goes well and these subjects have not been addressed, you may mention them toward the end of the interview.

8. Don't be negative about yourself or others. Never dwell on your liabilities.

9. Don't interrupt. It is not only impolite but also prevents you from hearing a complete question or remark.

10. Don't accept an offer until you have completed all your interviews.

Employment interviews are all about questions. And most of the questions are not new. You can actually anticipate 90 to 95 percent of all questions that will be asked before you ever walk into an interview room.[8]

The following questions represent all-time favorites asked of recent graduates and other job seekers. You'll find get-acquainted questions, experience and accomplishment questions, crystal-ball questions, squirm questions, and money questions. To get you thinking about how to respond, we've provided an answer or discussion for the first question in each group. As you read the remaining questions in each group, think about how you could respond most effectively.

You can anticipate 90 to 95 percent of all questions you will be asked in an interview.

Questions to Get Acquainted

After opening introductions, recruiters generally try to start the interviewing questioning period with personal questions that put the candidate at ease. They are also striving to gain a picture of the candidate to see if he or she will fit into the organization's culture.

1. Tell me about yourself.

    Experts agree that you must keep this answer short (1 to 2 minutes tops) but on target. Try practicing this formula: "My name is _____. I have completed _____ degree with a major in ____. Recently I worked for _____ as a _____. Before that I worked for _____ as a ____. My strengths are _____ (interpersonal) and _____ (technical)." Try rehearsing your response in 30-second segments devoted to your education, your work experience, and your qualities/skills. Some candidates end with, "Now that I've told you about myself, can you tell me a little more about the position?"

    Prepare for get-acquainted questions by practicing a short formula response.

2. What was your major in college, and why did you choose it?
3. If you had it to do over again, would you choose the same major? Why?
4. Tell me about your college (or your major) and why you chose it.
5. Do you prefer to work by yourself or with others? Why?
6. What are your key strengths?
7. What are some things you do in your spare time? Hobbies? Sports?
8. How did you happen to apply for this job?
9. What particular qualifications do you have for this job?
10. Do you consider yourself a team player? Describe your style as a team player.

Questions About Your Experience and Accomplishments

After questions about your background and education, the interview generally becomes more specific with questions about your experience and accomplishments.

1. Why should we hire you when we have applicants with more experience or better credentials?

    In answering this question, remember that employers often hire people who present themselves well instead of others with better credentials. Emphasize your personal strengths that could be an advantage with this employer. Are you a hard worker? How can you demonstrate it? Have you had recent training? Some people have had more years of experience but actually have less knowledge because they have done the same thing over and over. Stress your experience using the latest methods and equipment. Be sure to mention your computer training and use of the Internet and Web. Emphasize that you are open to new ideas and learn quickly.

    Employers will hire a candidate with less experience and fewer accomplishments if he or she can demonstrate the skills required.

2. Tell me about your part-time jobs, internships, or other experience.
3. What were your major accomplishments in each of your past jobs?
4. Why did you change jobs?
5. What was a typical work day like?
6. What job functions did you enjoy most? Least? Why?
7. Who was the toughest boss you ever worked for and why?
8. What were your major achievements in college?

Crystal Ball Gazing and Questions About the Future

Questions that look into the future tend to stump some candidates, especially those who have not prepared adequately. Some of these questions give you a chance to discuss your personal future goals, while others require you to think on your feet and tell how you would respond in hypothetical situations.

1. Where do you expect to be five years from now?

When asked about the future, show ambition and interest in succeeding with this company.

It's a sure kiss of death to respond that you'd like to have the interviewer's job! Instead, show an interest in the current job and in making a contribution to the organization. Talk about the levels of responsibility you'd like to achieve. One employment counselor suggests showing ambition but not committing to a specific job title. Suggest that you will have learned enough to have progressed to a position where you will continue to grow.

2. If you got this position, what would you do to be sure you fit in?
3. If your supervisor gave you an assignment and then left town for two weeks, what would you do?
4. This is a large (or small) organization. Do you think you'd like that environment?
5. If you were aware that a coworker was falsifying data, what would you do?
6. If your supervisor was dissatisfied with your work and you thought it was acceptable, how would you resolve the conflict?
7. Do you plan to continue your education?

Questions to Make You Squirm

The following questions may make you squirm, but the important thing to remember is to answer truthfully without dwelling on your weaknesses. As quickly as possible, convert any negative response into a discussion of your strengths.

1. What are your key weaknesses?

Strive to convert discussion of your weaknesses to topics that show your strengths.

It's amazing how many candidates knock themselves out of the competition by answering this question poorly. Actually, you have many choices. You can present a strength as a weakness (*Some people complain that I'm a workaholic or too attentive to details*). You can mention a corrected weakness (*I found that I really needed to learn about the Internet, so I took a course*). You could cite an unrelated skill (*I really need to brush up on my Spanish*). You can cite a learning objective (*One of my long-term goals is to learn more about international management. Does your company have any plans to expand overseas?*). Another possibility is to reaffirm your qualifications (*I have no weaknesses that affect my ability to do this job*).

2. If you could change one thing about your personality, what would it be and why?
3. What would your former boss say about you?
4. What do you want the most from your job? Money? Security? Power?

5. How did you prepare for this interview?
6. Do you feel you achieved the best grade-point average of which you were capable in college?
7. Have you ever used drugs?
8. Relate an incident in which you faced an ethical dilemma. How did you react? How did you feel?
9. If your supervisor told you to do something a certain way, and you knew that way was dead wrong, what would you do?

Questions About Money

Although money is a very important consideration, don't let it enter the interview process too soon. Some interviewers forget to mention money at all, while others ask what you think you are worth. Here are some typical money questions.

1. How much money are you looking for?

   One way to handle salary questions is to ask politely to defer the discussion until it's clear that a job will be offered to you. (*I'm sure when the time comes, we'll be able to work out a fair compensation package. Right now, I'd rather focus on whether we have a match*). Another possible response is to reply candidly that you can't know what to ask until you know more about the position and the company. If you continue to be pressed for a dollar figure, give a salary range. Be sure to do research before the interview so that you know what similar jobs are paying. For example, check weekly salary surveys published in the *National Business Employment Weekly*.

   Defer a discussion of salary until later in the interview when you know more about the job and whether it will be offered.

2. How much are you presently earning?
3. How did you finance your education?
4. How much money do you expect to earn at age ____?

For more tips on how to negotiate a salary, see the Communication Workshop for this chapter.

Questions for You to Ask

At some point in the interview, you will be asked if you have any questions. Your questions should not only help you gain information, but they should also impress the interviewer with your thoughtfulness and interest in the position. Remember, though, that this interview is a two-way street. You must be happy with

Your questions should impress the interviewer but also provide valuable information about the job.

GRANTLAND®

THE KEY TO A GOOD JOB INTERVIEW—

AS WITH MANY OTHER THINGS—

IS HAVING THE RIGHT ATTITUDE.

RECRUITER

© GRANTLAND ENTERPRISES, INC. ALL RIGHTS RESERVED.

www.grantland.net

the prospect of working for this organization. You want a position for which your skills and personality are matched. Use this opportunity to find out whether this job is right for you.

1. What will my duties be (if not already discussed)?
2. Tell me what it's like working here in terms of the people, management practices, work loads, expected performance, and rewards.
3. Why is this position open? Did the person who held it previously leave?
4. What training programs are available from this organization? What specific training will be given for this position?
5. What are the possibilities for promotion from this position?
6. Who would be my immediate supervisor?
7. What is the organizational structure, and where does this position fit in?
8. Is travel required in this position?
9. How is job performance evaluated?
10. Assuming my work is excellent, where do you see me in five years?
11. How long do employees generally stay with this organization?
12. What are the major challenges for a person in this position?
13. What can I do to make myself more employable to you?
14. What is the salary for this position?
15. When will I hear from you regarding further action on my application?

Fielding Illegal Questions

You may respond to an illegal question by asking tactfully how it relates to the responsibilities of the position.

Because federal laws prohibit discrimination, interviewers may not ask questions such as those in the following list. Nevertheless, you may face an inexperienced or unscrupulous interviewer who does ask some of these questions. How should you react? If you find the question harmless and if you want the job, go ahead and answer it. If you think that answering it would damage your chance to be hired, try to deflect the question tactfully with a response such as, *Could you tell me how my marital status relates to the responsibilities of this position?* Another option, of course, is to respond to any illegal question by confronting the interviewer and threatening a lawsuit. However, you could not expect to be hired under these circumstances. In any case, you might wish to reconsider working for an organization that sanctions such procedures.

Here are some illegal questions that you may or may not want to answer:

1. Are you married, divorced, separated, or single?
2. Do you have any disabilities that would prevent you from doing this job? (But it is legal to ask *Can you carry a 50-pound sack up a 10-foot ladder five times daily?*)
3. What is your corrected vision? (But it is legal to ask *Do you have 20/20 corrected vision?*)
4. Does stress ever affect your ability to be productive? (But it is legal to ask *How well can you handle stress?*)
5. How much alcohol do you drink per week? (But it is legal to ask *Do you drink alcohol?*)
6. Have you ever been arrested? (But it is legal to ask *Have you ever been convicted of a crime?*)
7. How old are you? What is your date of birth? (But it is legal to ask *Are you 18 years old or older?*)
8. Of what country are you a citizen? (But it is legal to ask *Are you a citizen of the U.S.?*)
9. What is your maiden name? (But it is legal to ask *What is your full name?*)
10. What is your religious preference?
11. Do you have children?

12. Are you practicing birth control?
13. Are you living with anyone?
14. Do you own or rent your home?
15. How much do you weigh? How tall are you?

Closing the Interview

After the recruiter tells you about the organization and after you have asked your questions, the interviewer will signal the end of the interview, usually by standing up or by expressing appreciation that you came. If not addressed earlier, you should at this time find out what action will follow. Too many candidates leave the interview without knowing their status or when they will hear from the recruiter.

You may learn that your résumé will be distributed to several departments for review. If this is the case, be sure to ask when you will be contacted. When you are ready to leave, briefly review your strengths for the position and thank the interviewer for telling you about the organization and for considering you for the position. Ask if you may leave an additional copy of your résumé or your list of references. If the recruiter says nothing about notifying you, ask ,"When can I expect to hear from you?" You can follow this by saying, "If I don't hear from you by then, may I call you?"

End the interview by thanking the interviewer, reviewing your strengths for this position, and asking what action will follow.

www.grantland.net

After leaving the interview, make notes of what was said in case you are called back for a second interview. Also, note your strengths and weaknesses so that you can work to improve in future interviews. Be sure to alert your references (whom you prepared in advance with a copy of your résumé, highlighted with sales points). Finally, write a thank-you letter, which will be discussed shortly.

If you don't hear from the recruiter within five days (or at the specified time), call him or her. Practice saying something like, "I'm wondering what else I can do to convince you that I'm the right person for this job."

Follow-Up Letters and Other Employment Documents

Although the résumé and letter of application are your major tasks, other important letters and documents are often required during the employment process. You may need to make requests, write follow-up letters, or fill out employment applications. Because each of these tasks reveals something about you and your communication skills, you'll want to put your best foot forward. These documents often subtly influence company officials to extend an interview or offer a job.

Reference Request

Most employers expect job candidates at some point to submit names of individuals who are willing to discuss the candidates' qualifications. Before you list anyone as a reference, however, be sure to ask permission. Try to do this in person. Ask an instructor, for example, if he or she would be willing and has the time to act as your recommender. If you detect any sign of reluctance, don't force the issue. Your goal is to find willing individuals who think well of you.

What your recommenders need most is information about you. What should they stress to prospective employers? Let's say you're applying for a specific job that requires a letter of recommendation. Professor Smith has already agreed to be a reference for you. To get the best letter of recommendation from Professor Smith, help her out. Write a letter telling her about the position, its requirements, and the recommendation deadline. Include a copy of your résumé. You might remind her of a positive experience with you (*You said my report was well organized*) that she could use in the recommendation. Remember that recommenders need evidence to support generalizations. Give them appropriate ammunition, as the student has done in the following request:

Dear Professor Smith:

Identify the target position and company. Tell immediately why you are writing.

Recently I applied for the position of administrative assistant in the Human Resources Department of Host International. Because you kindly agreed to help me, I am now asking you to write a letter of recommendation to Host.

Specify the job requirements so that the recommender knows what to stress in the letter.

The position calls for good organizational, interpersonal, and writing skills, as well as computer experience. To help you review my skills and training, I enclose my résumé. As you may recall, I earned an A in your business communication class; and you commended my long report for its clarity and organization.

Please send your letter before July 1 in the enclosed stamped, addressed envelope. I'm grateful for your support, and I promise to let you know the results of my job search.

Application Request Letter

Some organizations consider candidates only when they submit a completed application form. To secure a form, write a routine letter of request. But provide enough information about yourself, as shown in the following example, to assure the reader that you are a serious applicant:

Dear Mr. Adams:

Because you expect a positive response, announce your request immediately.

Please send me an application form for work in your Human Resources Department. In June I will be completing my studies in psychology and communications at Northwestern University in Evanston, Illinois. My program included courses in public relations, psychology, and communications.

Supply an end date, if it seems appropriate. End on a forward-looking note.

I would appreciate receiving this application by May 15 so that I may complete it before making a visit to your city in June. I'm looking forward to beginning a career in personnel management.

Application or Résumé Follow-Up Letter

If your letter or application generates no response within a reasonable time, you may decide to send a short follow-up letter such as the following. Doing so (1) jogs the memory of the personnel officer, (2) demonstrates your serious interest, and (3) allows you to emphasize your qualifications or to add new information.

Dear Ms. Lopez:

Please know I am still interested in becoming an administrative support specialist with Quad, Inc.

Since I submitted an application in May, I have completed my schooling and have been employed as a summer replacement for office workers in several downtown offices. This experience has honed my word processing and communication skills. It has also introduced me to a wide range of office procedures.

Please keep my application in your active file and let me know when I may put my formal training, technical skills, and practical experience to work for you.

Open by reminding the reader of your interest.

Use this opportunity to review your strengths or to add new qualifications.

Interview Follow-Up Letter

After a job interview you should always send a brief letter of thanks. This courtesy sets you apart from other applicants (most of whom will not bother). Your letter also reminds the interviewer of your visit as well as suggesting your good manners and genuine enthusiasm for the job.

Follow-up letters are most effective if sent immediately after the interview. In your letter refer to the date of the interview, the exact job title for which you were interviewed, and specific topics discussed. Avoid worn-out phrases, such as *Thank you for taking the time to interview me.* Be careful, too, about overusing *I*, especially to begin sentences. Most important, show that you really want the job and that you are qualified for it. Notice how the following letter conveys enthusiasm and confidence:

Dear Ms. Cogan:

Talking with you Thursday, May 23, about the graphic designer position was both informative and interesting.

Thanks for describing the position in such detail and for introducing me to Ms. Thomas, the senior designer. Her current project designing the annual report in four colors on a Macintosh sounds fascinating as well as quite challenging.

Now that I've learned in greater detail the specific tasks of your graphic designers, I'm more than ever convinced that my computer and creative skills can make a genuine contribution to your graphic productions. My training in Macintosh design and layout ensures that I could be immediately productive on your staff.

You will find me an enthusiastic and hard-working member of any team effort. I'm eager to join the graphics staff at your Santa Barbara headquarters, and I look forward to hearing from you soon.

Mention the interview date and specific position.

Show appreciation, good manners, and perseverance—traits that recruiters value.

Personalize your letter by mentioning topics discussed in the interview.

Rejection Follow-Up Letter

If you didn't get the job and you think it was perfect for you, don't give up. Employment consultant Patricia Windelspecht advises, "You should always respond to a rejection letter. . . . I've had four clients get jobs that way." In a rejection follow-up letter, it's okay to admit you're disappointed. Be sure to add, however, that you're still interested and will contact them again in a month in case a job opens up. Then follow through for a couple of months—but don't overdo it. "There's a fine line between being professional and persistent and being a pest," adds consultant Windelspecht.[9] Here's an example of an effective rejection follow-up letter:

Dear Mr. Crenshaw:

Although I'm disappointed that someone else was selected for your accounting position, I appreciate your promptness and courtesy in notifying me.

Subordinate your disappointment to your appreciation at being notified promptly and courteously.

Because I firmly believe that I have the technical and interpersonal skills needed to work in your fast-paced environment, I hope you will keep my résumé in your active file. My desire to become a productive member of your Transamerica staff remains strong.

I enjoyed our interview, and I especially appreciate the time you and Mr. Samson spent describing your company's expansion into international markets. To enhance my qualifications, I've enrolled in a course in International Accounting at CSU.

Should you have an opening for which I am qualified, you may reach me at (818) 719-3901. In the meantime, I will call you in a month to discuss employment possibilities.

Application Form

Some organizations require job candidates to fill out job application forms instead of submitting résumés. This practice permits them to gather and store standardized data about each applicant. Here are some tips for filling out such forms:

- Carry a card summarizing the vital statistics not included on your résumé. If you are asked to fill out an application form in an employer's office, you will need a handy reference to the following data: social security number, graduation dates, beginning and ending dates of all employment; salary history; full names, titles, and present work addresses of former supervisors; and full names, occupational titles, occupational addresses, and telephone numbers of persons who have agreed to serve as references.

- Look over all the questions before starting. Fill out the form neatly, printing if your handwriting is poor.

- Answer all questions. Write *Not applicable* if appropriate.

- Be prepared for a salary question. Unless you know what comparable employees are earning in the company, the best strategy is to suggest a salary range or to write *Negotiable* or *Open*.

- Ask if you may submit your résumé in addition to the application form.

Summing Up and Looking Forward

Whether you face a screening interview or a hiring/placement interview, you must be well prepared. You can increase your chances of success and reduce your sweaty palms considerably by knowing how interviews are typically conducted and by investigating the target company thoroughly. Practice answering typical questions, including legal and illegal ones. Consider tape recording or videotaping a mock interview so that you can check your body language and improve your answering techniques.

Close the interview by thanking the interviewer, reviewing your main strengths for this position, and asking what the next step is. Follow up with a thank-you letter and a call back, if appropriate.

You have now completed 14 chapters of rigorous instruction aimed at developing your skills so that you can be a successful business communicator in today's rapidly changing world of information. Remember that this is but a starting point. Your skills as a business communicator will continue to grow on the job as you apply the principles you have learned and expand your expertise.

1. Is it normal to be nervous about an employment interview, and what can be done to overcome this fear?
2. What can you do to improve the first impression you make at an interview?
3. In employment interviews, do you think that behavioral questions (such as, *Tell me about a business problem you have had and how you solved it*) are more effective than traditional questions (such as *Tell me what you are good at*)? Why?
4. Why is it important to avoid discussing salary early in an interview?
5. Why should a job candidate write a thank-you letter after an interview?

Chapter Review

6. If you have sent out your résumé to many companies, what information should you keep near your telephone and why?

7. Your first interview is with a small local company. What kind of information should you seek about this company and where could you expect to find it?

8. Name at least two ways in which you can practice for the interview and receive feedback on your performance.

9. Name at least six interviewing behaviors you can exhibit that send positive nonverbal messages.

10. What is your greatest fear of what you might do or what might happen to you during an employment interview? How can you overcome your fears?

11. Should you be candid with an interviewer when asked about your weaknesses?

12. How can you clarify vague questions from recruiters?

13. How should you respond if you are asked why a company should hire you when it has applicants with more experience or better credentials?

14. How should you respond to questions you feel are illegal?

15. List the various kinds of follow-up letters.

Activities and Cases

Web **14.1 Researching an Organization.** Select an organization where you would like to be employed. Assume you've been selected for an interview. Using resources described in this chapter, locate information about the organization's leaders and their business philosophy. Find out about the organization's accomplishments, setbacks, finances, products, customers, competition, and advertising. Prepare a summary report documenting your findings.

Related Web Site: <www.hoovers.com>

14.2 Building Interview Skills. Successful interviews require diligent preparation and repeated practice. To be best prepared, you need to know what skills are required for your targeted position. In addition to computer and communication skills, employers generally want to know whether a candidate works well with a team, accepts responsibility, solves problems, is efficient, meets deadlines, shows leadership, saves time and money, and is a hard worker.

Your Task. Consider a position for which you are eligible now or one for which you will be eligible when you complete your education. Identify the skills and traits necessary for this position. If you prepared a résumé in Chapter 13, be sure that it addresses these targeted areas. Now prepare interview worksheets listing at least ten technical and other skills or traits you think a recruiter will want to discuss in an interview for your targeted position.

14.3 Preparing Success Stories. You can best showcase your talents if you are ready with your own success stories that show how you have developed the skills or traits required for your targeted position.

Your Task. Using the worksheets you prepared in Activity 14.2, prepare success stories that highlight the required skills or traits. Select three to five stories to develop into answers to potential interview questions. For example, here's a typical question: "How does your background relate to the position we have open?" A possible response: "As you know, I have just completed an intensive training program in _____. In addition, I have over three years of part-time work experience in a variety of business settings. In one position I was selected to manage a small business in the absence of the owner. I developed responsibility and customer-service skills in filling orders efficiently, resolving shipping problems, and monitoring key accounts. I also inventoried and organized products worth over $200,000. When the owner returned from a vacation to Florida, I was commended for increasing sales and was given a bonus in recognition of his gratitude." People relate to and remember stories. Try to shape your answers into memorable stories.

14.4 Polishing Answers to Interview Questions. Practice makes perfect in interviewing. The more often you rehearse responses to typical interview questions, the closer you are to getting the job.

Your Task. Select three questions from each of the five question categories discussed in this chapter. Write your answers to each set of questions. Try to incorporate skills and traits required for the targeted position. Polish these answers and your delivery technique by practicing in front of a mirror or into a tape recorder.

14.5 Knowing What to Ask. When it is your turn to ask questions during the interview process, be ready.

Your Task. Decide on three to five questions that you would like to ask during an interview. Write these questions out and practice asking them so that you sound confident and sincere.

14.6 Practicing Answering Interview Questions. One of the best ways to understand interview dynamics and to develop confidence is to role-play the parts of interviewer and candidate.

Team

Your Task. Choose a partner from your team. Make a list of five interview questions from those presented in this chapter. In team sessions you and your partner will role-play an actual interview. One acts as interviewer; the other is the candidate. Prior to the interview, the candidate tells the interviewer what job and company he/she is applying to. For the interview, the interviewer and candidate should dress appropriately and sit in chairs facing each other. The interviewer greets the candidate and makes him/her comfortable. The candidate gives the interviewer a copy of his/her résumé. The interviewer asks three (or more depending on your instructor's time schedule) questions from the candidate's list. The interviewer may also ask follow-up questions if appropriate. When finished, the interviewer ends the meeting graciously. After one interview, reverse roles and repeat.

14.7 Videotaping an Interview. Seeing how you look during an interview can help you improve your body language and presentation style. Your instructor may act as interviewer, or an outside businessperson may be asked to conduct mock interviews in your classroom.

Your Task. Engage a student or campus specialist to videotape each interview. Review your performance and critique it looking for ways to improve. Your instructor may ask class members to offer comments and suggestions on individual interviews.

14.8 Handling Illegal Interview Questions. Although some questions are considered illegal by the government, many interviewers will ask them anyway—whether intentionally or unknowingly. Being prepared is important.

Your Task. How would you respond in the following scenario? Let's assume you are being interviewed at one of the top companies on your list of potential employers. The interviewing committee consists of a human resources manager and the supervising manager of the department where you would work. At various times during the interview the supervising manager has asked questions that made you feel uncomfortable. For example, he asked if you were married. You know this question is illegal, but you saw no harm in answering it. But then he asked how old you were. Since you started college early and graduated in three and a half years, you are worried that you may not be considered mature enough for this position. But you have most of the other qualifications required and you are convinced you could succeed on the job. How should you answer this question?

14.9 Requesting an Application Form. You decide to apply for a position with a company and you need an application form.

Your Task. Send a letter addressed to Douglas Tyson, Manager, Human Resources, KillerAp Software, 2443 Pacific Grove Drive, Cupertino, CA 94510. Request an employment application.

14.10 Saying Thanks for the Interview. You've just completed an exciting employment interview, and you want the interviewer to remember you.

Your Task. Write a follow-up thank-you letter to Ronald T. Ranson, Human Resources Development, Electronic Data Sources, 1328 Peachtree Plaza, Atlanta, GA 30314 (or a company of your choice).

14.11 Refusing to Take No for an Answer. After an excellent interview with Electronic Data Sources (or a company of your choice), you're depressed to learn that it hired someone else. But you really want to work for EDS.

Your Task. Write a follow-up letter to Ronald T. Ranson, Human Resources Development, Electronic Data Sources, 1328 Peachtree Plaza, Atlanta, GA 30314 (or a company of your choice). Indicate that you are disappointed but still interested.

 14.12 Answering Killer Questions in a Virtual Interview. The Monster.com Web site offers an entertaining on-line practice interview with questions "ranging from puff ball to killer." If this Web site is still available (pages are often removed), by all means try out your skills with this interactive tool that provides insightful and helpful feedback. Even an experienced interviewee is unlikely to get all of these questions right the first time.

Your Task. Visit the Monster.com Career Center and answer the virtual interview questions. Be prepared to discuss the advice for handling questions about salaries and your weaknesses. Do you agree with Monster's suggestions?

Related Web Site: To try "the world's hardest interview questions," visit <http://content.monster.com/jobinfo/interview/virtual>.

14.13 Searching for Advice. You can find wonderful, free, and sometimes entertaining information about job search strategies, career tips, and interview advice on the Web.

 Your Task. Use a search engine or visit the Guffey Web site to locate links to job search and résumé sites. From any Web site featuring interview information, make a list of at least five good interview pointers—ones that were not covered in this chapter. Send an e-mail message to your instructor describing your findings.

Related Web Site: At the www.meguffey.com site, click on "Job Search."

14.14 BusinessLink Video Case Study: Interviewing in Business. Dayton Hudson Corporation, with headquarters in Minneapolis, is the fourth largest retailer in the United States. It consists of Target, Dayton's, Hudson's, and Marshall Field's. In our video, members of Hudson's management team discuss hiring requirements as they begin staffing a new suburban store. Management team members discuss their hiring goals, what they look for during an interview, and how to follow up an interview.

Your Task. After viewing the Hudson's video, respond to these questions:

- How should a job candidate prepare for a job interview?
- How can a candidate send positive body language?
- What problems are typically suffered by job candidates during interviewing?
- What are the characteristics of a good résumé?
- What follow-up is expected after an interview?

Grammar/Mechanics Checkup—14

Punctuation Review

Review Sections 1.17 and 2.01–2.29 in the Grammar/Mechanics Handbook. Study the groups of sentences below. In the space provided write the letter of the one that is correctly punctuated. When you finish, compare your responses with those at the end of the book. If your responses differ, study carefully the principles in parentheses.

1. a. Our accounting team makes a point of analyzing your business operations, and getting to know what's working for you and what's not.
   b. We are dedicated to understanding your business needs over the long term, and taking an active role when it comes to creating solutions.
   c. We understand that you may be downsizing or moving into new markets, and we want to help you make a seamless transition.

2. a. If you are growing, or connecting to new markets, our team will help you accomplish your goals with minimal interruptions.
   b. When you look at our organization chart, you will find the customer at the top.
   c. Although we offer each customer a dedicated customer account team we also provide professional general services.

3. a. The competition is changing; therefore, we have to deliver our products and services more efficiently.
   b. Although delivery systems are changing; the essence of banking remains the same.
   c. Banks will continue to be available around the corner, and also with the click of a mouse.

4. a. One of the reasons we are decreasing the number of our ATMs, is that two thirds of the bank's customers depend on tellers for transactions.
   b. We are looking for an article entitled, "On-Line Banking."
   c. Banks are at this time competing with nontraditional rivals who can provide extensive financial services.

5. a. We care deeply about the environment; but we also care about safety and good customer service.
   b. The president worked with environmental concerns; the vice president focused on customer support.
   c. Our Web site increases our productivity, it also improves customer service.

6. a. Employees who will be receiving salary increases are: Terri, Mark, Rob, and Ellen.
   b. The following employees are eligible for bonuses: Robin, Jeff, Bill, and Jose.
   c. Our consulting firm is proud to offer Web services for: site design, market analysis, e-commerce, and hosting.

7. a. All secretaries' computers were equipped with Excel.
   b. Both attorneys statements confused the judge.
   c. Some members names and addresses must be rekeyed.

8. a. Our committee considered convention sites in Scottsdale, Arizona, Palm Springs, California; and Dallas, Texas.
   b. Serena was from Columbus, Ohio; Josh was from Denver, Colorado, and Rachel was from Seattle, Washington.
   c. The following engineers were approved: J. W. Ellis, civil; Dr. Thomas Lee, structural; and W. R. Verey, mechanical.

9. a. The package from Albany, New York was never delivered.
   b. We have scheduled an inspection tour on Tuesday, March 5, at 4 p.m.
   c. Send the check to M. E. Williams, 320 Summit Ridge, Ogden, Utah 84404 before the last mail pickup.

10. a. The best plan of action in my opinion, is a straightforward approach.
    b. Under the circumstances we could not have hoped for better results.
    c. Our department will, in the meantime, reduce its services.

11. a. If you demand reliable, competent service, you should come to us.
    b. We could not resist buying cookies from the enthusiastic, young Girl Scout.
    c. Our highly trained technicians, with years of experience are always available to evaluate and improve your network environment.

12. a. We guarantee same-day, not next-day, service.
    b. Our departmental budget requests are considerably reduced yet adequate.
    c. The nominating committee selected Todd Shimoyama, not Suzette Chase as its representative.

13. a. Their wealthy uncle left $1 million to be distributed to Bob, Carol, and Sue.
    b. Their wealthy uncle left $1 million to be distributed to Bob, Carol and Sue.
    c. Our agency will maintain and upgrade your computers, printers, copiers and fax machines.

14. a. Beginning June 1, we will service many top vendors, including: Compaq, Hewlett Packard, IBM, Dell and Mita.
    b. To promote our new business we are offering a 10 percent discount.
    c. In a period of only one month, we gained 150 new customers.

15. a. We specialize in network design, however we also offer troubleshooting and consulting.
    b. We realize that downtime is not an option; therefore, you can count on us for reliable, competent service.
    c. Our factory-trained and certified technicians perform repair at your location, or in our own repair depot for products under warranty and out of warranty.

Advanced Grammar/Mechanics Review—14

The following sentences contain errors in grammar, punctuation, capitalization, number style, usage, and spelling. Below each sentence write a corrected version.

1. City officials begged the two companys board of directors not to dessert they're locations, and not to abandon local employees.

2. One store listed its Seiko Watch at eighty dollars; while its competitor listed the same watch at seventy-five dollars.

3. Here are a group of participating manufactures who you may wish to contact regarding there Web cites.

4. If we are to remain friends this personal information must be kept strictly between you and I.

5. As soon as the merger is complete we will inform the entire staff, until then its business as usual.

6. Smart organizations can boost profit's allmost one hundred percent by retaining just five percent more of there customers.

7. Many companies sell better at home then abroad; because they lack overseas experience.

8. The quality of the e-mails, letters, memos and reports in this organization need to be improved.

9. The additional premium you were charged which amounted to fifty-five collars and 40 cents was issued because of you're recent accident.

10. The entire team of thirty-five managers were willing to procede with the proposal for asian expansion.

11. Several copys of the sales' report was sent to the CEO and I immediatley after we requested it.

12. Stored on open shelfs in room 17 is a group of office supplys and at least 7 reams of stationary.

13. Darren Highsmith who was recently appointed Sales Manager submitted 6 different suggestions for increasing sales.

14. China the worlds fastest growing country will be snapping up personal computers at a thirty percent rate by 2010.

15. Congratulations, your finished!

Grammar/Mechanics Challenge—14

Document for Revision

The following interview thank-you letter has faults in grammar, punctuation, spelling, wordiness, and word use. Use standard proofreading marks (see Appendix B) to correct the errors. When you finish, your instructor can show you the revised version of this letter.

4201 North Harrison

Shawnee, OK 74801

June 4, 200X

Mr. Anthony R. Masters

Human Resources Department

Biolage Enterprises

7246 South May Avenue

Oklahoma City, OK 73159

Dear Mr. Master:

I appriciate the opportunity for the interview yesterday for the newly-listed Position of Sales Trainee. It was really a pleasure meeting yourself and learning more about Biolage Enterprises, you have a fine staff and a sophisticated approach to marketing.

You're organization appears to be growing in a directional manner that parralels my interests' and career goals. The interview with yourself and your staff yesterday confirmed my initale positive impressions of Biolage Enterprises and I want to reiterate my strong interest in working with and for you. My prior Retail sales experience as a sales associate with Sears; plus my recent training in Microsoft Word and Excel would enable me to make progress steadily through your programs of training and become a productive member of your sales team in no time at all.

Again, thank-you for your kind and gracius consideration. In the event that you need any additional information from me, all you have to do is give me a call me at (405) 391-7792.

Sincerly yours,

_____

Let's Talk Money: Negotiating a Salary

When to talk about salary causes many job applicants concern. Some advisors recommend bringing the issue up immediately; others suggest avoiding the topic entirely. The best plan is probably to avoid discussing salary during a screening interview but be ready to discuss it later. The important thing to remember is that almost all salaries are negotiable. The following negotiating rules, recommended by career guru Ron Farr, can guide you to a better beginning salary.[10]

Rule No. 1: Never talk money until after the interviewing company decides it wants you.

Your goal is to avoid discussing salary until you know for sure that the interviewing company is making a job offer. If salary comes up and you are not sure whether the job is being offered to you, it's time for you to be blunt. Here are some things you could say:

Are you making me a job offer?
What salary range do you pay for positions with similar requirements?
I'm very interested in the position, and my salary would be negotiable.
Tell me what you have in mind for the salary range.

Rule No. 2: Know in advance the probable salary range for similar jobs in similar organizations.

Some job search Web sites provide salary information. But it's probably better for you to call around in your area to learn what similar jobs are paying. The important thing here is to think in terms of a wide range. Let's say you are hoping to start at between $26,000 and $32,000. To an interviewer, you might say, *I was looking for a salary in the high twenties to the low thirties.* This technique is called bracketing.

Rule No. 3: Always bracket your salary range to begin within their probable salary range and end a bit above what you expect to settle for.

Remember to be realistic. You probably have some idea of what the interviewing company is willing to pay for this position. If you guess that the salary for this position might be about $27,000, your bracketed range should begin with that figure and extend beyond what you expect to settle for.

Rule No. 4: Never say no to a job offer before it is offered.

Why would anyone refuse a job offer before it's made? It happens all the time. Let's say you were hoping for a salary of, say, $27,000. The interviewer tells you that the salary scheduled for this job is $24,000. You respond, *Oh, that's out of the question!* Before you were offered the job, you have, in effect, refused it.

Rule No. 5: Be ready to bargain if offered a low starting salary.

Many salaries are negotiable. Companies are often willing to pay more for someone who interviews well and fits their culture. If the company seems right to you and you are pleased with the sound of the open position but you have been offered a low salary, say, *That is somewhat lower than I had hoped but this position does sound exciting. If I were to consider this, what sorts of things could I do to quickly become more valuable to this organization?*

Even if the salary offered is an insult, don't kick the desk, grab your résumé, and stomp out. Hold your temper and say something like, *Thanks for the offer. The position is very much what I wanted in many ways, and I am delighted at your interest. If I start at this salary, may I be reviewed within six months with the goal of raising the salary to ____?*

Another possibility is to ask for more time to think about the low offer. Tell the interviewer that this is an important decision, and you need some time to consider the offer. The next day you can call and say, *I am flattered by your offer but I cannot accept because the salary is lower than I would like. Perhaps you could reconsider your offer or keep me in mind for future openings.*

Career Application

You've just passed the screening interview and have been asked to come in for a personal interview with the human resources representative and the hiring manager of a company where you are very eager to work. Although you are delighted with the company, you have promised yourself that you will not accept any position that pays less than $25,000 to start.

Your Task

- In teams of two, role-play the position of interviewer and interviewee.
- Interviewer: Set the interview scene. Discuss preliminaries, and then offer a salary of $22,500.
- Interviewee: Respond to preliminary questions and then to the salary offer of $22,500.
- Reverse roles so that the interviewee becomes the interviewer. Repeat the scenario.

A Reference Guide to Document Formats

Business documents carry two kinds of messages. Verbal messages are conveyed by the words chosen to express the writer's ideas. Nonverbal messages are conveyed largely by the appearance of a document. If you compare an assortment of letters and memos from various organizations, you will notice immediately that some look more attractive and more professional than others. The nonverbal message of the professional-looking documents suggests that they were sent by people who are careful, informed, intelligent, and successful. Understandably, you're more likely to take seriously documents that use attractive stationery and professional formatting techniques.

Over the years certain practices and conventions have arisen regarding the appearance and formatting of business documents. Although these conventions offer some choices (such as letter and punctuation styles), most business letters follow standardized formats. To ensure that your documents carry favorable nonverbal messages about you and your organization, you'll want to give special attention to the appearance and formatting of your letters, envelopes, memos, and fax cover sheets.

Appearance

To ensure that a message is read and valued, you need to give it a professional appearance. Two important elements in achieving a professional appearance are stationery and placement of the message on the page.

Stationery. Most organizations use high-quality stationery for business documents. This stationery is printed on select paper that meets two qualifications: weight and cotton-fiber content.

Paper is measured by weight and may range from 9 pounds (thin onionskin paper) to 32 pounds (thick card and cover stock). Most office stationery is in the 16- to 24-pound range. Lighter 16-pound paper is generally sufficient for internal documents including memos. Heavier 20- to 24-pound paper is used for printed letterhead stationery.

Paper is also judged by its cotton-fiber content. Cotton fiber makes paper stronger, softer in texture, and less likely to yellow. Good-quality stationery contains 25 percent or more cotton fiber.

Spacing After Punctuation. For some time typists left two spaces after end punctuation (periods, question marks, and so forth). This practice was necessary, it was thought, because typewriters did not have proportional spacing and sentences were easier to read if two spaces separated them. Professional typesetters, however, never followed this practice because they used proportional spacing, and readability was not a problem. Fortunately, today's word processors now make available the same fonts used by typesetters.

The question of how many spaces to leave after concluding punctuation is one of the most frequently asked questions at the Modern Language Association Web site <**http://www.mla.org**>. MLA experts point out that most publications in this country today have the same spacing after a punctuation mark as between words on the same line. Influenced by the look of typeset publications, many writers now leave only one space after end punctuation. As a practical matter, however, it is not wrong to use two spaces.

Letter Placement. The easiest way to place letters on the page is to use the defaults of your word processing program. These are usually set for side margins of 1 inch. Many companies today find these margins acceptable.

If you want to adjust your margins to better balance shorter letters, use the following chart:

Words in Body of Letter	Side Margins	Blank Lines After Date
Under 200	$1\frac{1}{2}$ inches	4 to 10
Over 200	1 inch	2 to 3

Experts say that a "ragged" right margin is easier to read than a justified (even) margin. You might want to turn off the justification feature of your word processing program if it automatically justifies the right margin.

Letter Parts

Professional-looking business letters are arranged in a conventional sequence with standard parts. Following is a discussion of how to use these letter parts properly. Figure A.1 illustrates the parts in a block-style letter. (See Chapter 6 for additional discussion of letters and their parts.)

Letterhead. Most business organizations use $8\frac{1}{2}$- × 11-inch paper printed with a letterhead displaying their official name, street address, Web address, e-mail address, and telephone and fax numbers. The letterhead may also include a logo and an advertising message such as *Frontier Bank: A new brand of banking.*

Dateline. On letterhead paper you should place the date two blank lines below the last line of the letterhead or 2 inches from the top edge of the paper (line 13). On plain paper place the date immediately below your return address. Since the date goes on line 13, start the return address an appropriate number of lines above it. The most common dateline format is as follows: *June 9, 2001.* Don't use *th* (or *rd*) when the date is written this way. For European or military correspondence, use the following dateline format: *9 June 2001.* Notice that no commas are used.

Addressee and Delivery Notations. Delivery notations such as *FAX TRANSMISSION, FEDERAL EXPRESS, MESSENGER DELIVERY, CONFIDENTIAL,* or *CERTIFIED MAIL* are typed in all capital letters two blank lines above the inside address.

Inside Address. Type the inside address—that is, the address of the organization or person receiving the letter—single-spaced, starting at the left margin. The number of lines between the dateline and the inside address depends on the size of the letter body, the type size (point or pitch size), and the length of the typing lines. Generally, one to nine blank lines are appropriate.

FIGURE A.1 **Block and Modified Block Letter Styles**

Letterhead ————————

island g r a p h i c s
8 9 3   D i l l i n g h a m   B o u l e v a r d   H o n o l u l u ,   H I   9 6 8 1 7 - 8 8 1 7

↓ line 13 or 1 blank line below letterhead

Dateline ————————— September 13, 200X

↓ 1 to 9 blank lines

Inside address ——————
Mr. T. M. Wilson, President
Visual Concept Enterprises
1901 Kaumualii Highway
Lihue, HI 96766

↓ 1 blank line

Salutation ——————— Dear Mr. Wilson

↓ 1 blank line

Subject line ——————— SUBJECT: BLOCK LETTER STYLE

↓ 1 blank line

This letter illustrates block letter style, about which you asked. All typed lines begin at the left margin. The date is usually placed two inches from the top edge of the paper or two lines below the last line of the letterhead, whichever position is lower.

This letter also shows open punctuation. No colon follows the salutation, and no comma follows the complimentary close. Although this punctuation style is efficient, we find that most of our customers prefer to include punctuation after the salutation and the complimentary close.

Body ——————————

If a subject line is included, it appears two lines below the salutation. The word *SUBJECT* is optional. Most readers will recognize a statement in this position as the subject without an identifying label. The complimentary close appears two lines below the end of the last paragraph.

↓ 1 blank line

Complimentary close
and signature block
Sincerely

Mark H. Wong

↓ 3 blank lines

Modified block style
Mixed punctuation
Mark H. Wong
Graphics Designer

↓ 1 blank line

MHW:pil

In block-style letters, as shown above, all lines begin at the left margin. In modified block-style letters, as shown at the left, the date is centered or aligned with the complimentary close and signature block, which start at the center. The date may also be backspaced from the right margin. Paragraphs may be blocked or indented. Mixed punctuation includes a colon after the salutation and a comma after the complimentary close. Open punctuation, shown above, omits the colon following the salutation and omits the comma following the complimentary closing.

Be careful to duplicate the exact wording and spelling of the recipient's name and address on your documents. Usually, you can copy this information from the letterhead of the correspondence you are answering. If, for example, you are responding to *Jackson & Perkins Company,* don't address your letter to *Jackson and Perkins Corp.*

Always be sure to include a courtesy title such as *Mr., Ms., Mrs., Dr.,* or *Professor* before a person's name in the inside address—for both the letter and the envelope. Although many women in business today favor *Ms.,* you'll want to use whatever title the addressee prefers.

Remember that the inside address is not included for readers (who already know who and where they are). It's there to help writers accurately file a copy of the message.

In general, avoid abbreviations (such as *Ave.* or *Co.*) unless they appear in the printed letterhead of the document being answered.

Attention Line. An attention line allows you to send your message officially to an organization but to direct it to a specific individual, officer, or department. However, if you know an individual's complete name, it's always better to use it as the first line of the inside address and avoid an attention line. Here are two common formats for attention lines:

MultiMedia Enterprises   MultiMedia Enterprises
931 Calkins Road   Attention: Marketing Director
Rochester, NY 14301   931 Calkins Road
                                          Rochester, NY 14301
ATTENTION MARKETING DIRECTOR

Attention lines may be typed in all caps or with upper- and lowercase letters. The colon following *Attention* is optional. Notice that an attention line may be placed two lines below the address block or printed as the second line of the inside address. You'll want to use the latter format if you're composing on a word processor because the address block may be copied to the envelope and the attention line will not interfere with the last-line placement of the zip code. (Mail can be sorted more easily if the zip code appears in the last line of a typed address.)

Whenever possible, use a person's name as the first line of an address instead of putting that name in an attention line. Some writers use an attention line because they fear that letters addressed to individuals at companies may be considered private. They worry that if the addressee is no longer with the company, the letter may be forwarded or not opened. Actually, unless a letter is marked "Personal" or "Confidential," it will very likely be opened as business mail.

Salutation. For most letter styles place the letter greeting, or salutation, one blank line below the last line of the inside address or the attention line (if used). If the letter is addressed to an individual, use that person's courtesy title and last name (*Dear Mr. Lanham*). Even if you are on a first-name basis (*Dear Leslie*), be sure to add a colon (not a comma or a semicolon) after the salutation. Do not use an individual's full name in the salutation (not *Dear Mr. Leslie Lanham*) unless you are unsure of gender (*Dear Leslie Lanham*).

For letters with attention lines or those addressed to organizations, the selection of an appropriate salutation has become more difficult. Formerly, *Gentlemen* was used generically for all organizations. With increasing numbers of women in business management today, however, *Gentlemen* is problematic. Because no universally acceptable salutation has emerged as yet, you'll probably be safest with *Ladies and Gentlemen* or *Gentlemen and Ladies.*

One way to avoid the salutation dilemma is to address a document to a specific person. Another alternative is to use the simplified letter style, which conveniently omits the salutation (and the complimentary close).

Subject and Reference Lines. Although experts suggest placing the subject line one blank line below the salutation, many businesses actually place it above the salutation. Use whatever style your organization prefers. Reference lines often show policy or file numbers; they generally appear two lines above the salutation.

Body. Most business letters and memorandums are single-spaced, with double line spacing between paragraphs. Very short messages may be double-spaced with indented paragraphs.

Complimentary Close. Typed one blank line below the last line of the letter, the complimentary close may be formal (*Very truly yours*) or informal (*Sincerely yours* or *Cordially*). The simplified letter style omits a complimentary close.

Signature Block. In most letter styles the writer's typed name and optional identification appear three to four blank lines below the complimentary close. The combination of name, title, and organization information should be arranged to achieve a balanced look. The name and title may appear on the same line or on separate lines, depending on the length of each. Use commas to separate categories within the same line, but not to conclude a line.

Sincerely yours,   Cordially yours,

Jeremy M. Wood   Casandra Baker-Murillo

Jeremy M. Wood, Manager   Casandra Baker-Murillo
Technical Sales and Services   Executive Vice President

Courtesy titles (*Ms., Mrs.,* or *Miss*) should be used before female names that are not readily distinguishable as male or female. They should also be used before names containing only initials and international names. The title is usually placed in parentheses, but it may appear without them.

Your truly,   Sincerely,

Ms. K.C. Tripton   Mr. Leslie Hill

(Ms.) K. C. Tripton   (Mr.) Leslie Hill
Project Manager   Public Policy Department

Some organizations include their names in the signature block. In such cases the organization name appears in all caps two lines below the complimentary close, as shown here.

Cordially,

LITTON COMPUTER SERVICES

Ms. Shelina A. Simpson

Ms. Shelina A. Simpson
Executive Assistant

Reference Initials. If used, the initials of the typist and writer are typed one blank line below the writer's name and title. Generally, the writer's initials are capitalized and the typist's are lowercased, but this format varies.

Enclosure Notation. When an enclosure or attachment accompanies a document, a notation to that effect appears one blank line below the reference initials. This notation reminds the typist to insert the enclosure in the envelope, and it reminds the recipient to look for the enclosure or attachment. The notation may be spelled out (*Enclosure, Attachment*), or it may be abbreviated (*Enc., Att.*). It may indicate the number of enclosures or attachments, and it may also identify a specific enclosure (*Enclosure: Form 1099*).

Copy Notation. If you make copies of correspondence for other individuals, you may use *cc* to indicate carbon copy, *pc* to indicate photocopy, or merely *c* for any kind of copy. A colon following the initial(s) is optional.

Second-page Heading. When a letter extends beyond one page, use plain paper of the same quality and color as the first page. Identify the second and succeeding pages with a heading consisting of the name of the addressee, the page number, and the date. Use either of the following two formats:

Ms. Rachel Ruiz   2   May 3, 2001

Ms. Rachel Ruiz
Page 2
May 3, 2001

Both headings appear on line 7 followed by two blank lines to separate them from the continuing text. Avoid using a second page if you have only one line or the complimentary close and signature block to fill that page.

Plain-Paper Return Address. If you prepare a personal or business letter on plain paper, place your address immediately above the date. Do not include your name; you will type (and sign) your name at the end of your letter. If your return address contains two lines, begin typing it on line 11 so that the date appears on line 13. Avoid abbreviations except for a two-letter state abbreviation.

580 East Leffels Street
Springfield, OH 45501
December 14, 2001

Ms. Ellen Siemens
Escrow Department
TransOhio First Federal
1220 Wooster Boulevard
Columbus, OH 43218-2900

Dear Ms. Siemens:

For letters prepared in the block style, type the return address at the left margin. For modified block-style letters, start the return address at the center to align with the complimentary close.

Letter Syles

Business letters are generally prepared in one of three formats. The most popular is the block style, but the simplified style has much to recommend it.

Block Style. In the block style, shown in Figure A.1, all lines begin at the left margin. This style is a favorite because it is easy to format.

Modified Block Style. The modified block style differs from block style in that the date and closing lines appear in the center, as shown at the bottom of Figure A.1. The date may be (1) centered, (2) begun at the center of the page (to align with the closing lines), or (3) backspaced from the right margin. The signature block—including the complimentary close, writer's name and title, or organization identification—begins at the center. The first line of each paragraph may begin at the left margin or may be indented five or ten spaces. All other lines begin at the left margin.

Simplified Style. Introduced by the Administrative Management Society a number of years ago, the simplified letter style, shown in Figure A.2, requires little formatting. Like the block style, all lines begin at the left margin. A subject line appears in all caps two blank lines below the inside address and two blank lines above the first paragraph. The salutation and complimentary close are omitted. The signer's name and identification appear in all caps four blank lines below the last paragraph. This letter style is efficient and avoids the problem of appropriate salutations and courtesy titles.

Punctuation Styles

Two punctuation styles are commonly used for letters. *Open* punctuation, shown with the block-style letter in Figure A.1, contains no punctuation after the salutation or complimentary close. *Mixed* punctuation, shown with the modified block style letter in Figure A.1, requires a colon after the salutation and a comma after the complimentary close. Many business organizations prefer mixed punctuation, even in a block style letter.

If you choose mixed punctuation, be sure to use a colon—not a comma or semicolon—after the salutation. Even when the salutation is a first name, the colon is appropriate.

Envelopes

An envelope should be of the same quality and color of stationery as the letter it carries. Because the envelope introduces your message and makes the first impression, you need to be especially careful in addressing it. Moreover, how you fold the letter is important.

Return Address. The return address is usually printed in the upper left corner of an envelope, as shown in Figure A.3. In large companies some form of identification (the writer's initials, name, or location) may be typed above the company name and return address. This identification helps return the letter to the sender in case of nondelivery.

On an envelope without a printed return address, single-space the return address in the upper left corner. Beginning on line 3 on the fourth space ($\frac{1}{2}$ inch) from the left edge, type the writer's name, title, company, and mailing address.

ABC ★ Automation Business Consultants
One Peachtree Plaza
Atlanta, GA 30312   (404) 369-1109

↓ line 13 or 1 blank line below letterhead

July 19, 2001

↓ 2 to 7 blank lines

FAX TRANSMISSION   ↓ 1 blank line   •————————— Identifies method of
                                                                      delivery

Ms. Sara Hendricks, Manager
American Land and Home Realty
P.O. Box 3392A
Atlanta, GA 30308

↓ 2 blank lines

SIMPLIFIED LETTER STYLE   •————————— Replaces salutation
                                                      with subject line
↓ 2 blank lines   •————————— Leaves 2 blank lines
                                                      above and below
                                                      subject line

You may be interested to learn, Ms. Hendricks, that some years ago the
Administrative Management Society recommended the simplified letter
format illustrated here. Notice the following efficient features:

1. All lines begin at the left margin.

2. The salutation and complimentary close are omitted.

3. A subject line in all caps appears 2 blank lines below the inside
   address and 2 blank lines above the first paragraph.

4. The writer's name and identification appear 4 blank lines below the
   last paragraph.

In addition to its efficiency, this letter style is helpful in dealing with the
problem of appropriate salutations. Since it has no salutation, your writers
need not worry about which to choose. For many reasons we recommend
this style to your staff.

Holly Higgins   •————————— Omits complimentary
                             ↓ 4 blank lines   close

HOLLY HIGGINS, MANAGER, OFFICE DIVISION   •————————— Highlights writer's
                                                      name and
HH:tlb   ↓ 1 blank line   identification
                             ↓ 1 blank line   with all caps

c John Fox   •————————— Identifies copy

Mailing Address. On legal-sized No. 10 envelopes ($4\frac{1}{8} \times 9\frac{1}{2}$ inches), begin the address on line 13 about $4\frac{1}{4}$ inches from the left edge, as shown in Figure A.3. For small envelopes ($3\frac{5}{8} \times 6\frac{1}{2}$ inches), begin typing on line 12 about $2\frac{1}{2}$ inches from the left edge.

The U.S. Postal Service recommends that addresses be typed in all caps without any punctuation. This Postal Service style, shown in the small envelope in Figure A.3, was originally developed to facilitate scanning by optical character readers.

FIGURE A.3 Envelope Formats

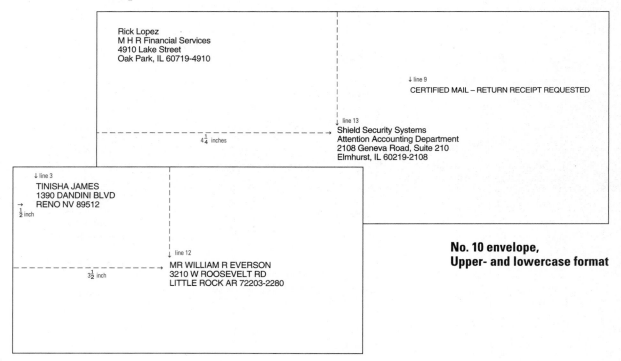

Rick Lopez
M H R Financial Services
4910 Lake Street
Oak Park, IL 60719-4910

↓ line 9
CERTIFIED MAIL – RETURN RECEIPT REQUESTED

↓ line 13
Shield Security Systems
Attention Accounting Department
2108 Geneva Road, Suite 210
Elmhurst, IL 60219-2108

$4\frac{1}{4}$ inches

**No. 10 envelope,
Upper- and lowercase format**

↓ line 3
TINISHA JAMES
1390 DANDINI BLVD
RENO NV 89512
→
$\frac{1}{2}$ inch

↓ line 12
MR WILLIAM R EVERSON
3210 W ROOSEVELT RD
LITTLE ROCK AR 72203-2280

$3\frac{1}{2}$ inch

No. $6\frac{3}{4}$ envelope, Postal Service uppercase format

Today's OCRs, however, are so sophisticated that they scan upper- and lowercase letters easily. Many companies today do not follow the Postal Service format because they prefer to use the same format for the envelope as for the inside address. If the same format is used, writers can take advantage of word processing programs to "copy" the inside address to the envelope, thus saving keystrokes and reducing errors. Having the same format on both the inside address and the envelope also looks more professional and consistent. For these reasons you may choose to use the familiar upper- and lowercase combination format. But you will want to check with your organization to learn its preference.

In addressing your envelopes for delivery in this country or in Canada, use the two-letter state and province abbreviations shown in Figure A.4. Notice that these abbreviations are in capital letters without periods.

Folding. The way a letter is folded and inserted into an envelope sends additional nonverbal messages about a writer's professionalism and carefulness. Most businesspeople follow the procedures shown here, which produce the least number of creases to distract readers.

For large No. 10 envelopes, begin with the letter face up. Fold slightly less than one third of the sheet toward the top, as shown in the following diagram. Then fold down the top third to within $\frac{1}{3}$ inch of the bottom fold. Insert the letter into the envelope with the last fold toward the bottom of the envelope.

FIGURE A.4 Abbreviations of States, Territories, and Provinces

State or Territory	Two-Letter Abbreviation	State or Territory	Two-Letter Abbreviation
Alabama	AL	North Dakota	ND
Alaska	AK	Ohio	OH
Arizona	AZ	Oklahoma	OK
Arkansas	AR	Oregon	OR
California	CA	Pennsylvania	PA
Canal Zone	CZ	Puerto Rico	PR
Colorado	CO	Rhode Island	RI
Connecticut	CT	South Carolina	SC
Delaware	DE	South Dakota	SD
District of Columbia	DC	Tennessee	TN
Florida	FL	Texas	TX
Georgia	GA	Utah	UT
Guam	GU	Vermont	VT
Hawaii	HI	Virgin Islands	VI
Idaho	ID	Virginia	VA
Illinois	IL	Washington	WA
Indiana	IN	West Virginia	WV
Iowa	IA	Wisconsin	WI
Kansas	KS	Wyoming	WY
Kentucky	KY		
Louisiana	LA		Two-Letter
Maine	ME	**Canadian Province**	Abbreviation
Maryland	MD	Alberta	AB
Massachusetts	MA	British Columbia	BC
Michigan	MI	Labrador	LB
Minnesota	MN	Manitoba	MB
Mississippi	MS	New Brunswick	NB
Missouri	MO	Newfoundland	NF
Montana	MT	Northwest Territories	NT
Nebraska	NE	Nova Scotia	NS
Nevada	NV	Ontario	ON
New Hampshire	NH	Prince Edward Island	PE
New Jersey	NJ	Quebec	PQ
New Mexico	NM	Saskatchewan	SK
New York	NY	Yukon Territory	YT
North Carolina	NC		

For small No. 6¾ envelopes, begin by folding the bottom up to within $\frac{1}{3}$ inch of the top edge. Then fold the right third over to the left. Fold the left third to within $\frac{1}{3}$ inch of the last fold. Insert the last fold into the envelope first.

Memorandums

As discussed in Chapter 5, memorandums deliver messages within organizations. Some offices use memo forms imprinted with the organization name and, optionally, the department or division names, as shown in Figure A.5. Although the design and arrangement of memo forms vary, they usually include the basic elements of *TO, FROM, DATE,* and *SUBJECT.* Large organizations may include other identifying headings, such as *FILE NUMBER, FLOOR, EXTENSION, LOCATION,* and *DISTRIBUTION.*

Because of the difficulty of aligning computer printers with preprinted forms, many business writers use a standardized memo template (sometimes called a "wizard"). This template automatically provides attractive headings with appropriate spacing and formatting. Other writers store their own preferred memo formats. Either method eliminates alignment problems.

If no printed or stored computer forms are available, memos may be typed on company letterhead or on plain paper, as shown in Figure A.6. On a full sheet of paper, start on line 13; on a half sheet, start on line 7. Double-space and type in all caps the guide words: *TO:, FROM:, DATE:, SUBJECT:.* Align all the fill-in information two spaces after the longest guide word (*SUBJECT:*). Leave 2 blank lines after the last line of the heading and begin typing the body of the memo. Like business letters, memos are single-spaced.

Memos are generally formatted with side margins of $1\frac{1}{4}$ inches, or they may conform to the printed memo form. (For more information about memos, see Chapter 5.)

E-Mail Messages

Because E-mail is a developing communication medium, formatting and usage are still fluid. The following suggestions, illustrated in Figure A.7 and also in Figure 5.2 in Chapter 5, may guide you in setting up the parts of an e-mail mes-

FIGURE A.5 Printed Memo Forms

FIRST FEDERAL BANK
Mortgage Department

Interoffice
Memorandum

DATE:

TO:

FROM:

SUBJECT:

PYRAMID, INC.
Internal Memo

TO: DATE:

FROM: FILE:

SUBJECT:

Appendix A Reference Guide to Document Formats

FIGURE A.6 Memo on Plain Paper

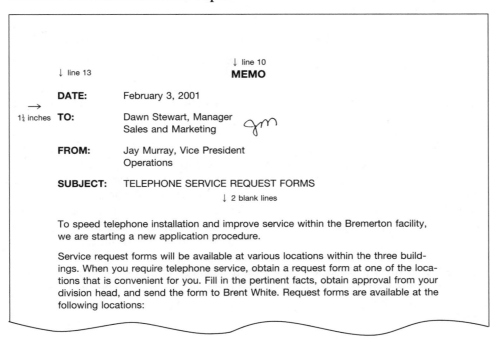

↓ line 10
MEMO

↓ line 13

DATE: February 3, 2001

→ 1½ inches **TO:** Dawn Stewart, Manager
Sales and Marketing

FROM: Jay Murray, Vice President
Operations

SUBJECT: TELEPHONE SERVICE REQUEST FORMS

↓ 2 blank lines

To speed telephone installation and improve service within the Bremerton facility, we are starting a new application procedure.

Service request forms will be available at various locations within the three buildings. When you require telephone service, obtain a request form at one of the locations that is convenient for you. Fill in the pertinent facts, obtain approval from your division head, and send the form to Brent White. Request forms are available at the following locations:

FIGURE A.7 E-Mail Message

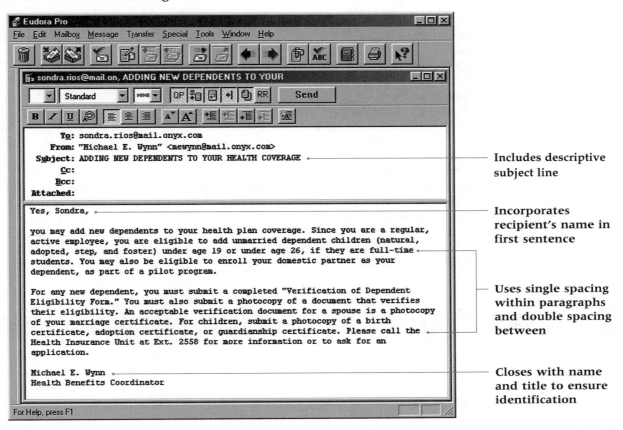

— Includes descriptive subject line

— Incorporates recipient's name in first sentence

— Uses single spacing within paragraphs and double spacing between

— Closes with name and title to ensure identification

sage. Always check, however, with your organization so that you can follow its practices.

To **Line.** Include the receiver's e-mail address after *To.* If the receiver's address is recorded in your address book, you just have to click on it. Be sure to enter all addresses very carefully since one mistyped letter prevents delivery.

From **Line.** Most mail programs automatically include your name and e-mail address after *From.*

Cc **and** *Bcc.* Insert the e-mail address of anyone who is to receive a copy of the message. *Cc* stands for carbon copy or courtesy copy. Don't be tempted, though, to send needless copies just because it's so easy. *Bcc* stands for *blind carbon copy.* Some writers use *bcc* to send a copy of the message without the addressee's knowledge. Writers are also using the *bcc* line for mailing lists. When a message is being sent to a number of people and their e-mail addresses should not be revealed, the *bcc* line works well to conceal the names and addresses of all receivers.

Subject. Identify the subject of the e-mail message with a brief but descriptive summary of the topic. Be sure to include enough information to be clear and compelling. Capitalize the initial letters of principal words, or capitalize the entire line if space permits.

Salutation. Include a brief greeting, if you like. Some writers use a salutation such as *Dear Sondra* followed by a comma or a colon. Others are more informal with *Hi, Sondra!,* or *Good morning* or *Greetings.* Some writers simulate a salutation by including the name of the receiver in an abbreviated first line, as shown in Figure A.7. Others writers treat an e-mail message like a memo and skip the salutation entirely.

Message. Cover just one topic in your message, and try to keep your total message under two screens in length. Single-space and be sure to use both upper- and lowercase letters. Double-space between paragraphs.

Closing. Conclude an external message, if you like, with *Cheers, Best wishes,* or *Warm regards,* followed by your name and e-mail address (because some programs and routers do not transmit your address automatically). If the recipient is unlikely to know you, it's not a bad idea to include your title and organization. Some veteran e-mail users include a *signature file* with identifying information embellished with keyboard art. Use restraint, however, because signature files take up precious space. Writers of e-mail messages sent within organizations may omit a closing and even skip their names at the ends of messages because receivers recognize them from identification in the opening lines.

Attachment. Use the attachment window or button to select the path and file name of any file you wish to send with your e-mail message. You can also attach a Web page to your message.

Fax Cover Sheet

Documents transmitted by fax are usually introduced by a cover sheet, such as that shown in Figure A.8. As with memos, the format varies considerably. Important items to include are (1) the name and fax number of the receiver, (2) the name and fax number of the sender, (3) the number of pages being sent, and (4) the name and telephone number of the person to notify in case of unsatisfactory transmission.

FAX TRANSMISSION

DATE: _____

FAX
TO: _____   NUMBER: _____
_____
_____

FAX
FROM: _____   NUMBER _____
_____
_____

NUMBER OF PAGES TRANSMITTED INCLUDING THIS COVER SHEET: ___

MESSAGE:

If any part of this fax transmission is missing or not clearly received, please call:

NAME: _____

PHONE: _____

When the document being transmitted requires little explanation, you may prefer to attach an adhesive note (such as a Post-it™ fax transmittal form) instead of a full cover sheet. These notes carry essentially the same information as shown in our printed fax cover sheet. They are perfectly acceptable in most business organizations and can save considerable paper and transmission costs.

B Proofreading Marks

PROOFREADING MARK	DRAFT COPY	FINAL COPY
⹀ Align horizontally	TO: Rick Munoz	TO: Rick Munoz
‖ Align vertically	166.32 132.45	166.32 132.45
Capitalize	Coca-cola	Coca-Cola
Close up space	runs on ms–dos	runs on MS-DOS
Center	meeting at 3 p. m.	meeting at 3 p.m.
Delete	⟧ Recommendations ⟦	Recommendations
Insert apostrophe	in my final judgement	in my judgment
Insert comma	our companys product	our company's product
Insert semicolon	you will of course	you will, of course,
Insert hyphen	value therefore, we feel	value; therefore, we feel
Insert period	tax free income	tax-free income
Insert quotation mark	Ms Holly Hines	Ms. Holly Hines
Insert space	shareholders receive a	shareholders receive a
Lowercase (remove capitals)	bonus	"bonus"
Move to left	wordprocessing program	word processing program
Move to right	the Vice President	the vice president
Spell out	HUMAN RESOURCES	Human Resources
Start new paragraph	I. Labor costs	I. Labor costs
Stet (don't delete)	A. Findings of study	A. Findings of study
Transpose	aimed at 2 depts	aimed at two departments
Use boldface	Keep the screen height at eye level.	Keep the screen height at eye level.
Use italics	officials talked openly	officials talked openly
Start new line	accounts recievable	accounts receivable
Run lines together	Conclusions	**Conclusions**
	The Perfect Résumé	*The Perfect Résumé*
	Globex, 23 Acorn Lane	Globex 23 Acorn Lane
	Invoice No., 122059	Invoice No. 122059

430

Documentation Formats

Careful writers take pains to document properly any data appearing in reports or messages for many reasons. Citing sources strengthens a writer's argument, as you learned in Chapter 11. Acknowledging sources also shields writers from charges of plagiarism. Moreover, good references help readers pursue further research. Fortunately, word processing programs have taken much of the pain out of documenting data, particularly for footnotes and endnotes.

Source and Content Notes

Before we discuss specific documentation formats, you should know the difference between source notes and content notes. Source notes identify quotations, paraphrased passages, and author references. They lead readers to the sources of cited information, and they must follow a consistent format. Content notes, on the other hand, enable writers to add comments, explain information not directly related to the text, or refer readers to other sections of a report. Because content notes are generally infrequent, most writers identify them in the text with a raised asterisk.* At the bottom of the page, the asterisk is repeated with the content note following. If two content notes appear on one page, a double asterisk identifies the second reference.

Your real concern, however, will be with source notes. These identify quotations or paraphrased ideas in the text, and they direct readers to a specific endnote or footnote or to the complete list (bibliography) of references at the end of your report.

Two Documentation Methods for Source Notes

Researchers have for years struggled to develop the perfect documentation system—one that is efficient for the writer and crystal clear to the reader. Most of these systems can be grouped into two methods: the footnote/endnote method and the parenthetic method.

Footnote/Endnote Method. Writers using footnotes or endnotes insert a small superscript (raised) figure into the text close to the place where a reference is mentioned. This number leads the reader to a footnote at the bottom of the page or to an endnote at the end of the report. Footnotes or endnotes contain a complete description of the source document. In this book we have used the endnote method. We chose this style because it least disrupts the text. Most of the individual citation formats in this book follow the traditional style suggested in *The Chicago Manual of Style*, 14e (Chicago: The University of Chicago Press, 1993, pp. 487–635).

---

*This is an example of a content note.

Parenthetic Method. Many writers, however, prefer to use a parenthetic style to cite references. In this method a reference to the author appears in parentheses close to the place where it is mentioned in the text. Some parenthetic styles show the author's last name and date of publication (e.g., *Smith 2000*), while others show the author's last name and page cited (e.g., *Smith 24*). One of the most well-known parenthetic systems is the Modern Language Association (MLA) format. The long report shown in Figure 11.15 illustrates this format. To provide guidance in preparing your academic and business papers, we'll focus on the MLA format in this textbook.

Which Method for Business? Students frequently ask, "But what documentation system is most used in business?" Actually no one method dominates. Many businesses have developed their own hybrid systems. These companies generally supply guidelines illustrating their in-house style to employees. Before starting any research project on the job, you'll want to inquire about your organization's preferred documentation style. You can also look in the files for examples of previous reports.

MLA Style—Modern Language Association

The MLA citation style uses parenthetic author references in the text. These in-text citations guide the reader to a bibliography called "Works Cited." Following are selected distinguishing characteristics of the MLA style. For more information, consult Joseph Gibaldi, *MLA Handbook for Writers of Research Papers*, 5e (New York: The Modern Language Association of America, 1999).

In-Text Citations

Within the text the author's last name and relevant page reference appear in parentheses, such as (*Jones 310*). In-text citations should be placed close to reference. Notice that no separating comma appears. If the author's name is mentioned in the text, cite only the page number in parentheses. Your goal is to avoid interrupting the flow of writing. Thus, you should strive to place the parenthetical reference where a pause would naturally occur, but as near as possible to the material documented. Note the following examples:

Author's Name in Text
Anthropologist E. T. Hall proposed the theory in 1958 (142–168).
Author's Name in Reference
The theory was first proposed in 1958 (Hall 142–168).
Authors' Names in Text
Others, like Bergstrom and Voorhees (243–251), support a competing theory.
Authors' Names in Reference
Others support a competing theory (e.g., Bergstrom and Voorhees 243–251).
Author's Name in Text
It may be true, as Hall contends, that "Americans view time as monochromatic" (17).

When citing films, television programs, or electronic references, MLA style recommends that you include in the text, rather than in a parenthetical reference, the name of the person or organization that begins the corresponding entry in the works-cited list.[1]

[1]Joseph Gibaldi, *MLA Handbook for Writers of Research Papers*, 5e (New York: The Modern Language Association, 1999), 208.

FIGURE C.1 Model MLA Bibliography of Sample References

Works Cited

American Airlines. <u>2000 Annual Report</u>. Fort Worth, TX: AMR   •————— **Annual report**
   Corporation.

Berss, Marcia. "Protein Man." <u>Forbes</u> 24 Oct. 1999: 64-66. •————— **Magazine article**

"Clementine@work." <u>SPSS Web Site</u>. Retrieved 7 Sept. 00.   •————— **World Wide Web**
   <http://www.spss.com/customer/clem_stories/>.

"Globalization Often Means That the Fast Track Leads Overseas." •———— **Newspaper article,**
   <u>The Washington Post</u> 16 June 1999: A10.   **no author**

Huang, Jerry Y. C. "Solid Waste Disposal," <u>Microsoft Encarta '95</u>. •—— **CD-ROM encyclope-**
   CD-ROM. Redmond, WA: Microsoft, 1994.   **dia article, one author**

Lancaster, Hal. "When Taking a Tip From a Job Network, Proceed   **Newspaper article,**
   With Caution." <u>The Wall Street Journal</u> 7 Feb. 2000: B1. •——— **one author**

Markoff, John. "Voluntary Rules Proposed to Help Insure Privacy
   for Internet Users." <u>The New York Times</u>. 5 June 1999,
   business sec., CyberTimes. Retrieved 9 June 1999 <http://www. •——— **On-line newspaper**
   times.com/library/cyber/week/y05dat.html>.   **article**

Mitchell, William J. <u>City of Bits: Space, Place, and the Informa-</u>
   <u>tionbahn</u>. Cambridge: MIT P, 1995. MIT P Electronic Books. •——— **On-line e-book**
   Retrieved 9 July 1998 <http://mitpress.mit.edu/e-books/
   City_of_Bits>.

Murphy, H. Lee. "Saturn's Orbit Still High With Consumers."
   <u>Marketing News Online</u>. 31 Aug. 1999. Retrieved 1 Sept. 1999 •——— **On-line magazine**
   <http://www.ama.org/pubs/mn/0818/n1.htm>.   **article**

Pinkerton Investigation Services. <u>The Employer's Guide to</u>
   <u>Investigation Services</u>, 2nd ed. Atlanta: Pinkerton   •——— **Brochure**
   Information Center, 1998.

Rivera, Francisco. Personal interview. 16 May 2000. •——— **Interview**

Rose, Richard C., and Echo Montgomery Garrett. <u>How to Make a Buck</u>
   <u>and Still Be a Decent Human Being</u>. New York: HarperCollins, •——— **Book, two authors**
   1998.

U.S. Dept. of Labor. <u>Child Care as a Workforce Issue: An Update</u>. •——— **Government**
   Washington, DC: GPO, 1999.   **publication**

Wetherbee, James C., Nicholas P. Vitalari, and Andrew Milner.
   "Key Trends in Systems Development in Europe and North   **Journal article with**
   America." <u>Journal of Global Information Management</u> 3.2 •——— **volume and issue**
   (1998): 5-20. ["3.2" signifies volume 3, issue 2]   **numbers**

Electronic Source With Author

William J. Mitchell's <u>City of Bits</u> discusses architecture and urban life in the context of the digital telecommunications revolution. *(In the works-cited list, the reader can find a complete reference under the author's name. See Figure C.1.)*

Electronic Source With Organization

More companies today are using data mining to unlock hidden value in their data. The data mining program "Clementine," described at the SPSS Web site, helps organizations predict market share and detect possible fraud. *(In the works-cited list, the reader can find a complete reference under "SPSS," the organization sponsoring the Web site. See Figure C.l)*

Works Cited

In-text citations lead the reader to complete bibliographical citations in the "Works Cited." This alphabetical listing may contain all works consulted or only those mentioned in the text. Check with your instructor or editor to learn what method is preferred. Below are selected guidelines summarizing important elements of the MLA format for "Works Cited," as shown in Figure C.1.

- **Hanging indented style.** Indent the second and succeeding line for each item. Single-space within entries and double-space between.

- **Book titles.** Underline the titles of books and use "headline style" (up style) for capitalization. This means that the initial letters of all main words are capitalized:

  Patrick S. O'Brien. <u>Making College Count for Career Search Success</u>. Cincinnati: South-Western College Publishing, 2000.

- **Magazine titles.** For the titles of magazine articles, include the date of publication but omit volume and issue numbers:

  Lee, Mary M. "Investing in International Relationships." <u>Business Monthly</u> 18 Feb. 2000, 23–24.

- **Journal articles.** For journal articles follow the same format as for magazine articles except include the volume number, issue number (if needed), and the year of publication inside parentheses:

  Taylor, Chris L. "Nonverbal Communication," <u>The Journal of Business Ethics</u> 10:2 (2000): 23–29. ["10:2" indicates volume 10, issue 2.]

- **Italics and underscoring.** MLA style recommends underscoring book, magazine, and journal titles because underscores are easier to read than italics. Italics, however, are preferred in many organizations. Check with your instructor or organization for the preferred style.

Electronic References

To refer to electronic sources, include print information, if available, along with as much other information as necessary for a reader to locate a source. Underline the title of a database, periodical, or professional or personal Web site. For sites without titles, underline a description such as <u>Home page</u>.

Although MLA style does not suggest including the word "Retrieved" before the access date, we include it to distinguish the retrieval date from the publication date. Figure C.1 illustrates the electronic and other formats for many different kinds of references. The MLA also posts some helpful guidelines for documenting electronic sources at its Web site. Visit **<www.mla.org>** and follow the prompts to "Documenting Sources From the World Wide Web."

For an updated list of citation formats for electronic references to typical business information sources, visit the Guffey Web site **<www.meguffey.com>** and click on "Documentation."

Grammar/Mechanics Handbook

Because many students need a quick review of basic grammar and mechanics, we provide a number of resources in condensed form. The Grammar/Mechanics Handbook, which offers you a rapid systematic review, consists of four parts:

- **Grammar/Mechanics Diagnostic Test.** This 65-point Grammar/Mechanics Diagnostic Test helps you assess your strengths and weaknesses in eight areas of grammar and mechanics.

- **Grammar/Mechanics Profile.** The G/M Profile enables you to pinpoint specific areas in which you need remedial instruction or review.

- **Grammar Review with Reinforcement and Editing Exercises.** A concise set of guidelines reviews basic principles of grammar, punctuation, capitalization, and number style. The review also provides reinforcement and quiz exercises that help you interact with the principles of grammar and test your comprehension. The guidelines not only provide a study guide for review but will also serve as a reference manual throughout the writing course. The grammar review can be used for classroom-centered instruction or for self-guided learning.

- **Confusing Words and Frequently Misspelled Words.** A selected list of confusing words, along with a list of 160 frequently misspelled words, completes the Grammar/Mechanics Handbook.

For additional assistance in helping you strengthen your language skills, we suggest the following resources:

- **On-line interactive skill builders.** At the Guffey Web Site <**www.meguffey. com**>, you will find sentence compentency drills that are similar to the grammar/mechanics exercises provided in this book. Click on "Book Support," "*Business English*," and "Skill Builders." You can also work on your spelling and vocabulary skills at this Web site.

- **Reference books.** More comprehensive treatment of grammar and punctuation guidelines can be found in Clark and Clark's *A Handbook for Office Workers* (South-Western College Publishing, 1998) and Guffey's *Business English* (South-Western, 1999).

The first step in your systematic review of grammar and mechanics involves completing a diagnostic test.

Grammar/Mechanics Diagnostic Test

Name _____

This diagnostic test is intended to reveal your strengths and weaknesses in using the following:

plural nouns	adjectives	punctuation
possessive nouns	adverbs	capitalization style
pronouns	prepositions	number style
verbs	conjunctions	

The test is organized into sections corresponding to these categories. In sections A–H, each sentence is either correct or has one error related to the category under which it is listed. If a sentence is correct, write *C*. If it has an error, underline the error and write the correct form in the space provided. Use ink to record your answers. When you finish, check your answers with your instructor and fill out the Grammar/Mechanics Profile at the end of the test.

A. Plural Nouns

<u>branches</u>

Example: The newspaper named editors in chief for both <u>branchs</u>.

1. Three of the attornies representing the defendants were from cities in other states.
2. Four freshmans discussed the pros and cons of attending colleges or universities.
3. Since the 1990s, most companys have begun to send bills of lading with shipments.
4. Neither the Johnsons nor the Morris's knew about the changes in beneficiaries.
5. The manager asked all secretaries to work on the next four Saturday's.

B. Possessive Nouns

6. We sincerely hope that the jurys judgment reflects the stories of all the witnesses.
7. In a little over two months time, the secretaries had finished three reports for the president.
8. Mr. Franklins staff is responsible for all accounts receivable contracted by customers purchasing electronics parts.
9. At the next stockholders meeting, we will discuss benefits for employees and dividends for shareholders.
10. Three months ago several employees in the sales department complained of Mrs. Smiths smoking.

C. Pronouns

<u>me</u>

Example: Whom did you ask to replace Tom and <u>I</u>?

11. My manager and myself were willing to send the copies to whoever needed them.
12. Some of the work for Mr. Benson and I had to be reassigned to Mark and him.
13. Although it's motor was damaged, the car started for the mechanic and me.
14. Just between you and me, only you and I know that she will be transferred.
15. My friend and I applied for employment at Reynolds, Inc., because of their excellent employee benefits.

D. Verb Agreement

<u>has</u>

Example: The list of arrangements <u>have</u> to be approved by Tim and her.

16. The keyboard, printer, and monitor costs less than I expected.

17. A description of the property, together with several other legal documents, were submitted by my attorney. _____
18. There was only two enclosures and the letter in the envelope. _____
19. Neither the manager nor the employees in the office think the solution is fair. _____
20. Because of the holiday, our committee prefer to delay its action. _____

E. Verb Mood, Voice, and Tense

21. If I was able to fill your order immediately, I certainly would. <u>**were**</u>_____
22. To operate the machine, first open the disk drive door and then you insert the diskette. _____
23. If I could chose any city, I would select Honolulu. _____
24. Those papers have laid on his desk for more than two weeks. _____
25. The auditors have went over these accounts carefully, and they have found no discrepancies. _____

F. Adjectives and Adverbs

26. Until we have a more clearer picture of the entire episode, we shall proceed cautiously. <u>**omit more**</u>_____
27. For about a week their newly repaired copier worked just beautiful. _____
28. The recently elected official benefited from his coast to coast campaign. _____
29. Mr. Snyder only has two days before he must complete the end-of-the-year report. _____
30. The architects submitted there drawings in a last-minute attempt to beat the deadline. _____

G. Prepositions and Conjunctions

31. Can you tell me where the meeting is scheduled at? _____
32. It seems like we have been taking this test forever. _____
33. Our investigation shows that the distribution department is more efficient then the sales department. _____
34. My courses this semester are totally different than last semester's. _____
35. Do you know where this shipment is going to? _____

H. Commas

For each of the following sentences, insert any necessary commas. Count the number of commas that you added. Write that number in the space provided. All punctuation must be correct to receive credit for the sentence. If a sentence requires no punctuation, write C.

Example: However, because of developments in theory and computer applications, management is becoming more of a science. <u>2_____</u>

36. For example management determines how orders assignments and responsibilities are delegated to employees. _____
37. Your order Mrs. Swift will be sent from Memphis Tennessee on July 1. _____
38. When you need service on any of your pieces of equipment we will be happy to help you Mr. Lopez. _____
39. Kevin Long who is the project manager at Techdata suggested that I call you. _____
40. You have purchased from us often and your payments in the past have always been prompt. _____

I. Commas and Semicolons 1

Add commas and semicolons to the following sentences. In the space provided, write the number of punctuation marks that you added.

_____ 41. The salesperson turned in his report however he did not indicate what time period it covered.

_____ 42. Interest payments on bonds are tax deductible dividend payments are not.

_____ 43. We are opening a branch office in Kettering and hope to be able to serve all your needs from that office by the middle of January.

_____ 44. As suggested by the committee we must first secure adequate funding then we may consider expansion.

_____ 45. When you begin to conduct research for a report consider the many library sources available namely books, periodicals, government publications, and databases.

J. Commas and Semicolons 2

_____ 46. After our office manager had the printer repaired it jammed again within the first week although we treated it carefully.

_____ 47. Our experienced courteous staff has been trained to anticipate your every need.

_____ 48. In view of the new law that went into effect April 1 our current liability insurance must be increased however we cannot immediately afford it.

_____ 49. As stipulated in our contract your agency will supervise our graphic arts and purchase our media time.

_____ 50. As you know Mrs. Simpson we aim for long-term business relationships not quick profits.

K. Other Punctuation

Each of the following sentences may require dashes, colons, question marks, quotation marks, periods, and underscores, as well as commas and semicolons. Add the appropriate punctuation to each sentence. Then, in the space provided, write the total number of marks that you added.

3_____ **Example:** Price, service, and reliability-these are our prime considerations.

_____ 51. The following members of the department volunteered to help on Saturday Kim Carlos Dan and Sylvia.

_____ 52. Mr Danner, Miss Reed, and Mrs Garcia usually arrived at the office by 8 30 am.

_____ 53. Three of our top managers Tim, Marcy, and Thomas received cash bonuses.

_____ 54. Did the vice president really say "All employees may take Friday off

_____ 55. We are trying to locate an edition of Newsweek that carried an article entitled Who Is Reading Your E-Mail

L. Capitalization

For each of the following sentences, circle any letter that should be capitalized. In the space provided, write the number of circles that you marked.

4_____ **Example:** vice president daniels devised a procedure for expediting purchase orders from area 4 warehouses.

_____ 56. although english was his native language, he also spoke spanish and could read french.

57. on a trip to the east coast, uncle henry visited the empire state building. _____
58. karen enrolled in classes in history, german, and sociology. _____
59. the business manager and the vice president each received a new compaq computer. _____
60. james lee, the president of kendrick, inc., will speak to our conference in the spring. _____

M. Number Style

Decide whether the numbers in the following sentences should be written as words or as figures. Each sentence either is correct or has one error. If it is correct, write C. If it has an error, underline it and write the correct form in the space provided.

Example: The bank had 5 branches in three suburbs.   five _____

61. More than 2,000,000 people have visited the White House in the past five years. _____
62. Of the 35 letters sent out, only three were returned. _____
63. We set aside forty dollars for petty cash, but by December 1 our fund was depleted. _____
64. The meeting is scheduled for May 5th at 3 p.m. _____
65. In the past 20 years, nearly 15 percent of the population changed residences at least once. _____

Grammar/Mechanics Profile

In the spaces at the right, place a check mark to indicate the number of correct answers you had in each category of the Grammar/Mechanics Diagnostic Test.

		NUMBER CORRECT*				
		5	4	3	2	1
1–5	Plural Nouns	_____	_____	_____	_____	_____
6–10	Possessive Nouns	_____	_____	_____	_____	_____
11–15	Pronouns	_____	_____	_____	_____	_____
16–20	Verb Agreement	_____	_____	_____	_____	_____
21–25	Verb Mood, Voice, and Tense	_____	_____	_____	_____	_____
26–30	Adjectives and Adverbs	_____	_____	_____	_____	_____
31–35	Prepositions and Conjunctions	_____	_____	_____	_____	_____
36–40	Commas	_____	_____	_____	_____	_____
41–45	Commas and Semicolons 1	_____	_____	_____	_____	_____
46–50	Commas and Semicolons 2	_____	_____	_____	_____	_____
51–55	Other Punctuation	_____	_____	_____	_____	_____
56–60	Capitalization	_____	_____	_____	_____	_____
61–65	Number Style	_____	_____	_____	_____	_____

*Note: 5 = have excellent skills; 4 = need light review; 3 = need careful review; 2 = need to study rules; 1 = need serious study and follow-up reinforcement.

Parts of Speech (1.01)

1.01 Functions. English has eight parts of speech. Knowing the functions of the parts of speech helps writers better understand how words are used and how sentences are formed.

a. *Nouns:* name persons, places, things, qualities, concepts, and activities (for example, *Kevin, Phoenix, computer, joy, work, banking*).
b. *Pronouns:* substitute for nouns (for example, *he, she, it, they*).
c. *Verbs:* show the action of a subject or join the subject to words that describe it (for example, *walk, heard, is, was jumping*).
d. *Adjectives:* describe or limit nouns and pronouns and often answer the questions *what kind? how many?* and *which one?* (for example, *red* car, *ten* items, *good* manager).
e. *Adverbs:* describe or limit verbs, adjectives, or other adverbs and frequently answer the questions *when? how? where?* or *to what extent?* (for example, *tomorrow, rapidly, here, very*).
f. *Prepositions:* join nouns or pronouns to other words in sentences (for example, desk *in* the office, ticket *for* me, letter *to* you).
g. *Conjunctions:* connect words or groups of words (for example, you *and* I, Mark *or* Jill).
h. *Interjections:* express strong feelings (for example, *Wow! Oh!*).

Nouns (1.02–1.06)

Nouns name persons, places, things, qualities, concepts, and activities. Nouns may be classified into a number of categories.

1.02 Concrete and Abstract. Concrete nouns name specific objects that can be seen, heard, felt, tasted, or smelled. Examples of concrete nouns are *telephone, dollar, IBM,* and *tangerine.* Abstract nouns name generalized ideas such as qualities or concepts that are not easily pictured. *Emotion, power,* and *tension* are typical examples of abstract nouns.

Business writing is most effective when concrete words predominate. It's clearer to write *We need 16-pound bond paper* than to write *We need office supplies.* Chapter 4 provides practice in developing skill in the use of concrete words.

1.03 Proper and Common. Proper nouns name specific persons, places, or things and are always capitalized (*General Electric, Baltimore, Jennifer*). All other nouns are common nouns and begin with lowercase letters (*company, city, student*). Rules for capitalization are presented in Sections 3.01–3.16.

1.04 Singular and Plural. Singular nouns name one item; plural nouns name more than one. From a practical view, writers seldom have difficulty with singular nouns. They may need help, however, with the formation and spelling of plural nouns.

1.05 Guidelines for Forming Noun Plurals
a. Add *s* to most nouns (*chair, chairs; mortgage, mortgages; Monday, Mondays*).
b. Add *es* to nouns ending in *s, x, z, ch,* or *sh* (*bench, benches; boss, bosses; box, boxes; Lopez, Lopezes*).
c. Change the spelling in irregular noun plurals (*man, men; foot, feet; mouse, mice; child, children*).

d. Add *s* to nouns that end in *y* when *y* is preceded by a vowel (*attorney, attorneys; valley, valleys; journey, journeys*).
e. Drop the *y* and add *ies* to nouns ending in *y* when *y* is preceded by a consonant (*company, companies; city, cities; secretary, secretaries*).
f. Add *s* to the principal word in most compound expressions (*editors in chief, fathers-in-law, bills of lading, runners-up*).
g. Add *s* to most numerals, letters of the alphabet, words referred to as words, degrees, and abbreviations (*5s, 1990s, Bs, ands, CPAs, qts.*).
h. Add *'s* only to clarify letters of the alphabet that might be misread, such as *A's, I's, M's,* and *U's* and *i's, p's,* and *q's*. An expression like *c.o.d.s* requires no apostrophe because it would not easily be misread.

1.06 Collective Nouns. Nouns such as *staff, faculty, committee, group,* and *herd* refer to a collection of people, animals, or objects. Collective nouns may be considered singular or plural depending upon their action. See Section 1.10i for a discussion of collective nouns and their agreement with verbs.

Review Exercise A—Nouns

In the space provided for each item, write *a* or *b* to complete the following statements accurately. When you finish, compare your responses with those provided. Answers are provided for odd-numbered items. Your instructor has the remaining answers. For each item on which you need review, consult the numbered principle shown in parentheses.

1. Nearly all (a) *editor in chiefs*, (b) *editors in chief* demand observance of standard punctuation. _____
2. Several (a) *attorneys*, (b) *attornies* worked on the case together. _____
3. Please write to the (a) *Davis's*, (b) *Davises* about the missing contract. _____
4. The industrial complex has space for nine additional (a) *companys*, (b) *companies*. _____
5. That accounting firm employs two (a) *secretaries*, (b) *secretarys* for five CPAs. _____
6. Four of the wooden (a) *benches*, (b) *benchs* must be repaired. _____
7. The home was constructed with numerous (a) *chimneys*, (b) *chimnies*. _____
8. Tours of the production facility are made only on (a) *Tuesdays*, (b) *Tuesday's*. _____
9. We asked the (a) *Lopez's*, (b) *Lopezes* to contribute to the fund-raising drive. _____
10. Both my (a) *sister-in-laws*, (b) *sisters-in-law* agreed to the settlement. _____
11. The stock market is experiencing abnormal (a) *ups and downs*, (b) *up's and down's*. _____
12. Three (a) *mouses*, (b) *mice* were seen near the trash cans. _____
13. This office is unusually quiet on (a) *Sundays*, (b) *Sunday's*. _____
14. Several news (a) *dispatchs*, (b) *dispatches* were released during the strike. _____
15. Two major (a) *countries*, (b) *countrys* will participate in arms negotiations. _____
16. Some young children have difficulty writing their (a) *bs and ds*, (b) *b's and d's*. _____
17. The (a) *board of directors*, (b) *boards of directors* of all the major companies participated in the surveys. _____
18. In their letter the (a) *Metzes*, (b) *Metzs* said they intended to purchase the property. _____
19. In shipping we are careful to include all (a) *bill of sales*, (b) *bills of sale*. _____
20. Over the holidays many (a) *turkies*, (b) *turkeys* were consumed. _____

---

1. b (1.05f)   3. b (1.05b)   5. a (1.05e)   7. a (1.05d)   9. b (1.05b)   11. a (1.05g)
13. a (1.05a)   15. a (1.05e)   17. b (1.05f)   19. b (1.05f) (Only odd-numbered answers are provided. Consult your instructor for the others.)

Pronouns (1.07–1.09)

Pronouns substitute for nouns. They are classified by case.

1.07 Case. Pronouns function in three cases, as shown in the following chart.

Nominative Case *(Used for subjects of verbs and subject complements)*	**Objective Case** *(Used for objects of prepositions and objects of verbs)*	**Possessive Case** *(Used to show possession)*
I	me	my, mine
we	us	our, ours
you	you	your, yours
he	him	his
she	her	her, hers
it	it	its
they	them	their, theirs
who, whoever	whom, whomever	whose

1.08 Guidelines for Selecting Pronoun Case

a. Pronouns that serve as subjects of verbs must be in the nominative case:

   He and *I* (not *Him* and *me*) decided to apply for the jobs.

b. Pronouns that follow linking verbs (such as *am, is, are, was, were, be, being, been*) and rename the words to which they refer must be in the nominative case.

   It must have been *she* (not *her*) who placed the order. (The nominative-case pronoun *she* follows the linking verb *been* and renames *it.*)

   If it was *he* (not *him*) who called, I have his number. (The nominative-case pronoun *he* follows the linking verb *was* and renames *it.*)

c. Pronouns that serve as objects of verbs or objects of prepositions must be in the objective case:

   Mr. Andrews asked *them* to complete the proposal. (The pronoun *them* is the object of the verb *asked.*)

   All computer printouts are sent to *him*. (The pronoun *him* is the object of the preposition *to.*)

   Just between you and *me*, profits are falling. (The pronoun *me* is one of the objects of the preposition *between.*)

Grammar/Mechanics Handbook

d. Pronouns that show ownership must be in the possessive case. Possessive pronouns (such as *hers, yours, ours, theirs,* and *its*) require no apostrophes:

We found my diskette, but *yours* (not *your's*) may be lost.

All parts of the machine, including *its* (not *it's*) motor, were examined.

The house and *its* (not *it's*) contents will be auctioned.

Don't confuse possessive pronouns and contractions. Contractions are shortened forms of subject-verb phrases (such as *it's* for *it is, there's* for *there is,* and *they're* for *they are*).

e. When a pronoun appears in combination with a noun or another pronoun, ignore the extra noun or pronoun and its conjunction. In this way pronoun case becomes more obvious:

The manager promoted Jeff and *me* (not *I*). (Ignore *Jeff and.*)

f. In statements of comparison, mentally finish the comparative by adding the implied missing words:

Next year I hope to earn as much as *she.* (The verb *earns* is implied here: . . . *as much as she earns.*)

g. Pronouns must be in the same case as the words they replace or rename. When pronouns are used with appositives, ignore the appositive:

A new contract was signed by *us* (not *we*) employees. (Temporarily ignore the appositive *employees* in selecting the pronoun.)

We (not *us*) citizens have formed our own organization. (Temporarily ignore the appositive *citizens* in selecting the pronoun.)

h. Pronouns ending in *self* should be used only when they refer to previously mentioned nouns or pronouns:

The CEO *himself* answered the telephone.

Robert and *I* (not *myself*) are in charge of the campaign.

i. Use objective-case pronouns as objects of the prepositions *between, but, like,* and *except:*

Everyone but John and *him* (not *he*) qualified for the bonus.

Employees like Miss Gillis and *her* (not *she*) are hard to replace.

j. Use *who* or *whoever* for nominative-case constructions and *whom* or *whomever* for objective-case constructions. In making the correct choice, it's sometimes helpful to substitute *he* for *who* or *whoever* and *him* for *whom* or *whomever:*

For *whom* was this book ordered? (*This book was ordered for him/whom?*)

Who did you say would drop by? (*Who/he . . . would drop by?*)

Deliver the package to *whoever* opens the door. (In this sentence the clause *whoever opens the door* functions as the object of the preposition *to.* Within the clause itself *whoever* is the subject of the verb *opens.* Again, substitution of *he* might be helpful: *He/Whoever opens the door.*)

1.09 Guidelines for Making Pronouns Agree With Their Antecedents. Pronouns must agree with the words to which they refer (their antecedents) in gender and in number.

a. Use masculine pronouns to refer to masculine antecedents, feminine pronouns to refer to feminine antecedents, and neuter pronouns to refer to antecedents without gender:

The man opened *his* office door. (Masculine gender applies.)

A woman sat at *her* desk. (Feminine gender applies.)

This computer and *its* programs fit our needs. (Neuter gender applies.)

b. Use singular pronouns to refer to singular antecedents:

Common-gender pronouns (such as *him* or *his*) traditionally have been used when the gender of the antecedent is unknown. Sensitive writers today, however, prefer to recast such constructions to avoid the need for common-gender pronouns. Study these examples for alternatives to the use of common-gender pronouns:*

Each student must submit a report on Monday.

All students must submit *their* reports on Monday.

Each student must submit *his* or *her* report on Monday. (This alternative is least acceptable since it is wordy and calls attention to itself.)

c. Use singular pronouns to refer to singular indefinite subjects and plural pronouns for plural indefinite subjects. Words such as *anyone, something,* and *anybody* are considered indefinite because they refer to no specific person or object. Some indefinite pronouns are always singular; others are always plural.

Always Singular			**Always Plural**
anybody	everyone	somebody	both
anyone	everything	someone	few
anything	neither		many
each	nobody		several
either	no one		

Somebody in the group of touring women left *her* (not *their*) purse in the museum.

Either of the companies has the right to exercise *its* (not *their*) option to sell stock.

d. Use singular pronouns to refer to collective nouns and organization names:

The engineering staff is moving *its* (not *their*) facilities on Friday. (The singular pronoun *its* agrees with the collective noun *staff* because the members of *staff* function as a single unit.)

Jones, Cohen, & James, Inc., has (not *have*) canceled *its* (not *their*) contract with us. (The singular pronoun *its* agrees with *Jones, Cohen, & James, Inc.,* because the members of the organization are operating as a single unit.)

e. Use a plural pronoun to refer to two antecedents joined by *and,* whether the antecedents are singular or plural:

Our company president and our vice president will be submitting *their* expenses shortly.

f. Ignore intervening phrases—introduced by expressions such as *together with, as well as,* and *in addition to*—that separate a pronoun from its antecedent:

One of our managers, along with several salespeople, is planning *his* retirement. (If you wish to emphasize both subjects equally, join them with *and:* One of our managers *and* several salespeople are planning *their* retirements.)

*See Chapter 2, page 39, for additional discussion of common-gender pronouns and inclusive language.

g. When antecedents are joined by *or* or *nor*, make the pronoun agree with the antecedent closest to it.

> Neither Jackie nor Kim wanted *her* (not *their*) desk moved.

Review Exercise B—Pronouns

In the space provided for each item, write *a*, *b*, or *c* to complete the statement accurately. When you finish, compare your responses with those provided. For each item on which you need review, consult the numbered principle shown in parentheses.

1. Mr. Behrens and (a) *I*, (b) *myself* will be visiting sales personnel in the Wilmington district next week. _____
2. James promised that he would call; was it (a) *him*, (b) *he* who left the message? _____
3. Much preparation for the seminar was made by Mrs. Washington and (a) *I*, (b) *me* before the brochures were sent out. _____
4. The Employee Benefits Committee can be justly proud of (a) *its*, (b) *their* achievements. _____
5. A number of inquiries were addressed to Jeff and (a) *I*, (b) *me*, (c) *myself*. _____
6. (a) *Who*, (b) *Whom* did you say the letter was addressed to? _____
7. When you visit Sears Savings Bank, inquire about (a) *its*, (b) *their* certificates. _____
8. Copies of all reports are to be reviewed by Mr. Sanders and (a) *I*, (b) *me*, (c) *myself*. _____
9. Apparently one of the female applicants forgot to sign (a) *her*, (b) *their* application. _____
10. Both the printer and (a) *it's*, (b) *its* cover are missing. _____
11. I've never known any man who could work as fast as (a) *him*, (b) *he*. _____
12. Just between you and (a) *I*, (b) *me*, the stock price will fall by afternoon. _____
13. Give the supplies to (a) *whoever*, (b) *whomever* ordered them. _____
14. (a) *Us*, (b) *We* employees have been given an unusual voice in choosing benefits. _____
15. On her return from Mexico, Mrs. Sanchez, along with many other passengers, had to open (a) *her*, (b) *their* luggage for inspection. _____
16. Either James or Robert will have (a) *his*, (b) *their* work reviewed next week. _____
17. Any woman who becomes a charter member of this organization will be able to have (a) *her*, (b) *their* name inscribed on a commemorative plaque. _____
18. We are certain that (a) *our's*, (b) *ours* is the smallest wristwatch available. _____
19. Everyone has completed the reports except Debbie and (a) *he*, (b) *him*. _____
20. Lack of work disturbs Mr. Thomas as much as (a) *I*, (b) *me*. _____

---

1. a (1.08h) 3. b (1.08c) 5. b (1.08c, 1.08e) 7. a (1.09d) 9. a (1.09b) 11. b (1.08f)
13. a (1.08j) 15. a (1.09f) 17. a (1.09b) 19. b (1.08i)

Cumulative Editing Quiz 1

Use proofreading marks (see Appendix B) to correct errors in the following sentences. All errors must be corrected to receive credit for the sentence. Check with your instructor for the answers.

Example: Nicholas and ~~him~~ *he* made all ~~there~~ *their* money in the 1990's.

1. Just between you and I, whom do you think would make the best manager?
2. Either Stacy or me is responsible for correcting all errors in news dispatchs.

3. Several attornies asked that there cases be postponed.

4. One of the secretarys warned Bill and I to get the name of whomever answered the phone.

5. The committee sent there decision to the president and I last week.

6. Who should Susan or me call to verify the three bill of sales received today?

7. Several of we employees complained that it's keyboard made the new computer difficult to use.

8. All the CEO's agreed that the low interest rates of the early 1990's could not continue.

9. Every customer has a right to expect there inquirys to be treated courteously.

10. You may send you're contribution to Eric or myself or to whomever is listed as your representative.

Verbs (1.10–1.15)

Verbs show the action of a subject or join the subject to words that describe it.

1.10 Guidelines for Agreement With Subjects. One of the most troublesome areas in English is subject-verb agreement. Consider the following guidelines for making verbs agree with subjects.

a. A singular subject requires a singular verb:

The stock market *opens* at 10 a.m. (The singular verb *opens* agrees with the singular subject *market.*)

He *doesn't* (not *don't*) work on Saturday.

b. A plural subject requires a plural verb:

On the packing slip several items *seem* (not *seems*) to be missing.

c. A verb agrees with its subject regardless of prepositional phrases that may intervene:

This list of management objectives *is* extensive. (The singular verb *is* agrees with the singular subject *list.*)

Every one of the letters *shows* (not *show*) proper form.

d. A verb agrees with its subject regardless of intervening phrases introduced by *as well as, in addition to, such as, including, together with,* and similar expressions:

An important memo, together with several letters, *was* misplaced. (The singular verb *was* agrees with the singular subject *memo.*)

The president as well as several other top-level executives *approves* of our proposal. (The singular verb *approves* agrees with the subject *president.*)

e. A verb agrees with its subject regardless of the location of the subject:

Here *is* one of the letters about which you asked. (The verb *is* agrees with its subject *one*, even though it precedes *one*. The adverb *here* cannot function as a subject.)

There *are* many problems yet to be resolved. (The verb *are* agrees with the subject *problems*. The adverb *there* cannot function as a subject.)

In the next office *are* several printers. (In this inverted sentence the verb *are* must agree with the subject *printers.*)

f.   Subjects joined by *and* require a plural verb:

Analyzing the reader and organizing a strategy *are* the first steps in letter writing. (The plural verb *are* agrees with the two subjects, *analyzing* and *organizing*.)

The tone and the wording of the letter *were* persuasive. (The plural verb *were* agrees with the two subjects, *tone* and *wording*.)

g.   Subjects joined by *or* or *nor* may require singular or plural verbs. Make the verb agree with the closer subject:

Neither the memo nor the report *is* ready. (The singular verb *is* agrees with *report*, the closer of the two subjects.)

h.   The following indefinite pronouns are singular and require singular verbs: *anyone, anybody, anything, each, either, every, everyone, everybody, everything, many a, neither, nobody, nothing, someone, somebody,* and *something*:

Either of the alternatives that you present *is* acceptable. (The verb *is* agrees with the singular subject *either*.)

i.   Collective nouns may take singular or plural verbs, depending on whether the members of the group are operating as a unit or individually:

Our management team *is* united in its goal.

The faculty *are* sharply *divided* on the tuition issue. (Although acceptable, this sentence sounds better recast: The faculty *members* are sharply divided on the tuition issue.)

j.   Organization names and titles of publications, although they may appear to be plural, are singular and require singular verbs.

Clark, Anderson, and Horne, Inc., *has* (not *have*) hired a marketing consultant.

Thousands of Investment Tips is (not *are*) again on the best-seller list.

1.11 Voice. Voice is that property of verbs that shows whether the subject of the verb acts or is acted upon. Active-voice verbs direct action from the subject toward the object of the verb. Passive-voice verbs direct action toward the subject.

Active voice: Our employees *write* excellent letters.
Passive voice: Excellent letters *are written* by our employees.

Business writing that emphasizes active-voice verbs is generally preferred because it is specific and forceful. However, passive-voice constructions can help a writer be tactful. Strategies for effective use of active- and passive-voice verbs are presented in Chapter 3.

1.12 Mood. Three verb moods express the attitude or thought of the speaker or writer toward a subject: (1) the indicative mood expresses a fact; (2) the imperative mood expresses a command; and (3) the subjunctive mood expresses a doubt, a conjecture, or a suggestion.

Indicative: I *am looking* for a job.
Imperative: *Begin* your job search with the want ads.
Subjunctive: I wish I *were* working.

Only the subjunctive mood creates problems for most speakers and writers. The most common use of subjunctive mood occurs in clauses including *if* or *wish.* In such clauses substitute the subjunctive verb *were* for the indicative verb *was:*

If he *were* (not *was*) in my position, he would understand.

Mr. Simon acts as if he *were* (not *was*) the boss.

We wish we *were* (not *was*) able to ship your order.

The subjunctive mood may be used to maintain goodwill while conveying negative information. The sentence *We wish we were able to ship your order* sounds more pleasing to a customer than *We cannot ship your order,* although, for all practical purposes, both sentences convey the same negative message.

1.13 Tense. Verbs show the time of an action by their tense. Speakers and writers can use six tenses to show the time of sentence action; for example:

Present tense:	I *work;* he *works.*
Past tense:	I *worked;* she *worked.*
Future tense:	I *will work;* he *will work.*
Present perfect tense:	I *have worked;* he *has worked.*
Past perfect tense:	I *had worked;* she *had worked.*
Future perfect tense:	I *will have worked;* he *will have worked.*

1.14 Guidelines for Verb Tense

a. Use present tense for statements that, although they may be introduced by past-tense verbs, continue to be true:

    What did you say his name *is*? (Use the present tense *is* if his name has not changed.)

b. Avoid unnecessary shifts in verb tenses:

    The manager *saw* (not *sees*) a great deal of work yet to be completed and *remained* to do it herself.

    Although unnecessary shifts in verb tense are to be avoided, not all the verbs within one sentence have to be in the same tense; for example:

    She *said* (past tense) that she *likes* (present tense) to work late.

1.15 Irregular Verbs. Irregular verbs cause difficulty for some writers and speakers. Unlike regular verbs, irregular verbs do not form the past tense and past participle by adding *-ed* to the present form. Here is a partial list of selected troublesome irregular verbs. Consult a dictionary if you are in doubt about a verb form.

TROUBLESOME IRREGULAR VERBS

Present	**Past**	**Past Participle** *(always use helping verbs)*
begin	began	begun
break	broke	broken
choose	chose	chosen
come	came	come
drink	drank	drunk
go	went	gone
lay (to place)	laid	laid
lie (to rest)	lay	lain
ring	rang	rung
see	saw	seen
write	wrote	written

a. Use only past-tense verbs to express past tense. Notice that no helping verbs are used to indicate simple past tense:

The auditors *went* (not *have went*) over our books carefully.

He *came* (not *come*) to see us yesterday.

b. Use past participle forms for actions completed before the present time. Notice that past participle forms require helping verbs:

Steve *had gone* (not *went*) before we called. (The past participle *gone* is used with the helping verb *had*.)

c. Avoid inconsistent shifts in subject, voice, and mood. Pay particular attention to this problem area, for undesirable shifts are often characteristic of student writing.

Inconsistent: When Mrs. Taswell read the report, the error was found. (The first clause is in the active voice; the second, passive.)

Improved: When Mrs. Taswell read the report, she found the error. (Both clauses are in the active voice.)

Inconsistent: The clerk should first conduct an inventory. Then supplies should be requisitioned. (The first sentence is in the active voice; the second, passive.)

Improved: The clerk should first conduct an inventory. Then he or she should requisition supplies. (Both sentences are in the active voice.)

Inconsistent: All workers must wear security badges, and you must also sign a daily time card. (This sentence contains an inconsistent shift in subject from *all workers* in first clause to *you* in second clause.)

Improved: All workers must wear security badges, and they must also sign a daily time card.

Inconsistent: Begin the transaction by opening an account; then you enter the customer's name. (This sentence contains an inconsistent shift from the imperative mood in first clause to the indicative mood in second clause.)

Improved: Begin the transaction by opening an account; then enter the customer's name. (Both clauses are now in the indicative mood.)

Review Exercise C—Verbs

In the space provided for each item, write *a* or *b* to complete the statement accurately. When you finish, compare your responses with those provided. For each item on which you need review, consult the numbered principle shown in parentheses.

1. A list of payroll deductions for our employees (a) *was,* (b) *were* sent to the personnel manager. _____
2. There (a) *is,* (b) *are* a customer service engineer and two salespeople waiting to see you. _____
3. Increased computer use and more complex automated systems (a) *is,* (b) *are* found in business today. _____
4. Crews, Meliotes, and Bove, Inc., (a) *has,* (b) *have* opened an office in Boston. _____
5. Yesterday Mrs. Phillips (a) *choose,* (b) *chose* a new office on the second floor. _____
6. The man who called said that his name (a) *is,* (b) *was* Johnson. _____
7. *Office Computing and Networks* (a) *is,* (b) *are* beginning a campaign to increase readership. _____
8. Either of the flight times (a) *appears,* (b) *appear* to fit my proposed itinerary. _____
9. If you had (a) *saw,* (b) *seen* the rough draft, you would better appreciate the final copy. _____

10. Across from our office (a) *is,* (b) *are* the parking structure and the information office.

11. Although we have (a) *began,* (b) *begun* to replace outmoded equipment, the pace is slow.

12. Specific training as well as ample experience (a) *is,* (b) *are* important for that position.

13. Inflation and increased job opportunities (a) *is,* (b) *are* resulting in increased numbers of working women.

14. Neither the organizing nor the staffing of the program (a) *has been,* (b) *have been* completed.

15. If I (a) *was,* (b) *were* you, I would ask for a raise.

16. If you had (a) *wrote,* (b) *written* last week, we could have sent a brochure.

17. The hydraulic equipment that you ordered (a) *is,* (b) *are* packed and will be shipped Friday.

18. One of the reasons that sales have declined in recent years (a) *is,* (b) *are* lack of effective advertising.

19. Either of the proposed laws (a) *is,* (b) *are* going to affect our business negatively.

20. Merger statutes (a) *requires,* (b) *require* that a failing company accept bids from several companies before merging with one.

---

1. a (1.10c)   3. b (1.10f)   5. b (1.15a)   7. a (1.10j)   9. b (1.15b)   11. b (1.15b)   13. b (1.10f)   15. b (1.12)   17. a (1.10a)   19. a (1.10h)

Review Exercise D—Verbs

In the following sentence pairs, choose the one that illustrates consistency in use of subject, voice, and mood. Write *a* or *b* in the space provided. When you finish, compare your responses with those provided. For each item on which you need review, consult the numbered principle shown in parentheses.

1. (a) You need more than a knowledge of equipment; one also must be able to interact well with people.
   (b) You need more than a knowledge of equipment; you also must be able to interact well with people.

2. (a) Tim and Jon were eager to continue, but Bob wanted to quit.
   (b) Tim and Jon were eager to continue, but Bob wants to quit.

3. (a) The salesperson should consult the price list; then you can give an accurate quote to a customer.
   (b) The salesperson should consult the price list; then he or she can give an accurate quote to a customer.

4. (a) Read all the instructions first; then you install the printer program.
   (b) Read all the instructions first, and then install the printer program.

5. (a) She was an enthusiastic manager who always had a smile for everyone.
   (b) She was an enthusiastic manager who always has a smile for everyone.

---

1. b (1.15c)   3. b (1.15c)   5. a (1.14b)

Cumulative Editing Quiz 2

Use proofreading marks (see Appendix B) to correct errors in the following sentences. All errors must be corrected to receive credit for the sentence. Check with your instructor for the answers.

1. Assets and liabilitys is what my partner and myself must investigate.

2. If I was you, I would ask whomever is in charge for their opinion.

3. The faculty agree that it's first concern is educating students.

4. The book and it's cover was printed in Japan.

5. Waiting to see you is a sales representative and a job applicant who you told to drop by.

6. Every employee could have picked up his ballot if he had went to the cafeteria.

7. Your choice of hospitals and physicians are reduced by this plan and it's restrictions.

8. My uncle and her come to visit my parents and myself last night.

9. According to both editor in chiefs, the tone and wording of all our letters needs revision.

10. The Davis'es, about who the article was written, said they were unconcerned with the up's and down's of the stock market.

Adjectives and Adverbs (1.16–1.17)

Adjectives describe or limit nouns and pronouns. They often answer the questions *what kind? how many?* or *which one?* Adverbs describe or limit verbs, adjectives, or other adverbs. They often answer the questions *when? how? where?* or *to what extent?*

1.16 Forms. Most adjectives and adverbs have three forms, or degrees: positive, comparative, and superlative.

	Positive	Comparative	Superlative
Adjective:	clear	clearer	clearest
Adverb:	clearly	more clearly	most clearly

Some adjectives and adverbs have irregular forms.

	Positive	Comparative	Superlative
Adjective:	good	better	best
	bad	worse	worst
Adverb:	well	better	best

Adjectives and adverbs composed of two or more syllables are usually compared by the use of *more* and *most;* for example:

The Payroll Department is *more efficient* than the Shipping Department.

Payroll is the *most efficient* department in our organization.

1.17 Guidelines for Use

a. Use the comparative degree of the adjective or adverb to compare two persons or things; use the superlative degree to compare three or more:

Of the two letters, which is *better* (not *best*)?

Of all the plans, we like this one *best* (not *better*).

b. Do not create a double comparative or superlative by using *-er* with *more* or *-est* with *most:*

His explanation couldn't have been *clearer* (not *more clearer*).

c. A linking verb (*is, are, look, seem, feel, sound, appear,* and so forth) may introduce a word that describes the verb's subject. In this case be certain to use an adjective, not an adverb:

The characters on the monitor look *bright* (not *brightly*). (Use the adjective *bright* because it follows the linking verb *look* and modifies the noun *characters.* It answers the question *What kind of characters?*)

The company's letter made the customer feel *bad* (not *badly*). (The adjective *bad* follows the linking verb *feel* and describes the noun *customer.*)

d. Use adverbs, not adjectives, to describe or limit the action of verbs:

The business is running *smoothly* (not *smooth*). (Use the adverb *smoothly* to describe the action of the verb *is running. Smoothly* tells how the business is running.)

Don't take his remark *personally* (not *personal*). (The adverb *personally* describes the action of the verb *take.*)

e. Two or more adjectives that are joined to create a compound modifier before a noun should be hyphenated:

The *four-year-old* child was tired.

Our agency is planning a *coast-to-coast* campaign.

Hyphenate a compound modifier following a noun only if your dictionary shows the hyphen(s):

Our speaker is very *well-known.* (Include the hyphen because most dictionaries do.)

The tired child was four years old. (Omit the hyphens because the expression follows the word it describes, *child,* and because dictionaries do not indicate hyphens.)

f. Keep adjectives and adverbs close to the words that they modify:

She asked for a cup of *hot* coffee (not a *hot cup of coffee*).

Patty had *only* two days of vacation left (not *Patty only had two days*).

Students may sit in the *first* five rows (not *in the five first rows*).

He has saved *almost* enough money for the trip (not *He has almost saved*).

g. Don't confuse the adverb *there* with the possessive pronoun *their* or the contraction *they're:*

Put the documents *there.* (The adverb *there* means "at that place or at that point.")

There are two reasons for the change. (The adverb *there* is used as filler preceding a linking verb.)

We already have *their* specifications. (The possessive pronoun *their* shows ownership.)

They're coming to inspect today. (The contraction *they're* is a shortened form of *they are.*)

Grammar/Mechanics Handbook

Review Exercise E—Adjectives and Adverbs

In the space provided for each item, write *a*, *b*, or *c* to complete the statement accurately. If two sentences are shown, select *a* or *b* to indicate the one expressed more effectively. When you finish, compare your responses with those provided. For each item on which you need review, consult the numbered principle shown in parentheses.

1. After the interview, Tim looked (a) *calm,* (b) *calmly.* _____
2. If you had been more (a) *careful,* (b) *carefuler,* the box might not have broken. _____
3. Because a new manager was appointed, the advertising campaign is running very (a) *smooth,* (b) *smoothly.* _____
4. To avoid a (a) *face to face,* (b) *face-to-face* confrontation, she wrote a letter. _____
5. Darren completed the employment test (a) *satisfactorily,* (b) *satisfactory.* _____
6. I felt (a) *bad,* (b) *badly* that he was not promoted. _____
7. Which is the (a) *more,* (b) *most* dependable of the two models? _____
8. Can you determine exactly what (a) *there,* (b) *their,* (c) *they're* company wants us to do? _____
9. Of all the copiers we tested, this one is the (a) *easier,* (b) *easiest* to operate. _____
10. (a) Mr. Aldron almost was ready to accept the offer.
    (b) Mr. Aldron was almost ready to accept the offer. _____
11. (a) We only thought that it would take two hours for the test.
    (b) We thought that it would take only two hours for the test. _____
12. (a) Please bring me a glass of cold water.
    (b) Please bring me a cold glass of water. _____
13. (a) The committee decided to retain the last ten tickets.
    (b) The committee decided to retain the ten last tickets. _____
14. New owners will receive a (a) *60-day,* (b) *60 day* trial period. _____
15. The time passed (a) *quicker,* (b) *more quickly* than we expected. _____
16. We offer a (a) *money back,* (b) *money-back* guarantee. _____
17. Today the financial news is (a) *worse,* (b) *worst* than yesterday. _____
18. Please don't take his comments (a) *personal,* (b) *personally.* _____
19. You must check the document (a) *page by page,* (b) *page-by-page.* _____
20. (a) We try to file only necessary paperwork.
    (b) We only try to file necessary paperwork. _____

---

1. a (1.17c) 3. b (1.17d) 5. a (1.17d) 7. a (1.17a) 9. b (1.17a) 11. b (1.17f) 13. a (1.17f) 15. b (1.17d) 17. a (1.17a) 19. a (1.17e)

Prepositions (1.18)

Prepositions are connecting words that join nouns or pronouns to other words in a sentence. The words *about, at, from, in,* and *to* are examples of prepositions.

1.18 Guidelines for Use

a. Include necessary prepositions:

What type *of* software do you need (not *what type software*)?

I graduated *from* high school two years ago (not *I graduated high school*).

b. Omit unnecessary prepositions:

Where is the meeting? (Not *Where is the meeting at?*)

Both printers work well. (Not *Both of the printers.*)

Where are you going? (Not *Where are you going to?*)

c. Avoid the overuse of prepositional phrases.

Weak: We have received your application for credit at our branch in the Fresno area.

Improved: We have received your Fresno credit application.

d. Repeat the preposition before the second of two related elements:

Applicants use the résumé effectively *by* summarizing their most important experiences and *by* relating their education to the jobs sought.

e. Include the second preposition when two prepositions modify a single object:

George's appreciation *of* and aptitude *for* computers led to a promising career.

www.grantland.net

Conjunctions (1.19)

Conjunctions connect words, phrases, and clauses. They act as signals, indicating when a thought is being added, contrasted, or altered. Coordinate conjunctions (such as *and, or, but*) and other words that act as connectors (such as *however, therefore, when, as*) tell the reader or listener in what direction a thought is heading. They're like road signs signaling what's ahead.

1.19 Guidelines for Use

a. Use coordinating conjunctions to connect only sentence elements that are parallel or balanced.

Weak: His report was correct and written in a concise manner.
Improved: His report was correct and concise.
Weak: Management has the capacity to increase fraud, or reduction can be achieved through the policies it adopts.
Improved: Management has the capacity to increase or reduce fraud through the policies it adopts.

b. Do not use the word *like* as a conjunction:

It seems as *if* (not *like*) this day will never end.

c. Avoid using *when* or *where* inappropriately. A common writing fault occurs in sentences with clauses introduced by *is when* and *is where*. Written English ordinarily requires a noun (or a group of words functioning as a noun) following the linking verb *is*. Instead of acting as conjunctions in these constructions, the words *where* and *when* function as adverbs, creating faulty grammatical equations (adverbs cannot complete equations set up by linking verbs). To avoid the problem, revise the sentence, eliminating *is when* or *is where*.

Weak: A bullish market is when prices are rising in the stock market.
Improved: A bullish market is created when prices are rising in the stock market.
Weak: A flowchart is when you make a diagram showing the step-by-step progression of a procedure.
Improved: A flowchart is a diagram showing the step-by-step progression of a procedure.
Weak: Word processing is where you use a computer and software to write.
Improved: Word processing involves the use of a computer and software to write.

A similar faulty construction occurs in the expression *I hate when*. English requires nouns, noun clauses, or pronouns to act as objects of verbs, not adverbs.

Weak: I hate when we're asked to work overtime.
Improved: I hate it when we're asked to work overtime.
Improved: I hate being asked to work overtime.

d. Don't confuse the adverb *then* with the conjunction *than*. *Then* means "at that time"; *than* indicates the second element in a comparison:

We would rather remodel *than* (not *then*) move.

First, the equipment is turned on; *then* (not *than*) the program is loaded.

Review Exercise F—Prepositions and Conjunctions

In the space provided for each item, write *a* or *b* to indicate the sentence that is expressed more effectively. When you finish, compare your responses with those provided. For each item on which you need review, consult the numbered principle shown in parentheses.

1. (a) Do you know where this shipment is being sent?
   (b) Do you know where this shipment is being sent to? _____
2. (a) She was not aware of nor interested in the company insurance plan.
   (b) She was not aware nor interested in the company insurance plan. _____
3. (a) Mr. Samuels graduated college last June.
   (b) Mr. Samuels graduated from college last June. _____
4. (a) "Flextime" is when employees arrive and depart at varying times.
   (b) "Flextime" is a method of scheduling worktime in which employees arrive and depart at varying times. _____
5. (a) Both employees enjoyed setting their own hours.
   (b) Both of the employees enjoyed setting their own hours. _____
6. (a) I hate when the tape sticks in my VCR.
   (b) I hate it when the tape sticks in my VCR. _____
7. (a) What style of typeface should we use?
   (b) What style typeface should we use? _____
8. (a) Business letters should be concise, correct, and written clearly.
   (b) Business letters should be concise, correct, and clear. _____

_____ 9. (a) Mediation in a labor dispute occurs when a neutral person helps union and management reach an agreement.
 (b) Mediation in a labor dispute is where a neutral person helps union and management reach an agreement.
_____ 10. (a) It looks as if the plant will open in early January.
 (b) It looks like the plant will open in early January.
_____ 11. (a) We expect to finish up the work soon.
 (b) We expect to finish the work soon.
_____ 12. (a) At the beginning of the program in the fall of the year at the central office, we experienced staffing difficulties.
 (b) When the program began last fall, the central office experienced staffing difficulties.
_____ 13. (a) Your client may respond by letter or a telephone call may be made.
 (b) Your client may respond by letter or by telephone.
_____ 14. (a) A résumé is when you make a written presentation of your education and experience for a prospective employer.
 (b) A résumé is a written presentation of your education and experience for a prospective employer.
_____ 15. (a) Stacy exhibited both an awareness of and talent for developing innovations.
 (b) Stacy exhibited both an awareness and talent for developing innovations.
_____ 16. (a) This course is harder then I expected.
 (b) This course is harder than I expected.
_____ 17. (a) An ombudsman is an individual hired by management to investigate and resolve employee complaints.
 (b) An ombudsman is when management hires an individual to investigate and resolve employee complaints.
_____ 18. (a) I'm uncertain where to take this document to.
 (b) I'm uncertain where to take this document.
_____ 19. (a) By including accurate data and by writing clearly, you will produce effective memos.
 (b) By including accurate data and writing clearly, you will produce effective memos.
_____ 20. (a) We need computer operators who can load software, monitor networks, and files must be duplicated.
 (b) We need computer operators who can load software, monitor networks, and duplicate files.

---

1. a (1.18b)   3. b (1.18a)   5. a (1.18b)   7. a (1.18a)   9. a (1.19c)   11. b (1.18b)   13. b (1.19a)   15. a (1.18e)   17. a (1.19c)   19. a (1.18d)

Cumulative Editing Quiz 3

Use proofreading marks (see Appendix B) to correct errors in the following sentences. All errors must be corrected to receive credit for the sentence. Check with your instructor for the answers.

1. If Cindy types faster then her, shouldn't Cindy be hired?

2. We felt badly that Mark's home was not chose for the tour.

3. Neither the company nor the workers is pleased at how slow the talks seems to be progressing.

4. Just between you and I, it's better not to take his remarks personal.

5. After completing there floor by floor inventory, managers will deliver there reports to Mr. Quinn and I.

6. If the telephone was working, Jean and myself could have completed our calls.

7. Powerful software and new hardware allows us to send the newsletter to whomever is currently listed in our database.

8. The eighteen year old girl and her mother was given hot cups of tea after there ordeal.

9. We begun the work two years ago, but personnel and equipment has been especially difficult to obtain.

10. Today's weather is worst then yesterday.

Punctuation Review

Commas 1 (2.01–2.04)

2.01 Series. Commas are used to separate three or more equal elements (words, phrases, or short clauses) in a series. To ensure separation of the last two elements, careful writers always use a comma before the conjunction in a series:

Business letters usually contain a dateline, address, salutation, body, and closing. (This series contains words.)

The job of an ombudsman is to examine employee complaints, resolve disagreements between management and employees, and ensure fair treatment. (This series contains phrases).

Trainees complete basic keyboarding tasks, technicians revise complex documents, and editors proofread completed projects. (This series contains short clauses.)

2.02 Direct Address. Commas are used to set off the names of individuals being addressed:

Your inquiry, *Mrs. Johnson,* has been referred to me.

We genuinely hope that we may serve you, *Mr. Lee.*

2.03 Parenthetical Expressions. Skilled writers use parenthetical words, phrases, and clauses to guide the reader from one thought to the next. When these expressions interrupt the flow of a sentence and are unnecessary for its grammatical completeness, they should be set off with commas. Examples of commonly used parenthetical expressions follow:

all things considered	however	needless to say
as a matter of fact	in addition	nevertheless
as a result	incidentally	no doubt
as a rule	in fact	of course
at the same time	in my opinion	on the contrary
consequently	in the first place	on the other hand
for example	in the meantime	therefore
furthermore	moreover	under the circumstances

As a matter of fact, I wrote to you just yesterday. (Phrase used at the beginning of a sentence.)

We will, *in the meantime,* send you a replacement order. (Phrase used in the middle of a sentence.)

Your satisfaction is our first concern, *needless to say.* (Phrase used at the end of a sentence.)

Do not use commas if the expression is necessary for the completeness of the sentence:

Kimberly had *no doubt* that she would finish the report. (Omit commas because the expression is necessary for the completeness of the sentence.)

2.04 Dates, Addresses, and Geographical Items. When dates, addresses, and geographical items contain more than one element, the second and succeeding elements are normally set off by commas.

a. Dates:

The conference was held February 2 at our home office. (No comma is needed for one element.)

The conference was held February 2, 2001, at our home office. (Two commas set off the second element.)

The conference was held Tuesday, February 2, 2001, at our home office. (Commas set off the second and third elements.)

In February 2001 the conference was held. (This alternate style omitting commas is acceptable if only the month and year are written.)

b. Addresses:

The letter addressed to Mr. Jim W. Ellman, 600 Via Novella, Agoura, CA 91306, should be sent today. (Commas are used between all elements except the state and zip code, which in this special instance are considered a single unit.)

c. Geographical items:

She moved from Toledo, Ohio, to Champaign, Illinois. (Commas set off the state unless it appears at the end of the sentence, in which case only one comma is used.)

In separating cities from states and days from years, many writers remember the initial comma but forget the final one, as in the examples that follow:

The package from Austin, Texas {,} was lost.

We opened June 1, 1995 {,} and have grown steadily since.

Review Exercise G—Commas 1

Insert necessary commas in the following sentences. In the space provided write the number of commas that you add. Write *C* if no commas are needed. When you finish, compare your responses with those provided. For each item on which you need review, consult the numbered principle shown in parentheses.

_____ 1. As a rule we do not provide complimentary tickets.

_____ 2. You may be certain Mr. Martinez that your policy will be issued immediately.

3. I have no doubt that your calculations are correct. _____
4. The safety hazard on the contrary can be greatly reduced if workers wear rubber gloves. _____
5. Every accredited TV newscaster radio broadcaster and newspaper reporter had access to the media room. _____
6. Deltech's main offices are located in Boulder Colorado and Seattle Washington. _____
7. The employees who are eligible for promotions are Terry Evelyn Vicki Rosanna and Steve. _____
8. During the warranty period of course you are protected from any parts or service charges. _____
9. Many of our customers include architects engineers attorneys and others who are interested in database management programs. _____
10. I wonder Mrs. Stevens if you would send my letter of recommendation as soon as possible. _____
11. The new book explains how to choose appropriate legal protection for ideas trade secrets copyrights patents and restrictive covenants. _____
12. The factory is scheduled to be moved to 2250 North Main Street Ann Arbor Michigan 48107 within two years. _____
13. You may however prefer to correspond directly with the manufacturer in Hong Kong. _____
14. Are there any alternatives in addition to those that we have already considered? _____
15. The rally has been scheduled for Monday January 12 in the football stadium. _____
16. A check for the full amount will be sent directly to your home Mr. Jefferson. _____
17. Goodstone Tire & Rubber for example recalled 400,000 steelbelted radial tires because some tires failed their rigorous tests. _____
18. Kevin agreed to unlock the office open the mail and check all the equipment in my absence. _____
19. In the meantime thank you for whatever assistance you are able to furnish. _____
20. Research facilities were moved from Austin Texas to Santa Cruz,California. _____

---

1. rule, (2.03)   3. C (2.03)   5. newscaster, radio broadcaster, (2.01)   7. Terry, Evelyn, Vicki, Rosanna, (2.01)   9. architects, engineers, attorneys, (2.01)   11. ideas, trade secrets, copyrights, patents, (2.01)   13. may, however, (2.03)   15. Monday, January 12, (2.04a)   17. Rubber, for example, (2.03)   19. meantime, (2.03)

Commas 2 (2.05–2.09)

2.05 Independent Clauses. An independent clause is a group of words that has a subject and a verb and that could stand as a complete sentence. When two such clauses are joined by *and, or, nor,* or *but,* use a comma before the conjunction:

We can ship your merchandise July 12, but we must have your payment first.

Net income before taxes is calculated, and this total is then combined with income from operations.

Notice that each independent clause in the preceding two examples could stand alone as a complete sentence. Do not use a comma unless each group of words is a complete thought (that is, has its own subject and verb).

Net income before taxes is calculated *and* is then combined with income from operations. (No comma is needed because no subject follows *and*.)

2.06 Dependent Clauses. Dependent clauses do not make sense by themselves; for their meaning they depend on independent clauses.

a. *Introductory clauses.* When a dependent clause precedes an independent clause, it is followed by a comma. Such clauses are often introduced by *when, if,* and *as:*

When your request came, we responded immediately.

As I mentioned earlier, Mrs. James is the manager.

b. *Terminal clauses.* If a dependent clause falls at the end of a sentence, use a comma only if the dependent clause is an afterthought:

The meeting has been rescheduled for October 23, *if this date meets with your approval.* (Comma used because dependent clause is an afterthought.)

We responded immediately *when we received your request.* (No comma is needed.)

c. *Essential versus nonessential clauses.* If a dependent clause provides information that is unneeded for the grammatical completeness of a sentence, use commas to set it off. In determining whether such a clause is essential or nonessential, ask yourself whether the reader needs the information contained in the clause to identify the word it explains:

Our district sales manager, *who just returned from a trip to the Southwest District,* prepared this report. (This construction assumes that there is only one district sales manager. Since the sales manager is clearly identified, the dependent clause is not essential and requires commas.)

The salesperson *who just returned from a trip to the Southwest District* prepared this report. (The dependent clause in this sentence is necessary to identify which salesperson prepared the report. Therefore, use no commas.)

The position of assistant sales manager, *which we discussed with you last week,* is still open. (Careful writers use *which* to introduce nonessential clauses. Commas are also necessary.)

The position *that we discussed with you last week* is still open. (Careful writers use *that* to introduce essential clauses. No commas are used.)

2.07 Phrases. A phrase is a group of related words that lacks both a subject and a verb. A phrase that precedes a main clause is followed by a comma only if the phrase contains a verb form or has five or more words:

Beginning November 1, Worldwide Savings will offer two new combination checking/savings plans. (A comma follows this introductory phrase because the phrase contains the verb form *beginning.*)

To promote their plan, we will conduct an extensive direct mail advertising campaign. (A comma follows this introductory phrase because the phrase contains the verb form *to promote.*)

In a period of only one year, we were able to improve our market share by 30 percent. (A comma follows the introductory phrase—actually two prepositional phrases—because its total length exceeds five words.)

In 1999 our organization installed a multiuser system that could transfer programs easily. (No comma needed after the short introductory phrase.)

2.08 Two or More Adjectives. Use a comma to separate two or more adjectives that equally describe a noun. A good way to test the need for a comma is this:

mentally insert the word *and* between the adjectives. If the resulting phrase sounds natural, a comma is used to show the omission of *and*:

> We're looking for a versatile, bug-free operating system. (Use a comma to separate *versatile* and *bug-free* because they independently describe *operating system*. *And* has been omitted.)

> Our *experienced, courteous* staff is ready to serve you. (Use a comma to separate *experienced* and *courteous* because they independently describe *staff*. *And* has been omitted.)

> It was difficult to refuse the *sincere young* telephone caller. (No commas are needed between *sincere* and *young* because and has not been omitted.)

2.09 Appositives. Words that rename or explain preceding nouns or pronouns are called *appositives*. An appositive that provides information not essential to the identification of the word it describes should be set off by commas:

> James Wilson, *the project director for Sperling's,* worked with our architect. (The appositive, *the project director for Sperling's,* adds nonessential information. Commas set it off.)

Review Exercise H—Commas 2

Insert only necessary commas in the following sentences. In the space provided, indicate the number of commas that you add for each sentence. If a sentence requires no commas, write *C*. When you finish, compare your responses with those provided. For each item on which you need review, consult the numbered principle shown in parentheses.

1. A corporation must be registered in the state in which it does business and it must operate within the laws of that state. _____
2. The manager made a point-by-point explanation of the distribution dilemma and then presented his plan to solve the problem. _____
3. If you will study the cost analysis you will see that our company offers the best system at the lowest price. _____
4. Molly Epperson who amassed the greatest number of sales points was awarded the bonus trip to Hawaii. _____
5. The salesperson who amasses the greatest number of sales points will be awarded the bonus trip to Hawaii. _____
6. To promote goodwill and to generate international trade we are opening offices in the Far East and in Europe. _____
7. On the basis of these findings I recommend that we retain Jane Rada as our counsel. _____
8. Mary Bantle is a dedicated hard-working employee for our company. _____
9. The bright young student who worked for us last summer will be able to return this summer. _____
10. When you return the completed form we will be able to process your application. _____
11. We will be able to process your application when you return the completed form. _____
12. The employees who have been with us over ten years automatically receive additional insurance benefits. _____
13. Knowing that you wanted this merchandise immediately I took the liberty of sending it by Express Parcel Services. _____
14. The central processing unit requires no scheduled maintenance and has a self-test function for reliable performance. _____

15. Foreign competition nearly ruined the American shoe industry but the textile industry remains strong.
16. Stacy Wilson our newly promoted office manager has made a number of worthwhile suggestions.
17. For the benefit of employees recently hired we are offering a two-hour seminar regarding employee benefit programs.
18. Please bring your suggestions and those of Mr. Mason when you attend our meeting next month.
19. The meeting has been rescheduled for September 30 if this date meets with your approval.
20. Some of the problems that you outline in your recent memo could be rectified through more stringent purchasing procedures.

---

1. business, (2.05) 3. analysis, (2.06a) 5. C (2.06c) 7. findings, (2.07) 9. C (2.08) 11. C (2.06b) 13. immediately, (2.07) 15. industry, (2.05) 17. hired, (2.07) 19. September 30, (2.06b)

Commas 3 (2.10–2.15)

2.10 Degrees and Abbreviations. Degrees following individuals' names are set off by commas. Abbreviations such as *Jr.* and *Sr.* are also set off by commas unless the individual referred to prefers to omit the commas:

Anne G. Turner, *M.B.A.*, joined the firm.

Michael Migliano, *Jr.*, and Michael Migliano, *Sr.*, work as a team.

Anthony A. Gensler *Jr.* wrote the report. (The individual referred to prefers to omit commas.)

The abbreviations *Inc.* and *Ltd.* are set off by commas only if a company's legal name has a comma just before this kind of abbreviation. To determine a company's practice, consult its stationery or a directory listing:

Firestone and Blythe, *Inc.*, is based in Canada. (Notice that two commas are used.)

Computers *Inc.* is extending its franchise system. (The company's legal name does not include a comma before *Inc.*)

2.11 Omitted Words. A comma is used to show the omission of words that are understood:

On Monday we received 15 applications; on Friday, only 3. (Comma shows the omission of *we received*.)

2.12 Contrasting Statements. Commas are used to set off contrasting or opposing expressions. These expressions are often introduced by such words as *not, never, but,* and *yet*:

The consultant recommended dual-tape storage, *not* floppy-disk storage, for our operations.

Our budget for the year is reduced, *yet* adequate.

The greater the effort, the greater the reward.

If increased emphasis is desired, use dashes instead of commas, as in *Only the sum of $100—not $1,000—was paid on this account.*

2.13 Clarity. Commas are used to separate words repeated for emphasis. Commas are also used to separate words that may be misread if not separated:

> The building is a long, long way from completion.

> Whatever is, is right.

> No matter what, you know we support you.

2.14 Quotations and Appended Questions

a. A comma is used to separate a short quotation from the rest of a sentence. If the quotation is divided into two parts, two commas are used:

> The manager asked, "Shouldn't the managers control the specialists?"

> "Not if the specialists," replied Tim, "have unique information."

b. A comma is used to separate a question appended (added) to a statement:

> You will confirm the shipment, won't you?

2.15 Comma Overuse. Do not use commas needlessly. For example, commas should not be inserted merely because you might drop your voice if you were speaking the sentence:

> One of the reasons for expanding our East Coast operations is {,} that we anticipate increased sales in that area. (Do not insert a needless comma before a clause.)

> I am looking for an article entitled {,} "State-of-the-Art Communications." (Do not insert a needless comma after the word *entitled*.)

> A number of food and nonfood items are carried in convenience stores *such as* {,} 7-Eleven and Stop-N-Go. (Do not insert a needless comma after *such as*.)

> We have {,} at this time {,} an adequate supply of parts. (Do not insert needless commas around prepositional phrases.)

Review Exercise I—Commas 3

Insert only necessary commas in the following sentences. Remove unnecessary commas with the delete sign (⌀). In the space provided, indicate the number of commas inserted or deleted in each sentence. If a sentence requires no changes, write C. When you finish, compare your responses with those provided. For each item on which you need review, consult the numbered principle shown in parentheses.

1. We expected Charles Bedford not Tiffany Richardson to conduct the audit. _____
2. Brian said "We simply must have a bigger budget to start this project." _____
3. "We simply must have " said Brian "a bigger budget to start this project." _____
4. In August customers opened at least 50 new accounts; in September,only about 20. _____
5. You returned the merchandise last month,didn't you? _____
6. In short employees will now be expected to contribute more to their own retirement funds. _____
7. The better our advertising and recruiting the stronger our personnel pool will be. _____
8. Mrs. Delgado investigated selling her stocks not her real estate to raise the necessary cash. _____
9. "On the contrary " said Mrs. Mercer "we will continue our present marketing strategies." _____

_____ 10. Our company will expand into surprising new areas such as, women's apparel and fast foods.

_____ 11. What we need is more not fewer suggestions for improvement.

_____ 12. Randall Clark Esq. and Jonathon Georges M.B.A. joined the firm.

_____ 13. "America is now entering " said President Saunders "the Age of Information."

_____ 14. One of the reasons that we are inquiring about the publisher of the software is, that we are concerned about whether that publisher will be in the market five years from now.

_____ 15. The talk by D. A. Spindler Ph.D. was particularly difficult to follow because of his technical and abstract vocabulary.

_____ 16. The month before a similar disruption occurred in distribution.

_____ 17. We are very fortunate to have, at our disposal, the services of excellent professionals.

_____ 18. No matter what you can count on us for support.

_____ 19. Mrs. Sandoval was named legislative counsel; Mr. Freeman executive adviser.

_____ 20. The data you are seeking can be found in an article entitled, "The Fastest Growing Game in Computers."

1. Bedford, Richardson, (2.12)   3. have," said Brian, (2.14a)   5. month, (2.14b)   7. recruiting, (2.12)   9. contrary," Mercer, (2.14a)   11. more, not fewer, (2.12)   13. entering," Saunders, (2.14a)   15. Spindler, Ph.D., (2.10)   17. have at our disposal (2.15)   19. Freeman, (2.11)

Cumulative Editing Quiz 4

Use proofreading marks (see Appendix B) to correct errors and omissions in the following sentences. All errors must be corrected to receive credit for the sentence. Check with your instructor for the answers.

1. Business documents must be written clear, to ensure that readers comprehend the message quick.

2. Needless to say the safety of our employees have always been most important to the president and I.

3. The Small Business Administration which provide disaster loans are setting up an office in Miami Florida.

4. Many entrepreneurs who want to expand there markets, have choosen to advertise heavy.

5. Our arbitration committee have unanimously agreed on a compromise package but management have been slow to respond.

6. Although the business was founded in the 1970's its real expansion took place in the 1990s.

7. According to the contract either the dealer or the distributor are responsible for repair of the product.

8. Next June, Lamont and Jones, Inc., are moving their headquarters to Denton Texas.

9. Our company is looking for intelligent, articulate, young, people who has a desire to grow with an expanding organization.

10. As you are aware each member of the jury were asked to avoid talking about the case.

Semicolons (2.16)

2.16 Independent Clauses, Series, Introductory Expressions

a. ***Independent clauses with conjunctive adverbs.*** Use a semicolon before a conjunctive adverb that separates two independent clauses. Some of the most common conjunctive adverbs are *therefore, consequently, however,* and *moveover:*

Business letters should sound conversational; *therefore,* familiar words and contractions are often used.

The bank closes its doors at 3 p.m.; *however,* the ATM is open 24 hours a day.

Notice that the word following a semicolon is *not* capitalized (unless, of course, that word is a proper noun).

b. ***Independent clauses without conjunctive adverbs.*** Use a semicolon to separate closely related independent clauses when no conjunctive adverb is used:

Bond interest payments are tax deductible; dividend payments are not.

Ambient lighting fills the room; task lighting illuminates each workstation.

Use a semicolon in *compound* sentences, not in *complex* sentences:

After one week the paper feeder jammed; we tried different kinds of paper. (Use a semicolon in a compound sentence.)

After one week the paper feeder jammed, although we tried different kinds of paper. (Use a comma in a complex sentence. Do not use a semicolon after *jammed.*)

The semicolon is very effective for joining two closely related thoughts. Don't use it, however, unless the ideas are truly related.

c. ***Independent clauses with other commas.*** Normally, a comma precedes *and, or,* and *but* when those conjunctions join independent clauses. However, if either clause contains commas, change the comma preceding the conjunction to a semicolon to ensure correct reading:

If you arrive in time, you may be able to purchase a ticket; but ticket sales close promptly at 8 p.m.

Our primary concern is financing; and we have discovered, as you warned us, that money sources are quite scarce.

d. ***Series with internal commas.*** Use semicolons to separate items in a series when one or more of the items contains internal commas:

Delegates from Miami, Florida; Freeport, Mississippi; and Chatsworth, California, attended the conference.

The speakers were Kevin Lang, manager, Riko Enterprises; Henry Holtz, vice president, Trendex, Inc.; and Margaret Slater, personnel director, West Coast Productions.

e. ***Introductory expressions.*** Use a semicolon when an introductory expression such as *namely, for instance, that is,* or *for example* introduces a list following an independent clause:

Switching to computerized billing are several local companies; namely, Ryson Electronics, Miller Vending Services, and Black Advertising.

The author of a report should consider many sources; for example, books, periodicals, databases, and newspapers.

Colons (2.17–2.19)

2.17 Listed Items

a. **With colon.** Use a colon after a complete thought that introduces a formal list of items. A formal list is often preceded by such words and phrases as *these, thus, the following,* and *as follows.* A colon is also used when words and phrases like these are implied but not stated:

> Additional costs in selling a house involve *the following*: title examination fee, title insurance costs, and closing fee. (Use a colon when a complete thought introduces formal list.)

> Collective bargaining focuses on several key issues: cost-of-living adjustments, fringe benefits, job security, and hours of work. (The introduction of the list is implied in the preceding clause.)

b. **Without colons.** Do not use a colon when the list immediately follows a *to be* verb or a preposition:

> The employees who should receive the preliminary plan are James Sears, Monica Spears, and Rose Lopez. (No colon is used after the verb *are.*)

> We expect to consider equipment for Accounting, Legal Services, and Payroll. (No colon is used after the preposition *for.*)

2.18 Quotations. Use a colon to introduce long one-sentence quotations and quotations of two or more sentences:

> Our consultant said: "This system can support up to 32 users. It can be used for decision support, computer-aided design, and software development operations at the same time."

2.19 Salutations. Use a colon after the salutation of a business letter:

> Gentlemen: Dear Mrs. Seaman: Dear Jamie:

Review Exercise J—Semicolons, Colons

In the following sentences, add semicolons, colons, and necessary commas. For each sentence indicate the number of punctuation marks that you add. If a sentence requires no punctuation, write C. When you finish, compare your responses with those provided. For each item on which you need review, consult the numbered principle shown in parentheses.

1. A strike in Canada has delayed shipments of parts consequently our production has fallen behind schedule.
2. Our branch in Sherman Oaks specializes in industrial real estate our branch in Canoga Park concentrates on residential real estate.
3. The sedan version of the automobile is available in these colors Olympic red metallic silver and Aztec gold.
4. If I can assist the new manager please call me however I will be gone from June 10 through June 15.
5. The individuals who should receive copies of this announcement are Jeff Doogan Alicia Green and Kim Wong.
6. We would hope of course to send personal letters to all prospective buyers but we have not yet decided just how to do this.
7. Many of our potential customers are in Southern California therefore our promotional effort will be strongest in that area.
8. Since the first of the year we have received inquiries from one attorney two accountants and one information systems analyst.

Grammar/Mechanics Handbook

9. Three dates have been reserved for initial interviews January 15 February 1 and February 12.   _____

10. Several staff members are near the top of their salary ranges and we must reclassify their jobs.   _____

11. Several staff members are near the top of their salary ranges we must reclassify their jobs.   _____

12. Several staff members are near the top of their salary ranges therefore we must reclassify their jobs.   _____

13. If you open an account within two weeks you will receive a free cookbook moreover your first 500 checks will be imprinted at no cost to you.   _____

14. Monthly reports from the following departments are missing Legal Department Human Resources Department and Engineering Department.   _____

15. Monthly reports are missing from the Legal Department Human Resources Department and Engineering Department.   _____

16. Since you became director of that division sales have tripled therefore I am recommending you for a bonus.   _____

17. The convention committee is considering Portland Oregon New Orleans Louisiana and Phoenix Arizona.   _____

18. Several large companies allow employees access to their personnel files namely General Electric Eastman Kodak and Infodata.   _____

19. Sherry first asked about salary next she inquired about benefits.   _____

20. Sherry first asked about the salary and she next inquired about benefits.   _____

---

1. parts; consequently, (2.16a)   3. colors: Olympic red, metallic silver, (2.01, 2.17a)
5. Doogan, Alicia Green, (2.01, 2.17b)   7. California; therefore, (2.16a)   9. interviews:
January 15, February 1, (2.01, 2.17a)   11. ranges; (2.16b)   13. weeks, cookbook; moreover, (206a, 2.16a)   15. Department, Human Resources Department, (2.01, 2.17b)
17. Portland, Oregon; New Orleans, Louisiana; Phoenix, (2.16d)   19. salary; (2.16b)

Apostrophes (2.20–2.22)

2.20 Basic Rule. The apostrophe is used to show ownership, origin, authorship, or measurement.

Ownership:	We are looking for *Brian's keys*.
Origin:	At the *president's* suggestion, we doubled the order.
Authorship:	The *accountant's annual report* was questioned.
Measurement:	In *two years' time* we expect to reach our goal.

a. *Ownership words not ending in* **s.** To place the apostrophe correctly, you must first determine whether the ownership word ends in an *s* sound. If it does not, add an apostrophe and an *s* to the ownership word. The following examples show ownership words that do not end in an *s* sound:

the employee's file	(the file of a single employee)
a member's address	(the address of a single member)
a year's time	(the time of a single year)
a month's notice	(notice of a single month)
the company's building	(the building of a single company)

b. *Ownership words ending in* **s.** If the ownership word does end in an *s* sound, usually add only an apostrophe:

several employees' files	(files of several employees)
ten members' addresses	(addresses of ten members)
five years' time	(time of five years)
several months' notice	(notice of several months)
many companies' buildings	(buildings of many companies)

A few singular nouns that end in s are pronounced with an extra syllable when they become possessive. To these words, add 's.
my boss's desk

the waitress's table

the actress's costume

Use no apostrophe if a noun is merely plural, not possessive:

All the sales representatives, as well as the secretaries and managers, had their names and telephone numbers listed in the directory.

2.21 Names. The writer may choose either traditional or popular style in making singular names that end in an *s* sound possessive. The traditional style uses the apostrophe plus an *s*, while the popular style uses just the apostrophe. Note that only with singular names ending in an *s* sound does this option exist.

Traditional style	**Popular style**
Russ's computer	Russ' computer
Mr. Jones's car	Mr. Jones' car
Mrs. Morris's desk	Mrs. Morris' desk
Ms. Horowitz's job	Ms. Horowitz' job

The possessive form of plural names is consistent: the Joneses' car, the Horowitzes' home, the Lopezes' daughter.

2.22 Gerunds. Use 's to make a noun possessive when it precedes a gerund, a verb form used as a noun:

Mr. Smith's smoking prompted a new office policy. (*Mr. Smith* is possessive because it modifies the gerund *smoking.*)

It was Betsy's careful proofreading that revealed the discrepancy.

Review Exercise K—Apostrophes

Insert necessary apostrophes in the following sentences. In the space provided for each sentence, indicate the number of apostrophes that you added. If none were added, write C. When you finish, compare your responses with those provided. For each item on which you need review, consult the numbered principle shown in parentheses.

1. Your account should have been credited with six months interest.
2. If you go to the third floor, you will find Mr. Londons office.
3. All the employees personnel folders must be updated.
4. In a little over a years time, that firm was able to double its sales.
5. The Harrises daughter lived in Florida for two years.
6. An inventors patent protects his or her patent for seventeen years.
7. Both companies headquarters will be moved within the next six months.
8. That position requires at least two years experience.
9. Some of their assets could be liquidated; therefore, a few of the creditors were satisfied.
10. All secretaries workstations were equipped with terminals.
11. The package of electronics parts arrived safely despite two weeks delay.
12. Many nurses believe that nurses notes are not admissable evidence.

13. According to Mr. Cortez [or Cortezs] latest proposal, all employees would _____ receive an additional holiday.
14. Many of our members names and addresses must be checked. _____
15. His supervisor frequently had to correct Jacks financial reports. _____
16. We believe that this firms service is much better than that firms. _____
17. Mr. Jackson estimated that he spent a years profits in reorganizing his staff. _____
18. After paying six months rent, we were given a receipt. _____
19. The contract is not valid without Mrs. Harris [or Harriss] signature. _____
20. It was Mr. Smiths signing of the contract that made us happy. _____

---

1. months' (2.20b)   3. employees' (2.20b)   5. Harrises' (2.21)   7. companies' (2.20b)
9. C (2.20b)   11. weeks' (2.20b)   13. Cortez' or Cortez's (2.21)   15. Jack's (2.21)
17. year's (2.20a)   19. Harris' or Harris's (2.21)

Cumulative Editing Quiz 5

Use proofreading marks (see Appendix B) to correct errors and omissions in the following sentences. All errors must be corrected to receive credit for the sentence. Check with your instructor for the answers.

1. The three C's of credit are the following character capacity and capital.

2. We hope that we will not have to sell the property however that may be our only option.

3. As soon as the supervisor and her can check this weeks sales they will place an order.

4. Any of the auditors are authorized to proceed with an independent action however only the CEO can alter the councils directives.

5. Although reluctant technicians sometimes must demonstrate there computer software skills.

6. On April 6 1994 we opened an innovative fully-equipped employee computer center.

7. A list of maintenance procedures and recommendations are in the owners manual.

8. The Morrises son lived in Flint Michigan however there daughter lived in Albany New York.

9. Employment interviews were held in Dallas Texas Miami Florida and Chicago Illinois.

10. Mr. Lees determination courage and sincerity could not be denied however his methods was often questioned.

Other Punctuation (2.23–2.29)

2.23 Periods

a. *Ends of sentences.* Use a period at the end of a statement, command, indirect question, or polite request. Although a polite request may have the same structure as a question, it ends with a period:

Corporate legal departments demand precise skills from their workforce. (End a statement with a period.)

Get the latest data by reading current periodicals. (End a command with a period.)

Mr. Rand wondered whether we had sent any follow-up literature. (End an indirect question with a period.)

Would you please reexamine my account and determine the current balance. (A polite request suggests an action rather than a verbal response.)

b. *Abbreviations and initials.* Use periods after initials and after many abbreviations.

R. M. Johnson	c.o.d.	Ms.
M.D.	a.m.	Mr.
Inc.	i.e.	Mrs.

Use just one period when an abbreviation falls at the end of a sentence:

Guests began arriving at 5:30 p.m.

2.24 Question Marks. Direct questions are followed by question marks:

Did you send your proposal to Datatronix, Inc.?

Statements with questions added are punctuated with question marks.

We have completed the proposal, haven't we?

2.25 Exclamation Points. Use an exclamation point after a word, phrase, or clause expressing strong emotion. In business writing, however, exclamation points should be used sparingly:

Incredible! Every terminal is down.

2.26 Dashes. The dash (constructed at a keyboard by striking the hyphen key twice in succession) is a legitimate and effective mark of punctuation when used according to accepted conventions. As an emphatic punctuation mark, however, the dash loses effectiveness when overused.

a. *Parenthetical elements.* Within a sentence a parenthetical element is usually set off by commas. If, however, the parenthetical element itself contains internal commas, use dashes (or parentheses) to set it off:

Three top salespeople—Tom Judkins, Tim Templeton, and Mary Yashimoto—received bonuses.

b. *Sentence interruptions.* Use a dash to show an interruption or abrupt change of thought:

News of the dramatic merger—no one believed it at first—shook the financial world.

Ship the materials Monday—no, we must have them sooner.

Sentences with abrupt changes of thought or with appended afterthoughts can usually be improved through rewriting.

c. *Summarizing statements.* Use a dash (not a colon) to separate an introductory list from a summarizing statement:

Sorting, merging, and computing—these are tasks that our data processing programs must perform.

2.27 Parentheses. One means of setting off nonessential sentence elements involves the use of parentheses. Nonessential sentence elements may be punctuated in one of three ways: (1) with commas, to make the lightest possible break

Grammar/Mechanics Handbook

in the normal flow of a sentence; (2) with dashes, to emphasize the enclosed material; and (3) with parentheses, to de-emphasize the enclosed material. Parentheses are frequently used to punctuate sentences with interpolated directions, explanations, questions, and references:

> The cost analysis (which appears on page 8 of the report) indicates that the copy machine should be leased.

> Units are lightweight (approximately 13 oz.) and come with a leather case and operating instructions.

> The IBM laser printer (have you heard about it?) will be demonstrated for us next week.

A parenthetical sentence that is not imbedded within another sentence should be capitalized and punctuated with end punctuation:

> The Model 20 has stronger construction. (You may order a Model 20 brochure by circling 304 on the reader service card.)

2.28 Quotation Marks

a. *Direct quotations.* Use double quotation marks to enclose the exact words of a speaker or writer:

> "Keep in mind," Mrs. Frank said, "that you'll have to justify the cost of automating our office."

> The boss said that automation was inevitable. (No quotation marks are needed because the exact words are not quoted.)

b. *Quotations within quotations.* Use single quotation marks (apostrophes on the typewriter) to enclose quoted passages within quoted passages:

> In her speech, Mrs. Deckman remarked, "I believe it was the poet Robert Frost who said, 'All the fun's in how you say a thing.' "

c. *Short expressions.* Slang, words used in a special sense, and words following *stamped* or *marked* are often enclosed within quotation marks:

> Jeffrey described the damaged shipment as "gross." (Quotation marks enclose slang.)

> Students often have trouble spelling the word "separate." (Quotation marks enclose words used in a special sense.)

> Jobs were divided into two categories: most stressful and least stressful. The jobs in the "most stressful" list involved high risk or responsibility. (Quotation marks enclose words used in a special sense.)

> The envelope marked "Confidential" was put aside. (Quotation marks enclose words following *marked.*)

In the four preceding sentences, the words enclosed within quotation marks can be set in italics, if italics are available.

d. *Definitions.* Double quotation marks are used to enclose definitions. The word or expression being defined should be underscored or set in italics:

> The term *penetration pricing* is defined as "the practice of introducing a product to the market at a low price."

e. ***Titles.*** Use double quotation marks to enclose titles of literary and artistic works, such as magazine and newspaper articles, chapters of books, movies, television shows, poems, lectures, and songs. Names of major publications—such as books, magazines, pamphlets, and newspapers—are set in italics (underscored) or typed in capital letters.

Particularly helpful was the chapter in Smith's EFFECTIVE WRITING TECHNIQUES entitled "Right Brain, Write On!"

In the <u>Los Angeles Times</u> appeared John's article, "E-Mail Blunders"; however, we could not locate it in a local library.

f. ***Additional considerations.*** Periods and commas are always placed inside closing quotation marks. Semicolons and colons, on the other hand, are always placed outside quotation marks:

Mrs. James said, "I could not find the article entitled 'Cell Phone Etiquette.'"

The president asked for "absolute security": all written messages were to be destroyed.

Question marks and exclamation points may go inside or outside closing quotation marks, as determined by the form of the quotation:

Sales Manager Martin said, "Who placed the order?" (The quotation is a question.)

When did the sales manager say, "Who placed the order?" (Both the incorporating sentence and the quotation are questions.)

Did the sales manager say, "Ryan placed the order"? (The incorporating sentence asks question; the quotation does not.)

"In the future," shouted Bob, "ask me first!" (The quotation is an exclamation.)

2.29 Brackets. Within quotations, brackets are used by the quoting writer to enclose his or her own inserted remarks. Such remarks may be corrective, illustrative, or explanatory:

Mrs. Cardillo said, "OSHA [Occupational Safety and Health Administration] has been one of the most widely criticized agencies of the federal government."

Review Exercise L—Other Punctuation

Insert necessary punctuation in the following sentences. In the space provided for each item, indicate the number of punctuation marks that you added. Count sets of parentheses and dashes as two marks. Emphasis or de-emphasis will be indicated for some parenthetical elements. When you finish, compare your responses with those provided. For each item on which you need review, consult the numbered principle shown in parentheses.

1. Will you please stop payment on my Check No. 233
2. (Emphasize.) Your order of October 16 will be on its way you have my word by October 20.
3. Mr Sirakides, Mrs Sylvester, and Miss Sanchez have not yet responded
4. Mrs Franklin asked if the order had been sent cod
5. Interviews have been scheduled for 3:15 p m, 4 p m, and 4:45 p m
6. (De-emphasize.) Three knowledgeable individuals the plant manager, the construction engineer, and the construction supervisor all expressed concern about soil settlement.
7. Fantastic The value of our stock just rose 10 points on the stock market exchange

8. The word de facto means exercising power as if legally constituted. _____

9. (De-emphasize.) Although the appliance now comes in limited colors brown, beige, and ivory, we expect to see new colors available in the next production run. _____

10. Was it the manager who said "What can't be altered must be endured _____

11. The stock market went bonkers over the news of the takeover. _____

12. Because the envelope was marked Personal, we did not open it. _____

13. Price, service, and reliability these are our prime considerations in equipment selection. _____

14. The lettercarrier said Would you believe that this package was marked Fragile _____

15. (Emphasize.) Three branch managers Carmen Lopez, Stan Meyers, and Ivan Sergo will be promoted. _____

16. (De-emphasize.) The difference between portable and transportable computers see Figure 4 for weight comparisons may be considerable. _____

17. All the folders marked Current Files should be sent to Human Resources. _____

18. I am trying to find the edition of Newsweek that carried an article entitled The Future Without Shock. _____

19. Martin Simon M D and Gail Nemire R.N were hired by Healthnet, Inc _____

20. The computer salesperson said This innovative, state-of-the-art laptop sells for a fraction of the cost of big-name computers.

---

1. 233. (2.23a) 3. Mr. Mrs. responded. (2.23a, 2.23b) 5. p.m. p.m. p.m. (2.23b)
7. Fantastic! exchange! (2.25) 9. (brown ivory) (2.27) 11. "bonkers" (2.28c)
13. reliability— (2.26c) 15. managers— Sergo— (2.26a) 17. "Current Files" (2.28c)
19. Simon, M.D., Nemire, R.N., Inc. (2.23b)

Cumulative Editing Quiz 6

Use proofreading marks (see Appendix B) to correct errors and omissions in the following sentences. All errors must be corrected to receive credit for the sentence. Check with your instructor for the answers.

1. Although the envelope was marked Confidential the vice presidents secretary thought it should be opened.

2. Would you please send my order c.o.d?

3. To be eligible for an apartment you must pay two months rent in advance.

4. We wanted to use Russ computer, but forgot to ask for permission.

5. Wasnt it Jeff Song not Eileen Lee who requested a 14 day leave.

6. Miss. Judith L. Beam is the employee who the employees council elected as their representative.

7. The Evening Post Dispatch our local newspaper featured an article entitled The Worlds Most Expensive Memo.

8. As soon as my manager or myself can verify Ricks totals we will call you, in the meantime you must continue to disburse funds.

9. Just inside the entrance, is the receptionists desk and a complete directory of all departments'.

10. Exports from small companys has increased thereby affecting this countrys trade balance positively.

Capitalization (3.01–3.16)

Capitalization is used to distinguish important words. However, writers are not free to capitalize all words they consider important. Rules or guidelines governing capitalization style have been established through custom and use. Mastering these guidelines will make your writing more readable and more comprehensible.

3.01 Proper Nouns. Capitalize proper nouns, including the *specific* names of persons, places, schools, streets, parks, buildings, religions, holidays, months, agreements, programs, services, and so forth. Do not capitalize common nouns that make only *general* references.

Proper nouns	Common nouns
Michael DeNiro	a salesperson in electronics
Germany, Japan	major trading partners of the United States
El Camino College	a community college
Sam Houston Park	a park in the city
Phoenix Room, Statler Inn	a meeting room in the hotel
Catholic, Presbyterian	two religions
Memorial Day, New Year's Day	two holidays
Express Mail	a special package delivery service
George Washington Bridge	a bridge
Consumer Product Safety Act	a law to protect consumers
Greater Orlando Chamber of Commerce	a chamber of commerce
Will Rogers World Airport	a municipal airport

3.02 Proper Adjectives. Capitalize most adjectives that are derived from proper nouns:

Greek symbol	British thermal unit
Roman numeral	Norwegian ship
Xerox copy	Hispanic markets

Do not capitalize the few adjectives that, although originally derived from proper nouns, have become common adjectives through usage. Consult your dictionary when in doubt:

manila folder	diesel engine
india ink	china dishes

3.03 Geographic Locations. Capitalize the names of *specific* places such as cities, states, mountains, valleys, lakes, rivers, oceans, and geographic regions:

New York City	Great Salt Lake
Allegheny Mountains	Pacific Ocean
San Fernando Valley	Delaware Bay
the East Coast	the Pacific Northwest

3.04 Organization Names. Capitalize the principal words in the names of all business, civic, educational, governmental, labor, military, philanthropic, political, professional, religious, and social organizations:

Inland Steel Company	Board of Directors, Midwest Bank
The Wall Street Journal*	San Antonio Museum of Art
New York Stock Exchange	Securities and Exchange Commission
United Way	National Association of Letter Carriers
Commission to Restore the Statue of Liberty	Association of Information Systems Professionals

3.05 Academic Courses and Degrees. Capitalize particular academic degrees and course titles. Do not capitalize references to general academic degrees and subject areas:

Professor Bernadette Ordian, *Ph.D.*, will teach *Accounting* 221 next fall.

Mrs. Snyder, who holds *bachelor's* and *master's* degrees, teaches *marketing* classes.

Jim enrolled in classes in *history, business English,* and *management.*

3.06 Personal and Business Titles

a. Capitalize personal and business titles when they precede names:

Vice President Ames	Uncle Edward
Board Chairman Frazier	Councilman Herbert
Governor G. W. Thurmond	Sales Manager Klein
Professor McLean	Dr. Samuel Washington

b. Capitalize titles in addresses, salutations, and closing lines:

Mr. Juan deSanto	Very truly yours,
Director of Purchasing	
Space Systems, Inc.	Clara J. Smith
Boxborough, MA 01719	Supervisor, Marketing

c. Generally, do not capitalize titles of high government rank or religious office when they stand alone or follow a person's name in running text.

Bill Clinton, former president of the U.S., supported Al Gore, his vice president.

The president conferred with the joint chiefs of staff and many senators.

Meeting with the chief justice of the Supreme Court were the senator from Ohio and the mayor of Cleveland.

Only the cardinal from Chicago had an audience with the pope.

d. Do not capitalize most common titles following names:

The speech was delivered by Timothy J. McEwen, *president*, South-Western College Publishing.

Lois Herndon, *chief executive officer*, signed the order.

e. Do not capitalize common titles appearing alone:

Please speak to the *supervisor* or to the *office manager.*

Neither the *president* nor the *vice president* was asked.

However, when the title of an official appears in that organization's minutes, bylaws, or other official document, it may be capitalized.

**Note:* Capitalize *the* only when it is part of the official name of an organization, as printed on the organization's stationery.

f. Do not capitalize titles when they are followed by appositives naming specific individuals:

   We must consult our *director of research*, Ronald E. West, before responding.

g. Do not capitalize family titles used with possessive pronouns:

   my mother   our aunt   your father   his cousin

h. Capitalize titles of close relatives used without pronouns:

   Both *Mother* and *Father* must sign the contract.

3.07 Numbered and Lettered Items. Capitalize nouns followed by numbers or letters (except in page, paragraph, line, and verse references):

Flight 34, Gate 12	Plan No. 2
Volume I, Part 3	Warehouse 33-A
Invoice No. 55489	Figure 8.3
Model A5673	Serial No. C22865404-2
State Highway 10	page 6, line 5

3.08 Points of the Compass. Capitalize *north, south, east, west,* and their derivatives when they represent *specific* geographical regions. Do not capitalize the points of the compass when they are used in directions or in general references.

Specific regions	**General references**
from the South	heading north on the highway
living in the Midwest	west of the city
Easterners, Southerners	western Nevada, southern Indiana
going to the Middle East	the northern part of the United States
from the East Coast	the east side of the street

3.09 Departments, Divisions, and Committees. Capitalize the names of departments, divisions, or committees within your own organization. Outside your organization capitalize only *specific* department, division, or committee names:

   The inquiry was addressed to the *Legal Department* in our *Consumer Products Division.*

   John was appointed to the *Employee Benefits Committee.*

   Send your résumé to their *human resources division.*

   A *planning committee* will be named shortly.

3.10 Governmental Terms. Do not capitalize the words *federal, government, nation,* or *state* unless they are part of a specific title:

   Unless *federal* support can be secured, the *state* project will be abandoned.

   The *Federal Deposit Insurance Corporation* protects depositors from bank failure.

3.11 Product Names. Capitalize product names only when they refer to trademarked items. Except in advertising, common names following manufacturers' names are not capitalized:

Magic Marker	Dell computer
Kleenex tissues	Swingline stapler
Q-tips	3M diskettes
Levi 501 jeans	Sony dictation machine
DuPont Teflon	Canon camera

3.12 Literary Titles. Capitalize the principal words in the titles of books, magazines, newspapers, articles, movies, plays, songs, poems, and reports. Do *not* capitalize articles (*a, an, the*), short conjunctions (*and, but, or, nor*), and prepositions of fewer than four letters (*in, to, by, for, etc.*) unless they begin or end the title:

Jackson's *What Job Is for You?* (Capitalize book titles.)

Gant's "Software for the Executive Suite" (Capitalize principal words in article titles.)

"Performance Standards to Go By" (Capitalize article titles.)

"The Improvement of Fuel Economy With Alternative Motors" (Capitalize report titles.)

3.13 Beginning Words. In addition to capitalizing the first word of a complete sentence, capitalize the first word in a quoted sentence, independent phrase, item in an enumerated list, and formal rule or principle following a colon:

The business manager said, "*All* purchases must have requisitions." (Capitalize first word in a quoted sentence.)

Yes, if you agree. (Capitalize an independent phrase.)

Some of the duties of the position are as follows:

1. *Editing* and formatting Word files

2. *Receiving* and routing telephone calls

3. *Verifying* records, reports, and applications (Capitalize items in an enumerated list.)

One rule has been established through the company: *No* smoking is allowed in open offices. (Capitalize a rule following a colon.)

3.14 Celestial Bodies. Capitalize the names of celestial bodies such as *Mars, Saturn,* and *Neptune.* Do not capitalize the terms *earth, sun,* or *moon* unless they appear in a context with other celestial bodies:

Where on *earth* did you find that manual *typewriter*?

Venus and *Mars* are the closest planets to *Earth.*

3.15 Ethnic References. Capitalize terms that refer to a particular culture, language, or race:

Oriental	Hebrew
Caucasian	Indian
Latino	Japanese
Persian	Judeo-Christian

3.16 Seasons. Do not capitalize seasons:

In the *fall* it appeared that *winter* and *spring* sales would increase.

Review Exercise M—Capitalization

In the following sentences correct any errors that you find in capitalization. Circle any lowercase letter that should be changed to a capital letter. Draw a slash (/) through a capital letter that you wish to change to a lowercase letter. In the space provided, indicate the total number of changes you have made in each sentence. If you make no changes, write *0.* When you finish, compare your responses with those provided. For each item on which you need review, consult the numbered principle shown in parentheses.

5 _____

Example: Bill McAdams, currently Assistant Manager in our Personnel department, will be promoted to Manager of the Employee Services division.

_____ 1. The social security act, passed in 1935, established the present system of social security.

_____ 2. Our company will soon be moving its operations to the west coast.

_____ 3. Marilyn Hunter, m.b.a., received her bachelor's degree from Ohio university in athens.

_____ 4. The President of Datatronics, Inc., delivered a speech entitled "Taking off into the future."

_____ 5. Please ask your Aunt and your Uncle if they will come to the Attorney's office at 5 p.m.

_____ 6. Your reservations are for flight 32 on american airlines leaving from gate 14 at 2:35 p.m.

_____ 7. Once we establish an organizing committee, arrangements can be made to rent holmby hall.

_____ 8. Bob was enrolled in history, spanish, business communications, and physical education courses.

_____ 9. Either the President or the Vice President of the company will make the decision about purchasing xerox copiers.

_____ 10. Rules for hiring and firing Employees are given on page 7, line 24, of the Contract.

_____ 11. Some individuals feel that american companies do not have the sense of loyalty to their employees that japanese companies do.

_____ 12. Where on Earth can we find better workers than Robots?

_____ 13. The secretary of state said, "we must protect our domestic economy from Foreign competition."

_____ 14. After crossing the sunshine skyway bridge, we drove to Southern Florida for our vacation.

_____ 15. All marketing representatives of our company will meet in the empire room of the red lion motor inn.

_____ 16. Richard Elkins, ph.d., has been named director of research for spaceage strategies, inc.

_____ 17. The special keyboard for the IBM Computer must contain greek symbols for Engineering equations.

_____ 18. After she received a master's degree in electrical engineering, Joanne Dudley was hired to work in our product development department.

_____ 19. In the Fall our organization will move its corporate headquarters to the franklin building in downtown los angeles.

_____ 20. Dean Amador has one cardinal rule: always be punctual.

---

1. Social Security Act (3.01) 3. M.B.A. University Athens (3.01, 3.05) 5. aunt uncle attorney's (3.06e, 3.06g) 7. Holmby Hall (3.01) 9. president vice president Xerox (3.06e, 3.11) 11. American Japanese (3.02) 13. We foreign (3.10, 3.13) 15. Empire Room Red Lion Motor Inn (3.01) 17. computer Greek engineering (3.01, 3.02, 3.11) 19. fall Franklin Building Los Angeles (3.01, 3.03, 3.16)

Cumulative Editing Quiz 7

Use proofreading marks (see Appendix B) to correct errors and omissions in the following sentences. All errors must be corrected to receive credit for the sentence. Check with your instructor for the answers.

Grammar/Mechanics Handbook

1. The Manager thinks that you attending the three day seminar is a good idea, however we must find a replacement.

2. We heard that professor watson invited edward peters, president of micro-pro, inc. to speak to our business law class.

3. Carla Jones a new systems programmer in our accounting department will start monday.

4. After year's of downsizing and restructuring the u.s. has now become one of the worlds most competitive producers.

5. When our company specialized in asian imports our main office was on the west coast.

6. Company's like amway discovered that there unique door to door selling methods was very successful in japan.

7. If you had given your sony camera to she or I before you got on the roller coaster it might have stayed dry.

8. Tracy recently finished a bachelors degree in accounting, consequently she is submitting many résumé's to companys across the country.

9. The Lopezs moved from San Antonio Texas to Urbana Illinois when mr lopez enrolled at the university of illinois.

10. When we open our office in montréal we will need employees whom are fluent in english and french.

Number Style (4.01–4.13)

Usage and custom determine whether numbers are expressed in the form of figures (for example, *5, 9*) or in the form of words (for example, *five, nine*). Numbers expressed as figures are shorter and more easily understood, yet numbers expressed as words are necessary in certain instances. The following guidelines are observed in expressing numbers in written sentences. Numbers that appear on business forms—such as invoices, monthly statements, and purchase orders—are always expressed as figures.

4.01 General Rules

a. The numbers *one* through *ten* are generally written as words. Numbers above *ten* are written as figures:

The bank had a total of *nine* branch offices in *three* suburbs.

All *58* employees received benefits in the *three* categories shown.

A shipment of *45,000* light bulbs was sent from *two* warehouses.

b. Numbers that begin sentences are written as words. If a number beginning a sentence involves more than two words, however, the sentence should be written so that the number does not fall at the beginning.

Fifteen different options were available in the annuity programs.

A total of 156 companies participated in the promotion (not *One hundred fifty-six companies participated in the promotion*).

4.02 Money. Sums of money $1 or greater are expressed as figures. If a sum is a whole dollar amount, omit the decimal and zeros (whether or not the amount appears in a sentence with additional fractional dollar amounts):

We budgeted *$30* for diskettes, but the actual cost was *$37.96.*

On the invoice were items for *$6.10, $8, $33.95,* and *$75.*

Sums less than $1 are written as figures that are followed by the word *cents*:

By shopping carefully, we can save *15 cents* per diskette.

4.03 Dates. In dates, numbers that appear after the name of the month are written as cardinal figures (*1, 2, 3,* etc.). Those that stand alone or appear before the name of a month are written as ordinal figures (*1st, 2d, 3d,** etc.):

The Personnel Practices Committee will meet *May 7.*

On the *5th* day of February and again on the *25th*, we placed orders.

In domestic business documents, dates generally take the following form: *January 4, 2001.* An alternative form, used primarily in military and foreign correspondence, begins with the day of the month and omits the comma: *4 January 2001.*

4.04 Clock Time. Figures are used when clock time is expressed with *a.m.* or *p.m.* Omit the colon and zeros in referring to whole hours. When exact clock time is expressed with the contraction *o'clock,* either figures or words may be used:

Mail deliveries are made at *11 a.m.* and *3:30 p.m.*

At *four* (or *4*) *o'clock* employees begin to leave.

4.05 Addresses and Telephone Numbers

a. Except for the number *one,* house numbers are expressed in figures:

540 Elm Street   17802 Washington Avenue
One Colorado Boulevard   2 Highland Street

b. Street names containing numbers *ten* or lower are written entirely as words. For street names involving numbers greater than *ten,* figures are used:

330 Third Street   3440 Seventh Avenue
6945 East 32 Avenue   4903 West 103 Street

If no compass direction (*North, South, East, West*) separates a house number from a street number, the street number is expressed in ordinal form (*-st, -d, -th*).

256 42d Street   1390 11th Avenue

c. Telephone numbers are expressed with figures. When used, the area code is placed in parentheses preceding the telephone number:

Please call us at *(818) 347-0551* to place an order.

Mr. Sims asked you to call *(619) 554-8923, Ext. 245,* after 10 a.m.

---

*Note: Some writers today are using the more efficient *2d* and *3d* instead of *2nd* and *3rd.*

4.06 Related Numbers. Numbers are related when they refer to similar items in a category within the same reference. All related numbers should be expressed as the largest number is expressed. Thus if the largest number is greater than *ten*, all the numbers should be expressed in figures:

> Only *5* of the original *25* applicants completed the processing. (Related numbers require figures.)

> The *two* plans affected *34* employees working in *three* sites. (Unrelated numbers use figures and words.)

> Getty Oil operated *86* rigs, of which *6* were rented. (Related numbers require figures.)

> The company hired *three* accountants, *one* customer service representative, and *nine* sales representatives. (Related numbers under ten use words.)

4.07 Consecutive Numbers. When two numbers appear consecutively and both modify a following noun, generally express the first number in words and the second in figures. If, however, the first number cannot be expressed in one or two words, place it in figures also (*120 34-cent* stamps). Do not use commas to separate the figures.

> Historians divided the era into *four 25-year* periods. (Use word form for the first number and figure form for the second.)

> We ordered *ten 30-page* color brochures. (Use word form for the first number and figure form for the second.)

> Did the manager request *150 100-watt* bulbs? (Use figure form for the first number since it would require more than two words.)

4.08 Periods of Time. Periods of time are generally expressed in word form. However, figures may be used to emphasize business concepts such as discount rates, interest rates, warranty periods, credit terms, loan or contract periods, and payment terms:

> This business was incorporated over *fifty* years ago. (Use words for a period of time.)

> Any purchaser may cancel a contract within *72* hours. (Use figures to explain a business concept.)

> The warranty period is *5* years. (Use figures for a business concept.)

> Cash discounts are given for payment within *30* days. (Use figures for a business concept.)

4.09 Ages. Ages are generally expressed in word form unless the age appears immediately after a name or is expressed in exact years and months:

> At the age of *twenty-one*, Elizabeth inherited the business.

> Wanda Tharp, *37*, was named acting president.

> At the age of *4 years and 7 months*, the child was adopted.

4.10 Round Numbers. Round numbers are approximations. They may be expressed in word or figure form, although figure form is shorter and easier to comprehend:

> About *600* (or *six hundred*) stock options were sold.

> It is estimated that *1,000* (or *one thousand*) people will attend.

For ease of reading, round numbers in the millions or billions should be expressed with a combination of figures and words:

At least *1.5 million* readers subscribe to the ten top magazines.

Deposits in money market accounts totaled more than *$115 billion.*

4.11 Weights and Measurements. Weights and measurements are expressed with figures:

The new deposit slip measures *2* by *6 inches.*

Her new suitcase weighed only *2 pounds 4 ounces.*

Toledo is *60 miles* from Detroit.

4.12 Fractions. Simple fractions are expressed as words. Complex fractions may be written either as figures or as a combination of figures and words:

Over *two thirds* of the stockholders voted.

This microcomputer will execute the command in *1 millionth* of a second. (Combination of words and numbers is easier to comprehend.)

She purchased a *one-fifth* share in the business.*

4.13 Percentages and Decimals. Percentages are expressed with figures that are followed by the word *percent.* The percent sign (%) is used only on business forms or in statistical presentations:

We had hoped for a *7 percent* interest rate, but we received a loan at *8 percent.*

Over *50 percent* of the residents supported the plan.

Decimals are expressed with figures. If a decimal expression does not contain a whole number (an integer) and does not begin with a zero, a zero should be placed before the decimal point:

The actuarial charts show that *1.74* out of *1,000* people will die in any given year.

Inspector Norris found the setting to be *.005* inch off. (Decimal begins with a zero and does not require a zero before the decimal point.)

Considerable savings will accrue if the unit production cost is reduced *0.1 percent.* (A zero is placed before a decimal that neither contains a whole number nor begins with a zero).

Quick Chart—Expression of Numbers

Use Words	Use Figures
Numbers *ten* and under	Numbers *11* and over
Numbers at beginning of sentence	Money
Periods of time	Dates
Ages	Addresses and telephone numbers
Fractions	Weights and measurements
	Percentages and decimals

Note: Fractions used as adjectives require hyphens.

Review Exercise N—Number Style

Circle *a* or *b* to indicate the preferred number style. Assume that these numbers appear in business correspondence. When you finish, compare your responses with those provided. For each item on which you need review, consult the numbered principle shown in parentheses.

1.	(a) 2 alternatives	(b) two alternatives	_____
2.	(a) Seventh Avenue	(b) 7th Avenue	_____
3.	(a) sixty sales reps	(b) 60 sales reps	_____
4.	(a) November ninth	(b) November 9	_____
5.	(a) forty dollars	(b) $40	_____
6.	(a) on the 23d of May	(b) on the twenty-third of May	_____
7.	(a) at 2:00 p.m.	(b) at 2 p.m.	_____
8.	(a) 4 two-hundred-page books	(b) four 200-page books	_____
9.	(a) at least 15 years ago	(b) at least fifteen years ago	_____
10.	(a) 1,000,000 viewers	(b) 1 million viewers	_____
11.	(a) twelve cents	(b) 12 cents	_____
12.	(a) a sixty-day warranty	(b) a 60-day warranty	_____
13.	(a) ten percent interest rate	(b) 10 percent interest rate	_____
14.	(a) 4/5 of the voters	(b) four fifths of the voters	_____
15.	(a) the rug measures four by six feet	(b) the rug measures 4 by 6 feet	_____
16.	(a) about five hundred people attended	(b) about 500 people attended	_____
17.	(a) at eight o'clock	(b) at 8 o'clock	_____
18.	(a) located at 1 Wilshire Boulevard	(b) located at One Wilshire Boulevard	_____
19.	(a) three computers for twelve people	(b) three computers for 12 people	_____
20.	(a) 4 out of every 100 licenses	(b) four out of every 100 licenses	_____

1. b (4.01a) 3. b (4.01a) 5. b (4.02) 7. b (4.04) 9. b (4.08) 11. b (4.02) 13. b (4.13)
15. b (4.11) 17. a or b (4.04) 19. b (4.06)

Cumulative Editing Quiz 8

Use proofreading marks (see Appendix B) to correct errors and omissions in the following sentences. All errors must be corrected to receive credit for the sentence. Check with your instructor for the answers.

1. The president of the U.S. recommended a 30 day cooling off period in the middle east peace negotiations.

2. Please meet at my attorneys office at four p.m. on May 10th to sign our papers of incorporation.

3. A Retail Store at 405 7th avenue had sales of over one million dollars last year.

4. Every new employee must receive their permit to park in lot 5-A or there car will be cited.

5. Mr thompson left three million dollars to be divided among his 4 children rachel, timothy, rebecca and kevin.

6. Most companys can boost profits almost one hundred percent by retaining only 5% more of there current customers.

7. Although the bill for coffee and doughnuts were only three dollars and forty cents Phillip and myself had trouble paying it.

8. Only six of the 19 employees, who filled out survey forms, would have went to hawaii as their vacation choice.

9. Danielles report is more easier to read then david because her's was better organized and had good headings.

10. At mcdonald's we devoured 4 big macs 3 orders of french fries and 5 coca colas for lunch.

Confusing Words

accede:	to agree or consent	*elicit:*	to draw out
exceed:	over a limit	*illicit:*	unlawful
accept	to receive	*every day:*	each single day
except	to exclude; (prep) but	*everyday:*	ordinary
advice:	suggestion, opinion	*farther:*	a greater distance
advise:	to counsel or recommend	*further:*	additional
		formally:	in a formal manner
affect:	to influence	*formerly:*	in the past
effect:	(n) outcome, result; (v) to bring about, to create	*hole:*	an opening
		whole:	complete
all ready:	prepared	*imply:*	to suggest indirectly
already:	by this time	*infer:*	to reach a conclusion
all right:	satisfactory	*liable:*	legally responsible
alright:	unacceptable variant spelling	*libel:*	damaging written statement
altar:	structure for worship	*loose:*	not fastened
alter:	to change	*lose:*	to misplace
appraise:	to estimate	*miner:*	person working in a mine
apprise:	to inform		
assure:	to promise	*minor:*	a lesser item; person under age
ensure:	to make certain		
insure:	to protect from loss	*patience:*	calm perseverance
capital:	(n) city that is seat of government; wealth of an individual; (adj) chief	*patients:*	people receiving medical treatment
		personal:	private, individual
		personnel:	employees
capitol:	building that houses state or national lawmakers	*precede:*	to go before
		proceed:	to continue
		precedence:	priority
cereal:	breakfast food	*precedents:*	events used as an example
serial:	arranged in sequence		
cite:	to quote; to summon	*principal:*	(n) capital sum; school official; (adj) chief
site:	location		
sight:	a view; to see	*principle:*	rule of action
complement:	that which completes	*stationary:*	immovable
compliment:	to praise or flatter	*stationery:*	writing material
conscience:	regard for fairness	*than:*	conjunction showing comparison
conscious:	aware		
council:	governing body	*then:*	adverb meaning "at that time"
counsel:	to give advice; advice		
desert:	arid land; to abandon	*their:*	possessive form of they
dessert:	sweet food	*there:*	at that place or point
device:	invention or mechanism	*they're:*	contraction of they are
devise:	to design or arrange		
disburse:	to pay out	*to:*	a preposition; the sign of the infinitive
disperse:	to scatter widely		

Grammar/Mechanics Handbook

too:	an adverb meaning "also" or "to an excessive extent"	*waiver:*	abandonment of a claim
two:	a number	*waver:*	to shake or fluctuate

160 Frequently Misspelled Words

absence	desirable	independent	prominent
accommodate	destroy	indispensable	qualify
achieve	development	interrupt	quantity
acknowledgment	disappoint	irrelevant	questionnaire
across	dissatisfied	itinerary	receipt
adequate	division	judgment	receive
advisable	efficient	knowledge	recognize
analyze	embarrass	legitimate	recommendation
annually	emphasis	library	referred
appointment	emphasize	license	regarding
argument	employee	maintenance	remittance
automatically	envelope	manageable	representative
bankruptcy	equipped	manufacturer	restaurant
becoming	especially	mileage	schedule
beneficial	evidently	miscellaneous	secretary
budget	exaggerate	mortgage	separate
business	excellent	necessary	similar
calendar	exempt	nevertheless	sincerely
canceled	existence	ninety	software
catalog	extraordinary	ninth	succeed
changeable	familiar	noticeable	sufficient
column	fascinate	occasionally	supervisor
committee	feasible	occurred	surprise
congratulate	February	offered	tenant
conscience	fiscal	omission	therefore
conscious	foreign	omitted	thorough
consecutive	forty	opportunity	though
consensus	fourth	opposite	through
consistent	friend	ordinarily	truly
control	genuine	paid	undoubtedly
convenient	government	pamphlet	unnecessarily
correspondence	grammar	permanent	usable
courteous	grateful	permitted	usage
criticize	guarantee	pleasant	using
decision	harass	practical	usually
deductible	height	prevalent	valuable
defendant	hoping	privilege	volume
definitely	immediate	probably	weekday
dependent	incidentally	procedure	writing
describe	incredible	profited	yield

Key to Grammar/ Mechanics Checkups

Chapter 1
1. attorneys (1.05d) **2.** Saturdays (1.05a) **3.** cities (1.05e) **4.** turkeys (1.05d) **5.** inventories (1.05e) **6.** Nashes (1.05b) **7.** 1990s (1.05g) **8.** editors in chief (1.05f) **9.** complexes (1.05b) **10.** counties (1.05e) **11.** Jennifers (1.05a) **12.** C (1.05d) **13.** liabilities (1.05e) **14.** C (1.05h) **15.** runners-up (1.05f)

Chapter 2
1. he (1.08b) **2.** his car (1.09b) **3.** him (1.08c) **4.** whom (1.08j) **5.** hers (1.08d) **6.** me (1.08c) **7.** I (1.08a) **8.** yours (1.08d) **9.** whoever (1.08j) **10.** me (1.08i) **11.** he (1.08f) **12.** us (1.08g) **13.** her (1.09c) **14.** its (1.09g) **15.** his or her (1.09b)

Chapter 3
1. *are* for *is* (1.10e) **2.** *has* for *have* (1.10c) **3.** *offers* for *offer* (1.10d) **4.** *is* for *are* (1.10g) **5.** C (1.10f) **6.** *is* for *are* (1.10i) **7.** C (1.10h) **8.** *chosen* (1.15) **9.** *lain* for *laid* (1.15) **10.** *were* for *was* (1.12) **11.** is for *are* (1.10c) **12.** b (1.15c) **13.** b (1.15c) **14.** a (1.15c) **15.** b (1.15c)

Chapter 4
1. long-time (1.17e) **2.** $50-per-year (1.17e) **3.** C (1.17e) **4.** quickly (1.17d) **5.** had only (1.17f) **6.** double-digit (1.17e) **7.** once-in-a-lifetime (1.17e) **8.** C (1.17e) **9.** better (1.17a) **10.** well-known (1.17e) **11.** up-to-the-minute (1.17e) **12.** after-tax (1.17e) **13.** couldn't have been clearer (1.17b) **14.** fifty-fifty (1.17e) **15.** feel bad (1.17c)

Chapter 5
1. b (1.19d) **2.** a (1.19d) **3.** b (1.18e) **4.** b (1.19c) **5.** a (1.19a) **6.** b (1.18a) **7.** b (1.19d) **8.** a (1.18c) **9.** b (1.18b) **10.** a (1.19c) **11.** b (1.19a) **12.** b (1.19b) **13.** a (1.19c) **14.** b (1.18c) **15.** b (1.19c)

Chapter 6
1. (2) not, as a rule, (2.03) **2.** (2) sure, Mrs. Schwartz, (2.02) **3.** (2) reliable, conscientious, (2.01) **4.** (0) **5.** (1) fact, (2.03) **6.** (3) Memphis, Tennessee, Des Moines, (2.04c) **7.** (1) meantime, (2.03) **8.** February 4, 1998, (2.04a) **9.** (2) Mr. Silver, Mrs. Adams, (2.01) **10.** (4) Holmes, Lane, San Diego, CA 92110, (2.04b) **11.** (2) feels, needless to say, (2.03) **12.** (2) supplies, replacing inventories, (2.01) **13.** (1) business, (2.02) **14.** (2) feels, however, (2.03) **15.** 0

Chapter 7
1. (1) warranty, (2.06a) **2.** (1) market, (2.05) **3.** (0) (2.05) **4.** (2) manufacturer, nameless, (2.06c) **5.** (1) imaginative, (2.08) **6.** (0) (2.06c) **7.** (2) Wilson, area, (2.09) **8.** (1) buyers, (2.05) **9.** (1) quality, (2.06a) **10.** (1) buyers, (2.07) **11.** (2) application, Monday, (2.06a, 2.04a) **12.** (2) hand, hard-working, (2.03, 2.08) **13.** (1) Concord, (2.06c) **14.** (3) telephone, Thursday, June 9, (2.06a, 2.04a) **15.** (1) classes, (2.05)

Chapter 8
1. (2) name," Zajdel, (2.14a) **2.** Cox, Ph.D., Merrikin, M.B.A., (2.10) **3.** (1) Monday, (2.14b) **4.** (0) (2.15) **5.** (1) investment, (2.12) **6.** (3) requested, cartridges, folders, (2.06a, 2.01) **7.** (2) think, however, (2.03) **8.** (2) period, Woodward, (2.07, 2.06c) **9.** (2) Diego, Monterey, (2.01, 2.15) **10.** (1) interviewed, (2.06a, 2.06c) **11.** (2) years, individuals, (2.07, 2.09) **12.** (2) Wall, week, (2.05c, 2.15) **13.** (0) (2.06c) **14.** (2) companies, robots, (2.01) **15.** (2) act, unprotected, (2.03, 2.08)

Chapter 9
1. (3) one year; long-term financing, hand, (2.03, 2.16b) **2.** (2) December; therefore, (2.16a) **3.** (3) months: September, October, (2.01, 2.17a) **4.** (1) are [omit comma] (2.17b) **5.** (1) money, (2.06a, 2.16b) **6.** (3) short-term credit; manufacturer, however, (2.03, 2.16a) **7.** (3) credit: accounts, promissory notes, (2.03, 2.16a) **8.** (9) businesspeople: Mary Ann Mahan, financial manager, Holmes Industries; Terry L. Buchanan, comptroller, Metropolitan Bank; and Mark Kendall, (2.16d, 2.17) **9.** (1) largest banks, (2.05) **10.** (5) customers; for example, retailers, service companies, manufacturers, (2.16e) **11.** (2) Inc., rating, (2.06c, 2.16c) **12.** (2) Federal, applications to: (2.06a, 2.17b) **13.** (2) high; therefore, (2.16) **14.** (2) 18 percent, prohibitive; (2.06a, 2.16c) **15.** (1) resources; (2.16b)

Chapter 10
1. Mr. Wilson's (2.20a, 2.21) **2.** year's (2.20a) **3.** weeks' (2.20b) **4.** Ms. Lanham's (2.21) **5.** boss's (2.20b) **6.** waitress's (2.20b) **7.** Kevin's (2.22) **8.** months' (2.20b) **9.** companies' (2.20b) **10.** month's (2.20a) **11.** lady's (2.20a) **12.** secretary's (2.20b) **13.** sellers" (2.20b) **14.** Mark's, David's (2.20a) **15.** Lisa's (2.20a)

Chapter 11

1. (2) managers—Jim Wong— (2.26a, 2.27) **2.** (3) please, Miss Sanchez, totals? (2.20, 2.23a) **3.** (2) variables (see Figure 13 on page 432) (2.27) **4.** (3) "recommendation" misspelled, (2.06a, 2.28c) **5.** (1) training— (2.26c) **6.** (2) said, "Who cartridges?" (2.28f) **7.** (3) "How You"? (2.28e, 2.28f) **8.** (2) states—Texas, California, and Alaska— (2.26a) **9.** (4) Mr. Ronald E. Harris, Miss Michelle Hale, and Ms. Sylvia (2.23b, 2.24) **10.** (3) "Trading Market" <u>Securities Markets</u> (2.28e) **11.** (2) over"; however, (2.16, 2.28f) **12.** (3) <u>liability</u> defined as "any future." (2.28d) **13.** (1) June 10; (2.06) **14.** (4) c.o.d. today? (2.23b, 2.24) **15.** (3) Hooray! checkup, haven't I? (2.24, 2.25)

Chapter 12

1. (5) American customs inspection International Airport (3.01, 3.02, 3.07) **2.** (6) Japanese international Japanese economics professor University (3.01, 3.02, 3.04, 3.06d) **3.** (4) business consumer business consumption (3.01, 3.13) **4.** (4) history sociology computer science (3.05) **5.** (5) Horticulture Are Nothing Sneeze At (3.12) **6.** (2) diskettes diskettes (3.11) **7.** (4) federal government state county (3.10) **8.** (4) United States This foreign (3.01, 3.06c, 3.13) **9.** (8) comptroller president board directors Internal Revenue Service company (3.01, 3.04, 3.06c) **10.** (2) mother sun's (3.03, 3.06g, 3.08, 3.14) **11.** (5) managing editor manager ad campaign (3.01, 3.06d, 3.06e, 3.09) **12.** (3) Austrian German Italian (3.02, 3.06a, 3.16) **13.** (4) Park island River Bridge (3.01, 3.03) **14.** (3) Computer Science Department (3.05, 3.07, 3.09) **15.** (5) Figure Chapter Census Bureau English (3.02, 3.04, 3.07)

Chapter 13

1. b (4.01a) **2.** a (4.05b) **3.** a (4.01a) **4.** b (4.03) **5.** b (4.02) **6.** a (4.03) **7.** b (4.04) **8.** b (4.07) **9.** b (4.08) **10.** b (4.10) **11.** b (4.02) **12.** b (4.08) **13.** b (4.12) **14.** a (4.06) **15.** a (4.06)

Chapter 14

1. c (2.05) **2.** b (2.06) **3.** a (2.16a) **4.** c (2.15) **5.** b (2.16b) **6.** b (2.17a) **7.** a (2.20) **8.** c (2.16d) **9.** b (2.04a) **10.** c (2.03) **11.** a (2.08) **12.** a (2.12) **13.** a (2.01) **14.** c (2.07) **15.** b (2.16)

Notes

Chapter 1

1. Paula Jacobs, "Strong Writing Skills Essential for Success, Even in IT," *InfoWorld,* 6 July 1998, 86.
2. "The Challenges Facing Workers in the Future," *HR Focus,* August 1999, 6.
3. Hal Buell and Amy Zuckerman, "Information, Please," *Journal for Quality and Participation,* May/June 1999, 52–55.
4. J. Burgoon, D. Coker, and R. Coker, "Communicative Explanations," *Human Communication Research,* 12, 1986, 463–494.
5. Ray Birdwhistell, *Kinesics and Context* (Philadelphia: University of Pennsylvania Press, 1970).
6. William E. Nolen, "Reading People," *Internal Auditor,* April 1995, 48–51.
7. E. T. Hall, *The Hidden Dimension* (Garden City, NY: Doubleday, 1966), 107–122.
8. Anne Russell, "Fine Tuning Your Corporate Image," *Black Enterprise,* May 1992, 80.
9. Anthony Patrick Carnevale and Susan Carol Stone, *The American Mosaic* (New York: McGraw-Hill, 1995), 160.
10. Lennie Copeland and Lewis Griggs, *Going International* (New York: Penguin Books, 1985), 12.
11. Nancy Rivera Brooks, "Exports Boom Softens Blow of Recession," *Los Angeles Times,* 29 May 1991, D1.
12. Figures compiled by Janice Hamilton Outtz, using *Outlook 1990–2005,* Bureau of Labor Statistics Bulletin 2402, p. 39, appearing in Carnevale and Stone, *The American Mosaic,* 36.
13. U.S. Department of Labor, Bureau of Labor Statistics, *Outlook 1990–2005,* 35.
14. Joel Makower, "Managing Diversity in the Workplace," *Business and Society Review,* Winter 1995.
15. Carnevale and Stone, *The American Mosaic,* 60.
16. Genevieve Capowski, "Managing Diversity," *Management Review,* June 1996, 13.
17. Makower, "Managing Diversity in the Workplace." See also Terry Lefton, "Bok in the Saddle Again," *Brandweek,* 8 February 1999, 26–31.
18. George Simons and Darlene Dunham, "Making Inclusion Happen," *Managing Diversity,* December 1995 <http://www.jalmc.org/mk-incl.htm> (Retrieved 9 August 1996).
19. John H. Bryan, CEO, Sara Lee Corporation, speech before the Corporate Affairs Communications Conference, 21 May 1990, Chicago.
20. "What's the Universal Hand Sign for 'I Goofed'?" *Santa Barbara News-Press,* 16 December 1996, D2.
21. Pete Engardio, "Hmm. Could Use a Little More Snake," *Business Week,* 15 March 1993, 53.
22. Makower, "Managing Diversity in the Workplace," 48–54.

Chapter 2

1. John Berlau, "Ebony's John H. Johnson," *Investor's Business Daily,* 26 March 1999, A1, A7.
2. Hugh Hay-Roe, "The Secret of Excess," *Executive Excellence,* January 1995, 20.
3. Earl N. Harbert, "Knowing Your Audience," in *The Handbook of Executive Communication,* ed. John L. Digaetani (Homewood, IL: Dow Jones/Irwin, 1986), 17.
4. Vanessa Dean Arnold, "Benjamin Franklin on Writing Well," *Personnel Journal,* August 1986, 17.
5. Mark Bacon, quoted in "Business Writing: One-on-One Speaks Best to the Masses," *Training,* April 1988, 95. See also Elizabeth Danziger, "Communicate Up," *Journal of Accountancy,* February 1998, 67.
6. Vern McKinley, "Keeping It Simple: Making Regulators Write in Plain English," *Regulation,* Fall 1998, 30–35.

Chapter 3

1. Malcolm Forbes, as quoted in Francis A. Corcell, "Why Don't Accountants Write Well," *Massachusetts CPA Review,* Winter 1995, 13–15.
2. Robert W. Goddard, "Communication: Use Language Effectively," *Personnel Journal,* April 1989, 32.

3. Andrew Fluegelman and Jeremy Joan Hewes, "The Word Processor and the Writing Process," in *Strategies for Business and Technical Writing*, 4th ed., Kevin J. Harty, ed. (San Diego: Harcourt Brace Jovanovich, 1989), 43. See also Lynn Quitman Troyka, *Simon & Schuster Handbook for Writers*, 4th ed. (Upper Saddle River, NJ: Prentice Hall, 1996), 49.

4. Maryann V. Piotrowski, *Effective Business Writing* (New York: HarperPerennial, 1996), 12.

Chapter 4

1. John S. Fielden, "What Do You Mean You Don't Like My Style?" *Harvard Business Review*, May/June 1982, 128.

2. Louise Lague, *People* Magazine editor, interview with Mary Ellen Guffey, 5 February 1992.

3. Barry Eckhouse, "Grammar Checkers Promise Better Writing, Improved Readability," *PC Week Labs Review*, 11 August 1995 <http://www.zdnet.com/pcweek/reviews/0807/tcheck.html> (Retrieved 13 September 1999). See also Steve R. Knowlton, "Grammar Aid Those Who/Whom Need it," *The New York Times*, 23 July 1998, D8.

Chapter 5

1. Eric Nee, "Interviews with Microsoft Executives," *Upside*, April 1995, 66–87; see also Sharon Gaudin, "CEOs See Gates' Vision of Future," *Computerworld*, 24 May 1999, 8.

2. Paula Jacobs, "Strong Writing Skills Essentials for Success, Even in IT," *InfoWorld*, 6 July 1998, 86.

3. G. Evans Witt, "You've Got Spam!" *American Demographics*, September 1999, 22.

4. Linda Himelstein, "Exhibit A: The Telltale Computer Tape," *Business Week*, 15 August 1994, 8; Lawrence Dietz, "E-Mail Is Wonderful But It Has Risks," *Bottom Line/Business* (published by Boardroom, Inc.), 15 June 1995, 3–4; Jenny C. McCune, "Get the Message," *Management Review*, January 1997.

5. Based on Charles Waltner, "Web Watchers," *Informationweek*, 27 April 1998, 121–126; and Howard Millman, "Easy EDI for Everyone," *InfoWorld*, 17 August 1998, 38–39.

6. Sharon R. King, "Video Game Industry Makes Push at Self-Policing," *The New York Times*, 13 October 1999, C1, C23.

7. Eleena de Lisser, "One-Click Commerce: What People Do Now to Goof Off at Work," *The Wall Street Journal*, 24 September 1999, B1.

8. Michael J. McCarthy, "Virtual Morality: A New Workplace Quandary," *The Wall Street Journal*, 21 October 1999, B1, B4.

Chapter 6

1. Cathy Trimble, coordinator, Wellness, Shore Memorial Hospital, interview with author, 1 October 1996.

2. Marcia Mascolini, "Another Look at Teaching the External Negative Message," *The Bulletin of the Association of Business Communication*, June 1994, 46.

3. Jeffrey Arlen, "Cleaning Up Kmart," *Discount Store News*, 6 May 1996, A3.

4. "Enforces Written Ethics Standards," *Discount Store News*, 6 May 1996, 3, 134.

Chapter 7

1. Cathy Dial, manager, Consumer Affairs, Frito-Lay, interview with author, 26 November 1996.

2. Mohan R. Limaye, "Further Conceptualization of Explanations in Negative Messages," *Business Communication Quarterly*, June 1997, 46.

3. Elizabeth M. Dorn, "Case Method Instruction in the Business Writing Classroom," *Business Communication Quarterly*, March 1999, 51–52.

4. Marcia Mascolini, "Another Look at Teaching the External Negative Message," *The Bulletin of the Association for Business Communication*, June 1994, 47.

5. "Letters to Lands' End," *February 1991 Catalog* (Dodgeville, WI: Lands' End, 1991), 100.

6. Michael Granberry, "Lingerie Chain Fined $100,000 for Gift Certificates," *Los Angeles Times*, 14 November 1992, D3.

7. Elizabeth M. Dorn, "Case Method Instruction," 51–52.

8. Andrew Ross Sorkin, "J. Crew Web Goof Results in Discount," *The New York Times*, 11 November 1999, D3.

9. Based on Robert L. Simison, "'Forget Paris,' GM Tells Journalists; Instead They Get to Visit Detroit," *The Wall Street Journal*, 12 August 1998, B1.

10. Laura Johannes, "Globe-Trotting Shutterbug Slaps Kodak With the Bill for a Reshoot," *The Wall Street Journal*, 24 April 1998, B1.

11. Elizabeth Douglass and Karen Kaplan, "GTE Admits Releasing Unlisted Numbers," *Los Angeles Times*, 17 April 1998, A1, A24.

12. Jeanette W. Gilsdorf, "Metacommunication Effects on International Business Negotiating in China," *Business Communication Quarterly*, June 1997, 27.

Chapter 8

1. René Nourse, vice president, Investments, Prudential Securities Incorporated, interview with author, 16 January 1995.

2. Hank Lavin, "Writing Business Letters That Sell," *Agency Sales Magazine*, June 1999, 36–38.

3. Stuart Elliott, "You've Got Mail, Indeed," *The New York Times*, 25 October 1999, C1, C25.

4. E. S. Browning, "In Pursuit of the Elusive Euroconsumer," *The Wall Street Journal*, 23 April 1992, B1.

5. Jackie Glick, "Automating Direct Marketing Campaigns," *Rough Notes*, January 1999, 56–58.

6. Laura Johannes, "Globe-Trotting Shutterbug Slaps Kodak With the Bill for a Reshoot," *The Wall Street Journal*, 24 April 1998, B1.

7. Edward O. Welles, "The Diva of Retail," *Inc.*, October 1999, 36–40.

8. Diana Booher, "Resolving Conflict," *Executive Excellence*, May 1999, 5.

9. Deborah DeVoe, "Don't Let Conflict Get You Off Course," *InfoWorld*, 9 August 1999, 69.

10. Devoe, "Don't Let Conflict," 70.

11. Nora Wood, "Singled Out," *Incentive*, July 1998, 20–23.

Chapter 9

1. Andrews S. Grove, "The Fine Art of Feedback," *Working Woman*, February 1992, 28.

2. Bob Urichuck, "Employee Recognition and Praise," *Canadian Manager*, Summer 1999, 27–29.

3. Amy Saltzman, "Suppose They Sue," *U.S. News & World Report*, 22 September 1997, 69.

4. Frances A. McMorris, "Ex-Bosses Face Less Peril Giving Honest Job References," *The Wall Street Journal*, 8 July 1996, B1.

5. Bob Rosner, "What Do You Say When You're Asked About an Ex-Employee?" Workforce, November 1999.

6. Based on Robert D. Ramsey, "Social Skills for Supervisors," *Supervision*, January 1997, 5–7 and Marjorie Brody, "Test Your Manners I.Q.," *Successful Meetings*, September 1999, 145–146.

7. Based on Edith Helmich, "Business Etiquette for a Technological Age" <http://www.hightechcareers.com/doc799/how-to799.html> (Accessed 8 December 1999).

Chapter 10

1. "Quotations from Chairman Powell: A Leadership Primer," *Management Review*, December 1996, 36.

Chapter 11

1. Thomas Sant, *Persuasive Business Proposals: Writing to Win Customers, Clients, and Contracts* (New York: American Management Association, 1992), vii.

2. Herman Holtz, *The Consultant's Guide to Proposal Writing* (New York: John Wiley, 1990), 188.

3. H. B. Koplowitz, "The Nature of Search Engines," *Link-Up*, September/October 1998, 28.

4. Based on Konnie G. Kustron, "Searching the World Wide Web," *Records Management Quarterly*, July 1997, 8–12.

5. Susan Feldman quoted in Annette Skov, "Internet Quality," *Database*, August/September 1998.

6. Gerald J. Alred, Walter E. Olin, and Charles T. Brusaw, *The Professional Writer* (New York: St. Martin's Press, 1992), 78.

7. M. Theodore Farries, II, Jeanne D. Maes, and Ulla K. Bunz, "References and Bibliography: Citing the Internet," *Journal of Applied Business Research*, Summer 1998, 33–36.

Chapter 12

1. Hal Lancaster, "Practice and Coaching Can Help You Improve Um, Y'Know, Speeches," *The Wall Street Journal*, 9 January 1996, B1.

2. Lancaster, "Practice and Coaching."

3. Dianna Booher, *Executive's Portfolio of Model Speeches for All Occasions* (Englewood Cliffs, NJ: Prentice Hall, 1991), 260.

4. Wharton Applied Research Center, "A Study of the Effects of the Use of Overhead Transparencies on Business Meetings, Final Report" cited in "Short, Snappy Guide to Meaningful Presentations," *Working Woman*, June 1991, 73.

5. Jim Endicott, "For Better Presentations, Avoid PowerPoint Pitfalls," *Presentations*, June 1998, 36–37.

6. Victoria Hall Smith, "Gigs by the Gigabyte," *Working Woman*, May 1998, 114.

7. Smith, "Gigs," 115.

8. Patricia A. LaRosa, "Voice Messaging Is Quality 'Lip Service,'" *The Office*, May 1992, 10.

9. "Did You know That . . .," *Boardroom Reports*, 15 August 1992, 15.

10. Hal Lancaster, "Learning Some Ways to Make Meetings Slightly Less Awful," *The Wall Street Journal*, 26 May 1998, B1.

11. Tom McDonald, "Minimizing Meetings," *Successful Meetings*, June 1996, 24.

12. Lancaster, "Learning Some Ways," B1.

13. John C. Bruening, "There's Good News About Meetings," *Managing Office Technology*, July 1996, 24–25.

14. Kirsten Schabacker, "A Short, Snappy Guide to Meaningful Meetings," *Working Woman*, June 1991, 73.

15. J. Keith Cook, "Try These Eight Guidelines for More Effective Meetings," *Communication Briefings* Bonus Item, April 1995, 8a. See also Morey Stettner, "How to Manage a Corporate Motormouth," *Investor's Business Daily*, 8 October 1998, A1.

16. Michael Jackson, quoted in "Garbage In, Garbage Out," *Consumer Reports*, December 1992, 755.

Chapter 13

1. Caitlin P. Williams, "The End of the Job As We Know It," *Training & Development*, January 1999, 52–54; Peter Cappelli, "Career Jobs Are Dead," *California Management Review*, Fall 1999, 146–167. See also Manuel London, "Redeployment and Continuous Learning in the 21st Century: Hard Lessons and Positive Examples from the Downsizing Era," *Academy of Management Executive*, November 1996, 67–79.

2. Maarten Mittner, "The Brave New World of Work," *Finance Week*, 30 October 1998, 77.

3. Cary L. Cooper, "The 1998 Crystal Lecture: The Future of Work—A Strategy for Managing the Pressures," *Journal of Applied Management Studies*, December 1998, 275–281.

4. George B. Weathersby, "Responding to Change," *Management Review*, October 1998, 5.

5. Sharon Voros, "Managing Your Career: The New Realities," *Communication World*, February 1997, 28–30.

6. Michele Pepe, "ResumeMaker Turns a Complete Circle," *Computer Reseller News*, 29 September 1997, 173.

7. Professor Mark Granovetter, quoted in Susan J. Wells, "Many Jobs on Web," *The New York Times*, 12 March 1998, A12.

8. George Crosby of the Human Resources Network, as quoted in Hal Lancaster, "When Taking a Tip From a Job Network, Proceed With Caution," *The Wall Street Journal,* 7 February 1995, B1.

9. Dan Moreau, "Write a Résumé That Works," *Changing Times,* June 1990, 91. See also Natalie Bortoli, "Resumes in the Right: New Rules Make Writing a Winner Easy," *Manage,* August 1997, 20–21.

10. Bortoli, "Resumes in the Right," 20.

11. H. B. Crandall, quoted in Jacqueline Trace, "Teaching Résumé Writing the Functional Way," *The Bulletin of the Association for Business Communication,* June 1985, 41.

12. Bortoli, "Resumes in the Right," 20.

13. Tom Washington, "Improve Your Résumé 100 Percent," **<http://www.nbew.com/archive/961001-001.html>** (Retrieved 27 September 1998).

14. Robert Lorentz, James W. Carland, and Jo Ann Carland, "The Résumé: What Value Is There in References?" *Journal of Technical Writing and Communication,* Fall 1993, 371.

15. "As Graduation Approaches . . .," *Personnel,* June 1991, 14.

16. Joyce Lain Kennedy and Thomas J. Morrow, *Electronic Résumé Revolution* (New York: John Wiley & Sons, 1994), Chapter 3.

17. Diane Cole, "Ethics: Companies Crack Down on Dishonesty," *The Wall Street Journal, Managing Your Career* supplement, Spring 1991, 8.

18. "Managing Your Career," *National Business Employment Weekly,* Fall 1989, 29.

19. Joan E. Rigdon, "Deceptive Resumes Can Be Door-Openers But Can Become an Employee's Undoing," *The Wall Street Journal,* 17 June 1992, B1. See also Barbara Solomon, "Too Good to be True?" *Management Review,* April 1998, 28.

20. Marc Silver, "Selling the Perfect You," *U.S. News & World Report,* 5 February 1990, 70–72.

21. Rhonda D. Findling, "The Résumé Fax-periment," *Résumé Pro Newsletter,* Fall 1994, 10.

22. Harriett M. Augustin, "The Written Job Search: A Comparison of the Traditional and a Nontraditional Approach," *The Bulletin of the Association for Business Communication,* September 1991, 13.

23. Sharon Voros, "Managing Your Career: The New Realities," *Communication World,* February 1997, 28–30.

Chapter 14

1. John D. Shingleton, *Successful Interviewing for College Seniors* (Lincolnwood, IL: VGM Career Horizons, 1992), x.

2. Scott Hays, "Kinko's Dials Into Automated Applicant Screening," *Workforce,* November 1999, 71–72.

3. Steve Alexander, "The Interview Spotlight," *InfoWorld,* 10 May 1999, 111–112.

4. Matt Richtel, "Online Revolution's Latest Twist: Job Interviews With a Computer," *The New York Times,* 6 February 2000, 1.

5. Linda Thornburg, "Computer-Aided Interviewing Shortens Hiring Cycle," *HR Magazine,* February 1998, 73–79.

6. Grant Faulkner, "Be Ready for Group Questioning," *InfoWorld,* 4 August 1997, 95.

7. Ron Fry, *Your First Interview* (Hawthorne, NJ: The Career Press, 1991), 16.

8. Caryl Rae Krannich and Ronald L. Krannich, *Dynamite Answers to Interview Questions* (Manassas Park, VA: Impact Publications, 1994), 46.

9. Julia Lawlor, "Networking Opens More Doors to Jobs," *USA Today,* 19 November 1990, B7.

10. J. Michael Farr, *The Very Quick Job Search* (Indianapolis: Jist Works, Inc., 1991), 177–178.

Index

Italic page numbers indicate illustrative information in figures.

I

idioms, 13–14, 21
illustration *see* clip art; graphic devices/highlighting;
    graphics; visual aids
in-text citations, 432–433
inclusive language, 39–40
independent clauses, 61, 64, 459, 465
indexes, bibliographic, 282
individualism, 11
inductive/deductive organizing methods *see* organizing
    data, direct/indirect pattern
information reports, 247, *252–253*, 253–254
information request letters, 135–137, *136*
information response letters, 139–141, *142*
information retrieval services, 42, 57
informational business messages, 115, *116*
initials, 470
interjections (grammatical), 440
internal communication *see* e-mail; memos
Internet, 42, 57
    learning to use, 26–27, 282–284
    personal use of, at work, 132–133
    see also Web
interviewing, 57, 58, 250
    on campus, 354
    career professionals, 353
    techniques (research), 285–286
    see also job interviews
introductory expressions, 465
inventories, 249
irregular verbs, 448–449
italics, *43, 63, 141*
    avoiding in e-mails, 110

J

jargon, 13–14, 16, 86
job application letters
    avoiding "I" dominance in, 378–379
    length of, 374
    parts of, 374–378
    purposes of, 373–374
    for solicited jobs, 374–375, *376*
    for unsolicited jobs, 375, *377*
job interviews, 390–401
    actions to avoid, *396*
    closing, 401
    computer interviews, 391
    conducting, 308
    dressing for, 394
    fighting fear, 395
    follow-up letters, 403
    hiring/placement interviews, 391–392
    nonverbal communication during, 394–395
    one-on-one, 391
    preparing and practicing for, 393
    questions, 396–401
        about experience/accomplishments, 397–398
        about the future, 398
        illegal, 400–401, 407–408

        salary, 399
        to get acquainted, 397
        to make you squirm, 398–399
        for you to ask, 399–400
    requesting, 378
    researching prior to, 392–393
    screening interviews, 391
    see also job search
    sequential and group interviews, 391–392
    steps in, *395*
    stress interviews, 392
job search, 350–356, *351*
    on-line, 26–27, 354–356, *355*
    traditional techniques, 354
    see also job interviews; résumés
junk mail, 200
    see also spam
justification reports, 247, 255, *258–259*

K

key ideas, repeating, 68–69
keywords (résumés), 365–366, *366*

L

labeling main ideas, 64
layout
    page, 248
    see also document formats
letterhead
    business, 417
    personal, *376, 379*
letters
    application/résumé follow-up, 402–403
    of appreciation, 223–224, *224, 225, 226*
    of authorization, 304
    bad-news follow-up, 167, *168*
    claim requests, 138–139, *140*
    claim responses, 145–148, *146*
    of congratulations, 224–227
    folding, 424–425
    form and guide, 232, *233*
    formatting, *136,* 416–422, *418, 423*
    information requests, 135–137, *136*
    information responses, 139–141, 142
    interview follow-up, 403
    job application, 373–379
    order requests, 137, *138*
    order responses, 141–143, *144*
    parts of, 417–422
    punctuation styles of, 422
    recommendation, 229–232, *231*
    rejection follow-up, 403–404
    requesting applications, 402
    requesting recommendations, 227–229, *228,* 402
    sales, 200–208, *205, 206*
    styles of, 422
    sympathy, 227
    transmittal, *296,* 304
    when to use, 34, 134–135